Sixth Edition

Managing Behavior in Organizations

Sixth Edition

Managing Behavior in Organizations

Jerald Greenberg

PEARSON

Boston   Columbus   Indianapolis   New York   San Francisco   Upper Saddle River   Amsterdam
Cape Town   Dubai   London   Madrid   Milan   Munich   Paris   Montréal   Toronto   Delhi   Mexico City
São Paulo   Sydney   Hong Kong   Seoul   Singapore   Taipei   Tokyo

Editor in Chief: Stephanie Wall
Director of Editorial Services:
  Ashley Santora
Editorial Project Manager: Sarah Holle
Editorial Assistant: Linda Albelli
Director of Marketing: Maggie Moylan
Senior Marketing Manager: Nikki
  Ayana Jones
Marketing Assistant: Gianna Sandri
Senior Managing Editor: Judy Leale
Production Project Manager: Ilene Kahn
Senior Operations Supervisor:
  Arnold Vila

Operations Specialist: Cathleen Petersen
Creative Director: Jayne Conte
Art Director: Suzanne Behnke
Cover Designer: Suzanne Behnke
Cover Photo: Shutterstock.com-LeksusTuss
Full-Service Project Management
and Composition: PreMediaGlobal
Printer/Binder: Edwards Brothers Malloy
Cover Printer: Lehigh-Phoenix Color/
  Hagerstown
Text Font: MinionPro

Credits and acknowledgments borrowed from other sources and reproduced, with permission, in this textbook appear on the appropriate page within text.

Many of the designations by manufacturers and sellers to distinguish their products are claimed as trademarks. Where those designations appear in this book, and the publisher was aware of a trademark claim, the designations have been printed in initial caps or all caps.

Library of Congress Cataloging-in-Publication Data
Greenberg, Jerald.
  Managing behavior in organizations / Jerald Greenberg. — 6th ed.
    p. cm.
  Includes bibliographical references and index.
  ISBN 978-0-13-272983-3 (alk. paper)—ISBN 978-0-13-274320-4 (coursesmart)
  1. Organizational behavior. I. Title.
  HD58.7.G7176 2012
  658.3—dc23

10 9 8 7 6 5 4 3 2 1

ISBN 10: 0-13-272983-0
ISBN 13: 978-0-13-272983-3

In loving memory of Bud, who left us much too soon.

J.G.

BRIEF CONTENTS

CONTENTS

PREFACE

Welcome to the sixth edition of *Managing Behavior in Organizations*. This book's relatively diminutive size and paperback format make it clear that it is not intended to be an in-depth account of the field of organizational behavior (OB, as it's called). Instead of covering every surface of the field's terrain, this book may be considered a tour of the scientific and practical highlights of OB housed in a succinct package.

It is with this in mind that I focus on the essential concepts and practices that students *really* must know. Fortunately, the thousands of students to whom I have taught this material over four decades in both physical and virtual university classrooms throughout the world have done a fine job (albeit sometimes with painful bluntness) of letting me know precisely what is wheat and what is chaff. It was with an eye toward answering their proverbial question, "What's the most important stuff?" that I wrote this book.

FOR WHOM IS THIS BOOK INTENDED?

In preparing this book, I was mindful of the needs of my dual-tiered target audiences—learners and those who are instructing them (i.e., students and teachers).

This book is aimed squarely at readers who have no special background or training in the social sciences. It is designed to be read by students taking their first class in management or organizational behavior. Specifically, these audiences include:

- Undergraduate students (in both two- and four-year colleges and universities)
- MBA students and those in related master's-level programs
- Practicing managers and executives in corporate training programs

Because this book is a stand-alone guide to the essentials of OB, instructors who have adopted previous editions have supplemented it with additional materials, such as cases, exercises, and readings that reflect their particular approaches to teaching OB. In fact, rather than attempting to be an all-inclusive package that dictates precisely what and how to teach, this book offers instructors the ultimate flexibility. Whether an instructor is teaching OB using the case method, an experiential approach, a seminar format, distance learning, or a traditional series of lectures, students must have knowledge of the field's basic assumptions, concepts, theories, research findings, and applications. It is this substantive knowledge that I strive to deliver in this book.

A BALANCED APPROACH TO RESEARCH, THEORY, AND PRACTICE

Many textbooks take intentionally narrow approaches to the subject matter they cover. Among OB texts, some focus primarily on research and theory whereas others focus primarily on managerial practice. In my opinion, these skewed orientations are misleading and do readers a disservice insofar as they fail to reflect the true nature of the field of OB.

By its very nature, OB is a deliberate blend of the scientific and the practical—an applied science in the truest sense. And this carefully balanced orientation is reflected in this book. Accordingly, I have prepared this book such that readers will come away with a firm understanding of *what* should be done (and what currently is being done) to improve the functioning of organizations and the satisfaction of people who work in them as well as the research and theory that shed light on *why* these practices are effective.

This orientation may be found throughout this book, but a few illustrations will make this explicit. Take Chapter 6, on motivation. Here, my treatment of the various classic theories of motivation is framed in terms of the central practical question: How do you motivate employees? The same may be said for Chapter 12 on organizational culture, creativity, and innovation. Readers of this chapter come away with not only a fundamental appreciation for the three concepts identified, but also a practical understanding of how to promote a culture in which individual creativity flourishes and organizational innovation abounds. Virtually every chapter captures this dual allegiance to theory and practice. Why? Because that's what OB—hence, this book—is all about!

MISSION: KEEPING ABREAST OF THE SHIFTING LANDSCAPE

Staying abreast of the ever-changing world of organizations is a full-time job. I know, because it's mine. For forty years, I have been a researcher, consultant, educator, and author probing into the world of *organizational behavior*. At social gatherings, I have been known to define it as the field that seeks to explain "what makes people tick" on the job. (By the way, to avoid ever being asked to assist in the delivery of a newborn, I never refer to being in the field of "OB.")

Over these years, various issues, topics, and theories once regarded as pivotal have faded into the background and their coverage in this book has been either reduced accordingly or deleted entirely. At the same time, new foci have received attention and now feature prominently on these pages. Keen sensitivity to the field's ebbs and flows has been critical to my mission of characterizing OB as it exists today. Several core issues have stood the test of time and are still covered in this book. However, what we know about them has changed—sometimes dramatically—in light of accumulated research, and the book's content has shifted accordingly, along with their breadth of coverage.

I can say without fear of contradiction that the nature of organizations today has made it more important than ever to pay attention to the topic of organizational behavior. The backdrop against which contemporary organizations function demands keen awareness of the dynamics of human behavior in organizations. Thanks to technology, the ways we work have been changing at a dizzying rate. Demographic shifts have altered the nature of the workforce with respect to members' values, languages, and backgrounds, resulting in unprecedented challenges and opportunities for everyone. At the same time, economic forces have driven a roller-coaster of shifting markets and unprecedented demands in the need for and availability of workforces. And as all this has been occurring, reductions in trade barriers, and highly efficient and relatively inexpensive transportation systems, and, of course, the ubiquity of the Internet, have made globalization a fact of life for all businesses, large and small.

The bottom line is clear: as potent forces have been altering the nature of organizations and the work people perform in them, so too has the field of organizational behavior been changing. And this has made the field of OB more vital and dynamic than ever—and my mission of chronicling it on these pages more challenging and exciting than ever.

NEW CONTENT

As you might imagine, the changing nature of OB has necessitated coverage of new topics in the present edition. Some topics covered in the past are now more abbreviated; others are discussed more extensively. Furthermore, quite a few topics appear in this edition for the first time. Among those making their premiere appearance are the following:

- Office hoteling (Chapter 1)
- Jellies (Chapter 1)
- Neurological responses to injustice (Chapter 2)
- Utilitarianism and natural rights perspectives on ethics (Chapter 2)
- Ethical relativism and imperialism (Chapter 2)
- Team halo effect (Chapter 3)
- Novel approaches to fighting stress (Chapter 4)
- Social support as a stress reducer (Chapter 4)
- Organizational demography (Chapter 5)
- Business case for diversity (Chapter 5)
- Motivational fit approach (Chapter 6)
- Emotion control and motivation control (Chapter 6)
- Need satisfaction as a source of rewards (Chapter 6)
- Swift trust (Chapter 7)

- Constructive versus destructive forms of organizational deviance (Chapter 7)
- Cyberloafing (Chapter 7)
- Informal communication using social media (e.g., Facebook, Twitter) (Chapter 8)
- Communicating in a multicultural workforce (Chapter 8)
- Peer-based normative control and peer-based rational control (Chapter 9)
- Gainsharing (Chapter 9)
- Implicit favorite bias in decision-making (Chapter 10)
- Hindsight bias and person sensitivity bias in decision making (Chapter 10)
- Servant leadership (Chapter 11)
- Core characteristics of organizational culture (Chapter 12)
- Immersion into Zappos's organizational culture (Chapter 12)
- Reorganization of GM's divisional structure (Chapter 13)
- Team-based organizations (Chapter 13)
- Action labs (Chapter 14)

These additions reflect growing interest in these topics in recent years. They were guided by informal feedback from professors and students using the previous edition of this book, formal feedback by reviewers, and my own assessment of what's happening in the field of OB. I resisted the temptation to include the latest fads. To have done otherwise would have triggered a departure from my mission of focusing on the essentials—in addition to dating the book prematurely and diminishing its usefulness for readers. As such, changes in content were evolutionary instead of revolutionary, and I trust that readers will welcome this approach.

NEW AND THOROUGHLY UPDATED FEATURES

In addition to the topics just identified, I added new features and thoroughly updated all content. These efforts may be seen in the several ways highlighted here.

New and Updated Company Examples

Although the ever-shifting terrain surely will make some of my efforts in vain, readers will find the book's examples as current as possible. Companies' practices come and go, as do their leaders, and even their existences. With this in mind, I offer this blanket apology for any references to such that are no longer applicable when this book is read.

New and Updated Practical Suggestions

In addition to updating company examples, readers should note that, however deemed necessary, I also updated references to research, theory, and conclusions drawn from them. In some cases, this required tweaking the nature of the practical advice our field is capable of offering. This is important to note because in all cases, the practical recommendations offered on these pages are guided by research findings. As such, they may be considered *evidence-based*, and their roots are valid. Knowing that the practices advocated in this book are driven by objective, empirical research should lead readers to accept them with confidence. And, unlike the recommendations found in some books, they are neither drawn out of thin air, nor the result of potentially biased, casual observations.

New and Updated Pedagogical Features

Readers familiar with the previous edition of this book will be pleased to find that two particularly popular features were retained but revised or updated as needed.

MAKING THE CASE   One of the features of which I speak here is the chapter-opening case. I call this *Making the Case* because it describes something going on in an organization that illustrates OB in action—thereby "making the case" for it as a topic worth studying. The chapter-opening cases in this book are either new to this edition or updated so as to ensure their continued relevance and pedagogical value. Some of the new *Making the Case* sections are as follows:

- *Edward Jones: Investing in People* (Chapter 1)
- *AIG: Bailout and Outrage* (Chapter 2)
- *Stressing Stress-Free Jobs at Kaiser Permanente* (Chapter 4)
- *Domino's Pizza Takes a Bite Out of Turnover* (Chapter 5)
- *Three Decisions Made, Then Quickly Unmade* (Chapter 10)
- *The Woman Who Saved the Chicken Fajitas* (Chapter 11)
- *"Welcome to Google, Here's Your Desk"* (Chapter 12)
- *Saving Campbell's from the Soup* (Chapter 14)

WINNING PRACTICES   These sections call readers' attention to current organizational practices that illustrate one or more key OB concepts from each chapter. They provide close-up examples of specific ways in which organizations have been using OB principles to improve a wide variety of different aspects of organizational functioning. New sections in this edition are as follows:

- *Feeling Sick? Your Doctor's Probably Got An App for That* (Chapter 1)
- *Three Novel Approaches to Fighting the Battle Against Stress* (Chapter 4)
- *Companies Stretch Goals in Two Directions* (Chapter 6)
- *"Virtual Troops" Usher Girl Scouts into the Digital Era* (Chapter 9)
- *Challenges of Leading in a Digital World* (Chapter 11)
- *Organizational Culture for Sale* (Chapter 12)
- *Making Changes Stick: How Three Successful Organizations Do It* (Chapter 14)

RETURN OF POPULAR PEDAGOGICAL FEATURES

Back by popular demand are the most useful pedagogical features from the previous edition of this book. These features appear at the front and back of each chapter.

Chapter-Opening Features

Preceding each chapter's opening case are two features designed to alert readers to the nature and significance of the material. These are as follows:

- *Learning Objectives.* At the beginning of each chapter, readers are provided with a list of six specific things they should be able to do after reading that chapter. These all begin with action words such as "define," "describe," "identify," and "distinguish."
- *Three Good Reasons You Should Care About....* Understandably, today's busy students may be prone to challenge the relevance of material, asking what value it has to them. Assuming that students are most receptive to learning about topics that have some recognizable benefits to themselves, these sections begin each chapter by indicating precisely why readers should care about the topic at hand.

End-of-Chapter Features Retained

At the close of each chapter are two different types of features designed to bring the material to life for readers.

APPLYING THE MATERIAL The first type of feature is intended to help students recognize and appreciate the practical implications of OB. Specifically, the following two features are designed to do this:

- *Back to the Case.* The end of each chapter contains a *Back to the Case* section in which readers are asked to answer three questions that require them to use the chapter material to explain specific aspects of the case. This drives home the relevance of the field of OB as a source of insight into the Making the Case sections.
- *You Be the Consultant.* These brief sections describe a hypothetical organizational problem and then challenge readers to draw on the material to find ways of solving it.

EXERCISES I have also retained the two skills-based exercises in each chapter that were so popular in earlier editions of this book. These are as follows:

- *Self-Assessment Exercise.* These exercises are designed to give readers insight into key aspects of their own individual attitudes and/or behavior relevant to the material covered.
- *Group Exercise.* These hands-on experiences require the joint efforts of small groups of students so as to help illustrate thinking about key phenomena described in the text.

These exercises can be an important part of students' learning experiences. They not only expose students to some of the phenomena described in the text on a firsthand basis, but they also stimulate critical thinking about those phenomena—and in ways that are intended to be highly engaging.

TEACHING AND LEARNING AIDS

This book is accompanied by very helpful teaching and learning aids for students and instructors that have been prepared especially for this book.

For Students

Students reading this book will benefit greatly by using several special features.

- *Interactive Study Guide.* The book's companion Web site can be found at www.pearsonhighered .com/greenberg. It contains a wide variety of features designed to help students organize and study the material in this book and to gain further insight into it.
- *Test questions.* Each chapter includes a set of questions (multiple-choice, true–false, and essay) based on the chapter material. To make the tests effective as a study aid, students receive instant feedback on them. And to stimulate thinking about each question, helpful "hints" are just a mouse-click away.

For Instructors

Professors who adopt this book have access to a complete set of instructional aids that consist of the following items:

- *Instructor's Manual.* Each chapter includes a chapter synopsis, lecture outline, and suggested answers to end-of-chapter questions.
- *The Test Item File.* Twenty-five multiple-choice questions, twenty-five true–false questions, and five to seven short-answer/essay questions based on the material in each chapter are included.
- *TestGenerator.* A comprehensive suite of software tools for testing and assessment is included in the *Test Manager* package to facilitate the process of creating exams.
- *PowerPoint Slides.* More than 100 full-color slides are available from the password-protected instructor's section of this book's Web site at www.pearsonhighered.com/greenberg.

To access these materials, instructors should contact their local Pearson sales representative.

ACKNOWLEDGMENTS: SOME SINCERE WORDS OF THANKS

Writing a book such as this is an endeavor one cannot undertake alone. Acknowledging this, I welcome the opportunity to thank the many hard-working reviewers, publishing professionals, and family members whose efforts have made this book possible.

Insightful Reviewers

To begin, I thank my colleagues who have provided valuable suggestions and comments in response to various drafts of this and earlier editions of this book. These include:

- Richard Grover, *University of Southern Maine*
- Jeffrey Miles, *University of the Pacific*
- Michael Buckley, *University of Oklahoma*
- Suzyn Ornstein, *Suffolk University*
- William A. Walker, *University of Houston*
- Henry Moon, *London Business School*
- Raymond T. LaManna, *New York Medical College*
- Charles Albano, *Fairleigh Dickinson University*
- Leonard Glick, *Northeastern University*
- Joe Rode, *Miami University*
- John Coleman, *University of Michigan*
- Melody Wollan, *Eastern Illinois University*

- Barbara McKintosh, *University of Vermont*
- Pat Sherrer, *Piedmont College*
- John Watt, *Purdue University*
- Morgan Milner, *Eastern Michigan University*
- Diane Denslow, *University of North Florida*
- Diane O'Brien, *Eastern Connecticut State University*

Talented Publishing Professionals

Second, I wish to thank the many hard-working individuals whose efforts made this book possible.

SUPPLEMENTARY MATERIALS I gratefully acknowledge several people for preparing the materials at this book's companion Web site. Specifically, I thank the talented staff members at Ansr Source for creating the very useful Student Study Guide, Veronica Horton for writing the Instructor Manual and making the beautiful PowerPoint slides, and Eileen Hogan for updating the Test Item File.

EDITORIAL STAFF Editorial director, Stephanie Wall, and her assistant, Linda Albelli, provided the steadfast support, along with the "gentle reminders," required to bring this book to fruition. Stephanie's contributions to shaping the form, tone, and direction of this book were immeasurable. I also thank her for assembling the best management and organizational behavior publishing team in the business.

Also working with me shoulder-to-shoulder on the many details that make this book a reality was Sarah Holle, project manager. I've never known more committed and kinder editorial staff. I am truly indebted to these outstanding professionals for lending their considerable talents to this project.

PRODUCTION AND MARKETING STAFF I am also indebted to Ilene Kahn, my production editor at Pearson Education, for guiding this book through the production process seemlessly. Copyeditor Cindy Bond and Haylee Schwenk at PreMediaGlobal worked tirelessly at transforming my ramblings into the coherent prose you have before you.

Nikki Jones, marketing manager, must be acknowledged for her insightful advice, which helped me make key decisions at various stages of this project. I also thank Maggie Moylan, director of marketing, for crafting a master plan for ensuring that this book reaches an ever-widening audience.

Supportive Family

In conclusion, I wish to thank members of my family for their support and for accepting without question my need to be isolated for long periods while I was working on this book. In Texas, Jack (a.k.a. "Paw Dawg"), David, James, and Raquel, and in New York, Ben and Sue have always been there for me. Their support has taken many forms and has been steadfast and invaluable.

As always, my wife Carolyn was with me every step of the way and has nurtured me with her love. I know I've been fortunate to have her in my life for over three decades, and I don't take her for granted. So, thanks, pal. I also benefitted from the joys of having Pepper around the house to sing, dance, and talk to me. As a parrot, he can also shred this book if he doesn't like it (or even if he does).

Jerald Greenberg

ABOUT THE AUTHOR

Jerald Greenberg has taught organizational behavior to thousands of students in universities throughout the world over almost 40 years. Most of this time he was at The Ohio State University's Fisher College of Business, where he won awards for excellence in teaching. He also has trained supervisors, managers, and executives in a wide variety of organizations. Dr. Greenberg is well known for his many contributions to organizational behavior research, especially his pioneering work on organizational justice. He has published widely on this topic and is regarded to be one of today's most influential management scholars. In recognition of sustained research excellence, Dr. Greenberg has won many prestigious awards. Among these are the Academy of Management's "Distinguished Scientific Contributions to Management Award" and the "Distinguished Scientific Achievement Award" from the Society for Industrial and Organizational Psychology (SIOP). When he is not lecturing, conducting research, or writing textbooks, Greenberg spends personal time in less successful endeavors—establishing his lack of talent as a rock musician and rooting for some of the NFL's most frustrating teams.

INTRODUCTION

1 | THE FIELD OF ORGANIZATIONAL BEHAVIOR

LEARNING OBJECTIVES

After reading this chapter, you will be able to:

1. **DEFINE** organizational behavior (OB).
2. **DESCRIBE** the major characteristics of the field of OB.
3. **DISTINGUISH** between the Theory X and Theory Y philosophies of management.
4. **IDENTIFY** the socioeconomic conditions that help shape the field of OB.
5. **DESCRIBE** the historical roots of the field of OB.
6. **CHARACTERIZE** the nature of the field of OB today.

THREE GOOD REASONS you should care about . . .

The Field of Organizational Behavior

1. Understanding the dynamics of behavior in organizations is essential to achieving personal success as a manager, regardless of your area of specialization.
2. Principles of organizational behavior are involved in making people both productive and happy on their jobs.
3. People can make or break their organizations, requiring successful companies to address a wide variety of OB-related issues.

Making the Case for...

The Field of Organizational Behavior

Edward Jones: Investing in People

With questionable practices and a global financial meltdown capturing headlines, it's no secret that the financial services industry has suffered in recent years. Although several once well-known competitors have succumbed to the storm, Edward Jones, the 90-year-old investment advising firm headquartered in St. Louis, didn't close any of its 12,615 offices nor did it lay off a single employee. In fact, it's grown its pool of 37,000 U.S.-based employees by eight percent.

Even in difficult market conditions, the firm's investment counselors have safeguarded—and, in many cases, grown—their customers' wealth. But the key to success at Edward Jones goes beyond skillfully investing clients' funds to wisely investing in the well-being of employees themselves. The company does this in several ways.

First, Edward Jones associates have strong incentives to work hard by earning opportunities to become limited or general partners in the firm. To date, some 12,000 associates have done so. As company officials acknowledge, this encourages everyone to cooperate with one another, building the sense that "we're all in this together" and "when one person succeeds, we all succeed."

To help promote this success, Edward Jones employees are given extensive training opportunities—95 hours per employee on average. The focus is on giving all associates—not just investment advisors—all the tools they need to chart their own careers and to advance along these paths. Not surprisingly, for eight consecutive years the firm has been recognized by *Training* magazine as having one of the best training programs for employees. This is in addition to earning top-ten rankings by *Fortune* magazine in recent years as one of the "top companies to work for."

Within Edward Jones, the firm's success and the way it treats its employees are considered to go hand-in-hand. The reasoning is straightforward: associates remain loyal to the firm because it treats them so very well (voluntary turnover is below the industry average at 9 percent). The resulting continuity allows customers to keep the same advisors for many years. This, in turn, enables investment counselors to know their customers well and customers to trust their counselors with their portfolios. This formula for success begets more success, as it attracts potential advisors to the firm and allows it to be very particular about whom it accepts. In fact, over 350 people on average apply for each new position that opens up. And with over $500 billion in clients' money entrusted to the firm, there's no such thing as being too selective.

It's clear that Edward Jones is doing something special, not only in investing its clients' money but also when it comes to investing in its own employees. The firm's associates are not only treated well but are given opportunities to shape their own destinies, both professionally and financially. And this is something that you don't find in all organizations. Edward Jones officials are convinced that its sharp focus on people has been paying dividends in customers'—and the firm's—bottom lines.

As you might imagine, behind these successes lies a management team whose members recognize the importance of the human side of work. After all, there can be no organizations without people. So, no matter how sophisticated Edward Jones' investment research may be, it's the firm's people that make the place special. With this in mind, it makes sense to realize that the human side of work is critical to the effective functioning—and basic existence—of organizations. This people-centered orientation is embraced in the field of *organizational behavior*—the topic of this book.

This chapter will introduce you to the field of organizational behavior. Specifically, I begin by describing the field's characteristics, the tools it uses to achieve its objectives, and the assumptions it makes about people. Following this, I present a capsule history of the field of organizational behavior, tracing its roots from its origins to its emergence as a modern science. Finally, I close this chapter by outlining what you can expect to find in the remainder of this book.

THE FIELD OF ORGANIZATIONAL BEHAVIOR: WHAT'S IT ALL ABOUT?

To help you fully appreciate the material in this book, it's useful to begin by explaining exactly what the field of organizational behavior is all about. I do this here by describing the field's defining characteristics.

Organizational Behavior: Its Defining Characteristics

The field of **organizational behavior** (or, **OB**, as it is commonly called) deals with human behavior in organizations. Formally defined, organizational behavior is the multidisciplinary field that seeks knowledge of behavior in organizational settings by systematically studying individual, group, and organizational processes.[1] This knowledge is used both by scientists interested in understanding human behavior and by practitioners interested in enhancing organizational effectiveness and individual well-being.

In this book, I will highlight these dual purposes, focusing both on explaining the nature of this scientific knowledge as well as how it has been—or may be—used for practical purposes. This dual focus is fundamental to the field of organizational behavior because it is considered an applied science. The definition of OB highlights four central characteristics of the field.

OB APPLIES THE SCIENTIFIC METHOD TO PRACTICAL MANAGERIAL PROBLEMS   Our definition of OB refers to seeking knowledge and to studying behavioral processes. Although it is neither as sophisticated as the study of physics or chemistry nor as mature as these disciplines, the orientation of the field of OB is still scientific in nature. Thus, like other scientific fields, OB seeks to develop a base of knowledge by using an empirical, research-based approach. That is, it is based on systematic observation and measurement of the phenomena of interest.[2] For an overview of some of the research techniques used in the field of organizational behavior, see Table 1.1.

Why is it so important to learn about behavior in organizational settings? To social scientists, learning about human behavior on the job—"what makes people tick" in organizations, so to speak—is valuable for its own sake. After all, scientists are interested in the generation of knowledge—in this case, insight into the effects of organizations on people and the effects of people on organizations. This is not to say, however, that such knowledge has no value outside of scientific circles. Far from it! OB specialists also apply knowledge from scientific studies, putting it to practical use. As they seek to improve organizational functioning and the quality of life of people working in organizations, as you will see throughout this book, they rely heavily on knowledge derived from OB research. Thus, there are both scientific and applied sides to the field of OB—facets that not only coexist but that complement each other as well. (Because we have all experienced OB phenomena, it sometimes seems commonsensical, leading us to wonder

TABLE 1.1	Research Methods Used in Organizational Behavior: A Summary

The field of organizational behavior is based on knowledge derived from scientific research. The major techniques used to conduct this research are summarized here.

Research Method	Description	Comments
Survey research	Questionnaires are developed and administered to people to measure how they feel about various aspects of themselves, their jobs, and their organizations. Responses to some questionnaires are compared to others, or to actual behaviors, to see how various concepts are interrelated.	This technique is the most widely used one in the field of OB.
Experimental research	Behavior is carefully studied—either in a controlled setting (a lab) or in an actual company (the field)—to see how a particular variable that is systematically varied affects other aspects of behavior.	This technique makes it possible to learn about cause–effect relationships.
Naturalistic observation	A nonempirical technique in which a scientist systematically records various events and behaviors observed in a work setting.	This technique is subject to the biases of the observer.
Case study	A thorough description of a series of events that occurred in a particular organization	Findings from case studies may not be generalizable to other organizations.

sometimes why the scientific approach is necessary. However, as you will see in the Group Exercise on p. 28, common sense is not always a reliable guide to the complexities of human behavior at work.)

OB FOCUSES ON THREE LEVELS OF ANALYSIS: INDIVIDUALS, GROUPS, AND ORGANIZATIONS

To best appreciate behavior in organizations, OB specialists do not focus exclusively on individuals acting alone. After all, in organizational settings, people frequently work together in groups and teams. Furthermore, people—alone and in groups—both influence and are influenced by their work environments. Considering this, it should not be surprising to learn that the field of OB focuses on three interrelated levels of analysis—individuals, groups, and organizations.

The field of OB recognizes that all three levels of analysis must be considered to comprehend fully the complex dynamics of behavior in organizations. Careful attention to all three levels of analysis is a central theme in modern OB and will be reflected fully throughout this text (see Figure 1.1). Consider these particulars.

- I will describe how OB scientists are concerned with individual perceptions, attitudes, and motives. This orientation, focusing primarily on the behavior of individuals, is known as the **micro approach** to OB. As indicated in the lower left corner of Figure 1.1, I cover this approach in Chapters 3–6 of this book.
- At the other extreme, the field of OB also examines organizations as a whole—the way they are structured and operate in their environments and the effects of their operations on the individuals and groups within them. As shown in the upper-right corner of Figure 1.1, this so-called macro approach to OB is covered in Chapters 12–14.

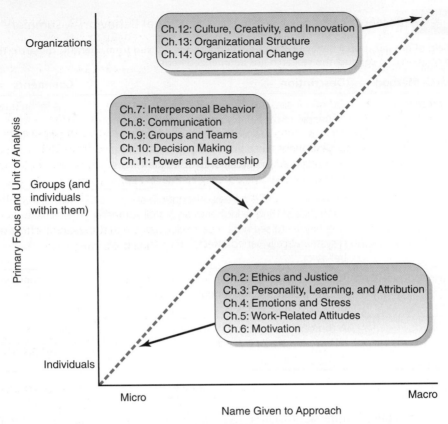

FIGURE 1.1   Levels of Analysis in the Field of Organizational Behavior
As indicated by the dashed line shown here, the topics studied in the field of OB (and hence, this book) vary along a continuum ranging from those focusing primarily on the behavior of individuals (known as the micro approach) to ones focusing primarily on organizations (known as the macro approach). Between these extremes, OB also focuses on the behavior of groups within organizations. The various chapters embracing these approaches are identified as they fall along this continuum.

- Between these two extremes, and sharing some characteristics of each, is the behavior of individuals in groups and of groups themselves. For example, in Chapters 7–11, I will describe such phenomena as how people communicate, make decisions, and influence others.

It is important to recognize that the lines between these approaches are not clear-cut, nor are they meant to be. Instead, they reflect the broad continuum of foci (indicated by the dashed line in Figure 1.1) that characterizes the field of OB.

OB IS MULTIDISCIPLINARY IN NATURE   When you consider the broad range of issues and approaches taken by the field of OB, it is easy to appreciate the fact that the field is multidisciplinary in nature. By this, I mean that it draws on a wide variety of social science disciplines. Rather than studying a topic from only one particular perspective, the field of OB is likely to consider a wide variety of approaches. These range from the highly individual-oriented approach of psychology, through the more group-oriented approach of sociology, to issues in organizational quality studied by management scientists.

For a summary of some of the key fields from which the field of OB draws, see Table 1.2. If, as you read this book, you recognize some particular theory or approach as familiar, chances are good that you already learned something about it in another class. What makes OB so special is that it combines these various orientations together into a single—very broad and very exciting—field.

OB SEEKS TO IMPROVE ORGANIZATIONAL EFFECTIVENESS AND THE QUALITY OF LIFE AT WORK   In the early part of the twentieth century, as railroads opened up the western portion of the United States and the nation's population rapidly grew (it doubled from 1880 to 1920!), the demand for manufactured products was great. New manufacturing plants were built, attracting waves of new immigrants in search of a living wage and laborers lured off farms by the employment prospects factory work offered. These individuals found that factories were gigantic, noisy, hot, and highly regimented—in short, brutal places in which to work. Bosses demanded more and more from their employees and treated them like disposable machines, replacing those who quit or who died from accidents with others who waited outside the factory gates.

TABLE 1.2   The Multidisciplinary Roots of OB

OB is a unique multidisciplinary field that draws on several different sciences. The most important parent disciplines are listed here, along with some of the OB topics with which they are associated and the chapters in this book where they are discussed.

Discipline	Relevant OB Topics	Associated Chapters
Psychology	Perception	Chapter 3
	Learning	Chapter 3
	Personality	Chapter 3
	Emotions	Chapter 4
	Stress	Chapter 4
	Attitudes	Chapter 5
Physiology	Motivation	Chapter 6
	Decision making	Chapter 10
Sociology	Group processes	Chapter 9
	Teams	Chapter 9
Anthropology	Group processes	Chapter 9
	Communication	Chapter 8
Political science	Leadership	Chapter 11
	Organizational culture	Chapter 12
Economics	Interpersonal conflict	Chapter 7
	Organizational power	Chapter 11
	Negotiation	Chapter 7
Management science	Decision making	Chapter 10
	Organizational power	Chapter 11
	Technology	Chapter 13
	Organizational change	Chapter 14

Clearly, the managers of a century ago held very negative views of employees. They assumed that people were basically lazy and irresponsible, and they treated workers with disrespect. This very negativistic approach, which has been around for many years, reflects the traditional view of management called the **Theory X** orientation. This philosophy of management assumes that people are basically lazy, dislike work, need direction, and will only work hard when they are pushed into doing so.

Today, however, if you asked corporate officials to describe their views of human nature, you'd probably find some more optimistic beliefs. Although some of today's managers still think that people are basically lazy, many others would disagree, arguing that it's not that simple. They would claim that most individuals are just as capable of working hard as they are of "goofing off." If employees are recognized for their efforts (such as by being fairly paid) and are given an opportunity to succeed (such as by being well trained), they may be expected to work very hard without being pushed. Thus, employees may put forth a great deal of effort simply because they want to. Management's job, then, is to create those conditions that make people want to perform as desired.

This approach, which assumes that people are not intrinsically lazy but willing to work hard when the right conditions prevail, is known as the **Theory Y** orientation. This philosophy assumes that people have a psychological need to work and seek achievement and responsibility. In contrast to the Theory X philosophy of management, which essentially demonstrates distrust for people on the job, the Theory Y approach is strongly associated with improving the quality of people's work lives (for a summary of the differences, see Figure 1.2).

The Theory Y perspective prevails within the field of organizational behavior today. It assumes that people are highly responsive to their work environments and that the ways they are treated will influence the ways they will act. In fact, OB scientists are very interested in learning

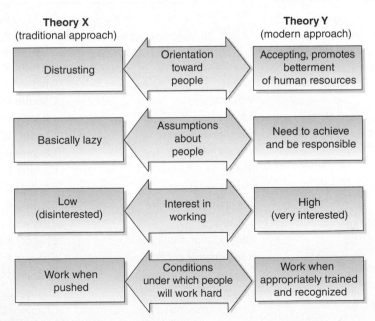

FIGURE 1.2   Theory X Versus Theory Y: A Summary
The traditional *Theory X* orientation toward people is far more negativistic than the contemporary *Theory Y* approach, which is widely accepted today. Some of the key differences between these management philosophies are summarized here.

exactly what conditions will lead people to behave most positively—that is, what makes work both productive for organizations and enjoyable for the people working in them. (Do your own assumptions about people at work more closely match a Theory X or Theory Y perspective? To find out, complete the Self-Assessment Exercise on p. 27.)

After reading this section, you may find yourself wondering about productivity and profitability. After all, the primary reason why businesses exist is to make a profit. What does all this talk about people have to do with the bottom line? The answer is simple. Yes, OB is concerned about the profit of organizations. In fact, making organizations more profitable is one of the field's key objectives. However, the way it goes about doing this is different than in other areas of business. OB doesn't deal with the design of machines used in manufacturing; it doesn't address a company's accounting and marketing procedures; and it has nothing to say about the pricing strategies that help sell products and services. Instead, OB seeks to make organizations more profitable by addressing the treatment of people and the way work is done. As you read this book, you will see exactly how vital this mission is and how the field goes about meeting it.

OB ASSUMES THAT THERE IS NO "ONE BEST" APPROACH What's the most effective way to motivate people? What style of leadership works best? Should groups of individuals be used to make important organizational decisions? Although these questions are quite reasonable, there is a basic problem with all of them. Namely, they all assume that there is a simple, unitary answer—that is, one best way to motivate, to lead, and to make decisions.

Today's specialists in the field of OB reject this simplistic approach and agree that there is no one best approach to such complex phenomena. To assume otherwise is not only overly simplistic and naive but, as you will see, also grossly inaccurate. When it comes to studying human behavior in organizations, there are no simple answers. Instead, OB scholars embrace a **contingency approach**—an orientation that recognizes that behavior in work settings is the complex result of many interacting forces. This orientation is a hallmark of modern OB, and you will see it throughout this book. Consider, for example, how an individual's personal characteristics (e.g., personal attitudes and beliefs) in conjunction with situational factors (e.g., an organization's culture, relations between coworkers) may all work together when it comes to influencing how a particular individual is likely to behave on the job.

Reflecting the popularity of the contingency approach, explaining OB phenomena often requires saying, "It depends." As our knowledge of work-related behavior becomes increasingly complex, it is difficult to give "straight answers." Rather, it is usually necessary to say that people will do certain things "under some conditions" or "when all other factors are equal." Such phrases provide a clear indication that the contingency approach is being used. In other words, a certain behavior is "contingent upon" the existence of specific conditions. And OB scientists are always striving to identify and understand these conditions.

Why Does OB Matter?

Now that you know the nature of the field, I will give you a preview of things to come by showing you the importance of just a few of the ways in which the field of OB matters to people and companies. With this in mind, I pose a question that asks you to draw on your personal experiences: Have you ever had a job where people didn't get along, nobody knew what to do, everyone goofed off, and your boss was—well, putting it politely—unpleasant? I can't imagine that you liked working in that company at all. In contrast, think of another position in which everyone was friendly, knowledgeable, hardworking, and pleasant. That's probably more to your liking. In such a situation you are likely to be interested in going to work, doing your best, and taking pride in what you do. At the heart of these differences are all issues that are of great concern to OB scientists and practitioners—and, as a result, they are the ones that will be covered in this book.

"Okay," you may be asking, "in some companies, things are nice and smooth, but in others, relationships are rocky—does it really matter?" As you will see throughout this book, the answer is a resounding *yes*! For now, here are just a few highlights of specific ways in which OB matters to people and the organizations in which they work.

- Companies whose managers accurately appraise the work of their subordinates enjoy lower costs and higher productivity than those that handle their appraisals less accurately.[3]
- People who are satisfied with the way they are treated on the job are generally more pleasant to their coworkers and bosses and are less likely to quit than those who are dissatisfied with the way others treat them.[4]
- People who are carefully trained to work together in teams tend to be happier and more productive than those who are simply thrown together without any definite organizational support.[5]
- Employees who believe they have been treated unfairly on the job are more likely to steal from their employers and to reject the policies of their organizations than those who believe they have been fairly treated.[6]
- People who are mistreated by their supervisors on the job experience more mental and physical illnesses than those who are treated with kindness, dignity, and respect.[7]
- Organizations that treat employees well with respect to pay and benefits, opportunities, job security, friendliness, fairness, and pride in company are, on average, twice as profitable as the Standard & Poor's 500 companies.[8]
- Companies that offer good employee benefits and that have friendly conditions are more profitable than those that are less people oriented.[9]

By now, you might be asking yourself: Why, if OB is so important, is there no one person in charge of it in an organization? After all, companies tend to have officials who are responsible for other basic areas such as finance, accounting, marketing, and production. Why not OB? If you've never heard of a vice president of OB or a manager of organizational behavior, it's because organizations do not have any such formal posts. So then, back to the question: Who is responsible for organizational behavior?

In a sense, the answer is *everyone*! Although OB is a separate area of study, it cuts across all areas of organizational functioning. Managers in all departments have to know how to motivate their employees, how to keep people satisfied with their jobs, how to communicate fairly, how to make teams function smoothly, and how to design jobs most effectively. In short, dealing with people at work is everybody's responsibility on the job. So, no matter what job you do in a company, knowing something about OB is sure to help you do it better. This is precisely why it's vitally important for you to know the material in this book.

OB IS RESPONSIVE TO SOCIOECONOMIC CONDITIONS

As the world changes, so too does the field of OB. In fact, many of the phenomena that OB scientists study are influenced by the ever-shifting nature of *socioeconomic* conditions—that is, changes in people and the business environment. In other words, ongoing changes in people and their environments take center stage in the field of OB. After all, people affect their environments (e.g., productive individuals strengthen the economy) and those environments affect people (e.g., foreign competition changes the nature of work performed). With this in mind, it is useful to recognize the changing conditions to which OB scientists and practitioners must be sensitive. Here, I begin by describing a fundamental fact of life in OB—namely, that organizations are dynamic in nature.

OB Recognizes the Dynamic Nature of Organizations

Thus far, our characterization of the field of OB has focused more on behavior than on organizations. Nonetheless, it is important to point out that both OB scientists and practitioners do pay a great deal of attention to the nature of organizations themselves. Under what conditions will organizations change? How are organizations structured? How do organizations interact with their environments? Questions such as these are of major interest to specialists in OB. But, before we can consider them (as we will do in Chapters 13 and 14), we must first clarify exactly what we mean by an *organization*.

Formally defined, an **organization** is a structured social system consisting of groups and individuals working together to meet some agreed-upon objectives. In other words, organizations consist of structured social units, such as individuals and/or work groups, who strive to attain a common goal. Typically, we think of making a profit as the primary goal of an organization—and indeed, for most business organizations, it is. However, different organizations may be guided by different goals. For example, charitable organizations may focus on the objective of helping people in need, political parties may be interested in electing candidates with certain ideas, and religious organizations may strive to save souls. Regardless of the specific goals sought, the structured social units working together toward them may be considered organizations.

OB scientists conceive of organizations as dynamic and ever-changing entities. In other words, they recognize that organizations are **open systems**—that is, self-sustaining systems that use energy to transform resources from the environment (such as raw materials) into some form of output (e.g., a finished product).[10] Figure 1.3 summarizes some of the key properties of open systems.

As this diagram makes clear, organizations receive input (i.e., raw materials) from their environments and continuously transform it into output (i.e., products or services). This output gets transformed back to input, and the cyclical operation continues. Because of the abstract nature of this description, let's now consider a real example, such as how organizations may tap the

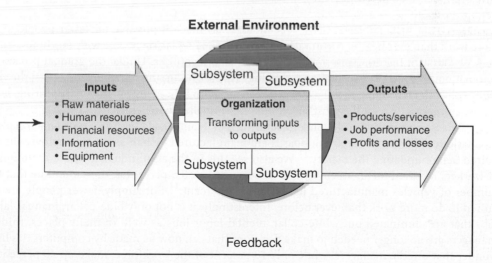

FIGURE 1.3 Organizations as Open Systems
The *open systems* approach is characteristic of modern-day thinking in the field of OB. It assumes that organizations are self-sustaining—that is, that they transform inputs to outputs in a continuous fashion. *Sources:* Based on suggestions by Scott, 2007, and Katz & Kahn, 1978; see Note 10.

human resources of the community by hiring and training people to do jobs. These individuals may work to provide a product in exchange for wages. They then spend these wages, putting money back into the community and allowing more people to afford their companies' products. This, in turn, creates the need for still more employees, and so on. If you think about it this way, it's easy to realize that organizations are dynamic and constantly changing.

The dynamic nature of organizations can be likened to the dynamic relationship between people and their environments. When we breathe, we take in oxygen and transform it into carbon dioxide. This, in turn, sustains the life of green plants that emit oxygen for people to breathe. The continuous nature of this open system—the so-called *oxygen-carbon dioxide life cycle*—characterizes not only life but the existence of organizations as well.

OB Responds to Advances in Technology

Since the industrial revolution, people had performed carefully prescribed sets of tasks—known as *jobs*—within large networks of people who answered to those above them—hierarchical arrangements known as *organizations*. This picture, although highly simplistic, does a good job of characterizing the working arrangements that most people had during much of the twentieth century. However, today, in the twenty-first century, the essential nature of jobs and organizations as we have known them is changing, and the major catalyst is rapidly advancing computer technology, especially the use of the Internet and wireless technology.[11] As you might imagine, this state of affairs has important implications for organizations—and, hence, the field of OB. (For a close-up look at how one particular group, medical doctors, have made successful use of technology in the form of iPads, see this chapter's Winning Practices section on p. 13.)

As more work is shifted to digital brains, some work that was once performed by human brains becomes obsolete. At the same time, new opportunities arise as people scurry to find their footing amid the shifting terrain of the high-tech revolution. The implications of this for OB are considerable. We will now review some of the most prominent trends in the world of work that have been identified in recent years.

AUTOMATION AND DOWNSIZING   Technology has made it possible for fewer people to do more work than ever before. **Automation**, the process of replacing people with machines, is not new, of course; it has gone on, slowly and steadily, for centuries. Unlike the gradual process of automation, advances in information technology (IT) are occurring so rapidly today that the very nature of work is changing as fast as we can keep up. With this, many jobs are disappearing, leaving organizations (at least the most successful ones!) smaller than before.[12]

This also occurs in product manufacturing. For example, at GE's Fanuc Automation plant in Charlottesville, Virginia, circuit boards are manufactured by half as many employees as required before updating the facility.[13] We also see this in the auto industry, where the number of workers required on an assembly line has dropped by 8.5 percent at the same time that the number of vehicles manufactured has risen by 5 percent.[14] Put simply, fewer people are required to do more work than ever before. Interestingly, it is not only blue-collar, manual-labor jobs that are eliminated but white-collar, mental-labor jobs as well. In many places, middle managers are no longer needed to make decisions that can now be made by computers. It's little wonder that middle managers, while only 10 percent of the workforce, make up 20 percent of recent layoffs.

As these figures suggest, organizations have been reducing the number of employees needed to operate effectively—a process known as **downsizing**.[15] Typically, this involves more than just laying off people in a move to save money. It is directed at adjusting the number of employees

Winning Practices

Feeling Sick? Your Doctor's Probably Got an App for That

Like millions of others, you may enjoy using your iPad to follow friends on Twitter, stream recent episodes of your favorite TV shows, and play *Angry Birds*. Chances are good, however, that your doctor is using his or her tablet for more serious purposes. Indeed, today's healthcare providers have been harnessing the power of this technology to enhance ready access to information that helps them streamline various aspects of their work.

Medical practitioners have access to a variety of apps that help them do their jobs. These tools fall into five categories.[16]

- *Apps for diagnosis.* The World Health Organization tells us that there are over 12,000 different diseases.[17] These present a bewildering combination of symptoms that can easily overwhelm even the most talented diagnosticians. Coming to their aid are apps in which doctors enter patients' clinical symptoms and laboratory findings and, drawing on detailed databases, the apps display possible diseases associated with this information, including maladies that may be easily overlooked. Such apps are available in several specialty areas, such as mental health, cardiology, and pediatrics.

- *Apps for prescribing drugs.* What doses of a particular pharmaceutical are available? What are the side effects? For what conditions has it been used, and how effectively? It is vital that physicians have answers to such questions when prescribing drugs for their patients. With this in mind, doctors traditionally consulted the 3,000-plus page *Physician's Desk Reference (PDR)* for information on over 1,100 commonly prescribed pharmaceuticals.[18] Because the *PDR* is so encyclopedic, however, doctors seeing patients often need to consult more streamlined databases of prescribing information. This has led to the development of several iPad apps that bring the latest prescribing information to doctors' fingertips. To stay current, many such apps are available on a subscription basis.

- *Apps for patient care.* Traditionally, doctors' examination rooms have been adorned with diagrams hung from walls that illustrate various parts of the human body. Physicians refer to these when explaining various anatomic structures to patients. Regardless of how richly illustrated these pictures may be, they are static and flat. Now, however, various apps are available that allow doctors to show patients pictures of bones and organs that show movement and that rotate 360 degrees, making it easier for doctors to communicate processes. Versions are available in English and Spanish.

- *Apps for reference.* Even the best doctors sometimes need to look up information, and apps exist that make such referencing a snap. Some of the most sophisticated ones show 3-D animations of various body functions and systems. Other apps show actual CT scans to which doctors can refer when interpreting the scans of their own patients.

- *Apps for recordkeeping.* Knowing how to treat patients requires access to information about their medical histories, and this begins with thorough notes about past conditions and treatments. Some apps make it possible for doctors to have access to this information at their fingertips and allow them to record new data quickly and easily. Unlike other apps, which work as stand-alones, these apps are user interfaces that are integrated into the computer networks of the offices, clinics, or hospitals where they're seeing patients.

When it comes to practicing medicine, there's no substitute for experience, of course, and computers—handheld or otherwise—will not be replacing physicians anytime soon. However, there's no mistaking the fact that tablet devices have found their way into the everyday tools of growing numbers of physicians. Doctors like the convenience that tablets provide, making it possible to tap the power of computers while avoiding trips to adjacent offices to look up information in books or computers. Although not all doctors use tablets (yet, at least), as increasingly powerful apps get developed, experts expect these devices to become as commonplace as the stethoscope. (Actually, at least one company has already developed a stethoscope app.)

needed to work in newly designed organizations and is, therefore, also known as **rightsizing**.[19] Whatever you call it, the bottom line is clear: many organizations need fewer people to operate today than in the past—sometimes far fewer. In one way or another, technology is involved in this process. For example, as technology reduces the number of people required to produce products, old jobs are eliminated. However, new jobs in the field of IT are created, ultimately changing not only the number of people working, but the very nature of what they do.

OUTSOURCING AND OFFSHORING   Another way in which technology has been changing organizations is by completely eliminating those departments that focus on noncore sectors of the business (i.e., tasks that are peripheral to the organization) and hiring outside firms to perform these functions instead. This is known as **outsourcing**.[20] Advances in communication technology, such as *VOIP (voice over Internet protocol),* make it feasible for individuals to stay in touch with people performing work for them in other locations. By outsourcing secondary activities, an organization can focus on what it does best. This key capability is known as its **core competency**. Companies like ServiceMaster, which provides janitorial services, and ADP, which provides payroll processing services, make it possible for their client organizations to concentrate on the business functions most central to their missions. So, for example, by outsourcing its maintenance work or its payroll processing, a manufacturing company may grow smaller and focus its resources on what it does best—manufacturing.

Some critics fear that outsourcing represents a "hollowing out" of companies—a reduction of functions that weakens organizations by making them more dependent on others.[21] It has been countered that outsourcing makes sense when the work that is outsourced is not highly critical to competitive success (e.g., janitorial services) or when it is so highly critical that it only can succeed by seeking outside assistance.[22] For example, it is widespread practice for companies selling personal computers today to outsource the manufacturing of various components (e.g., hard drives, optical disk drives, and chips) to other companies.[23] Although this practice may sound atypical compared to what occurs in most manufacturing companies, it isn't. In fact, the vast majority of organizations today outsource some portion of their business functions to outside firms.[24]

Often, the business that's outsourced is lost to companies in other nations. This process of shifting jobs to nations other than one's homeland is known as **offshoring**, which is short for offshore outsourcing. The most common use of offshoring occurs in the IT field, where some 69 percent of companies outsource their IT services, such as Web site hosting, network servicing, and help desks.[25] Because offshoring results in a loss of jobs in one's home country, the process of offshoring is frequently criticized. For example, General Electric's CEO, Jeff Immelt, has complained that American companies are moving too many job overseas, and that this process ultimately will be costly because the lost jobs at home result in lowered consumer spending.[26]

THE VIRTUAL CORPORATION   As more companies are outsourcing various organizational functions and are paring down to their core competencies, they might not be able to perform all the tasks required to complete a project. However, they can certainly perform their own highly specialized part of it very well. Now, if you put together several organizations whose competencies complement each other and have them work together on a special project, you'd have a very strong group of collaborators. This is the idea behind an organizational arrangement that is growing in popularity—the **virtual corporation**. A virtual corporation is a highly flexible, temporary organization formed by a group of companies that join forces to exploit a specific opportunity.[27]

For example, various companies often come together to work on special projects in the entertainment industry (e.g., to produce a motion picture) and in the field of construction (e.g., to build a shopping center). After all, technologies are changing so rapidly and skills are becoming so specialized these days that no one company can do everything by itself. And so, firms join forces temporarily to form virtual corporations—not permanent organizations, but temporary ones without their own offices or organization charts. Virtual corporations have been growing in popularity.[28] As one consultant put it, "It's not just a good idea; it's inevitable."[29]

TELECOMMUTING   In recent years, the practice of **telecommuting** (also known as **teleworking**) has grown in popularity. This is the practice of using communications technology (e.g., the Internet) to enable work to be performed from remote locations, such as the home. The underlying idea is that work is something you do, not someplace you go.[30]

Although we often think of home workers when discussing telecommuting, it's important to note that many workers opt for locations other than their homes or full-time company offices. Among these are the following practices.

- *Distributed work*—For many, the bulk of the work they do requires them to be outside the confines of traditional offices. Sales representatives, for example, spend lots of time meeting in their clients' offices. Such arrangements are known as **distributed work** because the work is distributed across various locations.
- *Office hoteling*—Once the offsite aspects of their jobs have been completed, employees may find it necessary to return to a home office. For such individuals, who work offsite more than onsite, it makes little sense to maintain permanent offices. Instead, many companies today allow employees to reserve offices on an as-needed basis. Because this reservation system works like getting a hotel room, the practice is called **office hoteling**.
- *Coworking spaces*—Many people are used to working with other people around them and don't like being alone. Sometimes, such individuals get together with others in shared offices or coffee shops so they can avoid isolation and benefit from the synergies of being around others. The places where this goes on are known as **coworking spaces**.
- *Jellies*—Sometimes, coworking spaces are provided in temporary special events referred to as "jellies."[31] A jelly is an informal gathering of people who desire one another's company while working independently. Jellies have been held in hundreds of places throughout the United States in diverse locations including various coffee houses and people's homes.

Statistics indicate that telecommuting is in full swing today but that its use is somewhat limited. Of approximately 130 million U.S. workers, only about 2.5 million (approximately 2 percent) use their homes as their primary workplaces and 17.2 million (approximately 13 percent) work offsite only occasionally.[32] In the private sector, full-time telecommuting is used most widely by call centers, where equipment is installed in people's homes that allows them to perform their jobs from there. And, with over 100,000 employees, the U.S. Office of Personnel Management has a vast network of teleworkers who can do their jobs without having to brave the frustrating commutes of Washington, DC.[33] This is only one of many possible benefits of telecommuting. For a summary of these, see Table 1.3.[34]

Despite these benefits, as you might imagine, telecommuting is not for everyone; it also has its limitations.[35] It works best on jobs that require concentration, have well-defined beginning and end points, are easily portable, call for minimal amounts of special equipment, and can be done with little supervision.[36] Fortunately, at least some aspects of most sales and professional

TABLE 1.3	Potential Benefits of Telecommuting

When its use is possible, the potential benefits of telecommuting are numerous and fall into the three categories summarized here.

Category	Benefit
Benefits to individuals	• Savings in commuting time • Savings of commuting expenses • Flexibility in working hours • Savings from not having to buy work clothes
Benefits to companies	• Attracts employees who desire telework • Makes it possible to hire some disabled employees • Savings in office expenses • Enhances compliance with Clean Air Act
Benefits to communities	• Reduces traffic congestion • Reduces greenhouse gas emissions that harm the environment

Sources: Based on information in Amigoni & Gurvis, 2009, and Truex, 2009; see Note 34.

jobs meet these standards. Even so, making telecommuting work requires careful adjustments in the way work is done. For a closer look at these considerations, see Figure 1.4.

OB Takes a Global Perspective

To understand behavior in organizations fully, we must appreciate the fact that today's organizations operate within an economic system that is truly international in scope.[37] The nations of the world are not isolated from one another economically; what happens in one country has effects on other countries. As an illustration, consider how losses in many European banks in 2011 sent economic shockwaves throughout the global financial community. This tendency for the world's countries to be influenced by one another is known as **globalization**—the process of interconnecting the world's people with respect to the cultural, economic, political, technological, and environmental aspects of their lives.[38]

The trend toward globalization, widespread in recent years, has been driven by three major forces. First, technology has been involved in several ways. Technology has drastically lowered the cost of transportation and communication, thereby enhancing opportunities for international commerce. Second, laws restricting trade generally have become liberalized throughout the world (e.g., in the United States and other heavily industrialized countries, free trade policies have been advocated). Third, developing nations have sought to expand their economies by promoting exports and opening their doors to foreign companies seeking investments.

If international trade is the major driver of globalization, then the primary vehicles are **multinational enterprises (MNEs)**—organizations that have significant operations (typically 25 percent or more of their output capacity) spread throughout various nations but headquartered in a single nation. As of 2011, the top five largest MNEs in the world were Walmart Stores, Royal Dutch Shell, ExxonMobil, British Petroleum (BP), and Sinopec (Chinese Petroleum

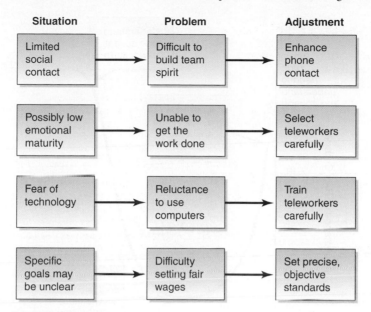

Situation	Problem	Adjustment
Limited social contact	Difficult to build team spirit	Enhance phone contact
Possibly low emotional maturity	Unable to get the work done	Select teleworkers carefully
Fear of technology	Reluctance to use computers	Train teleworkers carefully
Specific goals may be unclear	Difficulty setting fair wages	Set precise, objective standards

FIGURE 1.4 Adapting to Telecommuting

Jobs in which people engage in telecommuting often have to be adjusted in one way or another. Some of the major considerations are summarized here.

and Chemical Corporation).[39] Interestingly, not too many years ago, such lists also contained automakers (e.g., General Motors and Ford), but given their financial downturns in recent years, it's not surprising to find that they no longer appear. Still, the companies that sell oil and gasoline to fuel our cars dominate this list. This includes BP, despite losses suffered from its 2010 oil spill in the Gulf of Mexico.

As you might imagine, the rise of MNEs has resulted in large numbers of people who are citizens of one country but who live and work in another country for some extended periods of time. Such individuals are known as **expatriates,** or **expats** for short. Over the years, the number of expats throughout the world has risen, fallen, and changed direction along with shifts in economic development throughout the world. As economies grow in various countries, MNEs establish offices there to capitalize on the boom. By the same token, shrinking economies sometimes leave expats without jobs in their newly adopted nations. This occurred in Dubai in 2009 on a very large scale, as this once-booming Middle Eastern country went bust. Some 3.62 million expats had to return home after their formerly lucrative jobs dried up; it was impossible for them to maintain the lavish lifestyles they lived in Dubai during the good times.[40]

While working abroad, people are exposed to different **cultures**—the set of values, customs, and beliefs that people have in common with other members of a social unit (e.g., a nation).[41] And, when people are faced with new cultures, it is not unusual for them to become confused and disoriented—a phenomenon known as **culture shock**.[42] People also experience culture shock when they return to their native cultures after spending time away from them—a process of re-adjustment known as **repatriation**. In general, the phenomenon of culture shock results from people's recognition of the fact that others may be different from them in ways that they never imagined, and this takes some getting used to.

Scientists have observed that the process of adjusting to a foreign culture generally follows a U-shaped curve (see Figure 1.5).[43] That is, at first, people are optimistic and excited about

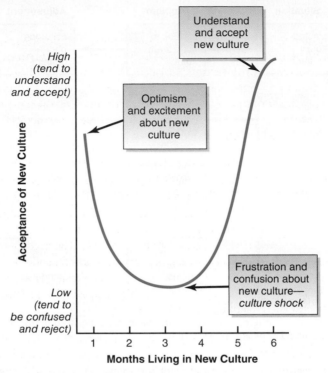

FIGURE 1.5   Adjusting to Foreign Culture: The General Stages
People's adjustment to new cultures generally follows the U-shaped curve illustrated here. After an initial period of excitement, *culture shock* often sets in. Then, after this period of adjustment (about six months), the more time spent in the new culture, the better it is accepted.

learning a new culture. This usually lasts about a month or so. Then, for the next several months, they become frustrated and confused as they struggle to learn their new cultures (i.e., culture shock occurs). Finally, after about six months, people adjust to their new cultures and become more accepting of and satisfied with them. These observations imply that feelings of culture shock are inevitable. Although some degree of frustration may be expected when you first enter a new country, the more time you spend learning its ways, the better you will come to understand and accept it.[44]

In general, culture shock results from the tendency for people to be highly *parochial* in their assumptions about others, taking a narrow view of the world by believing that there is one best way of doing things. They also tend to be highly *ethnocentric,* believing that their way of doing things is the best way. For example, Americans tend to be highly parochial by speaking only English (whereas most Europeans speak several languages), and ethnocentric by believing that everyone else in the world should learn their language.

As I just explained, over time, exposure to other cultures teaches people that there may be many different ways of doing the same thing (making them less parochial), and that these ways may be equally good, if not better (making them less ethnocentric). Although these biases may have been reasonable for Americans over 50 years ago, when the United States was the world's dominant economic power (producing three-quarters of its wealth), they would be extremely costly today. Indeed, because the world's economy is global in nature, suggesting that highly parochial and ethnocentric views have no place in contemporary organizations.

OB Embraces the Trend Toward Diversity

A broad range of people from both sexes, different races, ethnic groups, nationalities, and ages can be found throughout U.S. organizations. Indeed, the relative proportion of whites has dropped and is projected to drop further in the future. At the same time, the relative proportion of so-called minority groups has grown and is expected to grow further still in the years ahead.[45] Modern organizations have taken steps to accommodate—and capitalize on—growing levels of diversity within the workforce. This trend takes several forms, all of which have important implications for the field of OB.

MORE WOMEN ARE IN THE WORKFORCE THAN EVER BEFORE   In the 1950s, the "typical American family" was characterized by a man who went to work and his wife who stayed at home and watched the children. Although this profile still may be found, it is far from typical. In fact, over half of all women are employed outside the home, and half of all people in the workplace are women—and these figures have continued to rise steadily over the years.[46] This trend stems from not only economic necessity but also from the growing social acceptance of women working outside the home. As women, who traditionally have worked inside the home, have moved to working outside the home, companies have found it beneficial—or even necessary, in some cases—to make accommodations that help make this possible. The practice of making onsite childcare facilities available to employees is one such example.

RACIAL AND ETHNIC DIVERSITY IS REALITY   Just as yesterday's workers were primarily males, they also were primarily white. However, just as growing numbers of women have made men less of a majority, so too have increases in the numbers of people from different racial and ethnic groups made white people a smaller majority. Specifically, although white non-Hispanic workers are currently the dominant group, their proportion has been dropping and is expected to drop further in the years to come (see Figure 1.6 on p. 20).[47] At the same time, there have been increases in the proportions of African Americans, Hispanics, and Asians in the workforce, and these figures are expected to rise in the coming decades. Primarily because of a large influx of Latino and Hispanic immigrants, these individuals are projected to show the greatest proportional increase in the workforce. These trends are so strong that by 2050, today's so-called racial and ethnic minorities will make up about half of the U.S. population, altering what is meant by "minority group."[48]

PEOPLE ARE LIVING—AND WORKING—LONGER THAN EVER BEFORE   In the years after World War II, the peacetime economy flourished in the United States. With it, came a large increase in population as soldiers returned from war and began families. The generation of children born during this period is widely referred to as the **baby boom generation**. Today, the first of these baby boomers are turning 55 and are considered "older workers" by labor economists. In addition, only a few years from now, the number of older people in the workplace will swell dramatically. Living in a period in which retirement is no longer automatic at age 65, aged baby boomers will account for a growing part of the population in the years to come. In fact, people over 85 years old are already the fastest-growing segment of the U.S. population.[49] Clearly, this trend has profound implications on the traditional patterns of work and retirement that have developed over the years.

IMPLICATIONS FOR OB   The fact that more women, people of color, and older workers are in the workforce than ever before is not merely an idle sociological curiosity. It also has important implications for OB—ones that we will examine more closely in this book. After all, the more people differ from each other, the more challenges they are likely to face when interacting with one another. How these interactions play out is likely to be seen on the job in important ways. For example, as

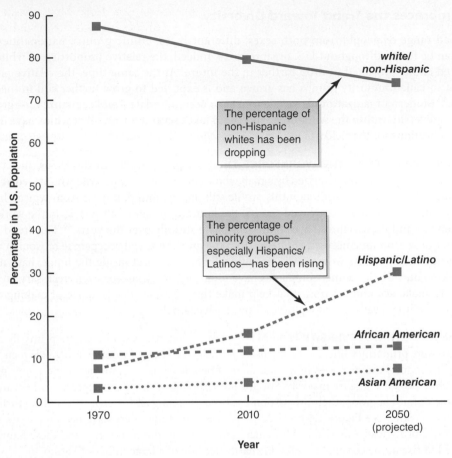

FIGURE 1.6 Minorities in the Workplace: Their Numbers Are Rising
Statistics reveal that the relative percentage of white non-Hispanics in the U.S. workforce, although currently highest, is dropping. However, the relative percentage of African Americans, Hispanics/Latinos, and Asian Americans is rising. As this trend continues, the term *minority* group will lose its meaning.
Source: Based on data reported by Bureau of Labor Statistics, 2012; see Note 45.

I will describe, differences in age, gender, and ethnic group membership are likely to bring with them differences in communication style that must be addressed for organizations to function effectively (see Chapter 8). It also is the case that people at different stages of their lives are likely to be motivated by different things (see Chapter 6) and to be satisfied with different aspects of their jobs (see Chapter 5). Furthermore, as workers adjust to a wider variety of people in the workplace, issues about their norms (see Chapter 9) are likely to come up, as well as their willingness to accept others who are different from themselves (see Chapter 5). This can have important implications for potential stress and conflict in the workplace (see Chapters 4 and 7), which may be expected to influence their capacity to work effectively as members of the same work teams (see Chapter 9).

HISTORICAL OVERVIEW OF THE FIELD OF OB

The importance of understanding the behavior of people at work has not always been as recognized as it is today. In fact, it was not until the early part of the twentieth century that the idea first developed, and it was only during the last few decades that it gained widespread acceptance. Now, in the twenty-first century, it is clear that the field has blossomed and matured. So that we can appreciate how the field of OB got to where it is today, I now briefly outline its history and describe some of the most influential forces in its development.

Scientific Management: The Roots of Organizational Behavior

The earliest attempts to study behavior in organizations came out of a desire by industrial efficiency experts to improve worker productivity. Their central question was straightforward: What could be done to get people do more work in less time? It's not particularly surprising that attempts to answer this question were made at the turn of the twentieth century. After all, this was a period of rapid industrialization and technological change in the United States. As engineers attempted to make machines more efficient, it was a natural extension of their efforts to work on the human side of the equation—making people more productive too. Given this history, it should not be too surprising that the earliest people we now credit for their contributions to OB were actually industrial engineers.

Frederick Winslow Taylor worked most of his life in steel mills, starting as a laborer and working his way up to the position of chief engineer. In the 1880s, while a foreman at Philadelphia's Midvale Steel Company, Taylor became aware of some of the inefficient practices of the employees.[50] Noticing, for example, that laborers wasted movements when shifting pig iron, Taylor studied the individual components of this task and identified a set of the most efficient motions needed to perform it. A few years later, while at Pittsburgh's Bethlehem Steel, Taylor similarly redesigned the job of loading and unloading railcars so that these tasks too could be done as efficiently as possible. On the heels of these experiences, Taylor published his groundbreaking book, *Scientific Management*. In this work, he argued that the objective of management is "to secure the maximum prosperity for the employer, coupled with the maximum prosperity of each employee."[51]

Beyond identifying ways in which manual-labor jobs can be performed more efficiently, Taylor's **scientific management** approach was unique in its focus on the role of employees as individuals. Specifically, his approach emphasized the importance of designing jobs as efficiently as possible. Taylor advocated two ideas that hardly seem special today but were quite new at the beginning of the twentieth century. First, he recommended that employees be carefully selected and trained to perform their jobs. Second, he believed that increasing workers' wages would raise their motivation and make them more productive. Although this idea is unsophisticated by today's standards—and not completely accurate (as we will see in Chapter 6)—Taylor may be credited with recognizing the important role of motivation in job performance.

It was contributions such as these that stimulated further study of behavior in organizations and created an intellectual climate that eventually paved the way for the development of the field of OB. Acknowledging these contributions, management theorist Peter Drucker described Taylor as "the first man in history who did not take work for granted, but who looked at it and studied it."[52]

The publication of *Scientific Management* stimulated several other scientists to pick up on and expand Taylor's ideas. Among the most strongly influenced were the industrial psychologists Frank and Lillian Gilbreth. This husband-and-wife team pioneered an approach known as **time-and-motion study**, a type of applied research designed to classify and streamline the individual movements needed to perform jobs with the intent of finding "the one best way" to perform them. Although this approach appears to be highly mechanical and dehumanizing, the Gilbreths, parents of 12 children, practiced "Taylorism" with a human face in their personal lives. (If this sounds at all familiar, it may be because you recall the classic film *Cheaper by the Dozen*, which tells the story of how the Gilbreths applied the principles of scientific management to their own rather large household.)

The Human Relations Movement and the Hawthorne Studies

Although scientific management highlighted the importance of the efficient performance of work, it did not go far enough in directing our attention to the wide variety of factors that might influence work behavior. In fact, many experts rejected Taylorism, favoring instead an approach that focused on employees' own views and emphasized respect for individuals.

At the forefront of this orientation was Elton W. Mayo, an organizational scientist and consultant widely regarded as the founder of what is called the **human relations movement**. This management philosophy rejects the primarily economic orientation of scientific management and focuses instead on the noneconomic, social factors operating in the workplace. Mayo and other proponents of the human relations movement recognized that task performance was greatly influenced by the social conditions that existed in organizations—that is, the way employees were treated by management and the relationships they had with each other. For a comparison between scientific management and the human relations movement, see Table 1.4.

In 1927, a series of studies was begun at Western Electric's Hawthorne Works outside Chicago. The researchers were interested in determining several things, including the effects of illumination on work productivity. How brightly or dimly lit should the work environment be for people to produce at their maximum level? Two groups of female employees took part in the study. One group, the control room condition, did their jobs without any changes in lighting; the other group, the test room condition, worked while the lighting was systematically varied, sometimes getting brighter and sometimes getting dimmer. The results were puzzling: productivity increased in both locations. Just as surprising, there was no clear connection between illumination and performance. In fact, output in the test room remained high even when the level of illumination was so low that workers could barely see what they were doing!

In another study conducted at the company's Bank Wiring Room, male members of various work groups were observed during regular working conditions and interviewed at length after work. In this investigation, no attempts were made to alter the work environment. What Mayo found here also was surprising. Namely, instead of improving their performance, employees deliberately restricted their output. Not only did the researchers actually see the men stopping work long before quitting time, but also in interviews the men admitted that they easily could have done more if they desired.

Why did this occur? Eventually, Mayo and his associates recognized that the answer resided in the fact that organizations are social systems. How effectively people worked depended, in great part, not only on the physical aspects of the working conditions experienced but also on the social conditions encountered. In the Hawthorne studies, Mayo noted, productivity rose simply because people responded favorably to the special attention they received. Knowing they were

---

TABLE 1.4 Scientific Management Versus the Human Relations Movement: A Summary

Although both are early approaches to the study of behavior in organizations, *scientific management* and the *human relations movement* are different in several key ways summarized here.

Basis of Difference	Scientific Management	Human Relations Movement
Primary focus	Human efficiency on the job	Social conditions in organizations
Objective	To improve productivity by minimizing wasted movements	To improve productivity by developing good working relationships
Major proponent	Frederick Winslow Taylor	Elton Mayo

being studied made them feel special and motivated them to do their best. Hence, it was these social factors more than the physical factors that had such profound effects on job performance.

The same explanation applied in the Bank Wiring Room study as well. Here the employees feared that, because they were being studied, the company would eventually raise the amount of work they were expected to do. So to guard against the imposition of unreasonable standards (and, hopefully, to keep their jobs!), the men agreed among themselves to keep output low. In other words, informal rules known as *norms* (a topic we will discuss more thoroughly in Chapter 9) were established about what constituted acceptable levels of job performance. These social forces at work in this setting proved to be much more potent determinants of job performance than the physical factors studied.

This conclusion, based on the surprising findings of the Hawthorne studies, is important because it ushered in a whole new way of thinking about behavior at work. It suggests that to understand behavior on the job, we must fully appreciate people's attitudes and the processes they use to communicate with each other. This way of thinking, so fundamental to modern OB, may be traced back to Elton Mayo's pioneering Hawthorne studies. Although the research was flawed in some important ways (e.g., conditions in the study rooms were not carefully controlled), what they revealed about the importance of human needs, attitudes, motives, and relationships in the workplace was quite influential and novel for its time.

Classical Organizational Theory

During the same time that proponents of scientific management got people to begin thinking about the interrelationships between workers and their jobs, another approach to managing people emerged. This perspective, known as **classical organizational theory**, focused on the efficient structuring of organizations. This is in contrast, of course, to scientific management, which sought to effectively organize the work of individuals.

Although several different theorists are identified with classical organizational theory, two of the best known are Henri Fayol and Max Weber. Fayol was a French industrialist who attributed his managerial success to various principles he developed, which included the following:

- A division of labor should be used because it allows people to specialize, doing only what they do best.
- Managers should have authority over their subordinates, the right to order them to do what's necessary for the organization.
- Lines of authority should be uninterrupted; that is, a clear chain of command should connect top management to the lowest-level employees.
- There should exist a clearly defined unity of command, such that employees receive directions from only one other person so as to avoid confusion.
- Subordinates should be allowed to formulate and implement their own plans.

Although many of these principles are still well accepted today, it is widely recognized that they should not always be applied in exactly the same way. For example, whereas some organizations thrive on being structured according to a unity of command, others require that some employees take directions from several different superiors. I will have more to say about this subject when we discuss various types of organizational designs in Chapter 13. For now, suffice it to say that current organizational theorists owe a debt of gratitude to Fayol for his pioneering and far-reaching ideas.

Probably the best-known classical organizational theorist is the German sociologist Max Weber. Among other things, Weber proposed a form of organizational structure well-known today—the **bureaucracy**. Weber's idea was that the bureaucracy is the one best way to efficiently

TABLE 1.5	Characteristics of an Ideal Bureaucracy

According to Max Weber, bureaucracies are the ideal organizational form. To function effectively, however, they must possess the characteristics identified here.

Characteristics	Description
Formal rules and regulations	Written guidelines are used to control all employees' behaviors.
Impersonal treatment	Favoritism is to be avoided; all work relationships are to be based on objective standards.
Division of labor	All duties are divided into specialized tasks and are performed by individuals with the appropriate skills.
Hierarchical structure	Positions are ranked by authority level in clear fashion from lower-level to upper-level ones.
Authority structure	The making of decisions is determined by one's position in the hierarchy; higher-ranking people have authority over those in lower-ranking positions.
Lifelong career commitment	Employment is viewed as a permanent, lifelong obligation on the part of the organization and its employees.
Rationality	The organization is committed to achieving its ends (e.g., profitability) in the most efficient manner possible.

organize work in all organizations—much as proponents of scientific management searched for the ideal way to perform a job.[53] The elements of an ideal bureaucracy are summarized in Table 1.5.

When you think about bureaucracies, negative images probably come to mind of lots of inflexible people getting bogged down in lots of red tape. Weber's "universal" view of bureaucratic structure lies in contrast to the more modern approaches to organizational design (see Chapter 13) in which it is recognized that different forms of organizational structure may be more or less appropriate under different situations. Although the bureaucracy may not have proven to be the perfect structure for organizing all work, many of Weber's ideas are still considered viable today.

Despite differences between Fayol's and Weber's principles for organizing work, both approaches assume that there is a single most effective way to structure organizations. Although, as noted earlier, such approaches seem simplistic by modern standards, we are indebted to Fayol, Weber, and other classical management theorists for calling our attention to the important effects of organizational design.

Organizational Behavior in the Modern Era

The pioneering contributions noted thus far set the stage for the emergence of the modern science of organizational behavior. Although the first doctoral degrees in OB were granted in the 1940s, the field's early growth was uneven. It was not until the late 1950s and early 1960s that OB became a going concern. By that time, active programs of research were occurring, including investigations of such key processes as motivation and leadership and of the impact of organizational structure on productivity.

Stimulated by a report by the Ford Foundation in the 1960s, which advocated that students trained in business receive firm grounding in the social sciences, the field of OB rapidly grew into one that borrowed heavily from other disciplines. In fact, the field of OB as we know it today may be characterized as a hybrid science that draws from many social science fields (recall Table 1.2 on p. 7). For example, studies of motivation and work-related attitudes, dealing as they do with the processes of learning and perception, draw on psychology. Similarly, the study of group dynamics and leadership relies heavily on sociology. The topic of organizational communication, obviously, draws on research in the field of communication. And OB scientists look to the field of management science to understand the design of organizational hierarchies and other structural arrangements. Taken together, it is clear that modern OB has become a truly multifaceted and interdisciplinary field.

Today, in the second decade of the twenty-first century, the field of OB has added a few new characteristics worth noting. These reflect both changes that are occurring in the world as a whole and that have occurred as a result of advances in the science over the years. Although there are too many new developments to mention them all, a few current trends deserve to be pointed out.

- In keeping with the ever-growing globalization of business, the field of OB has been paying more attention than ever to the *cross-cultural aspects of behavior*, acknowledging that our understanding of organizational phenomena may not be universal. Today, research that considers the international generalizability of OB phenomena is considered key to understanding organizational competitiveness in a global society. Acknowledging this trend, you will find multicultural examples of OB throughout this book.
- The study of *unethical behavior in organizations* is considered more important than ever before. Indeed, OB scientists are fascinated by understanding the factors that lead people to make ethical or unethical decisions and by their willingness to engage in such counterproductive behaviors as lying, cheating, stealing, and acting aggressively.[54] I will describe some of the factors that motivate people to behave unethically in Chapter 2 and various forms of counterproductive behavior in Chapter 7.
- That the body and mind are interconnected is well accepted in many scientific fields but until recently, organizational scientists have paid attention to human physiology in only one limited context—the study of workplace stress. Although bodily reactions to stress surely are important to understand (as we will discuss in Chapter 4), we now recognize that the human physiological systems are responsive to a wide variety of situations encountered in the workplace.[55] For example, as I will show in Chapter 2, research using fMRIs (machines that measure the flow of blood in people's brains) reveals that the portions of the brain associated with negative emotions are activated in individuals who believe that they have been treated unfairly.[56]
- OB scientists are interested in harnessing the power of diversity that has become a fact of organizational life today.[57] Racially and ethnically diverse employees help bring a wide variety of perspectives to the workplace that tend to improve the quality of organizational decisions. On the other hand, this benefit is too often threatened by prejudice and discrimination against such individuals. These issues are a major concern to today's OB specialists (see Chapter 5).
- The era of the employee who works from 9 to 5 and who stays with a single company all his or her life is rapidly fading. Today, many people are choosing to work part-time and to change jobs many times during their careers. These alternative work arrangements have important implications for the field of OB, as we will see in Chapter 4.
- Traditionally, people either worked alone or in small groups in which they had clear-cut responsibilities. Today, however, because it is common for people to work as members of teams, it is not only individuals but also entire team products for which individuals are responsible. As a result, employees tend to have more responsibilities than ever before and

are paid in ways that reflect their teams' accomplishments. Naturally, such developments are important to the field of OB, and I will discuss them more fully in Chapter 9.

- Organizations are facing *unrelenting change*—a fact that has not escaped the attention of OB scientists and practitioners. For example, as you will see in Chapter 14, the field pays a great deal of attention to how people cope with change, and it seeks ways of encouraging people to accept change. After all, unless people adapt to the changes, their organizations will find it difficult to thrive—or even to survive.

As you read this book, you will learn more about not only the traditional issues of concern in OB but also about these rapidly developing topics. One thing that makes the field of OB so interesting is that these trends, and many others, are all operating at once, making organizations highly concerned about a wide variety of OB principles and practices.

WHAT LIES AHEAD IN THIS BOOK?

Now that you know what the field of OB is all about, you are in a good position to appreciate what to expect as you continue reading this book. In the chapters ahead, you will learn about a wide variety of organizational behavior phenomena. My orientation will reflect the dual purposes of the field of OB—understanding and practical application. In other words, the focus will be on both basic processes as well as ways these can be applied to organizational practice. And, just to eliminate doubt about whether this material really matters in organizations, I will share lots of current examples to illustrate how OB principles have been followed within actual companies.

This book is organized around the three units of analysis described in this chapter— individuals, groups, and organizations. Specifically, Part II consists of Chapters 3–6, focusing on individual behavior. Part III, consisting of Chapters 7–11, examines group behavior. And finally, in Part IV, with Chapters 12–14, attention will be paid to organization-level processes.

In a sense, these distinctions are artificial because anything that happens in an organization is a blend of forces stemming from all three sources. With this in mind, you can expect to see several important connections between topics as you go through this book. These connections are indeed real and reflect the complexities of the field of OB as well as its multidisciplinary nature.

Rather than finding them frustrating, I believe you will come to appreciate the fascination they hold. After all, the field of OB can be no less complex than people themselves—and, as you know, we are not all that simple to understand! So with all this in mind, I hope you enjoy your tour of the field of OB presented in the next thirteen chapters.

Back to the Case

Answer the following questions based on this chapter's Making the Case (p. 3) to illustrate insights you have derived from the material in this chapter.

1. Going beyond the obvious rises and falls in stock prices, what other changing socioeconomic conditions in today's business environment may be expected to affect the nature of business at Edward Jones?
2. Does it appear that a Theory X or Theory Y approach is embraced at Edward Jones? On what do you base your answer?
3. How may advances in technology have changed the nature of work at Edward Jones? Consider changes that may have made things better and that may have made things worse.

You Be the Consultant

Designing the Office Environment

A large publishing company hires you to help design a new suite of offices in which proofreaders will be working. Your task is to determine the level of illumination that helps the proofreaders work most effectively. Answer the following questions relevant to this situation based on the material in this chapter.

1. What specific research method do you think would best provide an answer? Explain your answer.

2. How would managers adopting the Theory X philosophy differ from those adopting the Theory Y philosophy in approaching this issue?

3. What would be the major approach of Taylor's scientific management orientation to this matter? How would this differ from the approach taken by Mayo's human relations orientation?

Self-Assessment Exercise

TESTING YOUR ASSUMPTIONS ABOUT PEOPLE AT WORK: THEORY X OR THEORY Y?

What assumptions do you make about human nature? Are you inclined to think of people as primarily lazy and disinterested in working (a Theory X approach) or as willing to work hard under the right conditions (a Theory Y approach)? This exercise is designed to give you some insight into this question.

Directions

For each of the following eight pairs of statements, select the one that better reflects your feelings by marking the letter that corresponds to it.

1. (a) If you give people what they need to do their jobs, they will act very responsibly.
   (b) Giving people more information than they need will lead them to misuse it.
2. (c) People naturally want to get away with doing as little work as possible.
   (d) When people avoid working, it's probably because the work itself has been stripped of its meaning.
3. (e) It's not surprising to find that employees don't demonstrate much creativity on the job, because people tend not to have much of it to begin with.
   (f) Although many people are by nature very creative, they don't show it on the job, because they aren't given a chance.
4. (g) It doesn't pay to ask employees for their ideas, because their perspective is generally too limited to be of value.
   (h) When you ask employees for ideas, you are likely to get some useful suggestions.
5. (i) The more information people have about their jobs, the more closely their supervisors have to keep them in line.
   (j) The more information people have about their jobs, the less closely they have to be supervised.
6. (k) Once people are paid enough, the less they tend to care about being recognized for a job well done.
   (l) The more interesting the work is that people do, the less likely they care about their pay.
7. (m) Supervisors lose prestige when they admit that their subordinates may have been right whereas they were wrong.
   (n) Supervisors gain prestige when they admit that their subordinates may have been right whereas they were wrong.
8. (o) When people are held accountable for their mistakes, they raise their standards.
   (p) Unless people are punished for their mistakes, they will lower their standards.

Scoring

1. Give yourself one point for selecting b, c, e, g, i, k, m, and p. The sum of these points is your Theory X score.
2. Give yourself one point for selecting a, d, f, h, j, l, n, and o. The sum of these points is your Theory Y score.

Discussion Questions

1. Which perspective did this questionnaire indicate that you more strongly endorse, Theory X or Theory Y? Is this consistent with your own intuitive conclusion?
2. Do you tend to manage others in ways consistent with Theory X or Theory Y ideas?
3. Can you recall any experiences that may have been crucial in defining or reinforcing your Theory X or Theory Y philosophy?

Group Exercise

PUTTING YOUR COMMON SENSE ABOUT OB TO THE TEST

Even if you already have a good intuitive sense about behavior in organizations, some of what you think may be inconsistent with established research findings (many of which are noted in this book). So that you don't have to rely on your own judgments (which may be idiosyncratic), working with others in this exercise will give you a good sense of what our collective common sense has to say about behavior in organizations. You just may be enlightened.

Directions

Divide the class into groups of approximately five students. Then within these groups, discuss the following statements and reach a consensus as to whether each is true or false. Spend approximately 30 minutes on the entire discussion.

1. People who are satisfied with one job tend to be satisfied with other jobs too.
2. Because "two heads are better than one," groups make better decisions than individuals.
3. The best leaders always act the same ways in all situations they face.
4. Specific goals make people nervous; people work better when asked to do their best.
5. People get bored easily, leading them to welcome organizational change.
6. Money is the best motivator.
7. Interpersonal conflict is always disruptive and never facilitates the performance of work groups and teams.
8. People generally shy away from challenges on the job.

Scoring

Give your group one point for each item you scored as follows: 1 = True, 2 = False, 3 = False, 4 = False, 5 = False, 6 = False, 7 = False, and 8 = False. Should you have questions about these answers, information bearing on them appears in this book as follows: 1 = Chapter 5, 2 = Chapter 10, 3 = Chapter 11, 4 = Chapter 6, 5 = Chapter 14, 6 = Chapter 6, 7 = Chapter 7, and 8 = Chapter 6.

Discussion Questions

1. How well did your group do? Were you stumped on a few?
2. Comparing your experiences to those of other groups, did you find that there were some questions that proved trickier than others (i.e., ones where the scientific findings were more counterintuitive)? If you did poorly, don't be frustrated. These statements are a bit simplistic and need to be qualified to be fully understood. Have your instructor explain the statements that the class found most challenging.
3. Did this exercise give you a better understanding of the sometimes surprising (and complex) nature of behavior in organizations?

Notes

MAKING THE CASE NOTES

Fortune (2010). 100 best companies to work for. http://money.cnn.com/magazines/fortune/bestcompanies/2010/snapshots/2.html/. Edward Jones: Industry-leading training. (2011). http://www.careers.edwardjones.com/fa/StartingYourFinancialSalesCareer/Training/index.html/. 18th annual broker report card. *Registered Rep.* (2011). http://www.edwardjones.com/groups/ejw_content/documents/web_content/web088828.pdf. Edward Jones: Our culture (2011). http://www.careers.edwardjones.com/ca/wej/OurCulture/index.html.

CHAPTER NOTES

1. Barling, J., & Cooper, C. L. (2008). *Sage handbook of organizational behavior.* Thousand Oaks, CA: Sage. Miner, J. B. (2002). *Organizational behavior: Foundations, theories, analyses.* New York: Oxford University Press.
2. Thompson, L., Kern, M., & Loyd, D. L. (2003). Research methods of micro organizational behavior. In C. Sansone, C. Morf, & A. Panter (Eds.), *Handbook of methods in social psychology* (pp. 457–470). Thousand Oaks, CA: Sage. Rogelberg, S. G. (2002). *Handbook of research methods in industrial and organizational psychology.* Malden, MA: Blackwell.
3. Risher, H. (1999). *Aligning pay and results.* New York: AMACOM.
4. Judge, T. A., & Church, A. H. (2000). Job satisfaction: Research and practice. In C. A. Cooper & E. A. Locke (Eds.), *Industrial and organizational psychology: Linking theory to practice* (pp. 166–198). Malden, MA: Blackwell.
5. Hackman, J. R., Wageman, R., Ruddy, T. M., & Ray, C. L. (2000). Team effectiveness in theory and in practice. In C. A. Cooper & E. A. Locke (Eds.), *Industrial and organizational psychology: Linking theory to practice* (pp. 109–129). Malden, MA: Blackwell.
6. Greenberg, J. (2011). Organizational justice: The dynamics of fairness in the workplace. In S. Zedeck (Ed.), *APA handbook of industrial/organizational psychology* (Vol. 3, pp. 271–328). Washington, DC: American Psychological Association.
7. Greenberg, J. (2010). Organizational injustice as an occupational risk factor. In J. Walsh &

A. P. Brief (Eds.), *Academy of management annals* (Vol. 4, pp. 205–242). New York: Routledge.
8. The Corporate Research Foundation UK. (2000). *Britain's best employers: A guide to the 100 most attractive companies to work for.* New York: McGraw-Hill.
9. Bollinger, D. (1996). *Aiming higher: 25 stories of how companies prosper by combining sound management and social vision.* New York: AMACOM.
10. Scott, W. R. (2007). *Organizations and organizing: Rational, natural, and open systems.* Upper Saddle River, NJ: Pearson. Katz, D., & Kahn, R. (1978). *The social psychology of organizations.* New York: Wiley.
11. It all depends where you sit. (2000, August 14). *Business Week*, Frontier Section, p. F8.
12. Bridges, W. (1994). *Job shift: How to prosper in a workplace without jobs.* Reading, MA: Addison-Wesley.
13. General Electric. (2002). *GE Fanuc automation: Programmable control products.* http://support.ge-ip.com/support/resources/sites/ge_fanuc_support/content/live/document/0/do213/en_us/gfk1541b.pdf.
14. First Research. (2010). *Industry profiles.* http://www.firstresearch.com/industry-research/Automobile-Manufacture.html.
15. Tomasko, R. M. (1990). *Downsizing: Reshaping the corporation for the future.* New York: AMACOM.
16. The Health Hawk. (2010, May 18). *25 iPad apps revolutionizing healthcare.* http://masterofpublichealth.org/2010/25-ipad-apps-revolutionizing-healthcare/.
17. World Health Organization. (2011). *FAQ on ICD.* http://www.who.int/classifications/help/icdfaq/en/index.html.
18. Physician's Desk Reference. (2011). *PDR: Sixty-fifth edition.* Williston, VT: PDR Network.
19. Hendricks, C. F. (1992). *The rightsizing remedy.* Homewood, IL: Business One Irwin.
20. Tomasko, R. M. (1993). *Rethinking the corporation,* New York: AMACOM.
21. Bettis, R. A., Bradley, S. P., & Hamel, G. (1992). Outsourcing and industrial decline. *Academy of Management Review, 6*, 7–22.
22. Haapaniemi, P. (1993, Winter). Taking care of business. *Solutions*, pp. 6–8, 10–13.
23. See Note 22.

24. Stewart, T. A. (1993, December 13). Welcome to the revolution. *Fortune*, pp. 66–68, 70, 72, 76, 78.

25. QWS. (2011). *The costs and gains of outsourcing and offshoring*. http://www.quality-web-solutions.com/cost-gain-offshore-outsourcing.php.

26. Bailey, D., & Soyoung, K. (2009, June 26). GE's Immelt says U.S. economy needs industrial renewal. *UK Guardian*. http://www.guardian.co.uk/business/feedarticle/8578904.

27. Goranson, H. T. (1999). *The agile virtual enterprise*. Greenwich, CT: Quorum.

28. Davidow, W. H., & Malone, M. S. (1992). *The virtual corporation*. New York: Harper Business.

29. See Note 28 (quote, p. 99).

30. Woody, L. (2005). *The underground guide to telecommuting*. Boston: Addison-Wesley.

31. What is a Jelly? (2011). http://workatjelly.com/.

32. Undres4success.com. (2011). *Telework savings calculator*. http://undress4success.com/research/telework-savings-calculator/.

33. U.S. Office of Personnel Management. (2009, August). *Status of telework in the federal government: Report to the Congress*. Washington, DC: Author. http://undress4success.com/research/telework-savings-calculator/.

34. Amigoni, M., & Gurvis, S., (2009). *Managing the telecommuting employee*. Avon, MA: Adams Business. Truex, L. (2009). *The work at home success bible*. Avon, MA. Adams Media.

35. DuBrin, A. J. (1994). *Contemporary applied management: Skills for managers* (4th ed.). Burr Ridge, IL: Irwin.

36. Mariani, M. (2000, Fall). Telecommuters. *Occupational Outlook Quarterly*, pp. 10–17.

37. Deresky, H. (2007). *International management*, 6th ed. Upper Saddle River, NJ: Prentice Hall.

38. Lodge, G. C. (1995). *Managing globalization in the age of interdependence*. San Francisco, CA: Pfeifer.

39. Fortune. (2011, May). *Global 500*. http://money.cnn.com/magazines/fortune/global500/2011/index.html.

40. Triggs, J. (2009, February 7). British expats flee Dubai. *Express.Co.UK*: http://www.express.co.uk/posts/view/83804.

41. Ogbonna, E. (1993). Managing organizational culture: Fantasy or reality? *Human Resource Management Journal, 3*(2), 42–54.

42. DeCieri, H., & Dowling, P. J. (1995). Cross-cultural issues in organizational behavior. In C. L. Cooper & D. M. Rousseau (Eds.), *Trends in organizational behavior* (Vol. 2, pp. 127–145). New York: Wiley.

43. Hesketh, B., & Bochner, S. (1994). Technological change in a multicultural context: Implications for training and career planning. In Triandis, H. C., Dunnette, M. D., & Hough, L. (Eds.), *Handbook of industrial and organizational psychology* (Vol. 4, pp. 190–240). Palo Alto, CA: Consulting Psychologists Press.

44. Janssens, M. (1995). Intercultural interaction: A burden on international managers? *Journal of Organizational Behavior, 16*, 155–167.

45. Bureau of Labor Statistics. (2012). www.bls.gov.

46. U.S. Department of Commerce. (2011, March). *Women in America: Indications of social and economic well-being*. Washington, DC: Author.

47. See Note 45.

48. Carnevale, A. P., & Stone, S. C. (1995). *The American mosaic: An in-depth report on the future of diversity at work*. New York: McGraw Hill.

49. See Note 48.

50. Kanigel, R. (1997). *The one best way*. New York: Viking.

51. Taylor, F. W. (1947). *Scientific management*. New York: Harper & Row.

52. Drucker, P. F. (1974). *Management: Tasks, responsibilities, practices*. New York: Harper & Row.

53. Gormley, W. T., & Balla, S. J. (2012). *Bureaucracy and democracy: Accountability and performance* (3rd ed.). Washington, DC: CQ Press College.

54. Verschoor, C. C. (1998). A study of the link between a corporation's financial performance and its commitment to ethics. *Journal of Business Ethics, 17*, 1509–1516.

55. Heaphy, E. D., & Dutton, J. E. (2008). Positive social interactions and the human body at work: Linking organizations and physiology. *Academy of Management Review, 33*, 137–162.

56. Dulebohn, J. H., Conlon, D. E., Sarinopoulos, I., Davison, R. B., & McNamara, G. (2009). The biological bases of unfairness: Neuroimaging evidence for the distinctiveness of procedural and distributive justice. *Organizational Behavior and Human Decision Processes, 110*, 140–151.

57. Bureau of Labor Statistics (2012). www.bls.gov.

2 | ORGANIZATIONAL JUSTICE, ETHICS, AND CORPORATE SOCIAL RESPONSIBILITY

LEARNING OBJECTIVES

After reading this chapter, you will be able to:

1. **DESCRIBE** the various forms of organizational justice and how to promote them.
2. **IDENTIFY** the conditions under which people monitor the fairness of their organizations.
3. **EXPLAIN** what is meant by ethical behavior and why organizations should be concerned about ethics.
4. **DESCRIBE** the individual and situational factors responsible for unethical behavior in organizations and methods for minimizing such behavior.
5. **COMPARE** ethical relativism and ethical imperialism as orientations to ethics in the international arena.
6. **EXPLAIN** what is meant by corporate social responsibility and the nature of the relationship between responsible behavior and financial profitability.

THREE GOOD REASONS you should care about. . .

Organizational Justice, Ethics, and Corporate Social Responsibility

1. Treating employees unfairly adversely affects work attitudes and behaviors.
2. The public is growing increasingly intolerant of unethical corporate behavior, but managers can take steps to promote ethical behavior in their organizations.
3. Consumers and investors tend to support socially responsible companies, enhancing their financial performance.

Making the Case for. . .

Organizational Justice, Ethics, and Corporate Social Responsibility

AIG: Bailout and Outrage

For many years, American International Group (AIG) enjoyed a prominent position in the insurance business. Among its most lucrative products were "credit default swaps," insurance policies that protected banks and financial institutions from losses stemming from mortgage-backed securities (i.e., bundles of mortgages packaged as investments). Business boomed, earning executives at banks and AIG bonuses in the tens of millions of dollars, as banks issued record numbers of loans. Many of these were mortgages to individuals with low income and poor credit, so-called "subprime mortgages." Bankers considered the risk to be negligible because as houses appreciated in value, which they always had done, homeowners could refinance, paying off their original loans and taking out new ones. And because no one had ever seen anything other than continuous rises in real estate prices, there was no reason to fear that the cycle would not continue.

Then in September 2008, everything changed. Many variable interest loans—with initially low interest rates that got borrowers in the door, literally—rose to levels that home owners couldn't afford, and they began defaulting. This led the securities to nosedive in value. Banks lost money even faster than they were making it. Panicked by the prospect of failure, they turned to AIG, which guaranteed to protect them from such failures. But there was a problem: AIG suffered a "liquidity crisis," meaning that it didn't have the money to pay its obligations.

Recognizing that keeping the banks afloat was essential to preventing a major collapse of the financial system and a "Second Great Depression," the U.S. government intervened by launching the *Troubled Asset Relief Program* (*TARP*). Through this initiative, the Treasury Department was able to purchase $23 trillion in "troubled" assets and equity (e.g., losses stemming from home foreclosures) from financial institutions in an effort to stabilize them. As they regained health, the banks were to repay the government. AIG received $182.5 billion in aid from the federal government in exchange for a 77 percent stake in the company.

Although AIG was being kept afloat by government bailouts, company executives continued to receive the same enormous paychecks that they had been receiving before the bailout. The company was spending millions of taxpayer dollars on bonuses for the very executives whose poor judgment created the problem in the first place. It even spent $86,000 on an English hunting trip for top executives just one week after receiving a $37.8 billion loan from the Federal Reserve. Instead of being forced to resign in disgrace for causing such serious problems, these top officials were, in essence, being rewarded by their victims, the American people.

AIG officials countered that most of the company's leaders were not involved in the sub-prime mess and even those who were implicated needed to be paid well so they would stay aboard to remedy the situation. In March 2009, President Obama expressed indignation felt by many Americans. "People are rightly outraged about these particular bonuses," he said, adding, "But just as outrageous is the culture that these bonuses are a symptom of, that have existed for far too long—a situation where excess greed, excess compensation, excess risk-taking have all made us vulnerable and left us holding the bag."

From an economic and political standpoint, the AIG situation is far more complex than depicted in this case. However, from the perspective of OB, the principle involved appears rather straightforward. "A fair day's work for a fair day's wages" is a cherished value in the workplace. Those who do well deserve to be rewarded for their accomplishments, but those who fail do not deserve to benefit. It sounds simple enough, at least in principle. However, the AIG case seems to suggest that when it comes to bank or insurance executives, different rules apply. And as President Obama suggested in no uncertain terms, this is unacceptable.

As this case suggests, people are highly sensitive to unfairness in the workplace. In fact, among people asked to identify things that anger them most, both on the job and in life in general, "being treated unfairly" tops the list.[1] If you've ever received a very small pay raise despite having made enormous contributions to company success, you understand this only too well. OB scientists have studied these dynamics in the field of *organizational justice*, one of the major topics covered in this chapter.[2]

The quest to maintain justice in the workplace is part of a broader concern that people have for *ethics*—doing the right thing—the second major topic in this chapter. Given that philosophers over the years have not reached consensus about what constitutes "the right thing" to do, we shouldn't be surprised that distinguishing between right and wrong in the workplace is rarely a straightforward matter.[3] Yet it's clear from cases that have been in the news in the past few decades—the Enron case and the Bernard Madoff scandals being the most visible—we often know what's wrong when we see it.[4] And, as I will describe in this chapter, the field of OB provides a great deal of insight into why such unethical behavior occurs and can offer suggestions on how to curtail it.

As a natural outgrowth of their desires to behave ethically, many organizational leaders are going beyond merely doing what's right by proactively attempting to make things better in the communities in which they operate.[5] Indeed, many of today's organizations are demonstrating what is known as *corporate social responsibility*—not only attempting to meet prevailing legal and ethical standards but also exceeding them by embracing values that promote the greater welfare of society at large. Whether it involves donating money to charities, staffing community welfare projects, or taking steps to make our air and water clean, engaging in socially responsible behavior is of great concern to leaders of today's organizations. Here again, OB specialists have sought to explain this behavior, and their efforts are outlined in this chapter.

ORGANIZATIONAL JUSTICE: FAIRNESS MATTERS

Suppose that you received a failing grade in a course (hypothetically, of course). Naturally, you don't like it, but can you say that the grade is unfair? To answer this question, you would likely take several things into consideration. For example, does the grade accurately reflect how well you performed in the course? Were your scores added accurately and were they computed in an unbiased fashion? Has the professor treated you in a professional fashion? Finally, has the professor communicated the grading process to you adequately? In judging how fairly you have been treated, questions such as these are likely to be raised, and your answers are likely to have a considerable impact on how you feel about your grade, the professor, and even the school as a whole. Moreover, they are likely to have a profound effect on how you respond, such as whether you quietly accept the grade, complain about it to someone, or even quit school entirely.

Although this example involves you as a student, the same kinds of considerations are likely to arise in the workplace. In that context, instead of talking about grades from professors, concerns about justice may take analogous forms. Does your salary reflect your work accomplishments? How was your performance evaluation determined? Were you treated with dignity and respect by your boss? And have you been given important job information in a thorough and timely manner? Matters such as these are relevant to **organizational justice**—the study of people's perceptions of—and their reactions to—fairness in organizations.

The discussion of organizational justice that follows focuses on four important considerations. In the first two sections, I identify and describe the various forms of organizational justice that exist and the conditions under which people focus on each of these. Following this, I turn to an interesting new line of neurological research revealing that perceptions of injustice are associated with activity in various portions of our brains. Finally, I conclude this section of the chapter by offering useful tips for promoting justice in organizations.

Forms of Organizational Justice

The idea that justice is a multifaceted concept follows from the variety of questions just raised previously to everything from *how much* you get paid to how well you are treated by your boss. Not surprisingly, OB scientists have recognized that organizational justice takes several different forms, which I review here and summarize in Figure 2.1.[6]

DISTRIBUTIVE JUSTICE   On the job, people are concerned with getting their "fair share" of resources. We all want to be paid fairly for the work we do and we want to be adequately recognized for our efforts and any special contributions we bring to the job. **Distributive justice** is the form of organizational justice that focuses on people's beliefs that they get what they deserve—that is, that they have received appropriate amounts of valued outcomes (e.g., pay, recognition, etc.). For example, pay raises are considered to be distributed fairly when the best performers receive the largest raises.[7]

Distributive justice affects workers' feelings of satisfaction with their work outcomes, such as pay and job assignments. People will be dissatisfied with such important outcomes when

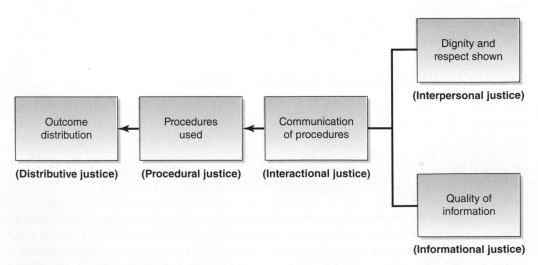

FIGURE 2.1   Forms of Organizational Justice
Organizational justice takes the various forms identified here.
Source: Based on suggestions by Greenberg, 2011; see Note 6.

these fall below expected levels. (Related to this, as you will see in the discussion of *equity theory* appearing in Chapter 6, feelings of distributive justice can have a great impact on people's motivation to perform their jobs.)

In an interesting study, researchers compared two groups of workers with respect to their feelings about distributive justice: a group of local workers from Singapore and a group of foreign workers, Chinese people who worked in Singapore.[8] In this setting, foreign workers tend to not be paid commensurate with their skills. Not surprisingly, the foreign workers expressed higher levels of distributive injustice and were less productive on their jobs.

PROCEDURAL JUSTICE   Recall our earlier example regarding receipt of a failing grade. In assessing the fairness of this situation you would want to know precisely how your grade was determined. After all, if the professor made an error in calculating your grade, it would be unfair for you to be penalized or to benefit as a result. The point is that fairness involves consideration of not only *how much* of various outcomes you receive (i.e., distributive justice) but also the process by which those outcomes are determined—that is, *procedural justice.*[9] In other words, **procedural justice** refers to people's perceptions of the fairness of the procedures used to determine the outcomes received.

Let's consider as an example an incident that occurred in New York City a few years ago. Cab drivers there went on strike to protest the mayor's imposition of new safety rules.[10] As it worked out, the drivers had little gripe with the rules themselves. However, they felt it was unfair for the mayor to impose the rules without consulting with them. In their eyes, fairness demanded having a voice in the decision-making process. This is a key consideration when judging procedural justice but it is only one of several standards that may be used. For an overview of the major factors that people take into account when forming judgments about procedural justice, see Table 2.1.

Concerns about procedural justice are likely to take different forms in various settings. Consider these examples from a variety of contexts.[11]

- *Formal performance appraisals*—Workers consider their job performance ratings to be fair to the extent that certain procedures are followed, such as when raters are assumed to be familiar with their work and when they believe that the standards used to judge them are applied to everyone equally and consistently.[12]
- *Classroom*—As a student, you want to make sure your professor uses fair procedures when grading your exams, such as by applying the same criteria to everyone's exams while grading essays and by not making any arithmetic errors when scoring exams.
- *Courtroom*—In the United States, laws require that evidence be ignored in court if it has been mishandled or if the police violated established rules to gather it. Likewise, entire cases may be thrown out if certain procedural rules have been violated.
- *Professional football*—To ensure that referees' calls are correct, the National Football League allows referees to review via videotape plays in which coaches believe that referees may have made an error.

It is important to note that following unfair procedures not only makes people dissatisfied with their outcomes (as in the case of distributive justice), but also leads them to reject the entire system as unfair.[13] Additionally, procedural justice affects people's tendencies to follow organizational rules: workers are not inclined to follow an organization's rules when they have reason to believe that its procedures are inherently unfair. And, of course, when this occurs, serious problems are likely to arise. Accordingly, everyone in an organization—especially top

TABLE 2.1   Procedural Justice Criteria

In making judgments about procedural justice, people take different factors into consideration. Some of the major ones are identified here, along with descriptions and examples of each.

Criterion	Description	Example
Voice in the making of decisions	Perceptions of procedural justice are enhanced to the extent that people are given a say in the decisions affecting them.	Workers are given an opportunity to explain their feelings about their own work to a supervisor who is evaluating their performance.
Consistency in applying rules	To be fair, the rules used as the basis for making a decision about one person must be applied equally to making a decision about others.	A professor must use the same exact standards in evaluating the term papers of each student in the class.
Accuracy in use of information	Fair decisions must be based on information that is accurate.	A manager calculating the amount of overtime pay a worker is to receive must add the numbers accurately.
Opportunity to be heard	Fair procedures are ones in which people have a readily available opportunity to correct any mistakes that have been made.	Litigants have an opportunity to have a judge's decision reconsidered in the event that an error was made in legal proceedings.
Safeguards against bias	A person making a decision must not have any opportunity to bias the results.	Lottery drawings are held in such a manner that each number is selected in a completely random, unbiased fashion.

Source: Based on information in Greenberg, 2011; see Note 6.

officials—would be well advised to adhere to the criteria for promoting procedural justice summarized in Table 2.1.

Although it is important to use fair procedures all of the time, they are especially important when the outcomes involved are unfavorable. Consider, for example, that you receive an A as the final grade in your OB course. Here, you're pleased to accept the favorable grade without asking any questions. However, if you were to receive a grade of D, you'd be far more interested in determining how this came about. Did the professor add your exam scores accurately? Were your essays scored in an unbiased manner? The negative outcome leads you to be concerned about the procedures and to ensure that procedures used to determine them were fair. This is known as the **fair process effect**. Research has shown that people are inclined to accept unfavorable outcomes when these were determined using fair procedures.

We see this most clearly in the case of people who have been involved in the legal system. Although people don't like losing their court cases, of course, such individuals generally accept even negative verdicts as fair to the extent that they believe that fair procedures were used in their cases. Among other things, this involves ensuring that the litigants had a say in determining the evidence to be used and that the judge was unbiased in rendering the verdict.[14]

The importance of the fair process effect is clear when you consider its practical implications. In organizations, after all, it is not always possible to give people the favorable outcomes they desire. However, this does not necessarily mean that they will respond negatively. The possibility of negative reactions may be minimized by following fair procedures (and, of course, by ensuring that everyone involved is well aware of the fairness of the procedures followed). To singer Mick Jagger's observation that, "you can't always get what you want," we add that you are inclined to accept what you get when it was determined in a procedurally fair manner.

INTERACTIONAL JUSTICE   People perceive fairness not only in terms of the outcomes they receive and the procedures used to determine those outcomes but also in terms of the way these outcomes and procedures are explained. This is known as **interactional justice**, which consists of the following two facets.

- **Informational justice**—The degree of information provided to explain outcomes and procedures. The more thorough and accurate the information is, the greater the degree of informational justice people will perceive
- **Interpersonal justice**—The degree of dignity and respect shown someone while explaining outcomes and procedures. People believe that they deserve to be treated in a respectful and dignified fashion, so the more this is done, the higher degree of interpersonal justice they will perceive.

Let's consider an example that illustrates interactional justice and why it's so important. Imagine that you were just laid off from your job. You're not happy about it, of course, but suppose that your boss explains this situation to you in a manner that shows a high degree of interactional justice. That is, she explains in considerable detail precisely why the layoff had to occur (e.g., she shares statistical analyses from the accounting department) and she does so in a manner that is highly professional and that shows concern for your feelings (e.g., she is very sensitive to the problems this causes you and expresses concern for you in a highly dignified manner).

Although none of this helps improve your resulting financial problems, the boss's treatment is inclined to take some of the sting out of the bad situation. This, in turn, helps eliminate the costly problem of wrongful termination lawsuits. Specifically, a study of layoff victims has shown that the more interactional justice they experienced during their jobs, the less inclined they were to sue their previous employers for wrongful termination.[15]

As you might expect, this is only one of the positive benefits associated with high levels of interactional justice. Among other things, people who experience high levels of interactional justice respond less negatively to a variety of other undesirable situations. Importantly, they are disinclined to resign their jobs when unfavorable policies are imposed and they are more inclined to follow those policies.[16] People who believe that they have been treated with high degrees of interactional justice also tend to be good organizational citizens by going out of their way to pitch in and help others even when they don't have to do so.[17] (To assess your perception of the various forms of organizational justice in an organization with which you may be familiar, see the Self-Assessment exercise on pp. 58–59.)

When Do People Assess Fairness?

Thus far, I have considered people's judgments of various types of justice but I haven't said anything about the conditions under which they pay attention to them. Exactly when do people look for information that allows them to assess fairness? As scientists put it, when do we engage in **fairness monitoring**? This is defined as the practice in which people gather and process information used to assess how fairly they are treated in their organizations.

We know, for example, that people look for information about fairness when conditions are uncertain, such as when one is new to an organization or when the organization has undergone changes.[18] Research also has suggested that people engage in monitoring different types of fairness depending on the nature of the managerial controls they perceive to be used in their organizations.[19] **Managerial controls** are the processes that managers use to communicate and monitor the performance of their subordinates to ensure that they are behaving as expected. Among these are the following major types.

- **Market controls**—The extent to which management emphasizes high levels of individual output and organizational productivity.
- **Bureaucratic controls**—The extent to which standards of performance are based on following established task procedures.
- **Clan controls**—The extent to which things get done by establishing warm and collegial relationships in an organization.

It was found that the type of fairness monitoring in which employees engaged depended on the type of managerial controls they perceived as predominating in their organizations. Specifically, three profiles emerged. First, individuals who perceived that they worked under market control conditions tended to monitor for distributive justice because information about rewards and performance were believed to be emphasized in their workplaces. Second, employees who perceived that high levels of bureaucratic controls existed in their workplaces focused on monitoring procedural justice because information about procedures was important to the functioning of their organizations. Third, people who perceived that clan controls predominated in their organizations showed high levels of interactional justice monitoring because interpersonal issues were perceived as being emphasized where they worked.

Of note, it also was found that individuals who conformed to these patterns—that is, whose perceptions of managerial controls matched the types of fairness monitoring most closely associated with them—tended to be the most productive and most satisfied with their jobs. These findings highlight the practical value of people's perceptions of organizational justice.

Neurological Responses to Injustice

Typically, OB scientists focus only on people's perceptions and their behaviors, especially when it comes to organizational justice. Interestingly, however, a recent study found that people's reactions to distributive injustice and procedural injustice may be seen in another way as well—activity inside people's brains.[20]

To establish this, a group of scientists had students play a game that involved bargaining with others in the hope of winning a financial award. While completing the bargaining game, participants were lying down inside a machine that used functional magnetic resonance imaging (fMRI) to scan their brains. This equipment uses large magnets to determine activation in the brain in terms of the flow of blood to certain regions while people are engaged in various activities. Here, the researchers were looking to determine the regions of the brain that were activated when participants were victimized by the other players' acts of distributive injustice (taking too much money) and procedural injustice (violating established rules).

Based on previous research, it was expected that different regions of people's brains would respond to procedural injustice and distributive injustice. Procedural injustice, the scientists reasoned, is highly cognitive, as people need to process information about what's going on to assess the extent to which various procedural rules have or have not been followed. As such, people

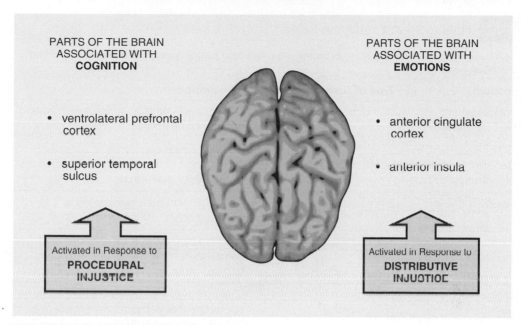

FIGURE 2.2 Neurological Reactions to Distributive Injustice and Procedural Injustice
Research using neurological imaging (fMRI) has found that people's brains respond differently when they are victims of distributive injustice and procedural injustice. As summarized here, different regions are activated in each case, suggesting that there are biological bases for reactions to unfairness.
Source: Based on suggestions by Dulebohn et al., 2009; see Note 20.

experiencing violations of procedural justice were predicted to show signs of activation in the portions of their brains associated with cognition. By contrast, they noted that people respond to distributive injustice in highly emotional ways. For example, they get angry when they believe that someone has not given them what they deserve. Accordingly, the researchers predicted that the brains of people experiencing distributive injustice would show signs of activation in regions known to be associated with emotion. As summarized in Figure 2.2, this is precisely what they found.

These findings are important because they suggest that differences in reactions to distributive injustice and procedural injustice are "real" in the sense that they may be traced neurologically. It looks like there is an actual biological basis for people's reactions to injustice. Another intriguing suggestion from the findings is that as a species, human beings' responses to injustice appear to be "hardwired."

Suggestions for Promoting Organizational Justice

The examples provided thus far make a compelling case for treating employees as fairly as possible. The results are beneficial not only for the employees themselves but for the companies for which they work. Illustrating this point, consider the dramatic findings of a study of 4,539 employees from 783 departments in 97 different hotels.[21] The researchers found that departments composed of employees who felt unfairly treated suffered significantly higher rates of turnover and lower levels of customer satisfaction than those composed of employees who felt fairly treated. And, of course, these factors have enormous impact on a hotel's success.

TABLE 2.2	How to Treat Employees Fairly	

Research has suggested various ways to promote organizational justice. Several of these are identified and described here.

Suggestion	Type of Justice Involved	Explanation
Pay workers what they deserve (use prevailing wages)	Distributive justice	This enhances motivation by demonstrating that the company doesn't want to cheat them
Pay workers in proportion to their accomplishments	Distributive justice	This establishes that those who succeed are rewarded for their efforts
Offer workers a voice	Procedural justice	This helps workers feel accepted by their organizations as valued individuals
Be "transparent" about how decisions are made	Procedural justice	Showing employees how decisions are made demonstrates that the company has nothing to hide
Explain decisions thoroughly	Interactional justice (informational)	Sharing lots of information helps employees appreciate that decisions were made in a serious, unbiased fashion
Train managers to treat others with dignity and respect	Interactional justice (interpersonal)	This establishes that company officials value their employees by showing that they are worthwhile individuals

In view of these findings, there is good reason for managers to go out of their way to promote justice in the workplace. Fortunately, what we know about organizational justice points to some useful suggestions for doing so, several of which are shown in Table 2.2.

ETHICAL BEHAVIOR IN ORGANIZATIONS: WHAT IS IT AND WHY DOES IT MATTER?

In recent years, we have been showered by headlines chronicling allegations of wrongdoing by individuals from all walks of life. Politicians, business leaders, athletic coaches, and even clergymen have been accused of engaging in acts widely considered to be immoral and unethical. Companies such as Enron and individuals such as Bernard Madoff have become icons of the epidemic of shameful behavior that rocked financial institutions in recent decades.[22] Ethically questionable business practices are nothing new, however.

Accounts of unethical behavior have been reported throughout the history of business.[23] Consider, for example, John D. Rockefeller, the nineteenth-century industrialist who founded the former industrial giant, Standard Oil. Rockefeller was known to have bribed politicians on a regular basis and to step on anyone who interfered with his quest to monopolize the oil industry.

It's clear that greed is a hallmark of human behavior, for many years leading people down a variety of unethical paths.[24] This appears to be changing, however, along with the public's tolerance of unethical behavior on the part of organizations.[25] Surveys have found that compared to managers from earlier years, today's top managers are more inclined to keep their promises, less inclined to engage in misconduct, less likely to feel pressure to be unethical, and perceive greater attention paid to practicing honesty and respect for others. At the same time, whatever ethical misdeeds they do witness are much more likely to be reported to organizational authorities.[26]

To the extent that people are increasingly intolerant of unethical business activity, it should not be surprising to learn that OB scientists are interested in understanding unethical practices and developing strategies for combating them. We will consider these issues in this section of the chapter. First, however, to prepare you for understanding ethical behavior in organizations, it helps to begin by addressing a fundamental question: What is ethics?

What Do We Mean by Ethics?

The answer to this question depends on whom you ask. Philosophers have long been interested in matters of ethics and so too are people in the field of management. As I will outline here, however, their orientations are fundamentally different.

THE PRESCRIPTIVE APPROACH OF PHILOSOPHERS Among philosophers, who have examined this question for hundreds of years, ethics is a complex matter, but one that may be understood from several distinct perspectives. The major philosophical approaches are known as *utilitarianism* and *natural rights*.

The philosophers Jeremy Bentham and John Stuart Mill proposed a doctrine known as **utilitarianism**. According to this approach, an action is considered ethical to the extent that it maximizes happiness among **stakeholders**—that is, everyone who is affected by the act in question. Thus, an act is considered ethical when it does the greatest good (and the least harm) to the greatest number of people. As you might imagine, this isn't easy to quantify, making utilitarianism an impractical approach to gauging ethics.

Another weakness of utilitarianism is that it argues that it would be acceptable to harm some people if doing so brings good to even more people. This would be the case, for example, if one or two people had to suffer or even die, in the course of developing a drug that would save many thousands of others. To some other great thinkers, such as the seventeenth-century English philosopher John Locke, this would be unethical because it violates the rights that everyone has simply because they are human beings. This is the idea behind the so-called **natural rights** approach to ethics, according to which all people are entitled to rights for life, liberty, and property. Thus, any practices that violate these rights, such as murder, slavery, and theft, would be considered unethical.

Despite their differences, these schools of thought have an important characteristic in common—namely, they focus on what it means to be ethical according to certain criteria (i.e., something is ethical when certain conditions exist). This is known as a **prescriptive orientation**, which is commonly adopted by philosophers. The prescriptive orientation focuses on the question, "What is ethical?"

THE DESCRIPTIVE APPROACH OF SOCIAL SCIENTISTS A different approach is adopted by most social scientists—including specialists in the field of OB—who are interested primarily in what people perceive as ethical and how they practice being ethical.[27] Known as a **descriptive orientation**, this approach focuses on such questions as "What do people believe to be ethical?" "How do people try to be ethical?" and "How do people respond to unethical behavior?" These questions will be considered in various ways in this chapter.

To understand precisely what OB scientists mean by ethics, we first must understand the concept of *moral values*. When social scientists speak of **moral values** they are referring to people's fundamental beliefs regarding what is right or wrong, good or bad. One of the most important sources of moral values is the religious background, beliefs, and training we receive. Although people's moral values may differ, several are widely accepted. For example, most people believe that helping someone in need (e.g., being charitable) is the right thing to do whereas harming someone (e.g., killing) is wrong.

Based on these beliefs, people are guided in ways that influence the decisions they make and the actions in which they engage. These standards are what we mean by *ethics*. Thus, **ethics** refers to standards of conduct that guide people's decisions and behavior (e.g., not stealing from others is one such ethical standard).[28]

With this in mind, organizational scientists acknowledge that it is not a company's place to teach employees values. After all, these come with people as they enter the workplace. However, it *is* a company's responsibility to set clear standards of behavior and to train employees in recognizing and following them.[29] (For a summary of the distinction between moral values and ethics, see Figure 2.3.)

Just as organizations prescribe other kinds of behavior that are expected in the workplace (e.g., when to arrive and leave), so too should they prescribe appropriate ethical behavior (e.g., how to complete expense reports and what precisely is considered a bribe). Not surprisingly, most top business leaders recognize that clearly prescribing ethical behavior is a fundamental part of good management. After all, says Kent Druyversteyn, former vice president of ethics at the aerospace giant General Dynamics, "Ethics is about conduct."[30]

In looking at Figure 2.3, please note the row of rounded boxes at the bottom. These identify some of the factors affecting moral values, ethics, decisions, and behavior. The ones corresponding to ethics and values are described in this section of the chapter. However, as indicated in the box in the lower right corner, the decisions people make and the behavior in which they engage are determined by a wide variety of considerations beyond ethics. Accordingly, these are discussed elsewhere throughout this book (note the references to the particular chapters in which those topics are discussed).

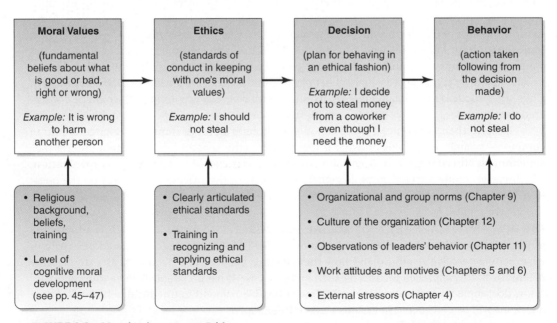

FIGURE 2.3   Moral Values Versus Ethics
As summarized here, *moral values* (which reside within an individual) provide the basis for *ethics* (which are standards of behavior that can be regulated by organizations). Ethical standards influence both decisions and behavior in the workplace, which also are affected by a host of other variables identified throughout this book.

Why Should Companies Care About Ethical Behavior?

It's obvious, of course, that companies *should* do things to promote ethical behavior among employees simply because they are morally appropriate. To some top executives, behaving ethically is an integral part of business. Take Levi Strauss & Co., for example, whose former chairman, Robert D. Haas, has observed as follows:

> Levi has always treated people fairly and cared about their welfare. . . . In the past, however, that tradition was viewed as something separate from how we ran the business. We always talked about the "hard stuff" and the "soft stuff." The soft stuff was the company's commitment to our work force. And the hard stuff was what really mattered; getting pants out the door. What we've learned is that the soft stuff and the hard stuff are becoming increasingly intertwined. A company's values—what it stands for, what its people believe in—are crucial to its competitive success. Indeed, values drive the business. . . . Values are where the hard stuff and the soft stuff come together.[31]

All too often, as you know, forces deter even good people from doing the right thing. Pressure to meet "the bottom line" sometimes encourages people to do whatever it takes to make money, at least in the short run, even if it leads them to behave unethically. For example, some unscrupulous stockbrokers have been known to boost their own sales commissions by encouraging clients to make investments they know are questionable. Corporate leaders need to be concerned about this, if not for moral reasons, then out of recognition of two critical business realities—by being ethical, companies can (1) reap various financial benefits and (2) adhere to legal regulations. I now explain how these factors help shape ethical behavior.

GOOD ETHICS IS GOOD BUSINESS   People promoting ethical behavior among businesses agree that good ethics is good business. In other words, although one may benefit in the short run by behaving unethically (e.g., the stockbroker in our example), being ethical pays off in the long run. These benefits take several forms, including the following:[32]

- *Improved financial performance*—Companies that make a clear commitment to ethics outperform those that make no such commitment on standard measures of financial success. In fact, one study reported that companies that make an explicit commitment to ethical behavior returned twice the value to shareholders than those that were more casual about ethical issues.[33]
- *Reduced operating costs*—Many efforts to reduce waste and to save energy designed to protect the natural environment also help save money.
- *Enhanced corporate reputation*—Many customers are loyal to companies that demonstrate their commitment to social causes. For example, The Body Shop has benefited by promoting the things it does to help the poor people from third-world nations from whom they buy raw materials, courting customers who share their values.
- *Increased ability to attract and retain employees*—People generally like working at companies that they can be proud of and that treat them well. When talented workers are difficult to find, socially responsible companies have an easier job of attracting potential employees—and retaining them once hired.

If this evidence is not sufficiently convincing, then consider the other side of the coin. The evidence also is compelling that "bad ethics is bad business." Companies that survive ethical scandals do so under diminished capacity in large part because "the black eye" makes the public shy away from them—both as consumers and as stockholders—at least for a while.[34]

Good examples from years past include Dow Corning (whose breast implants were found to be unsafe), BP (whose drilling rig exploded in the Gulf of Mexico, killing 11 men and spilling millions of gallons of oil), and the United Way (whose top official was accused of misusing agency funds). These misdeeds have cost their respective organizations dearly, and regaining the public's trust has proven to be a slow process. At the United Way, for example, although only one person, the president, was involved in the ethical scandal, completely independent and scrupulously ethical chapters of the esteemed philanthropic organization suffered severe reductions in donations (one-fifth of former donors stopped giving altogether and the remaining ones gave less) for at least five years.[35] The lesson is clear: even if company executives do not recognize the benefits of behaving ethically, they surely cannot afford to ignore the costs of behaving unethically.

LEGAL REGULATIONS   Being legal does not ensure being ethical. In fact, a useful way to think of the law is as providing the minimum acceptable standard to which companies must adhere. Being ethical typically involves following a higher standard. Vin Sarni, former CEO of PPG, put this well when he said, "It is not enough simply to say that our conduct is lawful. The law is the floor. Compliance with it will be the absolute minimum with respect to the PPG associate, no matter where he or she works. Our ethics go beyond the legal code."[36]

At the same time, it must be noted that the law plays a large role in governing ethical behavior within organizations. Some of the major laws enacted in the United States that influence ethical behavior in organizations are summarized in Table 2.3.

TABLE 2.3	Major U.S. Laws That Promote Ethical Behavior in Organizations

Businesses—and society at large—can be affected adversely by the unethical behavior of some people in organizations. As a safeguard, several laws have been enacted in the United States in recent decades. Some with the broadest impact are summarized here.

Year	Law	Description
1986	False Claims Act	Provides procedures for reporting fraudulent behavior against U.S. government agencies and protects whistleblowers (see Chapter 7) who do so.
1988	Foreign Corrupt Practices Act (revised)	Prohibits organizations from paying bribes to foreign officials for purposes of getting business.
1991, amended 2004	Federal Sentencing Guidelines for Organizations	Provides guidelines for federal judges to follow when imposing fines on organizations found guilty of committing federal crimes.
2002, revised 2007	Sarbanes-Oxley Act	Enacted to guard against fraudulent accounting practices (such as occurred at Enron), this law initiates reforms in the standards by which public companies report accounting data.
2003	Federal Prosecution of Business Organizations	To protect investors against unscrupulous acts by top executives (also in response to the Enron scandal), these revisions to the Federal Sentencing Guidelines for Organizations now focus on the role of boards of directors—the only parties in organizations with sufficient clout to prevent wrongdoing by high-ranking officials.

Although all the laws included in this table are important when it comes to minimizing unethical behavior in organizations, two have proven to be especially influential, the *Federal Sentencing Guidelines for Organizations* and the *Sarbanes-Oxley Act*.

- Established in 1991, the **Federal Sentencing Guidelines for Organizations** provide guidelines for federal judges to follow when imposing penalties on organizations (e.g., restitution, fines, etc.) found guilty of breaking federal laws. These specify that judges should take into account any efforts on the part of companies to prevent and detect violations of the law (thereby going lighter on companies that have tried to avoid violations). The "guidelines" identify various actions that companies can take in this regard.[37] These include developing compliance standards for which top executives are responsible, training employees to behave ethically, closely monitoring possible ethical violations, and punishing such violators. The Federal Sentencing Guidelines for Organizations have played a huge role in putting into place various mechanisms to help promote ethical behavior in organizations.
- Passed in the wake of the Enron scandal, the **Sarbanes-Oxley Act** (known widely as **SOX**) was an effort to avoid unscrupulous and fraudulent accounting practices by holding senior company officials personally accountable for their companies' accounting practices and reports. The rationale is simple: instead of just signing off on reports whose veracity is questionable because they can do so with impunity, making executives personally liable for these documents will encourage them to ensure that they are accurate and that the practices used to create them meet proper standards. SOX is very specific, requiring companies to analyze their risks for fraud, and to evaluate controls designed to safeguard against fraud and to detect it if it occurs.[38]

WHY DO SOME PEOPLE BEHAVE UNETHICALLY, AT LEAST SOMETIMES?

Management experts long have considered the matter of why some people behave unethically on at least some occasions. Put differently, is it a matter of good people who are led to behave unethically because of external forces acting on them (i.e., "good apples in bad barrels") or is it that bad people behave inappropriately in whatever setting they are in (i.e., "bad apples in good barrels")? Acknowledging the key role of leaders in determining the ethical climate of an organization, some scientists have considered the possibility that because of their profound influence, some unethical leaders (so-called "bad apples") have made their companies unethical as well (turning "good barrels into bad"), or poisoning the whole barrel, so to speak.[39]

Although the relative importance of "apples" and "barrels" has yet to be firmly decided, it is clear that ethical and unethical behavior is determined by *both* of these classes of factors—that is, individual factors (the person) and situational factors (the external forces people confront in the workplace). Here, I explore both sets of factors.

Individual Differences in Cognitive Moral Development

As you know from experience, people appear to differ with respect to their adherence to moral considerations. Some individuals, for example, refrain from padding their expense accounts, even if they believe they will not get caught, solely because they believe it is the wrong thing to do. They strongly consider ethical factors when making decisions. However, this is not true of everyone. Still others, as you know, would not think twice about padding their expense accounts, often rationalizing that the amounts of money in question are small and that "the company expects me to do it."

A key factor responsible for this difference is what psychologists refer to as **cognitive moral development**—that is, differences among people in their capacity to engage in the kind of reasoning that enables them to make moral judgments. (Scientists measure people's cognitive moral development by systematically analyzing how people say they would resolve various ethical dilemmas. For practice analyzing an ethical dilemma, complete the Group Exercise on pp. 59–60.)

The most well-known theory of cognitive moral development, introduced over four decades ago, is **Kohlberg's theory of cognitive moral development**.[40] According to this conceptualization, people develop over the years in their capacity to understand what is right. Specifically, the theory distinguishes among three levels of moral development (for a summary, see Figure 2.4).

The first level is referred to as the **preconventional level of moral reasoning**. People at this level (children and about one-third of all adults) haven't developed the capacity to assume the perspective of others. Accordingly, they interpret what is right solely with respect to themselves: it is wrong to do something if it leads one to be punished. Because their cognitive skills are not sufficiently advanced, such individuals generally cannot comprehend any arguments suggesting that something is wrong because it violates social obligations to others.

As we interact with other people over the years, most of us come to use higher level cognitive processes to judge morality. In a more sophisticated fashion, we judge right and wrong in terms of what is good for the others around us and for society as a whole. This second level is referred to as the **conventional level of moral reasoning**. Approximately two-thirds of adults fall into this category. What they do is governed strongly by what's expected of them by others,

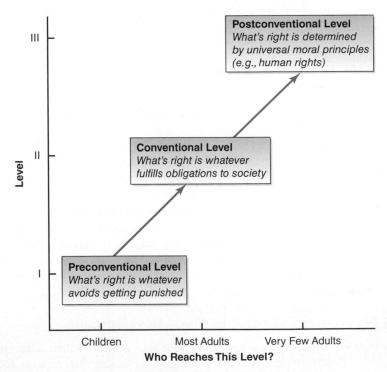

FIGURE 2.4 **Kohlberg's Theory of Cognitive Moral Development: A Summary**
According to *Kohlberg's theory of cognitive moral development*, people develop the capacity to make moral decisions as they develop over the years by interacting with others. The three major levels of cognitive moral development are identified here.
Source: Based on information in Kohlberg, 1976; see Note 40.

and they carefully scour the social environment for cues as to "what's right." People who engage in conventional moral reasoning obey the law not only because they fear the repercussions of not doing so, but also because they recognize that doing so is the right thing to do insofar as it promotes the safety and welfare of society as a whole.

Finally, Kohlberg's theory also identifies a third level of cognitive moral development, the **postconventional level of moral reasoning**. At this level, people judge what is right and wrong not solely in terms of their interpersonal and societal obligations but also in terms of complex philosophical principles of duty, justice, and rights. Very few people ever attain this level. Those who do, however, follow their own "moral compass," doing what they are convinced is truly right, even if others don't agree.

Research has found that people behave in very different ways as a function of their level of cognitive moral development. For example, as you might expect, people who are at higher levels of cognitive moral development (typically, conventional as opposed to preconventional) manifest their greater ethical behavior in several ways. Specifically, they are less inclined to harm others, less likely to misreport information even if it makes them look bad, and steal less from their employers.[41] Although efforts to raise people's level of moral reasoning through training have been successful, few such efforts have been used in organizations.[42] This is in large part because most workers already function at the conventional level, making them sensitive to efforts to promote ethical behavior predicated on changing the social norms that exist within organizations. We now will consider some of the key social dynamics that influence ethical behavior.

Situational Determinants of Unethical Behavior

As you might imagine, many different situational factors can lead people to behave unethically on the job. Although the list may be long, it is not too difficult to identify some of the major organizational influences on unethical behavior. Here, I consider three of the most important ones.

MANAGERIAL VALUES UNDERMINING INTEGRITY   Most managers appear to believe that "good ethics is good business." However, some managers have developed ways of thinking that lead them to make unethical decisions. Given how very influential top leaders are when it comes to influencing others in their organizations, it should not be surprising that unethical managerial values promote unethical organizational decisions.[43] Several well-known forms of unethical thinking are as follows:[44]

- **Bottom line mentality**—This line of thinking supports financial success as the only value to be considered. It promotes short-term decisions that are immediately financially sound, despite the fact that they may cause long-term problems for the organization.
- **Exploitative mentality**—This view encourages "using" people in a way that promotes stereotypes and undermines empathy and compassion. This highly selfish perspective sacrifices concern for others in favor of benefits to one's own immediate interests.
- **Madison Avenue mentality**—This perspective suggests that anything is right if the public can be made to see it as right. The idea is that executives may be more concerned that their decisions appear to be right than about their legitimate morality. This kind of thinking leads some companies to hide their unethical behavior (e.g., dumping toxic waste under cover of night) or to otherwise justify them as acceptable.

Recognizing the problems associated with these various orientations is not difficult. Their overemphasis on short-term monetary gain may lead to decisions that not only hurt individuals in the long run but also threaten the very existence of organizations.

ORGANIZATIONS SOMETIMES ENCOURAGE UNETHICAL BEHAVIOR   It is easy to understand that people may behave unethically on the job to the extent that they are encouraged to do so. Consider, for example, how some business executives are expected to say nothing about ethically dubious behavior they've witnessed in the company. In fact, in many companies it is considered not only acceptable but also desirable to be secretive and deceitful. For example, the practice of **stonewalling**—willingly hiding relevant information—is quite common.

A major reason for this is that organizations sometimes punish individuals who are too open and honest. As a case in point, consider that back in 1968, B.F. Goodrich allegedly rewarded employees who falsified and withheld data on the quality of aircraft brakes to win certification. This example illustrates how the *counternorms* of secrecy and deceitfulness were accepted and supported by the organization. By **counternorms**, I am referring to accepted organizational practices that run contrary to society's prevailing ethical standards. For a summary of some of the most common counternorms found in organizations, see Figure 2.5.[45]

WORKERS EMULATE THE UNETHICAL BEHAVIOR OF THEIR SUPERIORS   Probably very few organizational leaders condone and actively promote unethical behavior. However, many organizational officials promote unethical behavior unwittingly by way of the examples they set for their employees. For example, suppose a manager submits an expense report to her administrative assistant to prepare for submission to the accounting office. Included on it are several items the assistant knows are not legitimate (e.g., lavish meals with clients). Although the manager might not be thinking about it, by padding her expense account, she is sending a message to her administrative assistant that stealing from the company is an acceptable practice. Despite what she might say publicly about not stealing, her behind-the-scenes actions tell a different story. As a result, the administrative assistant might not think twice about taking a few dollars from the

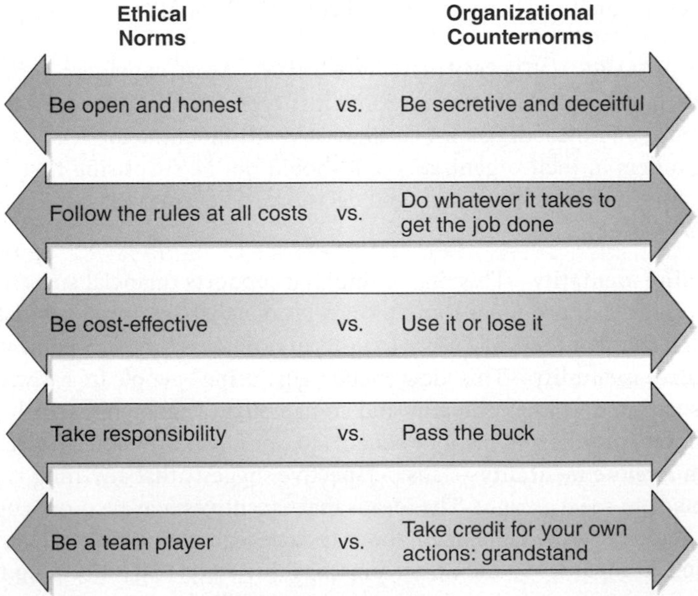

Ethical Norms		Organizational Counternorms
Be open and honest	vs.	Be secretive and deceitful
Follow the rules at all costs	vs.	Do whatever it takes to get the job done
Be cost-effective	vs.	Use it or lose it
Take responsibility	vs.	Pass the buck
Be a team player	vs.	Take credit for your own actions: grandstand

FIGURE 2.5   Ethical Norms Versus Organizational Counternorms
Although societal standards of ethics dictate the appropriateness of certain actions, counternorms that encourage and support opposite practices sometimes develop within organizations.
Source: Based on suggestions by Jansen & Von Glinow, 1985; see Note 45.

company's petty cash box to purchase her lunch. "After all," she may reason, "my boss takes a little extra money from the company, so it must be okay for me to do so too."

A survey of some 1,500 U.S. employees suggests that this is precisely what happens.[46] Specifically, employees who feel that the top managers in their organization act ethically themselves report seeing far less misconduct among their peers (15 percent) than those who feel that their top managers do not behave ethically themselves or who only talk about behaving ethically (56 percent). Obviously, when it comes to ethical conduct on the job, managers set an example by virtue of their own behavior, and their "actions speak louder than words." Putting it in the lingo of today's managers, to promote ethical behavior in their companies, it is essential for officials to "walk the talk."

Corporate Ethics Programs

Most companies today, particularly large ones, have in place some sort of formal, systematic mechanisms designed to promote ethics. These efforts, known as **corporate ethics programs**, are designed to create organizational cultures (see Chapter 12) that make people sensitive to potentially unethical behavior and that discourage them from engaging in such acts.

COMPONENTS OF CORPORATE ETHICS PROGRAMS   Typically, corporate ethics programs consist of some combination of several key components.[47]

- *A code of ethics*—A **code of ethics** is a document describing what an organization stands for and the general rules of conduct expected of employees (e.g., to avoid conflicts of interest, to be honest, and so on). Largely in reaction to federal laws such as those identified earlier (see pp. 44–45), just about all of today's large companies have codes of ethics in place. These documents differ considerably.[48] Some codes are highly specific, stating, for example, the maximum size of gifts that can be accepted; others are less precise, stating only general principles.
- *Ethics training*—Codes of ethics are especially effective when they are used in conjunction with training programs that reinforce a company's ethical values.[49] In the absence of such training, too many codes come across as "window dressing," and are ignored, if they are even read at all. Ethics training efforts consist of everything ranging from lectures, self-paced online courses, and case studies to more elaborate simulations. Citicorp, for example, has trained more than 40,000 employees in over 60 countries using an elaborate corporate ethics game, "The Work Ethic," that simulates ethical dilemmas that employees are likely to confront.[50]
- *Ethics audits*—Just as companies regularly audit their books to check on irregularities in their finances, they regularly should assess the morality of their employees' behavior so as to identify irregularities in this realm as well. Such assessments are known as **ethics audits**. These require actively investigating and documenting incidents of dubious ethical value, discussing them in an open and honest fashion, and developing a concrete plan to avoid such actions in the future. Conducting an ethics audit can be quite revealing. For some useful guidelines on how to do so, see Table 2.4.[51]
- *An ethics committee*—An **ethics committee** is a group of senior-level managers from various areas of the organization who assist an organization's CEO in making ethical decisions. Members of the committee develop and evaluate company-wide ethics policies.
- *An ethics officer*—An **ethics officer** is a high-ranking organizational official (e.g., the general counsel or vice president of ethics) who is expected to provide strategies for ensuring ethical conduct throughout an organization. Because the Federal Sentencing Guidelines for

TABLE 2.4	How to Conduct an Ethics Audit

A thorough ethics audit can reveal a great deal about a company's commitment to ethics and the extent to which its efforts to foster ethical behavior are effective. However, to recognize these benefits, it is crucial to conduct an ethics audit in an appropriate manner. The following guidelines will help.

1. Ensure that top executives, such as the CEO, are committed to the ethics audit and appoint a committee to guide it.
2. Create a diverse team of employees to write questions regarding the company's ethical performance. These should focus on existing practices (e.g., codes of ethics) as well as prevailing norms about company practices (e.g., billing clients for services not actually performed).
3. Carefully analyze official documents, such as ethical mission statements and codes of ethics, to see how clear and thorough they are.
4. Ask people questions about why they think various unethical behaviors have occurred.
5. Compare your company's ethical practices to those of other companies in the same industry.
6. Write a formal report summarizing these findings and present it to all concerned parties.

Source: Based on suggestions by Ferrell et al., 2010; see Note 51.

Organizations specify that a specific, high-level individual should be responsible for ethical behavior, many companies have such an individual in place.

- *A mechanism for communicating and clarifying ethical standards*—To be effective, ethics programs must clearly articulate—and reinforce—a company's ethical expectations to employees. With this in mind, growing numbers of companies are putting into place **ethics hotlines**, special phone lines that employees can call to ask questions about ethical behavior and to report any ethical misdeeds they may have observed. (For a particularly effective example of this, and other practices designed to encourage ethical behavior, see the Winning Practices section on p. 51.)

By themselves, codes of ethics have only limited effectiveness in regulating ethical behavior in organizations.[52] However, an integrated ethics program that combines a code of ethics with additional components (e.g., an ethics officer, ethics training, etc.) can be quite effective. Specifically, it has been found that compared to companies that don't have ethics programs in place, within those that do, employees (a) are more likely to report ethical misconduct to company authorities, (b) are considered more accountable for ethics violations, and (c) face less pressure to compromise standards of business conduct.[53] Clearly, the ethics programs are being felt.

ETHICS IN THE INTERNATIONAL ARENA

Our discussion thus far suggests that figuring out how to behave ethically isn't always easy. If that's the case when conducting business at home, then imagine how much more complex things become when conducting business in other countries. After all, people in different cultures often have different ethical standards. Consider these examples:

- In China, using pirated software is an acceptable practice.
- In Indonesia, bribing an official is considered an acceptable cost of doing business.
- In Japan, you cannot conduct business unless you give the other party a gift.

In North America, of course, all such acts would be frowned on and considered illegal or at least ethically questionable. Clearly, the implications for conducting business globally are

Winning Practices

Exelon Excels at Managing Ethics

The Exelon Corporation was formed by the merger of two electric utility companies, Unicom and PECO Energy. The creation of a new company provided an opportunity for an emphasis on ethics to be built into the company's structure from the ground floor. It was with this in mind that Eliecer Palacios, who was ethics and compliance director at Unicom at the time of the merger, got actively involved in the process of integrating the two companies.[54]

Palacios believed that this was important insofar as large utilities face ethical challenges along several fronts, such as stock trading practices (e.g., avoiding insider trading), protection of the environment (e.g., avoiding air and water pollution), procurement (e.g., avoiding bribes and kickbacks), and following fair labor practices (e.g., avoiding harassment and discrimination). And, given that the energy industry is deregulated, customers have the opportunity to express their dissatisfaction with any ethical missteps by taking their business elsewhere. To avoid any ethical scandals, Palacios built in several safeguards to ensure that Exelon would remain "squeaky clean."

At the heart of the company's ethics initiatives is an audit committee. One of the key things this body does is review Exelon's code of ethics on a quarterly basis. Members, consisting of vice presidents and lower-level employees from throughout the company as well as several attorneys, carefully review the extent to which the company is meeting its legal and ethical obligations. Is it obeying the law? Is it meeting its obligations to shareholders, employees, and the environment?

CEO John W. Rowe emphasizes the importance of the code. He introduces this document as follows.

We will be successful if we operate our Company, employ our people and finance our business in accordance with the highest ethical standards and with the law. We will destroy shareholder value if we do not. Our Exelon Code of Conduct provides the outline of what is expected of all of us to meet our important obligations, and gives us resources to understand these requirements and live up to them.[55]

Among the things on which the audit committee focuses are the company's efforts at training its tens of thousands of employees on proper ethical behavior. Like other big companies, Exelon has a code of ethics, but unlike many, it is actively involved in ensuring that its employees understand and follow it. With this in mind, Exelon employees are required annually to complete an intensive ethics training program using the company's Intranet. Also unlike many companies, everyone at Exelon, from the lowest-level employees up to the CEO, is required to participate in the ethics training.

In addition to its training efforts, Exelon maintains an active "helpline" that employees can call to lodge complaints about seemingly unethical behavior or to make inquiries about how to avoid unethical behavior. The helpline, staffed by Palacios and an assistant, receives about 300 calls per year. Most of these involve inquiries about behavior that is considered ethically appropriate (e.g., accepting gifts from a contractor valued at over $25 is considered inappropriate). Calls about allegations of waste, fraud, and abuse, although only about 10 to 15 percent of all received, also occur. All allegations are carefully investigated, and to ensure that these efforts are effective, the company strictly enforces a nonretaliation policy.

confusing. Given that a great deal of business conducted today is international in nature, it's important to consider the special ethical challenges this creates. Specifically, how does one behave ethically when conducting business abroad? The answer is complex and highly nuanced. However, problems may be avoided by adhering to several guiding principles that I now identify.

Ethical Relativism and Ethical Imperialism

Over the years, philosophers have approached international business ethics by distinguishing between two extreme approaches—*ethical relativism* and *ethical imperialism* (see Figure 2.6).

To some people, the matter of how to conduct oneself when doing business abroad is as easy as "when in Rome, do what the Romans do." This calls for adopting the ethics of whatever country in which one does business—an approach known as **ethical relativism**. The rationale is that one culture's ethics are no better than any other's, and that there are no internationally acceptable standards of right and wrong.

The problem with this approach is that it may lead to condoning acts that violate one's own sense of morality.[56] Consider this example. Some time ago, several European pharmaceutical companies and tanneries were looking for places where they could dispose of toxic chemical waste. Government officials from most countries they approached said no, fearing the health risks to their people. Nigeria, however, agreed to the business even though local workers, who didn't have any protective clothing, had a good chance of coming into contact with deadly substances as they moved the barrels that contained them. Despite the fact that the practice was permitted in Nigeria, it's easy to see how the risks to the workers make the practice ethically questionable. Just because one particular country was willing to assume the risk doesn't make it right.

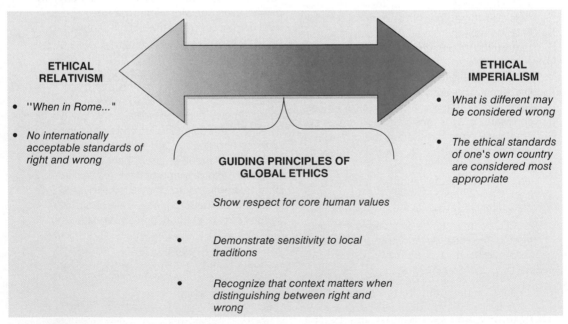

FIGURE 2.6   Approaches to Global Ethics: Two Extremes and a Middle Ground
Too often, people attempting to make ethical decisions in international settings follow one of the two ill-advised, extreme approaches identified here—*ethical relativism* and *ethical imperialism*. By adopting qualities of both approaches, a middle ground can be found in which people can be guided by three principles of global ethics.
Source: Based on suggestions by Donaldson, 1996; see Note 56.

Given that following ethical relativism may lead to moral transgressions, then how about the opposite approach? That is, what if, wherever they are, people use their own country's ethical standards? In other words, they do everywhere whatever they consider to be right while at home. This approach, which is the opposite of ethical relativism, is known as **ethical imperialism**.

It too has limitations. Highly absolute in its approach, ethical imperialism asserts that there is only a single set of rules regarding right and wrong—one's own. Thus, whatever is different is wrong. Obviously, this is very limiting because it fails to recognize cultural and situational differences that may influence ethical behavior. For example, North American–type training in avoiding sexual harassment likely would be questioned in Middle Eastern countries, where the treatment of women is highly regulated by social and religious customs.

Guiding Principles of Global Ethics

It has been recommended that company officials doing business abroad adopt a stance between the extremes of ethical relativism and ethical imperialism. In this connection, they may be guided by three key principles.[57]

SHOW RESPECT FOR CORE HUMAN VALUES   Certain practices, considered core human values, constitute the minimum ethical standards for organizations to follow. For example, ethical companies embrace people's rights to safe working conditions, rights to be free, and rights to be treated with dignity and respect.

It is with these considerations in mind that many companies refuse to work with suppliers who use *sweatshops*—factories, often located in developing countries, in which people (often children) are required to work long hours under dangerous conditions for extremely little pay and often live in squalid company-owned housing.[58]

DEMONSTRATE SENSITIVITY TO LOCAL TRADITIONS   Being ethical requires following local traditions, so long as these don't violate core human values, of course. As a case in point, consider the practice of gift-giving among business partners in Japan. Although many American companies frown on such acts because they fear that the giving of gifts might be a way of unfairly influencing someone by cultivating his or her favor, this is not the case in Japan. This is not to say that bribery is condoned there. Such acts are not meant to be bribes. Rather, the act of giving small gifts is a customary ritual that connotes politeness and trust between the parties. To not accept a gift from a business partner would be considered highly impolite and insulting. These days, because American companies conduct so much business in Japan, officials are coming to accept this practice as acceptable. After all, when you understand precisely what the act means in Japanese culture, it hardly can be considered unethical.

RECOGNIZE THAT CONTEXT MATTERS WHEN DISTINGUISHING BETWEEN RIGHT AND WRONG   Ethical rules are not hard and fast. Sometimes what's right in one context may be considered wrong in another. Being ethical requires taking into account the nature of the setting in which acts occur.

In the United States, for example, it would be considered unethical (and potentially illegal) to hire one's own relatives instead of a more qualified nonfamily member. By contrast, in India, such a practice makes sense. There, jobs are difficult to find, and some of the most successful companies offer as a perk to their employees the opportunity to hire their children once they graduate from school. This eases unemployment, thereby strengthening the economy. Additionally, Indians believe that keeping the family together is more important than pursuing economic opportunities. For these reasons, the practice of hiring relatives may be considered ethical—but only in India, where conditions are unique. That's the point: different contexts may require different ethical guidelines.

If, upon reading this, you realize the complexities of attempting to behave ethically in international settings, then you have reached the same conclusion as many a seasoned businessperson. As one business expert put it, "Managers living and working abroad who are not prepared to grapple with moral ambiguity and tension should pack their bags and come home."[59]

BEYOND ETHICS: CORPORATE SOCIAL RESPONSIBILITY

Usually, when we think of business organizations, we focus on their financial responsibilities to stockholders and investors—that is, to make money. Of course, this is not their only responsibility. To quote Henry Ford, "A business that makes nothing but money is a poor kind of business."[60] As we have been discussing, organizations also are responsible for obeying the law and answering to yet a higher standard, behaving ethically. In addition to these considerations, many of today's organizations are going beyond their legal and ethical responsibilities by taking proactive steps to help society at large by virtue of their philanthropic (i.e., charitable) contributions. Such organizations are, in a sense, repaying the communities that support them.

Collectively, four fundamental forms of responsibility—economic, legal, ethical, and philanthropic—comprise the so-called **pyramid of corporate social responsibility** (see Figure 2.7).[61]

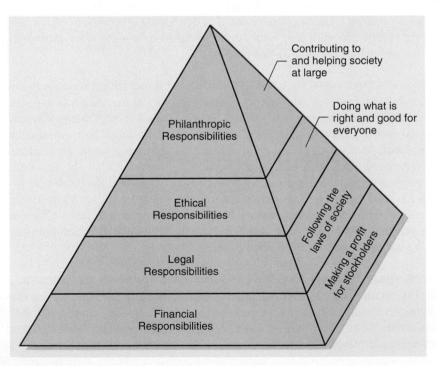

FIGURE 2.7   The Pyramid of Corporate Social Responsibility
To be socially responsible, companies must meet the four different types of responsibilities identified here. The most basic responsibilities, financial, are shown at the bottom because organizations would go out of business if they failed to meet their financial responsibilities.
Source: Based on suggestions by Schwartz, 2011; see Note 61.

The pyramid metaphor is used to reflect the fact that the most basic form of responsibility—financial responsibility—is at the base of the pyramid. After all, unless a company makes money, it will go out of business, making it impossible to attend to anything else.

The Nature and Forms of Corporate Social Responsibility

The term **corporate social responsibility** typically focuses at the top of the pyramid. It describes business practices that adhere to ethical values that comply with legal requirements, demonstrate respect for individuals, and promote the betterment of the community at large and the environment. It involves operating a business in a manner that meets or exceeds the ethical, legal, and public expectations that society has of businesses. Some examples of highly socially responsible actions from well-known companies are as follows:

- *Chiquita Brands International*—The world's top producer of bananas also is considered a leader in corporate social responsibility. This company avoids using toxic chemicals, and unlike some competitors, refrains from mistreating and underpaying its laborers.[62]
- *McDonald's*—So extensive is this international restaurant chain's commitment to social responsibility that it publishes an extensive *Worldwide Corporate Responsibility Report*. Among its many key activities is the Ronald McDonald House Charities, which works to improve the health and well-being of children and families around the world. The company also is engaged actively in protecting the environment by recycling and using innovative ways to conserve resources.
- *UPS*—For more than 50 years, this package delivery giant has operated a separate non-profit company, the UPS Foundation, designed to benefit the community. Recently, UPS has focused on sustaining the environment by deploying 245 new delivery trucks powered by compressed natural gas (CNG) to cities in Colorado and California. These so-called "green" trucks reflect the company's commitment to reducing emissions from fossil fuel and lowering its carbon footprint.

These three examples are noteworthy, but the companies are far from unique in their dedication to corporate social responsibility. In fact, many of the largest companies in the United States have been going out of their way to behave in a variety of socially responsible ways. This takes many forms, which I now describe.

HELPING THE COMMUNITY BY MAKING CHARITABLE CONTRIBUTIONS One of the most popular ways for companies to be socially responsible is by giving donations back to the communities in which they operate. Such acts are not only helpful and generous, of course, but also stand to be good business practices because helping the community promotes business and helps develop future employees.

PROMOTING ENVIRONMENTAL SUSTAINABILITY Many organizations are involved actively in efforts to preserve the natural environment. The three companies noted earlier (i.e., Chiquita Brands, McDonald's, and UPS) are among many that embrace **environmental sustainability**—that is, they engage in efforts to ensure that the earth's resources continue to endure.

Instead of considering environmental issues as an aside that diverts attention from an organization's primary objectives, companies that promote environmental sustainability demonstrate stewardship of the planet. Their leaders believe that this orientation is beneficial not only because it is good for our planet but also because it promotes opportunities for innovation (see Chapter 12), thereby creating an advantage over competitors.[63]

SOCIALLY RESPONSIBLE INVESTING Another way companies can be socially responsible is by adopting investment strategies that focus on social good in addition to financial gain—a practice known as **socially responsible investing**. Among other things, socially responsible companies (such as those identified on p. 55) concentrate on sustaining the environment, protecting consumers, preserving human rights, and promoting diversity. As I indicate below, such companies tend to be profitable investments.

PROMOTING THE WELFARE OF EMPLOYEES One of the most fundamental ways a company has of being socially responsible is by promoting the welfare of its own employees. Several companies have gone out of their way to avoid abusive labor practices even if they prevail in their industries. As an illustration, the Brazilian cosmetics firm Natura Cosméticos shows its support for human rights by not using child labor. It also gives generously to educational programs and encourages its employees to do volunteer work for nonprofit organizations.

It is important to realize that being socially responsible involves more than just a few isolated generous practices or occasional kind gestures. Moreover, it is not motivated by an interest in promoting a company's marketing or public relations efforts. It is far more integrative in nature and genuine in intent. Instead, corporate social responsibility is a comprehensive set of policies, practices, and programs that are integrated throughout business operations, and decision-making processes that are supported and rewarded by top management.

Profitability and Social Responsibility: The Virtuous Circle

Whenever corporate social responsibility is considered, the following question inevitably arises: Do socially responsible companies perform better financially than those that are less socially responsible? The answer is—generally, yes. A recent study compared the companies on the lists of the "100 Best Corporate Citizens" for the years 2001–2009 with a broad index of 1,000 companies with respect to total return on investments. The findings were impressive: companies in the 100 Best lists outperformed the others by 26 percent.[64] Although there are many possible explanations for these results, and conditions may change in the future, what they suggest about the potential benefits of investing in socially responsible companies appears to be considered seriously—especially since similar findings have been reported by other scientists as well.[65]

Although there are surely many different reasons for this link between social responsibility and profitability, a key one, which I also mentioned in connection with ethics, is that people often support the socially responsible activities of organizations with their patronage and investments. With this in mind, there exist mutual funds that invest only in socially responsible companies and books that provide detailed information on the socially responsible (and irresponsible) behavior of companies that consumers and investors can use to guide their decisions.[66] Today, individuals who desire to support socially responsible companies by "voting with their dollars" can find it easy to get the information they need on the Internet. That this may contribute to the financial well-being of a company is important, of course, since financial considerations are an organization's most basic responsibility (which is why they are at the base of the corporate social responsibility pyramid shown in Figure 2.7). That said, it is important to keep in mind that most companies engaging in socially responsible behavior do so for its own sake, and not as a path to profitability.

It is interesting to note that the connection between corporate social responsibility and profitability appears to be bidirectional in nature. The idea is straightforward: companies that are successful financially invest in social causes because they can afford to do so (i.e., they "do good by doing well") and as I noted previously, socially responsible companies tend to perform well financially (i.e., they "do well by doing good"). This relationship, which has been referred to as the **virtuous circle**, is shown in Figure 2.8.[67]

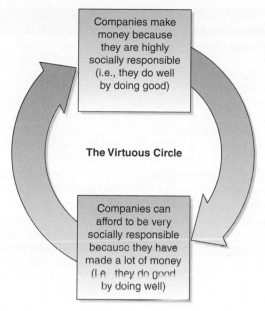

FIGURE 2.8   The Virtuous Circle
It is been suggested that socially responsible companies perform well financially because they are supported by customers and investors. As a result, they become wealthier, making it easier for them to become even more philanthropic. This is known as the *virtuous circle*.
Source: Based on suggestions by Treviño & Nelson, 2011; see Note 67.

With the virtuous circle in mind, it is not surprising to find that some of the world's most profitable organizations are also among the most philanthropic. As an example, let's consider ExxonMobil, which regularly is identified as one of the most profitable companies in the world. In one recent year alone, the ExxonMobil corporation, its divisions and affiliates, and the ExxonMobil foundation donated $189 million in cash, goods, and services worldwide ($111 million in the United States and $78 million in other countries).[68] By making these donations, the company is surely promoting goodwill. That this results in increased profits is a distinct possibility. And as this occurs, it becomes possible for ExxonMobil to make still more generous charitable contributions. In this manner, the cycle continues.

Back to the Case

Answer the following questions based on this chapter's Making the Case (p. 32) to illustrate insights you have derived from the material in this chapter.

1. What form(s) of justice were violated in this situation? What could have been done to avoid these injustices?
2. How do you think the ethics climate at AIG might change following the bailout and the public's outrage over the large bonuses paid to executives?
3. In view of this situation, do you believe that AIG will demonstrate higher levels of corporate social responsibility in the future? On what do you base this?

You Be the Consultant

Employee Theft in Convenience Stores

The district manager of a chain of 24-hour convenience stores is very concerned about her stores' rate of employee theft, which is currently about twice the industry average and rising rapidly. Because this problem has arisen suddenly, you and she suspect that it is in response to some recently introduced changes in the company's overtime policy. Managers who used to be paid time-and-a-half for each hour they worked over 40 are now paid a flat salary that typically results in lower total wages for the same amount of work. Answer the following questions based on the information in this chapter.

1. What form of justice appears to have been violated by the new pay policy? Explain your answer.

2. In this case, the new pay policy was implemented without first discussing it with store managers. Do you think that the theft rate might have been lower had this been done? Why is this, and what form of justice does this involve?

3. The company's code of ethics expressly prohibits theft, but other than being handed a copy along with other company documents and forms upon being hired, hardly anyone pays attention to it. What could be done to enhance the effectiveness of the code of ethics as a weapon for combating the theft problem?

Self-Assessment Exercise

ASSESSING ORGANIZATIONAL JUSTICE WHERE YOU WORK

To learn how workers respond to various types of injustices they may experience in the workplace, scientists have found it useful to use rating scales like the one shown. By completing this scale, you will gain some useful insight into your own feelings about the fairness experienced in the organization in which you work.

Directions

1. Using the following scale, respond to each of the questionnaire items by selecting a number from 1 to 5 to indicate the extent to which it applies to you.

    1 = almost never
    2 = slightly
    3 = moderately
    4 = greatly
    5 = almost always

2. In responding to each item, think about a particular organization in which you work or, if you are a student, think about a particular class.
3. Where you see the word "superior" (in the questionnaire), substitute a specific authority figure that is relevant to you (e.g., for a worker, one's supervisor; for a student, one's teacher).

Scale

To what extent . . .

1. _____ Are you encouraged to voice any concerns to your superiors?
2. _____ Are evaluations of your performance generally based on accurate information?
3. _____ Do you have opportunities to correct mistakes in the way your job performance is assessed?
4. _____ Do the rewards you receive (e.g., pay raises, recognition) reflect your relative contributions to the company?
5. _____ When people in your company are reprimanded, does the punishment received fit the crime?
6. _____ Do the best people in the company receive the most recognition for their accomplishments?
7. _____ Does your supervisor treat you in a polite manner?
8. _____ Does your superior demonstrate respect and dignity in the way he or she regularly treats you?
9. _____ Is your superior unlikely to make rude and demeaning statements?
10. _____ Does your superior communicate news to you in an open and unbiased fashion?
11. _____ Does your superior share important information in a timely manner?
12. _____ Is your superior likely to explain his or her decisions to you in a clear and thorough fashion?

Scoring

1. Add your responses to questions 1, 2, and 3. This is your *procedural justice* score.
2. Add your responses to questions 4, 5, and 6. This is your *distributive justice* score.
3. Add your responses to questions 7, 8, and 9. This is your *interpersonal justice* score.
4. Add your responses to questions 10, 11, and 12. This is your *informational justice* score.
5. For each score, higher numbers (e.g., 12–15) reflect higher perceived amounts of the type of fairness in question, whereas lower scores (e.g., 3–6) reflect lower perceived amounts of that type of fairness.

Discussion Questions

1. With respect to what particular type of fairness did you score highest? What specific experiences contributed to this assessment?
2. With respect to what particular type of fairness did you score lowest? What specific experiences contributed to this assessment?
3. What kinds of problems resulted from any violations of any type of organizational justice you may have experienced? What could have been done to avoid these violations?

Group Exercise

ANALYZING AN ETHICAL DILEMMA

More often than you might imagine, managers confront situations in which they have to decide the right thing to do. Such "ethical dilemmas," as they are known, are usually quite challenging. Discussing ethical dilemmas with others is often a useful way of shedding light on the ethical path by identifying ethical considerations that you may have overlooked on your own. This exercise will give you an opportunity to analyze an ethical dilemma.

Directions

1. Divide the class into multiple groups of three or four students.
2. Read the following ethical dilemma.
3. Working together with the others in your group, analyze the dilemma by answering the following questions:
   a. As the president in this situation, what do you think you *would do*? What factors enter into your decision?
   b. What do you think would be the *right thing* to do? Explain the basis for your answer.

Ethical Dilemma

You are president of a company that refurbishes rollers for presses used to print newspapers. Because the Internet has cut into newspaper circulation, your business is down considerably and it may be necessary to lay off part of your workforce. For many years, you've been using a laborious and inefficient mechanical method for stripping the rubber off old rollers. However, a far more efficient process involves using a particular chemical that would run off into a local stream. Currently, it's illegal to use this chemical because it was believed to pollute the water supply and to be harmful to wildlife. Today, however, research reveals that the chemical really is safe, at least in the quantities used by the company. Officials in your company who have connections in the EPA tell you that this agency is considering revising its regulations to allow industrial runoff to include certain amounts of this chemical. Depending on the level of chemical stipulated by the EPA, your company would be allowed to follow a far less expensive and time-consuming process that currently cannot be used. You can wait to see if and how the EPA will change its regulations, but this can take time that otherwise would allow you to become more profitable and to save jobs.

Discussion Questions

1. Did the members of your group generally agree or disagree about what they would do in the situation described? What new viewpoints, if any, did you learn from others in your group?
2. Did the members of your group generally agree or disagree about what they thought was the right thing to do? What were the major points of agreement and disagreement?
3. In judging the right thing to do, what factors were taken into account (e.g., possible legal ramifications, profitability, etc.) and in what manner were they considered? Did you gain any new insight into the ethical dilemma by virtue of the viewpoints expressed by others? Explain.

Notes

MAKING THE CASE NOTES

Ng, S. (2010, February 3). Despite critics, AIG sets bonuses. *WallStreetJournal.com*. http://online.wsj.com/article/SB10001424052748704022804575041300793298866.html. Gruenwald, M. (2010, January 15). Geithner gets a bad rap in the AIG scandal. *Time.com*. http://www.time.com/time/business/article/0,8599,1953864,00.html. Gentry, P. (2009, March 19). Obama outraged with AIG. *BET.com*. http://blogs.bet.com/news/pamela/2009/03/19/obama-outrage-with-aig. Board of Governors of the Federal Reserve System. (2009). Troubled asset relief program (TARP) information. http://www.federalreserve.gov/bankinforeg/tarpinfo.htm.

CHAPTER NOTES

1. Fitness, J. (2000). Anger in the workplace: An emotion script approach to anger episodes between workers and their superiors, co-workers and subordinates. *Journal of Organizational Behavior, 21,* 147–162. Törestad, B. (1990). What is anger provoking? A psychophysical study of perceived causes of anger. *Aggressive Behavior, 16,* 9–26.
2. Greenberg, J., & Colquitt, J. A. (2005). *Handbook of organizational justice.* Mahwah, NJ: Lawrence Erlbaum Associates.
3. Werhane, P., Radin, T. J., & Bowie, N. E. (2003). *Employment and employee rights.* Malden, MA: Blackwell.
4. Henriques, D. B. (2011). *The wizard of lies.* New York: Times Books. United States Senate, (2011). Collapse of Enron. Washington, DC: Author.
5. Harvard Business School Press. (2003). *Harvard Business Review on corporate responsibility.* Boston: Author.
6. Greenberg, J. (2011). Organizational justice: The dynamics of fairness in the workplace. In S. Zedeck (Ed.), *APA handbook of industrial/organizational psychology* (Vol. 3, pp. 271–328). Washington, DC: American Psychological Association. Colquitt, J. A. (2001). On the dimensionality of organizational justice: A construct validation of a measure. *Journal of Applied Psychology, 86,* 386–400.

7. Greenberg, J. (1996). *The quest for justice on the job: Essays and experiments.* Thousand Oaks, CA: Sage.

8. Ang, S., Van Dyne, L., & Begley, T. M. (2003). The employment relationships of foreign workers versus local employees: A field study of organizational justice, job satisfaction, performance, and OCB. *Journal of Organizational Behavior, 24,* 561–583.

9. Greenberg, J. (2000). Promote procedural justice to enhance acceptance of work outcomes. In E. A. Locke (Ed.), *The Blackwell handbook of principles of organizational behavior* (pp. 181–195). Malden, MA: Blackwell.

10. Allen, M. (1998, May 15). Giuliani threatens action if cabbies fail to cancel a protest. *New York Times,* p. C1.

11. See Note 10.

12. Halogen Software (2010). A sweet employee performance appraisal system for Jelly Belly. http://www.halogensoftware.com/customers/case-studies/services-manufacturing/study_jbelly.php.

13. Greenberg, J., & Cropanzano, R. A. (2001). *Advances in organizational justice.* Stanford, CA: Stanford University Press.

14. Tyler, T. (2005). *Procedural justice* (Vol. 1). London: Ashgate.

15. Lind, E. A., Greenberg, J., Scott, K. S., & Welchans, T. D. (2000). The winding road from employee to complainant: Situational and psychological determinants of wrongful termination claims. *Administrative Science Quarterly, 45,* 557–590.

16. Greenberg, J. (1994). Using socially fair procedures to promote acceptance of a work site smoking ban. *Journal of Applied Psychology, 79,* 288–297.

17. Tatlah, I. A., Saeed, M., & Iqbal, M. Z. (2011). Organizational behavior and procedural-interactive justice in HRM. A secondary school level study. *Journal of Emerging Trends in Economics and Managerial Behavior, 2,* 14–17.

18. Lind, A. E. 2001. Fairness heuristic theory: Justice judgments as pivotal cognitions in organizations. In J. Greenberg & R. Cropanzano (Eds.), *Advances in organizational justice* (pp. 56–88). Palo Alto, CA: Stanford University Press.

19. Long, C. P., Bendersky, C., & Morrill, C. (2011). Fairness monitoring Linking managerial controls and fairness judgments in organizations. *Academy of Management Journal, 54,* 1045–1068.

20. Dulebohn, J. H., Conlon, D. E., Sarinopoulos, I., Davidson, R. B., & McNamara, G. (2009). The biological bases of unfairness: Neuroimaging evidence for the distinctiveness of procedural and distributive justice. *Organizational Behavior and Human Decision Processes, 110,* 140–151.

21. Simons, T., & Roberson, Q. (2003). Why managers should care about fairness: The effects of aggregate justice perceptions on organizational outcomes. *Journal of Applied Psychology, 88,* 432–443.

22. McConahey, M. (2003, June 8). Ethics scandals reach epidemic level. *Press Democrat* (Santa Rosa, California), p. A8. (Also at www.jim-carroll.com/acrobat/publicity/pressdemocrat-1.pdf)

23. Alvey, J. E. (2012). *A short history of ethics and economics.* Northampton, MA: Edward Elgar.

24. Wang, L., & Murnighan, K. (2011). On greed. In J. P. Walsh & A. P. Brief (Eds.), *Academy of Management annals* (Vol 5, pp. 279–316). New York: Routledge.

25. Henderson, V. E. (1992). *What's ethical in business?* New York: McGraw-Hill.

26. Ethics Resources Center. (2003). *2003 National business ethics survey.* Washington, DC: Author.

27. DeCremer, D, & Tenbrunsel, A. E. (2012). *Behavioral business ethics.* New York: Routledge.

28. Ethics Resource Center. (2003). *What is ethics?* www.ethics.org/faq.html#eth_what.

29. Salopek, J. J. (2001, July). Do the right thing. *American Society for Training and Development.* www.astd.org/CMS/templates/index.html?template_id=1&articleid=26983.

30. Treviño, L. K., & Nelson, K. A. (1999). *Managing business ethics* (2nd ed.). New York: John Wiley & Sons. (quote, p. 14).

31. See Note 30 (quote, pp. 26–27).

32. MAALA Business for Social Responsibility. (2002). Corporate social responsibility. Tel Aviv, Israel: Author (also at www.maala.com.). Verschoor, C. C. (1998). A study of the link between a corporation's financial performance and its commitment to ethics. *Journal of Business Ethics, 17,* 1509–1516. Embley, L. L. (1993). *Doing well while doing good.* Upper Saddle River, NJ: Prentice Hall.

33. See Note 32.

34. See Note 32.

35. Johnson, D. C. (1997, November 9). United Way, faced with fewer donations, is giving away less. *New York Times*, p. A1.

36. See Note 30 (quote, pp. 30–31).

37. Ethics and Policy Integration Centre (2003). Toward an effective ethics and compliance program: The Federal Sentencing Guidelines for Organizations. Washington, DC: Author. http://www.ethicaledge.com/appendix1.html.

38. Public Company Accounting Oversight Board (2008, June 12). *Auditing standard number 5.* Washington, DC: Author.

39. Treviño, L. K., & Youngblood, S. A. (1990). Bad apples in bad barrels: A causal analysis of ethical decision-making behavior. *Journal of Applied Psychology, 75,* 378–385.

40. Kohlberg, L. (1976). Moral stages and moralization: The cognitive-developmental approach. In T. Lickona (Ed.), *Moral development and behavior: Theory, research, and social issues* (pp. 2–52). New York: Holt, Rinehart, and Winston. Kohlberg, L. (1969). Stage and sequence: The cognitive-developmental approach to socialization. In D. A. Goslin (Ed.), *Handbook of socialization theory and research* (pp. 347–380). Chicago: Rand McNally.

41. Greenberg, J. (2002). Who stole the money, and when? Individual and situational determinants of employee theft. *Organizational Behavior and Human Decision Processes, 89,* 895–1003. Blass, T. (1999). *Obedience to authority: Current perspectives on the Milgram paradigm.* Mahwah, NJ: Lawrence Erlbaum Associates. Grover, S. L. (1993). Why professionals lie: The impact of professional role conflict on reporting accuracy. *Organizational Behavior and Human Decision Processes, 55,* 251–272.

42. Treviño, L. K. (1992). Moral reasoning and business ethics. *Journal of Business Ethics, 11,* 445–459.

43. Brass, D. J., Butterfield, K. D., & Skaggs, B. C. (1998). Relationships and unethical behavior: A social-network perspective. *Academy of Management Review, 23,* 14–31.

44. Wolfe, D. M. (1988). Is there integrity in the bottom line: Managing obstacles to executive integrity. In S. Srivastava (Ed.), *Executive integrity: The search for high human values in organizational life* (pp. 140–171). San Francisco: Jossey-Bass.

45. Jansen, E., & Von Glinow, M. A. (1985). Ethical ambivalence and organizational reward systems. *Academy of Management Review, 10,* 814–822.

46. See Note 45.

47. Cassell, C., Johnson, P., & Smith, K. (1997). Opening the black box: Corporate codes of ethics in their organizational context. *Journal of Business Ethics, 16,* 1077–1093.

48. Parker, C., & Bielsen, V. L. (2012). *Explaining compliance: Business responses to regulation.* Northampton, MA: Edward Elgar.

49. Ethics Resource Center. (1994). *Ethics in American business: Policies, programs and perceptions.* Washington, DC: Author.

50. See Note 49.

51. Ferrell, O. C., Fraedrich, J., & Ferrell, L. (2010). *Business ethics* (8th ed.). Boston: Houghton Mifflin. Waddock, S., & Smith, N. (2000, Winter). Corporate responsibility audits: Doing well by doing good. *Sloan Management Review*, pp. 66–83.

52. Singer, A. (2003, May/June). Excelon excels at reaching out. *Ethikos, 16*(6), pp. 7–9, 13.

53. Excelon Corporation. (2011). Code of business conduct. http://www.exeloncorp.com/performance/governance/codeofconduct.aspx.

54. See Note 51.

55. Exelon Corporation. (2006. June 27). *Code of business conduct.* http://www.exeloncorp.com/assets/performance/docs/pdf_codeofconduct.pdf

56. Donaldson, T. (1996, September/October). Values in tension: Ethics away from home. *Harvard Business Review*, pp. 48–62.

57. See Note 56.

58. Gap, Inc. (2011). *Social responsibility report, 2010.* New York: Author. (Also at http://ccbn.mobular.net/ccbn/7/645/696/index.html.)

59. See Note 56 (quote, p. 55).

60. http://www.adviceonmanagement.com/advice_ethics.html

61. Carroll, A. B. (1991). The pyramid of corporate social responsibility: Toward the moral management of organizational stakeholders. *Business Horizons, 34*(4), 39–48. Schwartz, M. S. (2011). *Corporate social responsibility: An ethical approach.* Buffalo, NY: Broadview Press.

62. Business for Social Responsibility (2004). *Issue brief: Overview of corporate social responsibility.* http://www.bsr.org/CSRResources.

63. Laszio, C., & Zhexembayeva, N. (2011). *Embedded sustainability: The next big competitive advantage.* Palo Alto, CA: Stanford University Press.

64. Aguinis, H., & Glavas, A. (2012). What we know and don't know about corporate social responsibility: A review and research agenda. *Journal of Management, 38,* 932–968.

65. Orlitzky, M., Schmidt, F. L., & Rynes, S. L. (2003). Corporate social and financial performance: A meta-analysis. *Organization Studies, 24,* 403–441. Kelly, M. (2004, Winter). Holy Grail found: Absolute, definitive proof CSR pays off. *Business Ethics,* pp. 4–5.

66. McIntosh, M. (2003). *Raising a ladder to the moon: The complexities of corporate social and environmental responsibility.* New York: Palgrave Macmillan. Rayner, J. (2002). *Corporate social responsibility monitor.* London: Gee. Kinder, P. D., Lydenberg, S. D., & Domini, A. L. (1994). *Investing for good: Making money while being socially responsible.* New York: HarperCollins. Domini, A. L., Lydenberg, S. D., & Kinder, P. D. (1992). *The social investment almanac: A comprehensive guide to socially responsible investing.* New York: Henry Holt.

67. Treviño, L., & Nelson, K. (2011). *Managing business ethics: Straight talk about how to do it right* (5th ed.). New York: Wiley.

68. ExxonMobil. (2011). 2010 giving report. http://www.exxonmobil.com/Corporate/community_contributions_report.aspx.

PART

II

INDIVIDUAL BEHAVIOR

3 INDIVIDUAL PROCESSES: PERSONALITY, SOCIAL PERCEPTION, AND LEARNING

LEARNING OBJECTIVES

After reading this chapter, you will be able to:

1. **DEFINE** what is meant by personality and **DESCRIBE** its role in determining behavior.
2. **DESCRIBE** various personality dimensions that are responsible for individual differences in organizational behavior.
3. **DEFINE** social perception and **EXPLAIN** the processes by which people come to make judgments about what others are like.
4. **DESCRIBE** social identity theory and Kelley's theory of causal attribution and **IDENTIFY** the various biases that make the social perception process imperfect.
5. **DEFINE** *learning* and **DESCRIBE** the kinds of learning that occur in organizations.
6. **EXPLAIN** various ways in which principles of learning is used in organizations.

THREE GOOD REASONS you should care about. . .

Personality, Social Perception, and Learning

1. Understanding people's personalities helps us know what to expect of them, and understanding our own personalities provides valuable insight into our own behavior.
2. The process by which we perceive others is fundamental to a wide variety of organizational activities.
3. Effectively training, managing, and disciplining employees requires appreciating and applying fundamental principles of learning.

Making the Case for…

Personality, Social Perception, and Learning

The "Taylor-Made" Enterprise

In 1957, Jack Taylor, the sales manager of a Cadillac dealership in St. Louis, had an intriguing idea: instead of selling cars outright, it might be more profitable to rent them repeatedly on a short-term basis. Enterprise Rent-A-Car was born. Rather than competing with industry giants Hertz and Avis, who targeted business travelers by offering rentals at airports, Taylor aimed Enterprise toward a different market—individuals seeking temporary replacements for their damaged or stolen cars. From this modest start, Enterprise Rent-A-Car has grown into a company with more than 50,000 employees in 6,000 offices, making it now the largest car rental company in North America. And with locations within 15 miles of 90 percent of the U.S. population, it's arguably also the most convenient.

As the business was growing, Taylor's son Andy helped his father by working in rental branches, assisting customers, washing cars, and doing whatever was needed. Learning all he could about the business, Andy Taylor worked his way up the ladder, eventually becoming CEO in 1991. Under his leadership, Enterprise quickly became a multibillion-dollar company that expanded into Canada, the United Kingdom, Ireland, and Germany and acquired competitors such as Alamo and National.

The longer people work with Andy Taylor, the more convinced they become that it is not just his business savvy that has made Enterprise so successful, but also his special qualities—particularly, his infectious enthusiasm and his drive to succeed. He works tirelessly, acknowledging that "it doesn't matter how smart or talented you are if you are not willing to put in the work for future success." To ensure that they do, Taylor put a plan into place that rewards employees for their performance. From the assistant manager level upward, Enterprise employees are paid a salary plus a percentage of their branch's profits. As a result, they benefit directly from their hard work and that of their teammates with whom they work closely.

Taylor acknowledges that the business experience he picked up on the job was invaluable, saying, "Through my early experiences at Enterprise I was able to see firsthand the importance of customer service and employee development." So that today's employees can benefit from the same types of experiences, Enterprise promotes people from within the company. In fact almost all of the company's senior managers started out staffing rental offices and worked their way up the corporate ladder as management trainees. In fact, Taylor believes that advancing in Enterprise's training program is like earning a business degree while on the job—"an MBA without the IOU," as he puts it.

Taylor emphasizes that Enterprise's success does not come from an overarching focus on profit. Instead, he believes—and his company's history has shown—that profit follows naturally when you put people first. Indeed, making Enterprise a pleasant place for people to do business is the company's objective. One way Taylor does this is by visiting local offices to keep his finger on the pulse of the business—and by not passing up any opportunities to share his beliefs about the importance of keeping customers satisfied. He also puts people first by giving back to the community through generous donations (both personal and corporate) to local charities, such as the United Way. As Taylor put it, "It will be very satisfying if people say that no matter how big our company got, we always stayed true."

Within this tale of business success lies a backstory that illustrates several basic psychological processes responsible for key aspects of people's behavior in organizations. Collectively, these are the **individual processes** to which I am referring in the title of this chapter—psychological processes that occur within individuals that cannot be seen but whose existence can be inferred on the basis of people's behavior. In particular, my account of Andy Taylor of Enterprise Rent-A-Car highlights the role of the three individual processes discussed in this chapter—personality, social perception, and learning, which are responsible for several different forms of organizational behavior.

To begin, it is obvious that Andy Taylor is a very special individual. After all, it isn't everyone who works his way up from helping his father around the office to leading a multibillion-dollar business. But then again, like Andy Taylor, we all have our own special combination of characteristics that makes us distinct from others. It is this distinct pattern of traits that defines one's *personality*, the first topic I examine in this chapter.

Among the things that have contributed to Andy Taylor's success as an executive appears to be his sensitivity to what others think about the company, cultivating the impression that Enterprise is a "people-first," community-spirited company. The process by which people come to make judgments of other individuals (and companies) is known as *social perception*—a topic that I also cover in this chapter.

Finally, I conclude this chapter with a discussion of another important individual process, *learning*. The importance of learning is illustrated in the Enterprise case by the careful attention given to the management training program and, of course, the hands-on experiences that Andy received as he worked his way up the company.

As you will see from reading this chapter, the various individual processes touched on here are far broader in scope than this case suggests and account for a wide range of behavior in organizations. After reading this chapter, you will come away with a good understanding of the basic psychological processes that contributed to the success of Andy Taylor at Enterprise Rent-A-Car and, more importantly, that contribute to your own success in the workplace.

PERSONALITY: WHAT MAKES US EACH UNIQUE

If our experience with other people tells us anything, it is that we are all in some way *unique*, and at least to a degree, we are all *consistent*. That is, we each possess a distinct pattern of traits and characteristics not fully duplicated in any other person, and these are generally stable over time. Thus, if you know someone who is courteous and outgoing today, he or she probably showed these traits in the past and is likely to continue showing them in the future. Moreover, this person will tend to show them in many different situations over time. This is the essence of personality, the concept described in this section of the chapter. I begin by describing the general nature of personality— defining it formally and explaining its role in behavior. Following this, I identify and describe several different personality variables that are linked to organizational behavior in various ways.

What Is Personality and What Is Its Role in Behavior?

Scientists define **personality** as the unique and relatively stable pattern of behavior, thoughts, and emotions shown by individuals. In short, personality refers to the lasting ways in which any one person is different from all others. And, as you might imagine, personality characteristics play very important roles on the job.[1]

It is important to note, however, that personality by itself doesn't always determine how someone will behave. Suppose, for example, that you are a conscientious and hard-working

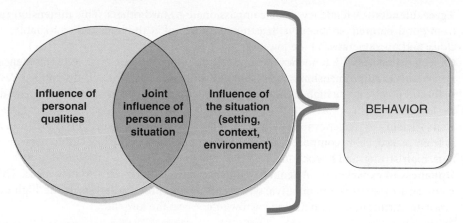

FIGURE 3.1 The Interactionist Perspective
According to the *interactionist perspective*, people's behavior is the result of the joint influence of personality and the situation or context in which the behavior occurs. On any particular occasion, either personality or the situation may predominate although some blend of both factors is almost always involved.

student who usually prepares thoroughly for exams. As a result, you generally perform quite well, earning high grades. On one particular occasion, however, you are ill and unable to study, leading you to perform poorly on an exam. In this example, something about the situation (your illness) counteracted your tendency to be well prepared, causing to the disappointing results. This example illustrates a key point—namely, that how a person behaves at any given time is affected by some combination of his or her personality in conjunction with various aspects of the situation being experienced.

This idea, known as the **interactionist perspective**, is summarized in Figure 3.1. The main point is that personality predisposes people to act in certain ways, but whether they do so depends on the situations in which they find themselves. It is important to keep this in mind as you read this chapter. Personality may affect behavior, but in different ways and in varying degrees in different situations. Throughout this book I will describe situational factors that affect behavior. Here in the first part of this chapter, however, I examine several key personality variables that play an important role in influencing people's behavior on the job.

The Big Five Dimensions of Personality: Our Most Fundamental Traits

How many different personality traits can you name? Some time ago, scientists combing through an English language dictionary identified almost 18,000 traits.[2] Fortunately, we don't have to consider anywhere near this many. A good number of these traits are very similar, and only a handful have been found to play a role in organizational behavior. In fact, evidence suggests that a more manageable five personality dimensions are especially influential. Because the importance of these particular dimensions has emerged in many different studies, they are referred to as the **Big Five dimensions of personality**.[3] These are as follows:

- **Extraversion**—A tendency to seek stimulation and to enjoy the company of other people. This reflects a dimension ranging from energetic, enthusiastic, sociable, and talkative at the high end to retiring, sober, reserved, silent, and cautious at the low end.

- **Agreeableness**—A tendency to be compassionate toward others. This dimension ranges from good-natured, cooperative, trusting, and helpful at the high end to irritable, suspicious, and uncooperative at the low end.
- **Conscientiousness**—A tendency to show self-discipline, and to strive for competence and achievement. This dimension ranges from well-organized, careful, self-disciplined, responsible, and precise at the high end to disorganized, impulsive, careless, and undependable at the low end.
- **Neuroticism**—A tendency to experience unpleasant emotions easily. This dimension ranges from poised, calm, composed, and not hypochondriacal at the low end to nervous, anxious, high-strung, and hypochondriacal at the high end.
- **Openness to experience**—A tendency to enjoy new experiences and new ideas. This dimension ranges from imaginative, witty, and having broad interests at the high end to down-to-earth, simple, and having narrow interests at the low end.

These five basic dimensions of personality are measured by means of questionnaires in which the people whose personalities are being assessed answer various questions about themselves. Some sample items similar to those on popular measures of the Big Five dimensions are shown in Table 3.1. By completing them, you gain a rough idea of where you stand on each of these dimensions.

TABLE 3.1   The Big Five Dimensions of Personality

The items listed here are similar to ones used to measure each of the *Big Five dimensions of personality*. Answering them may give you some insight into these key aspects of your personality.

Directions: Indicate the extent to which you agree or disagree with each item by entering a number in the space beside it. Enter 5 if you agree strongly with the item, 4 if you agree, 3 if you neither agree nor disagree, 2 if you disagree, and 1 if you disagree strongly.

Conscientiousness

_____ I keep my room neat and clean.
_____ People generally find me to be extremely reliable.

Extraversion

_____ I like lots of excitement in my life.
_____ I am usually very cheerful.

Agreeableness

_____ I am generally quite courteous to other people.
_____ People never think I am cold and sly.

Emotional Stability

_____ I often worry about things that are out of my control.
_____ I usually feel sad or "down."

Openness to Experience

_____ I have a lot of curiosity.
_____ I enjoy the challenge of change.

Scoring: Add your scores for each item. Higher scores reflect greater degrees of the personality characteristic being measured.

Research on the relationship between various Big Five dimensions of personality and specific forms of behavior has established some important connections. Overall, the Big Five dimensions are related strongly to work performance.[4] This is the case across many different occupational groups (e.g., professionals, police, managers, salespersons, skilled laborers), and several kinds of performance measures (e.g., ratings of individuals' performance by managers or others, performance during training programs, personnel records). Of all the dimensions, however, *conscientiousness* shows the strongest association with task performance: The higher individuals score on this dimension, the higher their performance.[5] The next strongest connection to job performance is for *emotional stability:* The more emotionally stable someone is, the better his or her task performance tends to be.[6]

Other dimensions of the Big Five also are linked to task performance, but in more specific ways. For instance, *agreeableness* is related positively to various interpersonal aspects of work (e.g., getting along well with others). And for some occupations—ones requiring individuals to interact with many other people during the course of the day (e.g., managers, police officers, salespeople)—*extraversion* is related positively to performance.

The Big Five dimensions also are related to team performance. Specifically, the higher the average scores of team members on conscientiousness, agreeableness, extraversion, and emotional stability, the better their teams perform.[7] Overall, then, it appears that the Big Five dimensions are a key determinant of job performance for teams as well as individuals.

In addition, the Big Five traits also are linked to other important organizational processes.[8] For example, several of the Big Five dimensions play an important role in determining who becomes a leader (see Chapter 11).[9] People scoring high in extraversion, in openness to experience, and in agreeableness (e.g., the tendency to trust others, at least initially) are more likely to become leaders than individuals who score low on these dimensions.[10]

Positive and Negative Affectivity: Tendencies Toward Feeling Good or Bad

As you probably know from experience, some people tend to be "up" most of the time whereas others tend to be more subdued or even depressed; these tendencies are apparent in a wide range of contexts. Such differences reflect the general ways in which individuals approach many events and experiences on their jobs and in their lives. People who approach life in an energetic, exhilarated, and passionate fashion are said to be high in **positive affectivity**. They tend to have an overall sense of well-being, see people and events in a positive light, and usually experience positive emotional states. By contrast, people who are low in positive affectivity are generally apathetic and listless.

Another personality dimension having to do with mood is known as **negative affectivity**. It is characterized at the high end by people who are generally angry, nervous, and anxious. In a survey of office workers 42 percent of respondents indicated that they worked with people who could be described as "negative"—perpetual pessimists who think everything will turn out badly, criticizers who find fault with everything, and people who are just plain negative—they are simply "down" all the time.[11] At the opposite end of the scale we find people who are low in negative affectivity. Such individuals are calm and relaxed most of the time.[12] As indicated in Figure 3.2, positive affectivity and negative affectivity are not the opposite of each other but, rather, two separate dimensions.

As you might suspect, people who are high in positive affectivity behave differently from those who are high in negative affectivity with respect to several key aspects of organizational behavior. In fact, individuals who are high in negative affectivity not only tend to perform poorly themselves, but their negativity also interferes with the performance of others. In other words,

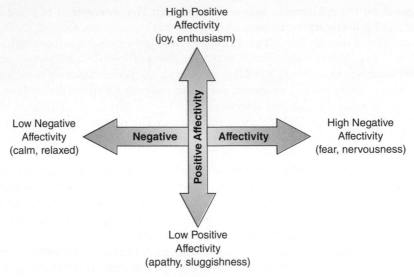

FIGURE 3.2   Positive and Negative Affectivity
Positive affectivity and negative affectivity are two independent dimensions. The mood states associated with high levels and low levels of each are shown here.

they create an atmosphere that reduces productivity and that, of course, can be costly. This comes across in terms of the following forms of behavior.

- *Decision making*—People with high levels of positive affectivity make superior decisions than those with high levels of negative affectivity.[13] (The topic of decision making is covered in Chapter 10.)
- *Team performance*—Work groups that have a positive affective tone (those in which the average level of positive affectivity is high) function more effectively than groups that have a negative affective tone (those in which the average level of negative affectivity is high).[14] (The performance of groups and teams is discussed in Chapter 9.)
- *Aggressive behavior*—Because they tend to be very passive in nature, people who are high in negative affectivity are likely to be targets of aggression from others in their organizations.[15] (Aggressive behavior is among the forms of counterproductive behavior presented in Chapter 7.)

In view of these findings, it's little wonder that positive and negative affectivity are considered important personality traits in the workplace.

Core Self-Evaluations: How Do We Think of Ourselves?

What is your image of yourself? To what extent is your self-concept positive or negative? Although most people view themselves in positive terms, not everybody does so to the same degree. Moreover, the particular way in which we view ourselves is not indicative of a single personality variable but, rather, four distinct elements of personality known as **core self-evaluations**. These refer to people's fundamental evaluations of themselves, their bottom-line conclusions about themselves.[16] Specifically, people's core self-evaluations are based on four particular personality traits. These are as follows:

- **Self-esteem**—The overall value one places on oneself as a person
- **Locus of control**—The extent to which individuals feel that they are able to control things in a manner that affects them
- **Emotional stability**—The tendency to see oneself as confident, secure, and steady (this is the opposite of *neuroticism,* one of the Big Five personality variables)
- **Generalized self-efficacy**—A person's beliefs about his or her capacity to perform specific tasks successfully

Individually, each of the four dimensions of core self-evaluations has been researched extensively, and each is associated with beneficial organizational outcomes.[17] Take self-esteem, for example. People with high levels of self-esteem tend to welcome opportunities to perform challenging jobs and enjoy rising to the occasion. Not surprisingly, they also put forth a great deal of effort and perform at high levels. By comparison, people who have low self-esteem perceive difficult work situations as threats and dislike them. As a result, they either try to avoid such tasks or don't give them their full effort because they expect to fail, and as a result, they tend to perform poorly.[18] Clearly, it's important to consider ways of boosting self-esteem. For some recommendations in this regard, see Table 3.2. (To get a sense of your own level of self-esteem, complete the Self-Assessment Exercise on pp. 93–94.)

Locus of control also is related positively to job satisfaction and performance. Specifically, someone with a highly internal locus of control is likely to believe that he or she can do what it takes to influence any situation. Such people feel confident of being able to bring about change. As a result, individuals with high internal locus of control tend to be satisfied with their jobs because they strive to improve any undesirable conditions or seek new positions (not remaining in jobs in which they believe their fates are sealed). And as a result of making situations better, they tend to perform at high levels as well.

Emotional stability also makes a difference. As we noted in conjunction with the Big Five dimensions of personality, emotional stability is the opposite of neuroticism (i.e., they are

TABLE 3.2 Suggestions for Boosting Self-Esteem

Although it is difficult to completely change key aspects of personality, such as self-esteem, without intensive psychological help, organizations can do various things to boost (and then maintain) the self-esteem of their employees.

Suggestion	Description
• Make people feel uniquely valuable.	Create opportunities for people to feel accepted by finding ways to make use of their unique skills and experiences.
• Make people feel competent.	Recognize the good things that people do and praise them accordingly. That is, "catch someone in the act of doing something right."
• Make people feel secure.	Employees' self-esteem will be enhanced when managers make their expectations clear and are forthright with them.
• Make people feel empowered.	People given opportunities to decide how to do their jobs feel good about themselves and their work.

opposite ends of the same personality dimension). People scoring high on emotional stability generally feel confident and secure, which makes them willing to take on job challenges and to work hard to meet them. Not surprisingly, such individuals not only perform their jobs well but also enjoy high levels of satisfaction in doing them.

Finally, let's consider generalized self-efficacy. Individuals who have high amounts of this trait are confident that they can do well at whatever they do. This, in turn, encourages them to take on such challenges: they believe they will succeed and are unlikely to give up when things get rough. As a result, they tend to be successful at these jobs. Then, because they associate the work with success, they are inclined to be satisfied with the jobs themselves. In view of this, it's important to consider how to raise self-efficacy on the job. (For some suggestions in this regard, see the Winning Practices section below.)

It's important to note that these individual effects tend to be particularly strong when taken together. In the aggregate, researchers consider core self-evaluations to be "among the best

Winning Practices

Boosting Employees' Self-Efficacy

When people believe that they can do a job and do it well, the chances that they really *can* succeed often increase. Why? Because heightened feelings of self-efficacy have important benefits. They increase both motivation and persistence ("Why give up? I know I can make it!") and encourage individuals to set challenging goals ("I know I can do much better than before"). So, encouraging high levels of self-efficacy among employees is worthwhile. With this in mind, here are three things that managers can do to boost self-efficacy among their employees.

Give constructive—not destructive—feedback. Probably the most important reason to give people feedback on their work is to help them improve. Other motives certainly exist (e.g., some managers give employees negative feedback to "put them in their place" or "even the score"), but these reasons are counterproductive from the point of view of increasing self-efficacy. On the other hand, constructive feedback that focuses on how an employee can improve his or her performance can elevate self-efficacy because it helps reassure recipients that they *can* get there—that they have or can soon acquire the skills or strategies necessary for success.

Expose employees to models of good performance—and success. How do people learn to do their jobs effectively? From direct practice, of course; but in addition, they acquire many skills and strategies from others. And the more of these they possess, the more likely they are to perform well—and so to experience increased self-efficacy. This suggests that companies that adopt carefully planned mentoring programs—programs in which inexperienced employees work closely with successful, experienced ones (see Chapter 11)—can help build self-efficacy among their employees.

Seek continuous improvement. Another technique for enhancing self-efficacy involves the quest for continuous improvement. GE's "Six Sigma" program, for instance, rests on the basic idea that "we can do it better—always!" The term *six sigma* is drawn from the field of statistics to refer to an outstanding level of performance, one that is far above average. Although some employees find this approach daunting at first, meetings and workshops soon convince them that they are part of a truly superb organization that will simply not settle for "average." The result? Employees come to view themselves as superior, boosting both their self-efficacy and their job performance.

Given the effectiveness of these practices in raising employees' levels of self-esteem, managers would be well advised to follow them closely.

dispositional predictors of job satisfaction and performance."[19] As a result, it's not surprising that OB scientists have paid a great deal of attention to core self-evaluations in recent years.[20]

SOCIAL PERCEPTION AND ATTRIBUTION: UNDERSTANDING AND JUDGING OTHERS

What do the following organizational situations have in common? (1) You are interviewing a prospective employee for a new position in your company. (2) You apologize profusely after spilling a cup of coffee on your boss. (3) You complete a form asking you to rate the strengths and weaknesses of your subordinates.

If you don't immediately see the connection, it's likely because these situations all involve a phenomenon that is so automatic that you probably never have thought about it before. Specifically, they all involve understanding and evaluating others—in other words, figuring out what they are like. In our three examples, you judge the applicant's qualifications, you make sure your boss's opinion of you is not negative, and you assess the extent to which your employees are doing their jobs properly. In each of these instances, you are engaging in **social perception**—the process of integrating and interpreting information about others so as to accurately understand them. As these examples illustrate, social perception is a fundamental process that is involved in many different organizational situations.[21] With this in mind, I now review several different approaches to the process of social perception.

Social Identity Theory: Answering the Question, "Who Are You?"

How would you answer if someone asked, "Who are you?" There are many things you could say. For example, you could focus on individual characteristics, such as your appearance, your personality, and your special skills and interests—that is, your **personal identity**. You also could answer in terms of the various groups to which you belong, saying, for example, that you are a student in a particular organizational behavior class, an employee of a certain company, or a citizen of a certain country— that is, your **social identity**. The conceptualization known as **social identity theory** recognizes that the way we perceive others and ourselves is based on both our unique characteristics (i.e., personal identity) and our membership in various groups (i.e., social identity).[22] For an overview of this approach, see Figure 3.3.

Social identity theory claims that the way we identify ourselves is likely to be based on our uniqueness in a group. Say, for example, that you are the only business major in an English class. In this situation, you will be likely to identify yourself as "the business major," and so too will others come to recognize you as such. In other words, that will become your identity in this particular setting. Because we belong to many groups, we are likely to have several unique aspects of ourselves to use as the basis for establishing our identities. For example, you may be the only left-handed person on a committee or the only one in your family to have graduated from college.

How do we know which particular bases for defining their personal identities people will choose? Given the natural desire to perceive ourselves positively and to get others to see us positively as well, we are likely to identify ourselves with groups we believe to be perceived positively by others. We know, for example, that people in highly regarded professions, such as doctors, are more inclined to identify themselves with their profession than those who have lower-status jobs.[23] Likewise, people tend to identify themselves with winning sports teams by wearing the colors and logos of those teams. In fact, the tendency to wear clothing that identifies oneself as a fan of a certain team depends on how successful that team has been: the better a team has performed, the more likely its fans are to sport apparel that publicly identifies them with that team.[24]

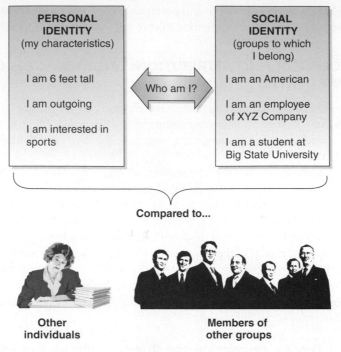

FIGURE 3.3   Social Identity Theory: An Overview
According to *social identity theory*, people identify themselves in terms of their individual characteristics and their group memberships. They then compare themselves to other individuals and groups to help define who they are, both to themselves and others.

In addition to explaining how we perceive ourselves, social identity theory also explains how we come to perceive others. Specifically, the theory claims that we focus on the differences between ourselves and other individuals as well as members of other groups (see the lower portion of Figure 3.3). In so doing, we tend to simplify things by assuming that people in different groups share certain qualities that make them different from ourselves—even if they really are not so different after all.

Not only do we perceive others as different from ourselves, but different in negative ways. This is particularly so when we are competing against them (see Chapter 7). Take athletic competitions, for example. If you ever heard the negative things that students from a particular college or university say about competitors from rival schools, then you know quite well the phenomenon I am describing here. Although such perceptions tend to be exaggerations—and inaccurate, as a result—most of us stick with these perceptions, nevertheless. The reason is simple. Making such categorizations helps bring order to the world. After all, distinguishing between "the good guys" and "the bad guys" makes otherwise complex judgments quite simple. And, after all, bringing simplicity to a complex world is what social perception is all about.

Attribution: Judging What People Are Like and Why They Do What They Do

A question we often ask about others is "why?" Why did the manager use the wrong data in his report? Why did the chief executive develop the policy she did? When we ask such questions, we're attempting to get at two different types of information: (1) What is someone really like? (2) What made the person behave as he or she did? People seek answers to these questions via the process of **attribution**—that is, the mechanisms by which individuals make judgments about what others are like (i.e., assessments of people's qualities and the reasons they behave as they do).

MAKING CORRESPONDENT INFERENCES: USING ACTS TO JUDGE DISPOSITIONS   Situations frequently arise in organizations in which we want to know what someone is like. Is your new boss inclined to be tough or kind-hearted? Are your coworkers prone to be punctual or late? The more you know about what people are like, the better equipped you are to know what to expect and how to deal with them. How, then, do we go about identifying another's traits?

Generally speaking, the answer is that we infer others' traits based on what we are able to observe of their behavior. The judgments we make about what people are like based on what we have seen them do are known as **correspondent inferences**. In other words, correspondent inferences are judgments about people's dispositions—their traits and characteristics—that correspond to what we have observed of their actions. For a summary and two examples of correspondent inferences that people might make, see Figure 3.4.

At first blush, this process seems deceptively simple. A person with a disorganized desk may be thought of as sloppy. Someone who slips on the shop floor may be considered clumsy. Such judgments might be accurate, but not necessarily! After all, the messy desk actually may be the result of a coworker rummaging through it to find some important documents. Similarly, the person who slipped could have encountered oily conditions under which anyone, even the most highly coordinated individual, would have fallen. In other words, it is important to recognize that the judgments we might make about someone may be inaccurate because there are many possible causes of behavior. For this reason, correspondent inferences may not always be accurate.

Another reason why correspondent inferences may be misleading is that people frequently conceal some of their traits—especially when these may be viewed as negative. So, for example, a sloppy individual may work hard in public to appear to be organized. Likewise, the unprincipled person may talk a good show about the importance of being ethical. In other words, people often

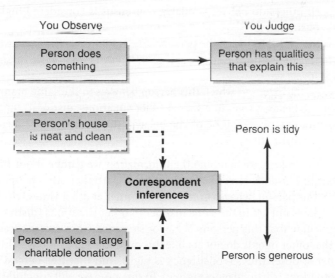

FIGURE 3.4   Correspondent Inferences: A Summary and Examples
Often, we base our judgments of people on what we observe about their behavior. Such judgments are known as correspondent inferences because what we infer about a person corresponds to what we observe about this individual's behavior. Consider the two examples shown here.

do their best to disguise some of their basic traits. Not surprisingly, this makes the business of forming correspondent inferences risky, at best.

Causal Attribution of Responsibility: Answering the Question "Why?"

Imagine finding out that your boss just fired one of your fellow employees. Naturally, you'd ask yourself, "Why did he do that?" Was it because your coworker violated the company's code of conduct? Or was it because changes in business made that person's job unnecessary. These two answers to the question "why?" represent two major classes of explanations for the causes of someone's behavior: *internal* causes, explanations based on actions for which the individual is responsible, and *external* causes, explanations based on situations over which the individual has no control. In this case, the internal cause would be the person's violation of the rules, and the external cause would be the financial need to eliminate the position.

Generally speaking, it is important to be able to determine whether an internal or an external cause was responsible for someone's behavior. Knowing why something happened to someone else might better help you prepare for what might happen to you. For example, in this case, if you believe that your colleague was fired because of something for which she was responsible herself, such as violating a company rule, then you might not feel as vulnerable as you would if you thought she was fired because her job was eliminated. In the first instance you might not feel vulnerable because you know that you wouldn't violate company rules. In the second case, however, you might take steps to secure your future by learning new skills or finding a new job before you are forced to do so. The key question of interest to social scientists is: How do people go about judging whether someone's actions were caused by internal or external factors?

An answer to this important question is provided by **Kelley's theory of causal attribution**. According to this conceptualization, we base our judgments of internal and external causality on three types of information. These are as follows:

- *Consensus*—the extent to which other people behave in the same manner as the person we're judging. If others do behave similarly, consensus is considered high; if they do not, consensus is considered low.
- *Consistency*—the extent to which the person we're judging acts the same way at other times. If the person acts the same at other times, consistency is high; if he or she does not, then consistency is low.
- *Distinctiveness*—the extent to which this person behaves in the same manner in other contexts. If he or she behaves the same way in other situations, distinctiveness is low (i.e., the behavior was not distinctive); if he or she behaves differently, distinctiveness is high (i.e., the behavior was distinctive).

According to the theory, we combine the information we gather about these three factors to make attributions of causality. Here's how. Suppose we learn that other people act like this one (consensus is high), this person behaves in the same manner at other times (consistency is high), and that this person does not act in the same manner in other situations (distinctiveness is high). We are likely to conclude that this person's behavior stemmed from *external* causes. In contrast, imagine learning that other people do not act like this one (consensus is low), this person behaves in the same manner at other times (consistency is high), and that this person acts in the same manner in other situations (distinctiveness is low). In this case, we will conclude that this person's behavior stemmed from *internal* causes.

This highly abstract description comes to life when you consider an example. Imagine that you're at a business lunch with several of your company's sales representatives when the sales

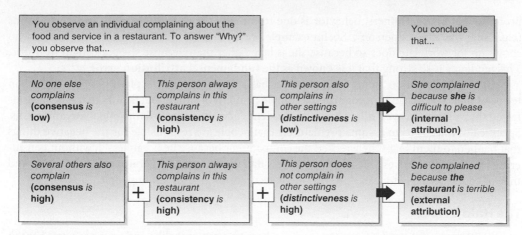

FIGURE 3.5   Kelley's Theory of Causal Attribution
In determining whether another's behavior stems mainly from internal or external causes, we rely on the three types of information identified here.

manager makes some critical remarks about the restaurant's food and service. Further imagine that no one else in your party acts this way (consensus is low), you have heard her say the same things during other visits to the restaurant (consistency is high), and that you have seen her acting critically in other settings, such as the regional sales meeting (distinctiveness is low). What would you conclude in this situation? Probably that her behavior stems from internal causes. In other words, she is a "picky" person, someone who is difficult to please.

Now, imagine the same setting but with different observations. Specifically, imagine that several other members of your group also complain about the restaurant (consensus is high), that you have seen this person complain in the same restaurant at other times (consistency is high), but that you have never seen her complain about anything else before (distinctiveness is high). By contrast, in this case, you probably would conclude that the sales manager's behavior stems from external causes: the restaurant really is inferior. For a summary of these contrasting conclusions, see Figure 3.5.

In closing this discussion, please note that although judgments about consensus and distinctiveness differ when internal and external judgments are made, consistency judgments are high in both cases. The reason for this is simple. Unless our observations of other people are highly consistent, we will be hard-pressed to make any judgments about them whatsoever. After all, if the things we observe about someone change all the time, it's difficult to get a handle on why they're doing what they do, whether these reasons are internal or external in nature.

THE BIASED NATURE OF SOCIAL PERCEPTION

As you might imagine, people are far from perfect when it comes to making judgments of others. In fact, researchers have noted that several important biases interfere with making completely accurate judgments of others.

The Fundamental Attribution Error

Despite what Kelley's theory suggests about internal and external attributions of causality, people are *not* equally predisposed to judging these types of attributions. Rather, we are more likely to explain others' actions in terms of internal rather than external causes. In other words, we are prone to assume that others' behavior is due to the way they are, their traits and dispositions (e.g., "she's that kind of person"). So, for example, we are more likely to assume that someone who shows up for work late does so because she is lazy rather than because she got caught in traffic. This tendency is so strong that it is known as the **fundamental attribution error**.

This phenomenon stems from the fact that it is far easier to explain people's actions in terms of their traits than to recognize the complex pattern of situational factors that may have affected their actions. As you might imagine, this tendency can be quite damaging in organizations. Specifically, it leads us to assume prematurely that people are responsible for the negative things that happen to them (e.g., "he wrecked the company car because he is careless"), without considering external alternatives, ones that may be less damning (e.g., "another driver hit the car"). And this, of course, is likely to lead us to making inaccurate judgments about people.

The Halo Effect

Imagine that you are a supervisor of a worker whom you generally like and who performs her job well. There is only one problem, however: She usually arrives to work late, causing others in her work team to have to cover for her. You are well aware of the problem, but despite this, when it comes to evaluating this employee's performance, you tend to give her high ratings, overlooking this one problem.

Why might you do this? The answer lies in what is called the **halo effect**. This refers to the tendency for a person's overall impression to bias his or her assessment of another on specific dimensions. This type of biased social perception is quite common. People want to have consistent perceptions of others and so they might tend to overlook the one characteristic that doesn't quite fit in. This occurs whether that characteristic is negative (as in this case) or positive. This might take the form of a manager giving a high rating to a subordinate on a particular dimension of performance because that worker is judged to be good on other characteristics. The result, of course, is that the rating given may not accurately reflect the worker's performance.

The halo effect applies not only to individuals but to work teams as well (a topic we will discuss in Chapter 9). Consider, for example, the way we tend to bias our perceptions of the teams for which we root as sports fans. Because we desire to see our team in a favorable light, we attribute positive characteristics to it when it wins ("this is the greatest team ever"). However, if our team loses, we tend to blame the loss on the mistakes or poor performance of one particular player ("the team is still good, but that one player ruined it for us"). This is known as the **team halo effect**—the tendency for people to credit teams for their successes but not to hold them accountable for their failures.[25] (For a summary of this effect, see Figure 3.6.) As members of the team in question, such judgments allow us to take credit for any successes that result ("I'm part of the reason for the team's success) while also deflecting blame for any failures ("the team's failure is someone else's fault").

Stereotypes: Fitting Others into Categories

Inaccurate judgments about people also can stem from the preconceived ideas we hold about certain groups. Here, I am referring to **stereotypes**—beliefs that all members of specific groups share similar traits and behaviors. Expressions of stereotypes usually take the form: "People from group *X* possess characteristic *Y*." For example, what comes to mind when you think about people who wear glasses? Are they studious? Eggheads? Although there is no evidence of such connections, it is interesting that for many people such an image lingers in their minds.

Deep down inside many of us know, and can articulate, that not all people from a specific group possess the characteristics—either negative or positive—with which we associate them. In

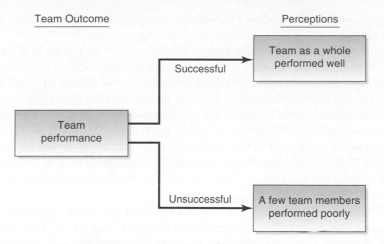

FIGURE 3.6 The Team Halo Effect: A Summary
According to the *team halo effect*, people tend to recognize teams more for their successes than for their failures. In other words, teams are credited for being successful, although a few individuals are blamed when teams are unsuccessful.

other words, most of us accept that the stereotypes we use are at least partially inaccurate. After all, not *all* X's are Y; there are exceptions (maybe even quite a few!).

If so, then why are stereotypes so prevalent? Why do we use them? To a great extent, the answer lies in the fact that people tend to do as little cognitive work as possible when it comes to thinking about others. That is, we tend to rely on mental shortcuts. If assigning people to groups allows us to assume that we know what they are like and how they may act, then we can save the tedious work of having to learn about them as individuals. After all, we come into contact with so many people that it's impractical—if not impossible—to learn everything about them we need to know. So, we rely on readily available information—such as someone's age, race, gender, or job type—as the basis for organizing our perceptions in a coherent way.

If you believe that members of group X tend to have trait Y, then simply observing that someone falls into category X becomes your basis for believing that he or she possesses Y. To the extent that the stereotype applies in this instance, your perception will be accurate. But in that case you would just be lucky. More likely than not, such mental shorthand will lead us to judgments about people that are inaccurate—the price we pay for using stereotypes. And, as is easy to imagine, such tendencies can be quite misleading in the workplace, making them very costly.

Because stereotypes are part of the root cause of prejudice, I will have more to say about them when discussing the topic of attitudes in Chapter 5. For now, however, it's important to keep in mind that stereotypes are a widespread source of bias in social perception. Of course, stereotypes hold not only for race, nationality, and gender, but for just about all ways in which people can be grouped together. (To get a feel for how stereotypes influence people's perceptions of various occupational groups, complete this chapter's Group Exercise on pp. 94–95.)

Self-Fulfilling Prophecies: The Pygmalion Effect and the Golem Effect

In case it isn't already apparent just how important perceptions are in the workplace, consider the fact that the way we perceive others actually can dictate how effectively people will work. Put differently, perceptions can influence reality! This is the idea behind what is known as the

self-fulfilling prophecy—the tendency for someone's expectations about another to cause that individual to behave in a manner consistent with those expectations.[26]

Self-fulfilling prophecies can take both positive and negative forms. In the positive case, holding high expectations of another tends to improve that individual's performance. This is known as the **Pygmalion effect**. This effect was demonstrated in a study of Israeli soldiers who were taking a combat command course.[27] The four instructors who taught the course were told that certain trainees had high potential for success, whereas the others had either normal potential or an unknown amount of potential. In reality, the trainees identified as belonging to each of these categories were assigned to that condition at random. Despite this, trainees who were believed to have high potential were found at the end of the training session to be more successful (e.g., they had higher test scores). This demonstrates the Pygmalion effect: trainees whose instructors expected them to do well actually did so.

Researchers also have found that the self-fulfilling prophecy works in the negative direction—that is, low expectations of success lead to poor performance. This is known as the **Golem effect**. Illustrating this phenomenon, researchers have found that paratroopers whose instructors expected them to perform poorly in their training class did, in fact, perform worse than those about whom instructors had no advance expectations. For an overview of the Pygmalion effect and the Golem effect, see Figure 3.7.

The lesson to be learned from this is clear: Managers should take concrete steps to promote the Pygmalion effect and to discourage the Golem effect. When leaders display enthusiasm toward people and express optimism about each person's potential, such positive expectations become contagious and spread throughout the organization. The impact on performance tends to be considerable.

As a classic demonstration of this, consider the case of Gordon Bethune, who took over the bankrupt Continental Airlines (now, part of United) back in 1995. Despite the carrier's troubled state, Mr. Bethune showed great enthusiasm and support toward its employees.[28] Although it would have been easy for him to be unsupportive and to show his disappointment with the

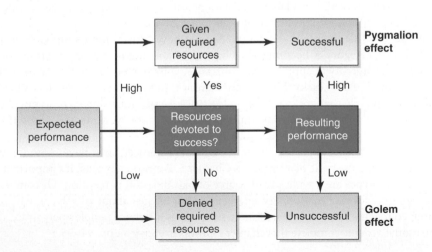

FIGURE 3.7   The Self-Fulfilling Prophecy: Two Forms
The *self-fulfilling prophecy* refers to the tendency for positive expectations to lead to positive results (known as the *Pygmalion effect*) and for negative expectation to lead to negative results (known as the *Golem effect*). To a large extent, this stems for the tendency to give people the resources needed to succeed when success is expected but to withhold these resources when success is not expected.

workforce, he did just the opposite. Only a few years later, Continental became one of the skies' most successful airlines. Although the changes he made to the airline's systems and equipment helped, these things alone would not have been enough if the employees had felt like failures. Indeed, Gordon Bethune's acceptance and enthusiasm toward Continental's workforce has been cited as a key cause of the airline's transformation "from worst to first."

Overcoming Bias in Social Perception: Some Guidelines

In most cases, people's biased perceptions of others are not the result of any malicious intent to inflict harm. Instead, biases in social perception tend to occur because we, as perceivers, are imperfect processors of information. We assume that people are internally responsible for their behavior because we cannot be aware of all the possible situational factors that may be involved—hence, we make the fundamental attribution error. Furthermore, it is highly impractical to be able to learn everything about someone that may guide our reactions—hence, we use stereotypes.

This does not mean, however, that we cannot minimize the impact of these biases. Indeed, there are several steps that can be taken to help promote the accurate perception of others in the workplace. For an overview of several such suggestions, see Table 3.3.

I recognize that many of these tactics are far easier to say than to do. However, to the extent that you conscientiously attempt to apply these suggestions to your everyday interaction with others in the workplace, you will stand a good chance of perceiving people more accurately. And this, of course, is a key ingredient in the recipe for managerial success.

| TABLE 3.3 | Guidelines for Overcoming Perceptual Biases |

Although perceptual biases are inevitable, the suggestions outlined here reflect useful ways of reducing their impact.

Recommendation	Explanation
Do not overlook external causes of others' behavior.	Ask yourself if anyone else may have performed just as poorly under the same conditions. If the answer is yes, then you should not automatically assume that the poor performer is to blame. Good managers need to make such judgments accurately so that they can decide whether to focus their efforts on developing employees or changing work conditions.
Identify and confront your stereotypes.	Although it is natural to rely on stereotypes, erroneous perceptions are bound to result—and quite possibly at the expense of someone else. For this reason, it's good to identify the stereotypes you hold. Doing so will help you become more aware of them, taking a giant step toward minimizing their impact on your behavior.
Evaluate people based on objective factors.	The more objective the information you use to judge others, the less your judgments will be subjected to perceptual distortion.
Avoid making rash judgments.	It is human nature to jump to conclusions about what people are like, even when we know very little about them. Take the time to get to know people better before convincing yourself that you already know all you need to know about them. What you learn may make a big difference in the opinion you form.

LEARNING: ADAPTING TO THE WORLD OF WORK

The process of *learning* is so basic to our lives that you probably already have a good sense of what it is. At the same time, though, you may find it difficult to define. Scientists, however, have studied learning extensively and they define it precisely as follows. **Learning** is a relatively permanent change in behavior occurring as a result of experience.

As straightforward as this definition may be, it incorporates three fundamental points. First, it's clear that learning requires that some kind of change occurs. Importantly, learning cannot be observed directly. Instead, it must be inferred on the basis of changes in behavior. Second, these changes must be more than temporary. This rules out changes that stem from such factors as illness or fatigue. Finally, learning is the result of experience—that is, continued contact with the world around us. As I illustrate in this chapter, these experiences may be direct—as occurs in the case of *operant conditioning*—or indirect—as occurs in the case of *observational learning*. I describe both forms of learning in this chapter along with ways in which they are used in organizations.

Operant Conditioning: Learning Through Rewards and Punishments

Imagine you are a chef working at a catering firm where you are planning a special menu for a fussy client. If your dinner menu is accepted and the meal is a hit, the company stands a good chance of adding a huge new account. You work hard at doing the best job possible and present your culinary creation to the skeptical client. Now, how does the story end? If the client loves your meal, your grateful boss gives you a huge raise and a promotion. However, if the client hates it, your boss asks you to turn in your chef's hat.

Regardless of which of these outcomes occurs, one thing is certain: Whatever you did in this situation, you will be sure to do again *if* it succeeded, or you will avoid doing it again *if* it failed.

This situation illustrates an important principle that lies behind a kind of learning known as **operant conditioning** (also called **instrumental conditioning**), namely, that our behavior produces consequences and that how we behave in the future will depend on what those consequences are. If our actions have pleasant effects, then we will be more likely to repeat them in the future. If, however, our actions have unpleasant effects, we are less likely to repeat them in the future.

This phenomenon, referred to as the **law of effect**, is fundamental to operant conditioning. Our knowledge of this phenomenon comes from the work of the famous social scientist B. F. Skinner.[29] Skinner's pioneering research has shown us that it is through the connections between our actions and their consequences that we learn to behave in certain ways. I summarize this process in Figure 3.8.

The various relationships between a person's behavior and the consequences resulting from it are known collectively as **contingencies of reinforcement**. We may identify four different contingencies, each of which describes the conditions under which rewards and punishments are either given or taken away. These are summarized in Table 3.4.

POSITIVE REINFORCEMENT　A great deal of behavior is learned because of the pleasurable outcomes that we associate with it. In organizations, for example, people usually find it pleasant and desirable to receive monetary bonuses, paid vacations, and various forms of recognition. The process by which people learn to perform acts leading to such desirable outcomes is known as **positive reinforcement**.

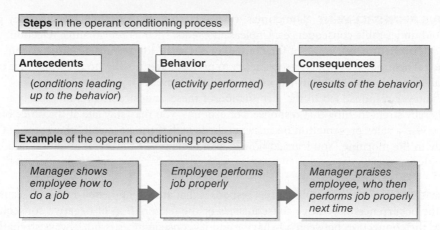

FIGURE 3.8   The Operant Conditioning Process
The basic premise of operant conditioning is that people learn by associating the consequences of their behavior with the behavior itself. In this example, the manager's praise increases the subordinate's tendency to perform the job properly in the future.

Whatever behavior led to the positive outcomes is likely to occur again, thereby strengthening that behavior. For a reward to serve as a positive reinforcer, it must be made contingent on the specific behavior sought. So, for example, if a sales representative is given a bonus after landing a huge account, the bonus will only reinforce the person's actions *if* he or she associates it with getting the account. When this occurs, the individual will be inclined in the future to do whatever it was that secured the account.

TABLE 3.4   Contingencies of Reinforcement

The four *contingencies of reinforcement* are defined in terms of the presentation or withdrawal of a pleasant or unpleasant stimulus. As summarized here, positively or negatively reinforced behaviors are strengthened, whereas punished or extinguished behaviors are weakened.

Stimulus Presented or Withdrawn	Desirability of Stimulus	Name of Contingency	Strength of Response	Example
Presented	Pleasant	Positive reinforcement	Increases	Praise from a supervisor encourages continuing the praised behavior.
	Unpleasant	Punishment	Decreases	Criticism from a supervisor discourages enacting the punished behavior.
Withdrawn	Pleasant	Extinction	Decreases	Failing to praise a helpful act reduces the odds of helping in the future.
	Unpleasant	Negative reinforcement	Increases	Future criticism is avoided by doing whatever the supervisor wants.

NEGATIVE REINFORCEMENT   Sometimes we also learn to perform acts because they permit us to avoid undesirable consequences. Unpleasant events, such as reprimands, rejection, probation, and termination, are some of the consequences faced for certain negative actions in the workplace. The process by which people learn to perform acts leading to the avoidance of such undesirable consequences is known as **negative reinforcement**.

Whatever response led to the termination of these undesirable events is likely to occur again, thereby strengthening that response. For example, you may stay late at the office one evening to revise a sales presentation because you believe that the boss will "chew you out" if it's not ready in the morning. You learned how to avoid this type of aversive situation and behave accordingly.

PUNISHMENT   Thus far, I have identified responses that are strengthened—either because they lead to the occurrence of positive consequences or the termination of negative consequences. However, the connection between a behavior and its consequences is not always strengthened; such links also may be weakened. This is what happens in the case of **punishment**. Specifically, punishment involves presenting an undesirable or aversive consequence in response to an unwanted behavior.

A behavior accompanied by an undesirable outcome is less likely to recur if the person associates the negative consequences with that behavior. For example, if you are chastised by your boss for taking excessively long coffee breaks, you are considered punished because being chastised is an undesirable consequence of your action. As a result, you will be less likely to take long breaks again in the future. As suggested by this example, punishment is the process responsible for the effectiveness of the practice of discipline described later in this chapter (pp. 90–93).

EXTINCTION   The link between a behavior and its consequences also may be weakened by withholding reward—a process known as **extinction**. When a response that was once rewarded is no longer rewarded, it tends to weaken and eventually die out—or be *extinguished*. Let's consider an example. Suppose for many months you brought boxes of donuts to your weekly staff meetings. Your colleagues always thanked you as they gobbled them down. You were positively reinforced by their approval, so you continued bringing the donuts. Now, after several months of eating donuts, your colleagues have begun dieting. So, although tempting, your donuts go uneaten. After going several times without being praised for your thoughtfulness, you will be unlikely to continue bringing donuts. Your once rewarded behavior will die out; it will be extinguished.

Observational Learning: Learning by Imitating Others

Although operant conditioning is based on the idea that we engage in behaviors for which we are directly reinforced, many of the things we learn on the job are *not* reinforced directly. Suppose, for example, on your new job you see many of your coworkers complimenting your boss on his attire. Each time someone says something flattering, the boss stops at his or her desk, smiles, and acts friendly. By complimenting the boss, they are reinforced by being granted his social approval.

Chances are, after observing this several times, you too will eventually learn to say something nice to the boss. Although you may not have directly experienced the boss's approval, you would expect to receive it based on what you have observed about the rewards or consequences experienced by others. This is an example of a kind of learning known as **observational learning**, or **modeling**. It occurs when someone acquires new knowledge *vicariously*—that is, by observing what happens to others.

A great deal of what is learned about how to behave in organizations results from observational learning. On the job, observational learning is a key part of many formal job instruction training programs. As I will explain in the next section, trainees given a chance to observe experts doing their jobs, followed by an opportunity to practice the desired skills, and then given feedback on their work tend to learn new job skills quite effectively.

Observational learning also occurs in a very informal, uncalculated manner. For example, people who witness the standards and traditions of their organizations and who subsequently incorporate these into their own behavior may be recognized as having learned through observation.

Finally, it is important to note that people learn not only what to do by observing others but also what *not* to do. Specifically, research has shown that people observing their coworkers getting punished for behaving inappropriately on the job tend to refrain from engaging in those same actions themselves. As you might imagine, this is a very effective and efficient way to learn how to behave because it keeps us from having to experience consequences on a first-hand basis. And because we're always observing others in the workplace, there's a great deal that may be learned observationally.

APPLICATIONS OF LEARNING IN ORGANIZATIONS

The principles of learning discussed thus far are used in organizations in many different ways. In the remainder of this chapter, I present four systematic approaches to incorporating learning in organizations.

Training: Learning and Developing Job Skills

Probably the most obvious use to which principles of learning may be applied in organizations is **training**—the process through which people systematically acquire and improve the skills and abilities needed to improve their job performance. Just as students learn basic educational skills in the classroom, employees must learn their job skills.

Training is used not only to prepare newly hired employees to meet the challenges of the jobs they will face but also to upgrade and refine the skills of existing employees on an ongoing basis. In fact, American companies spent approximately $171.5 billion on various types of employee training in 2010 alone.[30]

VARIETIES OF TRAINING METHODS   When we speak of training, we are referring to a variety of different activities. Some of the most widely used training methods are as follows:

- *Classroom training*—Just as students listen to lectures in classrooms, so too do employees receive information about work processes and procedures in **classroom training**. In this method, instructors describe various requirements of the job and provide tips on how to meet them. Typically, people learning new skills in the classroom are given an opportunity to practice these skills, either in a simulated work setting or on the job itself.
- *Apprenticeship programs*—Growing in popularity today are formal **apprenticeship programs**, in which classroom training is systematically combined with on-the-job instruction over a long period (often several years in the case of skilled tradespeople such as carpenters, electricians, and masons).[31] To ensure that people going into various trades are trained to appropriately high standards, many apprenticeship programs often are designed and regulated by professional trade associations. For example, the American Culinary Federation uses an apprenticeship program to ensure the proper training of future chefs.

- *Cross-cultural training*—In keeping with the global nature of today's business world, many companies are sending employees overseas to work. For these individuals to function effectively, they have to learn not only new languages but also the cultures and traditions of their host countries. This is accomplished in **cross-cultural training (CCT)**, a systematic way of preparing employees to live and work in another country.[32] This often involves briefing employees about their new cultures and using role-playing exercises to practice ways of interacting.
- *Corporate Universities*—Many companies are so serious about training that they have developed their own **corporate universities**—facilities devoted to handling a company's training needs on a full-time basis.[33] Among the best-known corporate universities is McDonald's "Hamburger University," in which McDonald's franchisees learn and/or polish the skills needed to successfully operate a McDonald's restaurant. Like several other companies, McDonald's has its own campus with full-time instructors.
- *Executive training programs*—Many companies rely on **executive training programs**—sessions in which companies systematically attempt to develop the leadership skills of their top leaders.[34] These programs often involves sending prospective executives to programs run by universities' business schools, where they learn how to develop their leadership skills and how to transform their organizations (topics that are covered in Chapters 11 and 14 of this book).
- *E-training*—These days, because the investment in computer technology required to reach people in remote locations is so small, the vast majority of companies conducting training do at least some of it online. The term **e-training** is used to describe training based on disseminating information online (e.g., through the Internet or a company's internal intranet network). Online training has been used in a wide variety of different industries.[35] Compared to traditional, classroom-based corporate training programs, the primary benefits of online training are (1) flexibility, (2) speed and efficiency, and (3) reduced cost. Given these considerations, it's not surprising that e-learning has been growing in popularity in recent years.[36]

PRINCIPLES OF LEARNING: KEYS TO EFFECTIVE TRAINING   In view of this staggering investment, it is important to consider ways of enhancing the effectiveness of employee training.[37] With this in mind, we now consider four factors that should be incorporated into training programs for them to be effective.

- *Promote active participation*—People not only learn more quickly but also retain the skills longer when they have actively participated in the learning process. The effectiveness of "learning by doing" applies to the learning of both motor tasks as well as cognitive skills. For example, when learning to swim, there's no substitute for actually getting in the water and moving your arms and legs. In the classroom, students who listen attentively to lectures, think about the material, and get involved in discussions tend to learn more effectively than those who just sit passively.
- *Encourage repetition*—If you know the old adage "practice makes perfect," you are already aware of the benefits of repetition on learning. Perhaps you learned the multiplication table, or a poem, or a foreign language phrase by going over it repeatedly. Scientists have not only established the benefits of repetition on learning but also have shown that these effects are even greater when practice is spread out over time rather than when it is lumped together. After all, when practice periods are too long, learning can suffer from fatigue, whereas learning a little bit at a time allows the material to sink in.
- *Capitalize on transfer of training*—As you might imagine, for training to be most effective, what is learned during training must be applied to the job. In general, the more closely a

training program matches the demands of a job, the more effective the training will be. A good example is the elaborate simulation devices used to train pilots and astronauts. At a more down-to-earth level is the equipment used in many technical schools for people to learn skilled trades such as welding, computer repair, and radiation technology.

- *Give feedback*—It is extremely difficult for learning to occur in the absence of feedback— that is, without being given knowledge about the results of one's actions. Feedback provides information about the effectiveness of one's training.[38] Of course, unless you learn what you already are doing well and what behaviors you need to correct, you will probably be unable to improve your skills. For example, it is critical for people being trained as word processing operators to know exactly how many words they correctly entered per minute if they are to be able to gauge their improvement. And, as anyone attempting to perfect a golf swing can tell you, it is necessary to know if one's drive was hooked or sliced if he or she has any hope of making proper adjustments.

Although the four principles of learning just described should be incorporated into any training programs, this alone does not guarantee success. For companies to reap the benefits of the considerable investments they make on training, it is essential for their training efforts to be integrated within their ongoing business practices and plans. For some specific suggestions in this regard, see Table 3.5.[39]

TABLE 3.5   Making Training Work: Some Best Practices

The most effective training programs used today are not a series of isolated practices. Rather, they are carefully integrated into a variety of organizational strategies, tasks, and objectives. Several of these are identified and described here.

Suggestion	Explanation
Align training priorities to business objectives	When deciding exactly what to train, it is important to select areas that are relevant to the organization's aims.
Make sure that investments in training yield rewards that justify the costs.	It's important to continuously assess the short-term and long-term benefits of training activities.
Investments in training must be supported by other organizational practices.	For training to pay off, it should be consistent with compensation systems, recruitment and staffing activities, and related practices.
Use a variety of different approaches to training.	Consider a broad variety of training techniques for various needs (e.g., lectures, on-the-job training, e-learning, etc.).
Encourage employees to identify their own training needs and desires.	Individualized learning plans can help motivate employees and develop otherwise untapped skills.
The job relevance of training should be clear.	Whatever training people receive should help save them time and enable them to improve in the long run, and not add to their workload burdens.
Training should not be considered a one-time event but an ongoing process.	The practice of doing something and reflecting on it should be a continuous one at all career stages.

Source: Based on suggestions by LSA Global (2009); see Note 39.

Organizational Behavior Management: Positively Reinforcing Desirable Actions

Earlier, in describing operant conditioning, we noted that the consequences of our behavior determine whether we repeat it or abandon it. Behaviors that are rewarded tend to be strengthened and repeated in the future. With this in mind, it is possible to administer rewards selectively to help reinforce behaviors that we wish to be repeated in the future. This is the basic principle behind **organizational behavior management** (also known as **organizational behavior modification**, or more simply, **OB mod**). Organizational behavior management may be defined as the systematic application of positive reinforcement principles in organizational settings for the purpose of raising the incidence of desirable organizational behaviors.

Organizational behavior management programs have been used successfully to stimulate a variety of behaviors in many different organizations.[40] For example, one manufacturer of Styrofoam egg cartons used OB mod to boost sagging productivity.[41] Here's how it operated: Any employee working for a full year without an industrial accident was given 20 points. Perfect attendance was given 25 points. Once a year, the points were totaled. When employees reached 100 points, they got a blue nylon jacket with the company's logo on it and a patch identifying their membership in the "100 Club." Those earning still more points received extra awards. For example, at 500 points, employees could select any of a number of small household appliances. These inexpensive prizes went a long way toward symbolizing for employees the company's appreciation for their good work.

Eventually, this simple program helped raise output by 16.5 percent, lowered errors by 40 percent, and lowered the accident rate by 43.7 percent. And, as you might expect, these results contributed to a significant boost in the company's profitability. Needless to say, this was a very simple and effective organizational behavior management program. Although not all such programs are equally successful, evidence suggests that they are generally quite beneficial.

Discipline: Eliminating Undesirable Behavior

Just as organizations systematically may use rewards to encourage desirable behavior, they also may use punishment to discourage undesirable behavior. Problems such as absenteeism, lateness, theft, and substance abuse cost companies vast sums of money, situations many companies attempt to manage by using **discipline**—the systematic administration of punishment.

By administering an unpleasant outcome (e.g., suspension without pay) in response to an undesirable behavior (e.g., excessive tardiness), companies seek to minimize the undesirable behavior. In one form or another, using discipline is a relatively common practice. In fact, 83 percent of companies use some form of discipline, or at least the threat of discipline, in response to undesirable behaviors. But, as you might imagine, disciplinary actions taken in organizations vary greatly. For a summary of commonly used disciplinary measures arranged in terms of severity, see Figure 3.9.[42]

The trick to disciplining effectively is to know how to administer punishment in a way that is considered fair and reasonable. Fortunately, research and theory have pointed to some effective principles that may be followed to maximize the effectiveness of discipline in organizations. I now describe several of these.

DELIVER PUNISHMENT SOON AFTER THE UNDESIRABLE RESPONSE OCCURS The less time that passes between the occurrence of an undesirable behavior and the administration of a negative consequence, the more strongly people will make the connection between them. When

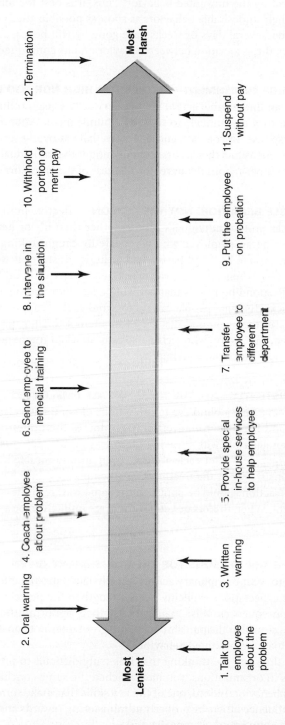

FIGURE 3.9 A Continuum of Disciplinary Measures

Ranked from mildest to most severe, these are the most common disciplinary tactics used by supervisors.

Source: Based on findings reported by Trahan & Steiner, 1994; see Note 42.

people make this association, the consequence is likely to serve as a punishment, thereby reducing the probability of repeating the unwanted behavior. Thus, it is best for managers to talk to their subordinates about their undesirable behaviors as soon as possible after committing them. Expressing disapproval after several days or weeks have gone by will be less effective since the passage of time will weaken the association between behavior and its consequences.

GIVE MODERATE LEVELS OF PUNISHMENT—NEITHER TOO HIGH NOR TOO LOW If the consequences for performing an undesirable action are not very severe (e.g., rolling one's eyes as a show of disapproval), then they are unlikely to serve as a punishment. After all, it is quite easy to live with such a mild response. In contrast, consequences that are overly severe might be perceived as unfair and inhumane. When this occurs, not only might the individual resign, but also a strong signal will be sent to others about the unreasonableness of the company's actions.

PUNISH THE UNDESIRABLE BEHAVIOR, NOT THE PERSON Effective punishment is impersonal in nature and focuses on the individual's actions rather than his or her personality. So, for example, when addressing an employee who is repeatedly caught taking excessively long breaks, it is unwise to say, "You're lazy and have a bad attitude." Instead, it would be better to say, "By not being at your desk when expected, you're making it more difficult for all of us to get our work done on time." Responding in this manner will be less humiliating for the individual. Additionally, focusing on exactly what people can do to avoid such disapproval (taking shorter breaks, in this case) increases the likelihood that they will attempt to alter their behavior in the desired fashion. By contrast, the person who feels personally attacked might not only "tune out" the message but also not know exactly how to improve.

USE PUNISHMENT CONSISTENTLY—ALL THE TIME, FOR ALL EMPLOYEES Sometimes managers attempting to be lenient turn a blind eye to infractions of company rules. Doing this may cause more harm than good because it inadvertently reinforces the undesirable behavior (by demonstrating that one can get away with breaking the rules). As a result, it is considered most effective to administer punishment after each occurrence of an undesirable behavior. Similarly, it is important to show consistency in the treatment of all employees. In other words, everyone who commits the same infraction should be punished the same way, regardless of the person administering the punishment. When this occurs, supervisors are unlikely to be accused of showing favoritism.

CLEARLY COMMUNICATE THE REASONS FOR THE PUNISHMENT GIVEN Making clear exactly what behaviors lead to what disciplinary actions greatly facilitates the effectiveness of punishment. Communicating expectations explicitly helps strengthen the perceived connection between behavior and its consequences. Wise managers use their opportunities to communicate with subordinates to make clear that the punishment being given does not constitute revenge but, rather, an attempt to eliminate an unwanted behavior.

If, after reading all this, you are thinking that it is truly difficult to properly administer rewards and punishments in organizations, you have reached the same conclusion as experts in the field of organizational behavior. Indeed, one of the key skills that make some managers so effective is their ability to influence others by properly administering rewards and punishments (to practice this skill, see the Group Exercise on pp. 94–95).

Back to the Case

Answer the following questions based on this chapter's Making the Case (p. 67) to illustrate insights you have derived from the material in this chapter.

1. How would you characterize Andy Taylor with respect to the personality variables described in this chapter? Which particular trait best seems to describe him?
2. What particular errors or biases in the attribution process are likely to be involved in the day-to-day running of the rental car business? Identify the specific form that these effects are likely to take and the conditions under which you expect them to occur.
3. What did Andy Taylor learn in the early days of Enterprise that helped him and the company become successful? How might learning be used in the company today?

You Be the Consultant

Selecting, Training, and Appraising Employees

As human resources manager for a large information technology firm, you are responsible for three key functions—selecting prospective employees, training current employees, and appraising employees' job performance. Because these processes have been far from perfect in the company, you decide to upgrade them in systematic fashion. Answer the following questions based on material in this chapter.

1. What personality characteristics would you recommend that the company seeks to find in its prospective employees? Which ones should it avoid? Explain your answers.
2. What types of biases and inaccuracies may be expected in the process of appraising employees' job performance? What can be done to minimize the impact of these factors?
3. Given that the company invests a great deal of money in its training program, you are interested in seeing that it works as effectively as possible. What specific steps can you take to ensure that learning of job skills occurs at a high level?

Self-Assessment Exercise

HOW MUCH SELF-ESTEEM DO YOU HAVE?

To objectively measure self-esteem (and most other personality variables), scientists rely on paper-and-pencil questionnaires. This scale, adapted from ones actually used by scientists to measure self-esteem, should give you some insight into this important aspect of your personality. Because this measure is brief and not scientifically validated, you shouldn't draw any definitive conclusions about yourself from it. Still, completing it will give you *some* insight into your own self-esteem. Moreover, this exercise will give you a good feel for what these paper-and-pencil measures of personality are like in general.

Directions

For each of the following items, indicate the degree to which you agree or disagree with each of the ten statements below by selecting one of the four following responses that best reflects your feelings.

Strongly disagree (SD)
Disagree (D)
Agree (A)
Strongly agree (SA)

Scale

_____ 1. I believe I am a worthwhile person, who is as good as others.
_____ 2. I have several positive qualities.
_____ 3. For the most part, I consider myself a failure.
_____ 4. Generally speaking, I can do things as well as others.
_____ 5. I cannot be proud of too many things about myself.
_____ 6. My feelings about myself are quite positive.
_____ 7. In general, I am very pleased with myself.
_____ 8. I really don't have a lot of self-respect.
_____ 9. There are times when I feel useless.
_____ 10. Sometimes I don't think I'm very good at all.

Scoring

1. For items 1, 2, 4, 6, and 7, assign points as follows: $SD = 1$; $D = 2$; $A = 3$; $SA = 4$.
2. For items 3, 5, 8, 9, and 10, assign points as follows: $SD = 4$; $D = 3$; $A = 2$; $SA = 1$.
3. Add the number of points in steps 1 and 2. This should range from 10 to 40. Higher scores reflect greater degrees of self-esteem.

Discussion Questions

1. Based on this questionnaire, how high or low is your self-esteem? Does your score make sense to you? In other words, does the questionnaire tell you something you already believed about yourself, or did it provide new insight?
2. Why do you think items 1, 2, 4, 6, and 7 are scored opposite from items 3, 5, 8, 9, and 10?
3. Do you think the techniques outlined in Table 3.2 on page 73 may help raise your self-esteem?

Group Exercise

DISCIPLINING A GENERALLY GOOD EMPLOYEE

Even the best employees sometimes behave inappropriately. When this occurs, managers confront a special challenge: How can they address the problem behavior without offending or turning off the employee in question? The following exercise will get you to think about handling this difficult, but not uncommon, type of dilemma.

Directions

1. Divide the class into two groups: a group of role-players and an audience.
2. One member of each role-playing group should read the role of Michael M. The other individual should read the role of Michael's supervisor. Members of the audience should read both roles.

3. After familiarizing themselves with their respective roles, the parties should discuss the situation as they would in a real organization. Spend approximately 15 minutes on this (but allow less time or more time as needed).

Role Descriptions

Michael M.

You have been a laborer with a home construction company for almost four years, during which time you have developed an excellent record. You are an outstanding craftsman who always does meticulous work and completes his projects ahead of schedule. You have always gotten along well with your coworkers, and customers have praised you for your kind and professional manner. You know that your boss likes you and is reluctant to fire you, so you have been taking advantage of him by showing up for work late—sometimes by as much as an hour. When your boss speaks to you about it, you admit to being late quite often but explain that this sometimes is necessary because you have to help get your children off to school in the morning. Besides, you explain that because you work so quickly, you make up for being late, so it shouldn't matter. However, you know that your company has a strict rule against being late ("three strikes and you're out"), and you are concerned about losing your job. You are worried about what your boss might say because you very much want to keep your job.

Michael M.'s Supervisor

Michael M. has been a laborer with your home construction company for almost four years, during which time he has developed an excellent record. He has been an outstanding craftsman who always does meticulous work and completes his projects ahead of schedule. Michael has always gotten along well with his coworkers, and customers have praised him for his kind and professional manner. Employees like Michael are hard to find, making you very interested in keeping him happy so that he will continue to work for you. There has been one recurrent problem, however. Because he knows he is so good and that you are reluctant to fire him, Michael has been taking advantage of you by showing up for work late—sometimes by as much as an hour. When you have spoken to him about this, he admits to being late quite often but says that this sometimes is necessary because he has to help get his children off to school in the morning. Besides, he claims that he works so quickly that he makes up for being late, so it shouldn't matter. However, your company has a strict rule against being late ("three strikes and you're out"), and you are concerned that by turning a blind eye to Michael, you are sending the message to the other employees that Michael is "above the law" and that you are "playing favorites" with him. You do not want to threaten your credibility by ignoring the problem, but you also don't want to risk making Michael quit.

Discussion Questions

1. Based on the guidelines for discipline described in this chapter, what specific steps should be taken to handle this situation?
2. As the roles were played out before you, what were the major strengths and weaknesses of the way Michael's supervisor handled the situation? Compare the reactions of audience members with reactions of the role players themselves.
3. As Michael's supervisor, how would you be affected, if at all, by the fact that Michael's lateness resulted from the need to take care of his children? Did this matter? If so, how, and what would you do about it? Compare the reactions of audience members with reactions of the role players themselves.

Notes

MAKING THE CASE NOTES

Enterprise. (2012). *About us*. http://aboutus.enterprise.com/. Schlereth, J. (2003, July–August). Putting people first. *BizEd*, pp. 16–20. *Hoover's Handbook of Private Companies* (2011). Enterprise Rent-A-Car (pp. 148–149). Austin, TX: Hoover's Online.

CHAPTER NOTES

1. Oswald, F. L., & Hough, L. M. (2011). Personality and its assessment in organizations: Theoretical and empirical developments. In S. Zedeck (Ed.), *Handbook of industrial and organizational psychology* (Vol. 1, pp. 333–376). Washington, DC: American Psychological Association. Barrick, M., & Ryan, A. M. (2003). *Personality at work: Reconsidering the role of personality in organizations*. San Francisco: Jossey-Bass. Roberts, B. W., & Hogan, R. (2001). *Personality psychology in the workplace*. Washington, DC: American Psychological Association.

2. Allport, G. W., & Odbert, H. S. (1936). Trait names: A psycholexical study. *Psychological Monographs, 47*, 211–214.

3. Costa, P. T., & McCrae, R. R. (1992). *The NEO-PI personality inventory*. Odessa, FL: Psychological Assessment Resources.

4. Oh, I.-S., Wang, G., & Mount, M. K. (2011). Validity of observer ratings of the five-factor model of personality traits: A meta-analysis. *Journal of Applied Psychology, 96*, 762–773. Salgado, J. F. (1997). The five-factor model of personality and job performance in the European community. *Journal of Applied Psychology, 82*, 30–43.

5. Hurtz, G. M., & Donovan, J. J. (2000). Personality and job performance: The Big Five revisited. *Journal of Applied Psychology, 85*, 869–879.

6. Chiaburu, D. S., Oh, I.-S., Berry, C. M., Li, N., & Gardner, R. G. (2011). The five-factor model of personality traits and organizational citizenship behavior: A meta-analysis. *Journal of Applied Psychology, 96*, 1140–1188. Mount, M. K., & Barrick, M. R. (1995). The Big Five personality dimensions: Implications for research and practice in human resources management. In K. M. Rowland & G. Ferris (Eds.), *Research in personnel and human resources management* (Vol. 13, pp. 153–200). Greenwich, CT: JAI Press.

7. Barrick, M. R., Stewart, G. L., Neubert, M. J., & Mount, M. K. (1998). Relating member ability and personality to work-team processes and team effectiveness. *Journal of Applied Psychology, 83*, 377–391.

8. Raja, U., Johns, G. J., & Ntalianis, F. (2004). The impact of personality on psychological contracts. *Academy of Management Journal, 47*, 350–367.

9. Watson, D., & Clark, L. A. (1997). Extraversion and its positive emotional core. In R. Hogan, J. A. Johnson, & S. R. Briggs (Eds.), *Handbook of personality psychology* (pp. 767–793). San Diego, CA: Academic Press.

10. Judge, T. A., Bono, J. E., Ilies, R., & Gerhardt, M. W. (2002). Personality and leadership: A qualitative and quantitative review. *Journal of Applied Psychology, 87*, 765–780.

11. Magruder, J. (2004, August 5). Negative employees costing companies money. *Arizona Republic*, p. B16.

12. Isen, A. M., & Baron, R. A. (1992). Positive affect as a factor in organizational behavior. In B. M. Staw & L. L. Cummings (Eds.), *Research in organizational behavior* (Vol. 13, pp. 1–54). Greenwich, CT: JAI Press.

13. Staw, B. M., & Barsade, S. G. (1993). Affect and managerial performance: A test of the sadder-but-wiser vs. happier-and-smarter hypotheses. *Administrative Science Quarterly, 38*, 304–331.

14. George, J. M. (1990). Personality, affect, and behavior in groups. *Journal of Applied Psychology, 75*, 107–116.

15. Aquino, K., Grover, S. L., Bradfield, M., & Allen, D. G. (1999). The effects of negative affectivity, hierarchical status, and self-determination on workplace victimization. *Academy of Management Journal, 42*, 260–272.

16. Judge, T. A., Locke, E. A., & Durham, C. C. (1997). The dispositional causes of job satisfaction: A core evaluations approach. *Research in Organizational Behavior, 19*, 151–188.

17. Grant, A. M., & Wrzesniewski, A. (2010). I won't let you down . . . or will I? Core self-evaluations, other orientation, anticipated guilt and gratitude, and job performance. *Journal of Applied Psychology, 95,* 108–121.

18. Judge, T. A., & Bono, J. E. (2001). Relationship of core self-evaluations traits—self-esteem, generalized self-efficacy, locus of control, and emotional stability—with job satisfaction and job performance: A meta-analysis. *Journal of Applied Psychology, 86,* 80–92.

19. See Note 18.

20. Grant, A. M., & Wrzesniewski, A. (2010). I won't let you down . . . or will I? Core self-evaluations, other orientation, anticipated guilt and gratitude, and job performance. *Journal of Applied Psychology, 95,* 108-121. Judge, T. A., Bono, J. E., Erez, A., & Locke, E. A. (2004). Core self-evaluations and job and life satisfaction: The role of self-concordance and goal attainment. *Journal of Applied Psychology, 90,* 257-268. Bono, J. E., & Judge, T. A. (2003). Core self-evaluations: A review of the trait and its role in job satisfaction and job performance. *European Journal of Personality, 17*(Suppl1), S5–S18.

21. Forgas, J. P. (2000). *Handbook of affect and social cognition.* Mahwah, NJ: Lawrence Erlbaum Associates.

22. Ashforth, B. E., & Mael, F. (1989). Social identity theory and the organization. *Academy of Management Review, 14,* 20–29.

23. LaTendresse, D. (2000). Social identity and intergroup relations within the hospital. *Journal of Social Distress and the Homeless, 9,* 51–69.

24. Cialdini, R. B., Borden, R. J., Thorne, A., Walker, M. R., Freeman, S., & Sloan, L. R. (1999). Basking in reflected glory: Three (football) field studies. In R. F. Baumeister (Ed.), *The self in social psychology* (pp. 436–445). New York: Psychology Press/Taylor & Francis.

25. Naquin, C. E., & Tynan, R. O. (2003). The team halo effect: Why teams are not blamed for their failures. *Journal of Applied Psychology, 88,* 332–340.

26. Eden, D. (2003). Self-fulfilling prophecies in organizations. In J. Greenberg (Ed.),

Organizational behavior: State of the science (2nd ed.) (pp. 91–122). Mahwah, NJ: Lawrence Erlbaum Associates.

27. Eden, D., & Shani, A. B. (1982). Pygmalion goes to boot camp: Expectancy, leadership, and trainee performance. *Journal of Applied Psychology, 67,* 194–199.

28. Bethune, G. (1999). *From worst to first: Behind the scenes of Continental's remarkable comeback.* New York: John Wiley & Sons.

29. Nye, R. D. (1992). *The legacy of B. F. Skinner: Concepts and perspectives, controversies and misunderstandings.* Belmont, CA: Brooks/Cole.

30. American Society for Training and Development. (2011). *The 2011 state of the industry: Increased commitment to workplace learning.* Alexandria, VA: Author.

31. Del Valle, C. (1993, April 26). From high schools to high skills. *BusinessWeek,* pp. 110, 113.

32. Francesco, A. M., & Gold, B. A. (1998). *International organizational behavior.* Upper Saddle River, NJ: Prentice Hall.

33. Jarvis, P. (2000). *Universities, corporate universities, and the higher learning industries.* London: Kogan Page. Meister, J. C. (1998). *Corporate universities.* New York: McGraw-Hill.

34. Gist, M. E., Stevens, C. K., & Bavetta, A. G. (1991). Effects of self-efficacy and post-training intervention on the acquisition and maintenance of complex interpersonal skills. *Personnel Psychology, 44,* 837-861.

35. Bell, B. S., & Kozlowski, S. W. J., (2008). Active leaning: Effects of core training design elements on self-regulatory processes, learning and adaptability. *Journal of Applied Psychology, 93,* 296–316.

36. See Note 35.

37. Arthur, W., Jr., Bennett, W., Jr., Edens, P. S., & Bell, S. T. (2003). Effectiveness of training in organizations: A meta-analysis of design and evaluation features. *Journal of Applied Psychology, 88,* 234–245. Kraiger, K. (2001). *Creating, implementing, and managing effective training and development: State-of-the-art lessons for practice.* San Francisco: Jossey-Bass.

38. Ilgen, D. R., & Moore, C. F. (1987). Types and choices of performance feedback. *Journal of Applied Psychology, 72,* 401–406.

39. LSA Global. (2009). Training best practices. http://www.lsaglobal.com/about/Training-Best-Practices.asp.

40. Stajkovic, A. D., & Luthans, F. (2003). Behavioral management and task performance in organizations: Conceptual background, meta-analysis, and test of alternative models. *Personnel Psychology, 56,* 155–194.

41. Doyle, D. C. (1992, October). Employee motivation that works: The 100 club employee program. *HR Magazine,* 33–41. http://findarticles.com/p/articles/mi_m3495/is_n10_v37/ai_13574940/.

42. Trahan, W. A., & Steiner, D. D. (1994). Factors affecting supervisors' use of disciplinary actions following poor performance. *Journal of Organizational Behavior, 15,* 129–139.

4 | COPING WITH ORGANIZATIONAL LIFE: EMOTIONS AND STRESS

LEARNING OBJECTIVES

After reading this chapter, you will be able to:

1. **DISTINGUISH** between emotions and moods.
2. **EXPLAIN** how emotions and moods influence behavior in organizations.
3. **DESCRIBE** ways in which people manage their emotions in the workplace.
4. **IDENTIFY** the major causes of organizational stress.
5. **DESCRIBE** the adverse effects of organizational stress.
6. **IDENTIFY** various ways of reducing stress in the workplace.

THREE GOOD REASONS you should care about ...

Emotions and Stress

1. Moods and emotions have potentially important effects on people's behavior in organizations.
2. Being sensitive to others' emotional states and knowing how to manage your own emotions are useful skills for people in the workplace to have.
3. Stress can have adverse effects on individuals and organizations but its impact can be reduced if you know how to manage it.

Making the Case for . . .

Emotions and Stress

Stressing Stress-Free Jobs at Kaiser Permanente

Wildfires spread through Southern California in 2011, creating high levels of stress in the lives of tens of thousands of citizens. Among them were health-care workers who had to cope with their own stress while caring for patients for whom the disaster took its toll. Although this was difficult for everyone, to be sure, employees of Kaiser Permanente benefitted from programs the large health maintenance organization put in place. Thanks to Dr. Kris Ludwigsen, a psychologist at a Kaiser Permanente medical facility in the San Francisco Bay Area, help already was available for employees suffering losses.

While counseling patients, Dr. Ludwigsen observed that many suffered illness stemming from the stressors in their lives. But it was not only her patients who needed treatment, she noted; so too did the doctors and nurses with whom she worked. Stressors in their personal lives (wildfires as well as less dramatic events) lead health-care professionals to become ill, as do conditions they routinely face on the job, such as making life-and-death decisions involving patients and pressures from administrators to lower costs while raising service quality. Dr. Ludwigsen wasn't at all surprised that her colleagues showed signs of stress-related illnesses. Many were forgetful, irritable, quick to cry, easily distracted, and had difficulty concentrating.

Unlike her patients, though, most of her colleagues didn't bother to seek treatment. Since they wouldn't come to her, she reached out to them. With this in mind, Dr. Ludwigsen launched a comprehensive multistep work stress program for both Kaiser Permanente patients and employees. Since many people—even medical professionals—don't recognize their stress-related symptoms, she began by building awareness. Group sessions were held (strictly confidential, of course) in which people were made aware of some of the signs of stress they were exhibiting. Fatigue, migraines, hypertension, stomach problems, and even panic attacks signaled that it was time to take action.

Since some of the most effective things to do involve getting the stress "out of your system," Dr. Ludwigsen enlisted Kaiser Permanente's help. For example, the company sponsors programs to improve employees' experiences off the job. These include fitness and health classes, and seminars designed to help enrich personal relationships. On the more active side, the company also has extensive new exercise facilities and sponsors a half-marathon in San Francisco. And to help people relax, it offers massages and yoga classes.

One of Dr. Ludwigsen's most important bits of advice has been to get people to avoid working long hours so they could rest and spend more time with their families. Although hospital officials were at first concerned that this would cut into the productivity of doctors and nurses, who routinely work long shifts, it wasn't a problem. Gains in productivity resulting from good health more than offset any increased costs linked to shorter shifts, creating benefits for everyone.

These various efforts suggest that Dr. Ludwigsen's message came across loud and clear: efforts at preventive health care are, in the long run, less expensive and more effective than treating disease. Although Kaiser Permanente may be said to be in the "pound of cure" business, it's also clear that it is committed strongly to offering far more than "an ounce of prevention."

There can be no mistaking the wisdom of Kaiser Permanente's efforts to preserve the health and well-being of its employees and of Dr. Ludwigsen's commitment to bringing this about. If you have any doubt about the value of such efforts, consider this: the workplace is the single greatest source of *stress* in people's lives. Over half of all employees report that stress lowers their workplace productivity, resulting in annual cost to American organizations estimated at a staggering $300 billion.[1] Stress makes a difference in how well people perform, the number of errors they make, and even whether or not they show up for work or remain on their jobs at all. Given that stress plays such an important role in the behavior of people in organizations, it clearly warrants the attention devoted to it in this chapter.

To understand stress fully, it helps to look more broadly at the wide range of emotions that people feel in everyday work situations and their reactions to them. Whether your experiences are positive (e.g., getting a raise), negative (e.g., receiving a poor performance appraisal), or neutral (e.g., doing your job as usual), these everyday feelings—*emotions* and *moods*—play an important role in how we think and act. If emotions and moods seem to be trivial, it's simply because their effects are so widespread that we take them for granted. However, as you will see in this chapter, their impact on the way we work can be considerable.[2]

I begin this chapter with an overview of emotions and mood in organizations, describing their basic nature and the important roles they play in organizations. Following this, I examine the nature of stress on the job, focusing closely on specific steps that can be taken to minimize its often harmful effects.

UNDERSTANDING EMOTIONS AND MOOD

Consider, for a moment, the following situations. Put yourself in the places of these characters, imagining how you would feel if you were them.

- After a gloomy winter, a beautiful, sunny day finally arrived, making Jessica happy. She is now inspired to come up with lots of new ideas for her clients.
- Hector is upset about not meeting his quarterly sales quota. Disappointed and worried about his future, he leaves the office to work out at the gym.
- It's a proud day for Demond. He's excited because that evening, he will receive a major award from the company in recognition of his achievements.

There's nothing special, here, right? Jessica is happy, Hector is upset, and Demond is excited. These are everyday situations to which people have typical reactions. You experience them all the time yourself. But don't let these rather ordinary feelings mislead you into thinking that they are unimportant, especially on the job. Indeed, scientists acknowledge that people's feelings at any given time are quite important. They also recognize that two different kinds of feelings are involved—*emotions* and *moods*. These states, as you will see, have far broader consequences than you might imagine, and they operate in highly complex ways.

Properties of Emotions

By definition, **emotions** are overt reactions that express feelings about events. You get angry when a colleague takes advantage of you. You become sad when your best friend leaves to take a new job. And you become afraid of what the future holds when a larger firm merges with the company in which you've worked for the last 15 years. These are all examples of emotional reactions. To understand them, I now examine the various properties of emotions and the different forms they take.

EMOTIONS ALWAYS HAVE AN OBJECT   Something or someone triggers emotions. For example, your boss may make you angry when she falsely accuses you of making a mistake or a change in company policy that prohibits overtime may leave you feeling worried. In each case, there is someone or something that caused your emotional reaction.

THE SPREAD OF EMOTIONS IS CONTAGIOUS   A key trigger of emotions in people is the emotions of others with whom we interact. This is described using the term **emotional contagion**, defined as the tendency to mimic others' emotional expressions, converging with them emotionally.[3] You may think of it as "catching" the emotions of others. This phenomenon is prevalent on the job, where workers frequently display the same emotional responses of the higher-ranking others with whom they interact.[4]

EXPRESSION OF EMOTIONS IS UNIVERSAL   People throughout the world generally portray particular emotions by using the same facial expressions. In fact, even people living in remote parts of the planet tend to express the same emotions in the same manner as those of us from developed regions.[5] As a result, we can do a pretty good (but not perfect) job of recognizing the emotional states of others if we pay attention to their facial expressions. We have to be careful, however, because as we will point out later, people do not always express the emotions they really feel. When they do, however, we are fairly good at recognizing them.

CULTURE DETERMINES HOW AND WHEN PEOPLE EXPRESS EMOTIONS   Although people throughout the world express emotions in similar fashion, individuals from various countries

---

TABLE 4.1   National Differences in Expressivity

In a survey of more than 5,000 people in 32 nations, researchers found that people in some countries are more inclined to express their emotions than those in other countries. Listed in order from most expressive (rank 1) to least expressive (rank 32), the findings are summarized here. The scores shown are an index created by the scientists to reflect each country's level of expressivity (higher scores reflect higher degrees of expressivity).

Rank	Nation	Score	Rank	Nation	Score	Rank	Nation	Score
1	Zimbabwe	523	10 tied	India	495	23 tied	Italy	451
2	Canada	520	13	Mexico	485	23 tied	Croatia	451
3	United States	519	14	Georgia	478	25	South Korea	449
4	Australia	510	15 tied	Poland	477	26 tied	Switzerland	446
5	Nigeria	506	15 tied	Portugal	477	26 tied	Malaysia	446
6	Denmark	505	17	People's Republic of China		28	Israel	442
7	New Zealand	502	18	Czech Republic	471	29	Russia	432
8	Belgium	498	19	Turkey	468	30	Bangladesh	422
9	Netherlands	496	20	Japan	467	31	Indonesia	420
10 tied	Brazil	495	21	Germany	464	32	Hong Kong	399
10 tied	Hungary	495	22	Greece	455			

Source: Based on data reported by Matsumoto et al., 2008; see Note 7.

differ in the degree to which it is considered acceptable to express those emotions.[6] These expectations are known as **display rules**.

For example, American and Canadian cultural norms accept public displays of emotion (e.g., hugging good-bye at the airport, or yelling at one another in public), whereas cultural norms frown on such public displays in Germany, encouraging people there to "tone down" their emotional displays. And, in several Asian nations, such as Hong Kong, Malaysia, and South Korea, people's willingness to express emotions is even lower. For an overview of some interesting national differences in people's willingness to express emotions, see Table 4.1 (on p. 102). [7]

Types of Emotions

Despite what you might think, people do not have an infinite (or even a very large) number of unrelated emotions. Rather, people's emotions may be categorized in just a few different ways. Depending on how you categorize them, different features of emotion are highlighted. I now describe two such ways of categorizing emotions.

SELF-CONSCIOUS EMOTIONS VERSUS SOCIAL EMOTIONS   A useful way of distinguishing between emotions is by comparing those that come from internal sources with those that come from external sources. This is the essence of the distinction between so-called *self-conscious emotions* and *social emotions*. As summarized in Figure 4.1, **self-conscious emotions** refer to feelings that stem from within. Examples include *shame, guilt, embarrassment, and pride.*[8] Scientists believe that self-conscious emotions developed within people to help them stay aware of and regulate their relationships with others. For example, we feel shame when we believe we have failed to meet expectations, and in such cases we are likely to humble ourselves to others, allowing them to have the upper hand. So if we have done something to harm a coworker, we are likely to demonstrate—and express—feelings of embarrassment and shame, which help appease the relationship with that individual.[9]

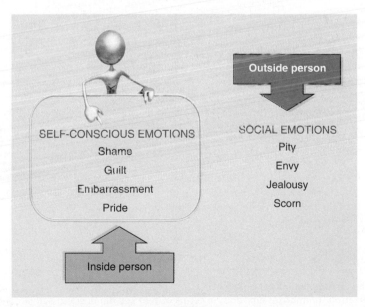

FIGURE 4.1   Self-Conscious Emotions Versus Social Emotions: A Summary
As indicated here, *self-conscious emotions* stem from within individuals, and *social emotions* refer to feelings stemming from outside individuals. Note the four examples in each category.

In contrast, **social emotions** refer to people's feelings based on information external to themselves. These include *pity, envy, jealousy,* and *scorn*. For example, a worker may experience envy if she covets something that another has (e.g., a better work assignment) or pity if she feels sorry for someone else (e.g., someone who was hurt in an accident). These are all emotions likely to be experienced in the workplace.[10]

THE CIRCUMPLEX MODEL OF AFFECT Another popular way for scientists to differentiate between emotions has been by combining two different dimensions—the degree to which emotions are pleasant or unpleasant, and the degree to which they make one feel alert and engaged (a variable known as *activation*). This two-dimensional perspective is incorporated in the **circumplex model of affect** (see Figure 4.2).[11] This diagram illustrates how various emotions are interrelated with respect to these two dimensions, resulting in four major categories.

To understand how to read this diagram (hence, to understand the circumplex model of affect), look, for example, at the upper right portion of Figure 4.2. It shows that being elated is a pleasant emotion (because it makes us feel good) and that it also is a highly activated emotion (because it encourages us to take action). They fall into the activated positive affect category. The same applies to the two other emotions in that part of the diagram (enthusiastic and excited).

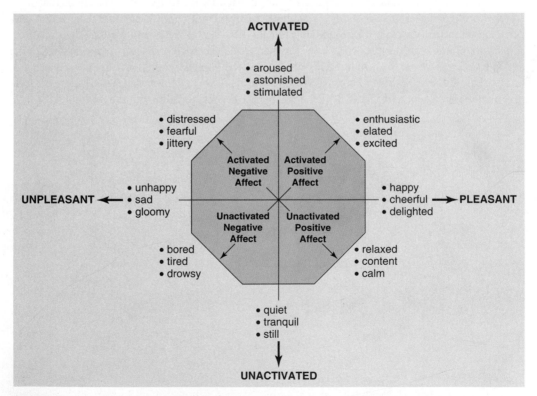

FIGURE 4.2 **The Circumplex Model of Affect**
This conceptualization summarizes emotions in terms of two key dimensions: activated–unactivated and pleasant–unpleasant. The emotions within each grouping are similar to one another. Those across from one another in this diagram are considered opposite emotions.
Source: Based On Huelsman et al., 2003; see Note 11.

Within the diagram, any emotions that lie directly opposite each other are characterized in the opposite manner. So, following through on our example, being bored, tired, and drowsy are emotions considered opposite to enthusiastic, elated, and excited. They are at the opposite ends of the two main dimensions—that is, they generate unactivated negative affect.

The Basic Nature of Mood

In contrast to emotions, which are highly specific and intense, we also have feelings that are more diffuse in scope, known as *moods*. Scientists define **mood** as an unfocused, relatively mild feeling that exists as background to our daily experiences. Whereas we are inclined to recognize the emotions we are feeling, moods are more subtle and difficult to detect. For example, you may say that you are in a good mood or a bad mood, but this isn't as focused as saying that you are experiencing a certain emotion, such as anger or sadness.

Moods fluctuate rapidly, sometimes widely, during the course of a day. For example, favorable feedback from the boss may make us feel good, but harsh criticism may put us in a bad mood. Such temporary shifts in feeling *states*—short-term differences in the way we feel—are only partly responsible for the moods that people demonstrate.

Superimposed over these passing conditions are also more stable personality *traits*—consistent differences between people's predispositions toward experiencing positive or negative affect, as we discussed in Chapter 3. Mood, in other words, is a combination of both who we are, personality-wise, and the conditions we encounter.[12]

Not surprisingly, then, the moods we experience can be based on our individual qualities (e.g., being depressed), as well as the general characteristics of our work groups or organizations (e.g., the extent to which people in them are upbeat, energetic, and enthusiastic). With this in mind, many companies today, including most of those appearing regularly on *Fortune* magazine's list of the "100 Best Companies to Work For," go out of their way to ensure that their employees have fun at work.[13] For an overview of some ways in which today's organizations are promoting fun in their workplaces, see Table 4.2.[14]

THE ROLE OF EMOTIONS AND MOOD IN ORGANIZATIONS

American statesman and inventor Benjamin Franklin is said to have observed that, "The Declaration of Independence only guarantees the American people the right to pursue happiness. You have to catch it yourself." This raises a question: What happens when people do, in fact, "catch" happiness? We certainly enjoy being happy, of course, but does this have any effect on work performance? We now consider these questions.

Are Happier People More Successful on Their Jobs?

Social scientists consider happy individuals to be ones who frequently experience positive emotions in their lives. And such persons, research suggests, enjoy several advantages over their less happy counterparts.[15] As I describe here, this takes two major forms.

JOB PERFORMANCE Happier people tend to outperform less happy people in several different ways. To begin, they tend to get better jobs—that is, ones that give them higher levels of autonomy, meaning, and variety.[16] Then, once on their jobs, they perform them more successfully.[17] This has been found to occur among people in jobs ranging from dormitory resident advisor to cricket player.[18] Interestingly, this same effect also occurs at the highest echelons of organizations. Happier CEOs of companies tend to have happier employees working for them. And,

TABLE 4.2	Having Fun on the Job: How Some Companies Are Doing It

Recognizing that they can take steps to enhance the positive moods of their employees, the companies identified here are among many that have initiated creative measures to ensure that their employees have fun on the job.

Company (Location)	Activity
Amy's Ice Cream (Austin, TX)	Before closing up the retail store on Wednesday nights, customers are asked to sing a silly song.
Capital One Services (Tampa, FL)	Large cakes made of Styrofoam were placed above the cubicles of employees celebrating birthdays.
Nokia Mobile Phones (San Diego, CA)	The company sponsors an all-employee band that puts on concerts once every three months.
Hasbro Toys (Pawtucket, RI)	Instead of frowning upon playing in the office, as many companies do, this maker of Nerf products encourages its employees to play with Nerf toys while on the job.
Home Depot (Atlanta, GA)	Some 4,300 key employees were flown to a huge party at the Georgia Dome, which included a private concert by Glen Frey and Joe Walsh of the Eagles.
Progressive Insurance (Cleveland, OH)	On Halloween, employees are encouraged to wear outrageous costumes to work.
S. C. Johnson & Son (Racine, WI)	Members of the customer service department are entitled to receive free back and shoulder massages.

Sources: Based on information reported in the various sources in Note 14.

importantly (as I will describe in Chapter 5), happy employees are inclined to remain on their jobs and not to seek new positions elsewhere.[19] In part because of this, organizations populated by happy individuals tend to be more successful—hence, profitable—than those consisting of less happy people.[20] Obviously, the importance of happiness cannot be overstated when it comes to job performance.

INCOME Do happier people earn higher incomes? Yes, they do. Research has found this to be the case in countries throughout the world. For example, high correlations between happiness and income were found among people in Germany and Russia.[21] This same relationship was found even among indigenous Malaysian farmers whose only income was the value of their property and belongings.[22] In these cases, because the relationships are correlational, it's unclear whether people make more money because they're happy or people become happy because they make more money. In either case, this connection is worth noting because it is quite strong.

Why Are Happier Workers More Successful?

What is behind these strong connections between happiness and work success? As in most OB phenomena, there are several answers.

DECISION QUALITY Research has found that people showing high positive affectivity do a better job of making decisions than those showing high negative affectivity.[23] Specifically, people with high positive affectivity make decisions that are more accurate and more important to their groups' effectiveness, and they have greater managerial potential. This ability to make better decisions is a particularly good reason why happy people tend to be successful.

EVALUATION   Mood also biases the way we evaluate people and things. For example, people report greater satisfaction with their jobs while they are in good moods than while they are in bad moods.[24] Being in a good mood also leads people to perceive (and admit to perceiving) the positive side of others' work. Because being in a good mood keeps managers from perceiving their subordinates' good behavior as bad (as might occur if they are biased or extremely tough), it leads them to offer the kind of encouraging feedback likely to help subordinates to improve (see Chapter 6). By contrast, managers whose bad moods lead them to evaluate their subordinates in an inappropriately negative fashion are unable to help those subordinates improve their work. This, of course, interferes with the performance of those workers and the effectiveness of their managers.

COOPERATION   Mood strongly affects the extent to which people help each other, cooperate with one another, and refrain from behaving aggressively (I will discuss these forms of behavior in more detail in Chapter 7). People who are in good moods also tend to be highly generous and are inclined to help fellow workers who need their assistance. People who are in good moods also are inclined to work carefully with others to resolve conflicts with them, whereas people in bad moods are likely to keep those conflicts brewing. Considering that conflict may disrupt team performance (see Chapter 7), this is yet another reason why being in a good mood enhances job performance.

Given that people's moods and emotions have profound effects on their performance in organizations, it's not surprising that scientists have developed theories that shed light on these effects. I now examine one particularly influential theory in this regard.

Affective Events Theory

One of the guiding forces in the study of emotions in organizations has been **affective events theory (AET)**.[25] This theory identifies various factors that lead to people's emotional reactions on the job and how these reactions affect those individuals (see Figure 4.3).[26]

Beginning on the left side of Figure 4.3, AET recognizes that people's emotions are determined, in part, by various features of the work environment. For example, the way we feel is likely to be determined by certain characteristics of the jobs we do (e.g., we are likely to feel good about jobs that are interesting and exciting), the demands we face (e.g., how pressured we are to meet deadlines), and by requirements for *emotional labor*.

The concept of **emotional labor** refers to the degree to which people have to work hard to display what they believe are appropriate emotions on their jobs. People in service professions (e.g., servers in restaurants and retail salesclerks), for example, often have to come across as being more pleasant than they really feel. As you might imagine, having to do this repeatedly can be very taxing. (I will return to this idea on pp. 110–111, in connection with the concept of *emotional dissonance*.)

These various features of the work environment are likely to lead to certain events. These include confronting **daily hassles**, unpleasant or undesirable events that put people in bad moods (e.g., having to deal with difficult bosses or coworkers). They also include experiencing more positive events known as **daily uplifts**. These are the opposite—namely, pleasant or desirable events that put people in good moods (e.g., enjoying feelings of recognition for the work they do).

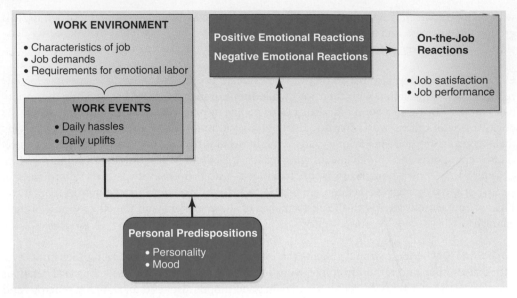

FIGURE 4.3 **Affective Events Theory**
According to affective events theory, people's job performance and job satisfaction are influenced by their positive and negative emotional reactions to events on the job. These events, in turn, are influenced by aspects of the work environment and various events that occur on the job. People's emotional reactions to these events depend on such individual characteristics as their moods and aspects of their personalities.
Source: Based on suggestions by Ashkanasy & Daus, 2002; see Note 26.

As Figure 4.3 reveals, people react to these various work events by displaying emotional reactions, both positive and negative. However, as the diagram also shows, the extent to which this occurs depends on each of two types of personal predispositions: personality and mood. As noted in Chapter 3, personality predisposes us to respond in varying degrees of intensity to the events that occur. In keeping with our discussion, for example, a person who has a high degree of positive affectivity is likely to perceive events in a positive manner, whereas one who has a high degree of negative affectivity is likely to perceive those same events more negatively.

Mood also influences the nature of the relationship between work events and emotional reactions, as Figure 4.3 suggests. This is in keeping with the point made earlier—that the mood we are in at any given time can exaggerate the nature of the emotions we experience in response to an event. So, for example, an event that leads a person to experience a negative emotional reaction (e.g., having a fight with a coworker) is likely to make that individual feel even worse if he or she is in a bad mood at the time.

Finally, the theory notes that these affective reactions have two important effects. First, they promote high levels of job performance. This should not be surprising, given that we already noted that happy people perform their jobs at high levels. Second, AET also notes that affective reactions are responsible for people's job performance and *job satisfaction*—that is, the extent to which they hold positive attitudes toward their jobs (I will discuss this in detail in Chapter 6). Indeed, research has established very strongly that people who are inclined to experience positive emotions are likely to be satisfied with their jobs.[27]

Putting this all together, consider the following example. You have been employed happily as a software engineer at a high-tech firm for about a year. You find the work pleasantly challenging and in line with your talents. Over the course of your workdays, you experience many enjoyable encounters with others. On this particular occasion, your boss has just given you a big pat on the back in recognition of your latest revenue-generating suggestion. And because you have a high degree of positive affect and are already in a good mood when this happened, you experience a very positive reaction to this event. As a result, you are strongly motivated to perform your job at a high level and you very much enjoy your work, taking pride in it as well.

AET has received considerable support from researchers.[28] Its importance rests on two key ideas—one for scientists and one for practicing managers.[29] First, unlike many other theories of OB (such as the others described in this book), this approach recognizes the important role of emotions. Second, AET sends a strong message to managers: Do not overlook the emotional reactions of your employees. They may be more important than you think. In fact, when they accumulate over time, their impact can be considerable. Thus, it is clear that anyone in a supervisory capacity has to pay attention to managing emotions in the workplace. We now turn to this topic.

MANAGING EMOTIONS IN ORGANIZATIONS

Although emotions occur naturally, people do not always display the emotions they feel. After all, it's not always to our advantage to let our true emotions show—especially on the job. For example, in the interest of keeping good relations with your boss, you probably would be reluctant to display any anger you feel toward him. This suggests that we make a conscious effort to manage the emotions we express. We now consider several ways that people go about doing this.

Developing Emotional Intelligence

If you think about the people you know, you probably realize that some are better than others at recognizing and regulating their own emotions, such as by holding their tempers in check when angry, and at recognizing the emotions of others, such as by figuring out who else around them is angry. These individuals are probably also highly adept at influencing the emotions of others, such as by being able to make people feel better when they are upset. Such individuals are said to be displaying a high degree of **emotional intelligence (EI)**.[30]

Specifically, EI consists of the four components shown in the corners of Figure 4.4.[31] These include awareness of one's own emotions (*self-awareness*) and the emotions of others (*social awareness*) as well as the ability to control one's own emotions (*self-management*) and to influence the emotions of others (*relationship management*). Each of these components is associated with a specific skill identified in the slices of the pie shown in the center of the diagram. Accordingly, people who are trained to enhance their EI learn the following:

- To develop *self-awareness*, they learn how to get in touch with their own emotional states, enhancing their capacity to appraise their feelings honestly and accurately.
- To develop *social awareness*, they learn to become sensitive to others and to show empathy for them.
- To develop *self-management*, they learn how to express their emotions naturally and how to keep any negative emotions in check.
- To develop *relationship management*, they learn how to collaborate closely with others, using emotions for constructive purposes.

Training programs that are used to develop EI incorporate case studies illustrating people with high levels of EI and comparing them to those with low EI. They also use exercises that provide models of appropriate behavior and exercises that give trainees practice in knowing what to

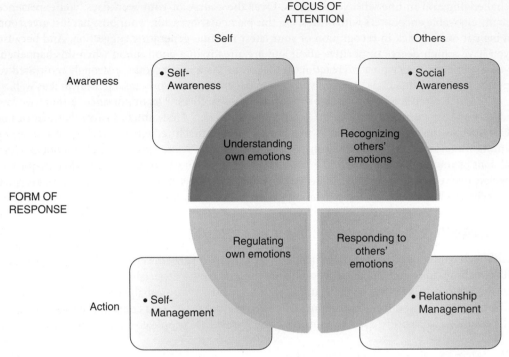

FIGURE 4.4 Components of Emotional Intelligence
EI consists of four components based on two distinct dimensions. These are summarized here, along with a specific skill required to develop each of the components.

do and say when interacting with others. Although the training techniques vary, they all begin by getting trainees to appreciate their existing levels of EI. To help you assess your own EI, complete the Self-Assessment Exercise on pp. 130–131.)

As you might imagine, individuals with high levels of EI have an important edge over others who are not so adept. As a case in point, sales representatives for the hair care and cosmetics giant L'Oréal who have high levels of EI outsell their colleagues who lack these skills. And after putting into place a training program to enhance everyone's EI, the company enjoyed an annual net revenue increase of over $2.5 million.[32] Such findings are not unusual. Many other companies also have seen big benefits stemming from efforts to enhance the EI levels of their employees.

Coping with Emotional Dissonance

Imagine that you are a flight attendant for a major airline. After a cross-country flight with rude passengers, you finally reach your destination. You feel tired and annoyed, but you do not have the option of expressing how you really feel. You don't even have the luxury of acting neutrally and expressing nothing at all. Instead, you are expected to act peppy and cheerful, smiling and thanking the passengers for choosing your airline and graciously bidding them farewell as they deplane. The conflict between the emotion you feel (anger) and the one you are required to express (happiness) may take its toll on your well-being. This example illustrates a kind of situation that is all too typical—one in which you are required to display emotions on the job that are inconsistent with how you actually feel.

This phenomenon, known as **emotional dissonance**, can be a significant source of work-related stress (the major topic discussed in the second half of this chapter).[33] Emotional dissonance is likely to occur in situations in which there are strong expectations regarding the emotions a person is expected to display by virtue of his or her job requirements. Our flight attendant example illustrates this point. The same applies to customer service representatives, bank tellers, entertainers—just about anyone who provides services to the public.

When emotional dissonance occurs, people often have to try very hard to ensure that they display the appropriate emotions. As noted earlier, the psychological effort involved in doing this is referred to as *emotional labor*. If you ever find yourself "biting your tongue"—that is, holding back from saying what you want to say—then you are expending a great deal of emotional labor.

Actually, not saying what you really think is only part of the situation. Emotional labor also is invested in saying things you don't really feel. For example, you would have to invest a great deal of emotional labor when confronting a coworker who comes to you asking you how you feel about her awful new hairdo. You don't like it at all, but you struggle to keep your feelings to yourself (and not to "leak" them nonverbally; see Chapter 8). When pressed to say something, you engage in "a little white lie" by telling her how very flattering it is. Although this is a form of dishonesty, it is considered widely appropriate to keep from hurting people's feelings by saying the polite thing.

This discussion underscores an important point: The emotions people actually experience, known as **felt emotions**, may be discrepant from the emotions they show others, known as **displayed emotions**. This is not at all surprising. After all, our jobs do not always give us the luxury of expressing how we truly feel. To do so, such as by expressing the anger you feel toward your boss, is likely to lead to problems. As sociologists tell us, social pressure compels people to conform to expectations about which particular emotions are appropriate to show in public and which are not. As noted earlier, such *display rules* vary among cultures. But they also appear to differ as a function of people's occupational positions.

It is an unspoken rule, for example, that an athletic coach is not supposed to be openly hostile and negative when speaking about an opponent (at least, when doing so in public). It also is expected that people considered "professionals," such as doctors and lawyers, demonstrate appropriate decorum and seriousness when interacting with their patients and clients. Should a physician observing your symptoms respond by saying, "What a disgusting condition you have; it sickens me to look at you," you probably would be seeking a new doctor right away.

Controlling Anger (Before It Controls You)

Although we all know what *anger* is, and we have experienced it many times (perhaps too many), a precise definition is in order. By **anger**, scientists are referring to a heightened state of emotional arousal (e.g., increased heart rate, rapid breathing, flushed face, sweaty palms, etc.) fueled by cognitive interpretations of situations. Anger reactions can run the gamut from irritation to outrage and fury.

Importantly, there are situations in which displaying anger can be purposeful and constructive. For example, to get a subordinate to take immediate action in a dangerous situation, a supervisor may express anger by raising her voice and looking that person straight in the eye. This would be the case should a military officer display her anger purposely to express urgency when ordering a soldier under her command to move immediately out of a combat zone. Because of its constructive and highly controlled nature, anger of this type is not problematic. In fact, it can be quite valuable. Where anger can be dangerous, however, is when it erupts violently and is out of control. We need to be concerned about this because aggression is a natural reaction to anger.

Quite often, behaving appropriately in business situations requires controlling anger. After all, to be successful, we cannot let the situations we face get the better of us. It's perfectly natural to get angry, particularly on the job, where there may be a great deal to anger us. However, it's considered inappropriate and unprofessional to show one's anger in public. Polite professionals in Western society are expected to show restraint. It is with this in mind that we almost never see politicians and business leaders lose their tempers when communicating in public. It's not that they don't get angry; far from it. It's simply that they have learned to control their emotional displays. And when this breaks down, causing them to "lose it," it's likely to be big news, with video clips of such incidents getting millions of hits on YouTube.

The challenge people face is to control their anger appropriately. This is the idea behind the practice of **anger management**—systematic efforts to reduce people's emotional feelings of anger and the physiological arousal it causes. Because we often cannot eliminate, avoid, or alter the things that anger us, it's important to learn to control our reactions. For some suggestions as to how to go about doing so, see Table 4.3.

STRESS: ITS BASIC NATURE

Stress is an unavoidable fact of organizational life today, taking its toll on both individuals and organizations. Specifically, 90 percent of American workers report feeling stressed at least once a week and 40 percent describe their jobs as very stressful most of the time.[34] What causes them stress? Lots of things, but having too much work to do and fear of being laid off are among people's most common concerns.

As you might imagine, these sources of stress are both harmful to individual workers and costly to their organizations. In fact, about half of all American workers report that stress has adversely affected their health.[35] Not surprisingly, stress on the job has been linked to increases in accidents, lost productivity, and of course, phenomenal boosts in

TABLE 4.3	Tips for Managing Anger in the Workplace

Controlling anger is easier said than done. However, several things can be done to accomplish this. Some tried-and-true techniques are summarized here.

Suggestion	Explanation
Practice relaxation	Learning to meditate is very useful because it helps make you calm, allowing you to cope effectively with situations that provoke anger. (You will find a description of this process in Table 4.11 on p. 128.)
Focus on facts	Angry people often think irrationally, making things worse. Instead, focus on the source of your anger and think things through logically, focusing on the facts of the situation.
Use humor	Laughter is incompatible with anger, so take the edge off your fury by focusing on something funny. For example, if you think someone is a "dirtbag," picture him with a big sack of dirt on top of his head.
Leave the room	When you feel anger welling up inside, move to another room or even leave the building. Changing your surroundings may help you escape whatever or whoever is causing you to be so angry—and this will keep you from saying something you regret later on.

medical insurance. Overall, work-related stress has been estimated as costing American companies $200 billion to $300 billion annually.[36]

In view of these sobering statistics, it is clearly important to understand the nature of organizational stress. Formally, scientists define **stress** as the pattern of emotional and physiological reactions occurring in response to demands from within or outside organizations. In this chapter, I will review the major causes and effects of stress. Importantly, I also will describe various ways of effectively managing stress so as to reduce its negative impact. Before doing this, however, I will describe the basic nature of stress in more detail.

Stressors in Organizations

What do the following situations have in common?

- You are selected to be an intern at a highly regarded Wall Street investment firm.
- You find out that your company is about to eliminate your department.
- Your boss tells you that you will not be getting a raise this year.
- You receive a major promotion that gives you more prestige and a higher salary.

The answer is that each situation involves events that put extreme demands on you. Stimuli of this type—both positive and negative, as illustrated in these four specific situations—are known as *stressors*. Specifically, **stressors** are defined as any demands, either physical or psychological in nature, encountered during the course of living. Scientists find it useful to distinguish stressors in terms of how long lasting they are. This results in the following three major categories (see Figure 4.5):

- **Acute stressors** are those that bring some form of sudden change that threatens us either physically or psychologically, requiring people to make unwanted adjustments. For example, you may be assigned to a different shift at work, requiring you to get up earlier in the morning and to eat meals at different times. As your body's equilibrium is disrupted, you respond physiologically (e.g., by being tired) and emotionally (e.g., by being grouchy).
- **Episodic stressors** are the result of experiencing lots of acute stressors in a short period of time, such as when you have "one of those days" in which everything goes wrong. In other words, you are experiencing particularly stressful episodes in life. This would be the case, for example, if within the course of a week you have a serious disagreement with one of your subordinates, you lose a major sales account, and then, to top it off, the pipes burst in your office, causing water to ruin your important papers and your computer. For a list of some of the most common episodic stressors, see Table 4.4.

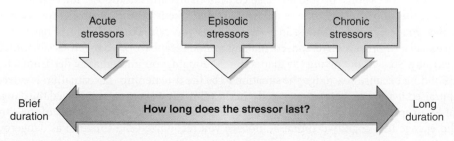

FIGURE 4.5   Different Types of Stressors
Whereas *acute stressors* tend to be of brief duration, *chronic stressors* endure for a long period of time. *Episodic stressors* generally last for intermediate periods of time.

TABLE 4.4	Common Episodic Stressors in the Workplace

Many of the most commonly encountered stressors in organizations are episodic in nature. If you think about these, it's not difficult to recognize how they actually are composed of several different acute stressors. For example, fear of losing one's job includes concerns over money, threats to self-esteem, embarrassment, and other acute stressors.

- Lack of involvement in making organizational decisions
- Unrelenting and unreasonable expectations for performance
- Poor communication with coworkers
- Fear of losing one's job
- Spending long amounts of time away from home
- Office politics and conflict
- Not being paid fairly given one's level of responsibility and performance

- **Chronic stressors** are the most extreme type of stressor because they are constant and unrelenting in nature, having a long-term effect on the body, mind, and spirit. For example, a person experiences chronic stressors if he or she is in a long-term abusive relationship with a boss or spouse or has a debilitating disease (e.g., arthritis or migraine headaches) that adversely affects his or her ability to work. In recent years, in which layoffs have been common, people have suffered stress due to considerable uncertainties about their futures.

The Cognitive Appraisal Process

The Roman emperor and philosopher Marcus Aurelius Antonious (A.D. 121–180) is quoted as saying, "If you are distressed by anything external, the pain is not due to the thing itself, but to your estimate of it; and this you have the power to revoke at any moment." This observation is as true today as it was over 2,000 years ago, when first spoken. The basic idea is that the mere presence of potentially harmful events or conditions in the environment is not enough for them to be stressors. For an event to become a stressor to someone, he or she must think of it as a stressor and acknowledge the danger and the difficulty of coping with it.

As you think about the events or conditions you encounter, some may be considered especially threatening (warranting your concern) whereas others pose less of a problem to you (and can be ignored safely). Your assessment of the dangers associated with any potential stressor is based on **cognitive appraisal**—the process of judging the extent to which an environmental event is a potential source of stress. Let's consider this process more closely.

On some occasions, people appraise conditions instantly. Suppose, for example, you are camping in the woods when you see a bear that looks like it's going to attack. You immediately assess that you are in danger and run away as fast as you can. This is a natural reaction, which biologists call a **flight response**. Indeed, making a rapid escape from a dangerous situation occurs automatically. So, without giving the matter much thought, you immediately flee from a burning office building because you judge the situation to be life threatening. The situation is extreme, so you appraised it as dangerous automatically. In the blink of an eye, you recognized the danger and sought to escape. Although you may not have deliberated all the pros and cons of the situation, you did engage in a cognitive appraisal process: you recognized the situation as dangerous and took action instantly.

Most of the situations managers face are neither as extreme nor as clear-cut. In fact, the vast majority of would-be stressors are stressors only if people perceive them as such. For example, if

TABLE 4.5	Tips for Assessing Potential Stressors Accurately

It is important to recognize potential stressors and to take appropriate action. However, it can be very disruptive to mistakenly assume that something is a stressor when, in reality, nothing is wrong. With this in mind, here are some useful guidelines for appraising potential stressors accurately.

Suggestion	Explanation
Check with others.	Ask around. If others are not concerned about a situation, then maybe you shouldn't be concerned either. Discussing the situation with people may alleviate any feelings of stress you may have had.
Look to the past.	Your best bet for deciding what to do may be to consider what has happened over the years. You may want to be concerned about something that has caused problems in the past, but worrying about conditions that haven't been problems before might only make things worse by distracting your attention from what really matters.
Gather all the facts.	It's too easy to jump to conclusions, seeing situations as problems that really aren't so bad. Instead of sensing a problem and assuming the worst, look for more objective information about the situation
Avoid negative mental monologues.	Too often, people talk themselves into perceiving situations as being worse than they really are, thereby adding to stress levels. You should avoid such negative mental monologues, focusing instead on the positive aspects of the situations you confront.

you are an expert at writing sales reports and really enjoy doing them, the prospect of having to work extra hours on preparing one is not likely to be a stressor for you. However, for someone else who finds the same task to be an obnoxious chore, confronting it may well be a stressor. Likewise, the deadline might not be a stressor if you perceive that it is highly flexible, that nobody takes it seriously, or if you can get an extension simply by asking. The point is straightforward: whether or not an environmental event is a stressor depends on how it is perceived. What might be a stressor for you under some circumstances might not be a stressor at other times or even for someone else under the same conditions. Remember, it's all just a matter of how things are appraised cognitively.

As you might imagine, it is important to appraise potential threats as accurately as possible. For example, to think that everyone in your department is happy when, in fact, they are all planning to quit surely would be a serious mistake. Likewise, interpreting a small dip in sales as a sign of economic collapse would cause you needless worry and may spark panic in others. As such, it is important to recognize what you can do as a manager to ensure that you and those around you are assessing potential stressors accurately. For some recommendations in this regard, see Table 4.5.

Bodily Responses to Stressors

When we encounter stressors, our bodies—in particular, the sympathetic nervous systems and endocrine systems—mobilize into action, elevating heart rate, blood pressure, and respiration.[37] Arousal rises quickly to high levels, and many physiological changes take place. If the stressors persist, the body's resources eventually may become depleted, at which point people's ability to cope (at least physically) decreases sharply, and severe biological damage may result.

To illustrate this, imagine that you are in an office building when you suddenly see a fire raging. How does your body react? As a natural, biological response, your body responds in

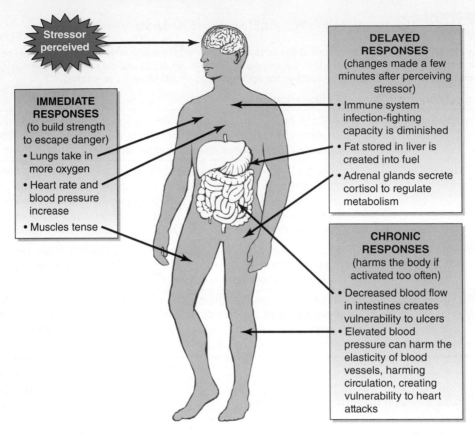

FIGURE 4.6 The Body's Reactions to Stress
As summarized here, the human body responds to stress in various ways involving several different physiological mechanisms. These responses differ based on whether they occur immediately after perceiving a stressor, a few minutes later (i.e., delayed responses), or after repeated exposure to stressors (i.e., chronic responses).

several ways—both immediately after experiencing the stressor, a few minutes later, and after repeated exposure (see Figure 4.6). For example, certain chemicals are released that make it possible for us to respond. Adrenaline boosts our metabolism, causing us to breathe faster, taking in more oxygen to help us be stronger and run faster. Aiding in this process, blood flows more rapidly (up to four times faster than normal) to prime the muscles, and other fluids are diverted from less essential parts of the body. As a result, people experiencing stressful conditions tend to experience dry mouths as well as cool, clammy, and sweaty skin. Other chemicals are activated that suppress the parts of the brain that control concentration, inhibition, and rational thought. (By the way, this is why people in emergency situations don't always think rationally or act politely.) In short, when exposed to stressors the body kicks into a self-protective mode, marshalling all its resources to preserve life. However, when this happens frequently, the chronic responses can be dangerous.

To the extent that people appraise various situations as stressors, they are likely to have stress reactions. And often these can have damaging behavioral, psychological, and/or medical effects. Indeed, physiological and psychological stress reactions can be so great that eventually they take their toll on the body and mind, resulting in such maladies as insomnia, cardiovascular disease, and depression. Such reactions are referred to as **strain**, defined as deviations from normal states of human function resulting from exposure to stressful events. (As you probably have seen in dealing with different people in your own lives, some individuals are far tougher than others. That is, they have the mental toughness to focus their minds and manage their emotions under stressful conditions.[38] To see how well you and others fare in this regard, complete the Group Exercise on pp. 131–132.[39])

Sometimes people find themselves worn down by chronic levels of stress. Such people are often described as suffering from **burnout**—a syndrome of emotional, physical, and mental exhaustion coupled with feelings of low self-esteem or low self-efficacy, resulting from prolonged exposure to intense stress and the strain reactions following from them.[40] Fortunately, some of the signs of burnout are clear, if you know what to look for. The distinct characteristics of burnout are summarized in Table 4.6.[41]

The symptoms of burnout identified in Table 4.6 may be organized into two categories, each of which reflects a different underlying process.[42] First, extreme job demands make people feel overtaxed, leading them to become *exhausted*. We see this, for example, among workers who are expected to perform at unreasonably high levels. While striving to do more than is possible, such individuals tend to become exhausted. A second process involved in burnout has to do with lacking the resources needed to meet job demands. This occurs, for example, among people experiencing budget cuts leading to shortages in the manpower (human resources) and/or the amount of time able to complete important projects. Such conditions lead people to withdraw from their jobs, feeling *disengaged*, which means that they are disinterested in their work, staying away (being absent and ultimately, resigning) and being cynical.

These important processes tend to operate in conjunction with one another, with the highest levels of burnout occurring among individuals who experience high job demands and limited resources at the same time. Research has found that this occurs among people from a wide variety of occupational groups, including individuals working in human services, industrial manufacturing, and transportation.[43]

| TABLE 4.6 | Major Symptoms of Burnout |

Burnout is a serious condition resulting from exposure to chronic levels of stress. The symptoms of burnout, summarized here, are important to recognize so as to avoid making an already bad state of affairs even worse.

Symptom	Description
Physical exhaustion	Victims of burnout have low energy and feel tired much of the time. They also report many symptoms of physical strain, such as frequent headaches, nausea, poor sleep, and changes in eating habits (e.g., loss of appetite).
Emotional exhaustion	Depression, feelings of helplessness, and feelings of being trapped in one's job are all part of burnout.
Depersonalization	People suffering from burnout often demonstrate a pattern of attitudinal exhaustion known as *depersonalization*. They become cynical about others, derogating them and themselves. Victims might focus on their jobs, their organizations, and even life in general.
Feelings of low personal accomplishment	People suffering from burnout conclude that they haven't been able to accomplish much in the past, and assume that they probably won't succeed in the future.

Source: Based on information in Bakker et al., 2000; see Note 40.

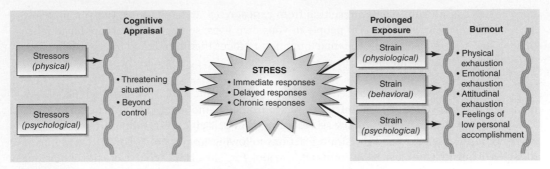

FIGURE 4.7   Stressors, Stress, and Strain: Recognizing the Distinctions

Stimuli known as *stressors* (which are both physical and psychological in nature) lead to stress reactions when they are cognitively appraised as being threatening and beyond one's control. The deviations from normal states resulting from stress are known as *strain*. Both physical and emotional ailments as well as impaired job performance result from strain.

Let's summarize where we have been thus far. I have identified physical and psychological causes of stress known as stressors. Through the cognitive appraisal process, these lead to various physical and mental stress reactions. With prolonged exposure, physiological, behavioral, and psychological strain reactions occur. Ultimately, in some cases, burnout occurs. For a summary of this process, see Figure 4.7.

MAJOR CAUSES OF STRESS IN THE WORKPLACE

Stress is caused by many different factors. For example, stress may be triggered by personal factors such as problems with family members, financial problems, and illness. Stress also may stem from societal factors, such as concerns over crime, terrorism, and downturns in the economy. However, in this book, we are concerned mostly about job-related stress. What causes stress in work settings? Unfortunately, as you will see, the list is quite long; many different factors play a role in creating stress in the workplace.

Occupational Demands

Some jobs, such as police officer and fire fighter, expose the people who hold them to high levels of stress. Others, such as jeweler and tailor, do not. This basic fact—that some jobs are much more stressful than others—has been confirmed in research surveying people in a wide variety of occupations.[44] Can you guess which particular jobs were found to be least and most stressful? For a listing of the top jobs in each category, see Table 4.7.

As you review this list, try to identify precisely what it is that makes the most stressful jobs different from the least stressful jobs. In other words, what particular characteristics of jobs create high levels of stress? Research addressing this question has shown that people experience greater stress the more their jobs require each of the following elements:

- Making decisions
- Constantly monitoring devices or materials (e.g., instruments and gauges)
- Repeatedly exchanging information with others
- Working in unpleasant physical conditions
- Performing unstructured rather than structured tasks

TABLE 4.7	The 10 Least Stressful and Most Stressful Jobs in America

Although very stressful situations can be found on just about any job, the ones shown here tend to have the lowest and highest overall levels of stress associated with them. Please note that these are generalizations; any particular individuals performing these jobs may experience higher or lower levels of stress than suggested here due to the unique conditions encountered.

Least Stressful Jobs	Most Stressful Jobs
1. Medical records technician	1. Enlisted military soldier
2. Jeweler	2. Fire fighter
3. Hair stylist	3. Airline pilot
4. Dressmaker/tailor	4. Military general
5. Medical laboratory technician	5. Police officer
6. Audiologist	6. Event coordinator
7. Precision assembler	7. Public relations executive
8. Dietitian	8. Senior corporate executive
9. Furniture upholsterer	9. Photo journalist
10. Electrical technician	10. Taxi driver

Sources: Based on CNBC. (2012); see Note 44.

The greater the extent to which a job possesses these characteristics, the greater the potential levels of stress those jobs are likely to trigger in the individuals holding them. Let's consider two particularly stressful jobs not identified in Table 4.7—nurses and long-distance bus drivers. If you think about the exact tasks these individuals routinely perform, you'll see that they match this profile quite well. Not surprisingly, people performing these jobs tend to suffer many adverse signs of stress (i.e., strain). This is not to imply, however, that people holding jobs that do not meet this profile are immune from stress. Instead, just about all jobs have potential to arouse stress. Illustrating this point, Table 4.8 identifies many potential sources of stress in a variety of widely held jobs.[45]

Conflict Between Work and Nonwork

If you've ever faced the demands of working while at the same time trying to raise a family, you are probably well aware of how difficult this situation can be. Not only must you confront the usual pressures to spend time at work while concentrating on what you're doing, but you also must pay attention to the demands placed on you by members of your family (e.g., to spend time with them). When people confront such incompatibilities in the various sets of obligations they have, they are said to experience **role conflict** (see Chapter 9 for a discussion of roles). As you might expect, when we experience conflicts between our work and nonwork lives, something has to give. Not surprisingly, the more time people devote to their jobs, the more events in their nonwork lives (e.g., personal errands) adversely affect their jobs (e.g., not being able to get the job done on time).

The stressful nature of role conflicts is particularly strong among a very large segment of the population, working parents. Such individuals are expected to switch back and forth rapidly between the demands of work and family, a feat known as **role juggling**.[46] As you may know

TABLE 4.8	Potential Sources of Stress in Many Common Jobs	

Although some jobs are inherently more stressful than others, even people holding everyday jobs in all fields confront significant sources of stress. Here are some examples.

Field	Typical Jobs	Common Source of Stress
Financial	Accountants, stock market traders, bank tellers, mortgage consultants	Clients are concerned about money, so they put lots of pressure on people working in this field.
Media	Newspaper, magazine, radio, or television journalists, reporters, editors	These people experience calm times followed by frantic activity as deadlines approach and as major events unfold.
Sales	Sales and marketing managers, advertising executives	These jobs create pressure to meet certain target objectives. Salespeople face pressure to always make good impressions.
Medical	Doctors, nurses, pharmacists, physical therapists	When human lives are at stake, the pressure to make the right decision is great. Also, dealing with human distress is very difficult on people.
Technology	Computer programmers and technicians, systems analysts	Workers in the information technology field face considerable pressure to stay abreast of very rapid changes.

Source: Based on information in Heller & Hindle, 1998; see Note 45.

from first-hand experience, role juggling is a potent source of stress. In fact, the more roles we are forced to juggle (i.e., the more balls we have in the air at any given time), the more stress we suffer in our lives. Interestingly, the same relationship occurs among student athletes: the more successfully such individuals are able to separate their distinct roles as students and as athletes, the less stress they suffer and the more well-being they experience.[47]

This suggests that stress may be reduced by limiting the number of incompatible roles we play. However, life would certainly be far less fulfilling for many individuals if they didn't have children or if they didn't play sports. Instead, the trick is to learn how to juggle the various roles we play successfully—that is, without dropping the ball. Although this isn't always easy, many people do it all the time. I will get you started on ways to do this yourself later in this chapter (pp. 127–129), where you will find a discussion of stress management.

Role Ambiguity: Stress Uncertainty

Even if individuals are able to avoid the stress associated with role conflict, they still may encounter another common source of job-related stress—**role ambiguity**. This occurs when people are uncertain about several aspects of their jobs (e.g., the scope of their responsibilities, what's expected of them, how to divide their time among various duties). Most people dislike such uncertainty and find it quite stressful, but it is difficult to avoid. In fact, role ambiguity is quite common: 35 to 60 percent of employees surveyed report experiencing it to some degree.[48] Clearly, managers who are interested in promoting a stress-free workplace should go out of their way to help employees understand precisely what they are expected to do. As obvious as this may sound, such advice is all too frequently ignored in actual practice.

Overload: So Much Work, So Little Time

When the phrase "work-related stress" is mentioned, most people envision scenes in which employees are asked to do more work than they possibly can handle. Such an image is indeed quite legitimate, for such *overload* is an important cause of stress in many work settings. In fact, in today's business environment, where many companies are trimming staff size (the phenomenon known as *downsizing*, which we will discuss in Chapter 14), fewer employees are required to do more work than ever before. A distinction needs to be made, however, between **quantitative overload**—the belief that one is required to do more work than possibly can be completed in a specific period—and **qualitative overload**—the belief that one lacks the required skills or abilities to perform a given job. Both are common sources of stress.

Today, as you know, overload is a problem when it comes to the management of information. Because we live in an information age, a period in which information is not only essential but also widely available, we are faced with more information than ever before. And with this comes pressure to store and process all that information in our heads as we strive to keep up with it all. This is known as **information anxiety**, an all-too-common fact of life in many contemporary workplaces.[49]

Responsibility for Others: A Heavy Burden

Some people, such as managers and supervisors, have jobs that require them to be responsible for others. And these others, as you probably suspect, can be a major source of stress for the individuals responsible for them. In general, individuals who are responsible for other people experience higher levels of stress than those who have no such responsibility. Such individuals are more likely to report feelings of tension and anxiety and are more likely to show overt symptoms of stress, such as ulcers or hypertension, than their counterparts in nonsupervisory positions.

This probably isn't too surprising if you think about it. After all, managers are often caught between the need to satisfy their staff members (e.g., giving them raises) while simultaneously meeting the demands of their own superiors (e.g., maintaining budgets). They also are often faced with meeting a wide variety of demands, creating responsibilities that often weigh heavily on them. Not surprisingly, many managers think of stress as a normal, everyday part of their jobs.

Importantly, managers who deal with people ineffectively—such as those who communicate poorly (see Chapter 8) and who treat people unfairly (see Chapter 2)—add stress to the lives of the people they supervise. As you surely know from your own experiences, a poor manager can be quite a significant source of stress. That said, it is clear that knowing and effectively practicing what you have learned about OB in this book can help alleviate stress among others in the workplace.

Lack of Social Support: The Costs of Isolation

According to an old saying, "misery loves company." With respect to stress, this statement implies that if we have to face stressful conditions, it's better to do so along with others (and with their support) rather than alone. Does this strategy actually work? In general, the answer is "yes." Research has shown that when individuals believe they have the friendship and support of others at work—that is, when they have **social support**—their ability to resist the adverse effects of stress increases. For example, a study found that police officers who felt they could talk to their colleagues about their reactions to a traumatic event (such as a shooting) experienced less stressful reactions than those who lacked such support.[50] Clearly, social support—or, simply even believing that it is available if needed—can be an important buffer against the effects of stress.[51]

Social support can come from many different sources. One of these is cultural norms (e.g., caring for the elderly is valued among the Japanese, thereby reducing the social isolation many elderly people otherwise experience). Another source of social support is social institutions (e.g., counseling from the church or school officials, help from the Red Cross). And, of course, probably the most important and valuable source of support comes from one's own friends and family members.

Regardless of its source, social support is beneficial for a variety of reasons. Specifically, some of the key processes through which social support may help reduce stress are as follows:[52]

- *Boosting self-esteem*—Others can help make us feel better about ourselves.
- *Sharing information*—Talking to other people can help us learn about ways of coping with problems and give us a new perspective on things.
- *Providing diversion*—Spending time with others can be a friendly diversion from life's stressors, taking your mind off them.
- *Giving needed resources*—Time spent with others can result in them offering to help by giving money, advice, or other resources needed to alleviate stress.

As shown here, not only does misery love company, but also company can help alleviate misery. This is something worth remembering the next time you feel stressed. Remember, don't go it alone. Friends can help, so seek them out.

ADVERSE EFFECTS OF ORGANIZATIONAL STRESS

By now, you probably are convinced that stress stems from many sources, and that it has important effects on the people who experience it. What may not yet be apparent, though, is just how powerful and far-reaching such effects can be. In fact, so widespread are the detrimental effects of stress (i.e., strain) that it has been estimated that their annual costs exceed 10 percent of the U.S. gross national product![53] With this in mind, I describe some of the specific problems linked to stress.

Lowered Task Performance—But Only Sometimes

The most current evidence available suggests that stress exerts mainly negative effects on task performance. For the most part, the greater the stress people encounter on the job, the more adversely affected their job performance tends to be.[54] In some cases, this is particularly serious. For example, one study reported that people who are experiencing higher levels of stress have significantly greater chances of having an auto accident than those experiencing lower levels of stress.[55]

It is important to note, however, that adverse job performance is not always linked to stress. Specifically, some people seem to "rise to the occasion" and turn in exceptional performances when confronted with potential stressors.

There appear to be two reasons for this. First, because some people are expert in the tasks being performed, they are highly confident in what they are doing. This leads them to appraise a situation that would be threatening to non-experts as merely challenging—and therefore, not at all stressful.

Second, some people are by nature high sensation-seekers and thrive on stress. These individuals find stress exhilarating and thrilling and are highly motivated to perform well under such conditions. Most people, however, are just the opposite. They find high levels of stress upsetting, which interferes with their job performance.

Desk Rage

A particularly unsettling manifestation of stress on the job that has become all too prevalent in recent years is known as **desk rage**—the lashing out at others in response to stressful encounters on the job. Just as angered drivers have been known to express their negative reactions to others in dangerous ways (commonly referred to as *road rage*), so too have office workers been known to behave violently toward others when feeling stress from long hours and difficult working conditions.

Desk rage is particularly frightening because it is shockingly commonplace: about half of all employees claim to have seen one or more colleagues explode into rage on at least one occasion. And, when this occurs, things may blow over but as suggested by accounts that fill the news, the consequences sometimes turn deadly. Obviously, it's wise for managers to be equipped to stop desk rage before it gets out of hand. For some suggestions in this regard, see Table 4.9.[56]

Stress and Health: The Silent Killer

How strong is the link between stress and personal health? The answer, say medical experts, is "very strong, indeed." In other words, physiological strain reactions can be quite severe. Some experts estimate that stress plays a role in anywhere from 50 to 70 percent of all forms of physical illness.[57] Included in these figures are some of the most serious and life-threatening ailments

---

TABLE 4.9   Addressing Desk Rage: Useful Tips for Managers

Because desk rage is all too prevalent, it's important for managers to recognize how to address it. Experts have offered the following tips.

Tip	Comment
Take control of your emotions whenever an employee seems to lose control.	Don't do anything that might keep the argument going or make it worse.
Carefully consider what led the person to be so angry.	By identifying the trigger, you are in a good position to straighten things out, such as by offering an explanation about something.
Immediately encourage everyone involved to take a deep breath.	Breathing deeply helps people calm down; doing so will help you to discuss the situation calmly.
Take the feud outside the workplace.	Discussing heated personal issues in the workplace may involve others, but going outside—to lunch, say—moves the discussion to neutral territory where calmer heads may prevail.
If someone seems to be having a particularly bad day, ask if there's anything you can do to help.	By intervening, you may be able to help with problems (e.g., overload), thereby eliminating conditions that promote anger.
Stay physically clear of someone who may be losing control.	By keeping an angry individual at arm's length, you may avoid a physical confrontation.
If you witness someone yelling at a coworker, intervene directly only if you are a supervisor. If you are a colleague, report this to your supervisor.	Direct intervention by a colleague may only make things worse by getting him or her involved as well. However, anyone witnessing acts of desk rage should report them at once to someone who has the authority to intervene.

Source: Lorenz, 2004; see Note 56.

known to medical science.[58] These ailments include such medical conditions as heart disease, stroke, backache, and ulcers. Stress also has psychological consequences, such as family conflict, depression, and sleep disorders. In addition, stress also has been linked to such behavioral problems as smoking, drug and alcohol abuse, and violence.

Such evidence makes it clear that the health-related effects of stress are not only wide-ranging in nature but also extremely serious. With this in mind, it's not surprising that many of today's companies are taking steps to keep stress in check. I review several of these in the remainder of this chapter.

REDUCING STRESS: WHAT CAN BE DONE?

Stress stems from so many different factors and conditions that to eliminate it entirely from our lives is impossible. However, there still are many things that both companies and individuals can do to reduce stress and to minimize its harmful effects.[59]

Employee Assistance Programs

Let's consider two important facts of organizational life. First, when companies hire individuals to do work, they get the whole person, problems and all. Second, whatever problems individuals may bring with them—be they medical, legal, social, or financial in nature—can and do influence how well they do their jobs. It is with this in mind that about two-thirds of today's companies have some kind of formal program in place to help employees with various problems they may face in their personal lives.[60] Such efforts are known as **employee assistance programs (EAPs)**. Sometimes, such programs are sponsored by trade unions, in which case, they are known as **member assistance programs (MAPs)**.

Interest in offering systematic ways of promoting the welfare of employees has grown so great that many companies today are seeking the assistance of specialized organizations with whom they contract to offer assistance programs for their employees. By outsourcing these services to firms that are expert in this area, companies are free to focus on their usual business while ensuring that they are taking care of their employees as needed. Privacy also is enhanced since using outsourced EAP services also helps ensure that personal information about employees is kept from their employers.

Importantly, EAPs are paying off. According to the Employee Assistance Professionals Association, a trade group for companies offering professional EAP services to organizations, employee work loss is avoided in 60 percent of the cases in which EAP services are provided.[61] EAPs have been of immense help to employees suffering stressful conditions in their lives, and the companies in which these individuals work have benefitted greatly as a result.

Stress Management Programs

Although EAPs can help address many sources of stress, it's inevitable that individuals still will encounter many stressors and that they will struggle to cope with them. It is with this in mind that many companies have introduced systematic programs designed to help employees reduce stress and to minimize its harmful effects. These are known as **stress management programs**. Such programs take many different forms but to some degree they focus on things to be done by the organizations, by individual employees, and by both individuals and organizations working together. For a summary of these techniques, see Table 4.10.[62] (And, for some novel examples of what three particular companies are doing in this regard, see the Winning Practices section on p. 126.)

The underlying assumption of such programs is that by minimizing employees' adverse reactions to stress, they will be healthier, less likely to be absent, and, consequently, more productive

TABLE 4.10	Overview of Stress Management Techniques Used in Organizations

Today's organizations use a variety of stress-management techniques focusing on individuals, organizations, and a combination of both. Some of the most popular ones in each category are summarized here.

Main Focus	Technique	Description
Organizations	Selection and placement	Put individuals in jobs that match their skills and interests.
	Training and education	Update workers' skills so that they are well suited to performing their jobs.
	Physical and environmental characteristics	Revise jobs so as to make them less dangerous (e.g., enhance safety of miners and police officers).
	Communication	Ensure that managers communicate job demands accurately and that they listen to concerns expressed by employees.
Individuals and organizations together	Person–environment fit	Regularly review individuals' abilities and ensure that they match the demands faced on the job.
	Role issues	Define jobs clearly to ensure that workers know precisely what they are expected to do (and not to do) on their jobs.
	Coworker support groups	Encourage workers to join groups in which they discuss work-related issues with their colleagues.
Individuals	Relaxation	Train employees in how to relax by controlling their breathing, especially in threatening situations.
	Meditation	Train employees in transcendental meditation, which allows them to relax while being attentive to what's going on.
	Biofeedback	Train people in ways to recognize signs of distress in their bodies, such as muscle and skin activity (see Table 4.11 on p. 128).
	Exercise	Building up the cardiovascular system helps people cope with potentially adverse bodily reactions to stress.

Source: Based on information in Giga et al., 2003; see Note 62.

on the job. This, in turn, is not only likely to have beneficial effects on the bottom lines of companies but also on the individual well-being of the employees who work in them.

Wellness Programs

Beyond helping employees reduce stress-related problems, about half of today's larger companies have **wellness programs** in place to keep them healthy. These are systematic efforts to train

Winning Practices

Three Novel Approaches to Fighting the Battle Against Stress

Although many companies are doing things to help their employees reduce the effects of stress, some are being particularly creative in this regard.[63] Given how successful they've been, it is worthwhile to know about some of these novel practices.

You've heard of teachers taking sabbaticals—time off—so they can recharge and/or learn new skills. What you might not know is that growing numbers of companies are offering sabbaticals to their employees as well. Take Arrow Electronics, for example, the Englewood, Colorado, company specializing in distributing electronic components to industrial and commercial customers. After working for seven years, employees are allowed to take a 10-week paid sabbatical during which they can do whatever they want. Company officials claim that the 1,400 employees who have taken advantage of this benefit return to their jobs refreshed and with greater appreciation for their work.

A quite different approach has been in use at Burmah Castrol, the multinational distributor of specialty lubricants and chemicals to businesses based in the United Kingdom. A few years ago, many of the company's top executives were asked to do more work in less time, resulting in signs of stress-related illness. To alleviate these problems, the company physician trained employees in various biomedical techniques that helped them recognize signs of stress (e.g., adrenaline rushes and increased heartbeat). The physician further showed them how to control these reactions by using various concentration techniques (i.e., "mind over matter"). Shortly thereafter, the signs of stress began to disappear.

Other companies take a far simpler approach. They help manage stress on a one-by-one basis by having employees look for signs that their colleagues may be suffering its adverse effects. For example, in the restaurant business, where very long hours are the rule, employees of Hard Rock Café International are encouraged to do whatever it takes to help their fellow employees avoid stress. Case in point: when the wife of the general manager of the Hard Rock in San Diego went into labor on the restaurant's opening night, executives told him to join his wife instead of staying for the festivities. Although his presence was critical to the event, execs realize that people are the company's top asset. They released him from his obligations so as to enhance his personal well-being at this important time in his life. This program appears to be working: Hard Rock has one of the lowest turnover rates in the restaurant industry today—about half the national average.

Despite their differences, these three examples illustrate an important point: companies that invest in efforts to reduce the stress of their employees generally reap considerable benefits.

employees in a variety of things they can do to promote healthy lifestyles. Very broad-based, wellness programs usually consist of workshops in which employees can learn ways to reduce stress and maintain their health. Exercise, nutrition, and weight-management counseling are among the most popular areas covered.

As an interesting example, Blue Cross Blue Shield of Oklahoma built a financial incentive into the wellness program it uses for its 1,300 employees.[64] The company offers "Weight Watchers at Work" meetings. Employees have to pay to participate in the 16-week program—but are reimbursed as in incentive if they attend at least 14 weekly sessions. In a recent five-year period, Blue Cross Blue Shield employees collectively have lost nearly 10 tons of excess weight.

As you might imagine, companies that have used such programs have found that they pay off handsomely. For example, at its industrial sites that offer wellness programs, DuPont has found that absenteeism is less than half of what it is at sites that do not offer such programs. Organizations such as The Travelers Companies and Union Pacific Railroad have enjoyed consistently high returns on each dollar they invest in employee wellness. And when it comes to saving money by promoting employee health, there is a lot at stake. Consider, for example, that annual health insurance costs in the United States due to obesity alone are $7.7 billion.[65]

As you might imagine, wellness programs help not only by reducing insurance costs, but also by reducing absenteeism due to illness. There's yet another way in which stress management efforts promise to help companies' bottom lines, and one of which most people are unaware. I am referring to the problem of **presenteeism**—the practice of showing up for work but being too sick to be able to work effectively.

Paying workers who are not performing well is not only costly on its own, but is also indirectly so, given that it may lower morale by sending the message that it's important to show up even if you're sick. And, of course, depending on the particular illness people have, it may spread disease throughout a workplace, compounding the problem. (For an overview of some possible motives for presenteeism and its results, see Figure 4.8). This phenomenon is especially problematic in view of estimates that about one in four employees engage in presenteeism.[66] Given that stress is one of the leading causes of illness, it follows that reducing stress can help minimize the problem of presenteeism (and many others too, of course).

Managing Your Own Stress

Even if you work for a company that doesn't have a formal program in place to help you manage stress, you're not out of luck. There still are several things you can do by yourself to help control the stress in your life. Some of the most effective ones are as follows.

MANAGE YOUR TIME WISELY People who don't use their time effectively find themselves easily overwhelmed, falling behind, not getting important things done, and having to work longer hours as a result. Not surprisingly, **time management**, the practice of taking control over how we spend time, is a valuable skill for reducing time pressure, which is a particularly widespread stressor. Three of the most effective time management practices involve setting priorities (doing the most important things first), allocating your time realistically (not overcommitting), and taking control over your time (e.g., by making "to do" lists).

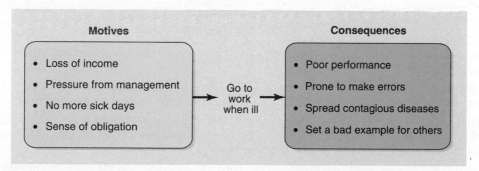

FIGURE 4.8 Presenteeism: Motives and Consequences
The opposite of absenteeism, *presenteeism,* can also be problematic for organizations. Some of the motives that people might have for going to work when ill are summarized here, along with the consequences.

EAT A HEALTHY DIET AND BE PHYSICALLY FIT   The evidence is clear that reduced intake of salt and saturated fats and increased consumption of fiber- and vitamin-rich fruits and vegetables greatly increases the body's ability to cope with the physiological effects of stress.[67] Regular exercise also helps. People who exercise regularly obtain many benefits closely related to resistance of the adverse effects of stress. For example, fitness reduces both the incidence of cardiovascular illness and the death rate from such diseases. Similarly, physical fitness lowers blood pressure, an important factor in many aspects of personal health.

RELAX AND MEDITATE   Many people find that it helps to relieve stress by engaging in **meditation**, the process of learning to clear one's mind of external thoughts, often by repeating slowly and rhythmically a single syllable (known as a *mantra*). Those who follow this systematic way of relaxing claim that it helps to relieve the many sources of stress in their lives. For an overview of general steps to follow while meditating, see Table 4.11.[68]

GET A GOOD NIGHT'S SLEEP   One of the most effective ways to alleviate stress-related problems is also one of the simplest: sleeping (if you can do it). We all need a certain amount of sleep to allow our bodies to recharge and function effectively. Eight hours per day is average, although some need more and others can function just fine on fewer. If you find that your worries are keeping you up at night, it may help to meditate (as outlined in Table 4.11).

AVOID INAPPROPRIATE SELF-TALK   Have you ever told yourself that things will be terrible if you fail at something, convincing yourself how awful things will be? Your answer is probably "yes," since many people do this kind of thing at least occasionally. Unfortunately, such thoughts can add to personal levels of stress, as we *awfulize* or *catastrophize* in our minds the

---

TABLE 4.11   How to Meditate

Meditation can help people gain better control of negative emotions, such as anger, and it also can help lessen negative reactions to stress. For these reasons, learning to meditate can be very useful. Although there are several different types of meditation, the relaxation approach outlined here is both easiest to learn and among the most effective. Give it a try.

1. Go to a quiet, dark place where you will not be disturbed. Sit in a comfortable position. Let your mind go blank and slowly relax your muscles.

2. Focus into space, slowly letting everything out of your mind. Do not let thoughts intrude. If they do, work at pushing them away.

3. Breathe slowly and in a regular rhythm. As you breathe in, slowly make the sound "haaah" as you would when slipping into a hot bath. Then, as you exhale, slowly produce the sound "saaah," sounding and feeling like a sigh.

4. Repeat this process, breathing slowly and naturally. When you do, inhale through your nose and pause for a few seconds. Then exhale through your mouth, again pausing for a few seconds.

5. Should thoughts enter your mind while attempting this process, don't feel badly about it. Instead, realize that this is natural and pick up the process once again. This will take time to master, so be patient. With practice, you will be able to do this more quickly.

6. Continue this process for what feels like about 20 minutes. Don't look at the clock, though. As the time draws to a close, maintain awareness of your breathing and sit quietly. Then, slowly becoming aware of where you are, open your eyes and get up gradually.

Sources: Based on suggestions by Rofe, 2012, Easwaran, 2011, and Novak, 2009; see Note 68.

horrors of not being successful, perfect, or loved. Fortunately, such thinking can be modified. Often, merely recognizing that we harbor such irrational and self-defeating beliefs is sufficient to get us to stop this kind of thinking, paving the way to more realistic—hence, less stress-arousing—thoughts.

TAKE A TIME-OUT When confronted with rising tension, people may find it useful to choose to insert a brief period of delay known as a **time-out**. This can involve taking a short break, going to the nearest restroom to splash cold water on your face, or any other action that yields a few moments of breathing space. Such actions interrupt the cycle of ever-rising tension that accompanies stress and can help to restore equilibrium and the feeling of being even partially in control of ongoing events. At the very least, this may keep you from saying or doing something for which you are sorry (or even in trouble) later on.

Back to the Case

Answer the following questions based on this chapter's Making the Case (p. 100) to illustrate insights you have derived from the material in this chapter.

1. In addition to the many things that Dr. Ludwigsen did to manage stress among Kaiser Permanente's employees, what else might have been done to help eliminate stressors or to reduce their adverse effects?
2. What particular sources of stress might nurses encounter routinely on their jobs at Kaiser Permanente and how might these differ from those in administrative jobs?
3. What emotional reactions might nurses experience on a daily basis and how might these differ while the community was ravaged by wildfires?

You Be the Consultant

Stressed-Out Employees Are Resigning

As the managing director of a large e-tail and catalog sales company, you are becoming alarmed about the growing levels of turnover your company has been experiencing lately among customer service representatives (CSRs). It already has passed the industry average, and you are worried about the company's capacity to staff the call center and the warehouse during the busy holiday period. In conducting exit interviews, you learned that the employees who are leaving generally like their work and the pay they are receiving. However, they are displeased with the rude way their customers are treating them, and this is creating stress in their lives. CSRs are quitting so they can take less stressful positions in other companies. Answer the following questions based on material in this chapter.

1. Assuming that levels of stress are high in the company, what problems would you expect to see in individuals, both physiologically and with respect to their job performance?
2. What steps can the company take to reduce the levels of stress encountered on the job?
3. You consider the possibility that the stress experienced stems also from additional sources that weren't mentioned in the exit interviews. What might such sources be? What could be done about them?

Self-Assessment Exercise

WHAT IS YOUR EI?

Various tests have been developed to measure the degree of emotional intelligence a person has, characterized as an emotional quotient (EQ score). The instrument presented here is similar to ones that some scientists have used to assess people's emotional intelligence. Although this contains just a sampling of items—and therefore, is not a definitive measure—completing this scale will give you a good sense of your own EQ.

Directions

The items on the following scale describe difficult situations that might be encountered on the job. For each, put a check mark next to the one response that best indicates what you would be most likely to do in that situation.

Scale

1. Someone with whom you work and who you consider to be a friend has borrowed one of your favorite screwdrivers. You asked him to return it to your toolbox, but so far he hasn't done so.

    _____ a. Who needs friends like this? I would end the friendship.
    _____ b. I'd ignore it. Keeping a friend is the most important thing.
    _____ c. Until he returns the screwdriver, I'd act cool toward him and hope he gets the message.
    _____ d. I'd explain to my friend why I really need to have the screwdriver back and politely ask him to return it.

2. After several months on the job, your boss finally assigns you an important project. This is your chance to show him how good you are, but only if you succeed. If you blow it, your future with the company will be bleak.

    _____ a. You spend several weeks working out the details of the project before telling anyone about this opportunity.
    _____ b. You put the project aside for now, planning to return to it some other time.
    _____ c. You get very nervous as you think about the implications.
    _____ d. You relax, think about the project, and then bounce some of your ideas off one of your colleagues before pursuing what you believe is the best one.

3. One of your coworkers in a nearby cubicle has an annoying habit of humming all the time, and it's really getting to you.

    _____ a. You just put up with it because it's not really so bad.
    _____ b. You explain to this person politely that his or her humming annoys you and explain the reasons why.
    _____ **c.** You take an indirect approach by making a joke about his or her annoying humming and hope that this person will get the hint.
    _____ d. You tell your boss that you'll quit your job if this person doesn't stop humming or if you aren't moved to a different cubicle.

4. You are in a business meeting with a client who, for no apparent reason, appears to be very uncomfortable talking to you.

    _____ a. You do your best to involve the client in a conversation so that the two of you can learn about one another.
    _____ b. You plan to schedule the next meeting at some other location.
    _____ c. You begin to worry that you've done something to ruin the business deal.
    _____ d. You assume that the client isn't interested in doing business with you so you don't pay much attention to the conversation and spend the time thinking about other things.

5. Walking through the office one day, you stumble and spill coffee all over the floor.

   _____ a. You get angry and mutter something to yourself about being so clumsy.

   _____ b. After cleaning up the mess, you laugh at yourself and go about your business.

   _____ c. You get extremely embarrassed and leave the office before anyone sees what you did.

   _____ d. You give a dirty look to anyone who happened to see what you did.

6. For several months, you were hoping to get an important promotion. You thought you were the ideal candidate, but your boss apparently didn't agree and recommended someone else instead.

   _____ a. You forget about it and convince yourself that the promotion really wasn't that important to you.

   _____ b. You keep on doing your best and realize that there will always be another opportunity to get promoted.

   _____ c. You feel so upset that you hide in the restroom and cry.

   _____ d. You keep thinking about what the promoted person has that you don't have and make yourself feel bad about what happened.

7. In the break room one day, one of your coworkers, Bob, began saying bad things about Cathy, a colleague whom you really admire, but who wasn't in the break room at the time.

   _____ a. Although you don't really mean them, you go along with Bob by adding a few negative remarks about Cathy yourself.

   _____ b. You don't say anything to Bob at the time but later tell him in private how you feel about his remarks.

   _____ c. You interrupt Bob, saying that you're uncomfortable talking behind someone's back, and then change the subject.

   _____ d. You keep quiet but then feel bad about not stopping Bob from talking negatively about Cathy.

Scoring Procedure and Interpretation

1. One of the responses for each situation shows a higher degree of emotional intelligence than the others because it reveals empathy and respect for others. With this in mind, try to identify these "answers"; that is, the responses that indicate the greatest amount of emotional intelligence.
2. Give yourself 1 point for answering the questions as follows. 1 = d, 2 = d, 3 = b, 4 = a, 5 = b, 6 = b, and 7 = c.
3. The higher your score, the higher your EQ.

Discussion Questions

1. How successful were you at being able to predict the one response in each set of alternatives that reflected high emotional intelligence? (In other words, how closely did your responses to scoring point number 1 match the correct responses indicated in scoring point number 2?)
2. How did your EQ compare to what you thought it would be? How did it compare to those of other people in your class?
3. For item 7, why do you think the high EI answer was alternative "c" instead of "b"? What does this scoring reveal about standing up for others as an aspect of emotional intelligence?

Group Exercise

ARE YOU AS TOUGH AS A NAVY SEAL?

Over the years, Olympic athletes and U.S. Navy Seals have been studied to see how effectively they can endure stress. This research uses a test known as the Attentional and Interpersonal Style (TAIS) inventory to assess the extent to which individuals can stay focused and keep their emotions under control, which is required for individuals to perform well under high-pressure conditions.[69] In this exercise, you will complete a questionnaire containing items similar to those used to study various elite teams to see how much stress they can endure. Completing this questionnaire will help you understand your own strengths and limitations in this regard. And, by discussing these scores with your teammates, you will come away with a good feel for the extent to which those with whom you work differ along this dimension as well.

Directions

1. Gather in groups of three or four people whom you know fairly well. If you are part of an intact group, such as a work team or a team of students working on a class project, meet with your fellow group members.
2. Individually, complete the following questionnaire by responding to each question using the scale below. Write the number corresponding to your response to each question in the space to the left of it.

   1 = Never
   2 = Rarely
   3 = Sometimes
   4 = Frequently
   5 = Always

Scale

_____ 1. When time is running out on an important project, I am the person who should be called on to take control of the schedule.
_____ 2. When listening to a piece of music, I can pick out a specific voice or instrument.
_____ 3. The people who know me think of me as being serious.
_____ 4. It is important to me to get a job completely right in every detail, even if it means being late.
_____ 5. When approaching a busy intersection, I easily get confused.
_____ 6. Just by looking at someone, I can figure out what he or she is like.
_____ 7. I am comfortable arguing with people.
_____ 8. At a cocktail party, I have no difficulty keeping track of several different conversations at once.

Scoring and Group Analysis

1. Compute your score by the eight numbers, resulting in a score between 8 and 40. Note that higher scores reflect a greater ability to focus.
2. Discuss your score with others in your group. In addition to the score numbers themselves, discuss your responses to each item, considering what each response indicates about the person's ability to focus.

Discussion Questions

1. What questions were easiest to interpret? Which were most difficult?
2. How did each individual's responses compare with the way you would assess his or her ability to focus under stress?
3. For what jobs is the ability to concentrate under stress particularly important? For what jobs is it not especially important? How important is this ability for the work you do currently (or, if you don't work now, for the kind of job you hope to do in the future)?

Notes

MAKING THE CASE NOTES

Kaiser Permanante. (2011). Managing stress related to the California fire storms. https://healthy.kaiserprtmanente.org. Dealing with stress on the job and elsewhere. (2006). *Schizophrenia .com Newsletter.* http://www.schizophrenia.com .newsletter/697/697stress.htm. Kaiser Permanente. (2006). Life outside of work. From http://www.kaiserpermanentejobs.org/workinghere/lifeoutside.asp. Jacobs, L. (2003, Winter). Discovering a remedy for physician work stress. *The Permanente Journal.* From http://xnet.kp.org/permanentejournal/winter03/group.html.

CHAPTER NOTES

1. American Institute of Stress. (2012). *Stress in the workplace.* http://www.stress.org/topic-workplace.htm. American Psychological Association Practice Organization. (2009). APA poll find economic stress taking a toll on men. http://www.apapracticecentral.org/news/2009/stress-men.aspx.

2. Lewis, M., Haviland-Jones, J. M., & Barrett, L. F. (2010). *Handbook of emotions* (3rd ed.). New York: Guilford.

3. Hatfield, E., Cacioppo, J. T., & Rhapson, R. L. (1994). *Emotional contagion.* New York: Cambridge University Press.

4. Barsade, S. G. (2002). The ripple effect: Emotional contagion and its influence on group behavior. *Administrative Science Quarterly, 47,* 644–675. Cherulnik, P. K., Donley, K. A., Wiewel, T. S. R., & Miller, S. R. (2001). Charisma is contagious: The effects of leaders' charisma on observers' affect. *Journal of Applied Social Psychology, 31,* 2149–2159.

5. Ekman, P., Friesen, W. V., & Ancoli, S. (2001). Facial signs of emotional experience. In W. G. Parrott (Ed.), *Emotions in social psychology* (pp. 255–264). Philadelphia, PA: Psychology Press.

6. Nakamura, N. (2000). Facial expression and communication of emotion: An analysis of display rules and a model of facial expression of emotion. *Japanese Psychological Review, 43,* 307–319.

7. Matsumoto, D., Yoo, S. H., & Fontaine, J. (2008). Mapping expressive differences around the world: The relationship between emotional display rules and individualism versus collectivism. *Journal of Cross-Cultural Psychology, 39,* 55–74.

8. Tangney, J. P., & Fischer, K. W. (Eds.), (1995). *Self-conscious emotions: The psychology of shame, guilt, embarrassment, and pride.* New York: Guilford Press. Tracy, J. L., & Robins, R. W. (2004). Putting the self into self-conscious emotions: A theoretical model. *Psychological Inquiry, 15,* 103–125.

9. Keltner, D., & Anderson, C. (2000). Saving face for Darwin: The functions and uses of embarrassment. *Current Directions in Psychological Science, 9,* 187–192.

10. Vecchio, R. P. (2005). Explorations of employee envy: Feeling envious and feeling envied. *Cognition and Emotion, 19,* 69–81. Poulson, C. F. II. (2000). Shame and work. In N. M. Ashkanasy, W. Zerbe, & C. E. J. Härtel (Eds.), *Emotions in the workplace: Research, theory, and practice* (pp. 490–541). Westport, CT: Quorum Books.

11. Huelsman, T. J., Furr, R. M., & Memanick, R. C., Jr. (2003). Measurement of dispositional affect: Construct validity and convergence with a circumplex model of affect. *Educational and Psychological Measurement, 63,* 655–673. Larsen, J., Diener, E., & Lucas, R. E. (2002). Emotion: Moods, measures, and differences. In R. G. Lord, R. J. Klimiski, & R. Kanfer (Eds.), *Emotions in the workplace* (pp. 64–113). San Francisco, CA: Jossey-Bass.

12. George, J. M., & Brief, A. P. (1996). Motivational agendas in the workplace: The effects of feelings on focus of attention and work motivation. In B. M. Staw & L. L. Cummings (Eds.), *Research in organizational behavior* (Vol. 18, pp. 75–109). Greenwich, CT: JAI Press.

13. 100 Best Companies to Work For. (2011). *Fortune.* http://money.cnn.com/magazines/fortune/bestcompanies/2011.html.

14. Hemsath, D., & Sivasubramaniam, J. (2001). *301 more ways to have fun at work.* San Francisco, CA: Berrett-Koehler. Hemsch, D., Hemsath, D., & Yerkes, L. (1997). *301 ways to have fun at work.* San Francisco, CA: Berrett-Koehler. Case, J. (1996, November 1). Corporate culture. *Inc. Magazine.* http://www.inc.com/magazine/19961101/1861.html.

15. Lyubomirsky, S., King, L., & Diener, E. (2005). The benefits of frequent positive affect: Does happiness lead to success? *Psychological Bulletin, 131,* 803–855.

16. Staw, B. M., Sutton, R. I., & Pelled, L. H. (1994). Employee positive emotion and favorable outcomes in the workplace. *Organization Science, 5,* 51–71.

17. Cropanzano, R., & Wright, T. A. (1999). A five-year study of change in the relationship between well-being and job performance. *Consulting Psychology Journal, 51,* 252–265. Wright, T. A., & Staw, B. M. (1999). Affect and favorable work outcomes: Two longitudinal tests of the happy-productive worker thesis. *Journal of Organizational Behavior, 20,* 1–23.

18. DeLuga, R. J., & Manson, S. (2000). Relationship of resident assistant conscientiousness, extraversion, and positive affect with rated performance. *Journal of Research in Personality, 34,* 225–235. Totterdell, P. (2000). Catching moods and hitting runs: Mood linkage and subjective performance in professional sports teams. *Journal of Applied Psychology, 83,* 848–859.

19. See Note 18.

20. Foster, J. B., Hebl, M. R., West, M., & Dawson, J. (2004, April). *Setting the tone for organizational success: The impact of CEO affect on organizational climate and firm-level outcomes.* Paper presented at the annual meeting of the Society for Industrial and Organizational Psychology, Toronto, Ontario, Canada. Pritzker, M. A. (2002). The relationship among CEO dispositional attributes, transformational leadership behavior and performance effectiveness. *Dissertation Abstracts International, 62*(12-B), 6008. (UMI No. AA13035464.)

21. Lucas, R. E., Clark, A. E., Georgellis, Y., & Deiner, E. (2004). Unemployment alters the set points for live satisfaction. *Psychological Science, 15,* 8–13. Graham, C., Eggers, A., & Sukhtanar, S. (in press). Does happiness pay: An exploration based on panel data from Russia. *Journal of Economic Behaviour and Organization.*

22. Howell, C. J., Howell, R. T., & Schwabe, K. A. (in press). Does wealth enhance life satisfaction for people who are materially deprived? Exploring the association among the Orang Asli of Peninsular Malaysia. *Social Indicators Research.*

23. Vohs, K. D., Baumeister, R. F., & Loewenstein, G. (in press). *Do emotions help or hurt decision making?* New York: Russell Sage Foundation Press.

24. Weiss, H. M., Nicholas, J. P., & Daus, C. S. (1999). An examination of the joint effects of affective experiences and job beliefs on job satisfaction and variations in affective experiences over time. *Organizational Behavior and Human Decision Processes, 78,* 1–24.

25. Weiss, H. M., & Beal, D. J. (2005). Reflections on affective events theory. *Research on Emotion in Organizations, 1,* 1-21. Weiss, H. M., & Cropanzano, R. (1996). An affective events approach to job satisfaction. In B. M. Staw & L. L. Cummings (Eds.), *Research in organizational behavior* (Vol. 18, pp. 1–74). Greenwich, CT: JAI Press.

26. Ashkanasy, N. M., & Daus, C. S. (2002). Emotion in the workplace: New challenges for managers. *Academy of Management Executive, 16,* 76–86.

27. See Note 26.

28. Wegge, J., Van Dick, R.,, Fisher, G. K., West, M. A., & Dawson, J. F. (2006). A test of basic assumptions of affective events theory (AET) in call centre work. *British Journal of Management, 17,* 237–254. Miner, A. G., & Hulin, C. L. (2000). *Affective experience at work: A test of affective events theory.* Poster presented at the 15th annual conference of the Society for Industrial and Organizational Psychology; New Orleans, LA. Fisher, C. (1998, August). *Mood and emotions while working: Missing pieces of job satisfaction?* Paper presented at the annual meeting of the Academy of Management. San Diego, CA.

29. Ashkanasy, N. M., Hartel, C. E. J., & Daus, C. S. (2002). Diversity and emotion: The new frontiers in organizational behavior research. *Journal of Management, 28,* 307–338.

30. Goleman, D. (1995). *Emotional intelligence*: New York: Bantam Books.

31. See Note 30.

32. Spencer, L. M., Jr., & Spencer, S. (1993). *Competence at work: Models of superior performance.* New York: John Wiley & Sons. Spencer, L. M., Jr., McClelland, D. C., & Kelner, S. (1997). *Competency assessment methods: History and state of the art.* Boston, MA: Hay McDer.

33. Morris, J. A., & Feldman, D. C. (1997). Managing emotions in the workplace. *Journal of Managerial Issues, 9,* 257–274.

34. Bolles, R. N. (2002). *What color is your parachute?* (2002 edition). Berkeley, CA: Ten Speed Press.

35. Northwestern National Life Insurance Company. (1999). *Employee burnout: America's newest epidemic.* Minneapolis, MN: Author.

36. Quick, J. C., Murphy, L. R., & Hurrell, J. J., Jr. (1992). *Stress and well-being at work.* Washington, DC: American Psychological Association.

37. Selye, H. (1976). *Stress in health and disease.* Boston: Butterworths.

38. Kane, K. (1997, October–November). Can you perform under pressure? *Fast Company,* pp. 54, 56. Enhanced Performance Web site: www.enhanced-performance.com.

39. Nideffer, R. M. (1976). Test of attentional and interpersonal style. *Journal of Personality and Social Psychology, 34,* 394-404.

40. Bakker, A. B., Schaufeli, W. B., Sixma, H. J., Bosveld, W., & Van Dierendonck, D. (2000). Patient demands, lack of reciprocity, and burnout: A five-year longitudinal study among general practitioners. *Journal of Organizational Behavior, 21,* 425–441.

41. See Note 40.

42. Demerouti, E., Bakker, A. B., Nachreiner, F., & Schaufeli, W. B. (2001). The job demands-resources model of burnout. *Journal of Applied Psychology, 86,* 499–512.

43. See Note 42.

44. CNBC. (2012, January). America's most stressful jobs. http://www.cnbc.com/id/45859959/America_s_Least_Stressful_Jobs_2012?CNBC. (2012, January). America's most stressful jobs. http://www.cnbc.com/id/45859025/America_s_Most_Stressful_Jobs_2012?

45. Heller, R., & Hindle, T. (1998). *Essential manager's manual.* New York: DK Publishing.

46. Gouldner., L., & Ofra, M. (2008). Juggling the roles of parents, therapists, friends and teachers: A working model for an integrative conception of mentoring. *Mentoring & Tutoring: Partnership in Learning, 16,* 412–428.

47. Settles, I. H., Sellers, R. M., & Damas, A., Jr. (2002). One role or two? The function of psychological separation in role conflict. *Journal of Applied Psychology, 87,* 574–582.

48. McGrath, J. E. (1976). Stress and behavior in organizations. In M. D. Dunnette (Ed.), *Handbook of industrial and organizational psychology* (pp. 1351–1398). Chicago: Rand McNally.

49. Shedroff, N. (2000, November 28). Forms of information anxiety. *Business 2.0,* p. 220.

50. Stephens, C., & Long, N. (2000). Communication with police supervisors and peers as a buffer of work-related traumatic stress. *Journal of Organizational Behavior, 21,* 407–424.

51. Beehr, T. A., Jex, S. M., Stacy, B. A., & Murray, M. A. (2000). Work stressors and coworker support as predictors of individual strain and job performance. *Journal of Organizational Behavior, 21,* 391 405.

52. Treharne, G. J., Lyons, A. C., & Tupling, R. E. (2001). The effects of optimism, pessimism, social support, and mood on the lagged relationship between stress and symptoms. *Current Research in Social Psychology, 7*(5), 60–81.

53. Sullivan, S. E., & Bhagat, R. S. (1992). Organizational stress, job satisfaction, and job performance: Where do we go from here? *Journal of Management, 18,* 353–374.

54. Cropanzano, R., Rupp, D. E., & Byrne, Z. S. (2003). The interrelationship of emotional exhaustion to work attitudes, job performance, and organizational citizenship behaviors. *Journal of Applied Psychology, 88,* 160 169. Motowidlo, S. J., Packard, J. S., & Manning, M. R. (1986). Occupational stress: Its causes and consequences for job performance. *Journal of Applied Psychology, 71,* 618–629.

55. Legree, P. J., Heffner, T. S., Psotka, J., Martin, D. E., & Medsker, G. J. (2003). Traffic crash involvement: Experiential driving knowledge and stressful contextual antecedents. *Journal of Applied Psychology, 88,* 5–26.

56. Daw, J. (2001, August). Road rage, air rage, and now desk rage. *Monitor on Psychology, 32*(7). 9–10. The list: Desk rage. *BusinessWeek* (2000, November 27), p. 12. Lorenz, I. (2004, December 20). 7 tips for combating desk rage. *CNN.com/CareerBuilder.com.* http://www.cnn.com/2004/US/Careers/08/13/boss.spying/index.html.

57. Frese, M. (1985). Stress at work and psychosomatic complaints: A causal interpretation. *Journal of Applied Psychology, 70,* 314–328. Quick, J. C., & Quick, J. D. (1984).

Organizational stress and preventive management. New York: McGraw-Hill.

58. Quick, J. C., Cooper, C, L., Gavin, J. H., & Quick, J. D. (2008). *Managing executive health.* New York: Cambridge University Press.

59. Latack, J. C., & Havlovic, S. J. (1992). Coping with job stress: A conceptual evaluation framework for coping measures. *Journal of Organizational Behavior, 13,* 479–508.

60. Society for Human Resource Management. (2006). *Annual benefits survey.* Alexandria, VA: SHRM.

61. Employee Assistance Professionals Association. (2006). Recent EAP cost/benefit statistics research: 2000–present. http://www.eapassn.org/public/articles/EAPcostbenefitstats.pdf.

62. Giga, S. I., Cooper, C. L., & Faragher, B. (2003). Development of a framework for a comprehensive approach to stress management interventions at work. *International Journal of Stress Management, 10,* 280–296.

63. See Note 62.

64. Flora, C. (2004, January/February). Keeping workers and companies fit. *Psychology Today,* pp. 36–40. Also available from http://www.psychologytoday.com/articles/pto-3285.html.

65. See Note 64.

66. Johns, G. (2011). Attendance dynamics at work: The antecedents and correlates of presenteeism, absenteeism, and productivity loss. *Journal of Occupational Health Psychology, 16,* 483–500. Robertson Cooper, Ltd. (2009, November). "Presenteeism" on the rise as an estimated quarter of UK employees admit to working when ill. http://www.robertsoncooper.com/news/presenteeism.aspx.

67. Shoshanna, B. (2005). *The anger diet.* Kansas City, MO: Andrews McMeel Publishing.

68. Rofe, R. J. (2012). *Meditation.* Seattle, WA: Create Space. Easwaran, E. (2011). *How to meditate.* Tomales, CA: Nilgiri Press. Novak, J. (2009). *How to meditate: A step-by-step guide to the art and science of meditation,* 3rd ed. Nevada City, CA: Crystal Clarity Press.

69. Winning Mind. (2012). http://taistest.com/

5 WORK-RELATED ATTITUDES: PREJUDICE, JOB SATISFACTION, AND ORGANIZATIONAL COMMITMENT

LEARNING OBJECTIVES

After reading this chapter, you will be able to:

1. **DISTINGUISH** among the concepts of prejudice, stereotypes, and discrimination.
2. **DISTINGUISH** between affirmative action plans and diversity management programs.
3. **DESCRIBE** various theories of job satisfaction.
4. **IDENTIFY** the consequences of having dissatisfied employees and **DESCRIBE** ways of boosting job satisfaction.
5. **DISTINGUISH** among fundamental forms of organizational commitment.
6. **IDENTIFY** the benefits of having a committed workforce and **DESCRIBE** ways of developing organizational commitment.

THREE GOOD REASONS you should care about. . .

Work-Related Attitudes

1. We are all potential victims of prejudice and discrimination on the job; nobody is immune.
2. The more people are satisfied with their jobs and committed to their organizations, the less likely they are to be absent and to voluntarily resign.
3. Changing attitudes is not impossible. There are specific things that practicing managers and their organizations can do to enhance the work-related attitudes of employees.

Making the Case for...

Work-Related Attitudes

Domino's Pizza Takes a Bite Out of Turnover

Ten million miles—that's how far you'd travel if you went to the moon and back 41 times. Coincidentally, that's also how far Domino's Pizza delivery drivers travel each week in more than 60 countries. The 200,000 employees who work in the 9,000 stores in these nations get 1.5 million pizzas out the door each day. And they've been doing this every day since 1960, when the founders, brothers Tom and James Monaghan, bought their first small pizzeria in Ypsilanti, Michigan.

The recipe for keeping these employees working happily at their jobs is something the company takes as seriously as its pizza recipe. And just as Domino's totally redesigned its pizzas "from the crust up" in 2010 to keep customers coming back for more, it also has been rethinking its approach to employees to keep them coming back to work.

This is no minor concern for Domino's Pizza, considering that annual turnover within stores has been more than 150 percent, resulting in an entirely new crew about every nine months. And given that it costs upward of $2,500 to replace an entry-level worker and 10 times more for a manager, it's no wonder that boosting employee retention has been a priority for the Domino's corporate management team in Ann Arbor. In 2005, under the leadership of David Brandon, Domino's launched several initiatives to tackle the turnover problem, which continued when Patrick Doyle assumed the CEO post in 2010.

Brandon initiated a three-pronged approach. This began with hiring new store managers who cared deeply about the company and who were committed to working with employees to ensure the quality of Domino's products. Then, once selected, managers were trained thoroughly in ways of effectively interviewing prospective employees who shared this commitment to quality and were interested in working hard to attain quality standards.

The second focus of the retention effort involved giving store managers tools to assess how well their employees were performing. This consisted of computerized tracking systems that enable them to learn precisely how long the pizza production process is taking as well as to identify star performers and those who need additional help. Brandon reasoned that employees needed to know precisely how well they were doing so that they could have a clear basis for being satisfied with their work, giving them opportunities to feel proud about meeting performance standards.

Third, although Brandon believed firmly in creating incentives for managers that reward them for outstanding performance. This led to a system of bonuses based on store profits and to stock options for managers whose store sales and customer satisfaction grew. The effect was to align the financial interests of the managers with those of Domino's Pizza, thereby retaining these valued employees by enhancing their commitment to the company.

Since these efforts were put in place, turnover at Domino's Pizza has been cut in half—a vast improvement whose impact has been felt on the bottom line. And in an era of crust-thin margins, such developments are welcomed, for sure. It is not surprising, therefore, that Domino's was named 2011's "Chain of the Year" by *Pizza Today* magazine.

It's certainly the case that Domino's Pizza's bottom line was boosted by increased sales in response to improved recipes of its products. But gaining customers by putting more cheese in the cheese bread is only part of the story. Brandon's recipe for corporate success also contained another essential ingredient. Specifically, enhancing employees' positive feelings about the company was key to controlling expenses by keeping employees on the job. What I'm talking about here is employees' *attitudes* toward their companies. Organizations are, of course, one focus of people's attitudes. We also have attitudes toward other people (e.g., how employees feel about their managers) and objects (e.g., how customers feel about pizza).

As you might imagine, attitudes are an important part of people's lives, particularly in the workplace. Indeed, people tend to have definite feelings about everything related to their jobs, whether it's the work itself, superiors, coworkers, subordinates, or even such mundane things as the decor in the company cafeteria. Feelings such as these are referred to as *work-related attitudes,* the topic of this chapter. As you might imagine, not only may our attitudes toward our jobs or organizations have profound effects on the way we perform, but also on the quality of life we experience while at work.

In view of their importance, I will examine these effects closely in this chapter. Specifically, this discussion of work-related attitudes has three major areas of focus. First, I will consider attitudes toward others, including that special—and problematic—kind of negative attitude known as *prejudice.* Second, I will look at attitudes toward the job, known as *job satisfaction.* Third, I will conclude this chapter by focusing on the kind of attitudes illustrated in our Domino's Pizza case—namely, people's attitudes toward the organizations in which they work, known as *organizational commitment.* Before getting to these specific work-related attitudes and to help you appreciate them fully, however, I begin by outlining the nature of attitudes in general.

ATTITUDES: WHAT ARE THEY?

To social scientists, **attitudes** are relatively stable clusters of feelings, beliefs, and behavioral predispositions (i.e., intentions) toward some specific object, person, or institution (i.e., the particular focus, known as an *attitude object*). By including the phrase *relatively stable* in the definition, attitudes reflect feelings that are not fleeting and that, once formed, tend to persist. Indeed, as I explain throughout this chapter (and again in Chapter 14), changing attitudes may require considerable effort.

When we speak of **work-related attitudes**, we are referring to those lasting feelings, beliefs, and behavioral tendencies toward various aspects of the job itself, the setting in which the work is conducted, the people involve, and/or the organization as a whole. As you will discover as you read this chapter, work-related attitudes are associated with many important aspects of organizational behavior, including job performance, absence from work, and as illustrated in our opening case about Domino's Pizza, voluntary turnover.

Regardless of exactly what they may be, all attitudes consist of three major components (see Figure 5.1).[1]

- **Evaluative component**—How you feel about the attitude object—that is, your liking or disliking of any particular person, thing, or institution. You may, for example, feel positively or negatively toward your boss, the sculpture in the lobby, or the fact that your company just landed a large contract.

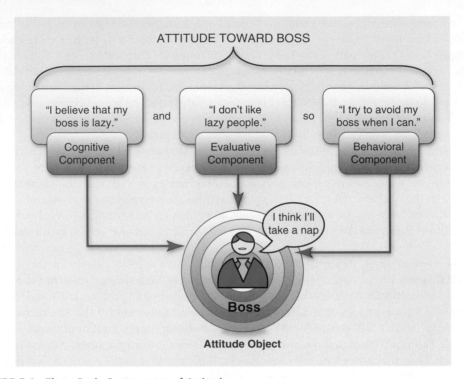

FIGURE 5.1 **Three Basic Components of Attitudes**
People's *attitudes* toward specific objects (the focus of attitudes) are composed of the three fundamental components shown here: the evaluative component, the cognitive component, and the behavioral component. This example illustrates how someone might have a negative attitude toward his or her boss.

- **Cognitive component**—What you believe about the attitude object—that is, the knowledge you have about a particular person, thing, or institution, whether or not it's correct. For example, you may believe that your boss is fair-minded, or that your company is moving in a particularly unwise direction. Even if you believe falsely that one of your coworkers is paid more than you, such a belief may factor into your attitude.
- **Behavioral component**—How you are predisposed to act in a particular situation. For example, a person who dislikes her job may be inclined to seek a new one. However, such predispositions do not predict behavior perfectly. After all, even people who are unhappy with their current positions might refrain from seeking new ones if they like their salary or if they believe that better jobs cannot be found.

Putting this all together, imagine a hypothetical retail store clerk named Carter. He believes that his store manager, Ava, is an honest, hard-working person (cognitive component), and he admires those kind of people (evaluative component). In line with this, he is predisposed to do things that don't let her down, such as showing up on time and working hard to boost sales (behavioral component). There's more to the story, however, as Carter holds additional attitudes. Specifically, he is dissatisfied with the work itself and believes that the company's incentive system keeps him from becoming successful no matter how hard he works.

This simple example illustrates a key point that will become apparent as you read this chapter: people may hold several different attitudes toward any particular attitude object and these may be inconsistent with one another. And since many factors are at work, it's not always possible to predict behavior accurately. Keep in mind that the behavioral component reflects a predisposition to behave a certain way but not a guarantee that a person actually will behave that way.

Now that you understand the basic nature of attitudes, the stage is set to examine the first of three work-related attitudes covered in this chapter—*prejudice,* negative attitudes toward other people.

PREJUDICE AND DISCRIMINATION: NEGATIVE ATTITUDES AND BEHAVIOR TOWARD OTHERS

It's not unusual to hear that someone is considered "prejudiced" because he or she speaks negatively about someone else; however, people often mean different things by this term. Fortunately, social scientists are very clear about what prejudice means. Specifically, **prejudice** is defined as negative feelings about people belonging to certain groups.

Members of racial or ethnic groups, for example, are victims of prejudice when they are believed to be disinterested in working, unprincipled, or inferior in one way or another. Prejudicial attitudes are problematic because they tend to be inaccurate, triggering potentially misleading perceptions of people (recall the discussion of stereotypes in Chapter 3) that potentially create barriers to their success. Given its importance, I examine the nature of prejudice here.

The Challenges of Organizational Demography

At the root of prejudicial feelings is the basic fact that people tend to be uncomfortable with others who are different from them. As chronicled in Chapter 1, demographic differences between people in the workplace today are not the exception, but the rule. For example, not so long ago the American workforce was composed predominantly of white males. But that is no longer the case. In fact, white men now represent less than half of the current American workforce, and most new entrants to the workforce are expected to be women and people of color.[2] This is the result of three major trends:[3]

- The birthrates of nonwhites are higher than those of whites
- Growing numbers of foreign nationals are entering the American workforce, making it more racially and ethnically diverse than ever
- We now have equal proportions of men and women in the workforce overall (although these figures vary considerably for different jobs)

The study of the composition of a workforce with respect to various characteristics (e.g., age, gender, ethnic makeup, etc.) is known as **organizational demography.**[4] As demographic characteristics change, challenges often result. Among white men, for example, there's a growing recognition that their era of dominance in the workplace is over, which many find threatening.[5] Not only white men, but everyone in the workplace must become aware that stereotypes and prejudicial attitudes (which I will examine in the next sections of this chapter) impose potential barriers to success. This is made difficult by the tendency for employees to feel uncomfortable working with others from whom they differ in key ways. When this occurs, disruptive interpersonal conflict sometimes results (see Chapter 7), potentially interfering with performance within work groups and teams.

Another likely reaction is that employees will distance themselves from those considered "different," triggering potentially serious disruptions to effective organizational communication (see Chapter 8). In some cases, as shown in research on top management teams, people even resign when they feel sufficiently uncomfortable as members of demographically diverse teams.[6] As some researchers have concluded, "the greater the dissimilarity (between group members), the more negative outcomes, such as conflicts, divisiveness, or turnover are likely to occur."[7]

When viewed in light of the fact that demographic diversity is the rule rather than the exception in contemporary organizations, it's imperative for everyone in the workplace to accept everybody else. Doing so helps avoid the costly problems of disharmony and communication failure just noted. But that's just the beginning. By going a step further—not just accepting people in the workplace, but *valuing* them and *embracing* their differences—organizations stand to benefit greatly.

Specifically, as I will describe later in this section of the chapter, important benefits are likely to result when working with people who bring different perspectives to the jobs they perform.[8] This is not surprising, given that people with diverse backgrounds have different experiences, and as a result, they can be expected to look at the world differently. Through these different lenses, ideas may emerge that might never have materialized in more homogeneous groups. And in today's highly competitive business environment, no organizations can afford to overlook leveraging these vital human resources. With this background in mind, I examine closely the nature of prejudicial attitudes in this section of the chapter.

Anatomy of Prejudice: Some Fundamental Distinctions

When people are prejudiced, they judge members of a group based on the qualities they attribute to that group. So, to the extent that we believe members of a certain group have various characteristics, learning that someone belongs to that group will lead us to believe that he or she also possesses those qualities. *Stereotype* is the term used to identify such beliefs.

PREJUDICIAL ATTITUDES: STEREOTYPES   As described in Chapter 3, a stereotype is a belief about someone based on the group to which that person belongs. Such beliefs, as you might imagine, are a key part of the prejudicial attitudes that people sometimes hold about others. Specifically, such beliefs reflect the cognitive component of the attitude in question. Whether they're positive or negative in nature, stereotypical beliefs are generally inaccurate. If we knew more about someone than simply whatever we assume based on his or her membership in various groups, we would likely make far more accurate judgments about that individual. However, to the extent that we often find it difficult or inconvenient to learn everything we need to know about someone, we frequently rely on stereotypes as mental shortcuts. So, for example, if you believe that individuals belonging to group X are not particularly bright, and you meet person A, who happens to belong to group X, you likely would assume that he or she is inclined to be unintelligent.

Although this may seem logical enough, by engaging in such stereotyping you run the risk of misjudging person A. After all, you don't really know this individual (although you made an assumption based on his or her group membership). The person in question actually might be quite brilliant, despite presuming just the opposite, which you judge negatively (the evaluative component). However, by drawing on the stereotype, you presupposed that person A wasn't too smart. Would you be willing to hire such an individual for a key post in your company? Probably not. Your predisposition against hiring A (the behavioral component) in

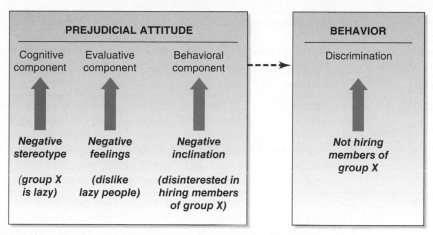

FIGURE 5.2 Prejudice Versus Discrimination: A Comparison
Prejudice is an *attitude* consisting of negative beliefs, such as *stereotypes* (cognitive component), negative feelings about those beliefs (evaluative component), and negative predispositions toward people described by those stereotypes (behavioral component). These attitudes sometimes (but not always) lead to behavior consistent with that attitude—that is, *discrimination*.

this situation reflects your prejudicial attitude. It also illustrates a potential cost of engaging in stereotyping.

DISCRIMINATION   Prejudicial attitudes are particularly harmful when they translate into actual behaviors. In such instances, people become the victims of others' prejudices—that is, **discrimination** occurs. Thus, as summarized in Figure 5.2, prejudice is an attitude, whereas discrimination is a form of behavior following from that attitude.

Completing our example, you may refrain from hiring person A, thereby behaving consistently with your attitude. This would be neither in your best interest nor that of the victim of your prejudicial attitudes and discriminatory behavior. For this reason, it is important to identify ways of overcoming the natural tendency to base our attitudes on stereotypes and to discriminate unfairly among people on this basis. Later in this chapter, I will outline some strategies that are effective in this regard. Before doing so, however, I outline the adverse effects of prejudice in organizations today. (Do discriminatory practices go on in the company where you work? To get a sense of this, complete the Group Exercise on p. 165.)

Everyone Can Be a Victim of Prejudice and Discrimination!

Unfortunate as it may be, this section's heading is painfully accurate: all of us are indeed potential victims of prejudice and discrimination. No matter what personal characteristics we may have, there very well may be people out there who harbor prejudice against us and who discriminate against us as a result. This is not surprising if you consider that people hold stereotypes about many different things.

Whatever you look like, wherever you're from, whatever your interests, chances are good that at least some people will approach you with predisposed beliefs about what you're like. For many groups of people, these beliefs have negative connotations, leading to potentially costly forms of discriminatory behavior. With this in mind, consider some of today's most prevalent targets of discrimination, profiled in Table 5.1.

TABLE 5.1	The Many Targets of Prejudice and Their Costs

As summarized here, people from many different groups are victimized by prejudicial attitudes that take a wide variety of forms.

Target Group	Profile
Elderly people	Although U.S. laws (e.g., the Age Discrimination in Employment Act) have done much to counter employment discrimination against older workers, prejudices continue to exist.[9] More elderly workers are in the workforce than ever before, but many such individuals are believed to be set in their ways and accident-prone. Not only is this false, but such individuals also bring well-needed experience to the job.
Younger people	Because they hold different worldviews than older people (e.g., they are inclined to question how things are done), and because they communicate differently than older people, younger people are sometimes not well understood by their superiors.[10]
Physically disabled people	The Americans With Disabilities Act requires companies to help people with physical and mental disabilities to make reasonable accommodations that help such individuals perform jobs for which they are qualified.[11] Still, only about one-third of such individuals find full-time employment.[12]
Women	Reflecting their raised educational levels over the years, women now account for 51 percent of all managerial and professional jobs. Although the figures differ in various professions, women earn only about 80 percent as much as men overall.[13] Women are still rare at the top of companies, accounting for only 12 of the CEOs of *Fortune* magazine's top 500 companies in 2011.[14] Legislation in the U.S. (e.g., the Equal Pay Act and the Equal Rights Act) and other nations (e.g., Canada, Australia, the U.K., and Hong Kong) explicitly prohibits discrimination based on gender.
Lesbian women, gay men, bisexuals, and transgendered people	In the U.S., members of the LGBT community are not protected by federal law, although discrimination based on sexual orientation is prohibited in growing numbers of municipalities. Still, discrimination exists. Research has found that heterosexuals have a 40 percent greater chance than openly gay men of being called when responding to recruitment ads.[15]
Members of racial and ethnic minority groups	The U.S. Equal Employment Opportunity Commission files lawsuits against companies that violate affirmative action laws. The number of complaints filed by employees who claim to be victims of discrimination has risen steadily, reaching almost 100,000 in 2011. Almost half of these claims are based on race and national origin.[16]
Members of various religious groups	Despite legal protection by the U.S. Civil Rights Act, members of some religious groups are made to feel unwelcome in their workplaces. In recent years, for example, some Muslims have been targets of intolerance.[17] Because it's not unusual for victims of religious intolerance to not report this to officials in their organizations, the problem is likely to be even more widespread than it appears.

STRATEGIES FOR REDUCING WORKPLACE PREJUDICE: MANAGING A DIVERSE WORKFORCE

It's one thing to identify prejudicial attitudes and quite another to eliminate them. Two major approaches have been taken toward doing precisely this—*affirmative action* and *diversity management.* As you'll see, their overall goals and orientations are quite different.

Affirmative Action

In the United States, **affirmative action** is a policy that has been used to promote the nondiscriminatory treatment of women and members of minority groups in the workplace. Derived from civil rights initiatives of the 1960s, affirmative action involves efforts to give employment opportunities to qualified individuals belonging to groups that traditionally have been disadvantaged.

The rationale is straightforward. The benefits of encouraging the hiring of qualified women and minority group members into positions in which they traditionally have been underrepresented are both immediate and long term. The immediate benefit, of course, is that such individuals will be given opportunities that they historically have been denied in the past. The long-term benefit comes about as people come to see that women and members of minority groups are able to succeed in the workplace, challenging their negative stereotypes. Then, eventually, as stereotypes begin to crumble, discrimination stands to be reduced, along with the prejudicial attitudes on which it is based.

Over the years, some confusion has arisen with respect to the objectives of affirmative action, so let's clarify.[18] What the U.S. government had in mind may be referred to as **nonpreferential affirmative action**—efforts to get companies to conduct ongoing appraisals of their rules and procedures and to eliminate those that exclude women and members of minority groups without sufficient justification. Typically, this involves the following:

1. Taking steps to ensure that there is a diverse pool of applicants.
2. Based on the racial composition of this pool, predicting what the workforce would look like if the selection of employees were nondiscriminatory (this is the so-called *affirmative-action goal*).
3. Comparing results with goals and revising procedures and policies to alleviate any discrepancies.

As affirmative action was implemented, controversies emerged with respect to the ideal of affirmative action goals because the language of the law was misleading. Although a goal is something you aim at, this is not what the government intended. What they had in mind was not a finite number that had to be met (despite the language used), but an image of what things *should* be like. Despite this, courts interpreted the law literally and held companies to specific numeric goals. So if, say, 20 percent of a company's broad labor pool consisted of African Americans, then courts required it to hire this percentage of African Americans. This form of affirmative action, known as **preferential affirmative action**, is generally what the public has in mind when it thinks of affirmative action. Today, although some people are enlightened, many remain unaware of the spirit of the law.

After over 40 years of experience with affirmative action programs, major gains have been made in the opportunities available for women and members of minority groups. Indeed, most problems with affirmative action have occurred in its preferential form.[19] However, nonpreferential affirmative action policies have been effective in increasing the attraction, selection, inclusion, and retention of underrepresented group members.

Diversity Management: Approach and Rationale

Over the past few decades, organizations have become increasingly proactive in their attempts to eliminate prejudice and have taken it upon themselves to go beyond affirmative action requirements. Their approach has involved not merely hiring a broader group of people than usual but creating an atmosphere in which diverse groups can flourish.[20] This is the idea behind **diversity management**.

UNDERLYING APPROACH Efforts to manage diversity are aimed at promoting supportive, not just neutral, work environments for women and minorities.[21] Diversity management calls not for simply treating everyone alike and ignoring their differences, but for recognizing and celebrating the differences between people with respect to the lifestyles and practices associated with their racial and ethnic heritages, their religions, their sexual orientation, and so on. The notion of **inclusion** is key—that is, making people feel valued as worthwhile members of the organization. And when people feel that they are welcomed, accepted, and valued instead of just tolerated, everyone benefits.[22] Diversity management may be distinguished from affirmative action in four key ways, as summarized in Table 5.2.[23]

THE BUSINESS CASE FOR DIVERSITY One cannot deny that companies are interested in managing diversity so that they can avoid becoming defendants in lawsuits claiming illegal discrimination. However, this generally is not the only reason, or even the main one. Instead, the primary motive is a traditional one—to improve business. With this in mind, we ask an important question: Can a "business case" be made for having a diverse workforce? In other words, do organizations with diverse workforces have advantages over those that don't?

Several studies reveal that the answer is yes.[24] One investigation, for example, examined the financial success of banks. Among these institutions, the more highly diverse their workforces, the better they performed financially.[25] This, in turn, added value to these banks, giving them advantages over their competitors. Another study, conducted among hospital workers in England, found that diversity also enhanced performance in another important way—namely, the level

---

TABLE 5.2 Comparing Affirmative Action and Diversity Management

Both *affirmative action* and *diversity management* are designed to promote positive attitudes and to reduce discrimination toward women and members of minority groups. As outlined here, however, their rationales and approaches differ with respect to several key dimensions.

Dimension	Affirmative Action	Diversity Management
Objective	Adherence to legal regulations and bureaucratic procedures	Systemic transformation of an organization's culture (see Chapter 12)
Focus	Avoiding penalties associated with discrimination	Positive images of people and celebration of what they can contribute to an organization
Motivation	Legal compliance	Belief that there's a good "business case" associated with promoting diversity
Groups targeted	Gender and race	Any and all differences between people (e.g., religion, sexual preference, etc.)

Source: Based on suggestions by Greene & Kirton, 2009; see Note 23.

of civility experienced by hospital patients.[26] The concept of civility refers to being treated in a pleasant, polite, respectful, and dignified manner (I will discuss this in more detail in Chapter 7). Specifically, the researchers found that patients experienced being treated with greater civility in hospitals in which the ethnic diversity of frontline staff members (i.e., those with whom patients come into contact) matched that of the community in which the hospitals were located.

Researchers conducting another study reasoned that when companies use their human resources effectively they can lower their costs and thereby perform better than their competitors.[27] To test this notion, they compared two groups of companies from 1986 through 1992. One group was composed of organizations that received awards from the U.S. Department of Labor for their exemplary efforts at managing diversity. The other group was composed of companies that had settled large claims against them for employment discrimination. To compare the performance of these organizations, the researchers relied on a key index of economic success—stock returns. Their findings were striking: companies that made special efforts to use their diverse human resources were considerably more profitable than those that discriminated against their employees.

The researchers explained that organizations that capitalized on the diversity of their workforces were better able to attract and retain the talented people needed for them to thrive. Indeed, this seems to be a major key to diversity. Organizations that effectively manage diversity are successful because they are especially adept at attracting and retaining pools of talented people from diverse backgrounds.[28] And, of course, it comes as no surprise that having the best people is essential to the success of any business.

Clearly, promoting diversity is a wise practice not only because it is the right way to treat people, but also because it makes good business sense! Indeed, as a recruiter for an executive search firm emphasized, "There is a strong business case [for diversity]. A diverse workplace isn't a luxury, it's a necessity."[29]

Diversity Management: What Are Companies Doing?

Considering the practical value of ethnic diversity, you probably won't be surprised that efforts to manage diversity are popular in today's organizations. This is evidenced in a survey revealing that the number of companies with diversity management policies in place has been growing rapidly, with 75 percent already having them and 14 percent planning to add them soon.[30] What exactly are these companies doing to promote diversity? I now identify four such tactics.

CONDUCT DIVERSITY TRAINING   Many companies conduct regular programs designed to develop people's skills with respect to managing diversity.[31] The best such programs do more than simply raise employees' awareness about the nature and importance of diversity, but train them in ways to interact effectively with people who are different from themselves. The main techniques used for this purpose are as follows:[32]

- *Cross-cultural understanding*—Understanding the cultural differences responsible for why different coworkers behave differently on the job.
- *Intercultural communication*—Learning to ensure that verbal and nonverbal barriers to communication across cultures are overcome.
- *Facilitation skills*—Training in how to help others alleviate misunderstandings that may result from cultural differences.
- *Flexibility and adaptability*—Cultivating the patience to take new and different approaches when dealing with others who are different.

As you might imagine, the nature and extent to which companies are involved in diversity management training vary widely. At some companies, training efforts are minimal and informal. However, others take diversity training very seriously and are highly methodical about assessing its impact. One such organization is Sodexo, the leading provider of food and facilities management services in North America. For example, after training has been conducted (that focuses on virtually all employees), the company administers a follow-up survey to assess the extent to which behavioral change is occurring (e.g., are members of minority groups being treated more respectfully?). The company also uses an extensive questionnaire known as the "Sodexo Diversity Index" to determine the extent to which its executives are demonstrating the company's diversity values. This measure assesses quantitatively and qualitatively both efforts and results (which, in turn, are used to determine compensation). As a result, when it comes to promoting diversity, Sodexo may be said to be "putting its money where its mouth is."

USE LEADERS TO SEND STRONG MESSAGES ABOUT DIVERSITY   In many of the most diversity-minded companies, top leaders are involved actively in diversity management initiatives. For example, at the pharmaceutical giant Merck & Co., there are many different **affinity groups**—that is, informal collections of individuals who share a common identity with respect to such factors as race, ethnicity, or sexual preference (e.g., Asian American, African American, Hispanic, Native Indigenous, lesbian/gay/bisexual/transgendered people, and others). Acknowledging that it's important to understand what diverse individuals have to say, Merck's CEO regularly sits-in on meetings of the company's affinity groups.

REQUIRE SUPPLIERS TO PROMOTE DIVERSITY   Several companies are not only content to promote diversity within their walls, but also use their influence to get their suppliers to promote diversity. For example, FedEx awards contracts to suppliers that promote diversity. As a corporate member of the National Minority Supplier Development Council (NMSDC), FedEx requires that all minority, woman, and small business suppliers obtain certification from a recognized third party such as the Small Business Administration (SBA), a supplier development council, or a state or local body.

MAKE DIVERSITY A TOP PRIORITY   Being truly effective at managing diversity means far more than conducting some training programs and having executives talk to various people. To make everyone feel included and welcome in an organization, diversity must be made a top priority. This may be done in the following ways.

- *Use ongoing diversity teams*—Devoting permanent teams to diversity helps ensure that any gaps between diversity initiatives (e.g., multicultural skills learning, affinity groups, etc.) are filled. This enables a company's diversity principles to be satisfied (i.e., attracting, developing, supporting a diverse workforce). Consider, for example, Convergys Corporation, a firm that provides customer service solutions to large corporate clients. This organization has permanent "Diversity Action Teams" that strive to identify and recommend solutions to diversity-related issues that arise anywhere in the company.
- *Create reporting relationships that emphasize diversity*—At Johnson & Johnson, for example, the company's chief diversity officer reports directly to its chairman and CEO, assuring that diversity is not overlooked. At the pharmaceutical firm Abbott, each of the 13 people who report to the CEO is responsible for attaining diversity goals. By putting diversity at the top levels of these organizations, its high priority is assured.
- *Establish accountability*—If an organization is going to be serious about promoting diversity, then its key people need to be held accountable for it. An effective way of doing this

is by using pay policies that reward accomplishments with respect to diversity. At IBM, for example, for a manager to receive the top performance evaluation, he or she must provide evidence of having fostered a spirit of inclusion among employees and of having promoted the company's diversity values.

As you might imagine, promoting diversity in an organization is a challenging and important objective that takes a considerable commitment from everyone. It doesn't just happen by itself. For a look at how it's being done at one particularly successful organization, see the Winning Practices section below.

Winning Practices

How the "Good Hands People" Use Diversity as a Competitive Weapon

The Allstate Insurance Company, the "good hands people," promotes diversity as a strategic weapon.[33] By reflecting the racial and ethnic diversity of its customers in its own workforce, Allstate is able to be sensitive to the needs of its employees. In the words of a former Allstate CEO, "Our competitive advantage is our people and our people are diverse. Nothing less than an integrated diversity strategy will allow the company to excel."[34]

Allstate's diversity management program takes a broad perspective. Not limited only to gender and ethnicity, it also pays attention to diversity with respect to age, religion, and sexual orientation. Specifically, it promotes diversity along three major fronts.

- Allstate recruiters visit Historically Black Colleges and Universities to attract members of the African American community. It also recruits from schools in Puerto Rico in an effort to expand its Hispanic customer base. The company has been recognized for these initiatives, suggesting that it has been successful and also helping attract more individuals from these groups.
- To help retain the diverse employees it hires, Allstate thoroughly trains them to know that they are expected to be unbiased toward others. The company also encourages development of minority candidates by showing them the routes to promotion and by seriously considering minority candidates when planning for succession up the ranks.

- Allstate employees receive diversity training within their first six months on the job (about a million person-hours have been invested thus far). This consists of classroom training that encourages people to recognize the way they see themselves and others as well as ways of building trusting environments among people who are different.

Allstate keeps careful statistical records of its diversity efforts and the company's financial success. Twice a year, the company's employees complete a questionnaire known as the "Diversity Index" asking them to indicate, among other things, the extent to which they witness insensitive or inappropriate behavior at work, the amount of dignity and respect they are shown, and their beliefs about the company's commitment to delivering services to customers regardless of their ethnic background.

Company records reveal that the higher the overall score on the Diversity Index, the more managers are successful in promoting a diverse work environment, and the more satisfied they are. And the company's statistics show that when this happens, Allstate does a better job of satisfying and retaining its customers. Indeed, Allstate is the top insurer of lives and automobiles among African Americans and also ranks as the top insurer of homes and lives among Hispanic Americans. Clearly, at Allstate, "good hands" come in many different colors, and making this happen is a highly successful business strategy.

JOB SATISFACTION: ITS NATURE AND MAJOR THEORIES

Some of the most widely studied of all workplace attitudes are those assessing people's feelings toward their jobs, referred to as **job satisfaction**. In this section of the chapter, I will address some fundamental issues about job satisfaction and describe several major theories that have been used to explain it.

The Nature of Job Satisfaction: Fundamental Issues

Would you say you are satisfied with your job? When tens of thousands of American workers were asked a similar question in a multiyear survey published in 2009, fewer than half reported that they were in fact satisfied. This number has dropped steadily since 1987 and is now at its lowest level (see Figure 5.3).[35]

How can this trend be explained? Two key factors appear to play a role. First, people's expectations have risen over the years, leading them to look for more and more from their jobs. And as the bar rises, it becomes increasingly difficult for companies to give employees what they want, resulting in dissatisfaction. Second, it's also likely that people find work less gratifying because the nature of jobs is changing.[36] In particular, many people find that their jobs have become so highly specialized and narrow that they are not especially gratifying.

As you might expect, the degree to which people are satisfied with their jobs depends on exactly what those jobs are. For example, as shown in Figure 5.4, the percentages of people who consider their jobs to be very satisfying vary considerably.[37] The least satisfying tend to

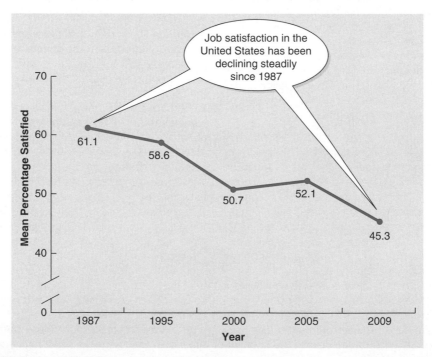

FIGURE 5.3   U.S. Job Satisfaction: Lowest Level in Over Two Decades
Systematic surveys of a broad spectrum of American workers have revealed that their job satisfaction has been declining regularly in recent decades. In fact, the current percentage who report feeling satisfied with their jobs is the lowest ever recorded in this survey.
Source: Based on data reported by Smith, 2009; see Note 35.

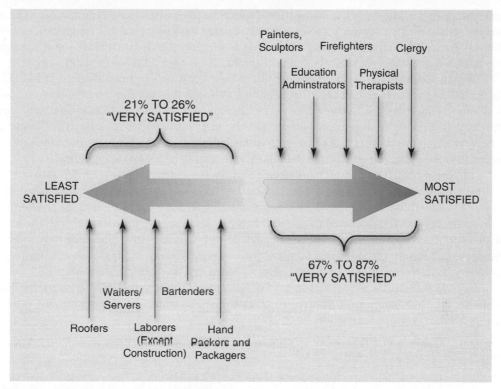

FIGURE 5.4 Who's Most and Least Satisfied with Their Jobs?
Systematic differences exist in the levels of job satisfaction expressed among people in different occupational groups. Those ranking highest and lowest in job satisfaction are shown here.
Source: Based on data reported by Smith, 2009; see Note 35.

be those jobs that are low level and require the most rudimentary skills, whereas the jobs that people find most satisfying tend to be more creatively fulfilling and give workers a greater sense of accomplishment.

This is only part of the story, however. Not everyone holding low-level jobs is dissatisfied with them, and not all holders of high-level jobs find them to be especially satisfying. For example, many doctors and lawyers do work that allows for considerable creative fulfillment, although the people who do these jobs tend to be neither especially satisfied nor dissatisfied with them. In short, it isn't easy to predict the level of satisfaction that people are likely to have solely on the basis of the jobs they hold, underscoring the inherently complex nature of job satisfaction.

In view of its complexities, it's probably not surprising that OB scientists have devoted a great deal of attention to studying job satisfaction. A major objective of such research is to develop ways of promoting job satisfaction among employees. To do this effectively, it's important for researchers to be guided by theories that focus on the processes that account for how job satisfaction operates. I now review several such theories.

The Dispositional Model of Job Satisfaction

Do you know some people who always seem to like their jobs, no matter what they are doing, while others always grumble about the work they do? If so, you are aware of the basic premise underlying what is known as the **dispositional model of job satisfaction**. This approach claims that job satisfaction is a relatively stable characteristic that stays with people through various situations.[38] According to this conceptualization, people who like the jobs they are doing at one time also tend to like the jobs they may be doing at another time, even if the jobs are different.

Supporting this approach, researchers have found that people are consistent in liking or disliking their jobs over as long as a 10-year period, although they may have had several different positions during that time. Such evidence is in keeping with the idea that job satisfaction operates much like the stable dispositions toward positive and negative affect described in Chapter 3. Indeed, research has shown that people who tend to be positive and cheerful most of the time do indeed express higher job satisfaction than those who tend to be "down" and gloomy.[39]

In keeping with this, research has shown that *genetic factors* play a role in job satisfaction. In other words, some people possess inherited tendencies to be either satisfied or dissatisfied with all aspects of their lives, including their jobs. Specifically, research has compared the levels of job satisfaction expressed by identical twins (who have the same genetic inheritance) with the levels of job satisfaction expressed by unrelated persons or by fraternal twins (who share only some of their genes).[40] Results indicated that identical twins expressed more similar levels of job satisfaction than did fraternal twins or unrelated persons. Moreover, this was true even when each member of a twin pair held a very different kind of job. Although these findings remain somewhat controversial, they have been replicated in other studies, so it does seem possible that genetic factors play a role in job satisfaction.[41]

Value Theory of Job Satisfaction

Another conceptualization, known as **value theory of job satisfaction**, takes a broader approach. This theory claims that almost any factor can be a source of job satisfaction as long as it is something that people value. The less people have of some aspect of the job (e.g., pay, learning opportunities) relative to the amount they desire, the more dissatisfied they will be—especially for those facets of the job that are highly valued. Thus, value theory focuses on discrepancies between what people have and what they want: the greater those discrepancies, the more dissatisfied they will be.

This approach to job satisfaction implies that an effective way to satisfy workers is to find out what they want and, to the extent possible, give it to them. However, because it often is unknown what employees want, this is easier said than done. In fact, organizations sometimes go through great pains to find out how to satisfy their employees. With this in mind, a growing number of companies, particularly big ones, survey their employees systematically. For example, FedEx is so interested in tracking the attitudes of its employees that it uses a fully automated online survey. The company relies on information gained from surveys of employees as the key to identifying sources of dissatisfaction and testing possible remedies.

Social Information Processing Model

It's your first day on a new job. You arrive at the office excited about what you will be doing but soon discover that your coworkers are far less enthusiastic. "This job stinks," they all say, and you hear all the details when you hang out with them during lunch. Soon, your own satisfaction with the job begins to fade. What once seemed exciting now seems boring, and your boss, who once seemed so pleasant, now looks more like an ogre. Your attitudes change not because of any objective changes in the job or your boss, but because you change your outlook based on the messages you receive from your coworkers.

The idea that people's attitudes toward their jobs are based on information they get from other people is inherent in the **social information processing model**. This approach specifies that people adopt attitudes and behaviors in keeping with the cues provided by others with whom they come into contact.[42] The social information processing model suggests that job satisfaction can be affected by such subtle things as the offhand comments others make.

With this in mind, it makes sense for managers to be very careful about what they say. A few well-chosen remarks may go a long way toward raising employees' job satisfaction. By the same token, a few offhand slips of the tongue may contribute to lowering morale. This applies both to in-person remarks as well as comments posted on social media sites (so watch those Tweets!).

JOB DISSATISFACTION: CONSEQUENCES AND WAYS TO REDUCE THEM

Thus far, I have alluded to the negative effects of job dissatisfaction, but without specifying exactly what these are. Now I ask: What consequences may be expected among workers who are dissatisfied with their jobs? I will examine these effects along with ways of avoiding, or at least, minimizing them.

Employee Withdrawal: Voluntary Turnover and Absenteeism

A few years ago, employees at a Safeway bakery in a small Oregon town were not particularly satisfied with their jobs. The bakery's 130 employees were so upset that they were frequently absent or quit their jobs. And these were no minor problems. At unpopular working times, such as Saturday nights, it was not unusual for as many as 8 percent of the workers to call in sick, leading production to suffer. Conditions were so bad that almost no one stayed in their jobs for more than a year.

As this situation reveals, all too extremely, people who are dissatisfied with their jobs want little to do with them—that is, they go out of their way to minimize the extent to which they are involved with them. This process is known as **employee withdrawal**. The two major forms of employee withdrawal are *voluntary turnover* and *absenteeism*, which are linked to job dissatisfaction.

VOLUNTARY TURNOVER   The most extreme form of employee withdrawal is quitting, formally ending the employee–employer relationship for good. This is referred to as **voluntary turnover**. When employees quit their jobs, the costs to their organizations can be substantial. Most prominent among these are costs due to lost productivity as well as the recruiting and training of replacements. These costs vary considerably for different jobs, as you might imagine. For example, these have been estimated as ranging from 30 to 50 percent of the annual base salary for unskilled, entry-level workers to 200 to 400 percent of the annual base salary for specialists in information technology (IT).[43] Beyond dollars and cents, companies also are concerned about the quality of their workforces when people leave.

This raises a very practical question—namely, why do employees quit their jobs? Knowing the answers promises to provide valuable insights into ways of reducing the problem of turnover (and, of course, its associated expenses). Scientists addressed this question a few years ago by interviewing a sample of employees who resigned from a variety of positions. Their findings, summarized in Table 5.3, reveal that employees left for eight key reasons.[44] As you review these reasons for quitting, you'll notice that several of the reasons cited (e.g., affective, constituent, calculative, and normative) may be considered direct expressions of job dissatisfaction.

TABLE 5.3	Why Do Employees Leave Their Organizations?

In a series of interviews with people who voluntarily quit their jobs, scientists found that the underlying reasons fit into the eight distinct categories shown here.

Reason	Explanation (the person . . .)
Affective	Does not enjoy the job or experiences in the organization
Contractual	Wants to get even with someone in the company who hasn't done something that was expected
Constituent	Wants to end relationships with one or more of the people in the workplace
Alternative	Has more attractive job opportunities outside the organization
Calculative	Believes that the future with the organization will be unpleasant in one or more ways
Normative	Faces pressure from within the company to leave
Behavioral	Believes that leaving the organization is easy because remaining there isn't highly valued by others
Moral	Believes that quitting is ethically appropriate because it avoids stagnation

Source: Based on suggestions by Maertz & Campion, 2004; see Note 44.

In general, low levels of job satisfaction are associated with high levels of turnover, but this relationship is complex. As suggested in Table 5.3, there are many factors at play, and only some of them are connected to job satisfaction. For example, if alternative positions are readily available, people may be expected to resign when feeling dissatisfied. However, when such options are limited—such as in recent years, when the economy is weak and companies are not hiring— voluntary turnover is a less viable option. In other words, knowing that one is dissatisfied with his or her job does not automatically suggest that he or she will quit. Indeed, many people stay on jobs that they dislike.

ABSENTEEISM In addition to voluntary turnover, employee withdrawal also takes the form of **absenteeism**—that is, the practice of staying away from the job when scheduled to work. Unscheduled absences are a less expensive form of withdrawal than turnover because they are temporary instead of permanent. This is not to say, however, that the costs of unscheduled absences are trivial. Far from it. A major human resources consulting firm estimates that absenteeism costs companies an average of 15 percent of their payroll expenses.[45]

As in the case of turnover, dissatisfaction with the job is a predominant reason for absenteeism.[46] (Recall the example of the Safeway bakery on p. 153.) However, absenteeism is linked even more strongly to low levels of job satisfaction. Specifically, research has shown that the more dissatisfied people are with their jobs, the more likely they are to be absent from work. This was demonstrated in a study of British health-care workers whose questionnaire responses on a measure of job satisfaction were compared to records of their absenteeism over a two-year period.[47] As summarized in Figure 5.5, workers whose levels of job satisfaction deteriorated over the study period showed an increase in absenteeism; those whose satisfaction increased over the study period showed a decrease in absenteeism. In view of the costly nature of absenteeism—especially in view of the fact that it can be highly disruptive to company operations—findings such as these are of great concern.

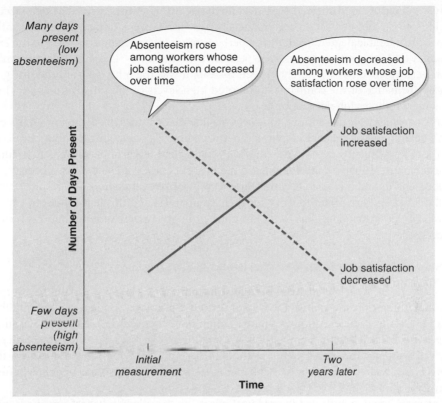

FIGURE 5.5   Relationship Between Job Satisfaction and Absence
A study tracing the levels of job satisfaction and absenteeism of health-care workers over a two-year period found the relationship depicted here. Absenteeism declined among those whose satisfaction rose, whereas absenteeism rose among those whose job satisfaction declined.
Source: Based on data reported by Hardy et al., 2003; see Note 47.

Job Performance: Are Dissatisfied Employees Poor Performers?

Although some dissatisfied employees leave their jobs, of course, not all do. What can be expected of those who remain? Does job performance suffer among dissatisfied employees? As in the case of turnover, the correlation between job performance and satisfaction is also positive, but relatively modest.[48] However, research shows that happier workers are in fact more productive.[49]

For some insight into why this relationship exists, let's consider a study that goes beyond individual performance to something that matters greatly to organizations—their financial success. The possibility of a connection between individual job satisfaction and the financial performance of companies was examined by a team of researchers who assessed the satisfaction of thousands of employees working over an eight-year period in some of the largest companies in the United States.[50] The scientists also computed the financial performance levels of the organizations in which these individuals worked, using two key indexes that are widely used by financial analysts: return on assets and earnings per share. Because the data were collected during a period in which the economy showed a variety of ups and downs (1987–1995), there was no reason to believe that the study's findings resulted from any fluke conditions that might have occurred.

By conducting sophisticated statistical analyses, the scientists arrived at two fascinating conclusions. First, job satisfaction and financial performance were, in fact, associated with each other to a considerable degree. Second, and perhaps more interestingly, this was *not* the result of the tendency for highly satisfied workers to perform at higher levels (i.e., job satisfaction enhances financial performance), as you might expect. Instead, it was the other way around: the good financial performance of the companies promoted high levels of job satisfaction (i.e., financial performance promotes job satisfaction).

Let's consider how this appears to work. Imagine that because the company adopts policies that have been found to enhance employees' performance (e.g., involving them in key decisions, paying them for acquiring new skills), employees show high levels of performance. In turn, this good performance enhances the company's financial success. And, since it is successful, it can offer good benefits and increased pay, and enjoy a very positive reputation. The result? Employees feel well treated and are proud to work for their companies, and this leads them to experience high levels of job satisfaction. This is not just conjecture: the research found that this is precisely what occurred.

Job Satisfaction and Injuries: Are Happy Workers Safe Workers?

Injuries at work are a serious matter—both for the employees who are hurt and their organizations. So anything that can reduce the risk of serious workplace accidents is, potentially, very valuable. Efforts to reduce workplace injuries often have focused on the design of equipment and jobs and on restricting the number of hours employees can work, so as to protect them from fatigue—all major factors in accidents. Although these practices are indeed effective, there is more involved. Evidence suggests that enhancing job satisfaction also has beneficial effects on job safety.

This has been demonstrated in organizations using so-called **high-performance work systems**.[51] These are organizations that offer employees opportunities to participate in decision-making, provide incentives for them to do so, and emphasize opportunities to develop skills. Not only are employees highly satisfied in such organizations, but within them, they also perform their jobs very safely.[52]

A team of researchers studying this phenomenon obtained ratings of work environments from several thousand employees to assess the extent to which their work environments were high-performance systems.[53] The researchers also obtained measures of job satisfaction from the same employees as well as records of occupational injuries from the companies in which these individuals worked. It was found that the greater the degree to which the organizations met the descriptions of high-performance organizations, the more the individuals who worked in them reported being highly satisfied with their jobs, and the lower were the levels of work-related accidents (see Figure 5.6). Further statistical analyses revealed also that to some extent, the low accident rates were the direct result of the high levels of job satisfaction experienced. In view of this, the importance of promoting job satisfaction cannot be overstated.

Job Satisfaction and Life Satisfaction

Do you think that people who are happy in their jobs also tend to be happy in their lives in general? You might not be surprised to learn that the answer is "yes." After all, work is a large part of life, and being happy on the job has a good chance of "spilling over" into other parts of our lives. Putting it differently, people who are happy with their jobs also tend to be happy with their lives in general.[54]

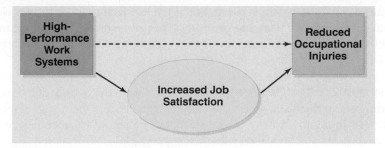

FIGURE 5.6 Job Satisfaction and Injuries at Work

Research indicates that high-performance work systems (i.e., those that provide employees with opportunities to participate in decision making, incentives that encourage them to do so, and human resource practices designed to ensure skill development) can increase performance and job satisfaction and offer the added benefit of reducing accidents. This effect appears to stem, at least in part, from enhanced job satisfaction among employees. Apparently, positive attitudes toward their work make employees more careful, thus helping them to avoid accidents.

Source: Based on suggestions by Barling et al., 2003; see Note 53.

Research suggests that mood, the positive and negative feelings we experience throughout the day (as discussed in Chapter 4), is involved in this relationship.[55] Consider, for example, a study conducted among university employees who rated their feelings of job satisfaction and their mood states several times each day.[56] Participants did this both on workdays and nonworkdays, rating their moods and job satisfaction at work and at home. Results indicated that job satisfaction and mood were closely linked at work; in fact, each influenced the other. High job satisfaction led to positive moods, and positive moods, in turn, triggered high job satisfaction.

Perhaps even more interesting, job satisfaction at work also influenced the moods these employees experienced at home. High job satisfaction at work generated positive moods away from work, whereas low job satisfaction at work generated negative moods. In other words, job satisfaction spilled over into employees' moods at home.

In summary, there is no doubt that job satisfaction is very important in organizations. Under some conditions, satisfied employees are more productive than dissatisfied employees. In addition, they are less likely to quit their jobs or to experience serious accidents and are more likely to experience positive feelings and moods at home. These reflect many practical reasons to promote job satisfaction. I now consider several of these.

Tips for Promoting Job Satisfaction

In view of the negative consequences of dissatisfaction, it makes sense to consider ways of raising satisfaction on the job. Although an employee's dissatisfaction might not account for all aspects of his or her performance, it is important to try to promote satisfaction if for no other reason than to make people happy. After all, satisfaction is a desirable end in itself. With this in mind, what can be done to promote job satisfaction? Based on the available research, I offer several suggestions.

PAY PEOPLE FAIRLY Workers who believe that their organizations' pay systems are inherently unfair tend to be dissatisfied with their jobs. (I discussed the importance of fairness in Chapter 2 and will revisit this topic in Chapter 6.) This not only applies to salary and hourly pay but also to fringe benefits. In fact, when people are given opportunities to select the fringe benefits they most desire, they believe that the system is fair and their job satisfaction tends to rise. Not only does this help people get what they want, but companies that give workers this opportunity send the message that they value their employees, contributing to their sense of the organization's fairness and to their individual satisfaction.

IMPROVE THE QUALITY OF SUPERVISION It has been shown that satisfaction is highest among employees who believe that their supervisors are competent, treat them with respect, and have their best interests in mind. Similarly, job satisfaction is enhanced when employees believe that they have open lines of communication with their superiors.

For example, in response to the dissatisfaction problems that plagued the Safeway bakery employees described on page 153, company officials responded by completely changing their management style. Traditionally, they were highly intimidating and controlling, leaving employees feeling powerless and discouraged. Realizing the problems caused by this iron-fisted style, they began loosening their highly autocratic ways, replacing them with a new openness and freedom. Employees were allowed to work together toward solving problems of sanitation and safety and were encouraged to make suggestions about ways to improve things. The results were dramatic: workdays lost to accidents dropped from 1,740 a year down to 2, absenteeism fell from 8 percent to 0.2 percent, and voluntary turnover was reduced from almost 100 percent annually to less than 10 percent. Clearly, improving the quality of supervision went a long way toward reversing the negative effects of satisfaction at this Safeway bakery.

DECENTRALIZE ORGANIZATIONAL POWER Although I will consider the concept of *decentralization* more fully later in this book (e.g., in Chapters 8 and 13), it is worth introducing here. **Decentralization** is the degree to which the capacity to make decisions resides in several people, as opposed to one or just a handful. When power is decentralized, people are allowed to participate freely in the process of decision making. This arrangement contributes to their feelings of satisfaction because it leads them to believe that they can have some important effects on their organizations. By contrast, when the power to make decisions is concentrated in the hands of just a few, employees tend to feel powerless and ineffective, thereby contributing to their feelings of dissatisfaction.

The changes in supervision made at the Safeway bakery also provides a good illustration of moving from a highly centralized style to a highly decentralized style. The power to make certain important decisions was shifted into the hands of those who were most affected by them. Because decentralizing power gives people greater opportunities to control aspects of the workplace that affect them, it makes it possible for workers to receive the outcomes they most desire, thereby enhancing their satisfaction. This dynamic appears to be at work in many of today's organizations.

MATCH PEOPLE TO JOBS THAT FIT THEIR INTERESTS People have many interests, and these are only sometimes fulfilled on the job. However, the more people find that they are able to fulfill their interests while on the job, the more satisfied they tend to be with those jobs. For example, a study found that college graduates were more satisfied with their jobs when the jobs were consistent with their college majors than when the jobs fell outside their fields of interest.

It is with this in mind that career counselors frequently find it useful to identify people's nonvocational interests. For example, several companies, such as AT&T, IBM, Ford Motor Company, and Shell Oil, systematically test and counsel their employees so they can effectively match their skills and interests to those positions to which they are best suited. Some companies, including Coca-Cola and Disneyland, go so far as to offer individualized counseling to employees so that their personal and professional interests can be identified and matched.

ORGANIZATIONAL COMMITMENT: ATTITUDES TOWARD COMPANIES

Just as people's attitudes toward their jobs are important, so too are their attitudes toward the organizations in which they work, known as **organizational commitment**. The concept of organizational commitment is concerned with the degree to which people feel psychological attachments, or bonds toward their organizations, being involved with them and interested in remaining a part of them.[57] A generation or two ago, most workers remained loyal to their companies throughout their working lives. However, today's workers are generally willing to hop from job to job to advance their careers.[58]

It is important to note that organizational commitment generally is independent of job satisfaction. Consider, for example, that a nurse may really like the kind of work she does, but dislike the hospital in which she works. This may lead her to seek a similar job elsewhere. By the same token, a waiter may have positive feelings about the restaurant in which he works, but may dislike waiting on tables. This may lead him to consider taking another position in the same restaurant, such as host or bartender. These complexities illustrate the importance of studying organizational commitment.

My discussion of this topic will begin by examining its different dimensions. I then review the impact of organizational commitment on organizational functioning, and conclude by presenting ways of enhancing commitment.

Varieties of Organizational Commitment

Being committed to an organization is not only a matter of "yes or no" or even "how much?" Distinctions also can be made with respect to various kinds of commitment. Specifically, scientists have distinguished among three distinct forms of commitment, which I review here (see the overview in Figure 5.7).[59]

CONTINUANCE COMMITMENT   Have you ever stayed in a job because you just didn't want to bother to find a new one? If so, you are already familiar with the concept of **continuance commitment**. This refers to the strength of a person's desire to remain working for an organization due to the belief that it will be costly to leave. The longer people remain in their organizations, the more they stand to lose what they have invested in them over the years (e.g., retirement plans,

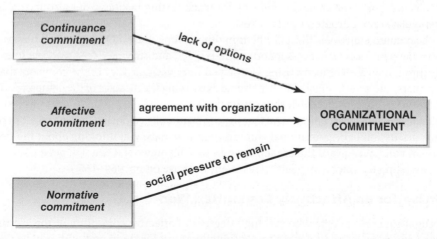

FIGURE 5.7   **Three Types of Organizational Commitment**
Scientists have distinguished among the three different types of organizational commitment summarized here.

close friendships). Many people are committed to staying in their jobs simply because they are unwilling to risk losing these things. They also may be unwilling to forego any job security they might have based on their seniority in their current organizations. This is a particular concern today, when many companies cut jobs regularly and new ones are hard to find. Individuals holding such beliefs may be said to have high degrees of continuance commitment.

NORMATIVE COMMITMENT   A second type of organizational commitment, known as **normative commitment**, refers to employees' feelings of obligation to stay with their organizations because of pressures from others. People who have high degrees of normative commitment are concerned greatly about what others would think of them for leaving. They would be reluctant to disappoint their employers and be concerned that their fellow employees might think poorly of them for resigning.

If you were a tax accountant who was thinking of taking a position in a new firm, for example, your colleagues may encourage you strongly not to leave until the busy season preceding the April 15 personal income tax filing deadline has passed. And if you have a high degree of normative commitment, you would be likely to satisfy their requests by not leaving your colleagues until they could find and train a suitable replacement.

AFFECTIVE COMMITMENT   The two types of commitment we've discussed thus far are not especially positive in that they do not suggest anything about an individual's connections to an organization based on his or her liking and attraction to it. However, the third type of organizational commitment, *affective commitment*, takes this into account. Specifically, **affective commitment** refers to the strength of people's desires to continue working for an organization because they regard it positively and agree with its underlying goals and values. People feeling high degrees of affective commitment desire to remain in their organizations because they endorse what these companies stand for and are interested in supporting their missions.

Sometimes, particularly when an organization is undergoing change, employees may wonder whether their personal values continue to be in line with those of the organizations in which they work. When this happens, they may question whether they still belong, and if they believe they do not, they resign. A few years ago, Ryder Truck Company successfully avoided losing employees on this basis by publicly reaffirming its corporate values. Ryder was facing a situation in which it was not only expanding beyond its core truck leasing business, but also facing changes due to deregulation (e.g., routes, tariffs, taxes).

To help guide employees through the tumultuous time, the CEO went out of his way to reinforce the company's core values—support, trust, respect, and striving. He spread the message far and wide throughout the company, using videotaped interviews, articles in the company magazine, plaques, posters, and even laminated wallet-size cards carrying the message of the company's core values. Ryder officials are convinced that showcasing the company's values in these ways was responsible for the high level of affective commitment that the company enjoyed during this turbulent period.

This discussion of organizational commitment may have you thinking about the degree of commitment you have toward the organization in which you work. (You will get a good sense of this by completing the interesting Self-Assessment Exercise on pp. 164–165.)

Why Strive for an Affectively Committed Workforce?

As you might imagine, people who feel high degrees of affective commitment toward their organizations experience strong desires to continue working for them and with a high degree of motivation (see Chapter 6).[60] In keeping with these feelings, several key aspects of work behavior have been linked to affective commitment.[61]

AFFECTIVELY COMMITTED EMPLOYEES CONTRIBUTE TO SUCCESSFUL ORGANIZATIONAL PERFORMANCE Naturally, officials are concerned greatly with how well their companies perform financially (e.g., with respect to such key factors as profit, sales growth, market share, etc.). Interestingly, a study conducted in the People's Republic of China found that these important indexes are linked to organizational commitment.[62] Surveying managers from 463 companies, the researchers distinguished between organizations in terms of the practices used to manage human resources. Some were oriented toward maximizing performance (such as by training employees in the latest developments in their fields), whereas others were geared more toward maintaining performance and stability (such as by retaining managers as long as they wish to remain in the company). The managers also completed scales assessing their degrees of affective commitment and continuance commitment to their companies.

The connections between these variables, as summarized in Figure 5.8, are quite interesting. As you might expect, the researchers found that companies using performance-oriented management practices were more successful financially than those focusing on merely maintaining the status quo. Organizational commitment played important roles in these relationships. Specifically, the reason why performance-oriented practices boosted performance was that these practices enhanced managers' feelings of affective commitment and these, in turn, led people to behave in ways that enhanced their companies' financial success.

However, companies using maintenance-oriented practices did not fare as well. Not feeling particularly inspired, managers in these companies did *not* experience high levels of affective commitment. Instead, maintenance-oriented practices raised feelings of continuance commitment, and of course, people who stay on their jobs while simply "going through the motions" and believing they have no better options are not especially productive. In fact, research has found that continuance commitment is *not* associated with high levels of job performance (sometimes, it even interferes with it, in fact).[63] Accordingly, companies in the Chinese study that used maintenance-oriented practices, and whose managers experienced

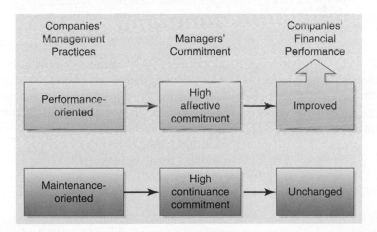

FIGURE 5.8   The Financial Benefits of Affective Commitment
Research has shown that when companies use performance-oriented management practices, it enhances affective commitment among managers. This in turn helps boost those companies' financial performance. In contrast, when companies use maintenance-oriented management practices, it enhances continuance commitment among managers. This in turn has no effect on the financial performance of those companies.
Source: Based on findings by Gong et al., 2009; see Note 62.

high levels of affective commitment as a result, were found *not* to be high performers financially. Based on this study, it's clear that managers will want to be keenly interested in promoting affective commitment. Later in this chapter, I will offer some suggestions about how to do so.

AFFECTIVELY COMMITTED EMPLOYEES ARE UNLIKELY TO WITHDRAW The higher degrees of affective commitment employees have for their organizations, the less likely they are to resign from them or to be absent from them (earlier referred to as withdrawal behavior). Affective commitment leads people to stay on their jobs and to show up ready to work when they are expected to do so.[64]

AFFECTIVELY COMMITTED EMPLOYEES ARE WILLING TO MAKE SACRIFICES FOR THEIR ORGANIZATIONS Beyond remaining in their organizations, people who are highly committed to them demonstrate a willingness to make sacrifices required for their organizations to thrive. We see this, for example, among the many employees in recent years who have remained with their companies despite reluctantly facing pay cuts. Airline employees are a good example, as many have endured several rounds of pay cuts but have remained on their jobs.

In view of these important benefits of affective commitment, organizations often take the steps necessary to enhance commitment among employees. I now describe various ways of doing this.

How to Promote Affective Commitment

Some determinants of organizational commitment fall outside of managers' spheres of control, giving them few opportunities to enhance these feelings. For example, commitment tends to be lower when the economy is such that employment opportunities are plentiful. An abundance of job options surely will lower continuance commitment, and there's not too much a company can do about it. However, although managers cannot control the economy, they can do several things to make employees want to stay working for the company—that is, to enhance affective commitment.

ENRICH JOBS People tend to be highly committed to their organizations when they believe they have a good chance to take control over the way they do their jobs and are recognized for making important contributions. When people get to perform jobs they believe are interesting and that provide opportunities to do work that challenges them mentally, they demonstrate their commitment to the organizations by working hard. This is the idea of *job enrichment*, an approach to motivating employees that I will examine fully in Chapter 6.

Enriching jobs worked well for Ford Motor Company, helping the automaker out of a crisis of organizational commitment in the face of budget cuts, layoffs, plant closings, lowered product quality, and other threats. In the words of the director of Ford's Employee Development Office:

> The only solution for Ford, we determined, was a total transformation of our company . . .
> To accomplish it, we had to earn the commitment of all Ford people. And to acquire that commitment, we had to change the way we managed people.[65]

With this in mind, Ford instituted its employee involvement program, a systematic way of involving employees in many aspects of corporate decision making. They not only got to perform a wide variety of tasks, but also enjoyed considerable autonomy in doing them (e.g., freedom to schedule work and to stop the assembly line, if needed). A few years after the program had been in place, Ford employees became more committed to the company—so much so, in fact, that the dissention between labor and management that usually resulted at contract renewal time all but vanished. Although employee involvement may not be the cure for all commitment ills, it was clearly highly effective in this case.

ALIGN THE INTERESTS OF THE COMPANY WITH THOSE OF THE EMPLOYEES Whenever making something good for a company also makes something good for its employees, those individuals are likely to become committed to their organizations. Many companies do this directly by introducing *profit-sharing plans*—that is, incentive programs in which employees receive bonuses in proportion to their company's profitability. Such plans are often quite effective in enhancing organizational commitment, especially when they are perceived to be administered fairly. A profit-sharing plan has been used to help retain executives and managers at UAL Corporation (the parent of United Airlines).[66] At some other companies, even lower-level employees get to enjoy profit-sharing. For example, the outdoor gear retailer, REI has a profit-sharing plan in place for its employees (including part-timers), making it a highly worker-friendly company.[67]

RECRUIT AND SELECT NEW EMPLOYEES WHOSE VALUES CLOSELY MATCH THOSE OF THE ORGANIZATION Recruiting new employees is important not only because it provides opportunities to find people whose values match those of the organization but also because of the dynamics of the recruitment process itself. Specifically, the more an organization invests in someone by working hard to lure him or her to the company, the more that individual is likely to return the same investment of energy by expressing commitment toward the organization. In other words, companies that show their employees they care enough to work hard to attract them are likely to find those individuals strongly committed to the company.

In conclusion, it is useful to think of organizational commitment as an attitude that may be influenced by managerial actions. Not only might people be selected who are predisposed to be committed to the organization, but also various things can be done to enhance the organizational commitment of employees once they are aboard.

Back to the Case

Answer the following questions based on this chapter's Making the Case (p. 138) to illustrate insights you have derived from the material in this chapter.

1. What did Domino's Pizza do to enhance its employees' job satisfaction and/or organizational commitment?
2. What benefits may be expected to result from these actions?
3. What additional steps might Domino's consider taking help tackle its turnover problem?

You Be the Consultant

Launching a Diversity Management Plan

The president of a medium-size manufacturing firm comes to you with a problem: he wants to raise the level of ethnic diversity of his workforce but is having trouble attracting and retaining minority employees. In addition, attitude surveys administered in the company reveal that a sizable number of employees believe that they have been victims of racial discrimination. You and the president agree that the time has come to launch a diversity management plan. Answer the following questions relevant to this situation based on the material in this chapter.

1. As suggested by the examples outlined in this chapter, what might the company do to help attract and retain members of racial and ethnic minority groups?

2. To justify introducing a diversity management plan, the president needs to make a strong business case. Drawing on the information in this chapter, how might a diversity management plan make good business sense?

3. What specific measures might the company take in its diversity management plan? What would you caution the president about the plan's potential problems?

Self-Assessment Exercise

HOW STRONGLY ARE YOU COMMITTED TO YOUR JOB?

Questionnaires similar to the one used here (which is based on established instruments) are used to assess three types of organizational commitment—continuance, affective, and normative.[68] Completing this scale will give you a good feel for your own level of job commitment and how this important construct is measured.

Directions

In the space to the left of each of the 12 statements that follow, write the number that reflects the extent to which you agree with it personally. Express your answers using the following scale:

    1 = not at all
    2 = slightly
    3 = moderately
    4 = a great deal
    5 = extremely

Scale

____ **1.** At this point, I stay on my job more because I have to than because I want to.
____ **2.** I feel I strongly belong to my organization.
____ **3.** I am reluctant to leave a company once I have been working there.
____ **4.** Leaving my job would entail a great deal of personal sacrifice.
____ **5.** I feel emotionally connected to the company for which I work.
____ **6.** My employer would be very disappointed if I left my job.
____ **7.** I don't have any other choice but to stay in my present job.
____ **8.** I feel like I am part of the family at the company in which I work.
____ **9.** I feel a strong obligation to stay in my job.
____ **10.** My life would be greatly disrupted if I left my present job.
____ **11.** I would be quite pleased to spend the rest of my life working for this organization.
____ **12.** I stay in my job because people would think poorly of me for leaving.

Scoring

1. Add the scores for items 1, 4, 7, and 10. This reflects your degree of *continuance commitment*.
2. Add the scores for items 2, 5, 8, and 11. This reflects your degree of *affective commitment*.
3. Add the scores for items 3, 6, 9, and 12. This reflects your degree of *normative commitment*.

Discussion Questions

1. Which form of commitment does the scale reveal you have most? Which do you have least? Are these differences great or are they highly similar?
2. Did the scale tell you something you didn't already know about yourself, or did it merely reinforce your intuitive beliefs about your own organizational commitment?
3. To what extent is your organizational commitment, as reflected by this scale, related to your interest in quitting your job and taking a new position?

Group Exercise

AUDITING ORGANIZATIONAL BIASES

Is your organization biased against certain groups of people? Even if you answer "no," chances are good that you may have missed some subtle and unintentional forms of prejudice lurking about. This exercise is designed to help you uncover some of these.

Directions

1. Reproduce the checklist that follows, making one copy for each member of the class.
2. Guided by this checklist, gather the information indicated for the organization in which you work (or, if you don't work, for any organization to which you have access) and check off all items that apply.
3. In answering, either use your existing knowledge of the company or ask those who might know. (If you do ask others, be sure to tell them that it's for a class project!)
4. Report back to the class after one week.

Checklist

Does your organization...

_____ Have signs and manuals in English only although several employees speak other languages?
_____ Ignore important holidays celebrated by people of certain cultures, such as Martin Luther King, Jr. Day, Yom Kippur, Cinco de Mayo, or Chinese New Year?
_____ Limit social events to married people?
_____ Restrict training opportunities available to women and people from minority groups?
_____ Emphasize male-oriented sporting events, such as football?
_____ Limit its recruitment efforts to colleges and universities that have predominately white students?
_____ Hire predominately females for secretarial positions?
_____ Discourage styles of dress that allow for the expression of varied cultural and ethnic backgrounds?

Discussion Questions

1. How many of the eight items did you check off? How about other members of the class? What was the class average?
2. What items represented the biggest sources of bias? What are the potential consequences of these actions?
3. What steps could be taken to change these practices? Do you think company officials would be willing to launch initiatives designed to turn things around? Why or why not?

Notes

MAKING THE CASE NOTES

White, J. (2011, June). Chain of the year: Domino's Pizza. *Pizza Today*, pp. 9–10. Domino's Pizza. (2012). Fun facts. http://www.dominosbiz.com/Biz-Public-EN/Site+Content/Secondary/About+Dominos/Fun+Facts. White, E. (2005, February 15). To keep employees, Domino's decides it's all about pay. *Wall Street Journal*, p. 1. Boorstin, J. (2005, February 7). Delivering at Domino's Pizza. *CNNMoney.com, Fortune*. http://money.cnn.com/magazines/fortune/fortune_archive/2005/02/07/8250433/index.htm. Coomes, S. (2005, May). Taming turnover. Pizza marketplace. From http://www.pizzamarketplace.com/article.php?id=4082. Domino's lowers corporate turnover with training program. *Nation's Restaurant News* (2005, April 5). http://findarticles.com/p/articles/mi_m3190/is_14_39/ai_n13596665.

CHAPTER NOTES

1. McGuire, W. J. (1985). Attitudes and attitude change. In G. Lindzey & E. Aronson (Eds.), *Handbook of social psychology* (3rd ed.) (Vol. 2, pp. 233–346). New York: Random House.
2. U.S. Bureau of Labor Statistics (2010). *Labor participation rates.* Washington, DC: Author.
3. U.S. Bureau of Labor Statistics (2009, November). *Labor force characteristics by race and ethnicity* (Report 1020). Washington, DC: Author.
4. Joshi, A. (2006). The influence of organizational demography on the external networking behavior of teams. *Academy of Management Review, 31,* 583–595. Nicholson, N. (1995). Organizational demography. In N. Nicholson (Ed.), *Blackwell encyclopedic dictionary of organizational behavior* (pp. 833–834). Malden, MA: Blackwell. Pfeffer, J. (1985). Organizational demography: Implications for management. *California Management Review, 38,* 67–81.
5. Tsui, A. S., Egan, T. D., & O'Reilly, C. A., III. (1992). Being different: Relational demography and organizational attachment. *Administrative Science Quarterly, 37,* 549–579.
6. Wagner, W. G., Pfeffer, J., & O'Reilly, C. A. (1984). Work group demography and turnover in top management groups. *Administrative Science Quarterly, 29,* 74–92. Godthelp, M., & Glunk, U. (2003). Turnover at the top: Demographic diversity as a determinant of executive turnover in the Netherlands. *European Management Journal, 21,* 614–626.
7. Watson, W., Stewart, W. H., Jr., & BarNir, A. (2003). The effects of human capital, organizational demography, and interpersonal processes on venture partner perceptions of firm profit and growth. *Journal of Business Venturing, 18,* 145–164.
8. Webber, S. S., & Donahue, L. M. (2001). Impact of highly and less job-related diversity on work group cohesion and performance: A meta-analysis. *Journal of Management, 27,* 141–162.
9. Gregory, R. F. (2001). *Age discrimination in the American workplace: Old at a young age.* New Brunswick, NJ: Rutgers University Press.
10. Lieberman, S., Simons, G., & Berardo, K. (2009). *Putting diversity to work.* Mississauga, Ontario, Canada: Crisp.
11. Magill, B. G. (1999). *Workplace accommodations under the ADA.* Washington, DC: Thomson Publishing Group.
12. Brault, M. (2008, February). *Disability status and the characteristics of people in group quarters.* U.S. Bureau of the Census. http://www.census.gov/hhes/www/disability/GQdisability.pdf.
13. U.S. Department of Commerce et al. (2011, March). *Women in America: Implications of social and economic well-being.* Washington, DC: Author.
14. Women CEOs (2011). *Fortune* 500. http://money.cnn.com/magazines/fortune/fortune500/2011/womenceos/.
15. Tilcsik, A. (2011). Pride and prejudice: Employment discrimination against openly gay men in the United States. *American Journal of Sociology, 117,* 586–626.
16. U.S. Equal Employment Opportunity Commission. (2012). Charge statistics: FY 1997 through FY 2011. http://eeoc.gov/eeoc/statistics/enforcement/charges.cfm.
17. Corrigan, J., & Neale, L. S. (2010). *Religious intolerance in America: A documentary history.* Charlotte, NC: University of North Carolina Press.

18. Philosophy and Public Policy. (2008). Civil rights and racial preferences: A legal history of affirmative action. http://www.puaf.umd.edu/IPPP/2QQ.HTM.

19. Kravitz, D. A. (2008). The diversity-validity dilemma: Beyond selection—the role of affirmative action. *Personnel Psychology, 61*, 173–193.

20. Ragins, B. R., & Gonzales, J. A. (2003). Understanding diversity in organizations: Getting a grip on a slippery construct. In J. Greenberg (Ed.), *Organizational behavior: The state of the science* (2nd ed.) (pp. 125–163). Mahwah, NJ: Erlbaum.

21. Murray, K. (1993, August 1). The unfortunate side effects of "diversity training." *New York Times*, pp. E1, E3.

22. Gottfredson, L. S. (1992). Dilemmas in developing diversity programs. In S. E. Jackson (Ed.), *Diversity in the workplace* (pp. 279–305). New York: Guilford Press.

23. Greene, A., & Kirton, G. (2009). *Diversity management in the UK*. New York: Routledge.

24. Klein, K. J., & Harrison, D. A. (2007). On the diversity of diversity: Tidy logic, messier realities. *Academic of Management Perspectives, 21*, 26–33. Harrison, D. A., & Klein, K. J. (2007). What's the difference? Diversity constructs as separation, variety, or disparity in organizations. *Academy of Management Review, 32*, 1199–1228.

25. Richard, O. C. (2000). Racial diversity, business strategy, and firm performance: A resource based view. *Academy of Management Journal, 43*, 164–177.

26. King, E. B., Dawson, J. F., West, M. A., Gilrane, V. L., Peddie, C. I., & Bastin, L. (2011). Why organizational and community diversity matter: Representativeness and the emergence of incivility and organizational performance. *Academy of Management Journal, 54*, 1103–1118.

27. Wright, P., Ferris, S. P., Hiller, J. S., & Kroll, M. (1995). Competitiveness through management of diversity: Effects of stock price valuation. *Academy of Management Journal, 38*, 272–287.

28. Kandola, R., & Fullerton, J. (1998). *Managing the mosaic: Diversity in action* (2nd ed.). London: Chartered Institute of Personnel and Development.

29. Kahn, J. (2001, July 9). Diversity trumps the downturn. *Fortune*, pp. 66–72 (quote, p. 70).

30. Fegley, S. (2006). *2006 workplace diversity and changes to the EEO-1 process: Survey report*. Alexandria, VA: Society for Human Resource Management.

31. Gardenswartz, L., & Rowe, A. (1994). *The managing diversity survival guide*. Burr Ridge, IL: Irwin.

32. Battaglia, B. (1992). Skills for managing multicultural teams. *Cultural Diversity at Work, 4*, 4–12.

33. Allstate Insurance Company. (2010). *Workforce diversity*. http://www.allstate.com/diversity/workplace.aspx. Allstate Insurance Company. (2008). *One company for us all*. http://www.allstate.com/Allstate/content/refresh-attachments/diversity_brochure.pdf.

34. What's it like to work at Allstate? Diversity. (2003). http://www.allstate.com/Careers/PageRender.asp?Page=diversity.htm.

35. Smith, T. W. (2009, April 17). *Job satisfaction in the United States*. Chicago, IL: National Opinion Research Center at the University of Chicago.

36. Burke, R. J., & Ng, E. (2006). The changing nature of work and organizations: Implications for human resource management. *Human Resource Management Review, 16*, 86–94.

37. See Note 35.

38. Judge, T. A. (1992). Dispositional perspective in human resources research. In G. R. Ferris & K. M. Rowland (Eds.), *Research in personality and human resources management* (Vol. 10, pp. 31–72). Greenwich, CT: JAI Press.

39. Judge, T. A., & Ilies, R. (2004). Affect and job satisfaction: A study of their relationships at home and at work. *Journal of Applied Psychology, 89*, 661–673.

40. Arvey, R. D., Bouchard, T. J., Jr., Segal, N. L., & Abraham, L. M. (1989). Job satisfaction: Genetic and environmental components. *Journal of Applied Psychology, 74*, 187–192.

41. Cropanzano, R., & James, K. (1990). Some methodological considerations for the behavioral-genetic analysis of work attitudes. *Journal of Applied Psychology, 71*, 433–439.

42. Salancik, G. R., & Pfeffer, J. R. (1978). A social information processing approach to job attitudes. *Administrative Science Quarterly, 23*, 224–252. Zalesny, M. D., & Ford, J. K. (1990). Extending the social information processing perspective: New links to attitudes, behaviors,

and perceptions. *Organizational Behavior and Human Decision Processes, 47,* 205–246.

43. Phillips, J. J., & O'Connell, A. (2003). *Managing employee retention: A strategic accountability approach.* San Diego, CA: Elsevier.

44. Maertz, C. P., & Campion, M. A., (2004). Profiles in quitting: Integrating process and content turnover theory. *Academy of Management Journal, 47,* 566–582.

45. Mercer Consulting. (2009). http://www .mercer.com/absenteeism.

46. Harrison, D. A., & Martocchio, J. J. (1998). Time for absenteeism: A 20-year review of origins, offshoots, and outcomes. *Journal of Management, 24,* 305–350.

47. Hardy, G. E., Woods, D., & Wall, T. D. (2003). The impact of psychological distress on absence from work. *Journal of Applied Psychology, 88,* 306–314.

48. Iaffaldano, M. R., & Murchinsky, P. M. (1985). Job satisfaction and job performance: A meta-analysis. *Psychological Bulletin, 97,* 251–273.

49. Judge, T. A., Thorenson, C. J., Bono, J. E., & Patton, G. K. (2001). The job satisfaction–job performance relationship: A qualitative and quantitative review. *Psychological Bulletin, 127,* 376–407.

50. Schneider, B., Hanges, P. J., Smith, D. B., & Salvaggio, A. N. (2004). Which comes first: Employee attitudes or organizational financial and market performance? *Journal of Applied Psychology, 88,* 836–851.

51. Goddard, J. (2001). High performance and the transformation of work: The implications of alternative work practices for the experience and outcomes of work. *Industrial and Labor Relations Review, 54,* 776–806.

52. Gyeke, S. A., & Salminen, S. (2006). Making sense of industrial accidents: The role of job satisfaction. *Journal of Social Sciences, 2,* 127–134.

53. Barling, J., Kelloway, E. K., & Iverson, R. D. (2003). High-quality work, job satisfaction, and occupational injuries. *Journal of Applied Psychology, 88,* 276–283.

54. Tait, M., Padgett, M. Y., & Baldwin, T. T. (1989). Job and life satisfaction: A reevaluation of the strength of the relationship and gender effects as a function of the date of the study. *Journal of Applied Psychology, 74,* 502–507.

55. Ilies, R., & Judge, T. A. (2002). Understanding the dynamic relationships among personality, mood, and job satisfaction: A field experience sampling study. *Organizational Behavior and Human Decision Processes, 89,* 1119–1139. Weiss, H. M. (2002). Deconstructing job satisfaction: Separating evaluations, beliefs, and affective experiences. *Human Resource Management Review, 12,* 173–194.

56. Judge, T. A., & Ilies, R. (2004). Affect and job satisfaction: A study of their relationship at work and at home. *Journal of Applied Psychology, 89,* 661–673.

57. Becker, T. E., Klein, H. J., & Meyer, J. P. (2009). Accumulated wisdom and new directions for workplace commitments. In H. J. Klein, T. E. Becker, & J. P. Meyer (Eds.), *Commitment in organizations: Accumulated wisdom and new directions* (pp. 419–452). New York: Routledge.

58. Reingold, J. (1999, March 1). Why your workers might jump ship. *Business Week,* p. 8. Anonymous. (1999, July–August). To attract talent, you've gotta give 'em all. *Management Review,* p. 10. Anonymous. (1999, July–August). Employee loyalty surprisingly strong. *Management Review,* p. 9. The list: Hot seat in the corner office (2000, February 14). *Business Week,* p. 8.

59. Meyer, J. P., Becker, T. E., & Vandenberghe, C. (2004). Employee commitment and motivation: Conceptual analysis and integrative model. *Journal of Applied Psychology, 89,* 991–1007. Meyer, J. P., Becker, T. E., & Van Dick, R. (2006). Social identities and commitments at work: Toward an integrative model. *Journal of Organizational Behavior, 27,* 665–683. Meyer, J. P., Allen, N. J., & Smith, C. A. (1993). Commitment to organizations and occupations: Extension and test of a three-component conceptualization. *Journal of Applied Psychology, 78,* 538–551.

60. Klein, H. J., Molloy, J. C., & Brinsfield, C. T. (2012). Reconceptualizing workplace commitment to redress a stretched construct: Revisiting assumptions and removing confounds. *Academy of Management Review, 37,* 130–151.

61. Lee, K., Carswell, J. J., & Allen, N. J. (2000). A meta-analytic review of occupational commitment: Relations with person- and work-related variables. *Journal of Applied Psychology, 85,* 799–811.

62. Gong, Y., Law, K. S., Chang, S., & Xin, K. R. (2009). Human resources management and firm performance: The differential role of managerial affective and continuance commitment. *Journal of Applied Psychology, 94,* 263–275.

63. Meyer, J. P., Stanley, D. J., Herscovitch, L., & Topolnytsky, L. (2002). Affective, continuance, and normative commitment to the organization: A meta-analysis of antecedents, correlates, and consequences. *Journal of Vocational Behavior, 61,* 20–52.

64. Clugston, M. (2000). The mediating effects of multidimensional commitment on job satisfaction and intent to leave. *Journal of Organizational Behavior, 21,* 477–486.

65. Rosen, R. H. (1991). *The healthy company.* Los Angeles: Jeremy P. Tarcher (quote, pp. 71–72).

66. FindLaw. (2012). Incentive compensation and profit sharing plan: UAL Corp. http://contracts.corporate.findlaw.com/compensation/incentive/4665.html.

67. REI. (2012). Pay and benefits: Total rewards at REI. http://www.rei.com/jobs/pay.html.

68. Meyer, J. P., & Allen, N. J. (1991). A three-component conceptualization of organizational commitment. *Human Resource Management Review, 1,* 61–89.

6 MOTIVATING PEOPLE TO WORK

LEARNING OBJECTIVES

After reading this chapter, you will be able to:

1. **DEFINE** motivation and **IDENTIFY** its fundamental components.
2. **DESCRIBE** the motivational-fit approach and what it suggests about how to improve motivation in organizations.
3. **EXPLAIN** how goals may be set to motivate workers to improve their job performance.
4. **DESCRIBE** equity theory and explain how it may be applied to motivating people in organizations.
5. **DESCRIBE** expectancy theory and **EXPLAIN** what it says about how to motivate people on the job.
6. **DISTINGUISH** among job enlargement, job enrichment and the job characteristics model as techniques for motivating employees.

THREE GOOD REASONS you should care about. . .

Motivating People to Work

1. Managers have a variety of opportunities to motivate employees by virtue of how they treat them.
2. The more highly motivated employees are, the more positively they respond in several different ways.
3. Jobs can be designed in ways that enhance employees' motivation to perform them.

Making the Case for...

Motivating People to Work

COSTCO: Doing Something Right

Not too many companies have the weight to push around Coca-Cola, but Costco has done just this. A few years ago, Costco dropped Coca-Cola products from its inventory after the soft drink giant raised its wholesale prices. The stalemate lasted only one month before Coca-Cola succumbed to the pressure of the largest wholesale club and seventh largest retailer in the world by rolling back its prices. Considering its willingness to take-on Coca-Cola instead of raising prices to its 64 million members, it's not surprising that shoppers love Costco. Low prices, wide selection, and outstanding service have kept satisfied customers returning to 600 Costco warehouse stores, bringing in nearly $89 billion in annual sales.

It's not only customers who like Costco but its 107,200 full-time and part-time employees, too. As evidence, consider the fierce loyalty of its workforce. In the retail sector, it's generally considered good to keep about half your employees annually, but Costco retains about 94 percent. What exactly is Costco doing that spurs its employees to keep coming to work? According to a former schoolteacher who now works at a Costco lunch counter, opportunities for promotion are key. Recognizing that the company prefers to develop new managers from within its workforce, she says, "I know that sooner or later, I'll be given a bigger job—perhaps one with management responsibility, and that excites me." Although it may be a huge leap from selling hotdogs to managing a department, advancements abound at Costco, making it not unrealistic for employees to aspire to bigger things.

This is only part of the story when it comes to motivating Costco employees. Better-than-average wages and benefits also are key. Because large retailers struggle to keep expenses low, the wages they pay tend to be low, and whatever benefits they offer are not especially generous. This isn't so at Costco. Although fewer than half of Walmart and Target employees receive health insurance, 85 percent of Costco's employees enjoy this valuable benefit. And because Costco saves money by keeping turnover low, it pays its employees relatively highly, up to $20 per hour for some nonsupervisory positions. This isn't quite as costly to Costco as it may seem because many employees, well aware of the stores' bargains, spend some of their paychecks at the very places they earn them. In fact, Costco's employees are among its most loyal shoppers.

Another key to Costco's success is its good customer service. Compared to many discount retail establishments, where surly clerks might bark one-word answers to your questions, if you even can find a clerk in the first place, most Costco employees are interested in helping. Officials are convinced that this is an extension of the company's friendly relations with its employees. Indeed, leaders demonstrate respect and concern for their employees, creating an atmosphere in which people desire to treat one another like family. Although none of this may be at the top of your mind when you visit your local Costco to stock up on a year's supply of paper towels or shaving cream, it just may give you a new appreciation for what's going on behind the scenes.

There's no doubt that Costco's success stems from its low prices and good service. As this case suggests, however, another important consideration is the high *motivation* of its employees. This factor, which leads people to work hard and remain loyal, is an invaluable asset for Costco—or any other business, for that matter. Companies strive to build their assets, and Costco has been actively committed to developing the motivation of its employees. With this in mind, it pays its employees well, it rewards them with promotions, and it treats them in a friendly and welcoming manner.

It's obvious that we certainly like these things, but do they really stimulate people into action? And if so, why? In other words, what psychological mechanisms explain what gets people to work hard? I focus on the answer to these important questions in this chapter. And in keeping with the simultaneously theoretical and applied orientation of the field of OB, I also examine how managers can put this information to practical use in attempting to motivate their employees.

Over the years, the question of what it takes to motivate workers has received a great deal of attention by organizational scientists.[1] In this chapter, I examine several of the most important approaches to the study of motivation, focusing on both the research bearing on them and their practical implications. Before getting to this, however, I will touch briefly on a fundamental matter—namely, what exactly is meant by motivation.

WHAT IS MOTIVATION?

Although motivation is a broad and complex concept, organizational scientists have agreed on its basic nature.[2] Specifically, **motivation** refers to the set of processes that arouse, direct, and maintain human behavior toward attaining some goal. The diagram in Figure 6.1 highlights the key elements of this definition.

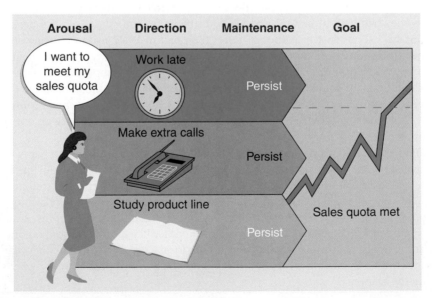

FIGURE 6.1   Basic Components of Motivation
Motivation involves the arousal, direction, and maintenance of action toward a goal.

Components of Motivation

My definition of motivation incorporates four distinct components that are fundamental to understanding its basic nature. These are as follows:

- *Goal*—This refers to the objective you are attempting to reach. For example, an investor may have a goal of amassing a certain amount of money, or a dieter may have a goal of losing a certain amount of weight.
- *Arousal*—This has to do with the drive or energy behind our actions. For example, people may be guided by their interest in building high-quality products, doing interesting work, being successful at what they do, and so on. This energizes them to do what it takes to meet these objectives.
- *Direction*—This refers to the choices people make—that is, how they direct their efforts to meet the goal. For example, employees interested in cultivating a favorable impression on their supervisors may do many different things: compliment them on their good work, do them special favors, work extra hard on an important project, and the like.
- *Maintenance*—This has to do with how long people persist at attempting to meet their goals. To give up in advance of goal attainment means not satisfying the need that motivated behavior in the first place. Obviously, people who do not persist at meeting their goals (e.g., salespeople who give up before reaching their quotas) cannot be said to be highly motivated.

By way of summarizing, let's consider an analogy. Imagine that you have been traveling and your goal is now to get home. The arousal part of motivation is like the energy created by the engine of the car you're driving. The direction component is like the steering wheel that takes you along the particular roads you have chosen for your trip. Finally, the maintenance aspect of the definition is the persistence that keeps you going, mile after mile, until you arrive home, reaching your goal. In both cases, any one missing part will keep you from getting where you want to go.

Three Key Points About Motivation

Now that I have defined motivation, I should note three important points you should keep in mind as you think about motivation on the job.

MOTIVATION AND JOB PERFORMANCE ARE NOT SYNONYMOUS Just because someone performs a task well does not mean that he or she is highly motivated. Motivation is just one of several possible determinants of job performance. The person who performs well may be very skillful but not put forth much effort at all (high performance but low motivation). If you're a mathematical genius, for example, you may breeze through your calculus class without trying. By contrast, someone who performs poorly may put forth a great deal of effort but fall short of a desired goal because he or she lacks the aptitude or skills needed to succeed (low performance but high motivation).

To appreciate this, recall something that you tried to learn but couldn't quite get the hang of, such as playing golf or the piano. Although you may have really wanted to succeed, it's possible that you lacked the skills needed to succeed no matter how hard you tried. In this case, you fell short despite your high motivation. However, of course, it's also possible that you failed because you gave up long before you were able to develop those skills. In this case, you simply weren't sufficiently motivated to devote the time needed to practice.

MOTIVATION IS MULTIFACETED   People are likely to have several different motives operating at once. Sometimes, these conflict with one another. For example, a word processing operator might be motivated to please her boss by being as productive as possible. However, being too productive may antagonize her coworkers, who fear that they're being made to look bad. The result is that the two motives may pull the individual in different directions, and the one that wins is the one that's stronger in that situation. Keeping this in mind makes it easy to see why simply knowing something that motivates a person doesn't allow you to predict perfectly how that individual will behave.

PEOPLE ARE MOTIVATED BY MORE THAN JUST MONEY   Suppose you struck it big in the lottery. Would you keep your current job? Interestingly, although some people make it clear that they would pack up and move to a tropical island where they would relax in the sun for the rest of their lives, most insist that they would continue to work. They might take a different job, but they'd continue to work even if they didn't need the money. Why? The answer is simple: money isn't people's only motive for working.

What is it, then, that motivates us, and where does money lie on this list? To some extent, the answers depend who you ask. Table 6.1 reveals the rankings of people found in surveys of lower- and mid-level employees[3] and of junior and senior executives.[4] The individuals surveyed represented a variety of companies in different industries. Despite some minor differences in orderings, the top four responses of both groups were remarkably similar. The top two factors for both groups were "doing challenging work" and "having a supportive, team-oriented atmosphere." Money came in consistently below these factors, ranking third among mid-lower-level employees and fourth among executives. As you will see in the rest of this chapter, the field of OB examines a variety of factors that motivate people—those indicated here as well as many others.

Having established these basic qualities of motivation, I now turn to the first of five different orientations to motivation discussed in this chapter. This particular approach, which focuses on motivating by enhancing fit with an organization, casts an interesting light on some issues already considered in this book.

TABLE 6.1   What Motivates People to Work?

Pay, although important, is not at the very top of the list of the most important sources of work motivation in people's lives. This applies to both lower- to mid-level employees and to junior and senior executives.

Factor	Lower- to Mid-Level Employees	Junior and Senior Executives
Challenging work	1	2
Supportive, team-oriented environment	2	1
Adequate compensation	3	4
Opportunities for promotion, achievement	4	6
Fit between life on and off the job	—	3
Incentives to succeed	5	—
Working at a company that has high values	—	5
Peer group respect	6	—

Sources: Robson, 2004; see Note 3; Gallinsky et al., 2009; see Note 4.

MOTIVATING BY ENHANCING FIT WITH AN ORGANIZATION

Imagine that you started a new job as a salesperson at an auto dealership. After a little while, however, you find that it's not really your thing. You're not the type of person to push someone into a sale, and as customers walk away, your self-confidence erodes. Realizing this about yourself makes you feel anxious as you approach a prospect on the floor or as you try to close a sale. And this, of course, interferes with your capacity to succeed. In turn, this lowers your motivation to work ("why even bother?"), further interfering with your performance, lowering your motivation, and so on. The downward cycle is spiraling you right out of the showroom and into a new job. Because your particular qualities are a poor match with the requirements of the job, your motivation and performance suffer.

In Chapter 3, I noted that many different personality traits and abilities influence job performance. In the context of motivation, however, scientists have found that a few particular traits and skills have especially profound effects. This is the basic idea behind a relatively new way of looking at motivation, known as the **motivational fit approach**.[5] Specifically, this framework stipulates that motivation is based on the connection between the qualities of individuals and the requirements of the jobs they perform in their organizations. The better people's traits and skills fit those requirements, the more highly motivated they will be (see Figure 6.2).

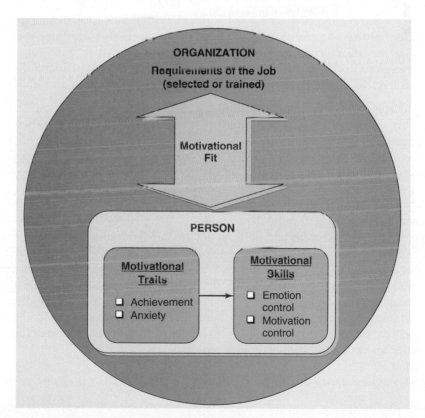

FIGURE 6.2 The Motivational Fit Approach: An Overview
According to the motivational fit approach, people are most highly motivated to perform when there is a good fit between various traits and skills they possess and certain important characteristics of the work they perform. These are summarized here.
Source: Based on suggestions by Kanfer & Heggestad, 1997; see Note 5.

Motivational Traits and Skills

The motivational fit approach specifies that two particular individual characteristics, referred to as **motivational traits**, are important. These are as follows:

- **Achievement**—a person's interests in excelling at what he or she does and in accomplishing desired objectives
- **Anxiety**—a person's tendency to be excessively apprehensive or nervous about things in everyday life

Because achievement and anxiety are considered traits, they are assumed to be relatively stable differences between people (see Chapter 3), making some individuals more successful than others. As it works out, the most highly motivated employees tend to be those characterized by high levels of achievement and low levels of anxiety. Such individuals not only are inclined to strive for excellence, but they also lack the emotional problems associated with being excessively worried.

In addition to the traits they possess, an individual's motivation also is determined by what are known as **motivational skills**—the particular strategies used when attempting to meet objectives. Unlike traits, which are relatively stable within individuals over time, people can be trained in skills, and these also develop naturally over time as people gain experience over their careers. Two particular motivational skills are important:

- **Emotion control**—a person's capacity to control his or her own emotions and to stay focused on the task at hand without allowing emotions to interfere
- **Motivation control**—a person's capacity to push himself or herself by directing attention to the job and to continue exerting effort even when his or her interest begins to wane

As you might expect, employees with highly developed motivational skills are not only more strongly motivated to succeed but ultimately also more successful on their jobs than those with less developed motivational skills. Specifically, individuals with high levels of emotional control and high levels of motivation control are more successful than those with low levels of these skills. This is probably not surprising, given that people with high levels of these skills are adept at overcoming key problems such as boredom and the frustration that inevitably occurs at work. Importantly, because these are skills rather than traits, anyone may develop them to some degree.

People's motivational traits and skills do not operate independently. Rather, traits influence skills. Consider, for example, someone with high amounts of the achievement trait. Such an individual is particularly likely to seek out challenging situations. And, because such situations present considerable opportunities for failure, the person has to learn to overcome the negative emotional reactions that are likely to result (emotion control) and is likely to be driven to continue even in the face of obstacles (motivation control). By contrast, because individuals who are low in the achievement trait are inclined to avoid challenging situations, they are unlikely to face conditions that allow them to develop motivational skills.

How to Motivate Workers According to the Motivational Fit Approach

Recognizing that people do not operate in a vacuum, the motivational fit approach specifies that it is important for people's motivational traits and skills to match the requirements of their work environments. Although this idea is admittedly abstract, we already considered a good illustration. Recall your unsuccessful attempt to make it as an auto salesperson? Given the nature of the work, it's understandable that you would be a bad fit with the organization. Fortunately, however, there's hope for you yet. Fit can be enhanced in two key ways.

PRESCREEN FOR DESIRED TRAITS AND SKILLS   First, the dealership can prescreen job applicants in a manner that keeps individuals with your particular profile out of such positions. This would save you, the company, and some unsuspecting customers a lot of grief. Indeed, research has shown that motivational fit is enhanced when people's characteristics match the unique requirements of the positions they seek.[6]

The underlying idea is that people's motivational traits and skills must fit has to do with the inherent nature of the job. On some jobs, such as research scientist, success requires the capacity to work independently, to innovate, and to persist when attempting to solve difficult problems. The individuals most highly motivated to pursue positions of this type are those with high amounts of achievement and strong motivational skills. By contrast, among people performing more routine jobs, such as factory worker or call center operator, such characteristics are not as likely to contribute to motivation. After all, the highly structured nature of these jobs is likely to make these traits and skills less important. Please note that "less important" does not mean "unimportant." Indeed, even among call center operators, motivational fit has been identified as a key to productivity.[7]

BUILD MOTIVATIONAL SKILLS   Second, the company can improve motivational fit by training people in ways of building their motivational skills. Although this might not come to you naturally at this time, becoming more of the way you have to be to perform the job is not out of the question. It involves learning a new skill, and you surely are capable of doing so. This may take the form, for example, of training you in building confidence so you can avoid the self-doubts that interfere with your motivation to perform this job.

Because the motivational fit approach is new, it has not received as much research attention as the other frameworks described in this chapter. However, studies conducted thus far have been highly supportive.[8] As a result, the motivational fit approach already has been acknowledged as an important and especially promising way of understanding motivation on the job.[9]

MOTIVATING BY SETTING GOALS

Just as people are motivated to fit with their organizations, they also are motivated by another very basic interest—to strive for, and to attain, goals. This process is known as **goal setting**, which is one of the most potent motivational forces acting on people.[10] In this section of the chapter, I describe the underlying psychological processes that make goal setting effective and identify some practical suggestions for setting goals on the job.

Goal-Setting Theory

Suppose that you are doing a task, such as word processing, when a performance goal is assigned. You are now expected to type 70 words per minute instead of the 60 words per minute you've been keyboarding all along. Would you work hard to meet this goal, or would you simply give up?

Some insight into the question of how people respond to assigned goals is provided by **goal-setting theory**, which is one of the most influential theories in the field of OB.[11] The basic idea behind this approach is that a goal serves as a motivator for three key reasons.

SELF-EFFICACY   When goals are set, people direct their attention to them and gauge how well they are doing. In other words, they compare their current capacity to perform with that required to succeed at the goal, thereby assessing their **self-efficacy**—that is, their beliefs about their capacity to succeed. To the extent that people believe they will fall short of a goal, they will feel dissatisfied and will work harder to attain it so long as they believe it is possible for them to do so. When they succeed at meeting a goal, they feel competent and successful.[12] Having a goal

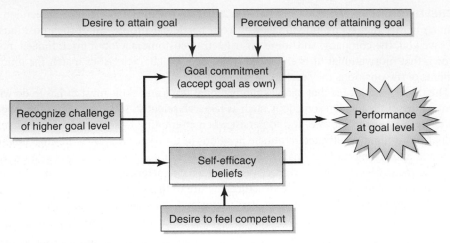

FIGURE 6.3 The Goal-Setting Process
When people are challenged to meet higher goals, several things happen. First, they assess their desire to attain the goal as well as their chances of attaining the goal. Together, these judgments affect their goal commitment. Second, they assess the extent to which meeting the goal will enhance their beliefs in their own self-efficacy. When levels of goal commitment and self-efficacy are high, people are motivated to perform at the goal level.

enhances performance in large part because the goal makes clear exactly what type and level of performance is expected (see Figure 6.3).

GOAL COMMITMENT   Goal-setting theory also claims that assigned goals will lead to the acceptance of those goals as personal goals.[13] In other words, they will be accepted as one's own. This is the idea of **goal commitment**—the extent to which people invest themselves in meeting a goal. Indeed, people become more committed to a goal to the extent that they desire to attain it and believe they have a reasonable chance of doing so. Likewise, the more strongly people believe they are capable of meeting a goal, the more strongly they will accept it as their own. By contrast, workers who perceive themselves as incapable of meeting goals will not be committed to meeting them, and as a result, will not strive to do so.

TASK PERFORMANCE   Finally, goal-setting theory claims that beliefs about both self-efficacy and goal commitment influence task performance. After all, people are willing to exert greater effort when they believe they will succeed than when they believe their efforts will be in vain.[14] Moreover, goals that are not personally accepted will have little capacity to guide behavior. In fact, the more strongly people are committed to meeting goals, the better they perform.[15]

AN EXAMPLE   Although this sounds fairly abstract, the ideas are really quite straightforward and they will come to life with an illustration. Let's use an example of a situation with which college students easily can relate. Suppose you don't care about getting good grades in school (i.e., you are not committed to achieving academic success). In this case, you would not work very hard regardless of how easy or difficult a course may be. By contrast, if you are highly committed to achieving success, then a difficult (but not impossible) goal (e.g., getting a good grade in a very challenging course) will have more meaning to you than an easy goal (e.g., getting a good grade in an easy course) because it enhances your self-efficacy. As a result, you will work harder to achieve it.

Guidelines for Setting Effective Performance Goals

Researchers have actively studied the goal-setting process, and their findings provide useful insight into precisely how to set goals so as to enhance motivation—and, importantly, the job performance that follows from it. I review these here in the form of recommendations about how to set goals effectively.

GOALS SHOULD BE SPECIFIC   Probably the best-established finding of research on goal setting is that people perform at higher levels when asked to meet a specific high-performance goal than when simply asked to "do your best," or when no goal at all is assigned. Generally, people find specific goals quite challenging and are motivated to meet them—not only to fulfill others' expectations but also to convince themselves that they have performed well.

A classic study conducted at an Oklahoma lumber camp provides a particularly dramatic demonstration of this principle.[16] The participants in this research were lumber camp crews who hauled logs from forests to their company's nearby sawmill. Over a three-month period before the study began, it was found that the crew loaded trucks to only about 60 percent of their legal capacities, wasting trips that cost the company money. Then a specific goal was set, challenging the loggers to load the trucks to 94 percent of their capacity before returning to the mill.

How effective was this goal in raising performance? The results, summarized in Figure 6.4, show that the goal was extremely effective. Not only was the specific goal effective in raising

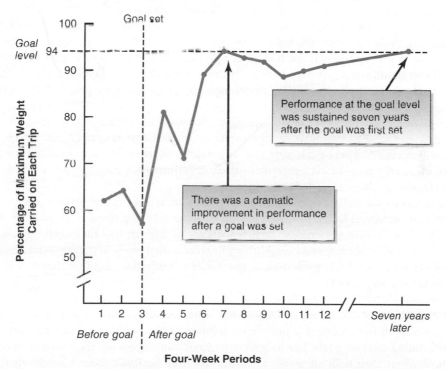

FIGURE 6.4   Goal Setting at a Logging Camp: An Impressive Demonstration
The performance of loggers loading timber onto trucks markedly improved after a specific, difficult goal was set. The percentage of the maximum possible weight loaded onto the trucks rose from approximately 60 percent before any goal was set to approximately 94 percent—the goal level—after the goal was set. Performance remained at this level as long as seven years.
Source: Adapted from Latham & Baldes, 1975; see Note 16.

performance to the goal level after just a few weeks, but these effects were also long-lasting: loggers sustained this level of performance throughout the next seven years. The resulting savings for the company were considerable.

GOALS SHOULD BE DIFFICULT   The goal set at the logging camp was successful not only because it was specific, but also because it pushed crew members to a higher standard. Obviously, a goal that is too easily attained will *not* bring about the desired increments in performance. For example, if you already type at 70 words per minute, the goal of 60 words per minute—although specific—would likely *lower* your performance because it is too easy. The key point is that a goal must be difficult as well as specific for it to raise performance.

It is interesting to consider *why* this occurs. The loggers were not paid any more for meeting the goal than for missing it. Still, they worked hard to meet it. Why? The answer is that the goal instilled purpose and meaning to the otherwise monotonous task of loading trucks. Loggers who met the goal took pride in doing so and found the task more interesting as a result. In fact, the challenge of meeting the goal made the job so much more fascinating that within a week after it was set, the loggers showed great improvements in attendance.[17]

GOALS SHOULD BE ATTAINABLE   As you might imagine, there is a limit to how difficult a goal should be. Although people will work hard to reach challenging goals, they only will do so when these goals fall within the limits of their capability. As goals become *too* difficult, performance suffers because people reject the goals as unrealistic and unattainable.[18]

Let's consider an example to which you can relate as a student. You may work much harder in a class that challenges your ability than one that is very easy. At the same time, however, you probably would give up trying if you had to get a perfect score on all exams to pass the course—a standard you would reject as unacceptable. The underlying principle applies in most situations. Specific goals are most effective if they are set high enough to challenge people, but not so high as to be rejected.

As examples of this, Bell Canada's telephone operators are required to handle calls within 23 seconds, and FedEx's customer service agents are expected to answer customers' questions within 140 seconds.[19] These goals were considered difficult when first imposed, but the people involved eventually met—or even exceeded—them over time. They were likely to enjoy the satisfaction of knowing they succeeded at doing so.

Sometimes, the difficult goals set by companies are so far beyond levels currently being achieved that employees lack a clear idea how to go about reaching them. Such goals are known as **stretch goals**. By their very nature, stretch goals are so difficult that they challenge people to rethink the way they work, thereby establishing unprecedented levels of performance. (For some effective examples of stretch goals used in one major organization, see this chapter's Winning Practices section on p. 181.)

PROVIDE FEEDBACK ON GOAL ATTAINMENT   Another suggestion for setting goals appears obvious, although in practice it is not always followed: Give people feedback on how closely they are coming to their goals. Just as golfers interested in improving their swings need feedback about where their balls are going, so do workers need feedback about how closely they are approaching their performance goals. In both instances, the feedback helps in two important ways. First, it helps people determine how well they are doing, which potentially enhances their feelings of self-efficacy. Second, feedback also helps people determine the specific ways in which their performance needs to be adjusted (e.g., seeing that they are "hooking" or "slicing" the ball

Winning Practices

Companies Stretch Goals in Two Directions

General Electric's former CEO, Jack Welch, regularly used stretch goals at his company to help it achieve vast improvements in quality and efficiency.[20] In describing them to his colleagues, Welch likened stretch goals to the bullet trains in Japan, which run at about 200 mph. Had engineers sought only modest speed improvements, they would have limited their thinking in ways leading to minor alterations in design. However, by specifying previously unheard of speeds, engineers were challenged to think completely differently—and therefore to achieve amazing results. Stretch goals of this type, in which higher levels of current activities are aggressively pursued (e.g., more speed, more profit, etc.), are known as **vertical stretch goals**.

Some other companies also use stretch goals for other purposes. At the investment firm Goldman Sachs, for example, stretch goals are used to aid professional development, such as by challenging managers to perform tasks that they never have done before. According to the firm's head of Global Investment Reach, "Our people thrive on change, stretch goals and tough circumstances."[21] Efforts of this type are known as **horizontal stretch goals**. Such initiatives help develop the company's most talented employees so they can be as

successful as possible in many different ways. Not only do horizontal stretch goals make employees' jobs more interesting, but they also increase the value of the individuals who achieve them as assets to their companies.

How can goals be stretched to acceptable levels without breaking—that is, in ways that will challenge employees without overwhelming them? Taking another page from General Electric's book of successful practices, the answer is straightforward: ask them. In other words, the company routinely involves employees in the goal-setting process, such as by using committees that include employees at various levels to establish new goals.

The experience at General Electric has been consistent with research on workers' participation in goal setting. Specifically, people better accept goals that they have been involved in setting than goals that have been assigned by their supervisors—and they work harder as a result.[22] This is particularly so in the case of stretch goals, where their extreme nature may make them appear to be unacceptably difficult. Not only does participation help people better understand and appreciate goals they had a hand in setting, but it also helps ensure that the goals set are not unreasonable.

down the fairway will prompt golfers to change their stance and club grip). (To demonstrate the effectiveness of goal setting for yourself, complete the Group Exercise on p. 197.)

MOTIVATION TO ACHIEVE EQUITY

Earlier in this chapter, I explained that although money isn't the top motivator for workers, it's still extremely important to them. It would be overly simplistic and misleading to suggest that people only want to earn as much money as possible. Even the highest-paid executives, sports figures, and celebrities sometimes complain about their pay despite receiving multimillion-dollar salaries.[23] Are they being greedy? Not necessarily. Often, the issue is not the actual amount of pay received, but rather, pay *equity*—that is, how one's pay compares to that of others doing similar work or to themselves at earlier times. This is in keeping with the notion of distributive justice discussed in Chapter 2. Here, I examine a particular approach to pay equity known as *equity theory*.

Equity Theory: Balancing Outcomes and Inputs

Equity theory proposes that people are motivated to maintain equitable (i.e., distributively fair) relationships between themselves and others and to avoid those relationships that are inequitable.[24] In judging equity, people compare themselves to others by focusing on two variables: **outcomes**— what we get out of our jobs (e.g., pay, fringe benefits, and prestige)—and **inputs**—the contributions made (e.g., time worked, effort exerted, units produced). It helps to think of these judgments in the form of ratios—that is, the outcomes received relative to the inputs contributed (e.g., $1,000 per week in exchange for working 40 hours). It is important to note that equity theory deals with out-comes and inputs as they are *perceived* by people, not necessarily objective standards. As you might imagine, well-intentioned people sometimes disagree about what constitutes equitable treatment.

According to equity theory, people make equity judgments by comparing their own outcome/input ratios to the corresponding outcome/input ratios of others. This so-called "other" may be someone else in one's work group, another employee in the organization, an individual working in the same field, or even oneself at an earlier point in time—in short, almost anyone against whom we compare ourselves. As shown in Figure 6.5, these comparisons can result in any of three different states: *overpayment inequity, underpayment inequity,* or *equitable payment.*

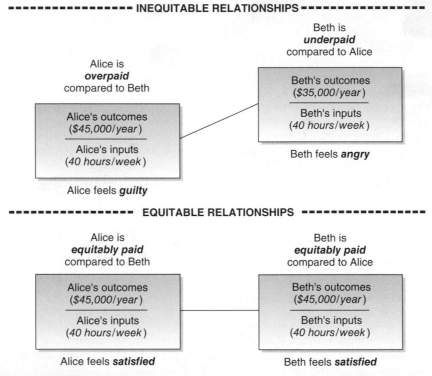

FIGURE 6.5   Equity Theory: A Summary and Example
According to *equity theory*, people make judgments of equity or inequity by comparing the ratios of their own outcomes/inputs to the corresponding ratios of others. People are motivated to change inequitable relationships (such as the one shown on top) to equitable ones (such as the one shown on the bottom). In this example, equitable conditions result when Beth's salary is raised from $35,000 to $45,000, thereby matching the salary of Alice, whose inputs are identical. This is only one possible way in which an equitable state can come about in this situation. Can you identify several others?

Let's consider a simple example that follows from Figure 6.5. Suppose Alice and Beth work together as paralegals in a law firm. Both women have equal amounts of experience, training, and education, and work equally long and hard at their jobs. In other words, their inputs are equivalent. But suppose Alice is paid an annual salary of $45,000 while Beth is paid only $35,000. In this case, Alice's ratio of outcomes/inputs is higher than Beth's, potentially creating a state of **overpayment inequity** for Alice (since the ratio of her outcomes/inputs is higher than Beth's), but **underpayment inequity** for Beth (since the ratio of her outcomes/inputs is lower than Alice's).

According to equity theory, Alice, realizing that she is paid more than an equally qualified person doing the same work, will feel *guilty* in response to her *overpayment*. By contrast, Beth, realizing that she is paid less than an equally qualified person for doing the same work, will feel *angry* in response to her *underpayment*. Guilt and anger are negative emotional states that people are motivated to change. As a result, they will seek to create a state of **equitable payment** in which their outcome/input ratios are equal, leading them to feel *satisfied*. (This is depicted in the bottom portion of Figure 6.5.)

CREATING EQUITY How can inequitable states be turned into equitable ones? The answer lies in adjusting the balance of outcomes and/or inputs. Among people who are underpaid, equity can be created by raising one's outcomes and/or lowering one's inputs. Likewise, those who are overpaid either may lower their outcomes or raise their inputs. Either action effectively would make the two outcome/input ratios equivalent.

Let's consider an example. Our underpaid person, Beth, might lower her inputs, such as by slacking off, arriving at work late, leaving early, taking longer breaks, or doing less work or lower quality work. This is precisely what professional basketball players do when they feel underpaid. Indeed, research has shown that NBA players who are paid less than others who perform equally well score fewer points than those who are equitably paid.[25]

In the case of Beth, the underpaid employee, there are other things she may do. Specifically, she may attempt to raise her outcomes, such as by asking for a raise. By contrast, the overpaid person, Alice, may do the opposite—raise her inputs or lower her outcomes. For example, she might put forth much more effort, work longer hours, and try to make a greater contribution to the company. She also might lower her outcomes, such as by working while on a paid vacation, or not taking advantage of fringe benefits the company offers.

These are all specific *behavioral* reactions to inequitable conditions—that is, things people can *do* to turn inequitable states into equitable ones. However, people may be unwilling to do some of the things necessary to respond behaviorally to inequities. In particular, they may be reluctant to restrict their productivity for fear of getting caught "goofing off." In such cases, people may attempt to resolve inequity *cognitively*, by changing the way they think about the situation. As noted earlier, because equity theory deals with perceptions, inequitable states may be redressed by altering one's thinking about one's own—and others'—outcomes and inputs.

For example, underpaid people may rationalize that others' inputs really are higher than their own (e.g., "I suppose she really *is* more qualified than me"), thereby convincing themselves that their higher outcomes are justified. Similarly, overpaid people may convince themselves that they really *are* better and deserve their relatively higher pay. Thus, by changing the way they see things, people can come to perceive inequitable situations as equitable, effectively relieving their feelings of guilt and anger, and transforming them into feelings of satisfaction. For a summary of behavioral and psychological reactions to inequity, see Table 6.2.

TABLE 6.2	Possible Reactions to Inequity: A Summary

People can respond to overpayment and underpayment inequities in behavioral and/or psychological ways. A few of these are summarized here. These reactions help change perceived inequities into states of perceived equity.

	Form of Reaction	
Type of Inequity	**Behavioral: What You Can Do Is …**	**Psychological: What You Can Think Is …**
Overpayment inequity	Raise your inputs (e.g., work harder) or lower your outcomes (e.g., work through a paid vacation).	Convince yourself that your outcomes are deserved based on your inputs (e.g., rationalize that you work harder than others and so you deserve higher pay).
Underpayment inequity	Lower your inputs (e.g., reduce effort) or raise your outcomes (e.g., get a raise in pay).	Convince yourself that others' inputs are really higher than your own (e.g., rationalize that the comparison worker is really more qualified and so deserves higher outcomes).

EXTREME RESPONSES TO WORKPLACE INEQUITIES Thus far, I have described rather ordinary and often subtle responses to inequity, such as raising or lowering outcomes or inputs either behaviorally or cognitively. Sometimes, however, people respond to inequitable conditions in rather extreme ways. Among these are the following.

- *Getting sick*—Research has confirmed that people find inequitable conditions to be highly distressing. And as described in Chapter 4, stress can be a source of illness. Indeed, such is the case for stress reactions stemming from perceived injustice. Specifically, research has shown that the more people believe they are unfairly paid, the more negative symptoms of stress they display, such as coronary heart disease, depression, and insomnia.[26]
- *Going on strike*—When employees go on **strike** they engage in a systematic stoppage of work designed as a protest against one or more organizations believed to have treated them unfairly. This practice has been used numerous times over the years. In fact, the first known strike in recorded history (recorded on papyrus, in this case) occurred well over 3,000 years ago when artisan tomb makers in ancient Egypt struck to protest low wages and poor working conditions.[27] Over the years and around the world, groups such as builders of railroad sleeping cars, miners, garment workers, teachers, autoworkers, airline pilots, and professional athletes (e.g., football, basketball hockey, and baseball players), among many others, have relied on strikes to send their messages of discontent to management.[28]
- *Stealing from employers*—To the extent that someone feels underpaid, that person sometimes raises his or her outcomes by stealing company property—that is, by taking what isn't given to him or her.[29] Although it's clearly unethical and illegal to steal company property, people often feel justified doing so on the grounds that they are "evening the score" with their companies.
- *Quitting the job*—Arguably the most extreme response to inequity involves quitting one's job and leaving the company responsible for the inequitable treatment.[30] This, of course, is a very costly thing to do. However, many who take this drastic step do so because they feel that their current situations are intolerable and hope that more equitable conditions can be found elsewhere.

Managerial Implications of Equity Theory

Equity theory has important implications for ways of motivating people.[31] I highlight three key ones here.

AVOID UNDERPAYMENT   Companies that attempt to save money by reducing employees' salaries may find that employees respond in many different ways so as to even the score. For example, they may steal, or they may shave a few minutes off their workdays, or otherwise withhold production. It's also not unusual for underpaid employees to quit their jobs. With these considerations in mind, companies that attempt to save money by underpaying their employees are taking a very short-sighted—and potentially dangerous—perspective.

AVOID OVERPAYMENT   You may think that because overpaid employees work hard to deserve their pay, it would be a useful motivational technique to pay people more than they merit. However, there are two key problems with this strategy.[32] First, it sends a dangerous message by reinforcing work behavior that doesn't warrant it. For example, giving a huge raise to an average performer sends the message that such average work is desirable (this follows from principles of instrumental conditioning described in Chapter 3). Second, by overpaying one individual you will be underpaying the others in his or her work group. And when the majority of employees feel underpaid, net reductions in job performance may be expected, along with overall declines in satisfaction that trigger turnover. For these reasons, overpayment should be avoided.

BE OPEN AND TRANSPARENT ABOUT PAY   One of the major challenges with attempting to treat people equitably is that people perceive things differently. To some extent, of course (as suggested in Chapter 3), the process of perception is bound to be imperfect. However, companies can do something to help everyone perceive things accurately: They can share information about pay openly. This is the notion of **transparency**, which refers to the practice of making information about pay available openly instead of keeping it secret.

Most companies are rather secretive about pay information, probably fearing backlash when employees learn what others are making. However, research has shown that it tends to work pretty much the opposite. People generally overestimate how much their superiors are paid and as a result they feel that their own pay is not as high as it should be.[33] However, when information about pay is shared, inequitable feelings are less likely to materialize. With this in mind, transparency can be useful because it helps employees understand the basis for their pay (recall the discussion of procedural justice in Chapter 2). This, in turn, leads people to trust their companies, motivating them to put forth the effort required to excel.[34]

EXPECTANCY THEORY: BELIEVING YOU CAN GET WHAT YOU WANT

Beyond seeking fair treatment on the job, people also are motivated by the belief that they can expect to achieve certain desired rewards by working hard to attain them. If you've ever put in long hours studying in the hopes of receiving an A in one of your classes, then you know what I mean. Believing that there may be a tasty carrot dangling at the end of the stick, and that it may be attained by putting forth the appropriate effort, can be a very effective motivator. This is the idea behind the well-known theory of motivation known as *expectancy theory*.

Basic Elements of Expectancy Theory

According to **expectancy theory**, motivation is the result of three different types of beliefs that people have.[35] I now describe these (see the overall summary in Figure 6.6).

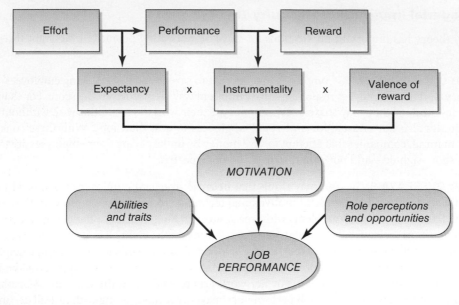

FIGURE 6.6 Overview of Expectancy Theory
Expectancy theory claims that motivation is the combined result of the three types of beliefs identified here—*expectancy*, *instrumentality*, and *valence of reward*. It also recognizes that motivation is only one of several determinants of job performance.

First, it sends a dangerous message by reinforcing work behavior that doesn't warrant it. For example, giving a huge raise to an average performer sends the message that such average work is desirable (this follows from principles of instrumental conditioning described in Chapter 3). Second, by overpaying one individual you will be underpaying the others in his or her work group. And when the majority of employees feel underpaid, net reductions in job performance may be expected, along with overall declines in satisfaction that trigger turnover. For these reasons, overpayment should be avoided.

EXPECTANCY   The concept of **expectancy**, refers to the belief that the effort we invest in performing a task will determine how well we perform that task. Sometimes people believe that putting forth a great deal of effort will allow them to get a lot accomplished (i.e., expectancy is high). However, at other times, we do not expect that our efforts will have much effect on how well we do (i.e., expectancy is low). For example, an employee operating a faulty piece of equipment may have a very low *expectancy* that his or her efforts will lead to high levels of performance. Naturally, someone working under such conditions would not be likely to exert much effort.

INSTRUMENTALITY   Even if an employee works hard, motivation may be lacking if that person believes that his or her performance is not going to be rewarded. This is the idea of **instrumentality**, the belief that we will be rewarded in a manner that reflects our performance. When people expect that they'll be suitably rewarded for what they do, their instrumentality beliefs are considered high. However, when people expect that they will not be rewarded for their performance, their instrumentality beliefs are considered low.

As an example, a worker who is extremely productive may be poorly motivated to perform if the pay system doesn't recognize his or her success. Often, this occurs among people who already have reached the top pay grades in their companies. Even if they have become more successful, because they cannot be paid at higher levels in recognition of this, their motivation suffers. In such cases, however, instrumentality beliefs may be high among people who believe that they will receive bonuses that reflect their accomplishments.

VALENCE Even if employees believe that hard work will lead to good performance *and* that they will be rewarded for their performance, motivation cannot be assured. Also considered must be the value of the rewards to the people receiving them—that is, its **valence**. Someone who doesn't care about the rewards offered by the organization will not be motivated to attain them. For example, a reward of $100 would be unlikely to motivate billionaires like Donald Trump and Warren Buffet because that amount of money is too small to matter to them. However, the same amount of money may be a very desirable reward for someone of more modest means. Only those rewards that have a high positive valence to their recipients have the potential to motivate those individuals' behavior.

One important factor that enhances the valence of rewards is the extent to which they satisfy people's fundamental *needs*. Psychologists have studied the nature of needs for many years and offer complex descriptions of their nature.[36] Most would agree, however, that **needs** are forces that motivate people to satisfy states that they inherently require for biological and/or social reasons. For example, we have a need to be satisfied physiologically, such as by having food and water, and socially, such as being admired and accepted by others. As suggested by the various needs summarized in Table 6.3, quite a few needs motivate people in the workplace.[37] While reviewing this list, please keep three things in mind.

- The list is not exhaustive. Various theorists focus on different needs, so you may think of others that are not on this list.
- Some needs overlap with others. Like anything else having to do with human beings, clear lines between needs cannot always be drawn.
- Scientists disagree on whether or not people's needs are universal in nature. Some believe that everyone has the same needs and they are relatively equal in importance all the time, whereas others argue that particular needs are important at certain times.[38]

What's important for our purposes in the field of OB, however, is much simpler. You should recognize the widespread nature and importance of these various needs, and that rewards that help satisfy human needs generally have high valence (i.e., they are considered most important and valuable to people). (To get a sense of the rewards that you personally value, complete the Self-Assessment Exercise on pp. 196–197.)

COMBINING ALL THREE TYPES OF BELIEFS Expectancy theory claims that motivation is a multiplicative function of all three components. This means that higher levels of motivation will result when expectancy, instrumentality, and valence are all high than when they are all low. The multiplicative assumption of the theory implies that if any one of these three components is zero, the overall level of motivation will be zero. So, for example, even if an employee believes that her effort will result in performance, which will result in reward, motivation will be zero if the valance of the reward she expects to receive is zero (i.e., if she believes that what she stands to receive in exchange for her effort has no value to her).

OTHER DETERMINANTS OF JOB PERFORMANCE Figure 6.6 also highlights a point I made in my opening remarks about motivation—that motivation is not equivalent to job performance. Specifically, expectancy theory recognizes that motivation is one of several important determinants of job performance.

TABLE 6.3	Human Needs in the Workplace

Our *needs* as human beings influence behavior in all life activities. On the job, these needs are often satisfied in a variety of ways, as summarized here. Expectancy theory recognizes that rewards with the most positive valence often are ones that satisfy needs.

Need	Description/Example	How Satisfied on the Job
Biological and physiological needs	Need for basic things such as air, food, water	Companies have cafeterias for employees.
Psychological and physiological safety needs	Need to feel protected from harsh environments or dangerous people	Safety (e.g., goggles) and security procedures (e.g. guards) are used.
Affiliation, relatedness, and intimacy needs	Need to feel that one has friends with whom they enjoy being and who appreciate and accept them	Companies sponsor social events (e.g., picnics).
Esteem needs	Need to feel recognized for accomplishing things	Companies conduct ceremonies in which employees receive awards (e.g., certificates, cash).
Cognitive needs	Need to feel that one has learned something new	Company training programs help employees acquire new knowledge.
Aesthetic needs	Need to experience and appreciate beautiful things	Companies put interesting pieces of art throughout their facilities.
Self-actualization needs	The need to realize one's personal potential	Companies offer ongoing opportunities for growth and development (e.g., exposure to new people and places).
Transcendence needs	The need to help others grow and develop	Companies provide opportunities to coach and mentor other employees.
Autonomy needs	The need to have the freedom to decide how to do things without interference	Some jobs are designed in an effort to give people this ultimate freedom (see pp. 192–193).
Competence and success needs	The need to believe that one has mastered some skill and is capable of succeeding when performing it	Companies provide ongoing training and give feedback to help people to recognize when they have succeeded (see Chapter 3).
Power needs	The need to have an impact on other people	Leading and managing others satisfies this need (see Chapter 11).

Sources: Maslow, 1998; Deci et al., 2001; see Note 37.

First, the theory assumes that *skills and abilities* also contribute to a person's job performance. It's no secret that some people are better suited to performing their jobs than others by virtue of their unique characteristics and special skills and abilities. For example, a tall, strong, well-coordinated person is likely to make a better professional basketball player than a very short, weak, uncoordinated one—even if the shorter person is highly motivated to succeed. Being highly motivated can help, of course, but it's not always enough to compensate for lack of physical or mental prowess. This is important for managers to keep in mind when diagnosing performance problems. If an employee is performing poorly, it might be a motivation problem (in which case, it's worth following the suggestions in the next section of this chapter) but it also may be due to a lack of skills (in which case the guidelines for training discussed in Chapter 3 should be followed).

Expectancy theory also recognizes that job performance will be influenced by people's *role perceptions*—in other words, what they believe is expected of them on the job. To the extent that there are disagreements about what one's job duties are, performance may suffer. For example, an assistant manager who believes her primary job duty is to train new employees may find that her performance is downgraded by a supervisor who believes she should be spending more time doing routine paperwork instead. In this case, the person's performance wouldn't suffer as a result of any deficit in motivation, but simply because of misunderstandings regarding what the job entails. As fundamental as this seems, many instances of poor job performance are, with surprising regularity, simply misunderstandings about role perceptions.

Finally, expectancy theory also recognizes the role of *opportunities to perform* one's job. Even the best employees may perform at low levels if their opportunities are limited. For example, a highly motivated salesperson may perform poorly if opportunities are restricted, such as if the territory is suffering from a financial downturn, or if the available inventory is limited. Here, once again, even a highly motivated person may perform poorly under certain (not too unusual) circumstances.

These examples underscore my point that motivation is just one of several determinants of job performance. The key thing to keep in mind is that motivation--combined with a person's skills and abilities, role perceptions, and opportunities--influences job performance.

Putting Expectancy Theory to Work: Key Managerial Implications

Expectancy theory is a very practical approach to motivation. It identifies several important things that can be done to motivate employees.

MAKE IT CLEAR THAT EFFORT IS LINKED TO PERFORMANCE   A useful way to enhance effort-performance expectancies is by following employees' suggestions about ways to change their jobs. Whenever employees are aware of factors that restrict their job performance, they should be encouraged to make the changes that alleviate these problems. Doing this makes desired performance attainable and showcases how to bring it about.

Good supervisors don't only make it clear to their employees what is expected of them, but they also help them attain that level of performance. When this occurs, workers will have a good understanding that working hard to perform the job correctly will lead to good performance. And this, as I noted, is one of the key forces behind motivation according to expectancy theory.

ADMINISTER REWARDS THAT HAVE POSITIVE VALENCE TO EMPLOYEES   These days, with a demographically diverse workforce, it would be misleading to assume that all employees care about having the same rewards. For example, younger workers might recognize the incentive value of a pay raise, while other benefits, such as additional vacation days, improved insurance benefits, day care, or elder-care facilities might be valued more by senior employees.

With this in mind, many companies have introduced **cafeteria-style benefit plans**—incentive systems allowing employees to select their fringe benefits from a menu of available alternatives. Given that fringe benefits constitute about 40 percent of payroll costs, more and more companies are recognizing the value of administering them flexibly. In fact, cafeteria-style benefit plans are in place in half of all larger companies (those employing more than 5,000) and about a quarter of smaller companies (those with less than 1,000 employees).

CLEARLY LINK VALUED REWARDS TO PERFORMANCE There are several ways companies can link reward to performance (supporting a principle of operant conditioning described in Chapter 3). Two popular ways of doing this are as follows:

- **Pay-for-performance plans**—These are compensation systems that reward people directly based on how well they perform their jobs. The *commission plans* used for salespeople or the *piece-rate systems* used to pay some factory workers and field hands are good examples.
- **Incentive stock option (ISO) plans**—These are programs that give employees the opportunity to purchase shares of their companies at a predetermined price in the future. So, over time, if the value of their companies' stock grows, the employee can "exercise the option" by selling the stock at a profit, and with certain income tax advantages.[39]

Despite their differences, both of these practices have something fundamental in common. They enhance employees' instrumentality beliefs by clearly linking their personal rewards to their job performance. And this, in keeping with expectancy theory, is a key ingredient for enhancing motivation.

Designing Jobs That Motivate

As you may recall from Chapter 1, Frederick W. Taylor's approach to stimulating work performance was to design jobs so that people worked as efficiently as possible. No wasted movements and no wasted time made for efficient performance, Taylor believed. The problem with Taylor's approach is that it failed to recognize that most people found highly repetitive machine-like movements to be so monotonous and boring that they frequently quit.

In contrast, today's organizational scientists have developed ways of designing jobs that people perform well not by requiring specific movements but by making them interesting and challenging. This is the basic principle behind **job design**, the process of creating jobs that people are motivated to perform because they are inherently appealing.[40] I now describe three well-established approaches to designing jobs so as to motivate employees.

Job Enlargement: Doing More of the Same Kind of Work

If you've ever purchased a greeting card, chances are good that you've picked up at least one made by American Greetings, one of the largest greeting card companies in the United States. What you might not know is that this Cleveland, Ohio–based organization redesigned some 400 jobs in its creative division. Now, rather than always working exclusively on, say, Christmas cards, employees move back and forth between different teams, such as those working on birthday ribbons, humorous mugs, and Valentine's Day gift bags.

This practice, known as **job enlargement**, involves giving employees more tasks to perform at the same level. There's no higher responsibility involved or any greater skills, just a wider variety of the same types of tasks. Enlarged jobs are said to be changed *horizontally* because people's level of responsibility stays the same. The idea behind job enlargement is simple: you can decrease boredom by assigning people to a wider variety of jobs.

Do job enlargement programs work? To answer this question, consider the results of a study comparing the job performance of people doing enlarged and unenlarged jobs.[41] In the unenlarged jobs, different employees performed separate paperwork tasks such as preparing, sorting, coding, and keypunching various forms. The enlarged jobs combined these various functions into larger jobs performed by the same people. Although it was more difficult and expensive to train people to perform the enlarged jobs than the separate jobs, important benefits resulted. In particular, employees expressed greater job satisfaction and less boredom. And, because one person followed the whole job all the way through, there were greater opportunities to correct errors. Not surprisingly, customers were satisfied with the results.

In a follow-up investigation of the same company conducted two years later, however, it was found that not all the beneficial effects continued.[42] Notably, employee satisfaction leveled off, and the rate of errors went up, suggesting that as employees got used to their enlarged jobs they found them less interesting and stopped paying attention to all the details. Hence, although job enlargement may help improve job performance, its effects may be short-lived. It appears that the problem with enlarging jobs is that after a while people get bored with them, and they need to be enlarged still further. Because it is impractical to continue enlarging jobs all the time, the value of this approach is rather limited.

Job Enrichment: Increasing Required Skills and Responsibilities

As an alternative, consider another approach taken to redesigning jobs. For many years, Procter & Gamble manufactured detergent by having large numbers of people perform a series of narrow tasks. Then, realizing that this rigid approach did little to utilize the full range of skills and abilities of employees, a P&G executive introduced a new way to make detergent in one of the company's plants. The technicians worked together in teams (see Chapter 9) to take control over large parts of the production process. They set production schedules, hired new coworkers, and took responsibility for evaluating each others' performance, including the process of deciding who was going to get raises. In short, they not only performed a wider variety of tasks, but ones requiring higher levels of skill and responsibility. This approach is referred to as **job enrichment**. Enriched jobs are said to be changed *vertically* because people's level of responsibility goes up. For a summary comparison between job enrichment and job enlargement, see Figure 6.7.

Overall, job enrichment programs have been successful in the organizations that have introduced them.[43] However, two key factors limit their popularity. First, there is the difficulty of implementation. Redesigning existing facilities so that jobs can be enriched is often prohibitively expensive. Besides, the technology needed to perform certain jobs makes it impractical for them to be redesigned. A second impediment is the lack of universal employee acceptance. Although many relish them, enriched jobs are not for everyone. A sizable number of people do *not* desire the additional responsibility associated with performing enriched jobs.

The Job Characteristics Model

This discussion thus far has neglected an important question—namely, how do you go about enriching a job? What elements of a job need to be enriched for it to be effective? An attempt to expand the idea of job enrichment, known as the **job characteristics model**, provides an answer to these important questions.[44]

BASIC ELEMENTS OF THE JOB CHARACTERISTICS MODEL This approach assumes that jobs can be designed to help people get enjoyment out of their jobs and care about the work they do. The model identifies how jobs can be designed to help people feel that they are doing meaningful and valuable work. In particular, it specifies that enriching certain elements of jobs alter people's psychological states in a manner that enhances their work effectiveness. Specifically, the job characteristics model identifies *core job dimensions* that help create three *critical psychological states*, leading, in turn, to several beneficial *personal and work outcomes* (see Figure 6.8 on p. 193).

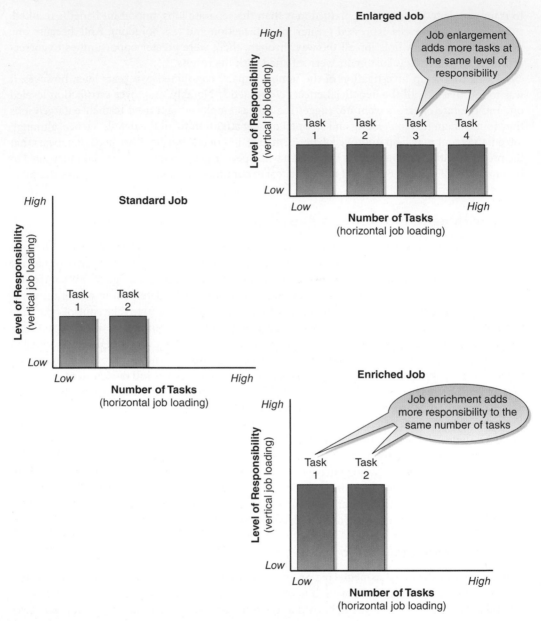

FIGURE 6.7 Job Enlargement and Job Enrichment: A Comparison
Redesigning jobs by increasing the number of tasks performed at the same level (*horizontal job loading*) is referred to as *job enlargement*. Redesigning jobs by increasing the employees' level of responsibility and control (*vertical job loading*) is referred to as *job enrichment*.

The five core job dimensions specified by the job characteristics model are as follows:

- **Skill variety**—the extent to which a job requires using several different skills and talents that an employee has. For example, a restaurant manager with high skill variety will perform many different tasks (e.g., maintaining sales records, handling customer complaints, scheduling staff, supervising repair work, and the like).

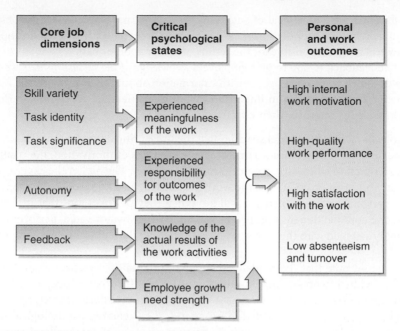

FIGURE 6.8 The Job Characteristics Model: Basic Components
The *job characteristics model* stipulates that certain *core job dimensions* lead to certain *critical psychological states*, which in turn lead to several beneficial *personal and work outcomes*. The model also recognizes that these relationships are strongest among individuals with high levels of *growth need strength*.
Source: Based on suggestions by Hackman & Oldham, 1980; see Note 44.

- **Task identity**– the degree to which a job requires doing a whole task from beginning to end. For example, tailors will have high task identity if they do everything associated with making an entire suit (e.g., measuring the client, selecting the fabric, cutting and sewing it, and altering it to fit).
- **Task significance**—the degree of impact a job is believed to have on others. For example, medical researchers working on a cure for a deadly disease surely recognize the importance of their work to the world at large. Even more modest contributions to the company can be recognized as being significant to the extent that employees understand the role of their jobs in the overall mission of the organization.
- **Autonomy**—the extent to which employees have the freedom and discretion to plan, schedule, and carry out their jobs as desired. For example, a team of Procter & Gamble employees was put in charge of making all the arrangements necessary for the building of a new $5 million facility for making concentrated Downy.
- **Feedback** – the extent to which the job allows people to have information about the effectiveness of their performance. For example, telemarketing representatives regularly receive information about how many calls they make per day and the monetary values of the sales made.

The job characteristics model specifies that these job dimensions have important effects on various critical psychological states as follows:

- Skill variety, task identity, and task significance jointly contribute to a task's *experienced meaningfulness*. A task is considered to be meaningful to the degree that it is experienced as being highly important, valuable, and worthwhile.

- Jobs that provide a great deal of autonomy are said to make people feel *personally responsible and accountable for their work*. When they are free to decide what to do and how to do it, they feel more responsible for the results, whether good or bad.
- Effective feedback is said to give employees *knowledge of the results of their work*. When a job is designed to provide people with information about the effects of their actions, they are better able to develop an understanding of how effectively they have performed and such knowledge improves their effectiveness.

The job characteristics model specifies that the three critical psychological states affect various personal and work outcomes—namely, people's feelings of motivation, the quality of work performed, satisfaction with work, absenteeism, and turnover. The higher the experienced meaningfulness of work, responsibility for the work performed, and knowledge of results, the more positive the personal and work benefits will be. When they perform jobs that incorporate high levels of the five core job dimensions, people should feel highly motivated, perform high-quality work, be highly satisfied with their jobs, be absent infrequently, and unlikely to resign from their jobs.

I also should note that the model is theorized to be especially effective in describing the behavior of individuals who are high in **growth need strength**—that is, people who have a high need for personal growth and development. People not particularly interested in improving themselves on the job are not expected to experience the theorized psychological reactions to the core job dimensions, nor consequently, to enjoy the beneficial personal and work outcomes predicted by the model. By introducing this variable, the job characteristics model recognizes the important limitation of job enrichment noted earlier—not everyone wants and benefits from enriched jobs.

ASSESSING THE MOTIVATING POTENTIAL OF JOBS   Based on the proposed relationship between the core job dimensions and their associated psychological reactions, the model claims that job motivation will be highest when the jobs performed rate high on the various dimensions. To assess this, a questionnaire known as the *Job Diagnostic Survey (JDS)* has been developed to measure the degree to which various job characteristics are present in a particular job. Based on responses to the JDS, we can make predictions about the degree to which a job motivates people who perform it.

The job characteristics model has been the focus of many empirical tests, most of which are supportive of many aspects of the model. One study conducted among a group of South African clerical workers found particularly strong support.[45] The jobs of employees in some of the offices in this company were enriched in accordance with techniques specified by the job characteristics model. Specifically, employees performing the enriched jobs were given opportunities to choose the kinds of tasks they perform (high skill variety), do the entire job (high task identity), receive instructions regarding how their job fit into the organization as a whole (high task significance), freely set their own schedules and inspect their own work (high autonomy), and keep records of their daily productivity (high feedback). Another group of employees, equivalent in all respects except that their jobs were not enriched, served as a control group.

After employees performed the newly designed jobs for six months, comparisons were made between them and their counterparts in the control group. With respect to most of the outcomes specified by the model, individuals performing redesigned jobs showed superior results. Specifically, they reported feeling more internally motivated and more satisfied with their jobs. There were also lower rates of absenteeism and turnover among employees performing the enriched jobs. The only outcome predicted by the model that was not found to differ was actual work performance; people performed equally well in enriched and unenriched jobs. Considering the many factors that are responsible for job performance (as discussed in connection with expectancy theory), this finding should not be too surprising.

SUGGESTIONS FOR ENHANCING THE MOTIVATING POTENTIAL OF JOBS The job characteristics model specifies several ways in which jobs can be designed to enhance their motivating potential. For example, instead of using several workers, each of whom performs a separate part of a whole job, it would be better to have each person perform the entire job. Doing so helps provide greater skill variety and task identity. For example, Corning Glass Works in Medford, Massachusetts, redesigned jobs so that people who assembled laboratory hot plates put together entire units instead of contributing a single part to the assembly process.

The job characteristics model also suggests that jobs should be set up so that the person performing a service (such as an auto mechanic) comes into contact with the recipient of the service (such as the car owner). Jobs designed in this manner will not only help the employee by providing feedback but also by enhancing skill variety (e.g., talking to customers in addition to fixing cars) and building autonomy (by giving people the freedom to manage their own relationships with clients). This suggestion has been implemented at Sea-Land Service, the large containerized ocean-shipping company. After this company's mechanics, clerks, and crane operators started meeting with customers, they became much more productive. Having faces to associate with the once abstract jobs they did clearly helped them take the jobs more seriously.

Another implication of the job characteristics model is that jobs should be designed to give employees as much feedback as possible. The more people know how well they're doing (be it from customers, supervisors, or coworkers), the better equipped they are to take appropriate corrective action (recall the discussion in Chapter 3 about the importance of feedback). It is with this in mind that many companies these days solicit customer feedback in questionnaires. We often see this, for example, among hospitals (which assess satisfaction among patients after being discharged), auto dealerships (which assess satisfaction with the sales and service experiences), and moving companies (which assess customers' satisfaction with the people who have packed household goods, loaded them onto vans, and driven trucks to new locations).

Back to the Case

Answer the following questions based on this chapter's Making the Case (p. 171) to illustrate insights you have derived from the material in this chapter.

1. What seem to be the strongest motivators of Costco employees? Which factors listed in Table 6.1 (p. 174) appear to be involved?
2. Which particular theory of motivation appears to best explain the high motivational level of Costco employees? What is your reason for this?
3. What else could be done to motivate Costco employees? What do you believe to be the limitations of this approach?

You Be the Consultant

Boosting Low Morale Among Employees

Suppose that you were just hired by executives of a large manufacturing company to help resolve problems of poor morale that have been plaguing the workforce. Turnover and absenteeism are high, and performance is at an all-time low. Answer the following questions relevant to this situation based on the material in this chapter.

1. Suppose, after interviewing the workers, you found that they believed that no one cared how well they were doing. What theories could help explain this problem? Applying these approaches, what would you recommend the company do to resolve this situation?

2. Company officials tell you that the employees are well paid, adding to their surprise about the low morale. However, your interviews reveal that the employees themselves feel otherwise. Theoretically, why is this a problem? What could be done to help?

3. "I'm bored with my job," an employee tells you, and you believe he speaks for many within the company. What could be done to make the jobs more interesting to those who perform them? What are the limitations of your plan? Would it work equally well for all employees?

Self-Assessment Exercise

WHAT REWARDS DO YOU VALUE?

According to expectancy theory, one thing companies can do to motivate employees is to give rewards that have positive valence to them. What work-related rewards have the greatest value to you? Completing this questionnaire will help you answer this question.

Directions

Following are 10 work-related rewards. For each, circle the number that best describes the value that particular reward has for you personally. Use the following scale to express your feelings: 1 = no value at all, 2 = slight value, 3 = moderate value, 4 = great value, 5 = extremely great value.

Scale

Reward	Personal Value				
Good pay	1	2	3	4	5
Prestigious title	1	2	3	4	5
Vacation time	1	2	3	4	5
Job security	1	2	3	4	5
Recognition	1	2	3	4	5
Interesting work	1	2	3	4	5
Pleasant conditions	1	2	3	4	5
Chances to advance	1	2	3	4	5
Flexible schedule	1	2	3	4	5
Friendly coworkers	1	2	3	4	5

Discussion Questions

1. Based on your answers, which rewards do you value most? Which do you value least? Do you think these preferences will change as you get older and perform different jobs? If so, how?
2. To what extent do you believe that you will be able to attain each of these rewards on your job? Do you expect that the chances of receiving these rewards will improve in the future? Why or why not?
3. Do you believe that the rewards you value most are also the ones valued by other people? Are these reward preferences likely to be the same for all people everywhere or at least for all workers performing the same job in the same company?

Group Exercise

DEMONSTRATING THE EFFECTIVENESS OF GOAL SETTING

The tendency for specific, difficult goals to enhance task performance is well established. The following exercise is designed to help you demonstrate this effect yourself. All you need is a class of students willing to participate and a few simple supplies.

Directions

1. Select a page of text from a book and make several photocopies. Then carefully count the words and number each word on one of the copies. This will be your score sheet.
2. Find another class of 30 or more students who don't know anything about goal setting. (We don't want their knowledge of the phenomenon to bias the results.) On a random basis, divide the students into three equal-size groups.
3. Ask the students in the first group (the "baseline" group) to copy as much of the text as they can onto another piece of paper, giving them exactly one minute to do so. Direct them to work at a fast pace. Using the score sheet created in step 1, identify the highest number of words counted by any one of the students. Then multiply this number by 2. This will be the specific, difficult goal level.
4. Ask the students in another group (the "specific goal" group) to copy the text on the same printed page for exactly one minute. Tell them to try to reach the specific goal number identified in step 3.
5. Repeat this process with the third group (the "do your best" group), but instead of giving them a specific goal, direct them to "try to do your best at this task."
6. Compute the average number of words copied in the "difficult goal" group and the "do your best" group. Have your instructor compute the appropriate statistical test (a t-test, in this case) to determine the statistical significance of the difference between the performance levels of the groups.

Discussion Questions

1. Was there, in fact, a statistically significant difference between the performance levels of the two groups? If so, did students in the "specific goal" group outperform those in the "do your best" group, as expected? What does this reveal about the effectiveness of goal setting?
2. If the predicted findings were not supported, why do you suppose this happened? What was it about the procedure that may have led to this failure? Was the specific goal (twice the fastest speed in the "baseline" group) too high, making the goal unreachable? Or was it too low, making the specific goal too easy?
3. What do you think would happen if the goal were lowered, making it easier, or raised, making it more difficult?

Notes

MAKING THE CASE NOTES

Costco Wholesale. (2012). Investor relations: Company profile. http://phx.corporate-ir.net/phoenix.zhtml?c=83830&p=irol-homeprofile. Costco Wholesale. (2012). Member relations. http://phx.corporate-ir.net/phoenix.zhtml?c=83830&p=irol-homeprofile. Costco Wholesale. (2008). Wikinvest. http://www.wikinvest.com/stock/.Costco_Wholesale_(COST). Yukl, G., & Lepsinger, R. (2005). Why integrating the leading and managing roles is essential for organizational effectiveness. *Organizational Dynamics*, 34(4), 361–375. Holmes, S., & Zellner, W. (2004, April 12). The Costco way: Higher wages mean higher profits; but try telling Wall Street. *BusinessWeek*, pp. 76–77. Kiel, F. (2008, October 6). Flaws in the selfish-worker theory. *BusinessWeek*, p. 78. Greenhouse, S. (2005, July 17). How Costco became the anti Walmart. *New York Times*. http://www.nytimes.com/2005/07/17/business/yourmoney/17costco.html.

CHAPTER NOTES

1. Latham, G. P. (2012). *Work motivation: History, theory, research, and practice* (2nd ed.). Thousand Oaks, CA: Sage. Pinder, C. C. (2008). *Work motivation in organizational behavior* (2nd ed.). New York: Psychology Press.
2. Mitchell, T. R., & Daniels, D. (2003). Motivation. In W. C. Borman, D. R. Ilgen, & R. J. Klimoski (Eds.), *Handbook of psychology, Vol. 12: Industrial and organizational psychology* (pp. 215–254). New York: Wiley.
3. Robson, C. (2004). What motivates workers today? London: Hays Office Support. http://www.hays.com/uk/index.jsp?Channel=office&Content=/uk/jobseekers/office/what-motivates-office-workers-today.htm.
4. Gallinsky, E., Carter, N., Bond, J. T., & Bloom, H. (2009). *Leaders in a global economy: Finding the fit for top talent*. New York: Families and Work Institute.
5. Kanfer, R., & Heggestad, E. D. (1997). Motivational traits and skills: A person-centered approach to work motivation. In L. L. Cummings & B. M. Staw (Eds.), *Research in organizational behavior* (Vol. 19, pp. 1–56). Greenwich, CT: JAI Press.
6. Kanfer, R., Wanberg, C. R., & Kantrowitz, T. M. (2001). Job search and employment: A personality-motivational analysis and meta-analytic review. *Journal of Applied Psychology, 86,* 837–855.
7. Cline, M. (2001, September). Cut agent turnover by hiring for motivational fit. *Call Center Management Review,* pp. 2–3.
8. Kanfer, R., & Ackerman, P. L. (2000). Individual differences in work motivation: Further explorations of a trait framework. *Applied Psychology: An International Review, 40,* 479–486.
9. See Note 8.
10. Latham, G. P. (2009). Motivate employee performance through goal setting. In E. A. Locke (Ed.), *Handbook of principles of organizational behavior* (pp. 161–178). Chichester, UK: Wiley. Locke, E. A. (2004). Goal-setting theory and its applications to the world of business. *Academy of Management Executive, 18,* 124–125. Miner, J. B. (2003). The rated importance, scientific validity, and practical usefulness of organizational behavior theories. *Academy of Management Executive, 2,* 250–268.
11. Locke, E. A., & Latham, G. P. (1990). *A theory of goal setting and task performance.* Englewood Cliffs, NJ: Prentice Hall.
12. Mento, A. J., Locke, E. A., & Klein, H. J. (1992). Relationship of goal level to valence and instrumentality. *Journal of Applied Psychology, 77,* 395–406.
13. Latham, G. P. (2004). The motivational benefits of goal-setting. *Academy of Management Executive, 18,* 126–129.
14. Gellatly, I. R., & Meyer, J. P. (1992). The effects of goal difficulty on physiological arousal, cognition, and task performance. *Journal of Applied Psychology, 77,* 696–704.
15. Latham, G. P., & Seijts, G. H. (1999). The effects of proximal and distal goals on performance on a moderately complex task. *Journal of Organizational Behavior, 20,* 421–429.
16. Latham, G., & Baldes, J. (1975). The practical significance of Locke's theory of goal setting. *Journal of Applied Psychology, 60,* 122–124.

17. See Note 16.

18. Wright, P. M., Hollenbeck, J. R., Wolf, S., & McMahan, G. C. (1995). The effects of varying goal difficulty operationalizations on goal setting outcomes and processes. *Organizational Behavior and Human Decision Processes, 61,* 28–43.

19. Bernstein, A. (1991, April 29). How to motivate workers: Don't watch 'em. *BusinessWeek,* p. 56.

20. Kerr, S., & Landauer, S. (2004). Using stretch goals to promote organizational effectiveness and personal growth: General Electric and Goldman Sachs. *Academy of Management Executive, 18,* 134–138.

21. Goldman Sachs Group. (2010). Global investment research: Who we look for. http://www2.goldmansachs.com/careers/our-firm/divisions/gir/who-we-look-for/index.html

22. Latham, G. P., Erez, M., & Locke, E. A. (1988). Resolving scientific disputes by the joint design of crucial experiments by the antagonists: Application to the Erez-Latham dispute regarding participation in goal setting. *Journal of Applied Psychology, 73,* 753–772.

23. Langley, M. (2003, June 9). Big companies get low marks for lavish executive pay. *Wall Street Journal,* p. C1.

24. Colquitt, J. A., & Greenberg, J. (2003). Organizational justice: A fair assessment of the state of the literature. In J. Greenberg (Ed.), *Organizational behavior: The state of the science* (2nd ed., pp. 165–210). Mahwah, NJ: Erlbaum. Adams, J. S. (1965). Inequity in social exchange. In L. Berkowitz (Ed.), *Advances in experimental social psychology* (Vol. 2, pp. 267–299). New York: Academic Press.

25. Harder, J. W. (1992). Play for pay: Effects of inequity in a pay-for-performance context. *Administrative Science Quarterly, 37,* 321–335.

26. Greenberg, J. (2010). Organizational injustice as an occupational health risk. In J. P. Walsh & A. P. Brief (Eds.), *Academy of management annals* (Vol. 4, pp. 205–243). Oxford, England: Routledge.

27. Romer, J. (1984). *Ancient lives: The story of the Pharaoh's tomb-makers.* London: Phoenix Press.

28. Dubofsky, M. (2000). *We shall be all: A history of the industrial workers of the world.* Champaign, IL: University of Illinois Press.

29. Greenberg, J. (1993). Stealing in the name of justice: Informational and interpersonal moderators of theft reactions to underpayment inequity. *Organizational Behavior and Human Decision Processes, 54,* 81–103.

30. Jones, D. A., & Skarlicki, D. P. (2003). The relationship between perceptions of fairness and voluntary turnover among retail employees. *Journal of Applied Social Psychology, 33,* 1226–1243.

31. Mowday, R. T., & Colwell, K. A. (2003). Employee reactions to unfair outcomes in the workplace: The contributions of Adams's equity theory to understanding work motivation. In L. W. Porter, G. A. Bigley, & R. M. Steers (Eds.), *Motivation and work behavior* (7th ed., pp. 65–82). Burr Ridge, IL: McGraw-Hill/Irwin.

32. Colquitt, J. A., Greenberg, J., & Zapata-Phelan, C. P. (2005). What is organizational justice? A historical overview. In J. Greenberg & J. A. Colquitt (Eds.), *Handbook of organizational justice* (pp. 3–55). Mahwah, NJ: Erlbaum.

33. Hodge, W. A., (2003). *The role of performance pay systems in comprehensive school reform.* Lanham, MD: University Press of America. Lawler, E. E., III. (1967). Secrecy about management compensation: Are there hidden costs? *Organizational Behavior and Human Performance, 2,* 182–189.

34. Lewicki, R. J., Wiethoff, C., & Tomlinson, E. C. (2005). What is the role of trust in organizational justice? In J. Greenberg & J. A. Colquitt (Eds.), *Handbook of organizational justice* (pp. 222–257). Mahwah, NJ: Erlbaum.

35. Porter, L. W., & Lawler, E. E., III. (1968). *Managerial attitudes and performance.* Homewood, IL: Irwin.

36. Hall, C. S., & Lindzey, G. (1966). *Theories of personality.* New York: Wiley.

37. Deci, E. L., Ryan, R. M., Gagné, M., Leone, D. R., Usunov, J., & Kornazheva, B. P. (2001). Need satisfaction, motivation, and well-being in the work organizations of a former Eastern Bloc country. *Personality and Social Psychology Bulletin, 27,* 930–942. Maslow, A. (1998). *Maslow on management.* New York: Wiley.

38. Heine, S. J., Lehman, D. R., Markus, H. R., & Kitayama, S. (1999). Is there a universal need for positive self-regard? *Psychological Review, 106,* 766–794.

39. Rodric, S. (2001). *The stock options book.* Oakland, CA: National Center for Employee Ownership.

40. Morgenson, F. P., & Campion, M. A. (2003). Work design. In W. C. Borman, D. R. Ilgen, & R. J. Klimoski (Eds.), *Handbook of psychology, Vol. 12: Industrial and organizational psychology* (pp. 423–452). New York: John Wiley & Sons.

41. Campion, M. A., & McClelland, C. L. (1991). Interdisciplinary examination of the costs and benefits of enlarged jobs: A job design quasi-experiment. *Journal of Applied Psychology, 76,* 186–198.

42. Campion, M. A., & McClelland, C. L. (1993). Follow-up and extension of the interdisciplinary costs and benefits of enlarged jobs. *Journal of Applied Psychology, 78,* 339–351.

43. Mohr, R. D., & Zoghi, C. (2006, January). *Is job enrichment really enriching.* Bureau of Labor Statistics working paper 389. http://www.bls.gov/osmr/pdf/ec060010.pdf

44. Hackman, J. R., & Oldham, G. R. (1980). *Work redesign.* Reading, MA: Addison-Wesley.

45. Orpen, C. (1979). The effects of job enrichment on employee satisfaction, motivation, involvement, and performance: A field experiment. *Human Relations, 32,* 189–217.

PART III

GROUP BEHAVIOR

7

INTERPERSONAL BEHAVIOR IN THE WORKPLACE: CONFLICT, COOPERATION, TRUST, AND DEVIANCE

LEARNING OBJECTIVES

After reading this chapter, you will be able to:

1. **DESCRIBE** two types of psychological contracts that develop in working relationships.
2. **DISTINGUISH** between various forms of trust that are likely to exist in the workplace.
3. **DESCRIBE** organizational citizenship behavior and ways in which it may be promoted.
4. **DISTINGUISH** between cooperation and competition as they occur in work organizations.
5. **DESCRIBE** the causes and effects of conflict in organizations.
6. **DISTINGUISH** between constructive and destructive types of workplace deviance and **DESCRIBE** various forms of each.

THREE GOOD REASONS you should care about. . .

Interpersonal Behavior in the Workplace

1. Cooperation between people can make life on the job not only more pleasant but more productive as well.
2. If managed properly, potentially harmful effects of conflict in the workplace can be avoided.
3. Managers can take several effective steps to reduce the likelihood of deviant organizational behavior, thereby avoiding its high costs.

Making the Case for...

Interpersonal Behavior in the Workplace

NASCAR: The Etiquette of Drafting

To the uninitiated, there's really not much to it. A commentator once described a NASCAR race as simply a matter of "go straight, turn left, go straight, turn left," round and round again. Do this faster than anyone else 200 times and you've won NASCAR's biggest, richest, and most prestigious race, the Daytona 500, pocketing about $1.5 million for your troubles. Ask Matt Kenseth, Daytona's 2012 winner or any of NASCAR's 75 million fans who are in the know, however, and they'll tell you that there's far more to the sport of racing high performance stock cars than meets the untrained eye.

A great car, a talented crew, and drivers with nerves of steel can be taken for granted as keys to success, but to win races, drivers also must know "how to compete by cooperating." And this, in a word, requires "drafting," the practice of following closely behind the car ahead of you so as to get sucked into its vacuum. Due to aerodynamics, this boosts the speed of both cars—not much, but enough to make all the difference in a long race such as the annual 500-mile events at Daytona and Talladega. The more cars in a drafting line—at any given time, these typically range from a pair of cars to about 10—the more each benefits.

Knowing that if they don't draft, they lose, the best NASCAR drivers are adept at working multicar draft lines and out-competing the others by out-cooperating them. Suppose a driver wants to pull ahead by swinging out of the pack, for example. He or she can do so, but unless another car pulls up behind, the absence of a draft will cause the driver's car to lose momentum and fall back several places. In the new draft line, both drivers benefit, but because each wants to win, these partnerships are fleeting. One moment, a driver may seek a nearby drafting partner to help move ahead, but inevitably, and just as quickly, he or she will defect in search of another. These ephemeral partnerships between rivals at 190 mph may last a few seconds or a few laps, but they are essential.

Winning drivers know when to join draft lines (or to invite others to join theirs) and when to defect. This interplay between cooperating and competing requires trusting other drivers to know and abide by the unspoken rules of the game. For this reason, veteran racers are wary of having rookies as draft partners until they have earned the confidence of the other drivers on the track. Trust also is an issue for allies—members of the same racing team. Confident that cooperation will be forthcoming, other cars from the driver's racing team are inclined to be multi-lap draft partners. Still, because drivers seek individual glory, even members of their own teams become rivals when the end of the race is near and the driver of the second-place car wants to "slingshot" ahead of the lead car to cross the finish line at the last second.

As you might imagine, having drafting partners enter a line requires close communication. Drivers sometimes have pre-race arrangements to cooperate with one another, but most drafting partnerships emerge on the fly. To broker these deals, drivers may use hand gestures, but these might be difficult to see and, of course, removing one's hands from the steering wheel for even a second can spell disaster. Instead, most deals are made by drivers communicating by radio with spotters, diplomatic envoys in the stands who negotiate drafting deals with the spotters of other drivers. These partnerships may last only the ten seconds required to pull ahead of another rival, but of course, the helping driver is expected to return the favor later in the race if needed. After all, on the racetrack, as in other things in life, "one hand washes the other."

Although you might be unaware of these dynamics as you watch a NASCAR race, they are potent illustrations that it involves far more than just driving around in circles. Being a winning NASCAR driver also requires good interpersonal relationships with other drivers. As one expert put it, "A driver's reputation as a trustworthy person may affect the outcome as much as his reputation as a driver."[1] Of course, the same could be said of people in many other lines of work, including ones that are less glamorous and far safer. Indeed, the themes highlighted here—trust, negotiation, cooperation, and competition—play prominent roles in just about any line of work. These processes of working with others and against them, broadly referred to as **interpersonal behavior**, are the focus of this chapter. Specifically, I will summarize an array of interpersonal behaviors that occur in the workplace, describing how they influence the way people work and their feelings about their jobs and organizations.

Figure 7.1 identifies the major forms of interpersonal behavior in the workplace that I will be discussing in this chapter. This diagram organizes interpersonal behaviors along a continuum, ranging from those that involve working with others (shown on the left) to those that involve working against others (shown on the right). This forms a useful road map for how I will proceed. Beginning on the left, I will first examine **prosocial behavior**—the tendency for people to help others on the job, sometimes even when there doesn't appear to be anything in it for them. Following this, I will discuss situations in which people help each other and receive help from them—that is, the tendency to *cooperate*. In NASCAR races and elsewhere in the world of business, as you know, people and entire companies don't always work with each other; they also *compete* against each other—that is, as one tries to win, it forces the other to lose. Under such circumstances, it is not unusual for *conflict* to emerge, breeding ill-will. And, when taken to the extreme, this results in *deviant* behavior—acts intended to bring harm, such as stealing from the company or even harming another person.

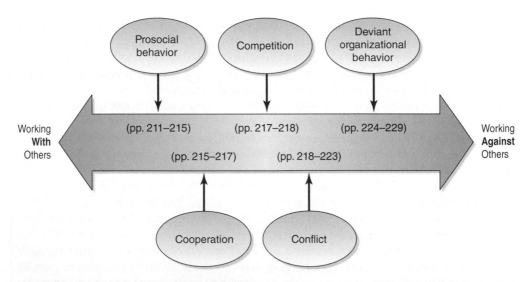

FIGURE 7.1 **Varieties of Interpersonal Behavior**
The five types of interpersonal behavior observed in organizations, and presented in this chapter, can be summarized as falling along a continuum ranging from those involving working with other people to those involving working against them.

Before examining these various forms of behavior, though, I consider two processes that play a role in all interpersonal relationships: developing *psychological contracts* and building *trust*. These processes are important because they often affect the extent to which people choose either to work with or against one another.

PSYCHOLOGICAL CONTRACTS: OUR EXPECTATIONS OF OTHERS

When people enter into relationships with each other, they quickly develop expectations about what these relationships will be like—what each side is expected to do. For instance, if you send a text message to a colleague asking a question, you expect that person to answer. If you report for work on a regular basis and do your job, you expect to be compensated at the end of the pay period. These examples illustrate what is known as the **psychological contract**—a person's perceptions and expectations about the mutual obligations in an employment relationship (or, for that matter, any other relationship).[2]

Although psychological contracts generally are not recorded formally on paper, they guide what we expect of others much as if they were. However, unlike legal contracts, in which the terms are made explicit, psychological contracts exist primarily in the beliefs and perceptions of the persons involved. Not surprisingly, there may well be differences of opinion regarding psychological contracts: What one person expects may not be exactly what another expects. As you know from experience, such disagreements often can lead to interpersonal friction.

Types of Psychological Contracts

Although psychological contracts can vary in many ways and are, in a sense, unique to each working relationship, most can be described in terms of two basic dimensions.[3]

- *Time frame*—how long the relationship is expected to last. These range from short term (as in temporary employees) to long term (as in the lifetime employment traditionally expected by employees of large Japanese companies).
- *Performance requirements*—how close the relationship is between performance demands (i.e., what employees are expected to do) and the rewards they receive.[4] These range, at one extreme, from jobs in which pay is related directly to output, to others in which the relationship is not defined purely in economic terms (e.g., employees expect emotional and social support from their companies as well as pay).

Together, these two dimensions point to the existence of three basic kinds of psychological contracts: *transactional, relational,* and *balanced*.[5] I summarize these in Figure 7.2.

TRANSACTIONAL CONTRACTS   Parties whose relationships are exclusively economic in nature and of relatively brief duration are said to have **transactional contracts**. Suppose, for example, that you are a student working at a summer job. You have been hired to take over for regular employees while they are on vacation. You know that your relationship with your employer is short term and that it is based on a clearly defined set of economic terms. You go to work each day as scheduled, you do your job, you get your paycheck, and at the end of the season, it's over—and you go back to school.[6]

RELATIONAL CONTRACTS   By contrast, **relational contracts** are informal expectations between individuals whose relationships are close and personal in nature. They are not tied to specific pay or other rewards and generally are longer term in nature. For example, if you have worked in the

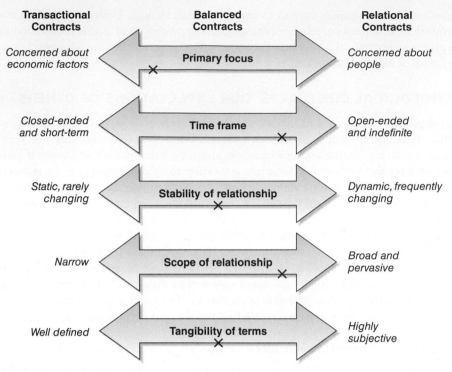

FIGURE 7.2 Three Forms of Psychological Contracts: A Summary
Psychological contracts may be considered either transactional, relational or balanced. The key characteristics of transactional and relational contracts are shown at opposite ends of the same continuum. Balanced contracts, however, combine various aspects of each, typically at the point indicated by "X" along each dimension.
Source: Based on suggestions by Dobos & Rousseau, 2004; see Note 2.

same company for the same boss for more than a decade, chances are good that your relationship is based not simply on an exchange of specific benefits and contributions that are largely economic in nature; rather, other factors, such as friendship, loyalty, and years of shared experiences matter, too. You expect that relationship to last well into the future, and you feel a sense of commitment to your boss, your job, and your company that no temporary employees, working under transactional psychological contracts, can share. It is precisely because of these feelings that employees tend to feel betrayed when their long-term employers find it necessary to lay off such, often highly paid, individuals.

BALANCED CONTRACTS   A third type of psychological contract combines the open-ended, long-term features of relational psychological contracts with the well-specified reward-performance contingencies of transactional contracts. Such **balanced contracts**, as they are known, are informal expectations between people that result in each side receiving some benefit from the other.[7] As an example, consider an individual who wants to start her own company. She may spend several years working in a large organization because this helps her develop the skills and contacts needed for founding a new venture. She is committed to staying in this company until she acquires these skills and contacts (perhaps for several years), and forms close relationships with the people who are helping her toward her goal. Clearly, then, she is exchanging her time, effort, and talent for pay and these other, less tangible benefits. The term "balanced contracts" reflects the fact that each side receives benefits from the arrangement between them. It is with this in mind that balanced relationships are depicted as falling between the two extremes shown in Figure 7.2.

Effects of Psychological Contracts

As you might expect, the three different kinds of psychological contracts have contrasting effects both for individuals and organizations. For instance, relational and balanced contracts encourage individuals to go beyond the basic requirements of their jobs, helping others or their companies on a voluntary basis (I will describe this kind of behavior, known as *organizational citizenship behavior,* in the section beginning on p. 211).[8]

Similarly, individuals with certain personal characteristics are inclined to form relational contracts, while people with other characteristics tend to form transactional ones. Specifically, people who are low in emotional stability (see Chapters 3 and 4) and who also are highly sensitive to being treated fairly (see Chapter 2) are inclined to form transactional contracts. However, people who are inclined to form long-term relational contracts possess different characteristics: they tend to have high degrees of conscientiousness and self-esteem (see Chapter 3).[9]

Can you see why? People who are low in emotional stability do not like long-term commitments, ones that demand high levels of social skills and trust.[10] On the other hand, individuals who are high in conscientiousness and self-esteem are more inclined to be concerned with doing a good job and with opportunities for growth and achievement than with purely economic benefits, especially short term ones. As a result, they tend to prefer—and to develop—relational contracts.

In sum, although psychological contracts aren't written on paper, they play important roles in many aspects of organizational behavior, including the ways in which different types of individuals work with or against each other—the main theme of this chapter.

TRUST IN WORKING RELATIONSHIPS

One thing that makes relationships based on transactional contracts so different from those based on relational contracts is the degree to which the parties *trust* one another. By **trust**, I am referring to the degree to which one person (a trustor) is willing to make himself or herself vulnerable to another (a trustee) based on the trustor's positive expectations about the trustee. In other words, trust reflects one person's degree of confidence in the words and actions of another.[11]

Suppose, for example, that your supervisor, the local sales manager of a retail store, will be talking to his boss, the district sales manager, about getting you transferred to a new location that you find more desirable. You are counting on your boss to come through for you because he says he will. To the extent that you believe that he will do what he promises—that is, make a strong case on your behalf—you trust him. However, if you believe that his recommendation will not be too enthusiastic or that he will not recommend you at all, you will trust him much less.

As you might expect, the concept of trust is more complex than suggested by this example. In fact, there are three distinct kinds of trust (for an overview, see Figure 7.3).

Calculus-Based Trust

One kind of trust, known as **calculus-based trust**, is based on the use of threats and deterrents.[12] Calculus-based trust exists whenever people believe that another person will behave as promised

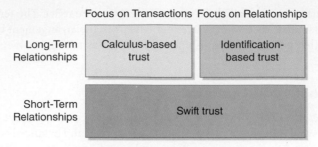

FIGURE 7.3 Three Major Forms of Trust: A Comparison
Different types of trust can be categorized with respect to whether their focus is on transactional or interpersonal factors and whether they exist in long-term or short-term relationships. Specifically, *calculus-based trust* exists in long-term relationships that focus on transactional considerations, whereas *identification-based trust* exists in long-term relationships that focus on interpersonal considerations. A third type of trust, *swift trust*, incorporates both transactional and interpersonal considerations but occurs only in short-term relationships (e.g., virtual teams).

out of fear of getting punished for doing otherwise. We trust our employers to contribute their shares to our Social Security accounts because they risk fines and penalties if they fail to do so. Similarly, if your company hires a catering firm to provide the food for an important social function, you trust this business to show up with the items you have ordered. If the caterer fails to do so, you won't pay for the food and you're likely to warn others not to hire that firm.

Calculus-based trust is characteristic of many business relationships—ones based on transactional contracts, in which each side knows what it is expected to deliver. Although calculus-based trust may not sound like the kind you would like others to have in you, it is essential for most businesses. It is the basis for a good reputation, and that, as everyone knows, often is the foundation for success. Various deterrents for the trustor help ensure the trustee that he or she is safe from exploitation. If you find yourself saying about a person, Y, "If Y messes with me, X will give it to him," then X provides your insurance policy, of sorts, that Y will not harm you. Such relationships are ones in which calculus-based trust is involved.

Identification-Based Trust

A very different kind of trust, and one that is grounded less in deterrents and more in the power of personal relations, is known as **identification-based trust**. This kind of trust is based on accepting and understanding another person's wants and desires. Identification-based trust occurs when people know and understand one another so well that they are willing to allow that individual to act on their behalf. The example described earlier, in which you allow your boss to discuss your transfer with a higher-ranking official, illustrates identification-based trust.

What is the foundation on which identification-based trust is based? In other words, what elements of a relationship between trustor and trustee must be established for the trustor to trust the trustee? Research has established that the most important factors are as follows:[13]

- *Familiarity*—The trustor knows something about the trustee based on having had a relationship in the past.
- *Shared experience*—Having spent time together, the trustor and the trustee have experienced many of the same things (i.e., they have a history with one another).

- *Reciprocal disclosure*—The trustor and the trustee have shared information about one another, which breeds closer interpersonal relationships between them. The parties come to trust one another as a result.
- *Fulfilled promises*—The trustee has already shown the trustor that he or she will do what was promised; there is a history of coming through for the trustee in the past.
- *Demonstrations of nonexploitation and vulnerability*—In the past, the trustor has had opportunities to exploit the trustee but has not taken advantage of them; despite having made himself or herself vulnerable to the trustor, the trustee was not harmed.

Swift Trust

The types of trust described thus far are ones that exist in ongoing, long-term relationships. This makes sense given that some degree of history between the parties would appear to be necessary for trust to develop. Interestingly, however, trust develops even within relationships that are short-term and temporary in nature—that is, ones that have a finite lifespan, whose members have a shared purpose, and in which activities are carefully coordinated. This would describe, for example, a crew of technicians from throughout the country who gather at a remote location to record a television commercial. The unit assembles for a day or two and then disbands, never to see one another again unless a job happens to bring them together sometime in the future.

Although it would appear that conditions don't exist for trust to develop in such temporary systems, it does, in fact, occur in them. It's not just a scaled-down version of what I've described earlier but something different, known as **swift trust**.[14] This refers to trust that occurs as a set of collective perceptions develops among members of temporary groups. In fact, various features of the temporary arrangement are responsible for this trust to develop. These are as follows:

- *Outcomes are interdependent*—In the type of temporary groups I am describing, people's successes or failures depend on one another. To meet your objectives, you have to help others meet theirs. People who are put "in the same boat" eventually "sink or swim" together, so they work together. Recognizing this leads people to develop trust in one another.
- *Time constraints exist*—Because time is limited and the pace of work is exaggerated in temporary groups, trust cannot develop in its usual, more leisurely manner. With little or no slack time, people are unlikely to engage in selfish activities that would make them untrustworthy. Believing this also encourages people to trust others.
- *Group members focus on task and professional roles*—Learning what someone is like (including his or her trustworthiness) usually takes time, making the development of such attributions (see Chapter 3) unlikely in temporary groups (unless, of course, someone does something out of the ordinary right away). Because individual information isn't available, people are inclined to judge their teammates in keeping with their professional roles. By focusing on individuals as professionals who contribute to the success of the joint task, people are unlikely to have any reasons to doubt their trustworthiness. To the contrary, their high professional regard for these individuals is likely to promote a willingness to trust them.
- *A trust broker is in place*—In temporary work units, the individual who hires and fires the team members is available to ensure that everyone involved will behave appropriately and not let others down. Such an individual is considered a **trust broker** because he or she plays a central role, overseeing the connections between people to ensure that everything goes smoothly. This likely would be the producer in the case of the television commercial—the

person to whom anyone can turn should concerns arise. The existence of such an individual offers a sort of "safety net" that provides a reason to trust strangers (who otherwise would not inspire trust).

As suggested in Figure 7.3, swift trust incorporates both the transactional aspects of calculus-based trust and the interpersonal aspects of identification-based trust. What's different, of course, is the focus on short-term relationships instead of long-term ones. Given that so many teams and groups are being formed virtually, for temporary purposes (see Chapter 9), it's not surprising that there have been many opportunities to conduct research on swift trust. Indeed, several studies have supported the notion that swift trust operates in a variety of temporary groups, including ones whose members come from all around the world.[15]

Developing Trustworthiness

What factors influence the development of trust? Although many play a role, research has established that three are especially important in promoting followers' trust in their leaders.[16] Each contributes somewhat, but trustworthiness develops most strongly when all three factors are combined. These are as follows:

- *Ability*—The term **ability** refers to one's knowledge and capacity to perform various tasks. In the case of trust, it's not only important to have knowledge about how to perform a particular job, but also general managerial ability—that is, knowing how to work effectively with people (such as described throughout this book). The role of ability in trustworthiness is straightforward: People are inclined to trust leaders whose abilities they recognize. This isn't all, of course, but subordinates can hardly trust leaders who they believe cannot perform their jobs well and who are ineffective in helping them do their own work.
- *Benevolence*—Some people are more inclined than others to be considerate and to demonstrate concern and support as necessary. Individuals who are especially sensitive in this manner are said to display high degrees of **benevolence**. Not surprisingly, the more benevolent leaders have been to their followers, the more likely those followers are to trust them. After all, we certainly wouldn't be willing to trust someone who is inconsiderate, unconcerned, and unsupportive of us.
- *Integrity*—As suggested in Chapter 2, people demonstrate high degrees of integrity when they adhere to moral and ethical principles (e.g., not stealing company property) and when they behave fairly. People are disinclined to put their trust in others who have revealed themselves to be not of high moral character. Why, for example, would you even think of trusting someone who has lied consistently?

Research has shown that when people perceive their leaders as being high in ability, benevolence, and integrity, they perceive them to be especially trustworthy.[17] And when this occurs, they behave in a variety of beneficial ways. Among other things, they are willing to go beyond their job descriptions and take risks required to succeed because they believe that their leaders will be supportive. They also perform their jobs particularly well because they are not worried about having to "watch their backs." For this same reason, people remain highly committed to organizations when they trust their leaders, which, as I discussed in Chapter 5, brings about several benefits, such as reducing turnover. Taking all these factors into account, precisely what can you do to promote trust in your own working relationships? For some useful suggestions in this regard, see Table 7.1.

| TABLE 7.1 | Guidelines for Promoting Trust in Working Relationships |

This discussion has identified several general factors that promote trustworthiness. However, what exactly can you do to put these ideas into practice? Several particular recommendations may be offered.

Suggestion	Explanation
Always meet deadlines.	If you promise to get something done on time, it is essential to meet that deadline. People who are chronically late in meeting deadlines rapidly gain a reputation for being untrustworthy. And, when others believe that you will not meet vital deadlines, they are unlikely to trust you with important assignments.
Follow through as promised.	It's not only important to do things on time, but also to perform those tasks in the manner in which others expect them to be done. If you do not (e.g., if you provide only part of what others expect you to do), you may acquire a reputation for being untrustworthy.
Share your personal values and goals with others.	Trusting someone requires a keen understanding and appreciation of that person. Gaining this understanding requires spending time together discussing common interests, common objectives, and so on.
"Walk the talk" (i.e., do what you say).	We certainly wouldn't trust someone who says one thing (e.g., "don't cheat") but does another (e.g., claims personal expenses on his business travel reimbursement form), so be sure to "walk the talk." By behaving as you tell others to behave, you send a strong message that such directives are to be taken seriously.
Give people a chance to express themselves.	When someone tells you something and you respond by having a warm and accepting conversation, you have revealed that you are benevolent, contributing to being considered as a confidant. Also, by inviting someone to express his or her ideas, you are likely to be seen as being procedurally fair (see Chapter 2) and, as a result, more trustworthy.
Make sure that people know about you.	We're unlikely to trust people with whom we've worked for some time but still don't know (you may wonder what they have to hide). Making an effort to ensure that people know who you are and what particular skills and abilities you bring to the table will make them feel comfortable with you—and more inclined to trust you, as a result.

ORGANIZATIONAL CITIZENSHIP BEHAVIOR: PROSOCIAL BEHAVIOR THAT GOES BEYOND FORMAL JOB REQUIREMENTS

Imagine the following situation. It's coming up on 5:00 p.m. and you're wrapping up your work for the day. You're eagerly looking forward to getting home and relaxing. While this is going on, the scene is quite different at the next cubicle. One of your colleagues has been working feverishly to complete an important report, but appears to have hit a snag. She now has little hope of getting the report on the boss's desk before he leaves for the day—that is, without your help. Pitching in to help your colleague is something you don't have to do. After all, there's nothing in your formal job description that makes it necessary for you to do so. What's more, you're quite weary after your own long day's work. However, when you see the bind your colleague is in, you put aside your own feelings and offer to stay and help her out.

In this case, although you're probably not going to win any medals for your generosity, you are being helpful, and you have gone "above and beyond the call of duty." Actions such as these, which exceed the formal requirements of one's job, reflect an important form of prosocial behavior known as **organizational citizenship behavior** (**OCB**, for short).[18] It is easy to imagine how such behaviors, although informal and sometimes minor in nature, may play an important role when it comes to the smooth functioning of organizations.

Forms of OCB

Volunteering to help a coworker in need, as in our example, may be recognized as OCB but it is not the only form that OCB can take. In fact, this is just one of five different forms of OCB. For a summary of these, along with examples of each, see Table 7.2.

As you look at the examples in Table 7.2, it will become apparent that some forms of organizational citizenship behavior are directed at *individuals*. In such cases it is referred to as **OCB-I**.[19] Some examples of OCB-I include the following:

- Doing a favor for someone
- Assisting a coworker with a personal problem
- Bringing in food to share with others
- Collecting money for flowers for sick coworkers or for funerals
- Sending birthday greetings to others in the office

TABLE 7.2 Organizational Citizenship Behavior: Specific Forms and Examples	
Organizational citizenship behavior (OCB) can take many different forms, most of which fall into the five major categories shown here. Also as indicated, these may be directed either at individuals (categorized as OCB-I) or organizations (categorized as OCB-O).	
Form of OCB	**Examples**
Altruism	• Helping a coworker with a project (OCB-I) • Switching vacation dates with another at his or her request (OCB-I) • Volunteering for companywide projects (OCB-O)
Conscientiousness	• Never missing a day of work (OCB-O) • Coming to work early if needed (OCB-O) • Not spending time on personal calls (OCB-O)
Civic virtue	• Attending voluntary meetings and functions (OCB-O) • Reading memos; keeping up with new information (OCB-O)
Sportsmanship	• Making do without complaint ("Grin and bear it!") (OCB-O) • Not finding fault with the organization (OCB-O)
Courtesy	• "Turning the other cheek" to avoid problems (OCB-I) • Not "blowing up" when provoked (OCB-I)

You'll also see in Table 7.2 that other forms of OCB are directed at *organizations* themselves. In such cases it is referred to as **OCB-O**. Some examples of OCB-O include the following:

- Speaking favorably about the organization to outsiders
- Being receptive to new ideas
- Being tolerant to temporary inconveniences without complaining
- Offering ideas to improve the functioning of the organization
- Expressing loyalty toward the organization

Why Does OCB Occur?

As you know, people sometimes are selfish and do not engage in OCB. What, then, lies behind the tendency to be a good organizational citizen? Although there are several factors involved, evidence strongly suggests that people's beliefs that they are being treated fairly by their organizations (especially their immediate supervisors) is a critical factor (recall the discussion of fairness in Chapter 2). Specifically, the more people believe they are treated fairly by their organizations, the more they trust its management, and the more willing they are to go the extra mile to help out when needed.[20] By contrast, people who feel that their organizations are taking advantage of them are untrusting and highly unlikely to engage in OCB.

OCB also occurs for other reasons. For example, OCB tends to occur when employees hold positive attitudes toward their organizations[21] and when they have good relationships with their supervisors.[22] It's interesting to note that not everyone is equally predisposed to engage in OCB. Personality characteristics also are linked to OCB. Specifically, individuals who are highly conscientious (see Chapter 3) and who are highly empathic (i.e., those who are inclined to take others' perspectives and to share their feelings and reactions) are inclined to engage in OCB.[23] This isn't too surprising, of course, since such individuals probably would be interested in "going the extra mile" to make others feel good.

Does OCB Really Matter?

OCB has several important effects on organizational functioning. Specifically, people's willingness to engage in various types of OCB is related to such work-related measures as job satisfaction and organizational commitment, which, as I described in Chapter 6, are related to organizational functioning in a number of complex ways.[24]

In addition, being a good organizational citizen can have important effects on recruiting efforts. After all, the more positive statements current employees make about the companies where they are employed, the more favorably those organizations will be regarded, thereby enhancing their capacities to attract the best new employees.[25]

As I have indicated, OCB is an unofficial aspect of people's jobs. It's considered *extra-role behavior* because it refers to things that people do that go beyond their formal job descriptions. However, because OCB can make such a big difference in job satisfaction and organizational commitment—not to mention just making life more pleasant for everyone—several companies do, in fact, take it into account as part of employees' formal performance appraisals.[26] This seems reasonable since even when OCB is *not* taken into account in a formal way, it still has great impact.

For example, research has shown that OCB has a greater impact on employees' performance appraisal ratings than such "official" factors as the knowledge, skills, and abilities people need to do their jobs.[27] As such, it's not surprising that many managers go out of their way to gather information about OCB so that they can take it into account in their performance ratings (even though they may have to make written comments about it since there's no official place for OCB on the evaluation form).[28]

This raises an interesting question: If OCB *were* to be incorporated into employees' formal performance appraisals, how heavily weighted should it be relative to **core task behavior (CTB)**—that is, the formal behaviors that traditionally are recognized as part of a particular job? If it's considered important by managers, then they would want to weight it highly since these ratings would send an official message to employees about how well they are performing as organizational citizens. Research suggests that this, in fact, is the case.[29] People believe that OCB should account for 30–50 percent of workers' formal performance ratings. With this in mind, it's not surprising that organizational officials are sensitive to the good citizenship of their employees.

Suggestions for Promoting OCB

Considering the importance of OCB, both actual and perceived, it would appear to be worthwhile for managers to consider ways of encouraging people to engage in OCB. Here are some recommendations for doing this.

- *Be a model of helpful behavior*—Helping, it appears, is contagious. Once it begins, it tends to increase. Managers can get the ball rolling by being helpful to their subordinates and to their peers. In this way, they become models of helpful behavior and encourage its occurrence.
- *Demonstrate courtesy*—Courtesy, too, is contagious, so managers always should be sure to demonstrate it in their own behavior. Show respect for employees, treat them politely—and the result will be that these aspects of OCB also will become the norm.
- *Make voluntary functions worth attending*—Why should employees attend voluntary meetings if these are dull and boring? Making meetings interesting and fun, on the other hand, may encourage employees to attend and to show the civic virtue aspect of OCB. For instance, if you are having a voluntary meeting in the morning, be sure to provide coffee and something to eat. There's nothing like food to draw a crowd!
- *Don't complain!*—If managers complain a lot, this sets the tone for similar behavior by employees—and OCB will go right out the window. So even if conditions are not ideal, be a "good sport" and refrain from complaining. This, too, will increase OCB in your work group.
- *Demonstrate conscientiousness*—If *you,* as manager, aren't willing to come in early, stay late, and go beyond the formal requirements of your position, you cannot expect your subordinates to do so. Thus, you should be sure to demonstrate these aspects of OCB clearly and openly yourself. Doing so will encourage your subordinates to do the same.
- *Don't stand on ceremony*—To expect others to pitch-in as needed, you should do this yourself. The phrase "it's not my job" should not be in your vocabulary. After all, going beyond formal roles is what OCB is all about.
- *Treat employees fairly*—Perhaps the single factor that exerts the strongest effects on OCB is perceived fairness: when employees perceive that they are being treated fairly, their willingness to engage in OCB increases. So it is *essential* to ensure that all actions and procedures in an organization lead to this conclusion (see Chapter 2). This may require considerable effort (e.g., to ensure that performance appraisals are conducted fairly), but it is well worthwhile in terms of the significant increases in OCB it will generate.

Although these suggestions may all seem like common sense, they certainly are *not* common practice. Often, managers do not set very good examples for their subordinates where OCB is concerned. They complain frequently, "pull rank" on subordinates, are discourteous, and take advantage of their positions such as by disappearing for two-hour lunches. Needless to say, such actions will discourage helpfulness by employees: Why should they go beyond the requirements of their jobs if their boss doesn't? The bottom line is clear: Promoting OCB begins by demonstrating it yourself.

COOPERATION: PROVIDING MUTUAL ASSISTANCE

Thus far, this discussion has focused on one person's giving help to another. However, it is probably even more common in organizations to find situations in which assistance is mutual, with two or more individuals, teams, or organizations working together toward some common goal. Such efforts are known as acts of **cooperation**. As you know from experience, people do not always cooperate with each other. As you might imagine, cooperation is essential to organizational success. Unless individuals, teams, and entire organizations cooperate with each other, all are likely to fall short of their objectives. With this in mind, it makes sense to consider the factors that bring about cooperation, both within organizations and between them as well.

Cooperation Within Organizations

Several factors affect the tendency for people to cooperate with each other within organizations. Let's now review some of the key ones.

THE RECIPROCITY PRINCIPLE We all know that "the golden rule" admonishes us to do unto others as we would have them do unto us. However, this doesn't describe exactly the way people behave. Instead of treating others as we would like to be treated, most people tend to treat others the way they have been treated in the past by them. In short, we are more inclined to follow a different principle: "an eye for an eye and a tooth for a tooth." Social scientists refer to this as the principle of **reciprocity**—the tendency to treat others as they have treated us.

To a great extent, the principle of reciprocity describes the way people behave when cooperating with others.[30] The key task in establishing cooperation in organizations is straightforward: getting it started. Once individuals or teams have begun to cooperate, the process may be largely self-sustaining. That is, one unit's cooperation encourages cooperation among the others. To encourage cooperation, therefore, managers should attempt to get the process under way.

PERSONAL ORIENTATION As you know from experience, some people tend to be more cooperative by nature than others. In contrast, other people tend to be far more competitive—interested in doing better than others in one way or another. Not surprisingly, scientists have found that people can be reliably classified into four different categories in terms of their natural predispositions toward working with or against others.[31] These are as follows:

- **Competitors**—People whose primary motive is doing better than others, besting them in open competition.
- **Individualists**—People who care primarily about maximizing their own gain regardless of whether others do better or worse than themselves.
- **Cooperators**—People who are concerned with maximizing joint outcomes, getting as much as possible for their team.
- **Equalizers**—People who are primarily interested in minimizing the differences between themselves and others.

Although there are individual differences, men as a whole tend to favor a competitive orientation, attempting to exploit others around them. By contrast, women tend to favor a cooperative orientation, preferring to work with other people rather than against them, and they also tend to develop friendly ties with others.[32] Still, it would be a mistake for managers to assume that men and women automatically fall into certain categories. Instead, it is widely recommended that managers take the time to get to know their individual workers' personal orientations and then match these to the kinds of tasks to which they may be best suited. For example, competitors may be most effective in negotiation situations, whereas cooperators may be most effective in teamwork situations. (To get a sense of which category best describes you, complete the Self-Assessment Exercise on pp. 230–231.)

ORGANIZATIONAL REWARD SYSTEMS It is not only differences between people that lead them to behave cooperatively but differences in the nature of organizational reward systems as well. Despite good intentions, companies all too often create reward systems that lead their employees to compete against each other. This would be the case, for example, in a company in which various divisions sell products that compete with each other. Sales representatives who receive commissions for selling their division's products have little incentive to help the company by attempting to sell another division's products. In other words, the company's reward system discourages cooperative behavior.

With an eye toward eliminating such problems and fostering cooperation, many of today's companies are adopting **team-based rewards**.[33] These are organizational reward systems in which at least a portion of an individual's compensation is based on the performance of his or her work group. The rationale behind these incentive systems is straightforward (and follows from the principle of reinforcement described in Chapter 3): People who are rewarded for contributing to their group's performance will focus their energies on group performance. In other words, they will cooperate with each other. Although there are many difficult challenges associated with setting up team-based reward programs that are manageable (e.g., based on measurable rewards that really matter) and that people find acceptable (e.g., ones that are administered fairly), companies that have met these challenges have reaped benefits in terms of increased job satisfaction and productivity.

Cooperation Between Organizations: Interorganizational Alliances

In business, competition is the natural order of things; company competing against company is the standard state of affairs. This does not mean, however, that it must always be the case. Sometimes, in fact, companies find it beneficial to work together to maximize their joint profits—that is, to cooperate. This occurs in several different ways that I now discuss.

PARTNERING WITH SUPPLIERS Years ago, companies used to think of suppliers (other companies from whom they purchase goods and services) as more or less interchangeable. They'd select the best one and ignore the others, and if the situation changed, they switched suppliers quickly. Today, however, companies are far more likely to work closely with their suppliers to ensure that they can provide high-quality products. For example, many auto companies have developed close, cooperative relationships with their suppliers (e.g., various manufacturing companies) to ensure a constant flow of high-quality components.

RESEARCH AND DEVELOPMENT (R&D) PARTNERSHIPS In certain industries, the costs of research and development can present a staggering burden to individual companies, especially those that are relatively small in size. Under these conditions, it often makes sense for two or more organizations to pool their resources and share in the potential rewards.[34]

This practice is widespread among small pharmaceutical companies that join forces to help bring new drugs to market. Because the process is usually far too expensive for any one company and requires more expertise than a firm can contribute by itself, they sometimes form partnerships in which each company brings something unique to the table. Examples may include special facilities, specific kinds of knowledge, useful ties with larger companies, and so on. The hope is that by cooperating in this manner, all participants in the partnership ultimately will benefit, accomplishing something together—bringing a drug to market—that they otherwise could not accomplish on their own.

Competition: The Opposite of Cooperation

Question: If cooperation is so beneficial, why does it not always occur? In other words, why do people or organizations with similar goals not always join forces? To a large extent, the answer is that some goals cannot be shared. There can be only one winner of the Super Bowl and one winner of the World Series; the teams cannot share these prizes. Similarly, when several large companies are courting the same small company as a takeover candidate, there can be only one winner as well. Such conditions breed **competition**—a pattern of behavior in which each person, group, or organization seeks to maximize its own gains, often at the expense of others. For a graphic summary of the differences between cooperation and competition, see Figure 7.4.

It is important to recognize that cooperation and competition might be occurring at the same time. That is, people may have **mixed motives**— the motive to cooperate and the motive to

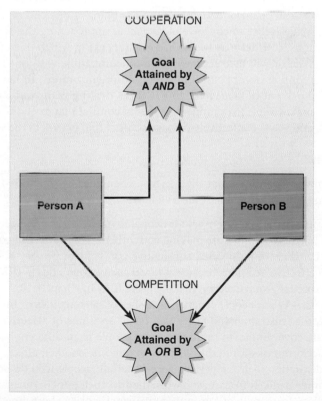

FIGURE 7.4 Cooperation Versus Competition: A Comparison
When *cooperating* with each other, people work together to attain the same goal that they share. However, when *competing* against one another, each person works to attain the same goal to the exclusion of the other.

compete may be operating simultaneously. Take the game of baseball, for example. Players may cooperate with each other, such as when it comes to getting a double play (where the shortstop might flip a ground ball to the second baseman, who then throws it to the first baseman). At the same time, these same players also may be competing against each other for individual batting records. And, of course, they are working together to compete against the other team. Clearly, there are a lot of things going on in such situations: The motives to cooperate and to compete often coexist within the same situation.

In business, competition is the natural order of things. Employees in the same company compete for a promotion, companies compete for the same government contract, and of course, retail businesses compete for the same customers. In recent years, for example, several start-up companies, such as Victory and Excelsior-Henderson, have made high-quality motorcycles that compete very favorably with "cruisers" from the legendary Harley-Davidson.[35] They are trying to attract customers by offering more bike for the money, while Harley fans continue to be attracted to something less tangible—that company's reputation. Although only time will tell the outcome of this competition, it is clear that no matter what happens, there will always be companies competing against other companies.

CONFLICT: THE INEVITABLE RESULT OF INCOMPATIBLE INTERESTS

If we conceive of prosocial behavior and cooperation as being at one end of a continuum (as in Figure 7.1), then it makes sense to conceive of *conflict* as approaching the opposite end. In the context of organizations, **conflict** may be defined as a process in which one party perceives that another party has taken or will take actions that are incompatible with one's own interests. As you might imagine, conflict occurs quite commonly in organizations. In fact, it has been estimated that about 20 percent of managers' time is spent dealing with conflict and its effects.[36] Considering this, it makes sense to examine the types of conflict that exist, the causes and consequences of conflict, and ways to effectively manage conflict that occurs in the workplace.

Types of Conflict

As you might imagine, all conflict is not alike. In fact, scientists have identified three major types of conflict that commonly occur.[37] These are as follows:

- *Substantive conflict*—It is not unusual for people to have different viewpoints and opinions with respect to a decision they are making with others. This variety of conflict is known as **substantive conflict**. In most cases, substantive conflict can be very beneficial to helping groups make effective decisions because it forces the various sides to clearly articulate their ideas. (I will discuss group decision making more fully in Chapter 10.)
- *Affective conflict*—When people experience clashes of personalities or interpersonal tension of some sort, the frustration and anger that result are signs of **affective conflict**. It is not unusual for affective conflict to result whenever people from different backgrounds are put together to perform tasks. Until they learn to accept one another, affective conflict is likely, resulting in disruption to group performance. After all, people who do not see the world in the same manner are likely to clash, and when they do, their joint performance tends to suffer.
- *Process conflict*—In many work groups, controversies arise about how they are going to operate—that is, how various duties and resources will be allocated and with whom various responsibilities will reside. This is known as **process conflict**. Generally, the more process conflict exists, the more group performance will suffer.[38]

As this discussion suggests, conflict takes several different forms and can have different effects—both positive and negative in nature. With this in mind, I now discuss the underlying causes of conflict.

Causes of Conflict

The conflicts we face in organizations may be viewed as stemming from a variety of causes, including both our interactions with other people and the organization itself. Here are just a few of the most important sources of organizational conflict.

GRUDGES   All too often, conflict is caused when people who have lost face in dealing with someone attempt to "get even" with that person by planning some form of revenge. Employees involved in this kind of activity are not only going out of their way to harm one of their coworkers, but by holding a grudge, they also are wasting energy that could be devoted to more productive organizational endeavors.

MALEVOLENT ATTRIBUTIONS   Why did someone do something that hurt us? To the extent that we believe that the harm we suffer is due to an individual's malevolent motives (e.g., the desire to hurt us), conflict is inevitable. However, whenever we believe that we suffered harm because of factors outside someone's control (e.g., an accident), conflict is less likely to occur. (You may recognize this as an example of the attribution process addressed in Chapter 3.) This causes problems in cases in which we falsely attribute the harm we suffer to another's negative intent when, in reality, the cause was externally based.

DESTRUCTIVE CRITICISM   Communicating negative feedback in organizations is inevitable. All too often, however, this process arouses unnecessary conflict. The problem is that some people make the mistake of using **destructive criticism**—that is, negative feedback that angers the recipient rather than helps this person do a better job. The most effective managers attempt to avoid conflict by using constructive criticism instead. For some important comparisons between these two forms of criticism, see Table 7.3.

DISTRUST   Based on the discussion of trust appearing earlier in this chapter (see pp. 207–211), it probably comes as no surprise that conflict may arise when trust is lacking. Specifically, the more strongly people suspect that some other individual or group does not have their best interests in mind, the more likely they are to have a relationship with that person or group that is riddled with conflict. In general, companies in which high levels of distrust predominate are considered to be undesirable places to work. This includes conflicts between labor and management as well as conflicts between coworkers at the same organizational levels.

COMPETITION OVER SCARCE RESOURCES   Because organizations almost never have unlimited resources (such as space, money, equipment, or personnel), it is inevitable that conflicts will arise over the distribution of those scarce resources. This occurs in large part because of a self-serving tendency in people's perceptions (see Chapter 3); that is, people tend to overestimate their own contributions to their organizations. Believing that we make greater contributions leads us to feel more deserving of resources than others. Inevitably, conflict results when others do not see it this way.

TABLE 7.3	Constructive Versus Destructive Criticism: A Comparison

The factors listed here distinguish constructive criticism (negative feedback that may be accepted by the recipient to improve his or her performance) from destructive criticism (negative feedback likely to be rejected by the recipient and unlikely to improve his or her performance).

Constructive Criticism	Destructive Criticism
Considerate—protects the recipient's self-esteem	Inconsiderate—harsh, sarcastic, biting
Does not contain threats	Contains threats
Timely—occurs as soon as possible after the substandard performance	Not timely—occurs after an inappropriate delay
Does not attribute poor performance to internal causes	Attributes poor performance to internal causes (e.g., lack of effort, motivation, ability)
Specific—focuses on aspects of performance that were inadequate	General—a sweeping condemnation of performance
Focuses on performance, not on the recipient	Focuses on the recipient—his or her personal characteristics
Motivated by desire to help the recipient improve	Motivated by anger, desire to assert dominance over the recipient, desire for revenge
Offers concrete suggestions for improvement	Offers no concrete suggestions for improvement

Consequences of Conflict: Both Good and Bad

The word *conflict* doubtlessly brings to mind negative images—thoughts of anger and confrontation. Indeed, there is no denying the many negative effects of conflict. But, as I have already noted—and as I will describe further—conflict has a positive side as well. With this in mind, I will now identify key consequences of conflict in organizations, both positive and negative.

NEGATIVE CONSEQUENCES OF CONFLICT   The major problem with conflict, as you know from experience, is that it yields strong negative emotions. However, these emotional reactions mark only the beginning of a chain of reactions that can have harmful effects in organizations.

The negative reactions, besides being quite stressful, are problematic in that they may divert people's attention from the task at hand. For example, people who are focused on getting even with a coworker and making him look bad in front of others are unlikely to be attending to the most important aspect of their jobs. In particular, communication between individuals or teams may be so adversely affected that any coordination of effort between them is compromised. Not surprisingly, such lowered coordination tends to lead to decrements in organizational functioning. In short, organizational conflict has costly effects on organizational performance. For some helpful suggestions on how to avoid many of these problems, see Table 7.4.[39]

POSITIVE CONSEQUENCES OF CONFLICT   Have you ever worked on a team project and found that you disagreed with someone on a key matter? If so, how did you react? Chances are good that you fell short of sabotaging that person's work or acting aggressively. In fact, the conflict may have brought the two of you to the table to have a productive discussion about the matter at hand. As a result of this discussion, you may have even improved relations between the two of you and the quality of the decisions that resulted from your joint efforts. If you can relate to this scenario, then you already recognize an important fact about organizational conflict—that some of its effects may be positive in nature.

TABLE 7.4	How to Manage Conflict Effectively

Although conflict is inevitable, there are concrete steps that managers can take to avoid the negative consequences that result from conflict between people in the workplace. Some of the most effective ones are identified here.

- Agree on a process for making decisions *before* a conflict arises. This way, when a conflict needs to be addressed, everyone knows how it is going to be handled.
- Make sure everyone knows his or her specific areas of responsibility, authority, and accountability. Clarifying these matters avoids potential conflicts when people either ignore their responsibilities or overstep their authority.
- Recognize conflicts stemming from faulty organizational systems, such as a pay system that rewards one department at the expense of another. In such cases, work to change the system rather than training employees.
- Recognize the emotional reactions to conflict. Conflicts will not go away until people's hurt feelings are addressed.
- Consider how to avoid problems rather than assign blame for them. Questions such as, "Why did you do that?" only make things worse. It is more helpful to ask, "How can we make things better?"
- Conflicts will not go away by making believe they don't exist; doing so will only make them worse. Avoid the temptation not to speak to the other party. Instead, discuss your misunderstandings with this individual thoroughly.

Sources: Based on suggestions by Scudder et al., 2012, and Bragg, 1999; see Note 39.

When asked about his management philosophy, Starbucks CEO and founder Howard Schultz touted the importance of conflict and debate, saying, "If there's no tension, I don't think you get the best result."[40] As this successful business leader suggests, organizational conflict can be the source of several benefits. Among these are the following:

- Conflict may improve the quality of organizational decisions (as in the preceding example).
- Conflict may bring out into the open problems that have been previously ignored.
- Conflict may motivate people to appreciate one another's positions more fully.
- Conflict may encourage people to consider new ideas, thereby facilitating change.

In view of these positive effects of conflict, the key is to make sure that more of these benefits occur as opposed to costs. It is with this goal in mind that managers work so diligently to effectively manage organizational conflict. I will now examine some of the ways they go about managing conflict successfully.

Managing Conflict Through Negotiation

When conflicts arise between individuals, groups, or even entire organizations, the most common way to resolve them is to work together to find a solution that is acceptable to all the parties involved. This process is known as **negotiation** (or **bargaining**), defined as the process in which two or more parties in dispute with each other exchange offers, counteroffers, and concessions in an attempt to find a mutually acceptable agreement.

Obviously, bargaining does not work when the parties rigidly adhere to their positions without budging—that is, when they "stick to their guns." For bargaining to be effective, the parties involved must be willing to adjust their stances on the issues at hand. And, for the people involved to be willing to make such adjustments, they must believe that they have found an acceptable outcome—one that allows them to claim victory in the negotiation process. For bargaining to be most effective in reducing conflict, this must be the case for all sides. That is, outcomes must be found for all sides that allow them to believe that they have "won" the negotiation process—results known as **win–win solutions**. In win–win solutions, everybody wins, precisely as the term implies. Solutions of this type are considered desirable because they allow each side to come away claiming that it has gained something through the negotiation process. And, with no "losers" involved, both bargaining parties can feel good and "save face" with their constituents (i.e., the groups on whose behalves bargainers are negotiating), thereby paving the way for harmony to result.

TIPS FOR NEGOTIATING WIN–WIN SOLUTIONS   Several effective ways of finding win–win solutions may be identified. (For practice in putting these techniques to use, see the Group Exercise on p. 231.)

1. *Avoid making unreasonable offers.* Imagine that a friend of yours is selling a used car with an asking price of $10,000—the car's established "book value." If you were to attempt to "lowball" the seller by offering only $1,000, your bad-faith offer might end the negotiations right there. A serious buyer would offer a more reasonable price, say $9,000—one that would allow both the buyer and the seller to come out ahead in the deal. In short, extreme offers tend to anger opponents, sometimes ending the negotiation process on a sour note and allowing none of the parties to get what they want.

2. *Seek the common ground.* All too often people in conflict with others assume that their interests and those of the other party are completely incompatible. When this occurs, they tend to overlook the fact that they actually might have several areas of interest in common. When parties focus on the areas of agreement between them, it helps bring them together on the areas of disagreement. So, for example, in negotiating the deal for purchasing the used car, you might establish the fact that you agree to the selling price of $9,000. This verifies that the interests of the buyer and the seller are not completely incompatible, thereby encouraging them to find a solution to the area in which they disagree, such as a payment schedule. By contrast, if either party believed that they were completely far apart on all aspects of the deal, they would be less likely to negotiate a win–win solution.

3. *Broaden the scope of issues considered.* Sometimes parties bargaining with each other have several issues on the table. When this occurs, it is often useful to consider the various issues together as a total package. Labor unions often do this in negotiating contracts with company management whenever they give in on one issue in exchange for compensation on another issue. So, for example, in return for not freezing wages, a company may agree to concede to the union's other interests, such as gaining representation on key corporate committees. In other words, compared to bargaining over single issues (e.g., the price of the used car), when the parties get to bargaining across a wide array of issues, it often is easier to find overall solutions that are acceptable to all sides.

4. *Uncover "the real" issues.* Frequently, people focus on the conflicts between them in only a single area although they may have multiple conflicts between them—some of which are hidden. Suppose, for example, that your friend is being extremely stubborn when it comes to negotiating the price of the used car. He's sticking firmly to his asking price, refusing to budge despite your reasonable offer, adding to the conflict between you. However, it may be the case that there are other issues involved. For example, he may be trying to "get even" with you for harming him several years ago. In other words, what may appear to be a simple conflict between two people may actually have multiple sources. Finding long-lasting solutions requires identifying all the important issues—even the hidden ones—and bringing them to the table.

As you might imagine, it is almost always far easier to say these things than to do them. Indeed, when people cannot come to agreement about something, they sometimes become irrational, not seeking common ground and not taking the other's perspective needed to find a win–win solution, but only thinking of themselves. In such circumstances, third parties can be useful to break the deadlock. (For a description of a popular approach for doing this, see the Winning Practices section below.)

Winning Practices

Settling Disputes Quickly and Inexpensively Out of Court: Alternative Dispute Resolution

When a customer canceled a $60,000 wedding reception, Anthony Capetola, a caterer from Long Island, New York, was only able to fill that time slot with an event bringing in half as much.[41] Although Capetola was harmed by the customer's actions, as you might imagine, that customer was unwilling to cough up the lost revenue. Many business owners in Capetola's shoes would seek restitution by taking the customer to court, resulting in a delay of many months, or even years, and a huge bill for litigation, not to mention lots of adverse publicity. Fortunately, in their contract, Capetola and the customer agreed to settle any future disagreements using what is known as **alternative dispute resolution** (**ADR**). This refers to a set of procedures in which disputing parties work together with a neutral party who helps them settle their disagreements out of court.

There are two popular forms of ADR—*mediation* and *arbitration*. **Mediation** involves having a neutral party (the *mediator*) work together with both sides to reach a settlement. Typically, mediators meet together and separately with each side and try to find a common ground that will satisfy everyone's concerns. Mediators do not consider who's wrong and who's right, but set the stage for finding a resolution. And that they do! In fact, by one recent estimate, mediators help disputing parties find solutions about 85 percent of the time. As you might imagine, however, for mediation to work, the two sides must be willing to communicate with each other. When this doesn't happen, ADR may take the form of **arbitration**. This involves having a neutral third party listen to the facts presented by each side and then make a final, binding decision.

ADR is very popular these days because it helps disputants reach agreements rapidly (often in a matter of a day or two, compared to typically far lengthier court trials) and inexpensively (usually for just a few thousand dollars split between the parties, compared to astronomical sums for attorney fees). Moreover, it keeps people who otherwise might end up in court out of the public eye, which could be damaging to their reputations—even the party in whose favor the judgment goes. Because it is low key and nonconfrontational, mediation is particularly valuable in cases in which the parties have an ongoing relationship (business or personal) that they do not want to go sour.[42] After all, the mediation process brings the parties together, helping them see each other's side—something that is usually lost for sure in the heat of a courtroom battle.

Not surprisingly, the popularity of ADR these days has led to the development of several companies specializing in rendering mediation and arbitration services. The largest of these, the American Arbitration Association, boasts offices in half the U.S. states, with a load pushing 80,000 cases per year. They maintain a file of some 18,000 arbitrators and mediators (typically lawyers, businesspeople, and former judges), enabling them to find a neutral party who is experienced in just about any kind of dispute that people are likely to have.

DEVIANT ORGANIZATIONAL BEHAVIOR

To this point, most forms of organizational behavior discussed in this book may be considered good, desirable, or beneficial to employees and/or the organizations in which they work. Unfortunately, however, some of the ways in which people behave have just the opposite effects—that is, they are harmful or counterproductive in one way or another. Such acts are referred to as **deviant organizational behavior**—and defined as actions on the part of employees that intentionally violate the standards of acceptable behavior in organizations and/or the formal rules of society.[43]

At first glance, you might assume that all forms of deviant organizational behavior produce negative effects. In fact, though, the issue is more complex. As you'll now see, deviant organizational behaviors can produce beneficial effects if, at the same time, they aid the broader society or culture. The distinction I am making here is between workplace deviance that is constructive as opposed to destructive in nature (see Figure 7.5).

Specifically, **destructive organizational deviance** is a form of behavior that violates both organizational and societal norms. By contrast, **constructive organizational deviance** refers to actions that deviate from organizational norms but are consistent with societal norms. With this as background, I now describe one well-known form of constructive deviance, whistle-blowing, and then review several all-too-prevalent forms of destructive deviance.

Whistle-Blowing: Constructive Workplace Deviance

Sometimes employees face situations in which they recognize that their organization is behaving improperly. To right the wrong, they reveal the improper or illegal practice to someone who may be able to correct it—an action known as *whistle-blowing*.[44] Formally, **whistle-blowing** is the disclosure by employees of illegal, immoral, or illegitimate practices by employers to people or organizations able to take action; these may be either internal to the organization, or when that doesn't work, external (e.g., to the press).

Is whistle-blowing a constructive action? Although some people in the organization might not think so, from the point of view of society, it usually is. In many instances, the actions of whistle-blowers can protect the health, safety, or security of the general public. For example,

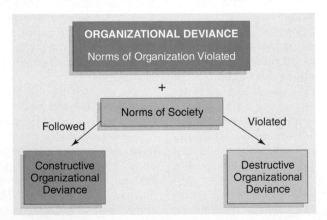

FIGURE 7.5 Constructive Versus Destructive Organizational Deviance
Behavior directed toward an organization is considered deviant if it violates its norms or rules, thereby bringing harm. If that behavior is consistent with the norms of society, it is considered *constructive organizational deviance*. However, if it is inconsistent with the norms of society and those of the organization, it is considered *destructive organizational deviance*.

an employee of a large bank who reports risky or illegal practices to an appropriate regulatory agency may be protecting thousands of depositors from considerable delay in recovering their savings. Similarly, an individual who blows the whistle on illegal dumping of toxic chemicals by his or her company may save many people from serious illness. This, of course, is in addition to keeping the natural environment from becoming polluted. For a summary of some actual cases of whistle-blowing, see Table 7.5.[45]

WHY DO THEY—AND DON'T THEY—DO IT? Why do people engage in whistle-blowing? There are several answers to this question. Sometimes, whistle-blowers desire to "get even" with a company they feel has treated them unfairly. Others, however, have more altruistic interests in mind, genuinely desiring to bring an end to the illegal and harmful actions they witness.[46]

TABLE 7.5 Whistle-Blowing: Some Examples

As these examples illustrate, employees blow the whistle on many different types of organizations accused of committing a wide range of questionable activities.

Whistle-Blower	Incident
Anonymous Accountant	In 2011, an accountant for a financial services firm notified the IRS that his or her employer was not paying income taxes. This netted the IRS $20 million in taxes and penalties and a $4.5 million award for the whistle-blower.
Harry Markopulos	In 2009, after having investigated the financial affairs of Bernard Madoff for almost eight years, he testified to authorities, providing details of Mr. Madoff's Ponzi scheme, and the Security and Exchange Commission's unresponsiveness to his many earlier efforts to convince them of the problem.
Bradley Birkenfeld	In 2007, this banker went to authorities about one of the largest tax fraud schemes in U.S. history, resulting in UBS bank paying a $780 million penalty and more than 14,000 "taxpayers" voluntarily disclosing their illegal offshore accounts.
Coleen Rowley	This special agent wrote a letter to the FBI director (with copies to two key members of Congress) about the bureau's failure to take action that could have prevented the terrorist attacks of September 11, 2001.
Sherron Watkins	In 2001, she notified the press about her letter to her boss at Enron identifying the company's fictitious accounting practices.
Tonya Atchinson	This former internal auditor at Columbia-HCA Healthcare Corp. charged the company with illegal Medicare billing.
Daniel Shannon	An in-house attorney for Intelligent Electronics protested the company's alleged misuse of marketing funds from computer manufacturers.
Robert Young	This agent for Prudential Insurance Co. in New Jersey accused company agents of encouraging customers to needlessly sell some policies and buy more expensive ones, boosting their commissions.
Bill Bush	This manager at the National Aeronautics and Space Administration (NASA) went public with the administration's policy of discouraging the promotion of employees older than 54 years of age.

Sources: See Note 45.

As you might imagine, blowing the whistle on one's employer is likely to be a very costly act for employees, as they often find themselves facing a long, uphill battle attempting to prove the wrongdoing. They also frequently face ostracism and job loss in response to their disloyalty. For example, five agents from State Farm Insurance were fired after they accused the company of various consumer abuses.[47] In another example, Jennifer P. Day was fired from her job as a Boston schoolteacher after she reported that the principal of her school gave answers to fourth-grade students taking a standardized statewide exam.[48]

It's not unusual for whistle-blowers to become targets of retaliation by their organizations. Several whistle-blowers have reported fearing for their lives, and a good many get fired for their actions. This, of course, is a major reason many people are highly reluctant to engage in this action.[49] Although various laws, such as the Whistleblower Protection Act in the United States, prevent employers from firing people directly because they blew the whistle, organizations frequently find alternative official grounds for dismissing "troublemakers."[50] It is not surprising, therefore, that six senior employees of the company that runs the 900-mile Trans-Alaska pipeline chose to remain anonymous when voicing their complaints about safety violations to BP.[51]

Despite the risks involved, of course, many individuals do decide to blow the whistle on their companies, and although they often are discarded by their organizations, they sometimes become true heroes and heroines to their societies. Illustrating this, Bradley Birkenfeld, who pointed to the tax-evasion practices of the asset management firm UBS, was named by the publication *Tax Notes* as its inaugural "Person of the Year," and the *NY Daily News* suggested that he be given a "statue on Wall Street."

Cyberloafing: Deviant Behavior Goes High-Tech

The advent of Internet technology has brought with it increased efficiency in accessing information and communicating with others—both of which are vital benefits. However, it also has created new ways for employees to loaf, or "goof off." Although workers have devised ways to slack off ever since people have been employed, access to the Internet and e-mail has provided more tempting opportunities than ever before. Employees who use their company's computers, such as its e-mail and/or Internet facilities, for personal use are considered to be engaged in **cyberloafing**.[52]

In the United States, approximately 40 million people have Internet and/or e-mail access at work, use it regularly, and are referred to as *online workers*. However, further statistics reveal that much of what online workers are doing while online is not work related. For example:

- According to an MSNBC survey, one-fifth of all people who have visited pornographic Web sites have done so while on the job.
- One-third of workers surveyed by the Society of Financial Service Professionals reported playing computer games while at work.
- Eighty-three percent of companies surveyed by the Privacy Foundation indicated that their employees were using e-mail for personal purposes.

These and other forms of cyberloafing are costing U.S. organizations, both private and public, untold millions of dollars a year. In fact, just one $40,000/year employee can cost his or her employer as much as $5,000 annually by playing around on the Internet for one hour a day.

DOES MONITORING HELP?   Executives are implicitly aware of this problem, and more than three-quarters believe that some types of online monitoring and filtering efforts are needed. Polls have found, however, that only about a third of online workers are monitored, and most of this monitoring is highly sporadic. In fact, only 38 percent of companies acknowledge monitoring the online work of employees who already have been suspected of cyberloafing. Bottom line: cyberloafing is a costly problem about which little is being done.

Although various software programs make it possible to monitor employees and such products are growing in popularity, this technology is not a panacea. Some problems are technical in nature, but the most notable ones are social–psychological. Specifically, employees believe that being monitored constitutes an invasion of their privacy and reject the practice as being unfair.

Decisions in federal courts are in agreement. A few years ago, for example, the 27-judge Judicial Conference of the United States repealed a proposed monitoring policy for their own employees, which they feared would violate their constitutional rights to privacy. Speaking for the group, federal appeals court judge Alex Kozinski objected to the policy's assertion that "court employees should have no expectation of privacy at any time while at work." The resulting policy permitted virtually no monitoring of employees' e-mail and only highly limited monitoring of their Internet use.

Where we stand now is quite interesting: Although cyberloafing is admittedly a widespread and costly problem, efforts aimed at addressing it that involve employee monitoring are not well accepted (or even legally permissible, in some cases). Clearly, the key is to find additional ways of discouraging people from cyberloafing. Admittedly, given the ancient problem of "goofing off" coupled with the vast opportunities to goof off provided by Internet access, cyberloafing looks like it's going to be a problem that stays around for years to come. Fortunately, organizational behavior specialists are now beginning to study this phenomenon, which hopefully will provide useful suggestions in the years to come.[53]

Workplace Aggression and Violence

Approximately 1.5 million Americans annually become victims of violence while on the job, resulting in direct and indirect costs to their companies of more than $4.2 billion.[54] Despite all the publicity given to such incidents, though, violence is actually a rare occurrence in workplaces. Only about 800 people are murdered at work each year in the United States, and most of these crimes are committed by outsiders, such as customers or criminals during robberies, not by fellow employees.[55] Although violence is relatively rare, other forms of **workplace aggression**—any efforts by individuals to harm others with whom they work or have worked in the past, or their organizations—are much more common.[56]

WORKPLACE AGGRESSION: ITS MANY FORMS When it comes to aggression, most people would like to maximize the harm they do their intended victims while simultaneously minimizing the likelihood of retaliation. In view of this, it's not surprising that many instances of workplace aggression are largely covert (hidden, disguised) in nature. This type of aggression is especially likely in workplaces because aggressors in such settings expect to interact with their intended victims frequently in the future. Using covert forms of aggression reduces the likelihood that the victims will retaliate against them.

Of course, not all forms of workplace aggression are covert. People do indeed sometimes assault others directly, either with words or in physical assaults. Overall, it appears that most aggression occurring in workplaces can be described as falling into three major categories.

- **Incivility and bullying**—Behaviors demonstrating a lack of regard for others, denying them the respect they are due. Often such acts are verbal or symbolic in nature (e.g., belittling others' opinions, talking behind their backs, spreading malicious rumors about them). For an overview of some of the most prevalent forms of bullying in the workplace, see Table 7.6.[57]

TABLE 7.6	Prevalent Forms of Workplace Bullying

Workplace bullying takes a variety of forms. Some of the most widely observed ones are summarized here.

Category	Examples
Constant Critic	• Uses insulting and belittling comments, engages in name-calling • Constantly harangues the victim about his or her incompetence • Makes aggressive eye contact
Two-Headed Snake	• Denies victims the resources needed to work • Demands that coworkers provide damning evidence against the victim • Assigns meaningless work as punishment
Vindictive Gatekeeper	• Isolates the victim, ignoring him or her with "the silent treatment" • Deliberately cuts the target out of the communication loop but expects the victim to have the missing information
Screaming Mimi	• Yells, screams, and curses • Makes loud, angry outbursts and throws tantrums • Intimidates by slamming things and throwing objects

Source: Based on information in Namie & Namie, 2011; see Note 57.

- **Obstructionism**—Behaviors designed to obstruct or impede the target's performance (e.g., failure to return phone calls or respond to memos, failure to transmit needed information, interfering with activities important to the target).
- **Overt aggression**—Behaviors that have typically been included under the heading "workplace violence" (e.g., physical assault, destruction of property, threats of physical violence, direct verbal abuse).

How common are these forms of behavior? More common than you might guess. In fact, a large proportion of employees report that they either have been on the receiving end of workplace aggression or that they have behaved aggressively toward others at some time during their careers. So, although overt violence involving physical assaults is relatively rare, other, less extreme forms of workplace aggression are quite common. In fact, in some workplaces, they are everyday occurrences.

WORKPLACE AGGRESSION: ITS CAUSES   What are the causes of workplace aggression? As is true of aggression in any context, many factors play a role. However, one that has emerged repeatedly in research on this topic is *perceived unfairness*.[58] When individuals feel that they have been treated unfairly by others in their organization—or by their organization itself—they experience intense feelings of anger and resentment, and often seek to "even the score" by harming the people they hold responsible in some manner (see Chapter 2).

In addition, the likelihood that a specific person will engage in workplace aggression is influenced by the overall level of aggression in his or her work group or organization.[59] In other words, to the extent that individuals work in environments in which aggression is common, they, too, are likely to engage in such behavior. Moreover, this seems to be true for aggression outside as well as inside organizations. For instance, one study found that the greater the incidence of violence in communities surrounding U.S. Post Offices, the higher were the rates of aggression within these facilities.[60] It was as if acceptance of violence in the surrounding communities paved the way for similar behavior inside this large organization.

Additional factors that play a role in workplace aggression involve changes that have been occurring in many workplaces: downsizing, layoffs, and increased use of part-time employees, to name a few. In fact, the greater the extent to which such changes have occurred, the greater is the level of stress and uncertainty experienced by employees. This, in turn, promotes workplace aggression. Since such changes have been widespread in recent years, it is quite likely that the incidence of workplace aggression is increasing as well. In sum, workplace aggression, like aggression in other contexts, derives from many different factors rather than a single dominant cause.

Employee Theft

Retail stores are very concerned with problems of shoplifting, as you know. What you might not know, however, is that companies lose more money and goods from their own employees than from customers. Specifically, they lose almost seven times more (about $969.14 per employee compared to $135.81 per shoplifter).[61] Although estimates of costs of employee theft are quite varied, it is clear that the figures are staggering, amounting to many billions of dollars per year.[62] Worse yet, theft by employees has been rising steadily in recent years in response to the weak economy. As one expert put it, "People not getting raises are starting to take them."[63]

To understand these statistics fully, it is important to recognize an important fact: almost everyone takes home some company property—a pencil, a note pad, some paper—for personal use, but in general, they don't consider this to be theft. Many consider this to be an accepted benefit of their jobs. Whether or not this is justified, taking company property for nonbusiness uses does indeed constitute **employee theft** in the legal sense of the term. Although taking home a few pens or pencils may seem innocent enough, *petty theft* or *pilferage,* as it is known, is widespread. It becomes a problem since so many people do it, and because they don't think it's wrong, they're disinclined to stop. However, the facts are clear: it costs companies more money when a lot of people steal small things than when just a few people steal large things (e.g., the embezzlers who capture headlines with their clever and bold antics).[64] To understand these dynamics, let's turn to a critical question: Why do employees steal?

WHY DO EMPLOYEES STEAL?   Some employees steal because they are troubled in some way (e.g., they are in serious debt or have a narcotics or gambling habit). But this appears to be the minority. Instead, many people engage in employee theft for a more innocuous reason—*they see their coworkers doing it.*

To the extent that everyone around you is taking home tools, office supplies, and even petty cash, it quickly seems appropriate for you to do it, too. Although this doesn't make it right, of course, and it clearly costs the company money, people are quick to rationalize that petty theft is "no big deal" and not worth worrying about. After all, we convince ourselves, "If everyone's doing it, it must be okay." Similarly, many employees engage in theft because in some companies, *not* stealing goes against the informal norms of the work group.[65] Unspoken rules go a long way toward determining how people behave on the job, and in some companies, an employee has to steal to feel accepted and to belong. In some retail stores, for example, so many clerks steal goods that those who don't go along are socially ostracized by their workmates.

Finally, employees frequently engage in theft because they want to "even the score" with employers who they believe have mistreated them. In fact, people who feel underpaid frequently steal from their employers because in so doing they are righting a wrong by taking what they believe they should have had all along. (This is in keeping with equity theory, described in Chapter 6.)

Back to the Case

Answer the following questions based on this chapter's Making the Case (p. 203) to illustrate insights you have derived from the material in this chapter.

1. In what particular ways do NASCAR drivers compete against one another and cooperate with each other?
2. How might trust be involved in the relationships between NASCAR drivers and within members of each team?
3. In what ways might conflict arise between NASCAR drivers from different teams? Is this conflict helpful or harmful? Why is this so?

You Be the Consultant

An Epidemic of Deviant Behavior in the Workplace

Life in your company has become tumultuous. Not only are people always on each other's backs, but also sometimes they are downright hostile to each other, sabotaging others' work. Even those who have not been sniping at one another are responding negatively, such as by stealing company property. With such a toxic atmosphere, it's not surprising that good employees are resigning. Answer the following questions using the material in this chapter.

1. What possible causes of the problem would you consider, and why?
2. Assuming that these causes are real, what advice would you offer about how to eliminate the problem?
3. How might various tactics aimed at reducing conflict be used to resolve the problems identified in this workplace?

Self-Assessment Exercise

ASSESSING YOUR PERSONAL ORIENTATION TOWARD OTHERS

On pages 215–216, you read descriptions of four different personal orientations toward others—*competitors, individualists, cooperators,* and *equalizers.* As you read them, you probably developed some ideas as to which orientation best describes you. This exercise is designed to help you find out.

Directions and Scale

Use the following scale to indicate how well each of the following statements describes you.

> 1 = Does not describe me at all/never
> 2 = Describes me somewhat/some of the time
> 3 = Describes me moderately/half of the time
> 4 = Describes me greatly/much of the time
> 5 = Describes me perfectly/all of the time

_____ 1. I don't care how much money one of my coworkers earns, as long as I make as much as I can.
_____ 2. When playing a game with a close friend, I always try to keep the score close.
_____ 3. So long as I do better than the next person, I'm happy.

_____ **4.** I will gladly give up something for myself if it can help my team get ahead.
_____ **5.** It's important to me to be the best in the class, even if I'm not doing my personal best.
_____ **6.** I feel bad if I do too much better than my friends on a class assignment.
_____ **7.** I want to get an A in this class regardless of what grade others might get.
_____ **8.** I enjoy it when the people on my work team all pitch in to beat other teams.

Scoring

Insert the number corresponding to your answer to each question in the spaces below. Then add the numbers in each column (these can range from 2 to 10). The higher your score, the more accurately the personal orientation heading that column describes you.

Competitor	**Individualist**	**Cooperator**	**Equalizer**
3. _____	1. _____	4. _____	2. _____
5. _____	7. _____	8. _____	6. _____
Total = _____	Total = _____	Total = _____	Total = _____

Discussion Questions

1. What did this exercise reveal to you about yourself?
2. Were you surprised at what you learned, or was it something you already knew?
3. Do you tend to maintain the same orientation most of the time, or are there occasions in which you change from one orientation to another? What do you think this means?

Group Exercise

NEGOTIATING THE PRICE OF A USED CAR

This exercise is designed to help you put into practice some of the skills associated with being a good negotiator. In completing this exercise, follow the guidelines for negotiating a win–win solution found on pages 222–223.

Steps

1. Find a thorough description of a recent-model used car in the newspaper.
2. Divide the class into groups of six. Within each group, assign three students to the role of buyer and three to the role of seller.
3. Each group of buyers and sellers should meet in advance to plan their strategies. Buyers should plan on getting the lowest possible price; sellers should seek the highest possible price.
4. Buyers and sellers should meet to negotiate the price of the car within the period of time specified by the instructor. Feel free to meet within your groups at any time to evaluate your strategy.
5. Write down the final agreed-upon price and any conditions that may be attached to it.

Discussion Questions

1. Did you reach an agreement? If so, how easy or difficult was this process?
2. Which side do you think "won" the negotiation? What might have changed the outcome?
3. How might the negotiation process or the outcome have been different had this been a real situation?

Notes

MAKING THE CASE NOTES

2012 Daytona 500 Results. (2012, February 26). http://www.daytonainternationalspeedway.com/ Articles/2012/02/daytona-500-results.aspx. Leslie-Pelecky, D. (2008). *The physics of NASCAR: How to make steel + gas + rubber = speed.* New York: Dutton/Penguin. Clarke, L. (2008). *One helluva ride: How NASCAR swept the nation.* New York: Villard/Random House. History of NASCAR. (2008, July 17). *NASCAR.com.* http://www.nascar .com/news/features/history. Ronfeldt, D. (2000, February). Social science at 190 mph on NASCAR's biggest speedways. *First Monday, 5(2).* http:// firstmonday.org/issues/issue5_2/ronfeldt/index .html. Daytona International Speedway. (2008). Brief history of the 500. Daytona 500. http:// www.daytona500.com/content-display.cfm/cat/ Brief-History-of-the-500.

CHAPTER NOTES

1. Ronfeldt, D. (2000, February). Social science at 190 mph on NASCAR's biggest speedways. *First Monday, 5(2).* http://firstmonday.org/ issues/issue5_2/ronfeldt/index.html

2. Dabos, G. E., & Rousseau, D. M. (2004). Mutuality and reciprocity in the psychological contracts of employees and employees. *Journal of Applied Psychology, 89,* 52–72.

3. Rousseau, D. M. (1995). *Psychological contracts in organizations: Understanding written and unwritten agreements.* Thousand Oaks, CA: Sage.

4. Rousseau, D. M. (2001). Schema, promise and mutuality: The building blocks of the psychological contract. *Journal of Occupational and Organizational Psychology, 74,* 511–541. Rousseau, D. M., & Schalk, R. (2000). *Psychological contracts in employment: Cross-national perspectives.* Thousand Oaks, CA: Sage.

5. See Note 2.

6. Rousseau, D. M., & Parks, J. M. (1993). The contracts of individuals and organizations. In L. L. Cummings & B. M. Staw (Eds.), *Research in organizational behavior* (Vol. 15, pp. 1–43). Greenwich, CT: JAI Press.

7. Hui, C., Lee, C., & Rousseau, D. M. (2004). Psychological contract and organizational citizenship behavior in China: Investigating generalizability and instrumentality. *Journal of Applied Psychology, 89,* 311–321.

8. See Note 4.

9. Raja, U., Johns, G., & Ntalianis, F. (2004). The impact of personality on psychological contracts. *Academy of Management Journal, 67,* 350–367.

10. Judge, T. A., Heller, D., & Mount, M. K. (2002). Five-factor model of personality and job satisfaction: A meta-analysis. *Journal of Applied Psychology, 87,* 530–541.

11. Schoorman, F. D., Mayer, R. C., & Davis, J. H. (2007). An integrative model of organizational trust: Past, present, and future. *Academy of Management Review, 32,* 344–354.

12. Lewicki, R. J., & Wiethoff, C. (2000). Trust, trust development, and trust repair. In M. Deutsch & P. T. Coleman (Eds.), *The handbook of conflict resolution* (pp. 86–107). San Francisco, CA: Jossey-Bass.

13. Bachman, R., & Zaheer, A. (2008). *Handbook of trust research.* Northampton, MA: Edgar Elgar.

14. Myerson, D., Weick, K. E., & Kramer, R. M. (1996). Swift trust in temporary groups. In R. M. Kramer & T. R. Tyler (Eds.), *Trust in organizations: Frontiers of theory and research* (pp. 166–195). Thousand Oaks, CA: Sage.

15. Peters, L., & Karren, R. J. (2009). An examination of the roles of trust and functional diversity performance ratings. *Group & Organization Management, 34,* 479–504. Henttonen, K., & Blomqvist, K. (2005). Managing distance in a global virtual team: The evolution of trust through technology-mediated relational communication. *Strategic Change, 14,* 107–119. Jarvenpaa, S. L., Knoll, K., & Leidner, D. E. (1998). Is anybody out there? Antecedents of trust in global virtual teams. *Journal of Management Information Systems, 14,* 29–64.

16. Colquitt, J. A., & Salam, S. C. (2009). Foster trust through ability, benevolence and integrity. In E. A. Locke (Ed.), *Handbook of principles of organizational behavior* (pp. 389–404). Chichester, UK: Wiley.

17. See Note 16.

18. Podsakoff, P. M., MacKenzie, S. B., Paine, J. B., & Bachrach, D. G. (2000). Organizational citizenship behaviors: A critical review of the theoretical and empirical literature and suggestions for future research. *Journal of Management, 26,* 513–563.

19. Settoon, R. P., & Mossholder, K. W. (2002). Relationship quality and relationship context as antecedents of person- and task-focused interpersonal citizenship behavior. *Journal of Applied Psychology, 87,* 255–267. McNeely, B. L., & Meglino, B. M. (1994). The role of dispositional and situational antecedents in prosocial organizational behavior: An examination of the intended beneficiaries of prosocial behavior. *Journal of Applied Psychology, 79,* 836–844.

20. Zellars, K. L., Tepper, B. J., & Duffy, M. K. (2002). Abusive supervision and subordinates' organizational citizenship behavior. *Journal of Applied Psychology, 87,* 1068–1076.

21. Podsakoff, P. M., MacKenzie, S. B., Paine, J. B., & Bachrach, D. G. (2000). Organizational citizenship behaviors: A crucial review of the theoretical and empirical literature and suggestions for future research. *Journal of Management, 26,* 513–563.

22. Tansky, J. W. (1993). Justice and organizational citizenship behavior: What is the relationship? *Employees' Responsibilities and Rights Journal, 6,* 195–207.

23. Ladd, D., & Henry, R. A. (2000). Helping coworkers and helping the organization: The role of support perceptions, exchange ideology, and conscientiousness. *Journal of Applied Social Psychology, 30,* 2028–2049.

24. See Note 1.

25. Fomburn, C. J. (1996). *Reputation.* Boston, MA: Harvard Business School Press.

26. Allen, T. D., & Rush, M. C. (1998). The effects of organizational citizenship behavior on performance judgments: A field study and laboratory experiment. *Journal of Applied Psychology, 83,* 247–260.

27. Johnson, J. (2001). The relative importance of task and contextual performance dimensions to supervisor judgments of overall performance. *Journal of Applied Psychology, 86,* 984–996.

28. Werner, J. M. (1994). Dimensions that make a difference: Examining the impact of in-role and extrarole behaviors on supervisory ratings. *Journal of Applied Psychology, 79,* 98–107.

29. Johnson, S. K., Holladay, C. L., & Quiñones, M. A. (2009). Organizational citizenship behavior in performance evaluations: Distributive justice or injustice? *Journal of Business and Psychology, 24,* 409–418.

30. Falk, A., Gachter, S., & Kovacs, J. (1999). Intrinsic motivation and extrinsic incentives in a repeated game with incomplete contracts. *Journal of Economic Psychology, 20,* 251–284.

31. Knight, G. P., Dubro, A. F., & Chao, C. (1985). Information processing and the development of cooperative, competitive, and individualistic social values. *Developmental Psychology, 21,* 37–45.

32. Knight, G. P., & Dubro, A. F. (1984). Cooperative, competitive, and individualistic social values: An individualized regression and clustering approach. *Journal of Personality and Social Psychology, 46,* 98–105.

33. Kirkman, B. L., & Shapiro, D. L. (2000). Understanding why team members won't share: An examination of factors related to employee receptivity to team-based rewards. *Small Group Research, 31,* 175–209. DeMatteo, J. S., Eby, L. T., & Sundstrom, E. (1998). Team-based rewards: Current empirical evidence and directions for future research. In B. M. Staw & L. L. Cummings (Eds.), *Research in organizational behavior* (Vol. 20, pp. 141–183). Greenwich, CT: JAI. Heneman, R.L. (2000). *Business-driven compensation policies.* New York: Amacom.

34. Koza, M., & Lewin, A. Y. (1998). The evolution of strategic alliances. *Organizational Science, 9,* 255–264.

35. Teerlink, R., & Ozley, L. (2000). *More than a motorcycle: The leadership journey at Harley-Davidson.* Boston: Harvard Business School Press.

36. Thomas, K. W., & Schmidt, W. H. (1976). A survey of managerial interests with respect to conflict. *Academy of Management Journal, 10,* 315–318.

37. Dirks, K. T., & McLean Parks, J. (2003). Conflicting stories: The state of the science of conflict. In J. Greenberg (Ed.), *Organizational behavior: The state of the science,* 2nd ed. (pp. 283–324). Mahwah, NJ: Lawrence Erlbaum Associates.

38. Jehn, K., & Mannix, E. (2001). The dynamic nature of conflict: A longitudinal study of intragroup conflict and performance. *Academy of Management Journal, 44,* 238–251.

39. Scudder, T., Patterson, M., & Mitchell, K. (2012). *Have a nice conflict.* San Francisco, CA: Jossey-Bass. Bragg, T. (1999, October). Ten ways to deal with conflict. *IIE Solutions,* pp. 36–37.

40. Resume: Howard Schultz (2002, September 9). *BusinessWeek Online.* www.businessweek.com/magazine/content/02_36/b3798005.htm

41. Bordwin, M. (1999). Do-it-yourself justice. *Management Review,* 56–58.

42. Greenberg, J. (2004). Deviance. In N. Nicholson, P. Audia, & M. Pillutla (Eds.), *Blackwell encyclopedia of organizational behavior* (2nd ed.). Malden, MA: Blackwell. Bennett, R. J., & Robinson, S. L. (2003). The past, present, and future of workplace deviance research. In J. Greenberg (Ed.), *Organizational behavior: The state of the science* (pp. 247–282). Mahwah, NJ: Lawrence Erlbaum Associates. Vardi, Y., & Weitz, E. (2003). *Misbehavior in organizations: Theory, research, management.* Mahwah, NJ: Lawrence Erlbaum Associates.

43. Bennett, R. J., & Robinson, S. L. (2003). The past, present, and future of workplace deviance research. In J. Greenberg (Ed.), *Organizational behavior: The state of the science* (pp. 52–70). Mahwah, NJ: Erlbaum.

44. Gundlach, M. J., Scott, D. S., & Martinko, M. J. (2003). The decision to blow the whistle: A social information processing framework. *Academy of Management Review, 28,* 107–123. Miceli, M., & Near, J. (1992). *Blowing the whistle.* Lexington, MA: New Lexington Press.

45. Fox News. (2011, April 8). IRS awards $4.5 million to whistleblower. FoxNews.com. http://www.foxnews.com/politics/2011/04/08/irs-awards-45m-whistleblower/. Edson, R. (2009, February 3). Madoff outrage: Whistleblower testimony rips SEC. *Foxbusiness.com.* http://www.foxbusiness.com/story/markets/industries/government/madoff-outrage-whistleblower-testimony-rips-sec. National Whistleblowers Center. (2010). Spotlight Bradley Birkenfeld. http://www.whistleblowers.org/index.php?option=com_content&task=blogcategory&id=71&Itemid=108. Fricker, D. G. (2002, March 27). Enron whistle-blower honored in Dearborn. www.freep.com/money/business/htm. Anonymous. (2000, April). Paul van Buitenen: Paying the price of accountability. *Accountancy, 125*(1), 280. Taylor, M. (1999, September 13). Another Columbia suit unsealed. *Modern Healthcare, 29*(37), 10. Ettore, B. (1994, May). Whistleblowers: Who's the real bad guy? *Management Review,* 18–23.

46. Australian Compliance Institute. (2004, July 16). Australians are reluctant whistleblowers. *The Age,* 112.

47. Gjersten, L. A. (1999). Five State Farm agents fired after accusing company of consumer abuse. *National Underwriter, 103*(51), 1, 23.

48. Rothstein, K. (2004, July 6). Class act for hire: Fired whistle-blowing teacher looks for work. *Boston Herald,* p. B7.

49. See Note 48.

50. Martucci, W. C., & Smith, E. W. (2000). Recent state legislative development concerning employment discrimination and whistle-blower protections. *Employment Relations Today, 27*(2), 89–99.

51. Jones, M., & Rowell, A. (1999). Safety whistleblowers intimidated. *Safety and Health Practitioner, 17*(8), 3.

52. Bidoli, M., & Eedes, J. (2001, February 16). Big Brother is watching you. *Future Company.* www.futurecompany.co.za/2001/02/16/covstory.htm

53. Mastrangelo, P., Everton, W., & Jolton, J. (2001). *Computer misuse in the workplace.* Unpublished manuscript. University of Baltimore. Lim, V. K. G., Loo, G. L., & Teo, T. S. H. (2001, August). *Perceived injustice, neutralization and cyberloafing at the workplace.* Paper presented at the annual meeting of the Academy of Management, Washington, DC.

54. Douglas, S. C., & Martinko, M. J. (2001). Exploring the role of individual differences in the prediction of workplace aggression. *Journal of Applied Psychology, 86,* 547–559.

55. National Institute for Occupational Safety and Health, Centers for Disease Control and Prevention. (1993). *Homicide in the workplace.* [Document # 705003]. Atlanta, GA: Author.

56. Baron, R.A. (2004). Workplace aggression and violence: Insights from basic research. In R.W. Griffin & V. O'Leary-Kelly (Eds.), *The dark side of organizational behavior* (pp. 23–61). San Francisco, CA: Jossey-Bass.

57. Namie, G., & Namie, R. (2011). *The bully-free workplace.* New York: Wiley.

58. Neuman, J. H. (2004). Injustice, stress, and aggression in organizations. In R. W. Griffin & V. O'Leary-Kelly (Eds.), *The dark side of organizational behavior* (pp. 62–102). San Francisco, CA: Jossey-Bass.

59. Glomb, T. M., & Liao, H. (2003). Interpersonal aggression in work groups: Social influence, reciprocal, and individual effects. *Academy of Management Journal, 46,* 386–396.

60. Dietz, J., Robinson, S. A., Folger, R., Baron, R. A., & Jones., T. (2003). The impact of societal violence and organizational justice climate on workplace aggression. *Academy of Management Journal, 46,* 317–326.

61. Jack L. Hays International. (2009). Theft surveys. http://www.hayesinternational.com/thft_srvys.html

62. Kooker, N. R. (2000, May 22). Taking aim at crime—stealing the profits: Tighter controls, higher morale may safeguard bottom line. *Nation's Restaurant News, 34*(21), 114–118.

63. Golden, A. (2009, November 6). As economy falters, employee theft on the rise. *Las Vegas Sun.* http://www.lasvegassun.com/news/2009/nov/06/managing-fraud-lesson-recession

64. Jabbkerm, A. (2000, March 29). Agrium seeks $30 million in damages in embezzlement case. *Chemical Week, 162*(13), 22.

65. Greenberg, J. (1998). The cognitive geometry of employee theft: Negotiating "the line" between taking and stealing. In R. W. Griffin, A. O'Leary-Kelly, & J. M. Collins (Eds.), *Dysfunctional behavior in organizations: Nonviolent dysfunctional behavior* (pp. 147–194). Greenwich, CT: JAI Press.

8 | ORGANIZATIONAL COMMUNICATION

LEARNING OBJECTIVES

After reading this chapter, you will be able to:

1. **DEFINE** communication and **DESCRIBE** the various steps in the communication process.
2. **RECOGNIZE** the differences between formal and informal communication in organizations.
3. **DISTINGUISH** between verbal communication—both traditional and computer mediated—and nonverbal communication, and the factors that make each effective.
4. **IDENTIFY** various inspirational techniques that can be used to enhance one's effectiveness as a communicator.
5. **DESCRIBE** what it takes to be a supportive communicator.
6. **EXPLAIN** how to meet the challenges associated with communicating with people from different cultures.

THREE GOOD REASONS you should care about. . .

Organizational Communication

1. Although managers spend a great deal of time communicating with others, they tend not to do so as effectively as possible.
2. Properly managing organizational communication is key to individual and organizational effectiveness.
3. There are several things you can do to enhance your organizational communication skills.

Making the Case for...

Organizational Communication

Reducing Interruptions High-Tech Style at Microsoft and IBM

Human beings are readily distracted, psychologists tell us, because distractions signal changes in the environment of which we must be aware. The doorbell rings and we answer it. Someone calls our name and we look up. This fact of nature wasn't a problem before we were busily multitasking and faced with e-mails, phone calls, instant messages, and people stopping by to chat. Today, however, the sheer number of distractions takes its toll on productivity. In fact, most people "switch gears" every few minutes, and when this occurs, it takes about a half hour to recover. Overall, people lose an average of 28 percent of their daily work hours due to disruptions, costing the U.S. economy some $650 billion each year.

As you might imagine, such an expensive problem has prompted a search for a solution. One fascinating fix comes from the company responsible for developing the technology that made possible many distractions in the first place—Microsoft. For more than 10 years, Microsoft scientist Eric Horvitz has been working on an artificial-intelligence system that emulates the behavior of people at work. His computer program, Priorities, tracks everything that people do at their computers and with handheld devices and then uses sophisticated statistical techniques to determine the costs and benefits of being interrupted by various e-mail messages.

If the program determines that it's too costly to interrupt you with a particular message, it will keep it from you until a time when the interruption is less expensive. So, for example, word of a corporate shake-up is more likely to be presented to you than, say, a message about the day's cafeteria offerings. For better or worse, Microsoft is considering including some version of this technology in a forthcoming version of its Windows operating system.

Not to be outdone, IBM is taking a different approach to the problem of disruption. Its program, IMSavvy, is like an answering machine for instant messages. Based on the nature and extent of keyboard activity, the program senses when you're busy or away from your desk and tells people who are demanding your attention that you are unavailable. There's still something important that the program hasn't yet worked out—namely, what if you're quiet because you are reading or thinking about something? Somehow, the silence or keyboard inactivity needs to be able to interpret this, but that's something for version 2.0.

Probably the most fascinating feature of IMSavvy is the way it gives people the opportunity to determine whether their message is sufficiently important to let the recipient decide if it warrants an interruption. The so-called "whisper" option is designed to emulate what might happen if someone knocks on your door while you're on the phone. You may wave the visitor away but listen to an important message whispered to you (e.g., "Hey, we closed the deal"). This way, people, rather than software, can determine the importance of any potential interruption. Of course, if this is abused, then we're back to the beginning by creating yet another (albeit softer) form of interruption.

Few among us are unable to relate to the problem of interruptions. After all, they threaten to affect our productivity adversely at work and at home, too. Then again, what you consider an interruption may simply be a message that you don't want to hear at that particular moment. The information, in reality, may be quite important to you or to someone else, although it might better be attended to at some later time. Matters of this nature are involved in the fundamental—and vital—process of *communication*.

I refer to it as vital because there can be no organizations without people communicating with one another. Waiters must take their customers' orders and pass them along to the chef. Store managers must describe special promotions to their sales staffs. And the football coach must tell his team what plays to run. Clearly, communication is the key to these attempts at coordination. Without it, people would not know what to do, and groups and organizations would not be able to operate effectively—if at all!

With this in mind, communication has been referred to as "the social glue ... that continues to keep organizations tied together,"[1] and "the essence of organizations."[2] Given its importance in the workplace, you may not be surprised to learn that managers spend as much as 80 percent of their time engaged in one form of communication or another (e.g., writing reports, sending e-mails, talking to others in person, etc.). Communication involves everyone in an organization (and outside it, too), from the lowest-level employee to the head of a large corporation.

Given the central role of communication in organizations, I will examine it closely in this chapter. I begin by defining the process of communication and characterizing its role in organizations. Following this, I describe two basic forms of communication: formal and informal. Next, I distinguish between two major types of communication in which we all engage—verbal communication and nonverbal communication. And because much of today's communication is high tech in nature, I highlight computer-mediated communication techniques. With these discussions as a foundation, I then offer practical suggestions about how to become a better communicator. Finally, recognizing the global nature of today's business environment, I conclude this chapter by examining the challenges of cross-national communication.

COMMUNICATION: ITS BASIC NATURE

To appreciate fully the process of organizational communication, I must address some fundamental issues. I begin by formally defining the concept of communication and then elaborating on the process by which it occurs. Following this, I describe the various purposes and levels of communication in organizations.

Defining Communication and Describing the Process

Although you probably already have a good idea of what communication entails, a formal definition will help orient you. With this in mind, I define **communication** as the process by which a person, group, or organization (the *sender*) transmits some type of information (the *message*) to another party (the *receiver*). To clarify this definition and to further elaborate on how the process works, I summarize it in Figure 8.1. You may find it useful to follow along with this diagram as you read about the various steps described here.

ENCODING   The communication process begins when one party has an idea that it wishes to transmit to another (either party may be an individual, a group, or an entire organization). It is the sender's mission to transform the idea into a form that can be sent to and understood by the receiver. This is what happens in the process of **encoding**—translating an idea into a form, such as written or spoken language, that can be recognized by a receiver. We encode information when

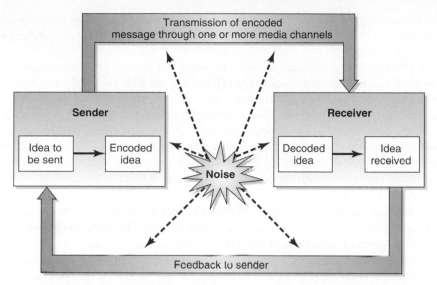

FIGURE 8.1 The Communication Process
Communication generally follows the steps outlined here. Senders *encode* messages and *transmit* them via one or more communication channels to receivers, who then *decode* these messages received. The process continues as the original receiver then sends *feedback* to the original sender. Factors distorting or limiting the flow of information—known collectively as *noise*—may enter into the process at any point.

we select the words we use to write a letter or speak to someone in person. This process is critical if we are to communicate our ideas clearly. If you've ever had difficulty finding the right words to express your ideas (and who hasn't!), then you know that people are far from perfect when it comes to encoding their ideas. Fortunately, as I will note later, this skill can be improved.

CHANNELS OF COMMUNICATION After a message is encoded, it is ready to be transmitted over one or more **channels of communication**—that is, the pathways along which information travels—to reach the desired receiver. Telephone lines, radio and television signals, fiber-optic cables, cell phone signals, mail routes, satellite transmissions to GPS devices, and even the air waves that carry the vibrations of our voices are all potential channels of communication.

Of course, the form of encoding largely determines the way information may be transmitted. Visual information—such as pictures and written words—may be mailed, delivered in person by a courier, shipped by an express delivery service, or sent electronically, such as via e-mail, instant message, uploaded onto a Web site, or faxed. Oral information may be transmitted over the telephone, via radio and television signals, using online sound files—and, of course, the old-fashioned way, in person. Whatever channel is used, the goal is the same: to send the encoded message accurately to the desired receiver.

DECODING Once a message is received, the recipient must begin the process of **decoding**—converting the message back into the sender's original ideas. This involves many different sub-processes, such as comprehending spoken and written words, interpreting facial expressions, and the like. To the extent that the sender's message is decoded accurately by the receiver, the ideas understood will be the ones intended. Of course, our ability to comprehend and interpret information received from others may be imperfect. For example, this may be restricted by unclear messages, by our own language skills, or by one's existing knowledge. Thus, as in the case of encoding, limitations in our ability to decode information represent another potential weakness in the communication process—but, as I will describe later in this chapter, it's one that can be developed.

FEEDBACK   Finally, once a message has been decoded, the process can continue, with the receiver transmitting a new message back to the original sender. This part of the process is known as **feedback**—in this context, defined as knowledge about the impact of messages on receivers. Receiving feedback allows senders to determine whether their messages have been understood properly. At the same time, giving feedback can help convince receivers that the sender really cares about what he or she has to say. Once received, feedback can trigger another idea from the sender, and another cycle of transferring information may begin. For this reason, I have characterized the process of communication summarized in Figure 8.1 as continuous.

NOISE   Despite the apparent simplicity of the communication process, it rarely operates as flawlessly as described here. As you will see, there are many potential barriers to effective communication. The name given to factors that distort the clarity of a message is **noise**. As I have suggested in Figure 8.1, noise can occur at any point along the communication process. For example, messages that are poorly encoded (e.g., written in an unclear way) or poorly decoded (e.g., not comprehended), or channels of communication that are too full of static (e.g., receivers' attentions are diverted from the message) may reduce communication's effectiveness.

One particularly prevalent source of noise in e-mail communication these days is **spam**, unsolicited commercial bulk e-mail messages. As much as 75 percent of e-mail messages received fall into this category, and despite efforts to stop it, the figure is rising.[3] In recent years, workers have been plagued by so much spam that it has been estimated that the average company loses about 10 days of productivity per year due to time lost by dealing with spam—even if employees spend as little as five seconds on each unwanted message.[4] Considering this, it probably comes as no surprise that spam, a modern form of noise, contributes greatly to the inefficiency of e-mail systems—bogging them down with unwanted information, making it difficult to search for desired messages, and often exposing people to distasteful material.

It's not only spam, of course; a variety of factors (e.g., time pressure, organizational politics) contribute to the distortion of information transmitted from one party to another. These factors and many others, as you will see in this chapter, make the process of organizational communication so very complex.

Purposes and Levels of Organizational Communication

In a sense, discussing the purpose of communication in organizations seems unnecessary since it's so obvious: You have to communicate with others to share information with them, which is necessary to get things done. This is true, of course, but communication actually serves a much broader range of purposes. In fact, communication serves at least eight critical functions in organizations.[5] These are as follows:

- *Directing action*—Communication between people is necessary to get others to behave in a desired fashion. Managers must communicate with subordinates to tell them what to do, to give them feedback on their performance, to discuss problems with them, to encourage them, and so on.
- *Linking and coordination*—For organizations to function effectively, individuals and groups must carefully coordinate their efforts and activities, and communication makes this possible. In a restaurant, for example, a waiter must take customers' orders and pass them along to the chef. This may occur orally (e.g., by shouting out the order), in writing (e.g., by viewing orders scribbled onto paper tickets), or electronically (e.g., by entering

orders on touch-screens that chefs can view on kitchen monitors). Despite these varied forms, the goal is identical: to communicate customers' requests to kitchen staff.

- *Building relationships*—Communication is essential to the development of interpersonal relationships. Building friendships and promoting trust (see Chapter 7) requires careful communication. Doing so can help create a pleasant atmosphere in the workplace. However opportunities to use technology for social networking can interfere with performing one's job, which is why visiting sites such as Facebook and Twitter while at work is frequently prohibited.[6]

- *Explaining organizational culture*—By communicating with others, employees come to understand how their companies operate, what is valued, and what matters most to people. In other words, they learn about the *culture* of their organizations (I will discuss organizational culture in detail in Chapter 12).

- *Interorganizational linking*—People communicate not only with others in their own organizations but also with representatives of other organizations. This makes it possible for companies to coordinate their efforts toward achieving mutual goals, such as occurs in *joint ventures* (see Chapter 13).

- *Presenting an organization's image*—Organizations send messages about themselves to broad groups of others. For example, companies publish information about goods and services to attract prospective customers. These forms of communication are designed to present certain images of the organization to the world.

- *Generating ideas*—Communication is used to generate ideas and to share them as necessary. When people brainstorm with one another, for example, the communication process helps create new ideas (see Chapter 10 for a discussion of the brainstorming process).

- *Promoting ideals and values*—Many organizations "stand for something" and have purposes that must be communicated clearly. For example, a stated purpose of the National Organization for Women (NOW) is to help women participate fully in society. Communication is required for word of this mission to reach people and for them to understand it. This is necessary, of course, if the stated objective is to be accomplished.

As these descriptions suggest, communication plays a vital role at all organizational levels. Specifically, organizational communication occurs at the five distinct levels summarized in Table 8.1. These range from *interpersonal communication* at one end, involving people on an individual basis, all the way to *mass communication*, in which information is shared with large numbers of people. This broad range of approaches lends itself to study by a variety of professional groups. Besides specialists in the field of OB, as this table suggests, communication also is of great interest to psychologists and sociologists, as well as scientists and practitioners in the fields of marketing, journalism, and political science. Among OB specialists, the focus primarily is on the three lowest levels, interpersonal communication, group-level communication, and organizational-level communication. You will see these various emphases in this chapter.

Now that I have established the nature of communication in organizations, I will continue by examining in the next two sections the two major varieties, *formal communication* and *informal communication*.

FORMAL COMMUNICATION IN ORGANIZATIONS

Imagine a CEO of a large conglomerate announcing plans for new products to a group of stockholders. Now, imagine a supervisor telling her subordinates what to do that day on the job. Both examples describe situations in which someone is sharing official information with others who need to know it. This is referred to as **formal communication**. As you might imagine, formal communication is aided by the use of technology.

TABLE 8.1	Levels of Organizational Communication	

As summarized here, communication occurs at many different levels. These range from the "micro level" communication between individuals through broader, "macro level" forms, involving communication within and between organizations, to societal-level communication, such as occurs in the case of mass communication.

Level of Communication	Description	Example
Interpersonal communication	Individuals sharing information, formally or informally	A supervisor meets with her direct report to discuss ways of improving this person's work.
Group-level communication	Sharing of information within groups or teams	The members of a sales team coordinate their efforts at developing a new sales campaign.
Organizational-level communication	Sharing of information between subunits of the same organization	Representatives of various company departments assemble to create a strategic plan.
Interorganizational communication	Sharing of information between organizations	Firms working together on a joint venture make plans for sharing resources required to create a new product.
Mass communication	A company broadcasting messages to large numbers of people	An automobile manufacturer notifies its dealers and owners of a safety recall.

Technology's Role in Formal Communication

Starting with the first time a boss scribbled a note to one of her employees, technology has been used for communication. Sure, a pencil or pen is quite low tech, but it's still technology. So too is the printing press, a marvel of technology that revolutionized communication in the fifteenth century. As time went on, and technology became more sophisticated the land-line telephone, the telegraph, and other such devices made it possible to send formal messages to one or more people who were physically distant. So, while it's clear that the use of technology to enhance formal organizational communication is not new, it is clear that the highly advanced nature of today's technology has greatly influenced the basic nature of organizational communication. As an illustration, consider the following ways in which technology has influenced the nature of organizational communication today.

- *Technology has sped up the pace of work*—As work gets done faster than ever, communication must be more effective because there is less time to correct errors or misunderstandings.
- *Teams enhance the need for coordination*—Because of the popularity of teams (as described in Chapter 9), people interact with lots of others who perform wide varieties of jobs. This requires coordinating information very carefully.
- *Employees are likely to be distributed geographically*—It's not unusual for people to work from home (see Chapter 1) and to keep in close contact with their offices while traveling on business. And, when people are out of sight, the normal opportunities to communicate when seeing someone in person are eliminated.
- *Knowledge and information are keys to success*—For today's organizations to be successful, they not only must be productive, but they also must stay abreast of rapidly

changing markets. This requires information to be accessed and shared in a coordinated fashion.
- *Technology has transformed the way people do their jobs*—In today's electronically sophisticated world, we count on a variety of communication media that have transformed the way people do their jobs. Using the Internet to access information and to communicate with others (e.g., via e-mail) is a prime example.

Having described these important qualities of formal communication today, I now expand this discussion by outlining its basic nature. Here, I focus on the *organization chart*, a tool used to describe formal communication and the various forms it takes.

Organization Charts and What They Reveal About Communication

The formally prescribed pattern of interrelationships existing between the various units of an organization is commonly described by using a diagram known as an **organization chart**. Such diagrams provide graphic representations of organizations' structures, outlines of the planned, formal connections between its various units—that is, who is supposed to communicate with whom.

An organization chart revealing the structure of a small part of a fictitious organization, and an overview of the types of communication expected to occur within it, are shown in Figure 8.2. Each box represents a particular job, as indicated by the job titles noted. The lines connecting the boxes show the formal lines of communication between the individuals performing those jobs—that is, who is supposed to communicate with whom. This particular organization chart is typical of most in that it shows that people communicate formally with those immediately above them and below them, as well as those at their own levels.

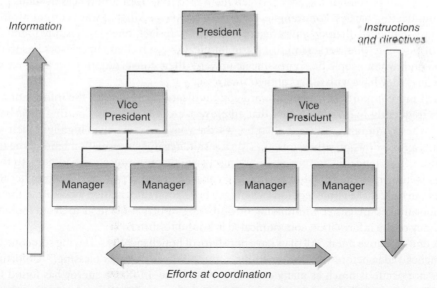

FIGURE 8.2   The Organization Chart: A Summary of Formal Communication Paths
Diagrams known as *organization charts* indicate the formal pattern of communication within an organization. They reveal which particular people, based on the jobs they hold, are required to communicate with each other. The types of messages generally communicated across different levels are identified here.

Downward Communication

Formal communication differs according to people's positions in an organization chart. Suppose, for example, that you are a supervisor. How would you characterize the formal communication that occurs between you and your subordinates—that is, communication down the organization chart? Typically, *downward communication* consists of instructions, directions, and orders—that is, messages telling subordinates what they should be doing. We also would expect to find feedback on past performance flowing in a downward direction. A sales manager, for example, may tell the members of her sales force what products they should be promoting.

As formal information slowly trickles down from one level of an organization to the next lowest level (as occurs when information is said to "go through channels"), it becomes less accurate. This is especially true when that information is spoken. In such cases, it is not unusual for at least part of the message to be distorted and/or omitted as it works its way down from one person to the next lowest-ranking person. (Anyone who has ever played the game of "telephone" has experienced this firsthand.) To avoid these problems, many companies have introduced programs in which they communicate formal information to large numbers of people at different levels all at one time.

Upward Communication

When information flows from lower levels to higher levels within an organization, such as messages from subordinates to their supervisors, it is known as *upward communication*. Typically, such messages involve information that managers need to do their jobs, such as data required to complete projects. This may include suggestions for improvement, status reports, reactions to work-related issues, and new ideas.

Although, logically, upward communication is the opposite of downward communication, there are some important differences between them resulting from differences in status between the communicating parties. For example, it has been established that upward communication occurs far less frequently than downward communication. In fact, one classic study found that 70 percent of assembly-line workers initiated communication with their supervisors less than once a month. And, when people do communicate upward, their conversations tend to be far shorter than the ones they have with others at their own level.

Even more importantly, when upward communication does occur, the information transmitted is frequently inaccurate. Given that employees are interested in "putting their best foot forward" when communicating with their bosses, they have a tendency to highlight their accomplishments and to downplay their mistakes. As a result, negative information tends to be ignored or disguised. This tendency for people to purposely avoid communicating bad news to their supervisors is known as the **MUM effect**. We are concerned about this phenomenon because supervisors can only make good decisions when they have good information available to them. And when subordinates are either withholding or distorting information so as to avoid looking bad, the accuracy of the information communicated is bound to suffer.

As one executive put it, "All of us have our share of bonehead ideas. Having someone tell you it's a bonehead idea before you do something about it is really a great blessing."[7] Unfortunately, this does not occur as much as many executives would like. In fact, a survey has found that although 95 percent of CEOs say that they have an open-door policy and will not harm those who communicate bad news, half of all employees fear that they will be jeopardizing their positions by sharing bad news, and frequently refrain from doing so.[8]

Horizontal Communication

Within organizations, messages don't only flow up and down the organization chart, but sideways as well. **Horizontal communication** is the term used to identify messages that flow laterally, at the same organizational level. Messages of this type are characterized by efforts at coordination, attempts to work together.

Consider, for example, how a vice president of marketing would have to coordinate her efforts with people in other departments when launching an advertising campaign for a new product. This would require the coordination of information with experts from manufacturing and production (to see when the products will be available) as well as those from research and development (to see what features people really want).

Unlike vertical communication, in which the parties are at different organizational levels, horizontal communication involves people at the same level. Therefore, it tends to be easier and friendlier. It is also more casual in tone and occurs more readily given that there are fewer social barriers between the parties. This is not to say that horizontal communication is without its potential pitfalls. Indeed, people in different departments sometimes feel that they are competing against each other for valued organizational resources, leading them to show resentment toward one another. And when an antagonistic, competitive orientation replaces a friendly, cooperative one, communication is bound to suffer.

INFORMAL COMMUNICATION: BEYOND THE ORGANIZATION CHART

Imagine a group of employees standing around the coffee machine chatting about how tough the big boss is or who was dancing with whom at the company party. These are also examples of organizational communication, but because they involve the sharing of unofficial information, they would be considered examples of **informal communication**. It's probably obvious to you that a great deal of information communicated in organizations goes far beyond sending formal messages up, down, or across organization charts. Such information is shared without any formally imposed obligations or restrictions.

Social Media and Informal Communication

Think for a moment about social media. If you consider the messages you may post on Twitter or Facebook, or videos you share on YouTube, it becomes clear just how prevalent—and far-reaching—informal communication may be. It's also apparent that today's technology has made the sharing of informal communication possible for anyone. Potentially, any blogger can reach as many readers as well-established media outlets, such as the *New York Times*.

To get a sense of the extensiveness of social media in informal communication, consider the following statistics regarding just one site, Facebook, today's most widely used social media site (Twitter, by the way, is fifth).[9] Specifically, it may be said that:

- *Facebook's reach is staggering*—One person out of every nine people on earth is registered on Facebook.
- *Facebook is international in scope*—Eighty percent of users are outside the United States and Canada and the site is available in 70 different languages.
- *Facebook is used widely*—By the end of December 2011, Facebook had 845 million active users per month and averaged 483 million active users per day.

- *Facebook has been growing rapidly*—Between 2010 and 2011, the number of registered users jumped by 82 percent.
- *Facebook is a wealth of shared information*—During the average 20-minute period in 2010, Facebook users posted 5.87 million wall posts, uploaded 2.72 million photos, and posted 10.21 million comments.

These statistics are fascinating, but don't lose sight of the point they are being used to illustrate—namely, Internet technology makes the sharing of informal communication more extensive than anyone ever could have imagined only a few years ago. This is worth keeping in mind if you consider the many times public figures such as athletes, politicians, and entertainers have embarrassed themselves or gotten into serious trouble by posting messages that they later wished they kept to themselves. Today, with the potential for our words to be broadcast to the whole world we all need to be mindful of the messages we put onto the blogosphere. Once a message is posted online, it's there for everyone to see forever. Keeping this in mind may give you pause (or, at least, it should) before clicking "send."

Hearing It "Through the Grapevine"

When people communicate informally, be it electronically or in person, they are not bound by their organizational positions. Anyone can tell anything to anyone else. Although it would clearly be inappropriate for a mail-room clerk to share his thoughts with a vice president about matters of corporate policy, both parties may be perfectly at ease exchanging thoughts about a local athletic team. The difference lies in the fact that the sports observations are unofficial in nature and are communicated informally—that is, without following the formal constraints imposed by the organization chart.

When anyone can tell something informally to anyone else, it results in a very rapid flow of information along what is commonly called **the grapevine**. This term refers to the pathways along which unofficial information travels. In contrast to formal organizational messages, which might take several days to reach their destinations, information traveling along the organizational grapevine tends to flow very rapidly. In fact, it is not unusual for some messages to reach everyone in a large organization in a matter of a few hours. This happens not only because informal communication crosses organizational boundaries and is open to everyone, but also because it is generally transmitted orally, and oral messages not only reach more people but also do so more quickly than written messages.

As I noted earlier, however, oral messages run the risk of becoming inaccurate as they flow between people. Because of the possible confusion that grapevines can cause, some people have sought to eliminate them. However, they are not necessarily bad. In fact, informally socializing with our coworkers can help make work groups more cohesive, and they also may provide excellent opportunities for the pleasant social contacts that make life at work enjoyable. Moreover, the grapevine remains one of the most efficient channels of communication. Indeed, about 70 percent of what people learn about their companies they pick up by chatting with coworkers in the cafeteria, at the coffee machine, in the corridors, or through social media.[10]

Rumors: The Downside of Informal Communication

Although the information communicated along the grapevine may be accurate in some respects, it may be inaccurate in others. In extreme cases, information may be transmitted that is almost totally without any basis in fact and is unverifiable. Such messages are known as **rumors**. Typically, rumors are based on speculation, someone's overactive imagination, and wishful thinking, rather than on facts.

Rumors race like wildfire through organizations because the information they contain is usually interesting and vague. This ambiguity leaves messages open to embellishment as they pass orally from one person to the next. Before you know it, almost everyone in the organization has heard the rumor, and its inaccurate message comes to be taken as fact ("Everyone knows it, so it must be true"). Hence, even if there may have been, at one point, some truth to a rumor, the message quickly grows untrue.

If you personally have ever been the victim of a rumor, you know just how troublesome it can be. Now, imagine how many times more serious the consequences may be when an organization falls victim to a rumor. Two extreme cases come to mind. In the late 1970s, a rumor circulated in Chicago that McDonald's hamburgers contained worms. And in June 1993, stories appeared in the press stating that people had found syringes in cans of Pepsi-Cola. Although both rumors were proven to be completely untrue, they cost both McDonald's and Pepsi considerable sums of money due to lost sales, not to mention the costs of investigation and advertising.

With this in mind, the question arises: What can be done to counter the effects of rumors? You may be tempted to consider directly refuting a rumor. This approach works best whenever a rumor is highly implausible and is challenged immediately by an independent source. This was precisely what occurred when the Food and Drug Administration (FDA) carefully investigated Pepsi-Cola and announced that there were not, nor could there have been, syringes in cans of Pepsi.

In the case of McDonald's, direct refutations (in the form of signs from the FDA stating that McDonald's used only wholesome ground beef in its burgers) had little effect because the rumor had spread so rapidly. In fact, directly challenging the rumor only led some customers to raise questions about why such official government statements were necessary in the first place, thereby fueling the rumor. What worked best at countering the rumor, research showed, was reminding people about other things they already believed about McDonald's (e.g., that it is a clean, family-oriented place).[11] In keeping with this, advertising campaigns (including public relations efforts by politicians rumored to be involved in various scandals) frequently devote more time to redirecting the public's attention away from negative thoughts and toward positive ones that they already have.

COMMUNICATING WITH AND WITHOUT WORDS: VERBAL AND NONVERBAL COMMUNICATION

By virtue of the fact that you are reading this book, I know that you are familiar with **verbal communication**—transmitting and receiving ideas using words. Verbal communication can be either oral—that is, using spoken language, such as face-to-face talks or telephone conversations—or written, such as faxes, letters, e-mail messages, instant messages, or postings on blogs. It also can occur either with the assistance of computers (in which case it is known as *computer-mediated communication*) or without such support (in which case it is known as *traditional communication*).

Despite their differences, these forms of communication share a key feature: they all involve words. As you know, however, people also communicate a great deal without words, non-verbally—that is, by way of their facial gestures, body language, the clothes they wear, and even where at a table they choose to sit. This is referred to as **nonverbal communication**. In this section of the chapter, I describe verbal communication media, both traditional and computer mediated, as well as nonverbal communication.

Traditional Verbal Media: Their Forms and Effectiveness

As you already know, organizations rely on a wide variety of verbal media. Some forms are considered *rich* because they are highly interactive and rely on a great deal of information. A face-to-face discussion is a good example. A telephone conversation may be considered a little less rich because it doesn't allow the parties to see each other. At the other end of the continuum are communications media that are considered lean because they are static (one way) and involve much less information. Flyers and bulletins are good examples because they are targeted broadly and focus on a specific issue. Letters also are a relatively lean form of communication. However, because letters are aimed at a specific individual, they may be considered not as lean as bulletins. For a summary of this continuum, please refer to Figure 8.3.[12]

FORMS OF WRITTEN COMMUNICATION   Although organizations rely on a wide variety of written media, two particular forms—*newsletters* and *employee handbooks*—deserve special mention because of the important roles they play. **Newsletters** are regularly published internal documents describing information of interest to employees regarding an array of business and nonbusiness issues. Traditionally, these were printed on paper, but most of today's company newsletters are published online, using the company's **intranet**—a Web site that only can be accessed by company employees.

 Employee handbooks also are important vehicles of internal organizational communication. These are formal documents describing basic information about the organization—its formal policies, mission, and underlying philosophy. Handbooks are widely used today. Not only are they effective ways of showing new employees "the ropes," but they also help clarify standards of acceptable behavior for all employees.

THE EFFECTIVENESS OF VERBAL MEDIA: MATCHING MEDIUM AND MESSAGE   Given that people in organizations spend so much of their time using both oral and written communication, it makes sense to ask: Which is more effective? As you might imagine, the answer is rather complex.

 One thing we know is that communication is most effective in organizations when it uses multiple channels—that is, *both* oral and written messages.[13] Oral messages help get people's immediate attention. Subsequent written follow-ups are helpful because they provide permanent documents to which people later can refer. Oral messages also have the benefit of allowing for immediate two-way communication between parties, whereas written messages frequently are

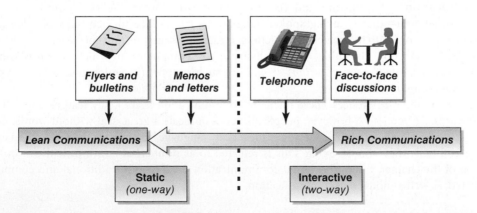

FIGURE 8.3   A Continuum of Traditional Verbal Communication Media
Traditional verbal communication media may be characterized along a continuum ranging from highly rich, interactive media (e.g., face-to-face discussions) to lean, static media (e.g., flyers and bulletins). *Source:* Based on information in Lengel & Daft, 1988; see Note 12.

either one-way or take too long for a response. As you might expect in organizations, two-way communications (such as face-to-face discussions and telephone calls) occur more frequently than one-way communications (e.g., memos).

The matter of how effectively a particular communications medium works depends on the kind of message being sent. According to **media richness theory**, managers will prefer using oral media when communicating ambiguous messages (e.g., directions on how to solve a complex technical problem) but written media for communicating clear messages (e.g., sharing a price list).[14] This makes sense if you think about it. After all, when a message is ambiguous, managers will find it easier to express themselves orally, especially given that spoken messages often provide immediate feedback, making it possible to tell how well the other person is getting the point. However, when it comes to clear messages, putting them in writing is more effective because it makes it easier for others to refer to them later on when needed.

Not surprisingly, research has shown that managers who follow this particular pattern of matching media with messages tend to be more effective on the job than those who do not do so.[15] This suggests that demonstrating sensitivity to communicating in the most appropriate fashion is an important determinant of managerial success.

Computer-Mediated Communication

Today, a great deal of the verbal communication in which we engage in organizations occurs with the assistance of computers, a process known as **computer-mediated communication**. Although people continue to talk to others in person, of course, various forms of online communication, such as e-mail, Web conferencing, and instant messaging, have become common in the workplace.[16] In fact, OB scientists have been involved in examining the nature and impact of this phenomenon.

COMPARING FACE-TO-FACE AND ONLINE COMMUNICATION   In recent years, our understanding of communication media has expanded from distinguishing between oral and written media to communication that occurs orally in one of two ways—either face-to-face or online. Comparing these two forms of communication is particularly important given the growing popularity of online conferencing, the practice of communicating with others virtually, using online technology that makes it possible to communicate with others live via Internet connections. Because the price of computer-based telecommunications equipment is relatively low, businesses have found online conferencing to be a highly cost-effective alternative to getting people together to discuss things in person. This leads to an important question: How do online communications between people differ from in-person discussions?

A study examined this question by comparing groups of people who were brought together to have in-person discussions on a defined topic with an approximately equal number of people who were brought together to discuss the same topic via an online conference.[17] This particular conference did not provide visual contact with others using Web cameras (it was not a videoconference). Rather, participants merely shared their remarks with others by typing them on a computer keyboard. Although both groups discussed the topic for approximately the same amount of time, one hour, the groups differed significantly in several different ways.

As summarized in Figure 8.4, compared to members of online groups, members of face-to-face groups made fewer comments, but the comments they made were longer and more detailed. In other words, online participants were generally less likely to elaborate on the statements they made, failing to share equally deep insight into their ideas. Also, because members of online groups could not be seen, they were more inclined to rely on simple statements of agreement (e.g., "that's a good idea") in situations in which members of face-to-face groups would just nod.

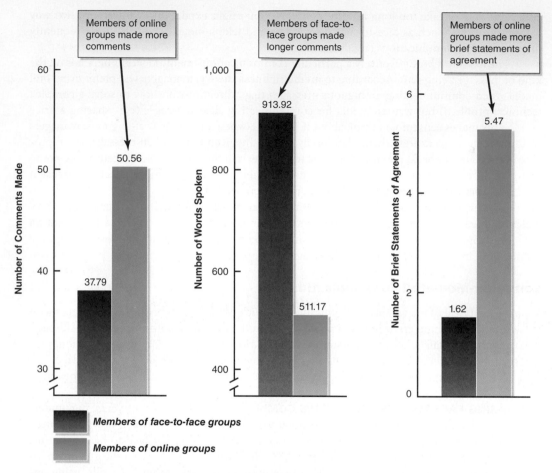

FIGURE 8.4 Face-to-Face Versus Online Communication: An Experimental Comparison
A study comparing the way people communicate with one another in person versus when having live online discussions revealed some interesting results. Specifically, it was found that although members of online groups made more comments, the comments made by members of face-to-face groups were longer and more detailed. Also, because online groups could not use nonverbal gestures to communicate their points, they relied more heavily on brief verbal statements to indicate their agreement with others.
Source: Based on data reported by Schneider et al., 2002; see Note 17.

These findings suggest that face-to-face and online discussions should be considered for different purposes. For example, market researchers may rely on online discussions to gather people's general and immediate reactions to new products. However, if they want to tap more detailed opinions, face-to-face discussions would appear to be a better choice.

USING "EMOTICONS" TO EXPRESS EMOTIONS IN E-MAIL E-mail is one of the most common forms of communication today, and some predict that it will even surpass face-to-face communication in popularity in the near future. As useful and as indispensable as e-mail has become, people sometimes find it frustrating to express their emotions through e-mail. After all, traditional e-mail is limited to alphanumeric characters and lacks the nonverbal information that makes face-to-face communication so rich. Although you can change the tone of your voice or make a face to express how you feel about something, it's harder to do this using only the tools of the keyboard.

In recent years, however, people have, rather ingeniously, developed simple graphic representations of facial expressions to express emotions. Known as **emoticons**, short for "emotional icons," these are created by typing characters such as commas, hyphens, and parentheses, which are best viewed by tilting one's head to the left. The most common emoticons are as follows:

:-) smile
:-(frown
;-) wink

People generally use emoticons to qualify their emotions in important ways, such as to communicate sarcasm. For example, the presence of the smiley face in the message, "he's really smart :-)" may be used to connote that the person in question is really not so smart at all.

However, research has revealed that emoticons do *not* always qualify the meanings of written messages.[18] For example, a negative message accompanied by a wink or a frown was not seen as being any more sarcastic or negative in tone than the words by themselves. For example, sending the message "That class was awful ;-)" was perceived to be as sarcastic as "That class was awful." Likewise, saying "That class was awful :-(" was perceived as negatively as "That class was awful."

In the case of positive statements, the effects were interesting. Saying "That class was great :-)" suggested that the speaker was happier than saying "that class was great," but it did not send the message that the class was any better. In other words, emoticons don't always have the effects that the communicator intended. One possible reason for this is that emoticons tend to be overused, and as a result, their impact has diminished over time.

Additional research has shown some interesting sex differences in the use of emoticons.[19] In general, women use emoticons more frequently than men. However, when men are communicating with women, they use emoticons more frequently than they do when they are communicating with other men. This is in keeping with research showing that in general, men feel more comfortable expressing their emotions to women than to other men. It's also interesting to note that men and women use emoticons for different purposes. In general, women tend to use emoticons to be humorous, but men use them to be teasing and sarcastic. Yeah, right ;-). In conclusion, you should be careful when using emoticons because they don't always do a good job of getting your message across.

Nonverbal Communication

It has been estimated that people communicate at least as much *nonverbally* (i.e., without words) as they do verbally.[20] Indeed, there can be no doubt that many of the messages we send others are transmitted without words. Here are just a few examples of how we communicate nonverbally in organizations and the messages sent by these nonverbal acts.

- *Mode of dress*—Much of what we say about ourselves to others comes from the way we dress. For example, despite the general trend toward casual clothing in the workplace, higher-status people tend to dress more formally than lower-ranking employees.[21]
- *Waiting time*—Higher-status people, such as managers and executives at all ranks, tend to communicate their organizational positions nonverbally by keeping lower-ranking

people waiting to see them—a gesture that sends the message that one's time is more important.[22]

- *Seating position*—Higher-ranking people also assert their higher status by sitting at the heads of rectangular tables, a position that not only has become associated with importance over the years but that also enables important people to maintain eye contact with those for whom they are responsible.[23]

As you read this, you may be asking yourself, "What can I do to present myself more favorably to those around me on the job?" Specifically, what can you do nonverbally to cultivate the impression that you have the qualities of a good leader and that you are worthy of promotion? Just as you can say certain things to enhance your image as a strong, effective employee, there also are several things you can do nonverbally that will enhance your image. For a summary of these, see Table 8.2.[24]

IMPROVING YOUR COMMUNICATION SKILLS

There can be no doubt that successful employees at all levels, from the lowest-ranking person to the CEO, stand to benefit by improving their verbal communication skills. Although there are far too many ways of improving your verbal communication than I can possibly review here, two particular approaches are worthy of mention. These include using inspirational tactics and being a supportive communicator.

Use Inspirational Communication Tactics

Effective leaders know how to inspire others when they communicate with them. To become an effective leader, or even a more effective employee, it helps to consider several key ways of inspiring others when communicating with them. These are as follows:

- *Project confidence and power with emotion-provoking words*—The most persuasive communicators attempt to inspire others by sprinkling their speech with words that provoke emotion. For example, it helps to use phrases such as "bonding with customers" instead of the more benign "being friendly." Effective communicators also use words in ways that highlight their power in an organization. For some linguistic tips in this regard, see Table 8.3.[25]

TABLE 8.2	How to Communicate Your Leadership Potential Nonverbally

People who are self-confident not only speak and write with assurance, but they also project their capacity to lead others in the various nonverbal ways summarized here.

- Stand and sit using an erect posture. Avoid slouching.
- When confronted, stand up straight. Do not cower.
- Nod your head to show that you are listening to someone talk.
- Maintain eye contact and smile at those with whom you are talking.
- Use hand gestures in a relaxed, nonmechanical way.
- Always be neat and well groomed and wear clean, well-pressed clothes.

Source: Based on suggestions by DuBrin, 2010; see Note 24.

TABLE 8.3	How to Project Confidence With Your Words

The most powerful and confident people tend to follow certain linguistic conventions. By emulating the way they speak, you, too, can enhance the confidence you project.

Rule	Explanation or Example
Always know exactly what you want.	The more committed you are to achieving a certain end, the more clearly and powerfully you will be able to sell your idea.
Use the pronoun *I* unless you are a part of a team.	This allows you to take individual credit for your ideas.
Downplay uncertainty.	If you are unsure of your opinion, make a broad but positive statement, such as "I am confident this new accounting procedure will make things more efficient."
Ask very few questions.	You may come across as being weak or unknowledgeable if you have to ask what something means or what's going on.
Don't display disappointment when your ideas are challenged.	It is better to act as though opposition is expected and to explain your viewpoint.
Make bold statements.	Be bold about ideas, but avoid attacking anyone personally.

Source: Based on suggestions by DuBrin, 2010; see Note 24.

- *Be credible*—Communicators are most effective when they are perceived to be credible. Such perceptions are enhanced when one is considered trustworthy, intelligent, and knowledgeable. Bill Joy, cofounder of Sun Microsystems (considered "the Thomas Edison of the Internet"), for example, has considerable credibility in the computer business because he is regarded to be so highly intelligent. At the very least, credibility is enhanced by backing up your claims with clear data. People might not believe you unless you support your ideas with objective information.
- *Pitch your message to the listener*—The most effective communicators go out of their way to send messages that are of interest to listeners. Assume that people will pay greatest attention when they are interested in answering the question, "How is what you are saying important to me?" People will attend most carefully to messages that have value to them.
- *Avoid "junk words" that dilute your message*—Nobody likes to listen to people who constantly use phrases such as "like," "know what I mean?" and "you know." Such phrases send the message that the speaker is ill-prepared to express himself or herself clearly and precisely. Because many of us use such phrases in our everyday language, it helps to practice by making a voice recording of what you are going to say so you can keep track of the number of times you say these things. Make a conscious effort to stop saying these words, and use your recording to monitor your progress.
- *Use front-loaded messages*—The most effective communicators come right out and say what they mean. They don't beat around the bush, and they don't embed their most

important message in a long speech or letter. Instead, they begin by making the point they are attempting to communicate and then use the remainder of the message to illustrate it and flesh out the details.

- *Cut through the clutter*—People are so busy these days that they easily become distracted by the many messages that come across their desks.[26] The most effective communicators attempt to cut through the clutter, such as by making their messages interesting, important, and special. Dull and uninspiring messages are likely to get lost in the shuffle.

Be a Supportive Communicator

Thus far, I have been describing a way of being an effective communicator by being forceful and inspiring people. Good communicators, as you know, are also highly people-oriented, requiring a low-key approach. To communicate effectively with others, we need to show that we are interested in what the other person has to say and respond in ways that strengthen the relationship between ourselves and the target of our messages. In short, we need to demonstrate what is called **supportive communication**. Doing this requires adhering to the following rules.[27]

- *Focus on the problem instead of the person*—Although people are generally receptive to ways of making things better, we all naturally resist suggestions that we somehow need to change ourselves. Saying, for example, "you need to be more creative," would lead most of us to become defensive and turn off the speaker. However, saying something more supportive, like "see if you can find a way of finding more solutions to this problem," is bound to meet with a far better reaction.
- *Match your words and your body language*—You can be a far more effective communicator when the things you say with your body match the words you use. For example, sending the message that you are excited about someone's idea is amplified by verbally explaining your satisfaction and nonverbally showing your excitement, such as by sitting up, looking alert, and opening your eyes widely. By contrast, crossing your arms, closing your eyes, and slumping while saying the same words would only detract from your message—if it even comes across at all.
- *Acknowledge the other person's ideas*—Even if you disagree with what someone is saying, you don't want to make that individual feel bad about expressing his or her ideas. Not only is this rude, but also it is a good way of getting people to keep their ideas to themselves, which interferes with effective management. So, for example, if you have to reject someone's recommendation for improving workplace operations, don't make that person feel bad by suggesting that the idea was silly and devoid of merit. Instead, it would be far more supportive to highlight the good aspects of that person's idea while at the same time explaining precisely why it should not be implemented right now.
- *Keep the conversation going*—One sure way to block the exchange of ideas is to say or do something that stops a conversation in its tracks. Long pauses may do this, as will saying things that change the topic. Effective communication requires keeping the conversation moving along, allowing ideas to get presented and discussed fully. This can be accomplished by listening carefully to what someone says and building on it when responding.

Encourage Open Feedback

In theory, it's simple: if accurate information is the key to effective communication, then organizations should encourage feedback since, after all, feedback is a prime source of information.

However, I say "in theory" because it is natural for workers to be afraid of the repercussions they may face when being extremely open with their superiors. Likewise, high-ranking officials may be somewhat apprehensive about hearing what's really on their subordinates' minds. In other words, people in organizations may be reluctant to give and to receive feedback—a situation that can wreak havoc on organizational communication.

These problems would be unlikely to occur in an organization in which top officials openly and honestly seek feedback and in which lower-level workers believe they can speak their minds with impunity. But how can this be accomplished? Although this is not easy, several successful techniques for opening feedback channels have been used by organizations. I now describe some of the more popular practices. (For a close-up look at one company's novel approach to addressing this problem, see the Winning Practices section on p 256.)

- **360-degree feedback**—Formal systems in which people at all levels give feedback to others at different levels and receive feedback from them, as well as outsiders—including customers and suppliers. This technique is used in such companies as Alcoa, BellSouth, General Mills, Hewlett-Packard, Merck, Motorola, and 3M.
- **Suggestion systems**—Programs that invite employees to submit ideas about how something may be improved. Employees are generally rewarded when their ideas are implemented. This practice has been used actively by Toyota, where it has generated over 20 million ideas since its inception in 1951
- **Corporate hotlines**—Telephone lines staffed by corporate officials ready to answer questions and listen to comments. These are particularly useful during times when employees are likely to be full of questions because their organizations are undergoing change. For example, AT&T used hotlines in the early 1980s during the period of its antitrust divestiture.

USE SIMPLE LANGUAGE   No matter what field you're in, chances are good that it has its own special language—its **jargon**. Although jargon may greatly help communication within specialized groups, it can severely interfere with communication among the uninitiated.

The trick to using jargon wisely is to know your audience. If the individuals with whom you are communicating understand the jargon, using it can facilitate communication. However, when addressing audiences whose members are unfamiliar with specialized language, simple, straightforward language is bound to be most effective. In either case, the rationale is the same: Communicators should speak the language of their audiences. Although you may be tempted to try to impress your audience by using big words, you may have little impact on them if they don't understand you. The advice is clear: Follow the **KISS principle**—that is, **keep it short and sweet** (sometimes also known as **keep it simple, stupid**).

AVOID OVERLOAD   Imagine this scene: You're up late one night at the end of the term. You're writing a term paper and studying (or trying to) for three finals all at the same time. Your desk is piled high with books. Then your roommate comes in to explain what you should do to prepare for the end-of-semester party. If this sounds familiar, then you probably know that it's unlikely that you'd be able to give everything you're doing your most careful attention. After all, when people are confronted with more information than they can process at any given time, their performance tends to suffer. This condition is known as **overload**.

As I noted earlier, these days we tend to be bombarded by messages so regularly that we take overload for granted. Staying competitive in today's hectic world often requires doing many things at once—but without threatening the performance that often results when communication channels are overloaded. Fortunately, several things can be done to avoid, or at least minimize, the

Winning Practices

Mistake of the Month

If your company has an important message to communicate to customers, the press, employees, financial analysts, or any such group, Delahaye Medialink can do research to help you find the most effective way of communicating with them. Given that this Portsmouth, New Hampshire–based company is in the communication research business, it probably comes as no surprise that it uses a particularly effective, yet counterintuitive, way of communicating within its ranks.[28]

It all started in 1989, when founder Katie Paine made a serious mistake: she overslept, causing her to miss a flight to an important meeting with a client. Despite her obvious embarrassment, Paine learned a vital lesson about the importance of getting up on time. But why, she thought, should this lesson be kept solely with her? After all, sharing it with others stood to benefit them as well. With this in mind, the next day Paine went to a staff meeting, where she put a $50 bill on the table and challenged her colleagues to tell a worse story about their own mistakes. That they did. One salesperson described how he went on a sales call without his business cards, and another admitted to having scheduled a presentation at Coca-Cola but left the presentation materials behind.

So many people learned so many things about ways to mess things up—and how to avoid them—that the "Mistake of the Month"

soon became a feature of staff meetings at Delahaye. It works like this. At each monthly staff meeting, a half-hour is devoted to identifying and discussing everyone's mistakes. Each is written on a board, and everyone gets to vote on two categories of mistakes—the one from which they learned the most and the one from which they learned the least. The person whose mistake is identified as helping the most is awarded a highly coveted downtown parking space for the next month. The person from whose mistake people learned the least are required to speak at the next meeting about what they are doing to ensure that it will never happen again. The time spent on this exercise is considered a wise investment because it allows all employees to learn from everyone else's mistakes.

Thus far, more than 2,000 mistakes have been identified—but few ever have been repeated, creating a positive effect on the company's work. Paine also notes that the program helps her identify steps she needs to take to improve things at Delahaye. She also notes that sharing mistakes has been "a bonding ritual," adding "once you go through it, you're a member of the club." This program has been so successful that ones like it are being used in several other companies.[29] Among these, is Keebler Cookies and Crackers, where the "mistake of the week" is celebrated.[30]

problem of overload. Among these are the following recommendations (which may be applied both to in-person communications and electronic communications):

- *Use gatekeepers*—People whose jobs require them to control the flow of information to potentially overloaded individuals, groups, or organizations are known as **gatekeepers**. In making appointments for top executives, for example, administrative assistants are providing a gatekeeping service.
- *Practice queuing*—A "queue" is a line. So, **queuing** involves lining up incoming information so that it can be attended to in an orderly fashion. Air traffic controllers do this when they "stack" incoming planes in a holding pattern so as to prevent them from tragically "overloading" the runway. And, as you know, physicians rely on queuing by requiring their nonemergency patients to make appointments and then seeing them only in the appointed order.

- *Screen phone calls*—The practice of screening phone calls is a good way to avoid overload: it allows you to take control over your time by taking the calls you want now and allowing the others to roll over into voice mail (which you can then answer at your convenience).
- *Filter your e-mail*—An easy way to become overloaded with information is by paying attention to unwanted e-mail messages. This refers both to *spam*, which I described earlier as a form of noise (see p. 240), and to any other messages that are legitimate but of lower priority.

Walk the Talk

When it comes to effective communication, actions definitely speak louder than words. Too often, communication is hampered by the practice of saying one thing but meaning another. And, whenever implicit messages (e.g., "we may be cutting jobs") contradict official messages (e.g., "don't worry, the company is stable"), confusion is bound to result.

This is especially problematic when the inconsistency comes from the top. In fact, one of the most effective ways of fostering effective organizational communication is for CEOs to "walk the talk," that is, to match their deeds to their words. After all, a boss would lose credibility if she told her employees that "my door is always open to you" but then was never available for consultation. Good communication demands consistency. And for the words to be heard as loud as the actions, they must match up.

Be a Good Listener

Effective communication involves more than just presenting messages clearly. It also involves doing a good job of comprehending others. Although most of us take listening for granted, effective listening is an important skill. In fact, given that managers spend about 40 percent of their time listening to others but are only 25 percent effective, listening is a skill that could stand to be developed in most of us. When I speak of *effective listening,* I am not referring to the passive act of just taking in information. Rather, effective listening involves three important elements.

- Being nonjudgmental while taking in information from others.
- Acknowledging speakers in ways that encourage them to continue speaking.
- Attempting to advance the speaker's ideas to the next step.

It is worthwhile to consider what we can do to improve our own effectiveness as listeners. Fortunately, experts have offered several good suggestions, some of which are summarized in Table 8.4.[31] Although it may require some effort, incorporating these suggestions into your own listening habits cannot help but make you a more effective listener.

Given its importance, it should not be surprising that many organizations are working hard to improve their employees' listening skills. For example, Unisys has long used seminars and self-training materials to teach effective listening skills to thousands of its employees. Such systematic efforts at improving listening skills represent a wise investment given that good listening definitely pays off. Indeed, research has shown that the more effective one is as a listener, the more likely he or she is to get promoted to a management position—and to perform effectively in that role. (To practice your own listening skills, and to help others do the same, see the Group Exercise on p. 265.)

COMMUNICATION IN TODAY'S GLOBAL ECONOMY

By this point in the chapter, you are likely to have reached the conclusion that effective communication in organizations cannot be taken for granted. Making things even more challenging are two fundamental facts of today's global economy: (1) business relationships span various national cultures and (2) the workforce within most countries is multilingual. As you might imagine, these

TABLE 8.4	Tips for Improving Your Listening Skills

Being a good listener is an important skill that can enhance the effectiveness of communication in organizations. Although it may be difficult to follow the suggestions outlined here, the resulting benefits make it worthwhile to try to do so.

Suggestion	Description
Do not talk while being spoken to.	It is difficult, if not impossible, to listen to someone while you are speaking to him or her.
Make the speaker feel at ease.	Help the speaker feel that he or she is free to talk as desired.
Eliminate distractions.	Don't focus on other things: pay attention only to the speaker.
Show empathy with the speaker.	Try to put yourself in the speaker's position, and make an effort to see his or her point of view.
Be as patient as possible.	Take the time needed to hear everything the speaker has to say.
Hold your arguments.	If you're busy forming your own arguments, you cannot focus on the speaker's points.
Ask questions.	By asking questions, you demonstrate that you are listening and make it possible to clarify areas of uncertainty.
Focus on what is being said instead of how you're going to respond.	Too often, when someone is speaking, we stop listening and begin planning what we're going to say when he or she finally stops talking.

Source: Based on suggestions from Gibson & Walker, 2011; see Note 31.

characteristics pose critical challenges that must be met for organizations to thrive—or even to survive. With this in mind, I now turn attention to the important challenges associated with communicating in today's global business environment.

Communicating Across National Cultures

It's no secret that businesses operate in a global economy. Approximately two-thirds of large companies in Europe, Australia, and New Zealand have employees in six or more countries (compared to 56 percent of Asian companies, 43 percent of North American companies, and 33 percent of Latin American companies).[32] Keeping this economy going requires a keen understanding of the complexities of communicating with people from different countries. This is far easier said than done—and mistakes readily can offend your hosts, even unintentionally.

Imagine, for example, that you are at home in a large U.S. city, where you are entertaining a group of potential business partners from abroad. As you enter a restaurant, you find it odd that your guests are reluctant to check their coats, taking them to the table instead, although the inside temperature is quite comfortable. Upon prompting, your guests admit that they heard all about the crime problem in the United States and were advised against ever letting something of value out of their sight. If you are not immediately offended, you would feel at the very least uncomfortable about the message your visitors are sending about their trust of Americans—a likely problem given that you are considering partnering with them.

Clearly, when visiting abroad, it pays to not only learn the language spoken there (even if only somewhat, as a gesture of politeness) but also to familiarize yourself carefully with the local

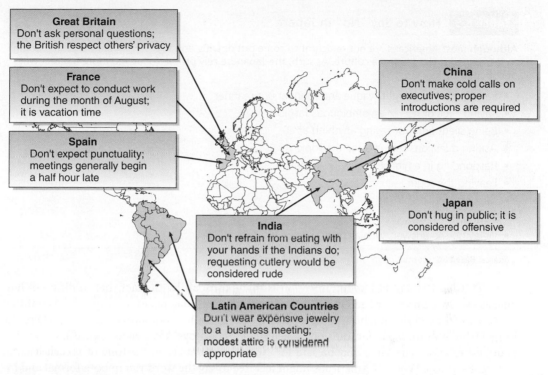

Great Britain
Don't ask personal questions; the British respect others' privacy

France
Don't expect to conduct work during the month of August; it is vacation time

China
Don't make cold calls on executives; proper introductions are required

Spain
Don't expect punctuality; meetings generally begin a half hour late

Japan
Don't hug in public; it is considered offensive

India
Don't refrain from eating with your hands if the Indians do; requesting cutlery would be considered rude

Latin American Countries
Don't wear expensive jewelry to a business meeting; modest attire is considered appropriate

FIGURE 8.5 "When in Rome": Understanding National Customs
Understanding differences in local customs is essential when conducting business in today's global economy. A few important customs that might come as a surprise to American businesspeople are summarized here. *Sources:* Based on information in Martin & Chaney, 2012, Marx, 2001, and Lewis, 2000; see Note 33.

customs.[33] As a quick summary of some of the most easily recognized pitfalls of international communication, see Figure 8.5. (And to see how familiar you are with the unique ways people from different cultures communicate, see the Self-Assessment Exercise on pp. 264–265.)

CHALLENGES OF CROSS-CULTURAL COMMUNICATION Three key factors make communicating with people from different cultures a difficult task. First, different words may mean different things to different people. For example, as hard as it might be for people from countries with long-standing capitalist economies to realize, Russians have difficulty understanding words such as *efficiency* and *free market*, which have no direct translation in their own language. People who have never known a free-market economy while they were growing up certainly may find it difficult to grasp the concept. Accordingly, it is not unusual for American executives to confront serious communication barriers when conducting business in Russia.[34]

Second, people in various nations sometimes have very different cultural norms about using certain words. Take the simple word *no*, for example. Although the term exists in the Japanese language, the Japanese people are reluctant to say no directly to someone because doing so is considered insulting. For this reason, they often rely on other ways of saying no that can be quite difficult for foreigners to understand (see Table 8.5).[35] As such, it is frequently considered wise for foreign visitors to other countries to learn not only the language of that country but the customs about using language as well.

TABLE 8.5	How to Say "No" in Japan

Although most Americans are not reluctant to come out directly and say "no" when necessary, doing so is frowned on by Japanese culture. As such, the Japanese rely on the following more indirect ways of communicating "no."

- Saying "no" in a highly vague and roundabout manner
- Saying "yes or no" in an ambiguous fashion
- Being silent and not saying anything at all
- Asking questions that change the topic
- Responding in a highly tangential manner
- Leaving the room
- Making a polite excuse
- Saying, "Yes, but…"
- Delaying the answer, such as by promising a future letter

Source: Based on information in Hodgson et al., 2000; see Note 35.

Third, cross-cultural communication is made difficult by the fact that in different languages even the same word can mean different things. Just imagine, for example, how confused an American executive might become when she speaks to her counterpart in Israel, where the same Hebrew word, *shalom*, means both "hello" and "good-bye" (as well as "peace"). Confusion is bound to arise. The same may be said for cultural differences in the tone of speech used in different settings. Whereas Americans might feel free to say the word *you* in both formal and informal situations, the Spanish have different words in each (*tú* for informal speech and *usted* for formal speech). To confuse these may be tantamount to misinterpreting the nature of the social setting, a potentially costly blunder—and all because of a failure to recognize the subtleties of cross-cultural communication.

GUIDELINES FOR AVOIDING PITFALLS IN CROSS-CULTURAL COMMUNICATIONS
Communication between people of different cultures can be promoted by taking into account several basic rules. To avoid misunderstandings that can ruin business relationships, it is especially important for people to follow these guidelines when conducting business with people from other countries.[36] These are as follows:

- *Learn local cultural rules*—By acknowledging that there are likely to be cultural differences between yourself and people from another country, learn what you can do to avoid embarrassing these people. Many Americans make this mistake, for example, when they publicly praise Asian visitors. Although this would be considered a very kind thing to do in American culture, Asians are likely to find it a source of discomfort because their cultures value group performance more highly than individual performance. Pay special attention to rules of etiquette regarding how to address people (by first name, last name, or title). To avoid embarrassment, it's a good idea to check with local experts to ensure that you are doing this correctly.
- *Don't take anything for granted*—It is important when communicating with people from other nations to challenge your cultural assumptions. Don't assume, for example, that everyone values the same things that you do. Although it may come as a shock to many Americans and Canadians, concepts such as equal achievement, autonomy, and individual accomplishment are not recognized as appropriate throughout the world.

- *Show respect for everyone*—We often find it funny when someone says or does something that runs counter to what we expect. However, giggling or telling someone that they have a funny accent is not only disrespectful, but also it imposes a tall barrier to effective communication. In this connection, it helps to focus on *what* people are saying rather than *how* they are saying it.
- *Speak slowly, clearly, and in straightforward language*—Even after you have studied a foreign language for a few years in high school or college, you may be surprised to find just how little you understand when you visit a country where that is the native language. "If they only spoke more slowly and clearly," you think to yourself, "I'd probably understand them." Indeed, you might. With this in mind, it's important for you to speak slowly and clearly (but not loudly!) when talking to people in languages that are not their native tongue. Moreover, it's important to avoid colloquial words or phrases that you take for granted but that they might not know.
- *Try to speak the local language (at least a little)*—People always appreciate the effort you make to speak their language, so give it a try. It's a good way to show goodwill and to break the barrier between you and someone from another nation. Whatever you do, however, check with a native speaker to make sure that your pronunciation is accurate and that you are not offending anyone by using the wrong words.
- *Beware of nonverbal differences*—The same gestures that mean one thing in one country may mean quite another in another country. For example, an American may not think twice about hugging a colleague who has done well or touching another's arm to acknowledge him or her. However, these same acts would be considered not only inappropriate but also offensive to people from Korea. Bottom line: You have not completely learned a foreign language until you have learned its nonverbal language as well.[37] For some examples of cross-cultural differences in nonverbal behavior, see Figure 8.6.

Communicating in a Multilingual Workforce: "You Say Tomato, I Say *Domates,* or *Pomidor,* or *Tomate*"

In the Book of Genesis, the Bible tells us of the Tower of Babel that Noah's descendants built to reach up to heaven. According to this tale, God prevented them from completing the tower by confusing their language so that they could no longer understand one another. From that time forward, according to the Bible, the peoples of the earth would speak different languages. Just as language differences kept the tower from completion in Biblical times, so too do language differences between people threaten to interfere with people's work today.

Just because you go to work at an American company in the United States, there's no assurance that everyone around you will be a native speaker of English. Especially in states like California and New York, where as many as one person in four is foreign born, there's good reason to expect that many of your coworkers will speak English with a foreign accent—if they speak it at all. The communication challenges this situation creates are not difficult to imagine. After all, business operations are sure to falter when people cannot understand each other because they are speaking different languages.

To combat this problem, several companies have implemented *English-only rules*, requiring all employees to speak only English while on the job. The underlying idea is that workplaces in which people speak only one language will be ones in which communications are clear and efficient and in which safety is enhanced as a result. In recent years, however, the courts have not looked favorably on such policies, claiming they interfere with an employee's rights to use whatever language he or she wishes. For example, a Washington court awarded a Cambodian-born

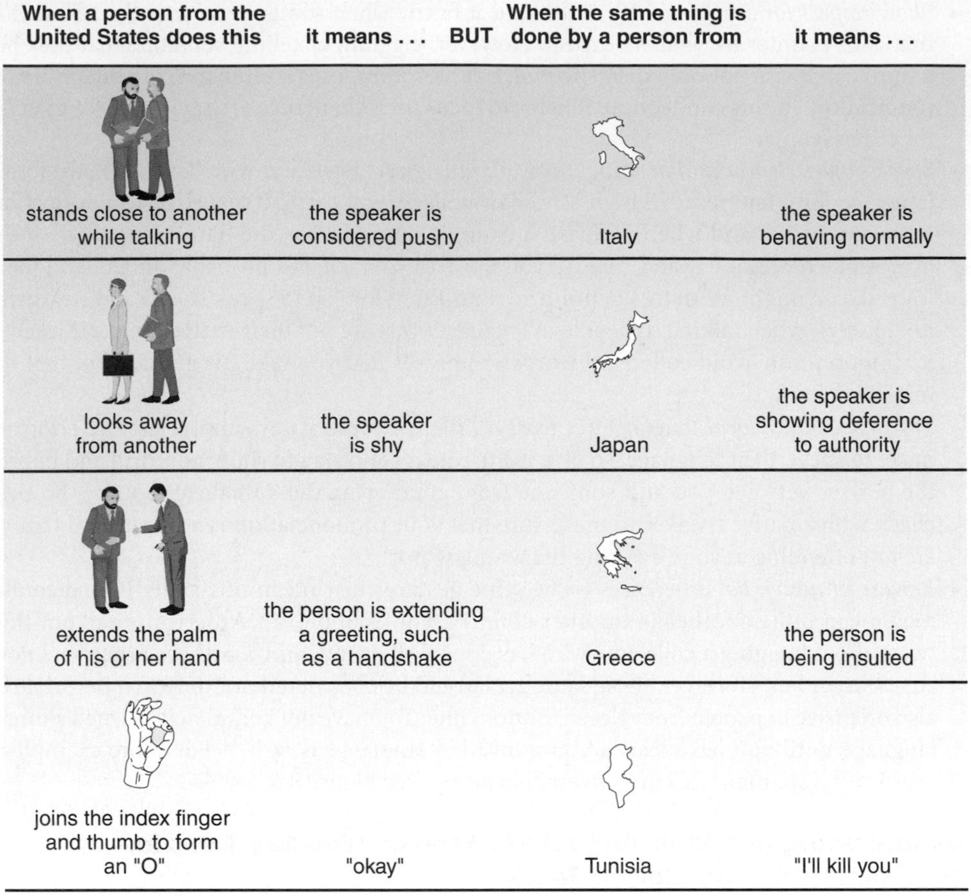

When a person from the United States does this	it means ...	BUT	When the same thing is done by a person from	it means ...
stands close to another while talking	the speaker is considered pushy		Italy	the speaker is behaving normally
looks away from another	the speaker is shy		Japan	the speaker is showing deference to authority
extends the palm of his or her hand	the person is extending a greeting, such as a handshake		Greece	the person is being insulted
joins the index finger and thumb to form an "O"	"okay"		Tunisia	"I'll kill you"

FIGURE 8.6   Beware of Nonverbal Miscommunication in Different Countries
Although people preparing to conduct business abroad may study their host country's language, they frequently fail to learn differences in the nonverbal language. As summarized here, this can lead to some serious miscommunication.
Sources: Based on information in Hossell, 2003, and Knapp & Hall, 2001; see Note 37.

immigrant $389,000 by the bank that employed him, ruling that he was unfairly denied a promotion because of his lack of fluency in English.[38] Legally, for companies to insist that their employees speak fluent English, they must establish clearly that an employee who cannot do so will perform poorly on the job.

Instead of insisting that everyone speak only English, companies with diverse customer bases are generally delighted to have employees who speak several different languages. For example, fluency in language other than English is important for sales associates at Longo Toyota in El Monte, California, where three-quarters of the sales staff speak at least one additional language (in fact, 20 different languages are spoken at Longo!). This has helped the dealership sell cars to people from the community who were not as well served by the competition, helping it become one of the top-grossing car dealerships in the United States.

Although it often is useful to be able to speak a second language, most U.S. companies find it necessary to ensure that its employees are sufficiently fluent in English to understand instructions, notices, and memos. With this in mind, many businesses have arranged for their employees to take classes in English as a second language. This is done at Kayem Foods, a meat processing and packaging company in Chelsea, Massachusetts, where English is a second language for 60 to 70 percent of the employees, most of whom have Spanish or Polish as their native tongues. This is so important that it's not relegated to something the company hopes workers will do on their own time off the job. Rather, teachers are brought into the facility to train workers during their shifts.

Learning to communicate in English is particularly important in the hospitality industry, where doing so is required to cater to American tourists. For example, before the Four Seasons Hotel and Resort opened on the southern tip of the island of Bali in Indonesia, none of the 10,000 applicants could speak English. In fact, nobody could pass a simple test of English required to perform any of the 580 jobs the resort was attempting to fill. The solution was intensive training in English language terms used in the hospitality industry—nine hours per day for almost a month. Although staff members might not be able to understand the entire language, they know enough English to serve its customers' needs.

In some locations, a company's customer base is so ethnically diverse that it must go out of its way to hire employees who speak foreign languages. What happens, however, if the one or two employees who speak an unusual language are not available? Detroit Edison, the electric utility company serving ethnically diverse southeast Michigan, has faced this challenge by using AT&T's Language Line service. This service provides around-the-clock translations in any of 140 different languages by accessing a toll-free phone number. Customers who speak a language that is unknown to any of Detroit Edison's service representatives are put on a conference call with someone from the company and the Language Line service. In conclusion, it's easy to see how very important it is for people to respond to the challenge of using language—be it one or many— to communicate effectively with coworkers and customers.

Back to the Case

Answer the following questions based on this chapter's Making the Case (p. 237) to illustrate insights you have derived from the material in this chapter.

1. What particular types of noise are likely to be reduced by the techniques developed by Microsoft and IBM?
2. Although these techniques are designed to improve communication, it's possible that they will impede it as well. What particular problems might result and how do you believe they could be overcome?
3. How might these tools lead to misunderstandings when it comes to cross-national communication? What problems might result and how do you believe they can be minimized?

You Be the Consultant

A Crisis in Communicating Coordination

"Everyone is moving in different directions; no one seems to have any sense of what the company is and where it is going. Making things worse, people around here aren't paying any attention to each other, and everyone is doing his or her own thing." These are the words of an operations director of a large credit card processing center, who asks you to look into these problems in your capacity as manager of human resources. Answer the following questions relevant to this situation based on the material in this chapter.

1. Casting the problem as one of poor communication between company officials and lower-level employees, what steps could be taken to fill everyone in on the company's plans, goals, and activities?
2. What specific tactics would you advise the company's management use to improve communication?
3. In what ways might differences in nationality be responsible for this state of affairs, and what can be done to help improve communication despite these differences?

Self-Assessment Exercise

HOW FAMILIAR ARE YOU WITH FOREIGN COMMUNICATION PRACTICES?

Expert communicators in today's global business world must have considerable familiarity with cultural differences in communication style around the world. This questionnaire is designed to assess your familiarity with many such communication practices. It is important to note that although people in any given country are not all alike, their cultural backgrounds lead them to share certain communication styles and practices.

Directions

Match the countries in the left-hand column to the communication characteristic that best describes its people, listed in the column on the right.

1. ___ Russia
2. ___ Brazil
3. ___ Germany
4. ___ Australia
5. ___ Japan
6. ___ Philippines
7. ___ Poland
8. ___ France
9. ___ Great Britain
10. ___ India

a. Chivalry and old-fashioned gallantry are important; first names are reserved for use only with close friends.

b. Show respect for speakers by being silent; tend to be shy and to refrain from open disagreement.

c. Women are deferent to men; good bargainers, who expect you to negotiate with them.

d. Raise their voice and use gestures when excited; formal dress and style are typical at meetings.

e. Punctuality is important; perfectionists, who demand lots of information from others.

f. Use humor a great deal, such as to break up tension; take time to make decisions.

g. Talk tough when they believe they have an advantage; tend to drink between meetings.

h. Being an hour or two late is not unusual; leadership is based on family name, age, and connections.

i. Very talkative and long-winded; tend to interrupt conversations with their own ideas.

j. Tend to be cynical and distrust people who praise them too enthusiastically.

Sources: Based on information in Rosen et al., 2000, see Note 32; Lewis, 2000, see Note 33.

Scoring

Using the following key, count how many correct matches you made.

1 = g, 2 = i, 3 = e, 4 = j, 5 = b, 6 = h, 7 = a, 8 = d, 9 = f, 10 = c

Discussion Questions

1. How many correct matches did you make? How does this figure compare to how you expected to score before you began this exercise?
2. Based on your own experiences, to what extent do you believe these descriptions are generally accurate?
3. How would you characterize your own culture relative to those described in this exercise?

Group Exercise

SHARPENING YOUR LISTENING SKILLS

Are you a good listener, a *really* good listener? Do you understand exactly what others are saying and get them to open up even more? Most of us tend to think that we are much better listeners than we really are. After all, we've been listening to people our whole lives—and, with that much practice, we must be at least reasonably acceptable. However, being a truly effective listener is an active skill, and it takes some practice to master. The following exercise will help you gain some insight into your own listening skills.

Directions

1. Divide the class into pairs of people who do not already know each other. Arrange the chairs so that the people within each pair are facing one another but are separated from the other pairs.
2. Within each pair, select one person as the speaker and one as the listener. The speaker should tell the listener about a specific incident on the job in which he or she was somehow harmed (e.g., disappointed by not getting a raise, embarrassed by another, getting fired, and so on), and how he or she felt about it. This discussion should last about 10 to 15 minutes.
3. Listeners should carefully attempt to follow the suggestions for good listening summarized in Table 8.4 (on p. 258). To help, the instructor should discuss these with the class.
4. After the conversations are over, review the suggestions with your partner. Discuss which ones the listener followed and which were ignored. Try to be as open and honest as possible about assessing your own and the other person's strengths and weaknesses. Speakers should consider the extent to which they felt the listeners were really paying careful attention to them.
5. Change roles and repeat steps 2 through 4. Speakers now become listeners, and listeners now become speakers.
6. As a class, share your experiences as speakers and listeners.

Discussion Questions

1. What did this exercise teach you about your own skills as a listener? Are you as good as you thought? Do you think you can improve?
2. Was there general agreement or disagreement in the class about each listener's strengths and weaknesses? Explain.
3. Which particular listening skills were easiest and which were most difficult for you to put into practice? Do you think there may be certain conditions under which good listening skills may be especially difficult to implement?

Notes

MAKING THE CASE NOTES

IBM. (2008, October 20). You've got (too much) mail. *IDEAS from IBM.* http://www.ibm.com/ibm/ideasfromibm/us/email/20081020/IFI_10202008.pdf. Jackson, M. (2008). *Distraction.* New York: Prometheus Books. Jackson, M. (2008, June 23). May we have your attention, please? *BusinessWeek*, pp. 55–56. Marcus, G. (2008). *Kluge: The haphazard construction of the human mind.* New York: Houghton Mifflin. Eric Horvitz. (2008). http://research.microsoft.com/~horvitz

CHAPTER NOTES

1. Tofanelli, D. (2012). *Communication in organizations.* Bloomington, IN: Author House. Roberts, K. H. (1984). *Communicating in organizations.* Chicago, IL: Science Research Associates (quote, p. 4).
2. Gillis, T. (2008). *The IABC handbook of organizational communication.* San Francisco, CA: Jossey-Bass. Weick, K. E. (1987). Theorizing about organizational communication. In F. M. Jablin, L. L. Putnam, K. H. Roberts, & L. W. Porter (Eds.), *Handbook of organizational communication* (pp. 97–122). Newbury Park, CA: Sage.
3. Spam Statistics and Facts. (2010). *Spamlaws.com.* http://www.spamlaws.com/spam-stats.html
4. Computer Mail Services. (2003). *Spam calculator.* www.cmsconnect.com
5. See Note 4.
6. Robert Half Technology. (2009, October 6). News release: *Whistle—but don't Tweet—while you work.* Menlo Park, CA: Author.
7. Daft, R. L., Lengel, R. H., & Trevino, L. K. (1987). Message equivocality, media selection, and manager performance: Implications for information systems. *MIS Quarterly, 11*, 355–366.
8. Stromberg, R. M. (1998, September). No, it couldn't happen here. *American Management Association International*, p. 70.
9. Facebook. (2012). Newsroom: Fact sheet. Facebook.com. http://newsroom.fb.com/content/default.aspx?NewsAreaId=22 Bullas, J. (2011, September 2). 20 stunning social media statistics plus infographic. *JeffBullas.com.* http://www.jeffbullas.com/2011/09/02/20-stunning-social-media-statistics/
10. Poe, R., & Courter, C. L. (1998, September). The great coffee grapevine. *Across the Board*, p. 7.
11. Walton, E. (1961). How efficient is the grapevine? *Personnel, 28*, 45–49.
12. Lengel, R. H., & Daft, R. L. (1988). The selection of communication media as an executive skill. *Academy of Management Executive, 2*, 225–232.
13. Jablin, F. M., & Putnam, L. L. (2000). *The new handbook of organizational communication: Advances in theory, research, and methods.* Thousand Oaks, CA: Sage.
14. Daft, R. L. & Lengel, R. H. (1984). Information richness: a new approach to managerial behavior and organizational design. In L. L. Cummings & B. M. Staw, B.M. (Eds.), *Research in organizational behavior* (Vol. 6, pp. 191–233). Homewood, IL: JAI Press. Daft, R.L., Lengel, R. H., & Trevino, L.K. (1987). Message equivocality, media selection, and manager performance: Implications for information systems. *MIS Quarterly, 12*, 355–366.
15. Lengel, R. H. & Daft, R. L. (1988). The selection of communication media as an executive skill. *Academy of Management Executive, 2*, 225–232.
16. Thurlow, C., Lengel, L., & Tomic, A. (2004). *Computer-mediated communication.* Thousand Oaks, CA: Sage.
17. Schneider, S. J., Kerwin, J., Frechtling, J., & Vivari, B. A. (2002). Characteristics of the discussion in online and face-to-face focus groups. *Social Science Computer Review, 20*, 31–42.
18. Walther, J. B., & Addario, K. P. (2001). The impacts of emoticons on message interpretation in computer-mediated communication. *Social Science Computer Review, 19*, 324–347.
19. Wolf, A. (2000). Emotional expression online: Gender differences in emoticon use. *CyberPsychology & Behavior, 3*, 827–833.
20. Hickson, M. L., Stacks, D. W., & Moore, N-J. (2003). *Nonverbal communication: Studies and applications* (4th ed.). Los Angeles, CA: Roxbury Publishing.
21. Rafaeli, A., Dutton, J. Harquail, C., & Mackie-Lewis, S. (1997). Navigating by

attire: The use of dress by female administrative employees. *Academy of Management Journal, 40*, 9–45.

22. Greenberg, J. (1989). The organizational waiting game: Time as a status-asserting or status-neutralizing tactic. *Basic and Applied Social Psychology, 10*, 13–26.

23. Zweigenhaft, R. L. (1976). Personal space in the faculty office: Desk placement and student–faculty interaction. *Journal of Applied Psychology, 61*, 628–632.

24. Dubrin, A. J. (2010). *Leadership* (6th ed.). Mason, OH: Cengage/South Western.

25. See Note 24.

26. Wurman, R. S. (2000). *Understanding.* Newport, RI: TED Conferences.

27. Whetten, D. E., & Cameron, K. S. (2002). *Developing management skills* (5th ed.). Upper Saddle River, NJ: Prentice Hall.

28. Labarre, P. (1998, November). Screw up, and get smart. *Fast Company*, p. 58.

29. Bapes, B. (2012). Mistake of the month club. *Presentation pointer.com.* http://www.presentation-pointers.com/show-article/articleid/225/ Davidson, E. (2011, December 29). Brogan & Partners featured for our mistake of the month. *Brogan & Partners Convergence Marketing.* http://www.brogan.com/blog/brogan-partners-featured-our-mistake-month

30. BusinessClassInc.com. (2009, August 31). Mistake of the week award at Keebler Cookies & Crackers. From http://www.business-classinc.com/2009/08/31/mistake-of-the-week-keebler-cookies-crackers/.

31. Gibson, J., & Walker, F. (2011). *The art of active listening.* Amazon Digital Services. http://www.amazon.com/Art-Active-Listening-Communication-ebook/dp/B005MSOIVM/ref=sr_1_1?s=books&ie=UTF8&qid=1328989744&sr=1-1 Morrison, K. E. (1994). *Leadership skills.* Tucson, AZ: Fisher Books.

32. Rosen, R., Digh, P., Singer, M., & Phillips, C. (2000). *Global literacies.* New York: Simon & Schuster.

33. Martin, J. S., & Chaney, L. H. (2012). *Global business etiquette: A guide to international communication and customs.* Santa Barbara, CA: ABC-CLIO. Marx, E. (2001). *Breaking through culture shock.* London: Nicholas Brealey Publishing. Lewis, R. D. (2000). *When cultures collide*, rev. ed. London: Nicholas Brealey Publishing.

34. Mellow, C. (1995, August 17). Russia: Making cash from chaos. *Fortune*, pp. 145–146, 148, 150–151.

35. Hodgson, J. D., Sango, Y., & Graham, J. L. (2000). *Doing business with the new Japan.* Oxford, England: Rowman & Littlefield. Ueda, K. (1974). Sixteen ways to avoid saying no in Japan. In J. C. Condon & M. Saito (Eds.), *International encounters with Japan* (pp. 185–192). Tokyo: Simul Press.

36. See Notes 26 and 27.

37. Hossell, K. P. (2003). *Body language.* Oxford, England: Heinemann Library. Knapp, M. L., & Hall, J. A. (2001). *Nonverbal communication in human interaction.* Belmont, CA: Wadsworth. Axtell, R. E. (1997). *Gestures: The do's and taboos of body language around the world.* New York: Wiley.

38. Dutton, G. (1998, December). One workforce, many languages. *Management Review*, pp. 42–47.

9 | GROUP PROCESSES AND WORK TEAMS

LEARNING OBJECTIVES

After reading this chapter, you will be able to:

1. **DEFINE** what is meant by a group and **IDENTIFY** different types of groups operating within organizations.
2. **DESCRIBE** the importance of norms, roles, status, and cohesiveness within organizations.
3. **EXPLAIN** how individual performance in groups is affected by the presence of others (social facilitation) and the number of others with whom one is working (social loafing).
4. **DEFINE** what teams are and **DESCRIBE** the various types of teams that exist in organizations.
5. **DESCRIBE** the evidence regarding the effectiveness of teams in organizations.
6. **EXPLAIN** why some teams fail to operate as effectively as possible and **DESCRIBE** steps that can be taken to build successful teams.

THREE GOOD REASONS you should care about. . .

Group Processes and Work Teams

1. The dynamics among people in groups is largely responsible for both the success and failure of many work groups, as well as the satisfaction of the individuals working in them.

2. Groups and teams can be very effective if you know how to manage them properly.

3. Teams are a fact of organizational life—one of the most popular ways of coordinating the activities of people on the job. Knowing how they operate and how to manage them effectively will give you a competitive advantage.

Making the Case for...

Group Processes and Work Teams

Making a "Better Place" in the World

Can a tiny company change the world? Although you might answer "no," this is precisely what Shai Agassi intends to do. As founder and CEO of Better Place, this Israeli visionary works with governments and auto manufacturers around the world to develop personal transportation systems that eliminate our dependence on oil, thereby reducing the environmental and economic damage that comes with it. His vehicle of choice to make the earth a "better place" is the electric vehicle (EV).

Better Place's business plan is straightforward: pay for the transportation you need as a sustainable service. This requires that automakers replace their gasoline-guzzling engines with powerful, but quiet and smooth-running, electric motors that run on batteries. Then, drivers pay a fee to access a network of charging spots. Better Place operates the electric recharge grid that makes this possible. As 2011 came to a close, partnering with the China Southern Power Grid, the company rolled its first EV in Asia onto the streets of Guangzhou, hoping to revolutionize automotive power in the world's largest market.

According to Chairman of the Board Idan Ofer, Better Place's strategy benefits everyone. Drivers benefit by getting to enjoy their cars in cleaner environments. The auto industry benefits by getting to service a brand new market segment. Energy companies benefit by getting to introduce new technologies. The world's nations benefit by aligning economic and environmental interests. And finally, of course, our planet benefits by being spared the pollution caused by the internal combustion engine.

Getting all this to work, as you might imagine, requires great teamwork, and Better Place has this covered. Jenny Cohen Derfel, vice president of global operations, works carefully with Sigi Eshel, vice president of marketing, to bring the company's ideas to international auto companies. They then hand off the plans to Agassi, who comes in to finalize the deal. It's like a relay race—and one they seem to be winning: Within the company's first six months, deals poured in.

Soon after Better Place's 2007 launch, Renault-Nissan signed on to develop a line of battery-powered electric cars. Then in January 2008, with the help of Moshe Kaplinsky, CEO of Better Place Israel, that nation became the first in the world to declare a plan for oil independence by 2020, using solar-powered electric recharge grids to power EVs. Only two months later, in March 2008, Denmark came onboard, working with Better Place to develop a recharge grid powered by energy from wind turbines. Since then, the United States (California and Hawaii, in particular), Canada, Australia, and Japan have gotten involved.

EVs are extremely quiet, reducing noise pollution, but some worry that they're actually *too* quiet. This makes the driving less than gratifying for some and takes away the auditory cues that blind pedestrians rely on when crossing the street. Better Place has a solution. Agassi has introduced "drivetones," which, like ringtones for your phone, can be downloaded and controlled through a dashboard switch. So, even if you don't have a Ferrari, with a little digital wizardry, your electric car can at least sound like one.

It's hard to say whether Better Place will ever change the world, but it's clear that Agassi and his team would be delighted to save it from pollution, making it truly a better place. And this, after all, is something special.

What's going on at Better Place is no doubt quite amazing. Few entrepreneurs can pull off the kind of successes that Agassi has enjoyed, creating an entirely new product that promises to revolutionize the world in such a short time. But he clearly isn't doing it alone. He is part of a hard-working team of talented individuals who share his vision and are willing to work with one another to make things happen. Indeed, *work teams* are extremely popular today in all kinds of organizations—and, considering Better Place's experiences, there's little wonder why. In the second half of the chapter, I will take a look at the nature of teams in the modern workplace. Acknowledging that they don't always operate as successfully as the team led by Agassi, I will describe the general effectiveness of teams and outline steps that can be taken to make them as productive as possible.

To help you understand the underlying factors that contribute to team success and failure, I first examine the basic nature of *groups* in general. As you know, a great deal of the work performed in organizations is done by people working together in groups. In view of this, it makes sense to understand the types of groups that exist and the variables governing the interrelationships between them and individuals—commonly referred to as *group dynamics*. The topic of **group dynamics** focuses on the nature of groups—the variables governing their formation and development, their structure, and their interrelationships with individuals, other groups, and the organizations within which they exist.[1] Because groups may be found in a variety of settings, the study of group dynamics has a long history in the social sciences—including OB.[2]

In the first half of this chapter, I will draw on this work. Specifically, I will describe the nature of groups by defining what groups are, identifying various types of groups and why they form, explaining the various stages through which groups develop, and describing the dynamics of the way groups are structured. Following this, I shift attention to how effectively groups operate. Specifically, I describe how people are affected by the presence of others, and the tendency for people to withhold their individual performance under certain conditions. Building on this, in the second half of this chapter, I focus on *teams*, special types of groups that are in widespread use in today's organizations. After distinguishing between groups and teams, I describe the factors that make teams effective along with ways to promote team success in the workplace.

GROUPS AT WORK: THEIR BASIC NATURE

To understand the dynamics of groups and their influences on individuals and organizations, I begin by specifying precisely what I mean by the term, *group*.

What Is a Group?

Imagine three people waiting in line at a supermarket checkout counter. Now compare them to the board of directors of a large corporation. Which collection would you consider to be a "group"? Although in our everyday language we may refer to the people waiting in line as a group, they clearly are not a group in the same sense as the members of the board. Obviously, a group is more than simply a collection of people. But what exactly is it that makes a group a group?

Social scientists define a **group** as a collection of two or more interacting individuals with a stable pattern of relationships between them who share common goals and who perceive themselves as being a group.[3] Let's now consider the key elements of this definition.

- *Social interaction*—One of the most obvious characteristics of groups is that they are composed of *two or more people in social interaction*. In other words, the members of a group must have some influence on each other. The interaction between the parties may be either in-person or virtual (electronic) in nature, but the individuals involved must have some impact on one another to be considered a group.

- *Stability*—Groups also must possess a *stable structure*. Although groups can change, and often do, they also have stable relationships that keep group members together and functioning as a unit. A collection of individuals that constantly changes (e.g., the people inside an office waiting room at any given time) cannot be thought of as a group. For it to be considered a group, a greater level of stability would be required.
- *Common interests or goals*—A third characteristic of groups is that their *members share common interests or goals*. For example, members of a stamp collecting club constitute a group that is sustained by the mutual interest of members. Some groups form because members with common interests help each other achieve a mutual goal. For example, the owners and employees of a sewing shop constitute a group formed around a common interest in sewing and the common goal of making money.
- *Recognition as being a group*—Finally, to be a group, the individuals involved must *perceive themselves as a group*. Groups are composed of people who recognize each other as a member of their group and can distinguish these individuals from nonmembers. The members of a corporate finance committee or a chess club, for example, know who is and is not in their group. In contrast, shoppers in a checkout line probably don't think of each other as being members of a group. Although they stand physically close to each other and may have passing conversations, they have little in common (except, perhaps, a shared interest in reaching the end of the line) and fail to identify themselves with the others in the line.

By defining groups in terms of these four characteristics, I have identified a group as a very special collection of individuals. As I shall explain, these characteristics are responsible for the important effects groups have on organizational behavior. To better understand these effects, I now review the wide variety of groups that operate within organizations.

Types of Groups

What do the following have in common: a military combat unit, three couples getting together for dinner, the board of directors of a large corporation, and the three-person cockpit crew of a commercial airliner? As you probably guessed, the answer is that they are all groups. But, of course, they are very different kinds of groups, ones people join for different reasons.

FORMAL GROUPS The most basic way of identifying types of groups is to distinguish between *formal groups* and *informal groups* (see Figure 9.1). **Formal groups** are created by an organization and are intentionally designed to direct members toward some important organizational goal.

One type of formal group is referred to as a **command group**—a group determined by the connections between individuals who are a formal part of the organization (i.e., those who legitimately can give orders to others). For example, a command group may be formed by the vice president of marketing who gathers her regional marketing directors from around the country to hear their ideas about a new national advertising campaign. The point is that command groups are determined by the organization's rules regarding who reports to whom and usually consist of a supervisor and his or her subordinates.

A formal organizational group also may be formed around some specific task. Such a group is referred to as a **task group**. Unlike command groups, a task group may be composed of individuals with some special interest or expertise in a specific area regardless of their positions in the organizational hierarchy. For example, a company may have a budget committee whose members make recommendations about how company funds should be spent. It may be composed of accounting and finance specialists, corporate vice presidents, and workers from the shop floor. Whether they are permanent committees, known as **standing committees**, or temporary ones

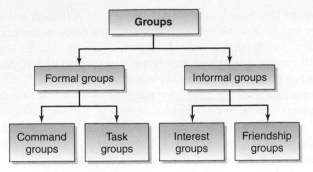

FIGURE 9.1 **Varieties of Groups in Organizations**
Within organizations, one may find formal groups (such as *command groups* and *task groups*)
and informal groups (such as *interest groups* and *friendship groups*).

formed for special purposes (such as a committee formed to recommend solutions to a parking problem), known as **ad hoc committees** or **task forces**, task groups are common in organizations.

INFORMAL GROUPS Of course, not all groups found in organizations are as formal as the ones described thus far. Many groups are informal in nature. **Informal groups** develop naturally among an organization's personnel without any direction from the management of the organization within which they operate.

A key factor in the formation of informal groups is a common interest shared by its members. For example, a group of employees who band together to seek union representation, or who march together to protest their company's pollution of the environment, may be called an **interest group**. The common goal sought by members of an interest group may unite workers at many different organizational levels. The key factor is that membership in an interest group is voluntary—it is not created by the organization but is encouraged by an expression of common interests.

Sometimes, the interests that bind individuals together are far more diffuse. Groups may develop out of a common interest in participating in sports, or going to the movies, or just getting together to chat. These kinds of informal groups are known as **friendship groups**. A group of coworkers who hang out together during lunch may also bowl or play cards together after work. Friendship groups extend beyond the workplace because they provide opportunities for satisfying the social needs of workers that are so important to their well-being.

Informal work groups are an important part of life in organizations. Although they develop without direct encouragement from management, friendships often originate out of formal organizational contact. For example, three employees working alongside each other on an assembly line may get to talking, discover their mutual interest in basketball, and decide to get together after work to shoot hoops. As you will see, such friendships can bind people together, helping them cooperate with each other and improving organizational functioning.

THE BASIC BUILDING BLOCKS OF GROUP DYNAMICS

Now that you understand exactly what a group is, you are prepared to appreciate the basic elements of group dynamics. These include *roles* (the various parts played by group members), *norms* (the rules and expectations that develop within groups), *status* (the prestige of group membership), and *cohesiveness* (the members' senses of belonging).

Roles: The Hats We Wear

One of the primary structural elements of groups is members' tendencies to play specific roles in group interaction, often more than one. Social scientists use the term *role* in much the same way as a director of a play would refer to a character playing a part. Indeed, the part one plays in the overall group structure is what I mean by a role. More formally, a **role** is defined as the typical behaviors that characterize a person in a social context.[4]

In organizations, many roles follow from people's positions within their companies. For example, a boss may be expected to give orders, and a teacher may be expected to lecture and to assign grades. These are behaviors expected of the individual in that role. The person holding the role is known as a **role incumbent**, and the behaviors expected of that person are known as **role expectations**. The person holding the office of the president of the United States (the role incumbent) has certain role expectations simply because he or she currently has that post. When a new president takes office, that person assumes the same role and has the same formal powers as the previous president. This is the case although the new president may have very different ideas about key issues facing the nation.

The roles discussed thus far reflect formal organizational positions, but not all roles are of this type. Indeed, many of the roles people assume in organizations are informal in nature. To appreciate this, think about committees on which you have served. Was there someone who joked and made people feel better, and another member who worked hard to get the group to focus on the issue at hand? This is not at all unusual. In fact, as groups develop, various members come to play different roles in the social structure—a process referred to as **role differentiation**. The emergence of different roles in groups is a naturally occurring process. In general, three roles commonly emerge in groups. These are as follows:

- The **task-oriented role**—the person who, more than anyone else, helps the group reach its goal.
- The **socioemotional role**—the group member who is highly supportive and nurturing, someone who makes everyone else feel good.
- The **self-oriented role**—the group member who does things for him- or herself, even at the expense of the group.

Norms: A Group's Unspoken Rules

One feature of groups that enhances their orderly functioning is the existence of *norms*. Defined, **norms** are generally agreed-upon informal rules that guide group members' behavior.[5] They represent shared ways of viewing the world. Norms differ from organizational rules in that they are not formal and written. Group members may be unaware of the subtle norms that influence them in important ways. For example, norms known as **injunctive norms** reflect people's views about what constitutes appropriate and inappropriate behavior in the workplace. If you recall the pressures placed on you by your peers as you grew up to dress or wear your hair in certain styles, you are well aware of the profound normative pressures exerted by groups as they attempt to enforce injunctive norms.

Some injunctive norms, known as **prescriptive norms**, dictate the behaviors that *should be performed*. For example, groups may develop prescriptive norms to follow their leader or to help a group member who needs assistance. Other injunctive norms, known as **proscriptive norms**, dictate specific behaviors that *should be avoided*. Proscriptive norms appear to be operating in groups whose members discourage one another from being absent. They also may account for the tendency for group members to refrain from telling each other's secrets to the boss.

TABLE 9.1	Group Norms: How Do They Develop?

Group norms develop in the various ways summarized here.

Basis of Norm Development	Example
Precedents set over time	Seating location of each group member around a table
Carryovers from other situations	Professional standards of conduct
Explicit statements from others	Working a certain way because you are told "that's how we do it around here"
Critical events in group history	After the organization suffers a loss due to one person's divulging company secrets, a norm develops to maintain secrecy

Source: Based on suggestions by Bicchieri, 2006, Feldman, 1984; see Note 6.

Sometimes the pressure to conform to norms is subtle, as in the dirty looks given to a manager by his peers for going to lunch with one of the assembly-line workers. At other times, normative pressures may be quite severe, such as when one production worker sabotages another's work because he is performing at too high a level and making his coworkers look bad. Although my examples emphasize the underlying social regulatory factors responsible for how groups develop norms, this is only one reason. There are, in fact, several factors responsible for the formation of norms.[6] For a summary of these, see Table 9.1.

Status: The Prestige of Group Membership

Have you ever been attracted to a group or organization because of the high esteem in which it is held by others? You may have wanted to join a certain fraternity or sorority because it is highly regarded by other students on campus. No doubt, members of championship-winning football teams proudly sport their Super Bowl rings to identify themselves as members of their prestigious organizations. Clearly, one potential reward of group membership is the status associated with being in that group. Even within social groups, different members are accorded different levels of prestige. Fraternity and sorority officers, and committee chairpersons, for example, may be recognized as more important members of their respective groups. This is the idea behind **status**— the relative social position or rank given to groups or group members by others.[7] Status may be recognized as both formal and informal in nature.

FORMAL AND INFORMAL STATUS In organizations, people differ with respect to the degrees of formal authority they have. This is the idea behind **formal status**, which refers to the prestige associated with formal organizational positions. So, for example, the formal status of a CEO is far higher than that of a mailroom clerk. The formal nature of many organizational hierarchies makes it possible to determine an individual's formal status.

Nowhere is this made clearer than in military organizations, where people wear bars and/or stars on their uniforms to demark their position in the military hierarchy. This leaves no question about the relative positions of the individuals involved, triggering clear protocol regarding how to behave toward one another.

Although what they convey about status may not be as clear-cut as in the military, material objects also are used in the private sector to send messages about the proper amount of formal status to be accorded someone. Such objects are known as **status symbols**, defined as objects reflecting the position of an individual within an organization's hierarchy. Popular examples of status symbols include job titles (e.g., director); perquisites, or perks (e.g., a reserved parking space); and luxurious working conditions (e.g., a large, private office that is lavishly decorated).[8]

Symbols of **informal status** within organizations also are widespread. These refer to the prestige accorded individuals with certain characteristics that are not formally recognized by the organization.[9] For example, employees who are older and more experienced may be perceived as higher in status by their coworkers. Those who have certain special skills (such as the home-run hitters on a baseball team) also may be regarded as having higher status than others on their teams. In some organizations, the lower value placed on the work of women and members of minority groups by prejudiced individuals, although highly inappropriate, is yet another example of informal status in operation.[10] In this case, however, it's low status that's being attributed to these individuals.

STATUS AND INFLUENCE: A KEY RELATIONSHIP One of the best-established findings in the study of group dynamics is that higher-status people tend to be more influential than lower-status people. By **influence**, I am referring to the capacity to affect others in some fashion. The connection between status and influence may be seen in a classic study of decision making in three-man bomber crews.[11] After the crews had difficulty solving a problem, the experimenter planted clues to the solution with either a low-status group member (the tail gunner) or a high-status group member (the pilot). It was found that the solutions offered by the pilots were far more likely to be adopted than the same solutions presented by the tail gunners. Apparently, the greater status accorded the pilots (because they tended to be more experienced and held higher military ranks) was responsible for the greater influence they wielded.

Cohesiveness: Getting the Team Spirit

One obvious determinant of any group's structure is its **cohesiveness**—the strength of group members' desires to remain part of their groups. Highly cohesive work groups are those in which members are attracted to each other, accept the group's goals, and help work toward meeting them. In very uncohesive groups, the members dislike each other and may even work at cross-purposes.[12] In essence, cohesiveness refers to a *we feeling*, an *esprit de corps*, or a sense of belonging to a group.

DETERMINANTS OF COHESIVENESS Several important factors have been shown to influence the extent to which group members tend to "stick together." These are as follows:

- *Severity of initiation*—The greater the difficulty people overcome to become a member of a group, the more cohesive the group will be.[13] The rigorous requirements for gaining entry into elite groups, such as the most prestigious medical schools and military training schools, are partly responsible for the high degree of camaraderie found in such groups. Having "passed the test" tends to keep individuals together and separates them from those who are unwilling or unable to "pay the price" of admission.
- *External threat*—Group cohesion also tends to be strengthened under conditions of high external threat or competition. When workers face a "common enemy," they tend to draw together. Such cohesion not only makes workers feel safer and better protected, but also aids them by encouraging them to work closely together and coordinate their efforts toward the common enemy. Good examples of cohesion in response to shared external threat may be

seen in the way employees of normally competing restaurants in New York City banded together to feed the hungry in the aftermath of the terrorist attacks of September 11, 2001.
- *Group size*—As you might imagine, cohesiveness tends to be greater in smaller groups.
Generally speaking, groups that are too large make it difficult for members to interact and,
therefore, for cohesiveness to reach a high level.
- *History of success*—"Nothing succeeds like success," as they say, and groups with a history
of success tend to be highly cohesive. It is often said that "everyone loves a winner," and the
success of a group tends to help unite its members as they rally around their success. For
this reason, employees tend to be loyal to successful companies—and sports fans tend to be
loyal to winning teams.

BEWARE—COHESIVENESS IS A DOUBLE-EDGED SWORD   Thus far, this discussion has implied
that cohesiveness is a positive thing. Indeed, it can be. For example, people are known to enjoy belonging to highly cohesive groups. Members of closely knit work groups participate more fully in
their group's activities, more readily accept their group's goals, and are absent from their jobs less
often than members of less cohesive groups.[14] Not surprisingly, cohesive groups tend to work together quite well and are sometimes exceptionally productive with low levels of voluntary turnover.[15]

However, highly cohesive groups also can be problematic. Consider, for example, what
would happen if a highly cohesive group's goals are contrary to the organization's goals. In this
case, that group is in a position to inflict a great deal of harm to an organization by working
against its interests.[16] Highly cohesive group members who conspire to sabotage their employers
are a good example. With this in mind, it's important to recognize that, when it comes to performance, group cohesiveness is a double-edge sword: its effects can be both helpful (if group norms
support the organization) or harmful (if group norms counter the organization's interests).

INDIVIDUAL PERFORMANCE IN GROUPS

Having reviewed the basic nature of groups, I now turn to an aspect of group dynamics that
is particularly relevant to the field of organizational behavior—the effects of groups on individual performance. Specifically, I focus on two issues in this connection: how people's work
performance is affected by the presence of others and how it is affected by the number of others
present—that is, group size.

Social Facilitation: Working in the Presence of Others

Imagine that you have been taking piano lessons for ten years and you now are about to go on
stage for your first major solo concert performance. You have been practicing diligently for several months, getting ready for the big night. Now, you are no longer alone in your living room but
on stage in front of hundreds of people. Your name is announced and silence breaks the applause
as you take your place in front of the concert grand. How will you perform now that you are in
front of an audience? Will you freeze, forgetting the piece you practiced, or will the audience spur
you on to your best performance yet? In other words, what impact will the presence of the audience have on your behavior?

THE SOCIAL FACILITATION EFFECT   After studying this question for over a century, using a
wide variety of tasks and situations, social scientists found that the answer to this question is
not straightforward.[17] Sometimes people were found to perform better in the presence of others
than when alone, and sometimes they were found to perform better alone than in the presence of

others. This tendency for the presence of others to enhance an individual's performance at times and to impair it at other times is known as **social facilitation**. (Although the word *facilitation* implies improvements in task performance, scientists use the term *social facilitation* to refer to both performance improvements and decrements stemming from the presence of others.)

The obvious question is this: Under what conditions will performance be helped by the presence of others and under what conditions will it be hindered? Research has shown that the answer depends on how well people know the task they are performing (for a summary, see Figure 9.2). When people are performing tasks they know quite well (e.g., a musical piece they have played for years), they generally perform better in front of an audience than alone. However, when people are performing tasks with which they are unfamiliar (e.g., a piece of music that is new to their repertoires), they generally perform better alone than in the presence of others.

SOCIAL FACILITATION AND PERFORMANCE MONITORING It's easy to imagine how the social facilitation effect may have a profound influence on organizational behavior. For example, consider the effects it may have on people whose work is monitored, either by others who are physically present or by connections made via computer networks. The rationale behind performance monitoring—the practice of supervisors observing subordinates while working—is that it will encourage people to perform at their best. But does it really work this way?

The concept of social facilitation suggests that monitoring should improve task performance only if the people monitored know their tasks extremely well. However, if they are relatively new to the job, their performance would suffer when monitored. In fact, research suggests that this is precisely what happens.[18] For employees who are not well practiced at their jobs, performance monitoring does not have the intended effects. Accordingly, supervisors seeking to raise employees' performance levels by introducing performance monitoring should carefully consider the effects of social facilitation before doing so. Specifically, monitoring is likely to boost the performance of people who are highly experienced at their jobs. Among other reasons, this may inspire them to show off how well they can do. However, among people who are not particularly

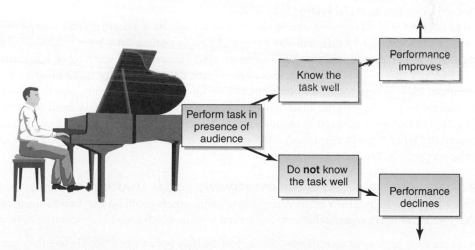

FIGURE 9.2 **The Social Facilitation Effect: A Summary**
According to the phenomenon of *social facilitation*, a person's performance on a task will be influenced by the presence of others. Compared to performance when doing the task alone, performance in front of an audience will be enhanced if that task is well learned but impaired if it is not well learned.

adept at their jobs (e.g., those who are new to the task), monitoring may make them nervous because it leads them to fear what their supervisors are thinking about them. This, in turn, may interfere with their job performance.

Social Loafing: "Free Riding" When Working With Others

Have you ever worked with several others to help a friend move into a new apartment, each carrying and transporting part of the load from the old place to the new one? Or how about sitting around a table with others, stuffing political campaign letters into envelopes and addressing them to potential donors? Although these tasks may seem quite different, they actually share an important common characteristic: performing each requires only a single individual, but several people's work can be pooled to yield greater outcomes. Because each person's contributions can be added together with another's, such tasks have been referred to as *additive tasks*.[19] The question of interest in this section of the chapter is an important one when it comes to organizing the way work is done: When a group of people get together to perform additive tasks, does each individual contribute as much work as when doing the same task alone?

THE SOCIAL LOAFING EFFECT   If you've ever performed additive tasks, such as the ones described here, you already may have a good sense of the answer to this question. In such situations, you may have found yourself working not quite as hard as you would have if you worked alone. Does this sound familiar? Indeed, research has established that when several people join forces on additive tasks, each individual contributes less than when performing the same task alone.[20]

As suggested by the old saying "Many hands make light the work," a group of people would be expected to be more productive than any one individual. However, when several people combine their efforts on additive tasks, each individual's contribution tends to be less. Five people working together raking leaves will *not* be five times more productive than a single individual working alone; there are always some who go along for a "free ride." In fact, the more individuals who are contributing to an additive task, the less each individual's contribution tends to be—a phenomenon known as **social loafing**.[21]

This effect was first noted almost seventy years ago by a scientist who compared the amount of force exerted by different size groups of people pulling on a rope.[22] Specifically, he found that one person pulling on a rope alone exerted an average of sixty-three kilograms of force. However, in groups of three, the per-person force dropped to fifty-three kilograms, and in groups of eight it was reduced to only thirty-one kilograms per person—less than half the effort exerted by people working alone! Social loafing effects of this type have been observed in many different studies conducted in recent years.[23] The general form of the social loafing effect is portrayed in Figure 9.3. (To demonstrate the social loafing effect firsthand, complete the Group Exercise on pp. 293–294.)

RESEARCH-BASED SUGGESTIONS FOR OVERCOMING SOCIAL LOAFING   Obviously, the tendency for people to reduce their effort when working with others could be a serious problem in organizations. Fortunately, research has revealed several ways in which social loafing can be overcome.

- *Make each performer identifiable*—Social loafing may occur when people feel they can get away with "taking it easy"—namely, under conditions in which each individual's contributions cannot be determined. A variety of studies on the practice of *public posting* support this idea.[24] This research has found that when each individual's contribution to a task is displayed where it can be seen by others (e.g., weekly sales figures posted on a chart), people

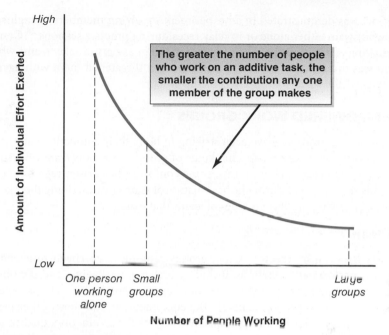

FIGURE 9.3 The Social Loafing Effect
When individuals work together on additive tasks, the greater the size of the group, the less effort each individual tends to exert. This phenomenon is known as *social loafing*.

are less likely to slack off than when only overall group (or company-wide) performance is made available. In other words, the more one's individual contribution to a group effort is highlighted, the more pressure each person feels to make a group contribution. Thus, social loafing can be overcome if one's contributions to an additive task are identified: potential loafers are not likely to loaf if they fear getting caught.

- *Make work tasks more important and interesting*—Research has revealed that people are unlikely to go along for a free ride when the task they are performing is believed to be vital to the organization.[25] For example, the less meaningful salespeople believe their jobs are, the more they engage in social loafing—especially when they think their supervisors know little about how well they are working.[26] To counteract this tendency, corporate officials should strive to make jobs more intrinsically interesting to employees. To the extent that jobs are interesting, people may be less likely to loaf. After all, if doing a job is fun, one would not want to slack off on it. (For some suggestions regarding how to bring this about, see Chapter 6.)
- *Reward individuals for contributing to their group's performance*—Social loafing may be overcome by encouraging people's interest in their group's performance.[27] Doing this (e.g., giving all salespeople in a territory a bonus if they jointly exceed their sales goal) may help employees focus more on collective concerns and less on individualistic concerns, increasing their obligations to their fellow group members. This is important, of course, in that the success of an organization is more likely to be influenced by the collective efforts of groups than by the individual contributions of any one member.
- *Threaten punishment*—To the extent that performance decrements may be controlled by threats of punishment for the individuals who are slacking off, loafing may be reduced.

This effect was demonstrated in an experiment involving members of high school swim teams who swam either alone or in relay races during practice sessions.[28] Confirming the social loafing effect, students swam faster alone than as part of relay teams when no punishment was threatened. However, when the coach threatened them with having to swim "penalty laps," the social loafing effect did not occur.

TEAMS: EMPOWERED WORK GROUPS

In recent years, as organizations have been striving to hone their competitive advantages, many have been organizing work around specific kinds of groups known as *teams*. Because the team movement frequently takes different forms, some confusion has arisen regarding exactly what teams are. In this section, I will clarify the basic nature of teams by describing their key characteristics and then identifying the various types of teams that exist.

What Is a Team?

At MillerCoors Brewing in Trenton, Ohio, groups ranging from six to nineteen employees work together to perform all operations, including brewing, packaging, and distributing Miller Genuine Draft beer. They schedule their own work assignments and vacations, conduct assessments of their peers' performance, maintain the equipment, and perform other key functions. Each group is responsible for meeting prespecified targets for production, quality, and safety—and to help, data regarding costs and performance are shared with them.

Clearly, these groups are different in key respects from those I have described thus far, such as a company's budget committee. The MillerCoors employees are all members of special kinds of groups known as *teams*. Formally defined, a **team** is a group whose members have complementary skills and are committed to a common purpose or set of performance goals for which they hold themselves mutually accountable. Applying this definition to the description of the way work is done at MillerCoors' Trenton plant, it's clear that teams are in use at this facility.

Given the unique and complex nature of teams, I will highlight some of their key characteristics and distinguish teams from the traditional ways in which work groups operate.[29] As you read these descriptions, you might find it useful to refer to Table 9.2 as a summary.

TABLE 9.2 Teams Versus Traditional Work Groups: Some Key Distinctions

Teams differ from traditional work groups in the various ways summarized here.

Traditional Work Groups	Teams
Designed around functions (e.g., marketing, engineering, etc.)	Design around work processes (e.g., developing and selling products)
Members have no sense of ownership over their work products	Members share ownership of the team's final products and services
Workers have single skills	Team members have multiple skills
Outside leaders govern workers	Team members govern themselves
Support staff and skills are found outside the group	Support staff and skills are built into teams
Organizational decisions are made by managers	Teams are involved in making organizational decisions for themselves

Source: Based on material in Bellman & Ryan, 2009; see Note 29.

TEAMS ARE ORGANIZED AROUND WORK PROCESSES RATHER THAN FUNCTIONS Instead of having traditional departments whose members focus on narrowly defined functions (e.g., finance, research and development, and so on), team members have many different skills and come together to perform several processes, such as designing and launching new products, manufacturing, and distribution. As an example, Sterling Winthrop, the pharmaceuticals company, used to have twenty-one different departments working on various aspects of the manufacturing process. Today, all facets of production (e.g., ordering supplies, blending the formulation, scheduling work, etc.) are carried out by members of teams who work together on the production process.

TEAMS "OWN" THE PRODUCT, SERVICE, OR PROCESSES ON WHICH THEY WORK By this, I mean that people feel part of something meaningful and understand how their work fits into the big picture (recall the discussion of the motivating properties of these kinds of beliefs described in Chapter 6). For example, employees at Florida's Cape Coral Hospital work in teams within four "mini hospitals" (surgical, general, specialty medical, and outpatient) —not only to boost efficiency but also to help them feel more responsible for their patients. By working in small units, team members have greater contact with patients and are more aware of the effects of their work on patient care. This is in contrast to the traditionally more distant ways of organizing hospital work into separate departments, in which employees tend to feel less connected to the results of their actions.

TEAM MEMBERS PERFORM A VARIETY OF TASKS Traditionally, insurance policies were processed by specialists from separate departments who did such things as score applications, underwrite policies, and enter information into online databases. Employees learned only how to perform their specialized tasks. In many insurance companies today, however, policies are processed by work teams in which members perform all these tasks. This, of course, requires employees to learn to perform a variety of different tasks, a process known as **cross-training**. This enables team members to help one another by pitching-in to do whatever may be required to get a job done.

Research has revealed that cross-training enhances team performance and that the processes responsible for this operate as outlined in Figure 9.4.[30] Specifically, when workers are cross-trained, they develop what are called **shared mental models**. These are common understandings of how a team operates, including how members are expected to work together and who does what at particular times. Shared mental models, in turn, help people understand how to coordinate their efforts with others and how to assist others who need help (i.e., how to back them up). Not surprisingly, such knowledge contributes to team success. By contrast, individuals who are not cross-trained fail to develop shared mental models with their teammates, thereby eliminating a key ingredient for team success.

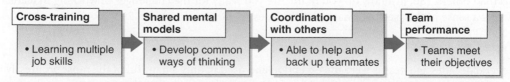

FIGURE 9.4 Cross-Training Improves Team Performance: How Does It Happen?
Research has found that cross-training members of work team raises the performance levels of those teams. The processes responsible for this effect are summarized here.
Source: Based on suggestions by Marks et al., 2002; see Note 30.

TEAMS GOVERN THEMSELVES—AT LEAST TO SOME EXTENT   Because team members tend to be so highly trained and involved in a variety of organizational activities, it is often unnecessary for them to be governed closely in the traditional manner in which bosses supervise their subordinates. Instead, many team leaders serve as *coaches* who help team members achieve their goals rather than as traditional, more authoritarian leaders (see Chapter 11). In other words, teams are **empowered** to make decisions on their own behalf.

As an example, consider the Texas Instrument defense electronics plant, where teams appoint their own leaders. Called "coordinators," these individuals do exactly what the name implies—they strive to ensure the smooth interaction between team members. In other organizations, such as the Mine Safety Appliances Company, team members take turns as "captains," handling all the paperwork for a few weeks until the job is rotated to someone else. It is important to note, however, that not all teams enjoy such total self-regulatory freedom.

As you might imagine, because many company officials are reluctant to give up power, complete self-governance by teams does not always occur. Still, at least some degree of self-governance tends to occur in today's work teams. (I will return to this issue in Chapter 11 when discussing leadership in teams.)

IN TEAMS, SUPPORT STAFF AND RESPONSIBILITIES ARE BUILT IN   Traditionally, such functions as maintenance, engineering, and human resources operate as separate departments that provide support to other groups requiring these services. Because this often causes delays, however, teams often include members who have expertise in these crucial support areas. For example, at most divisions of 3M, there are no quality inspectors. Instead, teams are used extensively in which all members are trained in ways of inspecting products and controlling quality. This is only one example of teams whose members perform tasks that traditionally were done by specialized organizational units, thereby making teams self-contained and self-sufficient.

TEAMS ARE INVOLVED IN MAKING COMPANY-WIDE DECISIONS   Traditionally, high level managers make important organizational decisions. In work teams, however, this responsibility falls on the shoulders of teams. For example, team members in some divisions of Eastman Chemical participate actively on company-level committees that develop policies and procedures affecting everyone. The underlying idea is that the people who are closest to the work performed should be the ones most involved in making the decisions. As noted earlier, the reluctance of some corporate leaders to completely empower teams may temper this process somewhat. In other words, although some companies may be reluctant to give teams complete decision-making power, the granting of at least some decision-making authority is a hallmark of modern teams.

Now that you know what teams are, you may be thinking that not all people are right for them. Indeed, this is so. The unique nature of teams makes them better suited to some individuals than others. (So, just how do you fit in? Are you ready for the challenges of working in teams? To get a sense of this, see this chapter's Self-Assessment Exercise on pp. 292–293.)

Types of Teams

Several decades ago, teams were the exception and used in only a handful of the most progressive organizations, such as Procter & Gamble and General Electric. Today, however, they are the rule. Within *Fortune* 500 companies, it has been estimated that approximately 80 percent rely on teams to perform at least some functions.[31] Considering their popularity, it should not be surprising that all teams are not alike but that they take a variety of different forms. I now summarize the major kinds of teams found in organizations.

WORK TEAMS AND IMPROVEMENT TEAMS   One way of distinguishing between teams has to do with their major *purpose* or *mission*. In this regard, some teams—known as **work teams**—are concerned primarily with the work done by the organization, such as developing and manufacturing new products, providing services for customers, and so on. Their principle focus is on using the organization's resources to effectively create its products (either goods or services). The examples I've given thus far fall into this category. Other teams—known as **improvement teams**—are oriented primarily toward the mission of increasing the effectiveness of the processes that are used by the organization. For example, Texas Instruments has relied on teams to help improve the quality of operations at its plant in Malaysia.

TEMPORARY AND PERMANENT TEAMS   A second way of distinguishing between types of teams has to do with *time*. Specifically, some teams are only **temporary** and are established for a specific project with a finite life span. For example, a team set up to develop a new product would be considered temporary because as soon as its job is done, it disbands. However, other kinds of teams are **permanent** and remain intact as long as the organization is operating. For example, teams focusing on providing effective customer service tend to be permanent parts of many organizations.

WORK GROUPS AND SELF-MANAGED WORK TEAMS   Teams also differ with respect to how much *autonomy* they have—that is, the degree to which they are free to make their own decisions. Typically, this is reflected in terms of two key factors: the degree of responsibility people have and the degree to which they are held accountable for their own work outcomes. Along the resulting continuum (see Figure 9.5), three kinds of groups and teams may be identified. These are as follows:

- At the low-autonomy extreme are **work groups**, in which leaders make decisions on behalf of group members, whose job it is to follow the leader's orders. This traditional form is becoming less popular, as more organizations are allowing employees to make their own key decisions.
- At the high-autonomy extreme are **self-managed work teams** (or **self-directed teams**). In such teams, small numbers (typically about ten) take on duties once performed by their supervisors, such as making work assignments, deciding on the pace of work, and so on.[32] In organizations where teams are used, only about 20 percent of the employees are involved in self-managed work teams.[33]
- Between these two extremes are **semiautonomous work groups**. These are groups whose members have some, but not complete, freedom to make decisions on their own behalf. Many companies making the move to self-managed work teams try using semiautonomous work groups along the way just to ensure that everyone involved is prepared for the freedom and responsibility that go with self-management.

INTACT AND CROSS-FUNCTIONAL TEAMS   Another way to distinguish teams is with respect to the team's connection to the organization's overall authority structure—that is, the connection between various formal job responsibilities. In some organizations, **intact teams** work together all the time and do not apply their special knowledge to a wide range of products. Teams in such organizations, such as Purina, the pet food company, do not have to stray from their areas of expertise.

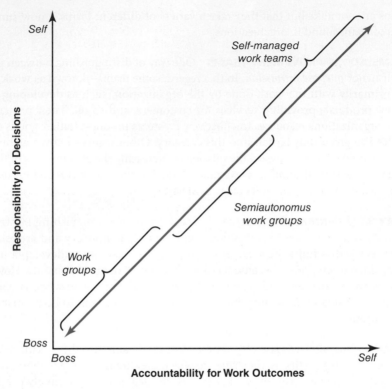

FIGURE 9.5 A Continuum of Autonomy
Work groups and teams differ with respect to the degree of autonomy they have. In *work groups*, bosses have responsibility over decisions and are accountable for work outcomes. The workers themselves have very little autonomy. By contrast, in *self-managed work groups*, the workers themselves have responsibility over decisions and are accountable for work outcomes. They are highly autonomous. *Semiautonomous work groups* fall between these two extremes.

With growing frequency, however, teams are crossing over various functional units (e.g., marketing, finance, human resources, and so on). Such teams, referred to as **cross-functional teams**, are composed of employees at identical organizational levels but from different specialty areas. Cross-functional teams are an effective way of bringing people together from throughout the organization to cooperate on large projects. To function effectively, the boundaries between cross-functional teams must be permeable—that is, employees must be members of more than one team. For example, members of an organization's manufacturing team must carefully coordinate their activities with members of its marketing team. To the extent that people are involved in several different kinds of teams, they may gain broader perspectives and make more contributions that are important to their various teams. As an example, Boeing used cross-functional teams to develop its 777 and 787 aircrafts.

PHYSICAL AND VIRTUAL TEAMS   The teams I have been describing thus far may be considered **physical teams** because they involve people who physically meet to work together. Although teams have operated this way for many years, and will continue to do so, technology has made it possible for teams to exist without members ever getting together physically.

Teams of this sort—that operate across space, time, and organizational boundaries, communicating with each other primarily through electronic technology—are known as **virtual teams**.[34] (For an example of a particularly successful virtual team, see the Winning Practices section below.)

Impressive Claims About Team Performance

In recent years, impressive claims about the success of teams in improving quality, customer service, productivity, and the bottom line have appeared in popular business publications.[35] For a sampling of these, see Table 9.3.

Winning Practices

"Virtual Troops" Usher Girl Scouts into the Digital Era

Think Girl Scouts and you probably think of cookies. But to the 50 million American women who enjoyed Girl Scouting during their childhoods, Girl Scouts of the USA is more than Thin Mints and Tagalongs. For over 100 years, Girl Scouts has remained steadfast in its commitment to empowering girls by developing their potential as leaders, improving their life skills, and learning how to cooperate with others.[36] And while the organization focuses on doing good for society and stewardship of our planet, Girl Scouting is also about having fun. This is why 2.3 million girls (and 880,000 women volunteers) today wear their Girl Scout badges with pride.

As impressive as these numbers may be, CEO Anna Maria Chávez hasn't been taking them for granted. Dedicated to maintaining membership by ensuring that the Girl Scouts is relevant to today's girls, Chávez has been committed to bringing the organization into the digital era.[37] Her primary vehicle has been a pilot program known as "virtual troops." This initiative uses Adobe's Web-conferencing service to bring girls together for monthly meetings. Not intending to do away with in-person troop meetings but to supplement them, Chávez wants virtual troops to involve girls for whom attending traditional meetings is impossible or inconvenient.

Virtual troops also appeal to Chávez because of the opportunities they provide to bring together girls from throughout the United States and the world who would ordinarily never have opportunities to interact. These networks are extensive: there are over 100 local Girl Scout councils in the United States, and Girl Scouts of the USA is part of a family of 10 million girls and adults in 145 countries assembled under the World Association of Girl Guides and Girl Scouts (WAGGGS). Only through Internet technology can there be any hope of extending the reach of members over the planet, and Chávez is hoping that virtual teams will help break down national barriers by bringing together girls with common interests.

In addition to the learning opportunities this offers, the new connections formed in virtual troops promise to help girls in two important ways: they introduce girls to the global nature of business, which they will encounter when they grow up; and they expose girls to technology businesses, which tend to be primarily led by men. Together, these experiences promote opportunities for girls to develop business and leadership skills, which long has been one of the key objectives of Girl Scouts.

If you consider that Girl Scouts of the USA sold some $700 million in cookies in 2011 and that 80 percent of women business owners in the United States are Girl Scouts alums, it's clear that the organization's business development mission is taken seriously.[38] To Chávez, virtual troops are another mechanism for of bringing this about, ensuring that the organization is more than simply crafts, camping, and cookies.

TABLE 9.3	The Effectiveness of Teams: Some Impressive Reports

Teams have been claimed to help many organizations enjoy dramatic gains in productivity, including the ones summarized here.

Company	Result
Wilson Sporting Goods	Average annual cost savings of $5 million
Kodak Customer Assistance Center	Accuracy of responses increased 100 percent
Corning	Defects dropped from 1,800 parts-per-million (ppm) to 3 ppm
Sealed Air	Waste reduced by 50 percent
Exxon	$10 million saved in six months
Carrier	Unit turnaround reduced from two weeks to two days
Xerox	Productivity increased by 30 percent
Westinghouse	Product costs down 60 percent
Texas Instruments	Costs reduced by more than 50 percent

Sources: Based on information in Wellington, 2012, and additional sources in Note 35.

Clearly, we are led to believe that teams in general can produce very impressive results. However, it is important to consider whether such claims are valid. In this section, I will examine evidence bearing on this question. Then I will focus on some of the obstacles to team success. In the final section of the chapter, I will consider some of the things that can be done to help promote highly successful teams. By way of launching this discussion, however, I begin by examining what it is about teams that stand to make them effective in the first place.

What Is It About Teams That May Make Them Effective?

To operate successfully, team members must coordinate their efforts in a manner that allows them to do what's necessary to accomplish team objectives. In the case of self-managed teams, the members take on this responsibility themselves. Two psychological mechanisms appear to be at work here. These are as follows:

- **Peer-based normative control**—Team members' longing for inclusion in their teams, the desire to be part of a community that pursues accepted goals.
- **Peer-based rational control**—Team members' motives to go along with their teams based on their beliefs that the team can reward them for doing what it deems appropriate.

These two forces emerge in varying degrees over time as teams operate. Members of self-managed teams experience these control mechanisms in the form of pressure from their fellow team members. These pressures to go along with whatever their teams value (e.g., a team's procedures and decisions) influence members because of what team membership offers. As specified here, this involves both the rewards team members offer (the rational form of peer-based control) as well as the interpersonal satisfaction that results from being part of a team (the normative form of peer-based control).

Recent research has demonstrated that both forms of peer-based control exist in work teams and that they play an important role in organizational functioning.[39] Specifically, a study examined the performance of 587 factory workers operating in 45 self-managed teams within three organizations. Systematic analyses of questionnaire responses revealed that higher levels of both individual performance and team performance occurred in teams in which greater degrees of peer-based rational control existed. Interestingly, these findings were more pronounced among teams in which levels of peer-based normative control also were high.

Overall, then, it's safe to conclude that for the potential benefits of teams to be realized, members have to be able to influence one another in both an instrumental fashion (i.e., through peer-based rational control) as well as an interpersonal fashion (i.e., through peer-based normative control). When these forms of control are weak or nonexistent, it appears that a key ingredient that makes teams so special is missing. Not surprisingly, this adversely affects job performance both individually and among teams as a whole.

How Successful Are Teams? Considering the Evidence

Now that you are familiar with the nature of teams, I move to the practical question that surely underscores their popularity: How effective are teams? Evidence suggests that they are successful in a variety of different ways.

The most straightforward way to learn about companies' experiences with work teams is to survey the officials of organizations that use them. One large-scale study did precisely this, sampling several hundred of the 1,000 largest companies in the United States.[40] Overall, companies that used teams reported successes—and in some cases, these were dramatic. For example, by using teams, FedEx was able to reduce incorrect billing errors by 13 percent in one year, and Procter & Gamble was able to trim manufacturing costs by 30 to 50 percent. Still other companies, such as General Electric, Best Foods, and Weyerhaeuser were able to boost production by more than 200 percent in some cases.

These impressive reports are further supported by in-depth case studies of numerous teams in many different organizations.[41] General Motors, for example, has used teams for many years. In 2010, as part of its financial reorganization plan, the company opened a new plant in Michigan, where it assembles battery packs for its electric car, the Chevy Volt. As in the conventional battery plants GM used to have, employees at the new facility operate in various teams. This includes managers working together in *support teams,* middle-level employees (e.g., technicians) working in *coordination teams,* and natural work units of various sizes performing specific tasks as members of *employee teams.* Although the teams work closely together, coordinating their activities, they function almost as separate businesses. By many measures, the traditional battery plant was very effective, and thus far, GE appears to be matching this success at its new facility.

Although case studies report successful experiences with teams, they are not entirely objective. After all, companies may be unwilling to broadcast their failures to the world. This suggests that more objective empirical research is needed. Overall, the results of such studies have been mixed. Some studies have shown that autonomous teams have significantly fewer accidents as well as lower rates of absenteeism and turnover than traditional work groups.[42] Other studies, however, have found that although many team members are satisfied with their arrangements, they are no more productive than when working individually.[43]

So, what's the conclusion? Are teams effective? Taken together, research suggests that teams are well received. Most people enjoy working in teams, at least after they have adjusted to them (which can take some time and effort). Certainly, teams help enhance commitment among employees, and as I described in Chapter 6, there are benefits to be derived from this (e.g., reduced absenteeism and turnover). From an organizational perspective, teams appear to be an effective way of eliminating layers of management, thereby allowing more work to be done by fewer people, making them more efficient and helping them respond to rapidly changing conditions (see Chapter 14). All of these benefits are tangible. However, it is important to keep in mind that teams do not always make individuals and organizations any more productive. Cases of companies becoming wildly successful after adopting teams, although compelling, cannot be generalized to all teams in all situations.

Potential Obstacles to Success: Why Some Teams Fail

Although I have reported many success stories about teams, I also have hinted at several possible problems and difficulties in implementing them. After all, working in a team demands a great deal, and not everyone is ready for them. Fortunately, we can learn from these experiences.[44] Analyses of failed attempts at introducing teams into the workplace suggest several obstacles to team success, pitfalls that can be avoided if you know them. I now discuss these (see summary in Figure 9.6).

UNWILLINGNESS TO COOPERATE Some teams fail because their members are unwilling to cooperate with one another. This is what happened once at Dow Chemical Company's plastics group in Midland, Michigan, where a team was put into place to create a new plastic resin.[45] Some members (those in the research field) wanted to spend several months developing and testing new options, while others (those on the manufacturing end) wanted to alter existing products slightly and start up production right away. Neither side budged, and the project eventually stalled. By contrast, when team members share a common vision and are committed to attaining it, they are generally very cooperative with each other, leading to success.

LACK OF MANAGEMENT SUPPORT A second reason why some teams are not effective is that they fail to receive support from management. Consider, for example, the experience at the Lenexa, Kansas, plant of the Puritan-Bennett Corporation, a manufacturer of respiratory equipment for medical patients.[46] After seven years of working to develop improved software for its respirators, product development teams failed to get the job done despite the fact that it should have taken only three years. According to Puritan-Bennett's director of research and development, the problem was that company officials never made the project a priority and refused to free up another key person needed to do the job. As he put it, "If top management doesn't buy into the idea . . . teams can go nowhere."[47]

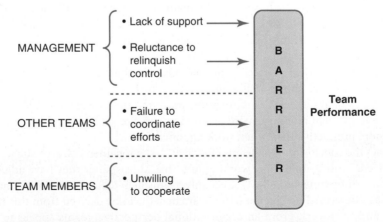

FIGURE 9.6 Barriers to Team Success: A Summary
As outlined here, the major barriers to successful teams come from management, other teams, and team members themselves.

MANAGERS' RELUCTANCE TO RELINQUISH CONTROL   A third obstacle to group success, and a relatively common one, is that some managers are unwilling to relinquish control. Good supervisors work their way up from the plant floor by giving orders and having them followed. However, team leaders have to build consensus and must allow team members to make decisions together. As you might expect, yielding control isn't always easy for some to do.

This was the problem some years back at Bausch & Lomb's sunglasses plant in Rochester, New York.[18] About 1,400 employees were put into 38 teams. After a few years, approximately half the supervisors failed to adjust to the change, despite receiving thorough training in how to work as part of a team. They argued bitterly with team members whenever their ideas were not accepted by the team, and eventually they were reassigned.

FAILURE TO COOPERATE BETWEEN TEAMS   Fourth, teams might fail not only because members do not cooperate with each other, but also because they fail to cooperate with other teams. This problem occurred in General Electric's medical systems division when it assigned two teams of engineers, one in Waukesha, Wisconsin, and another in Hino, Japan, the task of creating software for two new ultrasound devices.[49] Teams pushed features that made their products popular only in their own countries and duplicated each other's efforts. When teams met, language and cultural barriers separated them, further distancing the teams from one another. Without close cooperation between teams (as well as within them!), organizations are unlikely to reap the benefits they hoped for when creating teams in the first place.[50]

Guidelines for Developing Successful Teams

Now that you understand the track record of teams and some of the factors that make them fallible, you are in a good position to understand the various steps that can be taken to develop successful work teams. As you might imagine, making teams work effectively is no easy task. Success is not automatic. Rather, teams need to be carefully nurtured and maintained for them to accomplish their missions.[51] As one expert expressed it, "Teams are the Ferraris of work design. They're high performance but high maintenance and expensive."[52] What, then, could be done to help make teams as effective as possible? Based on analyses of high-performing work teams, several keys to success may be identified.[53]

PROVIDE TRAINING IN TEAM SKILLS   To be effective, team members must have the right blend of skills needed to satisfy their teams' objectives. Rather than simply putting teams together and hoping they will work, many companies are taking proactive steps to ensure that team members will get along and perform as they should. Formal efforts directed toward making teams effective are referred to as **team building**. Many of the particular skills on which team building focuses are summarized in Table 9.4.[54] As shown here, these various skills are touched upon in this book.

Team building usually is used when established teams are showing signs of trouble, such as when members lose sight of their objectives and when turnover is high. Workers having high degrees of freedom and anonymity require a depth of skills and knowledge that surpasses that of people performing narrower, traditional jobs. For this reason, successful teams are those in which investments are made in developing the skills of team members and leaders. In the words of one expert, "Good team members are trained, not born."

COMPENSATE TEAM PERFORMANCE   Traditionally, people are rewarded for performance levels they attain as individuals. In teams, however, it also is important to recognize group performance. Teams are no places for hot shots who want to make their individual marks—rather,

TABLE 9.4	Interpersonal Skills Required by Team Members	

Experts suggest that team members should be trained in a variety of interpersonal skills, including ones described elsewhere in this book.

Skill	Description	See Chapter(s)
Advocating	Ways of persuading others to accept one's point of view	7
Inquiring	Listening effectively to others and drawing information out of them	9
Tension management	Managing the tension that stems from conflict with others	7
Sharing responsibility	Learning to align personal and team objectives	9
Leadership	Understanding one's role in guiding the team to success	11
Valuing diversity	Acceptance—and taking advantage of—differences between members	5
Self-awareness	Willingness to criticize others constructively and to accept constructive criticism from others	7 and 8

Source: Based on information in DuFrene & Lehman, 2011, and Caudron, 1994; see Note 54.

teams require "team players." And the more organizations reward employees for their teams' successes, the more strongly team spirit is reinforced.

One popular way of accomplishing this is through **gainsharing**. This is the practice of encouraging team members to work together by rewarding them for developing procedures that lead to savings stemming from improved performance. That is, resulting gains are shared.

COMMUNICATE THE URGENCY OF THE TEAM'S MISSION   Team members are inclined to rally around challenges that compel them to meet high performance standards. As a result, the urgency of meeting those standards should be expressed.

For example, during the era of analogue recording, Ampex Corporation was the leading manufacturer of audio tape and videotape equipment for the broadcasting industry. Then, as storage of radio and television programs migrated to digital media (e.g., hard drives, solid state drives, and the like), it was necessary for Ampex to jump on the bandwagon if it was to survive. With this critical objective in mind, company officials worked hard to make their teams to recognize the urgency of the shift to digital technology. They emphasized that unless the company met these challenges, the plug surely would be pulled. Realizing that Ampex's very existence was at stake, work teams fast-forwarded the company into a position of prominence in its industry by ramping up development of digital recording technology.

PROMOTE COOPERATION WITHIN AND BETWEEN TEAMS   Team success requires not only cooperation within teams but between teams as well. As one expert put it, "Time and time again, teams fall short of their promise because companies don't know how to make them work together with other teams. If you don't get your teams into right constellations, the whole organization can stall."[55]

Boeing successfully avoided such problems in the course of developing its 777 passenger jet—a project involving some 200 teams. As you might imagine, on such a large project coordination of effort between teams is essential. To help, regular meetings were held between various team leaders who disseminated information to members. And team members could go wherever needed within the organization to get the information required to succeed. As one Boeing employee, a team leader, put it, "I can go to the chief engineer. Before, it was unusual even to see the chief engineer."[56] Just as importantly, if after getting the information they need, team members find problems, they are empowered to take action without getting management's approval. According to one Boeing engineer, "We have the no-messenger rule. Team members must make decisions on the spot. They can't run back to their functions [department heads] for permission."[57]

SELECT TEAM MEMBERS BASED ON THEIR SKILLS OR POTENTIAL SKILLS Because the success of teams demands that members work together closely on a wide variety of tasks, it is essential for them to have a complementary set of skills. This includes not only job skills but also interpersonal skills (especially since getting along with one's teammates is very important). With this in mind, at Ampex (noted earlier) three-person subsets of teams are used to select their own new members because they have the best idea about what skills are needed and who would best fit into the teams. It is also frequently important for teams to project future skills that may be needed and to train team members in these skills.

In an effort to keep team members' skills fresh, it is important to regularly confront members with new facts. Fresh approaches are likely to be prompted by fresh information, and introducing new facts may present the kind of challenges that teams need to be innovative (see Chapter 12). For example, when information about pending cutbacks in defense spending was introduced to teams at Harris Corporation (an electronics manufacturer), new technologies were developed that positioned the company to land large contracts in nonmilitary government organizations—including a $1.7 billion contract to upgrade the FAA's air traffic control system.

A Cautionary Note: Developing Successful Teams Requires Patience

It is important to caution that, although these suggestions are important, they alone do not ensure the success of work teams. Many other factors, such as the economy, the existence of competitors, and the company's financial picture, also are important determinants of organizational success. Still, the fact that these practices are followed in many highly successful teams certainly makes them worthy of consideration.

You should be aware that developing effective teams is difficult, and the path to success is riddled with obstacles. It is also time-consuming. According to management expert Peter Drucker, "You can't rush teams. It takes five years just to learn to build a team and decide what kind you want."[58] And it may take most organizations over a decade to make a complete transition to teams. Clearly, teams are not an overnight route to success. But with patience and careful attention to the suggestions outlined here, teams have ushered many companies into extraordinary gains in productivity. For this reason, they must be considered a viable option for organizing work groups.

Back to the Case

Answer the following questions based on this chapter's Making the Case (p. 269) to illustrate insights you have derived from the material in this chapter.

1. What types of groups and teams are likely to exist within Better Place?
2. What particular challenges may exist for teams within Better Place?
3. What could be done to improve the functioning of work teams in Better Place?

You Be the Consultant

Using Teams to Enhance Performance

A large manufacturing company has been doing quite well over the years but is now facing dramatic competition from overseas firms that are undercutting its prices and improving on the quality of its goods. The company president has read a lot about teams in popular business magazines and has called on you as a consultant to help implement a transition to teams for the organization. Answer the following questions relevant to this situation based on the material in this chapter.

1. What would you tell the company president about the overall record of teams—both successful and unsuccessful—in being able to improve organizational performance?

2. The company president notes that the current employees tend to have relatively poor skills and are generally disinterested in acquiring new ones. Will this be a problem when it comes to using teams? Why or why not?

3. The company president tells you that several people in the company—including some top executives—are a bit concerned about relinquishing some of their power to teams. Is this likely to be a problem, and if so, what can be done to help alleviate it?

Self-Assessment Exercise

ARE YOU READY FOR SOME TEAMWORK?

Because teams are special, it follows that the people who work in them have to be prepared for the unique situations they will face. Are you the kind of person who's ready for working in teams? This exercise will help you answer this question.

Directions

1. Read each of the following statements and carefully consider the degree to which it describes you.
2. In the space next to each statement write the number from 1 to 5 that best describes how well that statement describes you. Use the following alternatives to indicate your responses.

   1 = doesn't apply at all
   2 = applies a little
   3 = applies a fair amount
   4 = applies a great deal
   5 = applies perfectly

Scale

_____ 1. I prefer working on a variety of different tasks rather than one single task.
_____ 2. I relish opportunities to take credit for the work I do.
_____ 3. I enjoy opportunities to make decisions about how to get things accomplished.
_____ 4. Working along with others is something that's important to me.
_____ 5. I feel that I can get a lot accomplished without having someone look over my shoulder.
_____ 6. I welcome the opportunity to do whatever is best for my organization.

_____ 7. If necessary to get the job done, I am willing to learn new job skills.

_____ 8. I am not afraid of being my own boss.

_____ 9. I am interested in being retrained however necessary to meet new demands on my job.

_____ 10. I enjoy the challenge of making decisions that affect my entire organization.

_____ 11. I enjoy joining forces with others to get things accomplished.

_____ 12. Working together with people from different backgrounds is something I welcome.

_____ 13. I like to avoid leaning on management and prefer doing myself whatever it takes to get things done.

_____ 14. I take pride in the accomplishments of the others with whom I work.

_____ 15. I consider training in job skills to be an ongoing process, one that's necessary to keep up with changing times.

_____ 16. I believe that working with others doesn't always come naturally and is something that must be learned.

_____ 17. Instead of grabbing the spotlight, I am willing to share the credit for the work I perform with other people.

_____ 18. I prefer to work along with others instead of working on my own.

_____ 19. I believe that I can accomplish more when I cooperate with others than when I work by myself.

_____ 20. I like getting others to join me on projects.

Total _____

Scoring and Interpretation

1. Add together your responses. This will result in a number between 20 and 100.
2. To interpret your score, note the following:

   - Higher scores (e.g., 80–100) reflect a greater readiness to work in teams.
   - Lower scores (e.g., 20–40) reflect a lower readiness to work in teams.
   - Scores between 41 and 79 reflect an intermediate level of readiness to work in teams.

Discussion Questions

1. What was your score, and how did it compare to those of others in your class?
2. How well do you believe this questionnaire describes your readiness to work in teams?
3. What does this questionnaire reveal about the particular factors that would keep you from working well in teams? What do you think can be done to overcome these barriers?

Group Exercise

DEMONSTRATING THE SOCIAL LOAFING EFFECT

The social loafing effect is quite strong and is likely to occur in many situations in which people make individual contributions to an additive group task. This exercise is designed to demonstrate the effect firsthand in your own class.

Directions

1. Divide the class into groups of different sizes. Between five and ten people should work alone. In addition, there should be a group of two, a group of three, a group of four, and so on, until all members of the class have been assigned to a group. (If the class is small, omit intermediate size groups and assign students to only a few groups of very different sizes.) Form the groups by putting together at tables people from the same group.

2. Each person should be given a page or two from a telephone directory and a stack of index cards. Then have the individuals and the members of each group perform the same additive task—copying entries from the telephone directory onto index cards. Allow exactly ten minutes for the task to be performed, and encourage everyone to work as hard as they can.

3. After the time is up, count the number of entries copied.

4. For each group, and for all the individuals, compute the average per-person performance by dividing the total number of entries copied by the number of people in the group.

5. At the board, the instructor should graph the results. Along the vertical axis show the average number of entries copied per person. Along the horizontal axis show the size of the work groups—one, two, three, four, and so on. The graph should look like the one in Figure 9.3 (p. 279).

Discussion Questions

1. Was the social loafing effect demonstrated? What is the basis for your conclusion?

2. Did members of smaller groups feel more responsible for their group's performance than members of larger groups?

3. What could have been done to counteract any "free riding" that may have occurred in this demonstration?

Notes

MAKING THE CASE NOTES

Better Place. (2012). Press room. http://www.betterplace.com/the-company-pressroom. Schwartz, A. (2010, March 23). Better Place, by the numbers. *Fast Company.* http://www.fastcompany.com/1593916/better-place-by-the-numbers. Thompson, C. S. (2009, April 16). Batteries not included. *New York Times*, p. M44. Roth, D. (2008, August 18). Driven: Shai Agassi's audacious plan to put electric cars on the road. *Wired Magazine,* p. 16. http://www.wired.com/cars/futuretransport/magazine/16-09/ff_agassi. Ewing, J. (2008, September 1). My other car sounds like a Ferrari. *BusinessWeek,* p. 12. Better Place (2010). http://www.betterplace.com. Better Place enters electric car network partnership with Ontario. (2009). *Green Car Congress.* http://www.greencarcongress.com/2009/01/better-place-en.html. Agassi, S. (2008, July 26). Tom Friedman's Column. *The Long Tailpipe.* http://shaiagassi.typepad.com.

CHAPTER NOTES

1. Turner, M. E. (2000). *Groups at work: Theory and research.* Mahwah, NJ: Erlbaum. Cartwright, D., & Zander, A. (1968). Origins of group dynamics. In D. Cartwright & A. Zander (Eds.), *Group dynamics: Research and theory* (pp. 3–21). New York: Harper & Row.

2. Toothman, J. (2000). *Conducting the experiential group: An introduction to group dynamics.* New York: John Wiley & Sons. Bettenhausen, K. L. (1991). Five years of groups research: What we have learned and what needs to be addressed. *Journal of Management, 17,* 345–381.

3. Nowak, A., Vallacher, R. R., & Miller, M. E. (2003). Social influence and group dynamics. In T. Millon & M. J. Lerner (Eds.), *Handbook of psychology: Vol. 5, Personality and social psychology* (pp. 383–418). New York: John Wiley & Sons. Forsyth, D. L. (2009). *Group dynamics* (5th ed.). Belmont, CA: Wadsworth.

4. Podsakoff, P. M., & MacKenzie, S. B. (1997). Kerr and Jermier's substitutes for leadership model: Background, empirical assessment, and suggestions for future research. *Leadership Quarterly, 8,* 117–125. Biddle, B. J. (1979). *Role theory: Expectations, identities, and behavior.* New York: Academic Press.

5. Hackman, J. R. (1992). Group influences on individuals in organizations. In M. D. Dunnette & L. M. Hough (Eds.), *Handbook of industrial and organizational psychology* (2nd ed.) (Vol. 3, pp. 199–268). Palo Alto, CA: Consulting Psychologists Press.

6. Bicchieri, C. (2006). *The grammar of society: The nature and dynamics of social norms.*

New York: Cambridge University Press.
Feldman, D. C. (1984). The development and enforcement of group norms. *Academy of Management Review, 9,* 48–53.

7. Pearce, J. (2010). *Status, organization, and management.* New York: Cambridge University Press.

8. Greenberg, J. (1988). Equity and workplace status: A field experiment. *Journal of Applied Psychology, 73,* 606–613.

9. Wilson, S. (1978). *Informal groups: An introduction.* Upper Saddle River, NJ: Prentice Hall.

10. Jackson, L. A., & Grabski, S. V. (1988). Perceptions of fair pay and the gender wage gap. *Journal of Applied Social Psychology, 18,* 606–625.

11. Torrance, E. P. (1954). Some consequences of power differences on decision making in permanent and temporary three-man groups. *Research Studies: Washington State College, 22,* 130–140.

12. Hare, A. P. (1976). *Handbook of small group research* (2nd ed.). New York: Free Press.

13. Aronson, E., & Mills, J. (1959). The effects of severity of initiation on liking for a group. *Journal of Abnormal and Social Psychology, 59,* 178–181.

14. Cartwright, D. (1968). The nature of group cohesiveness. In D. Cartwright & A. Zander (Eds.), *Group dynamics: Research and theory* (3rd ed.) (pp. 91–109). New York: Harper & Row.

15. George, J. M., & Bettenhausen, K. (1990). Understanding prosocial behavior, sales performance, and turnover: A group-level analysis in a service context. *Journal of Applied Psychology, 75,* 698–709.

16. Douglas, T. (1983). *Groups: Understanding people gathered together.* New York: Tavistock.

17. Aiello, J. R., & Douthirt, E. A. (2001). Social facilitation from Triplett to electronic performance monitoring. *Group Dynamics, 5,* 163–180.

18. Aiello, J. R., & Svec, C. M. (1993). Computer monitoring of work performance: Extending to social facilitation framework to electronic presence. *Journal of Applied Social Psychology, 23,* 537–548.

19. Steiner, I. D. (1972). *Group processes and productivity.* New York: Academic Press.

20. Shepperd, J. A. (1993). Productivity loss in performance groups: A motivation analysis. *Psychological Bulletin, 113,* 68–81.

21. Latané, B., Williams, K., & Harkins, S. (1979). Many hands make light the work: The causes and consequences of social loafing. *Journal of Personality and Social Psychology, 37,* 822–832.

22. Kravitz, D. A., & Martin, B. (1986). Ringelmann rediscovered: The original article. *Journal of Personality and Social Psychology, 50,* 936–941.

23. Karau, S. J., & Williams, K. D. (1993). Social loafing: A meta-analytic review and theoretical integration. *Journal of Personality and Social Psychology, 65,* 681–706.

24. Nordstrom, R., Lorenzi, P., & Hall, R. V. (1990). A review of public posting of performance feedback in work settings. *Journal of Organizational Behavior Management, 11,* 101–123.

25. Bricker, M. A., Harkins, S. G., & Ostrom, T. M. (1986). Effects of personal involvement: Thought-provoking implications for social loafing. *Journal of Personality and Social Psychology, 51,* 763–769.

26. George, J. M. (1992). Extrinsic and intrinsic origins of perceived social loafing in organizations. *Academy of Management Journal, 35,* 191–202.

27. Albanese, R., & Van Fleet, D. D. (1985). Rational behavior in groups: The free-riding tendency. *Academy of Management Review, 10,* 244–255.

28. Miles, J. A., & Greenberg, J. (1993). Using punishment threats to attenuate social loafing effects among swimmers. *Organizational Behavior and Human Decision Processes, 56,* 246–265.

29. Bellman, G. M., & Ryan, K. D. (2009). Extraordinary groups: How ordinary teams achieve amazing results. San Francisco, CA: Jossey-Bass.

30. Marks, M. A., Sabella, M. J., Burke, C. S., & Zaccaro, S. J. (2002). The impact of cross-training on team effectiveness. *Journal of Applied Psychology, 87,* 3–13.

31. Rao, V. S. R. (2010, May 3). The popularity of teams. *Cite Man Network.* http://www.cite-man.com/9457-the-popularity-of-teams.html

32. Robbins, H., & Finley, M. (2000). *The new why teams don't work.* San Francisco: Barrett-Koehler.

33. Lawler, E. E., Mohrman, S. A., & Benson, G. S. (2001). *Organizing for high performance: The CEO report on employee involvement, TQM, reengineering, and knowledge management in Fortune 1000 companies.* San Francisco, CA: Jossey-Bass

34. Willmore, J. (2003). *Managing virtual teams.* London: Spiro Press. Hoefling, T. (2003). *Working virtually: Managing people for successful virtual teams and organizations.* London: Stylus Publications.

35. Wellington, P. (2012). *Managing successful teams.* Philadelphia, PA: Kogan Page. Sheridan, J. H. (1990, October 15). America's best plants. *Industry Week,* pp. 28–64. Holstein, W. J. (2008, May 30). Getting the most from management teams. *Bloomberg Businessweek.* http://www.businessweek.com/managing/content/may2008/ca20080530_775110.htm.

36. Girl Scouts of the USA. (2012). Empowering girls. *Girl Scout Facts.* http://www.girlscouts.org/who_we_are/facts/

37. Burnstein, D. D. (2012, February 20). Allow cookies: Girl Scouts enter the digital era with CEO Ana Maria Chavez. *FastCompany.* http://www.fastcompany.com/1817121/girl-scouts-ana-maria-chavez?partner=rss&utm_source=feedburner&utm_medium=feed&utm_campaign=Feed%3A+fastcompany%2Fheadlines+%28Fast+Company+Headlines%29&utm_content=Google+Feedfetcher.

38. See Note 37.

39. Stewart, G. L., Courtright, S. H., & Barrick, M. R. (2011). Peer-based control in self-managing teams: Linking rational and normative influences with individual and group performance. *Journal of Applied Psychology, 96,* 1279–1289.

40. See Note 39.

41. Hackman, J. R. (Ed.) (1990). *Groups that work (and those that don't).* San Francisco, CA: Jossey-Bass.

42. Pearson, C. A. L. (1992). Autonomous workgroups: An evaluation at an industrial site. *Human Relations, 45,* 905–936.

43. Wall, T. D., Kemp, N. J., Jackson, P. R., & Clegg, C. W. (1986). Outcomes of autonomous workgroups: A long-term field experiment. *Academy of Management Journal, 29,* 280–304.

44. See Note 43.

45. Stern, A. (1993, July 18). Managing by team is not always as easy as it looks. *New York Times,* p. B14.

46. Maginn, M. D. (1994). *Effective teamwork.* Burr Ridge, IL: Business One Irwin.

47. See Note 46.

48. See Note 46.

49. See Note 46.

50. See Note 46.

51. Salas, E., Edens, E., & Nowers, C. A. (2000). *Improving teamwork in organizations.* Mahwah, NJ: Lawrence Erlbaum Associates.

52. Dumaine, B. (1994, September 5). The trouble with teams. *Fortune,* pp. 86–88, 90, 92 (quote, p. 86).

53. Barner, R. W. (2001). *Team troubleshooter.* Palo Alto, CA: Davies Black. Maruca, R. F. (2000, November). Unit of one. *Fast Company,* pp. 109–140.

54. DuFrene, D. D., & Lehman, C. M. (2011). *Building high-performance teams* (4th ed.). Mason, OH: Cengage. Caudron, S. (1994, February). Teamwork takes work. *Personnel Journal,* pp. 41–46, 49.

55. See Note 52 (quote, p. 88).

56. See Note 52 (quote, p. 90).

57. See Note 52 (quote, p. 88).

58. Anonymous. (1994, December). The facts of life for teambuilding. *Human Resources Forum,* p. 3.

10 DECISION MAKING BY INDIVIDUALS AND GROUPS

LEARNING OBJECTIVES

After reading this chapter, you will be able to:

1. **IDENTIFY** the steps involved in the decision-making process.
2. **DESCRIBE** the different varieties of decisions people make in organizations.
3. **EXPLAIN** major approaches to individual decision making.
4. **IDENTIFY** various factors that contribute to imperfect decision making in organizations.
5. **DESCRIBE** the conditions under which individuals make better decisions than groups and groups make better decisions than individuals.
6. **EXPLAIN** how various techniques may be used to improve the quality of decisions made by groups.

THREE GOOD REASONS you should care about. . .

Decision Making by Individuals and Groups

1. Functioning effectively in today's business environment requires awareness of ways to improve the quality of decisions made in organizations.
2. Human decision making is inherently imperfect, although these imperfections can be overcome if you know what they are and how they operate.
3. Groups are widely used to make organizational decisions and although they have limitations, their effectiveness can be improved.

Making the Case for...

Decision Making by Individuals and Groups

Three Decisions Made, Then Quickly Unmade

A day doesn't go by when corporate executives fail to make decisions that have far-reaching effects. Some of these are received better than others by the public, of course. However, for public outcries over such decisions to be so loud that they would lead the organizations to rescind them almost immediately after they were announced is quite rare. Yet, this is precisely what happened in the fall of 2011 and winter of 2012—not once, but three times.

With some 24 million subscribers, you surely know Netflix, which delivers DVDs by mail and streams movies and TV shows online to customers for a flat monthly fee. What you probably never heard of, however, is Qwikster, the streaming-only digital entertainment service that Netflix unveiled in September 2011. This is because the service never got off the ground. Netflix CEO Reed Hastings believed that disk rental and online streaming needed to be two separate businesses. However, most customers enjoyed the flexibility and convenience of having both services for a single fee, making the prospect of subscribing to separate services at a higher total fee unappealing. Dissatisfied with this, Netflix customers rebelled, leading over 2 million to cancel their accounts. Fearing that the hemorrhaging wouldn't stop, Hastings withdrew plans for Qwikster only a few weeks after announcing it. Instead, Netflix restructured its plans such that customers had the option of subscribing to either or both services within a single account.

No sooner had the Netflix hubbub begun to subside, when consumers shifted their outrage to a new target—Verizon Wireless, the largest cellular carrier in the United States. On December 29, 2011, 108 million Verizon customers awoke to learn that the company was about to levy a $2 "convenience fee" on single bill payments made online or by telephone. The move was meant to encourage customers to use the company's auto-pay system instead of the costlier-to-process methods. However, the decision was not well received. The thought of paying a fee for paying a bill had customers up in arms. Protests, made over the blogosphere and in social networks, were loud. So outraged were Verizon customers that the company backed down just a day later—but not before using this incident to illustrate how it listens to its customers (especially when they shout so loudly that they cannot be ignored). Score another one for the customers.

Something may have been in the air then, because the public was only warming up for another round of protests. This time, though, the target was a nonprofit organization that made an unpopular policy decision. Susan G. Komen for the Cure has been highly successful at enhancing public awareness of breast cancer and funding research and other initiatives aimed at promoting women's health. In early 2012, officials of the renowned charity decided to cut funding to Planned Parenthood for breast cancer screening. Until then, Planned Parenthood had been serving thousands of at-risk women, thanks to its support from Komen. These cuts triggered an uproar throughout the United States. The backlash led Komen officials to reverse their decision less than two weeks later and forced the resignation of the executive responsible for making it. Again, the public spoke out—and organizational officials got the message, loud and clear.

There can be no mistaking the importance of many organizational decisions. That the public would respond as vociferously as described here, and that organizational officials would take heed and backtrack, underscores the central role of decision making in organizational functioning. Of course, not all organizational decisions are as monumental; most are more routine in nature and never come to the public's awareness. Whether far-reaching or mundane, *decision making* is woven into the tapestry of organizational life, thereby warranting a separate chapter in this book.

In the field of organizational behavior (OB), **decision making** is defined as the process of formulating problems, considering various solutions, selecting alternatives, and then implementing them. Making decisions is one of the most fundamental things that managers do.[1] It also is among the most widespread and most crucial activities performed by employees at all organizational levels.[2] Understanding how decisions are made and implemented is an important objective of the field of OB.

In this chapter, I will examine various theories of decision making, research bearing on these theories, and practical techniques designed to enhance the quality of organizational decisions. My focus will be on decisions made by both individuals and groups. Beginning with individuals, I will review various perspectives on how people go about making decisions. This discussion will consider factors that adversely affect the quality of individual decisions and ways of combating them—that is, techniques for improving the quality of individual decisions. I then shift the focus to group decisions, examining the conditions under which individuals and groups are each better suited to making decisions. Finally, I describe some of the factors that make group decisions imperfect, and various techniques used to overcome them, thereby improving the quality of group decisions. Before getting to this, however, I begin by outlining the general nature of the decision-making process and the wide variety of decisions made in organizations.

A GENERAL, ANALYTICAL MODEL OF DECISION MAKING

Scientists conceptualize the process of decision making as a **general, analytical model** that incorporates three phases (see Figure 10.1).[3] These are:

- *Decision Formulation*—The process of coming to understand the nature of the problem that is being confronted (steps 1–3 in Figure 10.1)
- *Decision Consideration*—The process of determining and selecting a possible decision to solve that problem (steps 4–6 in Figure 10.1)
- *Decision Implementation*—The process of carrying out the decision that has been made so as to solve the problem (steps 7–8 in Figure 10.1)

It is important to note that not all decisions fit neatly into the eight steps of the model, because some steps may be skipped and/or combined.[4] However, for the purpose of pointing out the *general* way in which the decision-making process operates, the model is quite useful. To show how it works, I'll use a simple running example: the owner of a small business finds that her cash reserves are insufficient to meet her company's payroll obligations.

Decision Formulation

The first three steps in the decision-making process involve decision formulation. It is through these steps that people think about and come to grips with the problem at hand.

1. **Identifying the problem.** To decide how to solve a problem, one first must acknowledge its existence. As obvious as this may be, people are not always aware of the problems they face because they may ignore them or misperceive them (see Chapter 3). In the case of the cash-short business owner, realizing the existence of a problem may be as easy as checking the bank balance, or having a bookkeeper or accountant point this out.

2. **Defining objectives.** After a problem is identified, the next step is to *define the objectives to be met in solving the problem.* It is important to conceive of problems in such a way that

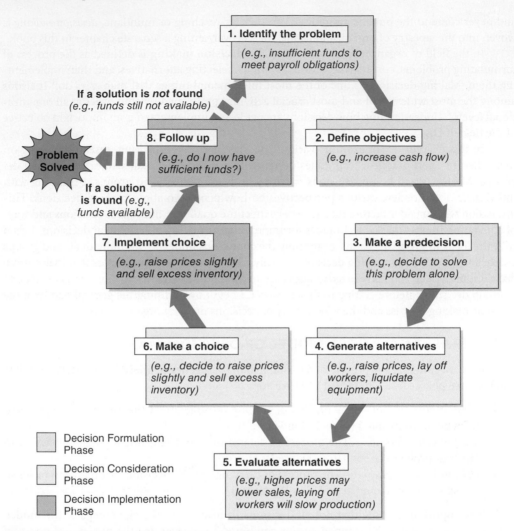

FIGURE 10.1 The General, Analytical Model of Decision-Making
The general, *analytical model of decision making* characterizes decisions as being made following the eight general steps (falling into three phases) shown here. Note how each step may be applied to a hypothetical organizational problem (in this example, not having sufficient funds to meet payroll obligations).
Source: Based on information in Wedley & Field, 1984; see Note 3.

possible solutions can be identified. Since the problem in the example is inadequate cash reserves, the objective may be to improve cash flow and a good solution is one that does this.

3. **Making a predecision.** A **predecision** is a decision about how to make a decision. Consider the options available to the manager in the example. She may assemble an ad hoc group to assess the problem (see Chapter 9); she may hire an outside consultant (an expensive option under the circumstances); she might delegate the decision to the company's accountant; or she may decide to take on the problem herself. In making such a decision she is likely to rely on software-based solutions known as **decision support systems (DSS)** that distill social science knowledge onto databases that are consulted to guide decisions.[5] In the example, let's say that the owner decides to make the decision herself.

Decision Consideration

The decision consideration phase of the process involves three steps through which people create, consider, and select alternatives to solve the problem at hand.

4. **Generating alternatives.** In this stage, possible solutions to the problem are identified. Often, people rely on previously used approaches that promise ready-made answers.[6] In the example, some possible ways of solving the revenue shortage problem would be to reduce the workforce, liquidate unnecessary equipment, take out a loan, or do something that increases sales immediately.

5. **Evaluating alternative solutions.** Now, the stage is set to select the best solution from among the alternatives in step 4. Upon considering the options, some may seem better than others. For example, although increasing sales would help solve the problem, it's much easier said than done. Borrowing money might help, but all it might do is forestall the problem until the next payroll period—and create even greater needs for cash when the time comes to repay the loan.

6. **Making a choice.** After several alternatives are evaluated, one is chosen. In this case, after carefully considering the alternatives, the business owner may decide to liquidate a lot of unused equipment (generating immediate cash), using some of it for payroll and the remainder to develop new products that are inclined to boost sales.

Decision Implementation

Once a problem has been identified and a decision has been made, it's time to carry out that decision and to assess its impact.

7. **Implementing the decision.** This step calls for carrying out the chosen decision. So now, the business owner would actually go about liquidating the equipment and developing the new products as decided upon in step 6.

8. **Following up.** The final step involves following up by assessing the current situation. Did the decision work as planned? If so, the problem is solved. If not, a new solution will have to be attempted and the process is repeated. For this reason, the decision-making process in Figure 10.1 is depicted as circular.

THE BROAD SPECTRUM OF ORGANIZATIONAL DECISIONS

Because decision making is so fundamental to organizations, decisions tend to be of many different kinds. I now identify three key ways of describing the varieties of decisions people make.

Programmed Versus Nonprogrammed Decisions

Think of a decision that is made repeatedly, according to a preestablished set of alternatives. For example, a word processing operator may decide to make a backup copy of the day's work on a network server, or an assistant manager of a fast-food restaurant may decide to order hamburger buns as the supply starts to dwindle. Decisions such as these are known as **programmed decisions**— routine decisions, made by lower-level personnel, that rely on predetermined courses of action.

By contrast, we may identify **nonprogrammed decisions**—ones for which there are no ready-made solutions. The decision maker confronts a unique situation in which the solutions are novel. A research scientist attempting to find a cure for a rare disease faces a problem that is poorly structured. Unlike the order clerk, whose course of action is clear when the supply of paper clips runs low, the scientist in this example must rely on creativity rather than preexisting answers to solve the problem at hand.

The differences between programmed and nonprogrammed decisions can be described with respect to three important questions (see Figure 10.2). As indicated, program decisions involve routine situations, allowing for guidance from past decisions, and are made by lower level personnel. In contrast, nonprogrammed decisions involve novel situations, in which no guidance from the past is possible, and are reserved for higher level executives.

Some nonprogrammed decisions are known as **strategic decisions**.[7] Such decisions typically are made by groups of high-level executives and have important long-term implications for the organization. Strategic decisions tend to reflect underlying organizational philosophies or missions. For example, an organization may make a strategic decision to grow at a specified yearly rate, or to be guided by a certain code of corporate ethics. Both decisions may be considered "strategic" because they guide the future direction of the organization in a specific, predetermined fashion. As suggested by this chapter's Making the Case (see p. 298), strategic decisions may not always work as planned.[8]

Certain Versus Uncertain Decisions

Just think of how easy it would be to make decisions if we knew what would happen tomorrow. Of course, we never know exactly what the future holds, but we can be more certain of some things than others. Having a degree of certainty about the factors on which decisions are made is highly desired in organizational decision making.

Degrees of certainty and uncertainty are expressed as statements of *risk*. All organizational decisions involve some degree of risk—ranging from complete certainty (no risk) to complete

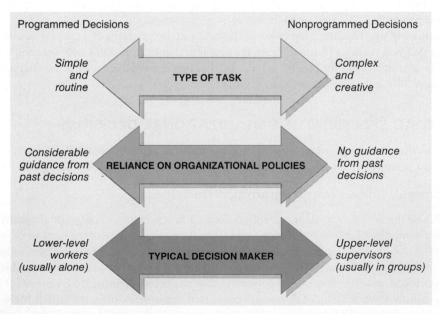

FIGURE 10.2 Comparing Programmed and Nonprogrammed Decisions
Two major types of organizational decisions—programmed decisions and nonprogrammed decisions—differ with respect to the three dimensions summarized here.

uncertainty, "a stab in the dark" (high risk). To make the best possible decisions in organizations, people seek to "manage" the risks they take—that is, minimizing the riskiness of a decision by accessing information germane to that decision.[9]

What makes an outcome risky or not is the *probability* of obtaining the desired outcome. Decision makers attempt to obtain information about the probabilities, or odds, of certain events occurring given that other events have occurred. For example, a financial analyst may report that a certain stock has risen 80 percent of the time that the prime interest rate has dropped, or a meteorologist may report that the precipitation probability is 50 percent (i.e., in the past it rained or snowed half the time certain atmospheric conditions existed). These may be considered reports of *objective probabilities* because they are based on concrete, verifiable data.

Decisions also are made using *subjective probabilities*—personal beliefs or hunches about what will happen. For example, a gambler who bets on a horse because it has a name similar to one of his children's, or a person who suspects it's going to rain because he just washed his car, is basing these judgments on subjective probabilities, or "gut feelings."

In general, what reduces uncertainty in decision-making situations? The answer is *information*. Knowledge about the past and the present can be used to help make projections about the future. Executives have access to two sources of relevant information. First, there are on-line information services (e.g., government reports and statistics, stock market filings) that provide valuable information. Second are the decision makers' past experiences and intuitions.[10] When it comes to making decisions, people often rely on what has worked for them in the past.[11] Individuals who have expertise in certain subjects know what information is best to use and how to interpret it once collected, when making decisions.

Top-Down Versus Empowered Decisions

In organizations, the job of making all but the most menial decisions traditionally belonged to managers. In fact, organizational scientist Herbert Simon, who won a Nobel Prize for his work on the economics of decision making, has gone so far as to describe decision making as synonymous with managing.[12] Subordinates collected information and gave it to superiors, who used it to make decisions. This approach, known as **top-down decision making**, puts decision-making power in the hands of managers and leaves lower-level workers little or no opportunities to make decisions. If this sounds familiar to you, it's probably because this is how most organizations have operated over the years.

Today, however, a different approach, known as **empowered decision making**, is in vogue. This approach gives individuals or teams the power to decide what they need to do so as to perform their jobs effectively. (For a comparison between top-down decision making and empowered decision making, see Figure 10.3.) The rationale is that the people who do the jobs know what's best, so having supervisors make decisions instead makes less sense. In addition, when people are empowered to make their own decisions, they tend to be highly committed to those decisions.

It is important to note that managers who empower their subordinates to make their own decisions are not abdicating their responsibility. Rather, they are delegating some of their power (see Chapter 11) to others who are capable of making decisions. When empowering workers, managers provide general guidance about how to make decisions, but they do not set up specific rules to be followed in each possible circumstance. This gives workers discretion about what to do. For example, a manager at a car rental agency may empower agents at rental counters to offer free upgrades or discounts as appeasement to customers who have reasonable complaints. In this case, the worker is making the decision as deemed necessary but within guidelines set by the

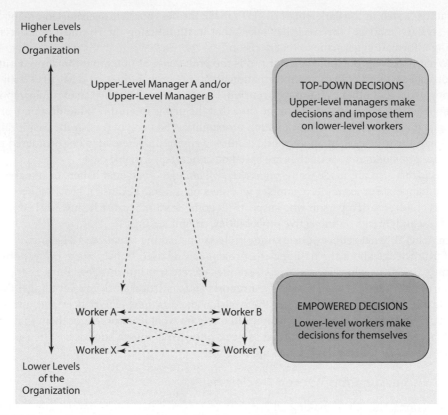

FIGURE 10.3 **Top-Down Versus Empowered Decisions: A Comparison**
Traditionally, decision making in organizations was a top-down practice. Upper-level workers made decisions, which they then imposed on lower-level workers, who carried them out. Although this still goes on, of course, many decisions today are made by lower-level workers who are empowered to make certain decisions for themselves.

manager (who, of course, is ultimately responsible). Not only does empowerment motivate many workers (as noted in Chapter 6) and serve as a source of job satisfaction (as noted in Chapter 5), but it also frees up the time of higher-level personnel. Instead of "micro-managing" by making small decisions, empowering lower-level workers enables higher-level managers to concentrate on making the higher-level decisions that only they themselves can make.

FACTORS INFLUENCING INDIVIDUAL DECISIONS IN ORGANIZATIONS

People's decisions are affected by factors associated with all three levels of analysis in the field of OB—individuals, groups, and organizations.

Individual Differences in Decision Making

People differ with respect to the way they make decisions. Specifically, research has found that they differ in terms of their *decision style* and their levels of *indecisiveness*.

DECISION STYLE The particular manner in which an individual approaches the decisions confronting him or her is known as **decision style**. Whereas some people are concerned primarily with achieving success at any cost, others are more concerned about the effects of their decisions on others. Furthermore, some individuals tend to be more logical and analytical in their approaches to problems, whereas others are more intuitive and creative. Clearly, important differences exist in the approaches decision makers take to problems. The **decision style model** classifies four major decision styles (see summary in Figure 10.4).[13]

- *Directive style*—Characterized by people who prefer simple, clear solutions to problems. Individuals with this style tend to make decisions rapidly because they use little information and do not consider many alternatives. They generally rely on existing rules to make their decisions and aggressively use their status to achieve results.

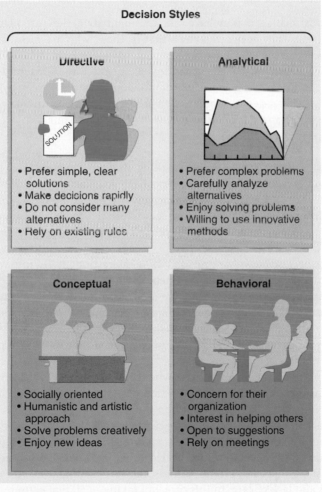

Decision Styles

Directive
- Prefer simple, clear solutions
- Make decisions rapidly
- Do not consider many alternatives
- Rely on existing rules

Analytical
- Prefer complex problems
- Carefully analyze alternatives
- Enjoy solving problems
- Willing to use innovative methods

Conceptual
- Socially oriented
- Humanistic and artistic approach
- Solve problems creatively
- Enjoy new ideas

Behavioral
- Concern for their organization
- Interest in helping others
- Open to suggestions
- Rely on meetings

FIGURE 10.4 Decision Style Model: A Summary
According to the *decision style model*, people may be characterized as adhering to one of the four decision styles summarized here.
Source: Based on information in Rowe et al., 1984; see Note 13.

- *Analytical style*—Individuals who are willing to consider complex solutions based on ambiguous information. People with this style carefully analyze their decisions using as much data as possible. Such individuals tend to enjoy solving problems. They want the best possible answers and are willing to use innovative methods to achieve them.
- *Conceptual style*—People who are socially oriented in their approach to problems. Their approach is humanistic and artistic. Such individuals tend to consider many broad alternatives when dealing with problems and to solve them creatively. They have a strong future orientation and enjoy initiating new ideas.
- *Behavioral style*—People who are concerned deeply about the organizations in which they work and about the personal development of their coworkers. They are highly supportive of others and very concerned about others' achievements, frequently helping them meet their goals. Such individuals tend to be open to suggestions from others and therefore tend to rely on meetings for making decisions.

Although most managers may have one dominant style, they use many different styles. In fact, those who can shift between styles—that is, those who are most flexible in their approaches to decision making—have highly complex, individualistic styles of their own. Despite this, people's dominant styles reveal a great deal about the way they tend to make decisions. Not surprisingly, conflicts often occur between individuals with different styles. For example, a manager with a highly directive style may have a hard time accepting the slow, deliberate actions of a subordinate with an analytical style. (To give you a feel for your own decision style, see the Self-Assessment Exercise on p. 328.)

INDECISIVENESS Do you have difficulty making choices? Do you take a long time to make decisions? Do you delay the making of decisions? Do you change your mind frequently? The more of these questions to which you answer yes, the more *indecisive* you are likely to be. Researchers are interested in a personality characteristic known as **indecisiveness**, which looks at the degree to which individuals approach decisions eagerly as opposed to putting them off.[14]

Research on indecisiveness has provided some interesting insight into why indecisive people take longer to make decisions. For one, people who are highly indecisive tend to be perfectionists—but not in a good way.[15] They are inclined to be overly concerned about making mistakes and to have doubts about the quality of their decisions. Indecisive people also tend to be more inefficient in the ways they scan their environments for relevant information. Studies tracing their eye movements reveal that indecisive people spend time looking at irrelevant information or looking at nothing at all.[16]

It's interesting to consider how people who differ in levels of indecisiveness may behave when making decisions on the job. As in the case of most personality variables (as I noted in Chapter 3), their impact is likely to depend on the nature of the situations they're facing. It's easy to envision jobs in which being indecisive can be problematic, such as when quick action is required. This would be the case, for example, among airline pilots, astronauts, and soldiers in combat, where indecisiveness could be deadly. However, in some other positions, such as executives making decisions about important business matters, making decisions too quickly may be a sign of hastiness and lack of care. In this case, not taking in all that extra information can be a serious liability, because it may interfere with making effective decisions. Of course, one also can take too much time to make a decision. This may cause potential problems, such as forcing other important decisions to be delayed.

Group Influences: A Matter of Trade-Offs

As you might imagine, groups influence organizational decisions in a vast array of ways, potentially positive and negative. I now consider these.

POTENTIAL BENEFITS OF DECISION-MAKING GROUPS Much can be gained by using decision-making groups. For example, bringing people together may increase the amount of knowledge and information available for making good decisions. In other words, there may be a *pooling of resources* in which everyone involved contributes something to the joint effort.

A related benefit is that in decision-making groups, there can be a *specialization of labor*. In other words, with enough people around to share the workload, individuals can perform only those tasks at which they are best, thereby potentially improving the quality of the group's efforts.

Another benefit is that group decisions are likely to enjoy *greater acceptance* than individual decisions. People involved in making decisions generally understand those decisions better and are more committed to carrying them out than decisions made for them by someone else.[17]

POTENTIAL PROBLEMS OF DECISION-MAKING GROUPS Despite these potential benefits, there also are some possible problems associated with using groups to make decisions. These are as follows:

- Groups are inclined to *waste time*. The time spent socializing before getting down to business, for example, may distract groups from the tasks at hand and be very costly to organizations as a result.
- Disagreement over important matters may breed ill will and *group conflict*. Although constructive disagreement may lead to better group outcomes, as discussed in Chapter 7, disruptive conflict may interfere with group decisions.
- There may be *intimidation by group leaders*. It is not unusual for lower-ranking employees to cultivate the favor of higher-ranking leaders by conforming to the opinions with which they believe those leaders approve. This is problematic because in groups where "yes-men" or "yes-women" focus on pleasing a dominant leader, open and honest discussion of solutions to problems is discouraged.

GROUPTHINK: TOO MUCH COHESIVENESS CAN BE A DANGEROUS THING As I described in Chapter 9, members of groups sometimes become so concerned about not "rocking the boat" that they are reluctant to challenge their groups' decisions. When this happens, group members tend to isolate themselves from outside information, and the process of critical thinking deteriorates. This phenomenon is referred to as **groupthink**.[18]

To illustrate the phenomenon of groupthink, consider the tragic decision to launch the space shuttle *Challenger* in January 1986. Analyses of conversations between key personnel suggested that NASA officials made the decision to launch the shuttle under freezing conditions while ignoring admonitions from engineers.[19] Given that NASA had such a successful history, the decision makers operated with a sense of invulnerability. They also worked so closely together and were under such intense pressure to launch the shuttle without further delay that they all collectively went along with the launch decision, creating the illusion of unanimous agreement. For a more precise description of groupthink and a practical guide to recognizing its symptoms, see Figure 10.5.

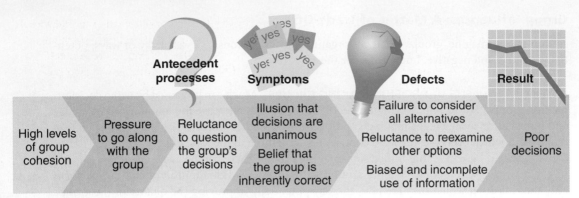

FIGURE 10.5 Groupthink: An Overview
Groupthink occurs when highly cohesive conditions in groups discourage members from challenging their group's overall decision. Poor-quality decisions result.

Organizational Influences on Individual Decisions

In addition to individual and group forces that affect people's decisions, factors associated with organizations themselves also are involved. I now examine these.

POLITICAL PRESSURE   Sometimes, the quality of decisions people make in organizations is limited by the pressures they face to look good to others (i.e., to "save face") even though the resulting decisions might not be in the best interest of their organizations. Imagine, for example, how an employee might distort the available information needed to make a decision if the correct information would jeopardize his job. This would be the case if a sales rep inflated his quarterly sales figures to make himself look good although this might lead to an overly optimistic picture of a product's popularity. Unfortunately, such misuses of information to support desired decisions are all too common.

In an interesting case, a proponent of medical inoculation for the flu was so interested in advancing his pro-inoculation position that he proceeded with the inoculation program although there was only a 2 percent chance of an epidemic, a fact that he conveniently ignored because it failed to serve his true purpose.[20] This case reveals that people may make the decisions needed to cultivate favorable impressions of themselves in the short term even if they have good reason to doubt the ultimate effectiveness of these decisions. And when political concerns rather than quality concerns drive decisions, it's not surprising that poor outcomes may result.

TIME PRESSURE   It's a reality that people often have only limited amounts of time to make important decisions. Among firefighters, emergency room doctors, and fighter pilots, it's clear that time is of the essence. But even those of us who toil in less dramatic settings also face the need to make good decisions quickly. The practice of thoroughly collecting information, carefully analyzing it, and then leisurely reviewing the alternatives is a luxury few modern decision makers can afford. This is especially so given the rapidly accelerating pace of many jobs these days.[21] And this, unfortunately, often leads to the making of bad—and inevitably, costly—decisions.

When it comes to making decisions about things you know well, a lack of time is not necessarily problematic. Highly experienced experts are able to make good decisions quickly because they draw on a wealth of experiences collected over the years.[22] Whereas novices are very deliberate in their decision making, considering one option at a time, experts are able to make decisions quickly because they are able to assess the situations they face and compare them to experiences they have had earlier in their careers. They know what matters, what to look for, and what pitfalls to avoid. What is so often considered "gut instinct" is really nothing more than the wealth of accumulated experiences.

HOW ARE INDIVIDUAL DECISIONS MADE?

Now that I have described the types of decisions people make in organizations and the factors that influence them, you are prepared to consider *how* people go about making decisions. Here, I review three major approaches.

The Rational-Economic Model: In Search of the Ideal Decision

We all like to think that we are "rational" people who make the best possible decisions. But what exactly does it mean to make a *rational* decision? Organizational scientists view **rational decisions** as those that maximize the attainment of goals, whether they are the goals of a person, a group, or an entire organization.[23] What is the most rational way for an individual to go about making a decision?

Economists interested in predicting market conditions and prices have relied on a **rational-economic model** of decision making, which assumes that decisions are optimal in every way. An economically rational decision maker will attempt to maximize his or her profits by searching systematically for the *optimum* solution to a problem. For this to occur, the decision maker must have complete and perfect information and be able to process all this information in an accurate and unbiased fashion.[24]

In many respects, rational-economic decisions follow the same steps outlined in the general, analytical model of decision making (recall Figure 10.1, on p. 300). However, what makes the rational-economic approach special is that it calls for the decision maker to recognize *all* alternative courses of action (step 4), and to evaluate each one accurately and completely (step 5). In other words, it views decision makers as attempting to make *optimal* decisions.

Of course, the rational-economic approach to decision making does not take into account the fallibility of the human decision maker. Based on the assumption that people have access to complete and perfect information and use it to make perfect decisions, the model can be considered a *normative* (also called *prescriptive*) approach—one that describes how decision makers ideally ought to behave so as to make the best possible decisions. (Many conceptualizations of decision making used by economists are of this type.) It does not describe how decision makers actually behave in most circumstances. This task is undertaken by the next major approach to individual decision making, one that is more in keeping with the approaches of OB scientists, known as the *administrative model*.

The Administrative Model: Acknowledging the Limits of Human Rationality

As personal experience undoubtedly tells you, people do not act in a completely rational-economic manner. In fact, we cannot—we're just not built for it. To illustrate this point, consider how a company's human resources manager might go about selecting a new receptionist. After several applicants are interviewed, the manager might choose the best candidate seen so far and stop interviewing. Had the manager been following a rational-economic model, he or she would have had to interview *all* possible candidates before deciding on the best one. This is impractical, of course, making it impossible to ever fill the position. However, by ending the search after finding someone considered reasonably good enough to do the job, the manager is using a much simpler approach.

The process used in this example characterizes an orientation to decision making known as the **administrative model**.[25] This conceptualization recognizes that decision makers may have a limited and imperfect view of the problems confronting them. The number of solutions that can be recognized or implemented is limited by the innate capabilities of decision makers and the resources available to them. For example, decision makers rarely have enough time to consider all the information available to them before having to make a decision. Even if they did, the information available is often too limited or too imperfect to predict the consequences of many decisions, making it difficult or impossible to determine which is best.

How, then, are decisions made according to the administrative model? The answer is that instead of considering all possible solutions, decision makers consider solutions as they become available. Then they decide on the first alternative that meets their criteria for acceptability. Thus, the decision maker selects a solution that may be just good enough, although not optimal. Such decisions are referred to as **satisficing decisions**. Of course, a satisficing decision is much easier to make than an optimal decision. In most decision-making situations, people consider satisficing decisions to be acceptable and strive to make them instead of trying to make the optimal decision.[26] Think of it this way: Making an optimal decision is like searching a haystack for the sharpest needle, but making a satisficing decision is like searching a haystack for a needle just sharp enough with which to sew.

One major factor that contributes to less than optimal decisions has to do with limitations in people's innate cognitive capacities. In other words, the administrative model recognizes the **bounded rationality** under which most organizational decision makers must operate. The idea is that people lack the cognitive skills required to formulate and solve highly complex business problems in a completely objective, rational way.[27] Although computers help a great deal when it comes to organizing information, of course, it's ultimately human beings who attempt to make sense out of what all the information means and what courses of action to take. And let's face it, we're just not perfect.

Another factor that keeps people from making decisions that maximize some important criteria, such as profitability, is their tendency to conform to moral and ethical standards. Using the terminology of the administrative model, people use **bounded discretion**.[28] In other words, people limit their consideration of decision options to ones that fall within ethical and legal boundaries. For example, although a grocery store might take in more money if it doctored scales at the deli counter to display higher than actual weights, most proprietors, wanting to treat their customers ethically, would be unwilling to do so—even if they had no chance of getting caught. If people were motivated solely by interest in maximizing outcomes, they wouldn't let these ethical considerations interfere with their decision making. But they do—at least in most cases, although certainly not all (as I chronicled in Chapter 2).

It should not be surprising that the administrative model does a better job than the rational-economic model of describing what decision makers really do. The administrative approach is considered *descriptive* (also called *proscriptive*) because it depicts what actually occurs. This interest in examining the real, imperfect behavior of decision makers, rather than specifying the ideal, economically rational behaviors that decision makers ought to engage in, lies at the heart of the distinction between the administrative and rational-economic models. My point is not that decision makers do not want to behave rationally, but that restrictions imposed by their innate capabilities and by the environments in which they work keep them from making "perfect" decisions.

Image Theory: An Intuitive Approach to Decision Making

If you think about it, you'll probably realize that some, but certainly not all, decisions are made following the logical steps of the general, analytical model of decision making. Consider Elizabeth Barrett Browning's poetic question, "How do I love thee? Let me count the ways."[29] It's unlikely that anyone would ultimately answer the question by carefully counting what one loves about another even if many such characteristics could be enumerated. Instead, a more intuitive-based decision making is likely, not only for matters of the heart, but for a variety of important organizational decisions as well.[30]

The point is that selecting the best alternative by weighing all the options is not always a major concern when making a decision. People also consider how various decision alternatives fit with their personal standards as well as their personal goals and plans. The best decision for someone might not be the best for someone else. In other words, people may make decisions in a more automatic, intuitive fashion than traditionally is recognized. Representative of this approach is **image theory**.[31] This conceptualization is summarized in Figure 10.6.

Image theory deals primarily with decisions about adopting a certain course of action (e.g., should the company develop a new product line?) or changing a current course of action (e.g., should

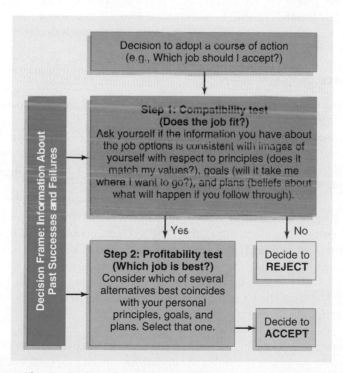

FIGURE 10.6 Image Theory: An Overview and Example
According to *image theory*, decisions are made in a relatively automatic, intuitive fashion following the two steps outlined here.
Source: Adapted from Beach & Mitchell, 1990; see Note 31.

the company drop a current product line?). According to the theory, people make decisions on the basis of a simple, two-step process. The first step is the *compatibility test,* a comparison of the degree to which a particular course of action is consistent with various images—particularly individual principles, current goals, and plans for the future. If any lack of compatibility exists with respect to these considerations, a rejection decision is made.

If the compatibility test is passed, then the *profitability test* is carried out. That is, people consider the extent to which using various alternatives best fits their values, goals, and plans. The decision is then made to accept the best available candidate. These tests are used within a certain *decision frame*—that is, with consideration of meaningful information about the decision context (such as past experiences). The basic idea is that we learn from the past and are guided by it when making decisions. The example shown in Figure 10.6 highlights this approach to decision making.

According to image theory, the decision-making process is very rapid and simple. The theory suggests that people do not ponder and reflect over decisions, but make them using a smooth, intuitive process with minimal cognitive processing. If you've ever found yourself saying that something "seemed like the right thing to do," or "something doesn't feel right," you're probably well aware of the kind of intuitive thinking that goes on in a great deal of decision making.

THE IMPERFECT NATURE OF INDIVIDUAL DECISIONS

As I have suggested, people are less than perfect when it comes to making decisions. Unlike computers, we have only limited capacity. In addition, we also fail to perceive the world in an objective manner. Instead, we tend to be biased in the ways we approach decisions. Here, I describe several such biases in decision making.

Framing Effects

Have you ever found yourself changing your mind about something because of *how* someone explained it to you? If so, you might have said something like, "Now that you put it that way, I agree." This may sound familiar to you because it describes a well-established decision-making characteristic known as **framing**—the tendency for people to make different decisions based on how a problem is presented to them. I now describe three major forms of framing effects that occur when people make decisions (see summary in Figure 10.7).[32]

RISKY CHOICE FRAMING   For many years, scientists have noted that when problems are framed in a manner that emphasizes the positive gains to be received, people tend to shy away from taking risks and go for the sure thing (i.e., decision makers are said to be *risk-averse*). However, when problems are framed in a manner that emphasizes the potential losses to be suffered, people are more willing to take risks so as to avoid those losses (i.e., decision makers are said to make *risk-seeking* decisions).[33] This is known as the **risky choice framing effect**. To illustrate this phenomenon, consider the following example:

> The government is preparing to combat a rare disease expected to take 600 lives. Two alternative programs to combat the disease have been proposed, each of which, scientists believe, will have certain consequences. *Program A* will save 200 people, if adopted. *Program B* has a one-third chance of saving all 600 people, but a two-thirds chance of saving no one. Which program do you prefer?

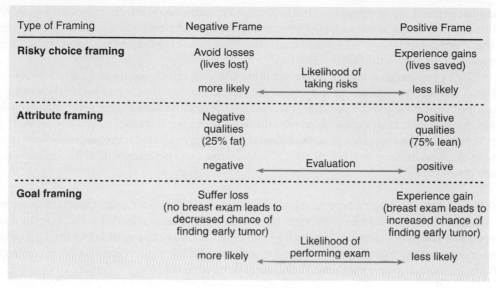

Type of Framing	Negative Frame		Positive Frame
Risky choice framing	Avoid losses (lives lost)	Likelihood of taking risks	Experience gains (lives saved)
	more likely ←	→	less likely
Attribute framing	Negative qualities (25% fat)	Evaluation	Positive qualities (75% lean)
	negative ←	→	positive
Goal framing	Suffer loss (no breast exam leads to decreased chance of finding early tumor)	Likelihood of performing exam	Experience gain (breast exam leads to increased chance of finding early tumor)
	more likely ←	→	less likely

FIGURE 10.7   Framing Effects: A Summary of Three Types
Information presented (i.e., framed) negatively is perceived differently than the same information presented positively. This takes the three different forms summarized here—*risky choice framing, attribute framing,* and *goal framing.*
Source: Based on suggestions by Levin et al., 1998; see Note 32.

When such a problem was presented to people, 72 percent expressed a preference for Program A, and 28 percent for Program B. In other words, they preferred the "sure thing" of saving 200 people over the one-third possibility of saving them all.

However, this did not occur when the description of the programs was framed in negative terms such as the following:

> *Program C* was described as allowing 400 people to die, if adopted. *Program D* was described as allowing a one-third probability that no one would die, and a two-thirds probability that all 600 would die. Now which program would you prefer?

Compare these four programs. Program C is just another way of stating the outcomes of Program A, and Program D is just another way of stating the outcomes of Program B. However, Programs C and D are framed in negative terms, which led to opposite preferences: 22 percent favored Program C and 78 percent favored Program D. In other words, people tended to avoid risk when the problem was framed in terms of "lives saved" (i.e., in positive terms), but to seek risk when the problem was framed in terms of "lives lost" (i.e., in negative terms). This classic effect has been replicated in several studies.[34]

ATTRIBUTE FRAMING   Risky choice frames involve making decisions about which course of action is preferred. However, the same basic idea applies to situations not involving risk, but involving evaluations. Suppose, for example, you're walking down the meat aisle of your local supermarket when you spot a package of ground beef labeled "75% lean." Of course, if the same package were to say "25% fat," it would mean exactly the same thing. However, you probably wouldn't perceive these situations identically. In fact, consumer marketing research has shown that people rated the same sample of ground beef as being better tasting and less greasy when it was framed with respect to a positive attribute (i.e., 75% lean) than when it was framed with respect to a negative attribute (i.e., 25% fat).[35]

This phenomenon, known as the **attribute framing effect**, occurs in a variety of organizational settings. Specifically, people evaluate the same characteristic more positively when it is described in positive terms than when it is described in negative terms. Take performance evaluation, for example. In this context, people whose performance is framed in positive terms (e.g., percentage of shots made by a basketball player) tend to be evaluated more positively than those whose identical performance is framed in negative terms (e.g., percentage of shots missed by that same player).[36]

GOAL FRAMING   A third type of framing, *goal framing*, focuses on an important question: When attempting to persuade someone to do something, is it more effective to focus on the positive consequences of doing it or the negative consequences of not doing it? For example, suppose you are attempting to get women to engage in self-examination of their breasts to check for signs of cancer. You may frame the desired behavior in positive terms:

> "Research shows that women who *do* breast self-examinations have an *increased* chance of finding a tumor in the early, more treatable stages of the disease."

Or you may frame it in negative terms:

> "Research shows that women who *do not* do breast self-examinations have a *decreased* chance of finding a tumor in the early, more treatable stages of the disease."

Which approach is more effective? Research has shown that women were significantly more likely to engage in breast self-examinations when they were presented with the consequences of not doing it rather than the benefits of doing it.[37] This is an example of the **goal framing effect** in action. According to this phenomenon, people are more strongly persuaded by the negatively framed information than by the positively framed information.

A GENERAL CONCLUSION ABOUT FRAMING   Scientists believe that framing effects are due to the tendency for people to perceive equivalent situations framed differently as not really equivalent.[38] In other words, focusing on the glass as "half full" leads people to think about it differently than when it is presented as being "half empty," although they might recognize intellectually that the two are really the same. Such findings illustrate the point that people are not completely rational decision makers, but are systematically biased by the cognitive distortions created by simple differences in the way situations are framed.

Reliance on Heuristics

Another type of cognitive bias that influences decision makers reflects the fact that people seek to simplify the complex decisions they face. A way they do this is by using **heuristics**— simple rules of thumb that guide them through a complex array of decision alternatives.[39] Although heuristics are potentially useful to decision makers, they also represent potential impediments to decision making. I now consider two commonly used heuristics (see the summary in Figure 10.8).

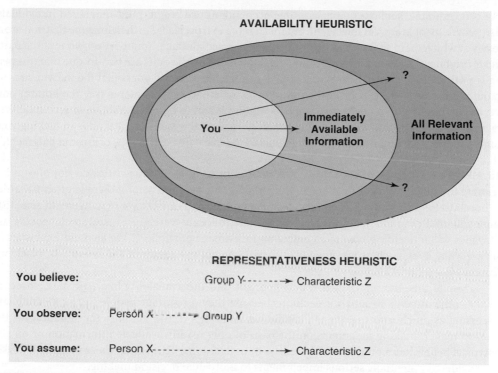

FIGURE 10.8 The Availability Heuristic and the Representativeness Heuristic
People making decisions often rely on simple rules of thumb, known as *heuristics*, to help them. Sometimes, however, these actually hinder decision-making quality. This occurs in the case of the *availability heuristic,* in which people are inclined to consider immediately available information (e.g., what they already know) instead of all relevant information. The *representativeness heuristic* is another example. Here, decision makers are likely to assume that people possess the characteristics they associate with others in those individuals' groups—that is, that people we meet are representative of the groups to which they belong.

THE AVAILABILITY HEURISTIC   Sometimes, people believe that a decision based on some information, even if imperfect, may be better than a decision based on no information at all. This is the idea behind the **availability heuristic**. Specifically, this refers to the tendency for people to base their judgments on information that is readily available to them—even though it might not be accurate.

Suppose, for example, that a real estate executive needs to know the percentage of available houses in a particular neighborhood. There is not enough time to gather the appropriate statistics, so she bases her judgments on her knowledge of available property nationwide. If the neighborhood in question is atypical, her estimate will be off accordingly (see the top portion of Figure 10.8). In other words, basing judgments solely on information that just happens to be available increases the possibility of making inaccurate decisions. Yet people use the availability heuristic on a regular basis when making decisions.[40]

THE REPRESENTATIVENESS HEURISTIC   The **representativeness heuristic** refers to the tendency to perceive others in stereotypical ways if they appear to be typical representatives of the category to which they belong.

For example, suppose you believe that accountants are bright, mild-mannered individuals, whereas salespeople are less intelligent, but much more extroverted. Further, imagine that you are at a party at which there are twice as many salespeople as accountants. You meet someone at the party who is bright and mild-mannered. Although mathematically the odds are two-to-one that this person is a salesperson rather than an accountant, chances are you will guess that the individual is an accountant because she possesses the traits you associate with accountants (see the bottom portion of Figure 10.8). In other words, you believe this person to be representative of accountants in general—so much so that you would knowingly go against the mathematical odds in making your judgment. Research reveals that it is not unusual for people to make this type of error in judgment.[41]

THE HELPFUL SIDE OF HEURISTICS   It is important to note that heuristics do not *always* deteriorate the quality of decisions made. In fact, they can be quite helpful. People often use rules of thumb to help simplify the complex decisions they face. For example, management scientists employ heuristics to aid decisions regarding where to locate warehouses, and stock brokers use heuristics when deciding how to assemble an investment portfolio.[42] We also use heuristics in our everyday lives, such as when we play chess ("control the center of the board") or blackjack ("hit on 16, stick on 17").

Despite this, the representativeness heuristic and the availability heuristic may be recognized as impediments to superior decisions because they discourage people from collecting and processing as much information as they should. Although it may simplify the situation for the decision maker, making judgments on the basis of only readily available information or on stereotypical beliefs has a potentially high cost—poor decisions. This is why these systematic biases are considered potentially serious impediments to individual decision making.

The Inherently Biased Nature of Individual Decisions

As individuals, we make imperfect decisions not only because of our overreliance on heuristics but also because of certain inherent biases that we bring to the various decision-making situations we face. Among the several biases people have when making decisions, four have received special attention by OB scientists. I describe them here.

BIAS TOWARD IMPLICIT FAVORITES   Don was about to receive his MBA. This was going to be his big chance to move to San Francisco, the city by the bay. Don long had dreamed of living there, and his first "real" job, he hoped, would be his ticket. As the corporate recruiters made their annual migration to campus, Don eagerly signed up for several interviews. One of his first was with a highly regarded consulting firm in San Francisco. The salary was right and the people seemed nice, a combination that pleased Don very much. Apparently the interest was mutual; soon Don was offered a position.

The story doesn't end here, however. It was only March, and Don felt he shouldn't jump at the first job to come along, even though he really wanted it. So, to do "the sensible thing," he signed up for more interviews. Shortly thereafter, a local firm made Don a more attractive offer. Not only was the salary higher, but there was every indication that the job promised a much brighter future than the one in San Francisco.

What would he do? Would he accept the better local job or go to the one in San Francisco? Actually, Don didn't consider it much of a dilemma. After thinking it over, he convinced himself that the work at the local firm was fairly low level and lacked an exciting client base to challenge him. And the starting salary, he reasoned, wasn't really all that much better than it was at the firm in San Francisco. The day after graduation Don was packing for his new office overlooking the Golden Gate Bridge.

Do you think the way Don made his decision was atypical? He seemed to have his mind made up in advance about the job in San Francisco, and didn't really give the other one a chance (even though it was better in several ways). Research suggests that people make decisions in this way all the time. That is, people tend to pick an **implicit favorite** option (i.e., a preferred alternative) very early in the decision-making process and do not give serious consideration to subsequent options.[43]

Instead, people use those other options to convince themselves that the implicit favorite is indeed the best choice. An alternative considered for this purpose is known as a **confirmation candidate**. It is not unusual to find that people psychologically distort their beliefs about confirmation candidates in order to justify selecting their implicit favorites. Don did this when he convinced himself that the job offered by the local firm really wasn't as good as it seemed. (For an outline of some steps likely to occur in this process, see Table 10.1.)

Research shows that people make decisions very early in the decision process. For example, in one study of the job recruitment process, investigators found that they could predict 87 percent of the jobs that students would take as early as two months before the students acknowledged that they actually had made a decision.[44] Apparently, people's decisions are biased by a tendency to not consider all the relevant information available to them. In fact, their judgments tend to be biased by the strengths and weaknesses of various alternatives so as to make them fit their already-made decision—that is, to select their implicit favorite.[45]

This phenomenon clearly suggests that people not only fail to consider all possible alternatives when making decisions, but that they even fail to consider all readily available alternatives. Instead, they tend to make up their minds very early and convince themselves that they are right about this decision. As you might imagine, this bias toward implicit favorites is likely to severely limit the quality of decisions that are made.

TABLE 10.1   Bias Toward Implicit Favorites: Some Likely Steps

Although the bias toward implicit favorites may take many forms, it usually follows a pattern of steps similar to those outlined in this example involving the selection of a new job.

Step	I think this . . .	And so I do this . . .	Job referred to as . . .
1	I need a job and I heard that Job A is great, so I . . .		
2		Look at Job A	Implicit favorite
3	I like Job A, as I thought I would. But I shouldn't take the first job, so I . . .		
4		Look at Job B	Confirmation candidate 1
5	Job B has several advantages, but I'll keep looking just to make sure that Job A is the best one for me, so I . . .		
6		Look at Job C	Confirmation candidate 2
7	I also recognize advantages of Job C, but I have now considered alternatives (confirmation candidates) to convince myself that Job A really is the best, so I am ready to . . .		
8		Accept Job A (finally)	My job

HINDSIGHT BIAS   "Hindsight is 20–20," so they say. This means that when we look back on past decisions, we know better what we should have done. Indeed, this phenomenon is quite pervasive. For example, people tend to distort the way they see things to conform to what they already know about the past. This effect, known as the **hindsight bias**, refers to the tendency for people to perceive outcomes as more inevitable after they have occurred (i.e., in hindsight) than before they occurred (i.e., with foresight). A sign of hindsight bias is when people believe that they could have predicted past events better than they actually did—that is, when they say, "I knew it all along."

The hindsight bias occurs because people feel good about being able to judge things accurately. As such, people are more willing to say that they expected past positive events to have occurred than past negative events. After all, we look good when we can take credit for predicting successes but look bad when we anticipated negative outcomes without doing anything to stop them.

PERSON SENSITIVITY BIAS   U.S. President George W. Bush first took office in January 2001, following a highly controversial election that many didn't believe he won fairly. As time went on, many people disapproved of his foreign policy, claiming that he was ill suited to the position of president. Then, only eight months later, following the September 11 terrorist attacks, President Bush unified the country with impassioned speeches that sent his approval ratings into the stratosphere. His stance with respect to foreign policy was now widely praised. Years later, when the war in Iraq faltered, his approval rating plummeted. This mini history lesson nicely illustrates an interesting aspect of human nature (beyond the fickle nature of politics, that is): When things are going poorly, nobody likes you, but when things are going well, everyone's your friend.

Scientists refer to this as **person sensitivity bias**. Formally, this is the tendency for people to blame others too much when things are going poorly and to give them too much credit when things are going well. The person sensitivity bias suggests that the decisions we make about others are unlikely to be completely objective. As people, we need to understand others (as I emphasized in Chapter 3), and it makes things easier for us if we keep our perceptions consistent: what's good is very good; what's bad is very bad. With such a bias underlying our judgments of others, it's little wonder that the decisions we make about them may be highly imperfect. After all, to the extent that effective decisions rely on accurate information, biases such as the person sensitivity bias predispose us to perceive others in less than objective ways.

ESCALATION OF COMMITMENT BIAS   Because decisions are made all the time in organizations, it's inevitable that some of these will be unsuccessful. What would you say is the rational thing to do when a poor decision has been made? You might assume that the ineffective action should be stopped or reversed. In other words, it would make sense to "cut your losses and run." However, people don't always respond in this manner. In fact, they often do the opposite—that is, they follow up their ineffective decisions by sticking with them, making still more ineffective decisions.

Let's illustrate this phenomenon in an example. Suppose you are an executive of a company that has invested in a new product that, despite everyone's best efforts, is not selling as well as projected. What would you do? Since the product is faltering, it may make sense to kill it off, cutting your losses. However, you may not do this at all. Instead of losing your initial investment, you may invest still more money in the hope of salvaging your first investment. The more you invest, the more you may be tempted to save those earlier investments by making later investments. That is to say, people sometimes "throw good money after bad" because they have "too much invested to quit." This is known as the **escalation of commitment phenomenon**—the tendency for people

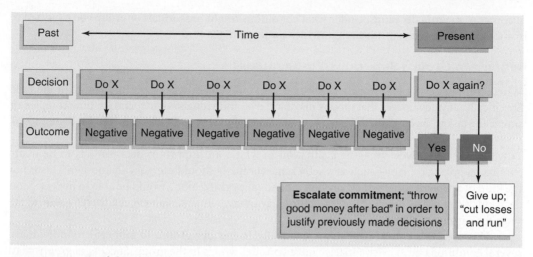

FIGURE 10.9 Escalation of Commitment: An Overview
According to the escalation of commitment phenomenon, people who have repeatedly made poor decisions continue to support those failing courses of action to justify their earlier decisions. Under some conditions, however, as summarized here, this effect will not occur.

to continue to support previously unsuccessful courses of action because they have sunk costs invested in them (see Figure 10.9).[46]

To get a sense of why people escalate commitment to failing courses of action, a team of scientists recently conducted a systematic analysis of all the research on this phenomenon.[47] Among their findings was that people's decisions to follow up on failing courses of action was motivated by the desire to justify their initial decisions as good ones. Specifically, people seek to "save face" and maintain their reputations as good decision makers by suggesting that they didn't waste time or money on their initial decisions. The scientists also found that the escalation of commitment phenomenon is particularly strong within groups in which the authority to make decisions is shared among several individuals. In these circumstances, each of the group members wants to preserve his or her image in the eyes of the others, resulting in multiple voices favoring the escalation of commitment.

Because the escalation of commitment bias is both widespread and potent, it's important to consider how to overcome it. The best way of doing this appears to involve making exceptionally clear to decision makers the actual costs of failed decisions. It's easy for these costs to be ignored when they are overshadowed by the desire to protect one's reputation. However, when the true costs are emphasized (e.g., in explanations highlighting clear dollars-and-cents costs) along with opportunity costs (i.e., the costs of not taking other, more successful actions), they are hard to ignore. And when this occurs, the stage is set to counter the otherwise potent tendency to escalate commitment to failing courses of action.

GROUP DECISIONS: DO TOO MANY COOKS SPOIL THE BROTH?

Decision-making groups are well-established facts of modern organizational life. Groups such as committees, study teams, task forces, and review panels are often charged with the responsibility for making important business decisions.[48] They are so common, in fact, that some administrators have been estimated to spend as much as 80 percent of their time in committee meetings.[49] In view of this, it is important to consider the effectiveness of groups relative to individuals when it comes to making decisions. Under what conditions might individuals or groups be expected to make superior decisions? Research provides some good answers.[50]

When Are Groups Superior to Individuals?

Whether groups will perform better or worse than individuals depends on the nature of the task. Specifically, any advantages that groups may have over individuals will depend on how complex or simple the task is. As I explain this here, you may find it useful to follow the summary in Figure 10.10.

COMPLEX PROBLEMS   Imagine a situation in which an important decision has to be made about a complex problem—such as whether one company should merge with another. This is not the kind of problem about which any one individual working alone would be able to make a good decision. After all, its highly complex nature may overwhelm even an expert, thereby setting the stage for a group to do a better job.

However, this doesn't happen automatically. In fact, for groups to outperform individuals, several conditions must exist. First, we must consider who is in the group. Successful groups tend to be composed of *heterogeneous group members with complementary skills*. So, for example, a group composed of lawyers, accountants, real estate agents, and other experts may make much better decisions on the merger problem than would a group composed of specialists in only one field. Indeed, research has shown that the diversity of opinions offered by group members is one of the major advantages of using groups to make decisions.[51]

As you might imagine, it is not enough simply to have skills. For a group to be successful, its members must also be able to freely communicate their ideas to each other in an open, nonhostile manner. Conditions under which one individual (or group) intimidates another from contributing his or her expertise can easily negate any potential gain associated with composing groups of heterogeneous experts. After all, *having* expertise and being able to make a contribution by *using*

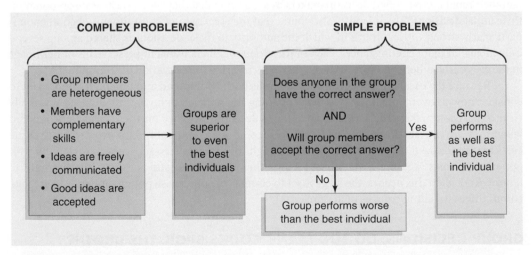

FIGURE 10.10   When Are Group Decisions Superior to Individual Decisions?
When performing complex problems, groups are superior to individuals if certain conditions prevail (e.g., when members have heterogeneous and complementary skills, when they can freely share ideas, and when their good ideas are accepted by others). However, when dealing with simple problems, groups perform only as well as the best individual group member—and then, only if that person has the correct answer and if that answer is accepted by others in the group.

that expertise are two different things. Indeed, research has shown that only when the contributions of the most qualified group members are given the greatest weight does the group derive any benefit from that member's presence.[52] In summary, then, for groups to be superior to individuals, they must be composed of a heterogeneous collection of experts with complementary skills who can freely and openly contribute to their group's product.

SIMPLE PROBLEMS   In contrast to complex decision tasks, imagine a situation in which a judgment is required on a simple problem with a readily verifiable answer. For example, make believe that you are asked to translate a phrase from a relatively obscure language into English.

Groups might do better than individuals on such a task, but primarily because the odds are increased that someone in the group knows the language and can perform the translation on behalf of the group. However, there is no reason to expect that even a large group will be able to carry out such a task better than a single individual who has the required expertise even if someone in the group can perform the task. In fact, an expert working alone may do even better than a group. This is because an expert individual performing a simple task may be distracted by others and suffer from having to convince them of the correctness of his or her solution. For this reason, exceptional individuals tend to outperform entire groups on simple tasks.[53] In such cases, for groups to benefit from a pooling of resources, there must be some resources to pool. The pooling of ignorance does not help.

So, how can we answer the proverbial question: Are two heads better than one? The answer depends on the nature of the problem that's being addressed. Specifically, two heads may be better than one if at least one of those heads contains what it takes to succeed and if others allow that head to prevail. Thus, whether groups perform better than individuals depends on the nature of the task performed and the expertise of the people involved. Recall the graphic summary of these considerations in Figure 10.10 (p. 320).

When Are Individuals Superior to Groups?

As I have described thus far, groups may be expected to perform better than the average or even the exceptional individual under certain conditions. However, there are also conditions under which individuals are superior to groups.

Most of the problems faced by organizations require a great deal of creative thinking. For example, a company deciding how to use a newly developed adhesive in its consumer products is facing decisions on a poorly structured task. Although you would expect that the complexity of such creative problems would give groups a natural advantage, this is not the case. In fact, research has shown that on poorly structured, creative tasks, individuals perform better than groups.[54]

Despite this, groups tend to be used widely for making decisions on these kinds of tasks. Accordingly, it is important to ask: How can the quality of group decisions be improved when carrying out poorly structured, creative tasks? One commonly used approach is known as **brainstorming**. This technique was developed by an advertising executive as a tool for coming up with creative, new ideas.[55] When brainstorming, group members are encouraged to present their ideas in an uncritical way and to discuss freely and openly all ideas presented by others. Specifically, members of brainstorming groups are required to follow four main rules:

- Avoid criticizing others' ideas.
- Share even far-out suggestions.
- Offer as many comments as possible.
- Build on others' ideas to create your own.

Does brainstorming improve the quality of creative decisions? To answer this question, researchers compared the effectiveness of individuals and brainstorming groups working on creative problems.[56] Specifically, participants were given thirty-five minutes to consider the consequences of situations such as, "What would happen if everybody went blind?" or "What would the world be like if everybody grew an extra thumb on each hand?" Clearly, the novel nature of such problems requires a great deal of creativity. The researchers compared the number of solutions generated by groups of four or seven people and a like number of individuals who worked on the same problems alone. They also had a panel of experts assess the quality of the responses without knowing which groups they came from. The results were clear: with respect to both quantity and quality, individuals were significantly more effective than groups on creative tasks.

In summary, groups perform worse than individuals when working on creative tasks. A great part of the problem is that some individuals feel inhibited by the presence of others even though one rule of brainstorming is that all ideas may be shared, including those that are far out. To the extent that people wish to avoid feeling foolish as a result of saying silly things, their creativity may be inhibited when in groups. Groups also may inhibit creativity in another way—by slowing down the process of bringing ideas to fruition. Despite these limitations, many creative professionals (e.g., advertising executives) strongly believe in the power of brainstorming and remain committed to using it.[57] What then could be done to make brainstorming more effective? For some specific suggestions on how to reap the potential benefits of brainstorming, see Table 10.2.[58]

TABLE 10.2   Tips for Brainstorming Successfully

The rules of brainstorming are simple enough, but doing it effectively requires some guidance. Many brainstorming sessions fail because people don't fully appreciate the finer points of how to conduct them. Following the guidelines summarized here promises to make your own brainstorming sessions more effective. All may be considered refinements or tweaks of the four basic rules of brainstorming.

Suggestion	Explanation
Brainstorm frequently, at least once per month.	Practice makes perfect. The more frequently people engage in brainstorming, the more comfortable they are with it—hence, the more effective it becomes.
Keep brainstorming sessions brief, less than an hour in length.	Brainstorming effectively can be very exhausting, so limit the time dedicated to it. After about an hour, people become too inefficient to make it worthwhile to continue.
Focus on the problem at hand.	The best brainstorming sessions begin with a clear statement of the exact problem to be addressed. These shouldn't be too broad or too narrow.
Don't forget to "build" and "jump."	The best ideas to result from brainstorming sessions build on other ideas. Everyone should be encouraged to jump from one idea to another as they build on earlier ones.
Prepare for the session.	Brainstorming is much more effective when people prepare in advance by reading up on the topic than when they come in "cold."
Don't limit yourself to words—use props.	Some of the most effective brainstorming sessions result when people introduce objects to help model their ideas.

Sources: Based on suggestions by Miller, 2012, Coyne & Coyne, 2011, and Kelley, 2001; see Note 57.

TECHNIQUES FOR IMPROVING THE EFFECTIVENESS OF DECISIONS

As suggested in this chapter, certain advantages can be gained from sometimes using individuals and sometimes using groups to make decisions. A decision-making technique that combines the best features of groups and individuals, while minimizing their disadvantages, would be ideal. Several techniques designed to realize the "best of both worlds" have been used widely in organizations. I review such techniques here.

Training Individuals to Improve Group Performance

Earlier in this chapter, I noted that how well groups solve problems depends in part on the composition of those groups. If at least one group member is capable of coming up with a solution, groups may benefit by that individual's expertise. Based on this reasoning, it follows that the more qualified individual group members are to solve problems, the better their groups as a whole will perform. What, then, might individuals do to improve the nature of the decisions they make?

Researchers looking into this question have found that people tend to make four types of mistakes when attempting to make creative decisions, and that they make better decisions when trained to avoid these errors.[59] Here are the four common mistakes and suggestions for avoiding them.

HYPERVIGILANCE The state of **hypervigilance** involves frantically searching for quick solutions to problems, going from one idea to another out of a sense of desperation that one idea isn't working and that another needs to be considered before time runs out. A poor, "last chance" solution may be adopted to relieve anxiety. This problem may be avoided by keeping in mind that it is best to stick with one suggestion and work it out thoroughly, and reassuring the person solving the problem that his or her level of skill and education is adequate to perform the task at hand.

UNCONFLICTED ADHERENCE Many decision makers make the mistake of sticking to the first idea that comes into their heads without more deeply evaluating the consequences, a mistake known as **unconflicted adherence**. As a result, such people are unlikely to become aware of any problems associated with their ideas or to consider other possibilities. To avoid unconflicted adherence, decision makers are urged (1) to think about the difficulties associated with their ideas, (2) to force themselves to consider different ideas, and (3) to consider the special and unique characteristics of the problem they are facing and avoid carrying over assumptions from previous problems.

UNCONFLICTED CHANGE Sometimes people are very quick to change their minds and adopt the first new idea to come along—a problem known as **unconflicted change**. Decision makers are trained to avoid unconflicted change by focusing on (1) the risks and problems of adopting that solution, (2) the good points of the first idea, and (3) the relative strengths and weaknesses of both ideas.

DEFENSIVE AVOIDANCE Too often, decision makers fail to solve problems effectively because they go out of their way to avoid working on the task at hand. This is known as **defensive avoidance**. People can do the following things to minimize this problem.

- *Avoid procrastination*—Don't put off the problem indefinitely just because you cannot come up with a solution right away. Continue to budget some of your time on even the most frustrating problems.

- *Avoid disowning responsibility*—It is easy to minimize the importance of a problem by saying, "It doesn't matter, so who cares?" Avoid giving up so soon.
- *Don't ignore potentially corrective information*—It is tempting to put your nagging doubts about the quality of a solution to rest in order to be finished with it. Good decision makers would not do so. Rather, they use their doubts to test and potentially improve the quality of their ideas.

Structuring Groups to Enhance Group Decisions

Just as there are various things individuals can do to improve decision making, there are also steps that groups can take to enhance the quality of their decisions. The basic idea underlying these techniques is identical: structure the group experience so as to enable the many benefits of groups to occur while limiting the weaknesses. Two such techniques have been popular for some time and remain widely used today.

THE DELPHI TECHNIQUE: DECISIONS BY EXPERT CONSENSUS   According to Greek mythology, people interested in seeing what fate the future held for them could seek the counsel of the Delphic oracle. Today's organizational decision makers sometimes consult experts to help them make the best decisions as well. A technique developed by the RAND Corporation, known as the **Delphi technique**, represents a systematic way of collecting and organizing the opinions of several experts into a single decision.[60] For a summary of the steps in this process, see Figure 10.11.

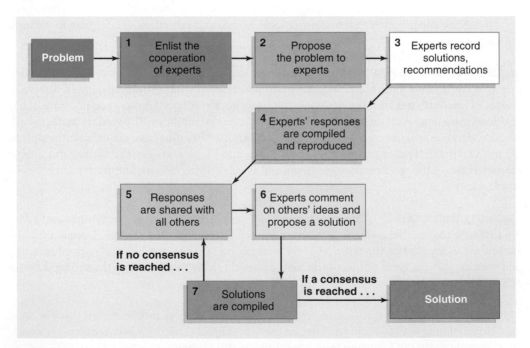

FIGURE 10.11   The Delphi Technique
The Delphi technique allows decisions to be made by several experts while avoiding many of the pitfalls of face-to-face group interaction. Its general steps are outlined here.

The Delphi process starts by enlisting the cooperation of experts and presenting the problem to them, usually in a letter or e-mail message. Each expert then proposes what he or she believes is the most appropriate solution. The group leader compiles these individual responses and reproduces them so they can be shared with all the other experts in a second mailing. At this point, each expert comments on the others' ideas and proposes another solution. These individual solutions are returned to the leader, who compiles them and looks for a consensus of opinions. If a consensus is reached, the decision is made. If not, the process of sharing reactions with others is repeated until a consensus eventually is obtained.

The obvious advantage of using the Delphi technique to make decisions is that it allows expert judgments to be collected without the great costs and logistical difficulties of bringing experts together for a face-to-face meeting. However, the technique is not without limitations. As you might imagine, the Delphi process can be very time-consuming. Sending out letters or e-mail messages, waiting for everyone to respond, transcribing and disseminating the responses, and repeating the process until a consensus is reached can take quite a long time. Experts have estimated that the minimum time required to use the Delphi technique would be more than forty-four days. In one case (using regular postal mail), the process took five months to complete.[61] With the widespread use of Web technology, the Delphi approach can be sped up considerably, but it is still slow—if for no other reason than it requires input from people who are already quite busy.

Obviously, the Delphi approach is not appropriate for making decisions in crisis situations, or whenever else time is of the essence. However, the approach has been successfully employed to make decisions such as what items to put on a conference agenda and what the potential impact of implementing new land-use policies would be.[62]

THE NOMINAL GROUP TECHNIQUE: A STRUCTURED GROUP MEETING When there are only a few hours available to make a decision, group discussion sessions can be held in which members interact with each other in an orderly, focused fashion aimed at solving problems. The **nominal group technique (NGT)** brings together a small number of individuals (usually about seven to ten) who systematically offer their individual solutions to a problem and share their personal reactions to others' solutions.[63] The technique is referred to as *nominal* because the individuals involved form a group in name only. The participants do not attempt to agree as a group on any solution, but rather vote on all the solutions proposed. For a summary of this process, see Figure 10.12.

As shown in Figure 10.12, the nominal group process begins by gathering the group members together around a table and identifying the problem at hand. Then each member writes down his or her solutions. Next, one at a time, each member presents his or her solutions to the group as the leader writes them down on a chart. This process continues until all the ideas have been expressed. Following this, each solution is discussed, clarified, and evaluated by the group members. Each member is given a chance to voice his or her reactions to each idea. Once all the ideas have been evaluated, the group members privately rank order their preferred solutions. Finally, the idea that receives the highest rank is taken as the group's decision. (To experience the NGT firsthand, complete the Group Exercise on p. 329.)

The NGT has several advantages and disadvantages.[64] I have already noted that it can be used to arrive at group decisions in only a few hours. This can be useful for many types of decisions—but, of course, not for urgent decisions that have to be made on the spot. The benefit of the technique is that it discourages any pressure to conform to the wishes of a high-status

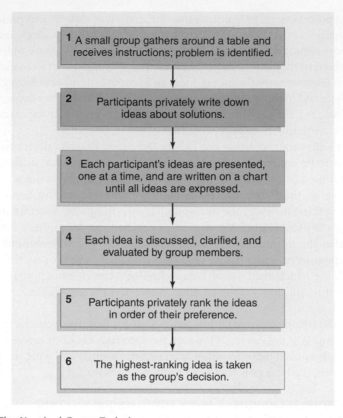

FIGURE 10.12 **The Nominal Group Technique**
The nominal group technique structures face-to-face group meetings in such a way that the open expression and evaluation of ideas are encouraged. It follows the six steps summarized here.

group member because all ideas are evaluated openly and the preferences are expressed in private balloting. The technique must be considered limited, however, in that it requires the use of a trained group leader. In addition, using NGT successfully requires that only one narrowly defined problem be considered at a time. So, for very complex problems, many NGT sessions would have to be run—and only *if* the problem under consideration could be broken down into smaller parts.

The techniques presented to this point may make only limited use of Internet technology, if they do so at all. They were used long before the Internet existed. However, growing numbers of organizations are harnessing the power of the Internet as a means of improving group decision making. (For a look at one such approach that is gaining in popularity, see this chapter's Winning Practices section on p. 327.)

Winning Practices

Group Decision Support Systems

Suppose you need to collaborate with people located in different places who cannot meet at the same time. Today, this is not such an unusual situation. A solution that has been growing in popularity involves leveraging the power of the Internet to allow people to meet virtually, using what are known as **group decision support systems (GDSS)**.[65] These are interactive computer-based systems that combine communication, computer, and decision technologies to improve the effectiveness of group problem-solving meetings. Typically, they involve having people type their ideas into a networked program so that they can be "discussed" with others online. This may be done in real time among individuals who happen to be available. When this isn't possible, a record of all discussions is left for others to examine as needed when they join in.

Some software vendors have been claiming that using their products promotes the efficiency of group decision meetings. Although scientific research on this is limited, it is a reasonable claim given the nature of the process. Additionally, users of GDSS expect that it will improve the quality of group decisions by removing some of the impediments to decision making that I identified earlier. Specifically, it may accomplish this in three key ways:

- GDSS helps meetings stay focused, and participants avoid overload because the software directs the flow of information.
- GDSS sessions allow the appropriate experts to contribute to meetings at their convenience—even though they may be far away—instead of receiving input only from those who physically can attend the meeting.
- Because GDSS sessions can be configured so as to keep contributors anonymous, no participants have to worry about getting "put down" for sharing certain points. Intimidation by powerful leaders is all but eliminated as a result. Also, because even unpopular ideas can be shared with impunity, the problem of groupthink is reduced.

Research has found that GDSS has, in fact, improved group decisions. Specifically, compared to face-to-face groups, groups using GDSS not only shared considerably more information but also made far better decisions as a result. For now, it seems that group decision support systems appear to be quite effective. However, because they are very new, we don't yet know all the conditions under which they will continue to be successful. As OB researchers conduct further research on this topic, we surely will learn more about this promising technique in the future.

Back to the Case

Answer the following questions based on this chapter's Making the Case (p. 298) to illustrate insights you have derived from the material in this chapter.

1. What biases or limitations in the decision-making process might have accounted for the three organizational decisions that proved so unpopular with the public? How might they have applied to these particular cases?
2. How might groupthink have accounted for the failed decisions made in these three cases?
3. How might the various techniques used to improve decision making have been applied to avoid the three unpopular decisions described in this case?

You Be the Consultant

Making Decisions Effectively

A business associate refers you to the president of a growing environmental management firm. The fact that the company is new and operates in a changing business environment makes all of its decisions especially crucial. As such, you are hired to assist in guiding the president in helping the company make decisions in the most effective possible way. Answer the following questions relevant to this situation based on the material in this chapter.

1. The president has been making decisions about how to deal with governmental regulations all by himself. Should he consider delegating this task to a group instead? Why or why not?
2. What individual biases would be expected to interfere with the quality of the decisions made by individuals in this company?
3. In what ways might the group interaction limit the quality of decisions made? What steps can be taken to overcome these problems?

Self-Assessment Exercise

ARE YOU RISK-SEEKING OR RISK-AVERSE?

It's one thing to read about the effects of framing on riskiness but quite another to experience it firsthand. This exercise will help you demonstrate the effects of framing for yourself.

Directions

Read the following descriptions of hypothetical situations. Then answer the following question for each: *Which project will you select: Alpha or Beta?*

Situation 1: You are an executive whose policies have resulted in a $1 million loss for your company. Now you are considering two new projects. One of them, Alpha, will provide a definite return of $500,000. The other, Beta, will provide a 50–50 chance of obtaining either a $1 million return or a $0 return.

Situation 2: You are considering one of two new projects to conduct in your company. One of them, Alpha, will provide a definite return of $500,000. The other, Beta, will provide a 50–50 chance of obtaining either a $1 million return or a $0 return.

Discussion Questions

1. What choice did you make in Situation 1? Most people would select Beta in such a situation because it gives them a 50–50 chance of undoing the loss completely. Such a risk-seeking decision is likely in a situation in which people are focusing on undoing loss.
2. What choice did you make in Situation 2? Most people would select Alpha in such a situation because it gives them a sure thing, a "bird in the hand." Such a risk-averse decision is likely in a situation in which people are focusing on gains received.
3. Given that both situations are mathematically identical, why should people prefer one or the other?

Group Exercise

RUNNING A NOMINAL GROUP: TRY IT YOURSELF

A great deal can be learned about nominal groups by running one—or, at least, by participating in one—yourself. Doing so will not only help illustrate the procedure but also how effectively it works.

Directions

1. Select a topic suitable for discussion in a nominal group composed of students in your class. It should be a topic that is narrowly defined and on which people have many different opinions (these work best in nominal groups). Some possible examples include:

   - What should your school's student leaders be doing for you?
   - What can be done to improve the quality of instruction in your institution?
   - What can be done to improve the quality of jobs that students obtain after they graduate from your school?

2. Divide the class into groups of ten or so students. Arrange each group in a circle (or around a table, if possible). Select one person in each group to serve as the facilitator.
3. Following the steps outlined in Figure 10.12 (see p. 326), facilitators should guide their groups in discussions regarding the focal question identified in step 1. Allow approximately forty-five minutes to one hour to complete this process.
4. If time allows, select a different focal question and a different group leader, and repeat the procedure.

Discussion Questions

1. Collectively, how did the group answer the question? Do you believe that this answer accurately reflected the feelings of the group? How do you think your group experiences would have differed had you used a totally unstructured, traditional face-to-face group instead of a nominal group?
2. How did the various groups' answers compare? Were they similar or different? Why?
3. What were the major problems, if any, associated with the nominal group experience? For example, were there any group members who were reluctant to wait their turns before speaking up?

Notes

MAKING THE CASE NOTES

Munarriz, R. A. (2012, February 13). Netflix blows it this time. *The Motley Fool.* http://www.fool.com/investing/general/2012/02/13/netflix-blew-it-this-time.aspx. Hastings. R. (2011, September 18). An explanation and some reflections. *Netflix US and Canada Blog.* http://blog.netflix.com/2011/09/explanation-and-some-reflections.html. Verizon Wireless. (2011, December 29). Customers encouraged to use options to avoid single payment fee that starts January 15. *News Center.* http://news.verizonwireless.com/news/2011/12/pr2011-12-29b.html. Verizon Wireless. (2011, December 30). Verizon Wireless will not institute single payment fee. *News Center.* http://news.verizonwireless.com/news/2011/12/pr2011-12-30.html. Libor, R., & Chan, B. X. (2011, December 29). An uproar on the Web over $2 fee by Verizon. *New York Times.* http://www.nytimes.com/2011/12/30/business/media/an-uproar-on-the-web-over-2-fee-by-verizon.html. Gawker (2012, February 7). Komen Foundation VP resigns in wake of Planned Parenthood dispute. http://gawker.com/5882990/komen-foundation-vp-resigns-in-wake-of-planned-parenthood-dispute. Preston, J. (2012, February 7). After outcry, a senior official resigns at Komen. *New York Times.* http://www.nytimes.com/2012/02/08/us/after-outcry-a-top-official-resigns-at-komen-cancer-charity.html.

CHAPTER NOTES

1. Mintzberg, H. J. (1988). *Mintzberg on management: Inside our strange world of organizations.* New York: Free Press.
2. Drucker, P. F. (2006). Brainy quote. http://www.brainyquote.com/quotes/authors/p/peter_f_drucker.html.
3. Wedley, W. C., & Field, R. H. G. (1984). A predecision support system. *Academy of Management Review, 9,* 696–703. Nutt, P. C. (1993). The formulation process and tactics used in organizational decision making. *Organization Science, 4,* 226–251.
4. Nutt, P. (1984). Types of organizational decision processes. *Administrative Science Quarterly, 29,* 414–450.
5. Fulk, J., & Boyd, B. (1991). Emerging theories of communication in organizations. *Journal of Management, 17,* 407–446.
6. Stevenson, M. K., Busemeyer, J. R., & Naylor, J. C. (1990). Judgment and decision-making theory. In M. D. Dunnette & L. M. Hough (Eds.), *Handbook of industrial and organizational psychology* (2nd ed., Vol. 1, pp. 283–374). Palo Alto, CA: Consulting Psychologists Press.
7. Dutta, A. (2001). Business planning for network services: A systems thinking approach. *Information Systems Research, 12,* 260–283. Hill, C. W., & Jones, G. R. (1989). *Strategic management.* Boston, MA: Houghton Mifflin.
8. Crainer, S. (1998, November). The 75 greatest management decisions ever made. *Management Review,* pp. 16–23.
9. Amit, R., & Wernerfelt, B. (1990). Why do firms reduce business risk? *Academy of Management Journal, 33,* 520–533.
10. Simon, H. A. (1987). Making management decisions: The role of intuition and emotion. *Academy of Management Executive, 1,* 57–64.
11. Kirschenbaum, S. S. (1992). Influence of experience on information-gathering strategies. *Journal of Applied Psychology, 77,* 343–352.
12. Simon, H. (1977). *The new science of management decisions* (2nd ed.). Englewood Cliffs, NJ: Prentice Hall.
13. Rowe, A. J., Boulgaides, J. D., & McGrath, M. R. (1984). *Managerial decision making.* Chicago, IL: Science Research Associates.
14. Frost, R. O., & Shows, D. L. (1993). The nature and measurement of compulsive indecisiveness. *Behavioral Research and Theory, 31,* 683–692.
15. See Note 14.
16. Patalano, A. L., Juhasz, B. J., & Dicke, J. (2009). The relationship between indecisiveness and eye movement patterns in a decision making informational search task. *Journal of Behavioral Decision Making, 22,* 560–560.
17. Murninghan, J. K. (1981). Group decision making: What strategies should you use? *Management Review, 25,* 56–62.
18. Janis, I. L. (1982). *Groupthink: Psychological studies of policy decisions and fiascoes* (2nd ed.). Boston, MA: Houghton Mifflin.
19. Morehead, G., Ference, R., & Neck, C. P. (1991). Group decision fiascoes continue: Space shuttle *Challenger* and a revised groupthink framework. *Human Relations, 44,* 531–550.
20. Neustadt, R. E., & Fineberg, H. (1978). *The swine flu affair: Decision making on a slippery disease.* Washington, DC: U.S. Department of Health, Education and Welfare.
21. Hurry up and decide (2001, May 14). *BusinessWeek,* p. 16.
22. Breen, B. (2000, September). What's your intuition? *Fast Company,* pp. 290–294, 296, 298, 300. Klein, G. (1999). *Sources of power.* Cambridge, MA: MIT Press.
23. Linstone, H. A. (1984). *Multiple perspectives for decision making.* New York: North-Holland.
24. Simon, H. A. (1979). Rational decision making in organizations. *American Economic Review, 69,* 493–513.
25. March, J. G., & Simon, H. A. (1958). *Organizations.* New York: Wiley.
26. See Note 25.
27. Simon, H. A. (1957). *Models of man.* New York: Wiley.
28. Shull, F. A., Delbecq, A. L., & Cummings, L. L. (1970). *Organizational decision making.* New York: McGraw-Hill.
29. Browning, E. B. (1850/1950). *Sonnets from the Portuguese.* New York: Ratchford and Fulton.
30. Mitchell, T. R., & Beach, L. R. (1990). " . . . Do I love thee? Let me count . . . " Toward an understanding of intuitive and automatic decision making. *Organizational Behavior and Human Decision Processes, 47,* 1–20.
31. Beach, L. R., & Mitchell, T. R. (1990). Image theory: A behavioral theory of image

making in organizations. In B. Staw and L. L. Cummings (Eds.), *Research in organizational behavior* (Vol. 12, pp. 1–41). Greenwich, CT: JAI Press.

32. Levin, I. P., Schneider, S. L., & Gaeth, G. J. (1998). All frames are not created equal: A typology and critical analysis of framing effects. *Organizational Behavior and Human Decision Processes, 76,* 141–188. Levin, I. P. (1987). Associative effects of information framing. *Bulletin of the Psychonomic Society, 25,* 85–86.

33. Kahneman, D., & Tversky, A. (1984). Choices, values, and frames. *American Psychologist, 39,* 341–350.

34. Highhouse, S., & Yüce, P. (1996). Perspectives, perceptions, and risk-taking behavior. *Organizational Behavior and Human Decision Processes, 65,* 151–167.

35. Levin, I. P., & Gaeth, G. J. (1988). Framing of attribute information before and after consuming the product. *Journal of Consumer Research, 15,* 374–378.

36. See Note 35.

37. Meyerowitz, B. E., & Chaiken, S. (1987). The effects of message framing on breast self-examination attitudes, intentions, and behavior. *Journal of Personality and Social Psychology, 52,* 500–510.

38. Frisch, D. (1993). Reasons for framing effects. *Organizational Behavior and Human Decision Processes, 54,* 391–429.

39. Nisbett, R. E., & Ross, L. (1980). *Human inference: Strategies and shortcomings of social judgment.* Englewood Cliffs, NJ: Prentice Hall.

40. Maule, A. J., & Hodgkinson, G. (2002). Heuristics, biases and strategic decision making. *Psychologist, 15,* 68–71.

41. Kahneman, D., & Tversky, A. (1973). On the psychology of prediction. *Psychological Review, 80,* 251–273.

42. Gaeth, G. J., & Shanteau, J. (1984). Reducing the influence of irrelevant information on experienced decision makers. *Organizational Behavior and Human Performance, 33,* 187–203.

43. Power, D. J., & Aldag, R. J. (1985). Soelberg's job search and choice model: A clarification, review, and critique. *Academy of Management Review, 10,* 48–58.

44. Soelberg, P. O. (1967). Unprogrammed decision making. *Industrial Management Review, 8,* 110–129.

45. Langer, E., & Schank, R. C. (1994). *Belief, reasoning, and decision making.* Hillsdale, NJ: Erlbaum.

46. Conlon, D. E., & Garland, H. (1993). The role of project completion information in resource allocation decisions. *Academy of Management Journal, 36,* 402–413.

47. Sleesman, D. J., Conlon, D. E., McNamara, G., & Miles, J. E. (2012) Cleaning up the big muddy: A meta-analytic review of the determinants of escalation of commitment. *Academy of Management Journal, 55,* 541–562.

48. Davis, J. H. (1992). Introduction to the special issue on group decision making. *Organizational Behavior and Human Decision Processes, 52,* 1–2.

49. Delbecq, A. L., Van de Ven, A. H., & Gustafson, D. H. (1975). *Group techniques for program planning.* Glenview, IL: Scott Foresman.

50. Hill, G. W. (1982). Group versus individual performance: Are N + 1 heads better than one? *Psychological Bulletin, 91,* 517–539.

51. Wanous, J. P., & Youtz, M. A. (1986). Solution diversity and the quality of group decisions. *Academy of Management Journal, 29,* 141–159.

52. Yetton, P., & Bottger, P. (1983). The relationships among group size, member ability, social decision schemes, and performance. *Organizational Behavior and Human Performance, 32,* 145–149.

53. See Note 52.

54. See Note 52.

55. Osborn, A. F. (1957). *Applied imagination.* New York: Scribner's.

56. Bouchard, T. J., Jr., Barsaloux, J., & Drauden, G. (1974). Brainstorming procedure, group size, and sex as determinants of the problem-solving effectiveness of groups and individuals. *Journal of Applied Psychology, 59,* 135–138.

57. Miller, B. C. (2012). *Quick brainstorming activities for busy managers.* New York: AMACOM. Coyne, K. B., & Coyne, S. T. (2011). *Brainstorming: A better approach to breakthrough ideas.* New York: HarperBusiness. Kelley, T. (2001, June–July). Reaping the whirlwind. *Context,* pp. 56–58.

58. See Note 57.

59. Bottger, P. C., & Yetton, P. W. (1987). Improving group performance by training in individual problem solving. *Journal of Applied Psychology, 72,* 651–657.

60. Dalkey, N. (1969). *The Delphi method: An experimental study of group decisions.* Santa Monica, CA: RAND Corporation.

61. Van de Ven, A. H., & Delbecq, A. L. (1971). Nominal versus interacting group processes for committee decision making effectiveness. *Academy of Management Journal, 14,* 203–212.

62. See Note 61.

63. Gustafson, D. H., Shulka, R. K., Delbecq, A., & Walster, W. G. (1973). A comparative study of differences in subjective likelihood estimates made by individuals, interacting groups, Delphi groups, and nominal groups. *Organizational Behavior and Human Performance, 9,* 280–291.

64. Ulshak, F. L., Nathanson, L., & Gillan, P. B. (1981). *Small group problem solving: An aid to organizational effectiveness.* Reading, MA: Addison-Wesley.

65. Sauter, V. (2010). *Decision support systems for business intelligence.* Hoboken, NJ: Wiley. Fuks, H., Lukosch, S., & Salgado, A. C. (2005). *Groupware: Design, implementation, and use.* New York: Springer Verlag.

11 | THE QUEST FOR LEADERSHIP

LEARNING OBJECTIVES

After reading this chapter, you will be able to:

1. **DEFINE** leadership and **EXPLAIN** the major sources of power leaders have at their disposal.
2. **DESCRIBE** the trait approach to leadership and **IDENTIFY** the major characteristics of effective leaders.
3. **IDENTIFY** the types of behavior that have been most strongly associated with effective leadership.
4. **EXPLAIN** the relationship between leaders and followers as characterized in various conceptualizations of the process of leadership.
5. **DESCRIBE** the basic tenets of contingency theories of leadership and how they may be applied.
6. **DESCRIBE** various approaches that can be taken to develop leaders in organizations.

THREE GOOD REASONS you should care about. . .

Leadership

1. An organization's success is greatly determined by the quality of its leadership.
2. There are steps that anyone can take to enhance his or her effectiveness as a leader.
3. Several leadership development techniques are widely used to enhance leaders' effectiveness.

Making the Case for. . .

Leadership

The Woman Who Saved the Chicken Fajitas

With only eighty-three restaurants in seventeen states, Houlihan's doesn't have the presence of its larger competitors in the $190 billion casual-dining market, which include Applebee's, Chili's, and T.G.I. Friday's. Nor does it have their multimillion dollar advertising budgets to lure customers. What Houlihan's does have, though, is a particularly valuable human asset—Jen Gulvik, a leader who listens.

As vice president of marketing, Gulvik realized that it was necessary to bring new customers through Houlihans' doors, which required delivering precisely what diners were looking for. This, in turn, meant listening to prospective customers. Comment cards on the tables reached only current diners. What Gulvik needed was to reach out to the broader community, especially younger "Millennials," among whom the restaurant had the most appeal. Her mission became to move people from recognizing the appeal of Houlihan's to becoming its customers.

As her major weapon in this battle, Gulvik relied on one of the favorite communication tools of her target market: social networking. In the summer of 2009, she invited 100,000 visitors to the restaurant's Web site, to join its private, by-invitation-only social networking site, HQ. This was to be a brand community that could serve as a "virtual comment card." It became wildly popular. Today, HQ consists of some 10,500 "Houlifans," as the community's members call themselves.

The feedback from Houlifans has proven invaluable in transforming the previously stodgy, pub-style restaurants into hipper, suburban-chic spots, complete with indie pop and modern soul background music and even new forks on the tables. Their input has enabled Houlihan's to change menu items on-the-fly, such as when Houlifans made it clear that several of the restaurant's new tapas-style (small plate) items needed work. The white bean hummus and pita, for example, was described as "thick and spongy." Because Gulvik spends at least an hour a day online with the Houlihan's community, her ears perked up when she heard about this problem. Immediately, she got word to Chef Dan that some tweaking was required. Today, the tapas menu—containing all high-profit margin items—accounts for about a quarter of total sales.

In the eyes (and taste buds) of many, the single most important benefit from HQ has been its capacity to share concerns directly with Gulvik. When one revision of the menu led to the removal of the chicken fajitas, a low-profit item, customers who loved them began purchasing the fajitas sauce from the restaurants to take home. However, many guests came to Houlihan's just for the fajitas and weren't interested in other menu offerings. Acknowledging the importance of giving customers what they want—and reinforcing contributions to HQ as well—Gulvik put the chicken fajitas back on the menu. The HQ community was abuzz, and excited customers tweeted photos of the dish to their friends as proof if its return. One customer who had come to the restaurant in search of the fajitas spotted Gulvik and introduced her to her dining companion as "the woman who saved the chicken fajitas." And so she forever will be known.

Although Jen Gulvik might not be famous (yet, at least), her story is likely quite similar to that of untold thousands of other leaders who toil in relative anonymity every day. They are known within their organizations, of course, and maybe in their industries, but theirs are not household names. This does not make them any less vital as leaders. Their organizations count on them to bring them huge successes. Indeed, it is widely believed in the world of business that *leadership* is the key ingredient in the recipe for corporate achievement. And this view is by no means restricted to business organizations. As you know from experience, leadership also is important when it comes to politics, sports, religion, and many other activities.[1]

Is this view justified? Do leaders really play crucial roles in shaping the fates and fortunes of businesses? Over a century of research on this topic suggests that they do. Effective leadership is indeed a key determinant of organizational success.[2] Given its importance, it makes sense that leadership has been one of the most widely studied phenomena in the social sciences.[3] In view of this, I devote this chapter to describing various approaches to the study of leadership as well as their implications for managerial practice. Before doing this, however, I begin by closely examining the fundamental nature of leadership.

THE NATURE OF LEADERSHIP

In a sense, leadership resembles love. Most people can recognize it, but they find it difficult to define. So what precisely is leadership and how do leaders go about influencing others? I now focus on these essential issues regarding the fundamental nature of leadership.

A Definition: What Leadership Is—and Is Not

Imagine that you have accepted a new job and entered a new work group. How do you recognize its leader? One possibility, of course, is through the formal titles and assigned roles each person in the group holds. In short, you would identify the individual designated as department head or project manager as the group's leader. Now, however, imagine that after several staff meetings, you have noticed that this person is really not the most influential. Although she or he has formal authority, these meetings have been dominated by another individual who, ostensibly, is the top person's subordinate. What might you conclude about leadership then? You may say that the real leader is the person who actually runs things—not the one with the formal title and the apparent authority.

In many cases, of course, the disparity I have just described does not exist. The individual possessing the greatest amount of formal authority is also the most influential. In some situations, however, this is not so. And in such cases, we typically identify the person who actually exercises the most influence over the group as its **leader**. These observations point to the following definition of leadership, one accepted by many experts on this topic: **Leadership** is the process whereby one individual influences other group members in a noncoercive manner toward the attainment of defined group or organizational goals.[4] I summarize this process in Figure 11.1.

As you read about leadership in this chapter, you will come to appreciate four of its key characteristics. These are as follows:

- *Leadership involves noncoercive influence*—Dictators may use force to get others to behave as desired, but leaders do not. As former U.S. President Dwight D. Eisenhower put it, "You do not lead by hitting people over the head; that's assault, not leadership."

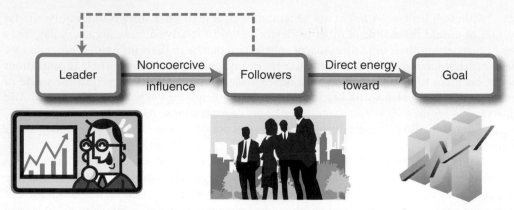

FIGURE 11.1   The Leadership Process: A Summary
Leadership is a process in which one person, a *leader*, influences a follower in a noncoercive manner to attain a goal. Note, of course, that leaders also may be influenced by their followers.

- *Leadership influence is goal-directed*—Leaders typically aren't interested in changing everything. Instead, they focus on altering those actions or attitudes of their subordinates that are related to specific objectives (e.g., meeting quotas).
- *Leadership requires followers*—Leaders influence subordinates, of course, but they are also influenced by them. In fact, leadership exists only in relation to followers. After all, one cannot lead without followers!
- *Leaders and managers are distinct—at least, in theory*—The primary function of a *leader* is to envision and articulate the essential purpose or mission of an organization and the strategy for attaining it. By contrast, the job of the *manager* is to implement that vision. In actual practice, however, the lines may be blurred; these two functions are not always distinct. For some differences between leaders and managers, see Table 11.1.[5]

How Do Leaders Influence Others? Sources of Leadership Power

As our definition suggests, leaders influence others. To understand fully how leaders operate, it is necessary to identify how exactly they come by the power to exert influence. As outlined here, the basis for a leader's power resides in his or her formal position as well as the way followers respond to his or her personal qualities.[6]

POSITION POWER   A great deal of the power that people have in organizations comes from the posts they hold in those organizations. In other words, they are able to influence others because of the formal power associated with their jobs. This is known as **position power**. For example, there are certain powers that the president of the United States has simply due to the authority given to the officeholder (e.g., signing bills into law, making treaties, and so on). These formal powers remain vested in the position and are available to anyone who holds it. When the president's term is up, these powers transfer to the new officeholder. There are four bases of position power. These are as follows:

- **Legitimate power**—The power that someone has because others recognize and accept his or her authority. For example, students recognize that their instructors have the legitimate power (i.e., authority) to make class policies and to determine grades.
- **Reward power**—The power to control the rewards others receive. For example, a supervisor has the power to reward one of her subordinates by recommending a large pay raise.

TABLE 11.1	Leaders Versus Managers: A Summary Comparison

The distinction between managers and leaders is reflected in the points identified here. Because some managers do the things in the "leaders" column and some leaders do the things in the "managers" column, the practical distinctions between them are sometimes blurred in actual practice. Note that several of the activities identified are discussed elsewhere in this book (where indicated in parentheses).

Managers do this . . .	Leaders do this . . .
• Figure out how to get things done	• Determine what and when things should be accomplished
• Pay close attention to work procedures and follow them precisely	• Focus on inspiring other people with creative new ideas (Chapter 12)
• Follow the rules	
• Maintain the status quo, keeping things as they are	• Follow ethical principles (Chapter 2)
	• Introduce new changes (Chapter 14) and innovation (Chapter 12)
• Control people by rewarding and punishing them appropriately (Chapter 3)	• Energize people and earn their trust (Chapter 7)
• Focus on short-term results	• Attend to the long-term, big picture
• Make decisions based on what has been done in the past (Chapter 10)	• Make decisions that follow new and original courses of action (Chapter 10)

Source: Based on suggestions by Bennis, 2009; see Note 5.

- **Coercive power**—The capacity to control punishment. For example, a boss may tell you to do something "my way or else." As noted earlier, dictators are inclined to use coercive power, whereas leaders limit its use to only the mildest forms. For example, leaders do not attempt to manage subordinates by being abusive. Individuals who rely on such tactics are more inclined to be considered bullies than leaders, regardless of whatever formal titles they may hold.
- **Information power**—The power a person has by virtue of his or her access to valuable data or knowledge. Traditionally, people in top positions have access to unique sources of information that are not available to others (e.g., knowledge of company performance, market trends, and so on). As they say, "knowledge is power," and such information greatly contributes to the power of people in many jobs. However, because the Internet puts vast amounts of information at everybody's fingertips, the potential for today's leaders to wield power because of their access to unique information isn't as great as it may have been only a few decades ago.

PERSONAL POWER In addition to the power leaders derive from their formal positions in organizations, they also derive power from their own unique qualities or characteristics. This is known as **personal power**. There are four sources of personal power, as follows:

- **Rational persuasion**—The power leaders have by virtue of the logical arguments and factual evidence they provide to support their arguments. Rational persuasion is widely used by top executives, such as when they present detailed reports in making a case as to why certain policies should be changed.
- **Expert power**—The power leaders have to the extent that others recognize their expert knowledge on a topic. For example, athletes do what their coaches tell them in large part because they recognize and respect their coaches' expertise.
- **Referent power**—The power that individuals have because they are liked and admired by others. For example, senior managers who possess desirable qualities and good reputations may have referent power over younger managers who identify with them and wish to emulate them.

- **Charisma**—The power someone has over others because of his or her engaging and magnetic personality. As I will describe later in this chapter, people with this characteristic are highly influential and inspire others to do things.

As outlined here, leaders derive power from a variety of sources. In the remainder of this chapter, I describe various approaches to understanding how leaders rely on these sources of power to attain group and organizational goals.

THE TRAIT APPROACH TO LEADERSHIP: HAVING THE RIGHT STUFF

At one time or another, many of us dream about being leaders. We may fantasize about taking charge of large groups whose members view us with great awe and respect. Despite such daydreams, however, relatively few of us actually become leaders. And among those who do, even fewer are particularly effective in this role.

This raises an intriguing question: What sets effective leaders apart from most others? Why, in short, do some people, but not others, become good leaders? One of the most widely studied approaches to this question suggests that effective leadership is based on the characteristics that people have. In other words, people become leaders because they are different from others in some special ways.[7]

The Great Person Theory

Are some people born to lead? Common sense suggests that this is so. Great leaders of the past, such as Alexander the Great, Queen Elizabeth I, and Abraham Lincoln do seem to differ from ordinary people in several respects. The same could also be said of various contemporary leaders, including some politicians, military personnel, and business executives. Such individuals are inclined to possess high levels of ambition coupled with clear visions of precisely where they want to go. One scientist expressed this idea as follows:

> [I]t is unequivocally clear that *leaders are not like other people.* Leaders do not have to be great men or women by being intellectual geniuses or omniscient prophets to succeed, but they do need to have the "right stuff" and this stuff is not equally present in all people. Leadership is a demanding, unrelenting job with enormous pressures and grave responsibilities. It would be a profound disservice to leaders to suggest that they are ordinary people who happened to be in the right place at the right time . . . In the realm of leadership (and in every other realm), the individual does matter.[8]

This orientation expresses an approach to the study of leadership known as the **great person theory**. According to this perspective, great leaders possess stable traits that set them apart from most other people. What are these traits? Researchers have identified several such characteristics, and these are listed in Table 11.2.[9] As you review these, you will readily recognize and understand most of them. However, because several are not particularly obvious, we review these here.[10] (To get a sense of your own beliefs about the characteristics of great leaders, complete the Group Exercise on p. 360.)

LEADERSHIP MOTIVATION: THE DESIRE TO LEAD   The concept of **leadership motivation** refers to leaders' desires to influence others—in essence, to lead.[11] Such motivation takes two distinct forms. These are as follows:

- **Personalized power motivation**—People's desires to dominate others, which tend to be reflected in extreme levels of concern about status.

TABLE 11.2	Characteristics of Successful Leaders

Research indicates that successful leaders possess high degrees of the traits listed here.

Trait or Characteristic	Description
Drive	Desire for achievement; ambition; high energy; tenacity; initiative
Honesty and integrity	Trustworthy; reliable; open
Leadership motivation	Desire to exercise influence over others to reach shared goals
Self-confidence	Trust in own abilities
Cognitive ability	Intelligence; ability to integrate and interpret large amounts of information
Knowledge of the business	Knowledge of industry and relevant technical matters
Creativity	Originality
Flexibility	Ability to adapt to needs of followers and requirements of situation

- **Socialized power motivation**—People's desires for power as a means of achieving shared goals, which they do by cooperating with others (see Chapter 7), such as through developing networks (see p. 355) and coalitions

FLEXIBILITY   Effective leaders demonstrate *flexibility*—that is, the ability to recognize the particular actions required in a given situation and then to act accordingly. Evidence suggests that the most effective leaders do not behave in the same ways all the time. Instead, they tend to be adaptive, matching their styles to the needs of followers and the demands of the situations they face.[12]

FOCUS ON MORALITY   In view of all the attention that has been paid to the dishonest dealings of many top business leaders in recent years (see Chapter 2), it's important to note that successful leaders do, in fact, place considerable emphasis on ethics and morality. This is in keeping with what has been called *authentic leadership*. **Authentic leaders** are highly moral individuals who are confident, hopeful, optimistic, and resilient and are highly aware of the contexts in which they operate.[13] Such individuals are passionate about their purposes in the organizations and consistent in the ways they practice their values. And, reflecting their tendencies to "lead with their hearts as well as their heads," authentic leaders develop long-term relationships with others and demonstrate the discipline needed to get things done. Not surprisingly, authentic leaders play key roles in promoting the growth and development of their subordinates and, as a result, the sustained performance of their organizations.

MULTIPLE DOMAINS OF INTELLIGENCE   Scientists have acknowledged that leaders have to "be smart" in a variety of ways. In other words, they have to demonstrate what is known as **multiple domains of intelligence**.[14] In particular, leaders need to be intelligent in at least three special ways. These are as follows:

- **Cognitive intelligence**—The capacity to process great deals of information accurately. Effective leaders don't have to be geniuses, but they do have to be smart enough to understand the big picture and to carry out the many tasks they perform.

- **Emotional intelligence**—The capacity to be sensitive to one's own emotions and the emotional states of others (recall the discussion of this concept in Chapter 4).
- **Cultural intelligence**—Knowledge of the cultural norms of the countries in which a company conducts business.[15] This is more important than ever in today's global economy, which is why the largest organizations actively train key personnel in the cultural nuances of the nations in which they operate (recall the discussion of cross-cultural training on pp. 87–88).[16]

Transformational Leaders: Special People Who Make Things Happen

For a moment, think about two of the greatest leaders throughout history, the Reverend Dr. Martin Luther King, Jr. and U.S. President John F. Kennedy. Despite their different roles in history, these individuals had something important in common: both articulated clear visions about changing society, and they brought these visions to reality. Rev. King's famous "I have a dream" speech inspired people to adopt the civil rights movement, and President Kennedy's shared vision of "landing a man on the moon and returning him safely to earth" before 1970 inspired the "space race" of the 1960s. Such individuals—that is, people who do things that make monumental changes in society or in organizations—are known as **transformational leaders**.[17] Simply put, they transform the worlds in which they operate.

Exactly what is it that makes a leader transformational? Their key characteristics are as follows:

- *Charisma*—Transformational leaders have a mission and inspire others to follow them, often in a highly emotional manner (recall this concept from p. 338).
- *Self-confidence*—They are highly confident in their ability and judgment, and others readily become aware of this.
- *Vision*—Transformational leaders have ideas about how to improve the status quo and do what it takes to change things for the better, even if it means making personal sacrifices.
- *Environmental sensitivity*—These leaders are highly realistic about the constraints imposed on them and the resources needed to effect change. They know what they can and cannot do.
- *Intellectual stimulation*—Transformational leaders help followers recognize problems and identify ways of solving them.
- *Interpersonal consideration*—These leaders give followers the support, encouragement, and attention they need to perform their jobs well.
- *Inspiration*—They clearly communicate the importance of the company's mission and rely on symbols (e.g., pins and slogans) to help focus their efforts.
- *Morality*—Transformational leaders tend to make decisions in a manner showing advanced levels of moral reasoning (recall this concept from Chapter 2).[18]

In the world of business, Jack Welch, the former CEO of General Electric (GE), is a classic example of a transformational leader in the corporate world.[19] Under Welch's leadership, GE underwent a series of major changes with respect to the way it does business.[20] At the individual level, GE abandoned its highly bureaucratic ways and now does a good job of listening to its employees. Not surprisingly, GE has consistently ranked among the most admired companies in its industry in *Fortune* magazine's annual survey of corporate reputations (including a number-one ranking for several years!). In the 1980s, Welch bought and sold many businesses for GE, using as his guideline that GE would only keep a company if it placed either number one or number two in market share. If this meant closing plants, selling assets, and laying off personnel, he did it, earning him the nickname "Neutron Jack." Did Welch transform and revitalize GE? Having added well over $100 billion to the company's coffers, making it the most valuable company in the United States at the time, there can be no doubt about it.[21]

Research paints a clear picture of the effectiveness of transformational leadership.[22] For example, managers at FedEx who are rated by their subordinates as being highly transformational tend to be better performers and are recognized by their superiors as being highly promotable.[23] Consider also a study of platoon leaders in the U.S. Army, which revealed that the more strongly leaders demonstrated transformational characteristics, the more successfully their platoons performed.[24] This same research also offered insight into why this occurred. Specifically, the soldiers' perceptions of the degree of cohesiveness in their platoons were a key factor (recall the discussion of group cohesiveness in Chapter 9). The more platoon leaders were recognized as being transformational, the more cohesive were their platoons, and this, in turn, was a key determinant of how well those platoons performed. Thus, cohesiveness is a partial explanation for the successful impact of transformational leaders.

Another factor that makes transformational leaders potentially successful is that their behavior stands to have beneficial effects on others. Transformational leaders generate excitement by inspiring followers to work hard and to think beyond themselves. They also share visions that stand to benefit others in their organizations. Recent research shows that a key factor in the success of transformational leaders is their contact with individuals who benefit from their actions, even if these beneficiaries are from other departments in the organization.[25] The transformational leaders in this situation become successful because the beneficiaries help bring the leader's vision to life for the followers. In other words, they illustrate the leader's positive impact in the eyes of followers, thereby demonstrating to followers that the leader is doing a good job (for a summary of this process, see Figure 11.2).

As you read this, you may be wondering how to become a transformational leader. Although it surely isn't easy and there are no simple formulas to follow, the suggestions offered in Table 11.3 may be considered useful places to begin your quest.[26]

LEADERSHIP BEHAVIOR: WHAT DO LEADERS DO?

Thus far, I have focused on the qualities that leaders possess—that is, *who leaders are*. Additional insight into leadership can be derived from looking at leadership behavior—that is, by examining *what leaders do*. What exactly are these things? What do leaders do that makes them effective as leaders? I now describe several answers to this question.

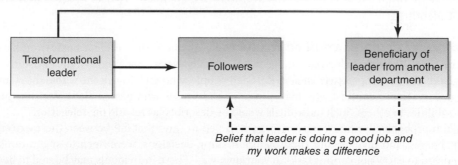

FIGURE 11.2   Transformational Leadership: The Important Role of Beneficiaries
Recent research has revealed that a key reason for the effectiveness of transformational leaders has to do with their contact with the beneficiaries of their actions. The underlying process is summarized here.
Source: Based on suggestions by Grant, 2012; see Note 25.

TABLE 11.3	Suggestions for Becoming a Transformational Leader

Becoming a transformational leader is not easy, but following the recommendations outlined here may help leaders change and revitalize their organizations.

Suggestion	Explanation
Develop a vision that is both clear and highly appealing to followers.	A clear vision will guide followers toward achieving organizational goals and make them feel good about doing so.
Articulate a strategy for bringing your vision to life.	Don't present an elaborate plan; rather, state the best path toward achieving the mission.
State your vision clearly and promote it to others.	Visions should not only be clear but also compelling, such as by using anecdotes.
Show confidence and optimism about your vision.	If a leader lacks confidence about success, followers will not try very hard to achieve that vision.
Express confidence in followers' capacities to carry out the strategy.	Followers must believe that they are capable of implementing a leader's vision and leaders should build subordinates' self-confidence.
Build confidence by recognizing small accomplishments toward the goal.	If a group experiences early success, it will be motivated to continue working hard.
Celebrate successes and accomplishments.	Formal or informal ceremonies are useful for celebrating success, thereby building optimism and commitment.
Take dramatic action to symbolize key organizational values.	Visions are reinforced by things leaders do to symbolize them. For example, one leader demonstrated concern for quality by destroying work that was not up to standards.
Set an example; actions speak louder than words.	Leaders serve as role models. If they want followers to make sacrifices, for example, they should do so themselves.

Sources: Based on suggestions by Yukl, 2012; see Note 1; Bass & Riggio, 2008; see Note 26.

Participative Versus Autocratic Leadership Behaviors

When it comes to describing the behavior of leaders, a key variable involves how much influence they allow subordinates to have over the decisions that are made. Two approaches to doing this may be identified.

THE AUTOCRATIC–DELEGATION CONTINUUM Think about the different bosses you have had over the years. Some probably wanted to control virtually everything, made all the decisions themselves, and told people precisely what to do. Such people, who seek to run the whole show, are said to be **autocratic**. In contrast, you may also have had bosses who passed along decision-making responsibilities to others. Such individuals would be described as relying on **delegation**.

You probably also know supervisors who acted in ways that fall between these extremes— that is, bosses who invited your input before making decisions, were open to suggestions, and allowed you to carry out various tasks in your own way. These individuals may be said to be using a **participative leadership style**.[27] More precisely, they may be *consulting* with you or involving you in a *joint decision* of some sort. In either case, you were more involved than you would have been in the case of an autocratic leader but less involved than with a leader who delegated all responsibility to you. (For a summary of the autocratic–delegation continuum, see Figure 11.3.)

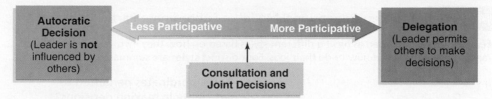

FIGURE 11.3 The Autocratic–Delegation Continuum
Traditionally, the amount of influence leaders give followers has been summarized as a continuum ranging from autocratic behavior (no influence) to delegation behavior (high influence). Consultation and joint decisions are intermediate forms of participation in decision making.
Source: Based on suggestions by Yukl, 2012; see Note 1.

Although the autocratic–delegation continuum does a reasonable job of describing the role of the leader in organizational decision making, it is regarded as being overly simplistic. In fact, upon more carefully studying the way leaders make decisions, researchers have observed that describing a leader's participation in decision making involves two separate dimensions.[28] I now describe these.

THE TWO-DIMENSIONAL MODEL OF SUBORDINATE PARTICIPATION Acknowledging the need for a more sophisticated approach, scientists have proposed the **two-dimensional model of subordinate participation**. As the name implies, this conceptualization describes subordinates' participation in decisions in terms of two dimensions.

- The *autocratic–democratic dimension* characterizes the extent to which leaders permit subordinates to take part in decisions. The autocratic extreme is marked by no participation; the democratic extreme is marked by high participation.
- The *permissive–directive dimension* reflects the extent to which leaders direct the activities of subordinates and tell them how to carry out their jobs. The permissive extreme is marked by not telling subordinates how to do their jobs; the directive extreme is marked by telling subordinates precisely how to do their jobs.

Combining these two dimensions yields the four possible leadership styles identified in Table 11.4. Of these, does any one have a clear-cut edge over the others? Is one pattern superior in most situations? Existing evidence suggests that this is doubtful. All four styles involve a mixed pattern of advantages and disadvantages. Moreover—and this is the crucial point—the relative success of each depends heavily on conditions existing within a given organization.

To illustrate this point, consider a manager who is a *directive autocrat*. Such a person makes decisions without consulting subordinates and supervises their work activities very closely. Not surprisingly, such individuals are not very popular. However, there are conditions under which they are well suited to leading, such as when employees are inexperienced or underqualified for their jobs, or when subordinates adopt an adversarial stance toward management and must be closely supervised.

In contrast, consider the *permissive autocrat*—a leader who combines permissive supervision with an autocratic style of making decisions. This pattern may be useful in dealing with employees who have high levels of technical skill and who want to be left alone to manage their own jobs (e.g., scientists, engineers, computer programmers), but who have little desire to participate in routine decision making.

The remaining two patterns (*directive democrat* and *permissive democrat*) also are well suited to specific organizational conditions. The key task for leaders, then, is to match their own style to the needs of their organization and to change as these needs shift and evolve.

| TABLE 11.4 | The Two-Dimensional Model of Subordinate Participation |

Leaders can be described as having different styles based on how they involve subordinates in making decisions about how to do their jobs. Four distinct styles are summarized here.

Are subordinates told exactly how to do their jobs?	Are subordinates permitted to participate in making decisions?	
	Yes *(Democratic)*	No *(Autocratic)*
Yes *(directive)*	**Directive Democrat** *(makes decisions participatively; closely supervises subordinates)*	**Directive Autocrat** *(makes decisions unilaterally; closely supervises subordinates)*
No *(permissive)*	**Permissive Democrat** *(makes decisions participatively; gives subordinates latitude in carrying out their work)*	**Permissive Autocrat** *(makes decisions unilaterally; gives subordinates latitude in carrying out their work)*

Source: Based on suggestions by Muczyk & Reimann, 1987; see Note 28.

What happens when leaders lack such flexibility? Events in one now-defunct and short-lived company—People Express Airlines—are instructive.[29] Don Burr, the founder and CEO, had a very clear managerial style: He was a highly permissive democrat. He involved employees in many aspects of company decision making and emphasized autonomy in work activities. Indeed, he felt that everyone at People Express should be viewed as a "manager."

This style worked well while the company was young, but as it grew and increased in complexity, such practices created mounting difficulties. New employees were not necessarily as committed as older ones, so permissive supervision didn't work well with them. And as decisions increased in both complexity and number, a participative approach became less effective. Unfortunately, top management was reluctant to alter its style; after all, it seemed to have been instrumental in the company's early success. This poor match between the style of top leaders and changing conditions seems to have contributed (along with many other factors, of course) to People Express's ultimate demise.

To conclude, no single leadership style is best under all conditions or in every situation. Specific ideas regarding the most appropriate style for a given situation are described in the discussion of so-called *contingency theories of leader effectiveness*, beginning on page 351.

Person-Oriented Versus Production-Oriented Leaders

Think about all the leaders you've known in your career. Now divide them into two categories—those who were relatively effective and those who were ineffective. How do the two groups differ?

If you think about this carefully, your answers are likely to take one of two forms. First, you might reply, "My most effective bosses helped me get the job done. They gave me advice, answered my questions, and let me know exactly what was expected of me. My most ineffective bosses didn't do this." Second, you might answer, "My most effective bosses seemed to care about me as a person. They were friendly, listened to me when I had problems or questions, and seemed to help me toward my personal goals. My ineffective bosses didn't do this." These observations reflect two important dimensions.

INITIATING STRUCTURE   A large body of research suggests that leaders do, in fact, differ greatly along these two dimensions.[30] Those at the high end of the first dimension, known as **initiating structure** (or **production centered**), focus mainly on production and on getting the job done. They engage in actions such as organizing work, inducing subordinates to follow rules, setting goals, and making leader and subordinate roles explicit. In contrast, leaders at the lower end of this dimension show less of a tendency to engage in these actions.

CONSIDERATION   Leaders at the high end of the second dimension, known as **consideration** (or **person centered**), are concerned primarily with establishing good relations with their subordinates and being liked by them. They engage in actions such as doing favors for subordinates, explaining things to them, and ensuring their welfare. In contrast, leaders at the low end of this dimension don't care much about how they get along with subordinates.

WHAT WORKS BEST?   At first glance, you might assume that initiating structure and consideration are linked so that people at the high end of one of these dimensions are automatically at the low end of the other. However, this is not the case. The two dimensions are largely independent.[31] Thus, a leader may have a high degree of concern for production and concern for people, a low degree of both dimensions, a high degree of one dimension and a low degree of the other, moderate degrees of each, and so on (see Figure 11.4).

Is any one of these possible patterns better than the others? Systematic research suggests that the answer is yes. Specifically, the best results occur when leaders demonstrate high degrees of concern with both people and production.[32] Indeed, high amounts of concern with people (showing consideration) *and* concern with productivity (initiating structure) are not incompatible. Rather, skillful leaders combine both of these orientations into their overall styles to produce favorable results. Thus, although no one leadership style is best, leaders who combine these two concerns may often have an important edge over leaders who show only one or

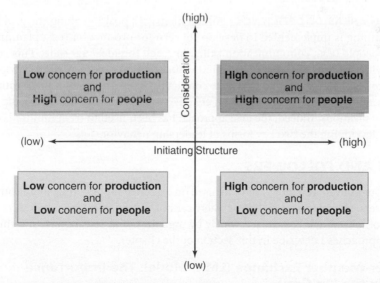

FIGURE 11.4   **Two Key Dimensions of Leader Behavior**
Leaders' behavior can vary from low to high with respect to *consideration* (person orientation) and *initiating structure* (task orientation). Patterns of leader behavior produced by variations along these two dimensions are illustrated here.

the other. This idea was expressed nicely by a former U.S. army general and a business executive when he said:

> To lead successfully, a person must demonstrate . . . expertise and empathy. In my experience, both of these traits can be deliberately and systematically cultivated; this personal development is the first important building block of leadership.[33]

Developing Successful Leader Behavior: Grid Training

How can one go about developing these two forms of leadership behavior—demonstrating concern for production and concern for people? A technique known as **grid training** uses a process designed to cultivate these two important skills.[34] Its major steps involve assessment followed up with training.

ASSESSMENT IN A GRID SEMINAR   The initial step consists of a *grid seminar*—a session in which an organization's managers (who have previously been trained in the appropriate theory and skills) help organization members analyze their own management styles. This is done using a specially designed questionnaire that allows managers to determine how they stand with respect to their *concern for production* and their *concern for people*. Each participant's approach on each dimension is scored using a number ranging from 1 (low) to 9 (high).

Managers who score low on both concern for production and concern for people are scored 1,1—evidence of what is called *impoverished management.* A manager who is highly concerned about production but shows little interest in people, scores 9,1 and is said to have a *task management* style. In contrast, those who show the opposite pattern—high concern with people but little concern for production—are described as having a *country club* style of management; they score 1,9. Those who score moderately on both dimensions, with a 5,5, are said to follow a *middle-of-the-road* management style. Finally, there are individuals who are highly concerned with both production and people. They score 9,9. This is the most desirable pattern, representing what is known as *team management.* These various patterns are known as the *managerial grid*® and are illustrated in Figure 11.5.

DEVELOPING AREAS OF DEFICIENCY   After a manager's position along the grid has been determined, training is implemented to develop concern for production (e.g., planning skills) and concern for people (e.g., communication skills) to reach the ideal 9,9 state. This consists of organization-wide sessions aimed at helping individuals interact more effectively with each other. Then these concepts are expanded to reduce conflict between groups that work with each other.

Grid training is widely considered an effective way to improve the leadership behaviors of people in organizations. Indeed, the grid approach has been used to train hundreds of thousands of people in developing the two key forms of leadership behavior.

LEADERS AND FOLLOWERS

Thus far throughout this chapter, I have focused on leaders but paid only passing attention to the role of followers. However, in a real sense, there cannot be leaders without followers. As such, the importance of followers is recognized widely by organizational researchers, and this is apparent in the two approaches I describe in this section of the chapter.

The Leader–Member Exchange (LMX) Model: The Importance of Being in the "In-Group"

Informal observation suggests that leaders do not treat all their subordinates in the same manner. Some followers are favored more than others. This important fact lies at the heart of the **leader–member exchange (LMX) model.**[35]

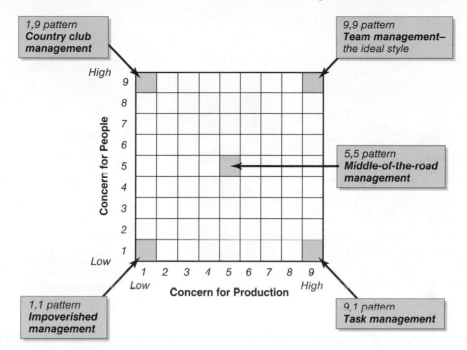

FIGURE 11.5 The Managerial Grid®
A manager's standing along two basic dimensions, concern for production and for people, can be illustrated by means of a diagram such as this, known as the *managerial grid.*® In *grid training*, people learn to be effective leaders by demonstrating high amounts of both dimensions.
Source: Based on suggestions by Blake & Mouton, 1969; see Note 34.

This conceptualization suggests that for various reasons, leaders form different kinds of relationships with various groups of subordinates. One group, referred to as the *in-group*, is favored by the leader. Members of in-groups receive considerably more attention from the leader and larger shares of the resources they have to offer (such as time and recognition). By contrast, other subordinates fall into the *out-group*. These individuals are disfavored by leaders. As such, they receive fewer valued resources from their leaders.

Leaders distinguish between in-group and out-group members very early in their relationships with followers—and on the basis of surprisingly little information. Sometimes, perceived similarity with respect to personal characteristics such as age, gender, or personality is sufficient to categorize followers into a leader's in-group.[36] Similarly, a particular follower may be granted in-group status if the leader believes that person to be especially competent at performing his or her job.[37]

Research has supported the idea that leaders favor members of their in-groups. For example, one study found that supervisors inflated the ratings they gave poorly performing employees when these individuals were members of the in-group, but not when they were members of the out-group.[38] Given the favoritism shown toward in-group members, it follows that such individuals would perform their jobs better and would hold more positive attitudes toward their jobs than members of out-groups.

In general, research supports this prediction. For example, it has been found that in-group members are more satisfied with their jobs and more effective in performing them than out-group members.[39] In-group members are also less likely to resign from their jobs than out-group members.[40] And, as you might imagine, members of in-groups tend to receive more mentoring from their superiors than do members of out-groups, helping them become more successful in their careers (for a summary, see Figure 11.6).[41]

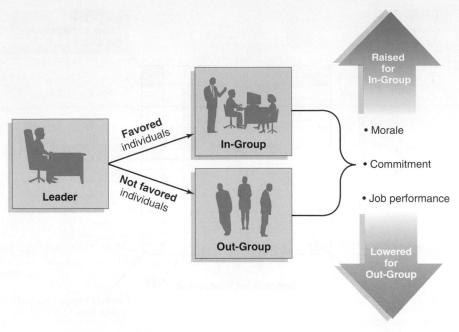

FIGURE 11.6 The LMX Model: A Summary
According to the *leader–member exchange* (*LMX*) *model,* leaders distinguish between groups they favor (in-groups) and those they do not (out-groups). Members of in-groups generally enjoy higher levels of morale, commitment, and job performance than members of out-groups.

Together, these studies provide good support for the LMX model. Such findings suggest that paying attention to the relations between leaders and their followers can be very useful. The nature of such relationships can strongly affect the morale, commitment, and performance of employees. Helping leaders improve such relations, such as through training, therefore, can be extremely valuable in these key respects.

The Challenge of Leading Work Teams

Traditionally, leaders make strategic decisions on behalf of followers, who are responsible for carrying them out. In many of today's organizations, however, where *teams* are used (see Chapter 9), leaders play a somewhat different role. For the most part, they are called upon to provide special resources to team members, who are empowered to implement their own missions in their own ways. Instead of "calling the shots," team leaders help subordinates take responsibility for their own work. As such, they are quite different from the traditional "command and control" leadership role I have been discussing.[42] Table 11.5 summarizes the key differences.

When most people think of leaders, they tend to think of individuals who make strategic decisions on behalf of followers who are responsible for carrying them out. In many of today's organizations, however, where the movement toward *self-managed teams* predominates, it is less likely than ever that leaders are responsible for getting others to implement their orders to help fulfill their visions. Instead, team leaders may be called upon to provide special resources to groups empowered to implement their own missions in their own ways. They don't call all the shots, but help subordinates take responsibility for their own work.

In this sense, instead of thinking of subordinates as existing to serve leaders, this thinking works the other way around—that is, leaders exist to serve the needs of team members. Such an orientation is known as **servant leadership**. A servant leader is an individual who focuses on the

TABLE 11.5	Leading Groups Versus Leading Teams

The popularity of teams in today's organizations has important implications for how leaders go about fulfilling their roles. Some of the key differences between leading traditional work groups and leading teams are summarized here.

In traditional work groups, leaders . . .	But in teams, leaders . . .
Tell people what to do.	Ask people what they think and share responsibility for organizing and doing the work.
Take all the credit.	Share the limelight with all their teammates.
Focus on training employees.	Concentrate on expanding their team's capabilities by functioning primarily as coaches who build confidence in team members, cultivating their untapped potential.
Relate to others individually.	Create a team identity by helping it set and meet goals, and celebrating when met.
Work at reducing conflict between individuals.	Make the most of team differences by building respect for diverse points of view and ensuring that all team members' views are expressed.
React to change.	Foresee changes, better preparing the organization to make appropriate adaptations.

needs of his or her team members and considers how to help solve their problems and to promote their personal development.[43]

Because leading teams differs from the traditional approach to leadership in hierarchical organizations, many leaders are ill-prepared to assume this role.[44] To help meet this challenge, here are a few guidelines that may be followed to achieve success as a team leader.

- Instead of directing people, *team leaders work at building trust and inspiring teamwork.* One way this can be done is by encouraging interaction among all members of the team as well as between the team and its customers and suppliers.
- Rather than focusing simply on training individuals, effective *team leaders concentrate on expanding team capabilities.* In this connection, team leaders function primarily as *coaches*, helping the team by providing all members with the skills needed to perform the task, removing barriers that might interfere with success, and finding the necessary resources required to get the job done.
- Instead of managing one-on-one, *team leaders attempt to create a team identity.* In other words, leaders must help teams understand their missions and recognize what they're doing to help fulfill them.
- Although traditional leaders work at preventing conflict between individuals, *team leaders are encouraged to make the most of differences between members.* This can be done by (a) building respect for diverse points of view, (b) making sure that all team members are encouraged to present their views, and (c) respecting these ideas once they are expressed.
- Unlike traditional leaders who simply react to change, team leaders try to *foresee and influence change.* To the extent that leaders recognize that change is inevitable (a point I will emphasize in Chapter 14), they may be better prepared to make the various adaptations required.

In conclusion, leading teams is a far cry from leading individuals in the traditional directive (or even participative) manner. The special nature of teams makes the leader's job very different. Although appreciating these differences is easy, making the appropriate adjustments may be extremely challenging—especially for individuals who are well practiced in the ways of traditional, hierarchical leadership. However, given the prevalence of teams in today's work environment, the importance of making the adjustments cannot be overstated. Leading new teams using old methods is a surefire formula for failure. (The use of teams is one of the hallmarks of leadership in today's digital era. To understand how the nature of leadership has been changing in companies that have adapted successfully to the dominance of information technology, see the Winning Practices section below.)

Winning Practices

Challenges of Leading in a Digital World

As you might imagine, today's Internet-driven economy creates new realities that present challenges for contemporary leaders. Some of the most formidable ones are as follows:[45]

- *Growth occurs so quickly that strategies have to be changed constantly.* For example, at eBay, growth has been so dramatic over the years (sometimes 40 to 50 percent each quarter!) that it became an entirely different company every few months.[46] Leaders couldn't think of taking anything for granted, except the fact that whatever they decided to do yesterday may need to be changed tomorrow.

- *Leaders of Internet companies are not expected to have all the answers.* The highly technical nature of business and the rapid pace of change make it impossible for just one or two people to make all the right decisions. As one executive of an e-commerce business put it, today's leaders "must be evangelists for changing the system, not preserving it."[47]

- *Showing restraint is critical.* There are so many opportunities available to Internet companies today that executives can too easily enter into bad deals. Andrew Jarecki, cofounder and CEO of Moviefone, Inc., seemed to be aware of this when he ignored the many offers to buy the company that came along until 1999, when AOL approached with a $400 million deal. The restraint he showed by not accepting earlier offers proved beneficial.

- *Hiring and retaining the right people is more important than ever.* In the world of the Internet, the average tenure of a senior executive is only eighteen months. Constant change means that the people who are hired for today's jobs must meet the demands of tomorrow's jobs as well. As Jay Walker, founder and vice chairman of Priceline.com, put it, "You've got to hire ahead of the curve," adding, "If you wait until you're actually doing [as much business as you expect] to hire the necessary talent, then you'll be too late."[48]

- *Today's leaders must not take anything for granted.* When Mark Cuban and his partner founded Broadcast.com (before selling it to Yahoo! four years later for $5.7 billion), they made lots of incorrect decisions. Instead of sticking by them, they quickly adjusted their game plan to fit the realities they faced.

- *Internet leaders must focus on real-time decision making.* Leaders have traditionally been trained to gather lots of data before making carefully researched decisions. According to Ruthann Quindlen, partner in Institutional Venture Partners, leaders can no longer afford to do so: "If your instinct is to wait, ponder, and perfect, then you're dead.... Leaders have to hit the undo key without flinching."[49]

As outlined here, many of the traditional ways of leading need to be adjusted to accommodate today's Internet economy. However, this does not require that we rewrite all the rules of good leadership. Showing concern for people and concern for production, for example, have not gone out of style! In fact, to successfully accommodate the fast-paced, modern era, they may be more important than ever.

CONTINGENCY THEORIES OF LEADER EFFECTIVENESS

By this point in the chapter, it should be apparent that there is no one best approach to leadership. Instead, different leadership styles may contribute to the effective functioning of organizations under certain conditions. Recognition of this basic point lies behind approaches to leadership referred to as **contingency theories of leader effectiveness**. I now examine two such theories.[50]

LPC Contingency Theory: Matching Leaders and Tasks

Earlier, I explained that the behaviors associated with effective leadership fall into two major categories—concern for people and concern for production. Both types of behavior contribute to a leader's success. However, a more refined look at this issue leads us to ask exactly *when* each type of behavior works best. That is, under what conditions are leaders more successful when they demonstrate a concern for people compared to a concern for production?

THE BASICS OF THE THEORY   This question is addressed by a widely studied approach to leadership known as **LPC contingency theory**. The underlying assumption of this conceptualization is that a leader's contribution to the successful performance of his or her group is determined both by the leader's own traits together with various features of the situation. Different levels of leader effectiveness occur under different combinations of conditions. To fully understand leader effectiveness, both types of factors must be considered.

According to the theory, a variable known as **LPC** (short for liking for least preferred coworker) is the most important personal characteristic. This refers to a leader's tendency to evaluate in a favorable or unfavorable manner the person with whom she or he has found it most difficult to work. Leaders who perceive this person in negative terms (low LPC leaders) are concerned primarily with attaining successful task performance. In contrast, those who perceive their least preferred coworker in a positive light (high LPC leaders) are mainly concerned with establishing good relations with subordinates. A questionnaire is used to measure one's LPC score. It is important to note that the theory views LPC as being fixed—that is, an aspect of an individual's leadership style that cannot be changed. As I will explain, this has important implications for applying the theory so as to improve leader effectiveness.

Which type of leader—one low in LPC or one high in LPC— is more effective? As suggested by the word *contingency*, the answer is: "It depends." And what it depends upon is the degree to which the situation is favorable to the leader—that is, how much it allows the leaders to have control over their subordinates. This, in turn, is determined largely by three factors:

- The nature of the *leader's relations with group members*—the extent to which he or she enjoys their support and loyalty
- The *degree of structure* in the task being performed—the extent to which task goals and subordinates' roles are clearly defined
- The leader's *position power*—as described on pages 336–337, this refers to his or her formal capacity to enforce compliance by subordinates

Combining these three factors, the leader's situational control can range from very high (positive relations with group members, a highly structured task, and high position power) to very low (negative relations, an unstructured task, and low position power).

What types of leaders are most effective under these various conditions? According to the theory, low LPC leaders (ones who are task oriented) are superior to high LPC leaders (ones who are relations oriented) when situational control is either very low or very high. In contrast, high LPC leaders have an edge when situational control falls within the moderate range (refer to Figure 11.7).

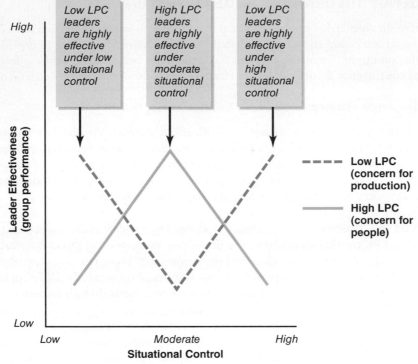

FIGURE 11.7 **LPC Contingency Theory: An Overview**
LPC contingency theory predicts that low LPC leaders (ones who are primarily task oriented) will be more effective than high LPC leaders (ones who are primarily people oriented) when situational control is either very low or very high. However, the opposite is true when situational control is moderate.

The rationale for these predictions is as follows: Under conditions of low situational control, groups need considerable guidance to accomplish their tasks. Without such direction, nothing would get done. For example, imagine a military combat group led by an unpopular platoon leader under battle conditions in which things are falling apart and the troops are thinking of mutinying. Any chance of effectiveness this person has would result from paying careful attention to the task at hand, rather than hoping to establish better relations with the group. Since low LPC leaders are more likely to provide structure than high LPC leaders, they are expected to be more effective under such conditions.

Similarly, low LPC leaders are also superior under conditions that offer them a high degree of situational control. Indeed, when leaders are liked, their power is not challenged. When the demands of the task make it clear what leaders should be doing, it is perfectly acceptable for them to focus on the job at hand. Subordinates expect their leaders to exercise control under such conditions and accept it when they do so, and this leads to task success. For example, an airline pilot leading a cockpit crew is expected to take charge and not to seek the consensus of others as she guides the plane onto the runway for a landing. Surely, she would be less effective if she didn't take charge but instead asked the co-pilot what he thought she should do. In other words, this is not the proper occasion to consult with others and take their opinions into account but instead to tell them what to do.

Things are different, however, between these two extremes—that is, when circumstances offer leaders moderate situational control. Consider, for example, a condition in which a leader's relations with subordinates are good, but the task is unstructured and the leader's power is somewhat restricted. This describes what might be found within a research and development team attempting to find creative new uses for a company's products. Here, it clearly would be inappropriate for a low LPC leader to tell people what to do. Rather, a highly nurturing leader who is considerate of the feelings of others would likely be most effective—that is, a high LPC leader.

It is important to note that a considerable amount of research supports LPC contingency theory. That is, the performance of work groups does, in fact, tend to be highest under the conditions specified by the theory: (1) when low LPC leaders work under especially favorable and unfavorable conditions, and (2) when high LPC leaders work under moderately favorable conditions.

APPLYING LPC CONTINGENCY THEORY Practitioners have found LPC contingency theory to be quite useful when it comes to suggesting ways of enhancing leader effectiveness. Because the theory assumes that certain kinds of leaders perform best under certain kinds of situations, and that leadership style is fixed, the best way to enhance effectiveness is to fit the right kind of leaders to the situations they face.

Doing this involves completing questionnaires that can be used to assess both the LPC score of the leader and the amount of control he or she faces on the job. Then, using these indexes, a match can be made such that leaders are put into situations that best suit their leadership styles—a technique known as **leader match**. For example, a high LPC leader may be moved to a job in which situational control is either extremely high or extremely low.

Sometimes, however, it is impractical to reassign leaders within an organization. Under such conditions, it is recommended to focus on changing the situational control variables—leader–member relations, task structure, and leader position power. For example, this may point to attempting to improve relations between leaders and group members. It also may suggest the need to raise or lower the degree to which leaders have formal control over their subordinates.

Several companies—most notably, Sears—have used the leader match approach with some success. In fact, several studies have found it to be effective in improving group performance on at least some occasions.

Situational Leadership Theory: Adapting Leadership Style to the Situation

Another conceptualization, **situational leadership theory**, also is considered a contingency theory because it focuses on the best leadership style for a given situation. Specifically, the scientists who developed this theory argue that leaders are effective when they select the right leadership style for the conditions they face.[51] This depends on the *maturity* of followers—that is, their readiness to take responsibility for their own behavior. This, in turn, is based on two important variables with which you already are familiar (although they were described earlier using different terminology):

- *Task behavior*—the degree to which followers have the appropriate job knowledge and skills (i.e., the degree to which they require guidance and direction)
- *Relationship behavior*—the degree to which followers are willing to work without taking direction from others (i.e., their need for emotional support)

By combining high and low levels of these independent dimensions, four different situations are identified, each of which is associated with the particular leadership style that is most effective in that situation. These are as follows:

- *Telling*—Situations in which followers need a great deal of direction from their leaders but don't need much emotional support from them. The practice of *telling* followers what to do is most useful in such circumstances. That is, giving followers specific instructions and closely supervising their work may be the best approach.

- *Selling*—Followers still lack the skill to be able to succeed, although in this case, they require more emotional support. Under these conditions, *selling* works best. Being very directive may make up for the follower's lack of ability, while being very supportive will help get them go along with what the leader is asking of them.
- *Participating*—Followers need very little guidance in performing their jobs, but require considerable emotional hand-holding and support to motivate them. That is, low levels of task behavior, but high levels of relationship (supportive) behavior are required. A *participating* style of leadership works well in such situations because it allows followers to share their expertise while enhancing their desire to perform.
- *Delegating*—Followers are both willing and able to do what is asked of them. In other words, low levels of task behavior and low levels of relationship behavior are required. Under such conditions, *delegating* is the best way to treat followers—that is, turning over to them the responsibility for making and implementing their own decisions.

According to situational leadership theory, leaders must be able (1) to diagnose the situations they face, (2) to identify the appropriate behavioral style, and then (3) to implement that response. Because the situations leaders face may change all the time, they must constantly reassess them, paying special attention to followers' needs for guidance and emotional support. To the extent that they do so, they are likely to be effective.

Specialized training in these skills has been found to be quite useful. In fact, the approach has been used to train leaders at such corporate giants as Xerox, Mobil Oil, and Caterpillar, as well as in the U.S. military services. (Which style of leadership are you most prone to follow in your own treatment of others? To give you some insight into this question, complete the Self-Assessment Exercise on p. 359.)

LEADERSHIP DEVELOPMENT: BRINGING OUT THE LEADER WITHIN YOU

In case it's not clear by now, being an effective leader isn't easy. It helps if you happen to be fortunate enough to be born with "the right stuff." It is also beneficial to find yourself in the kind of situation in which an opportunity exists to demonstrate your capacity as a leader. However, anyone can improve his or her leadership skills, honing his or her capacity to inspire others in an organization. This is the idea behind **leadership development**, the systematic process of training people to expand their capacity to function effectively in leadership roles.

All leadership development programs are based on two key assumptions: (1) that leadership makes a difference in an organization's performance, and (2) that it is possible for leaders to be developed (i.e., made, if not born).[52] However, the various leadership development tools go about the mission of promoting leaders' skills in different ways. I now identify some of the most widely used techniques.[53]

360-Degree Feedback

In Chapter 3, I described **360-degree feedback**, the process of using multiple sources from inside and outside an organization to evaluate the work of an individual. This practice has proven to be an effective way for leaders to learn what key others, such as peers, direct reports, and supervisors, think about them.[54] This is a useful means of identifying aspects of one's leadership style that are in need of change. Its basic assumption is that various people will be able to provide different perspectives on one's leadership.

The practice of collecting 360-degree feedback is extremely popular these days. In fact, nearly all of the *Fortune* 500 companies rely on this technique in one way or another.[55] However, collecting feedback and taking appropriate action based on it are two entirely different things. After all, many people are threatened by negative feedback and defend against it psychologically by dismissing it as invalid. Even those who agree with it might not be willing to change their behavior (a topic I will revisit in Chapter 14). Furthermore, even the most well-intentioned leaders may fail to take action on the feedback they receive if that information is too complex or inconsistent, which is not too unusual. To help in this regard, many companies have found that leaders who have face-to-face meetings with others in which they get to discuss the feedback they receive are particularly inclined to follow up in an effective manner.

It's not at all unusual for 360-degree feedback to be given within exercises conducted in **assessment centers**.[56] These are sessions (lasting from only a few hours to several days) in which a variety of techniques are used to determine how people behave under various standardized conditions. For example, people in assessment centers often participate in *role-playing exercises*. Typically, the individual being assessed assumes the role of a person in a particular job who is asked to respond to various things being said by a trainer who is playing another role. The way the individual responds can provide insight into what he or she is like. Discussing this insight is part of the assessment.[57] This information can be extremely useful to leaders because it opens the door to gaining valuable insight into their own behavior and how it may be changed so as to make them better leaders.

Networking

Far too often, leaders find themselves isolated from things that are going on in other departments. As a result, when they need help, they don't know where to go to get it. As a leadership development tool, **networking** is designed to break down these barriers. Specifically, it is aimed at helping leaders learn to whom they should turn for information, finding what problem-solving resources are available to them.

Networking is beneficial to leadership development because it promotes peer relationships in work settings. These are valuable because they involve mutual obligations, thereby promoting cooperation. What's more, they tend to be long lasting. In fact, it is not unusual for some peer relationships to span an entire career. Importantly, personal networks tend to be effective because they transcend organizational boundaries, thereby bringing together people from different parts of an organization who otherwise would not normally come into contact with one another.

Executive Coaching

A highly effective method of developing leaders involves custom-tailored, one-on-one learning aimed at improving an individual leader's performance, an approach known as **executive coaching**. This can be either a one-time process aimed at addressing some specific issues, or it can be an ongoing process. In either case, executive coaching typically includes an integrative assessment of a leader's strengths and weaknesses along with a comprehensive plan for improvement. These programs tend to follow the specific steps outlined in Figure 11.8.

In some organizations, being assigned a coach is seen as a remedial measure, a sign of weakness. In such cases, any benefits of coaching may be minimized as leaders fail to get involved in the process out of embarrassment. For this reason, organizations that use coaches are advised to

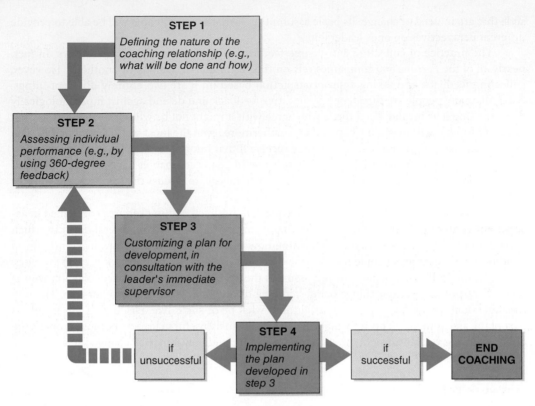

FIGURE 11.8   **Steps in the Executive Coaching Process**
The process of executive coaching generally follows the four steps outlined here.

provide these services to an entire executive group, thereby removing any stigma and putting all leaders on an equal footing. Research has found that this approach is particularly effective when it is used following a formal training program. In fact, the customized, one-on-one coaching provided after a standardized training program was found to increase leaders' productivity by 88 percent.[58]

Mentoring

In Chapter 5, I discussed how minority group members stand to benefit by having relationships with *mentors,* more senior associates who help show them the ropes. Mentors also may be useful when it comes to developing leaders by having experienced leaders—either from inside or outside the organization—help new ones. Although this approach is unlikely to include a formal assessment of a leader's strengths and limitations, it tends to focus on personal and professional support. Research has found that officials from a wide array of organizations consider mentoring one of the most effective forms of leadership development they have in place.[59]

A potential problem with mentoring is that protégés (i.e., the individuals helped by mentors) may become so highly connected to their mentors that they fail to think independently. Soon, what a mentored employee does is just what the mentor would have done. Although this is beneficial, it also can be potentially limiting, leading to a narrowness of thought. This problem is especially likely to occur in the case of executive mentoring because individuals making important decisions may fear straying from the tried-and-true solutions of their mentors. And whenever this occurs, the organization is denied any fresh new perspective that the less seasoned executive might be able to provide.

Job Assignments

When it comes to leadership, the phrase "experience is the best teacher" holds true. Indeed, one of the most effective ways of training leaders is by assigning them to positions that allow them to gain "on the job" experience.

With this in mind, many companies assign personnel to relatively unfamiliar positions in other countries so they can broaden their experiences by developing new areas of familiarity. For example, the Coca-Cola Company recently transferred more than 300 professional and managerial employees from the United States to facilities abroad for one year in an effort to develop leadership skills before returning them home to assume new leadership positions. Procter & Gamble does the same thing on a regular basis, assigning prospective leaders to positions at foreign affiliates for periods of one to three years. In many ways, this is akin to the practice of developing players by sending them to a team's minor league "farm teams" used in Major League Baseball.

For job assignments to serve their developmental function, it is necessary for the newly assigned positions to provide the kind of opportunities that make learning possible. Ideally, these jobs give newly developing leaders opportunities to try out different approaches to leadership so they can determine what works for them. In other words, they should be given the latitude to try different approaches, even if they fail. It is important to keep in mind that the purpose of the job assignment is to facilitate learning, in which case some degree of failure is inevitable (as is the case for all students). However, should an emphasis be placed on job performance instead, it's unlikely that the new assignment will have the intended benefits, and it is destined to be looked upon unfavorably.

Action Learning

Traditionally, much of the learning that takes place when people are taught to lead occurs in the classroom. The problem with this approach, however, is that shortly after the formal training sessions are over, people revert to their old ways when back at their jobs, resulting in little if any developmental progress. To combat this problem, many organizations have been turning to **action learning**, a continuous process of learning and reflection that is supported by colleagues and that emphasizes getting things done.[60] The underlying assumption of action learning is that leaders develop most effectively when they are working on real organizational problems.[61]

Citibank has used action learning to help develop its leaders who were having difficulty thinking about problems from a broad perspective.[62] Specifically, they took the following steps.

1. The issues to be worked on were selected by heads of business units. These had to be ones that affected total Citibank performance.
2. Participants were selected from throughout the world based on a thorough review of their talents.
3. A three-day orientation session was held off-site in which team-building skills were practiced (these are discussed in Chapter 9).
4. For two to three weeks, data were collected about effective banking practices from both inside and outside Citibank.
5. These findings were analyzed systematically and recommendations were developed.
6. Findings were presented to area heads and the CEO in 90-minute meetings.
7. A one-day debriefing session was held with a coach. These focused on the recommendations, team processes, and individual development opportunities.
8. One to two weeks later, senior managers followed up and made decisions regarding the various recommendations.

Although the business imperatives that drive action learning differ from case to case, the general process used tends to follow the steps outlined here. Action learning has been used not only at Citibank, but also at such organizations as General Electric (to develop new markets), ARAMARK (to promote cross-cultural opportunities), Shell Oil (to alter perceptions of the company's financial strength), and the U.S. Army (to share lessons from battlefield experiences).[63] Because action learning is a general idea that takes different forms in various organizations, its effectiveness has been difficult to assess. However, research generally confirms the effectiveness of training leaders by using the kind of active approaches described here instead of more passive, classroom training (see also the discussion of the factors that make training effective in Chapter 3).

The various leadership development techniques I have described in this section of the chapter are useful for developing a variety of characteristics and skills in leaders or potential leaders. These focus on many of the topics considered elsewhere in this book (e.g., communication, motivation, etc.) as well as ones addressed in this chapter (e.g., when it's best to delegate, how to be people centered and production centered, etc.). With this in mind, it's best to conceive of leadership development as an extremely broad endeavor that takes a variety of forms and has several different objectives. Considering the broad nature of leadership behavior, this certainly is understandable.

Back to the Case

Answer the following questions based on this chapter's Making the Case (p. 334) to illustrate insights you have derived from the material in this chapter.

1. Of the various leadership styles described in this chapter, which particular one best seems to describe Ms. Gulvik? On what do you base your opinion?
2. Of the various characteristics or traits of leaders with "the right stuff," does Ms. Gulvik appear to have any? If so, which ones?
3. Does Ms. Gulvik appear to be engaging in any of the various behaviors associated with effective leadership? If so, which ones? How else might she behave so as to enhance her effectiveness as a leader?

You Be the Consultant

A Controlling Leadership Style

The president and founder of a large office furniture manufacturer tells you, "Nobody around here has any respect for me. The only reason they listen to me is because this is my company." Many employees report that he is a highly controlling individual who does not let anyone do anything for themselves.

1. What behaviors should the president attempt to emulate to improve his leadership style? How may he go about doing so?

2. Under what conditions would you expect the president's leadership style to be most effective? Do you think that these conditions might exist in his company?

3. Would your advice be any different if he were in charge of a small Internet start-up firm instead of a large manufacturing company? If so, what different recommendations would you make and why?

Self-Assessment Exercise

DETERMINING YOUR LEADERSHIP STYLE

As noted on pages 353–354, *situational leadership theory* identifies four basic leadership styles. To be able to identify and enact the most appropriate style of leadership in any given situation, it is first useful to understand the style to which you are most strongly predisposed. This exercise will help you gain such insight into your own leadership style.

Directions

Following are eight hypothetical situations in which you have to make a decision that will affect you and members of your work group. For each, indicate which of the following actions you are most likely to take by writing the letter corresponding to that action in the space provided.

- *Action A.*   Let the members of the group decide themselves what to do.
- *Action B.*   Ask the members of the group what to do but make the final decision yourself.
- *Action C.*   Make the decision yourself but explain your reasons.
- *Action D.*   Make the decision yourself, telling the group exactly what to do.

_____ 1. In the face of financial pressures, you are forced to make budget cuts for your unit. Where do you cut?

_____ 2. To meet an impending deadline, someone in your secretarial pool will have to work late one evening to finish typing an important report. Who will it be?

_____ 3. As coach of a company softball team, you are required to trim your squad to twenty-five players from thirty currently on the roster. Who goes?

_____ 4. Employees in your department have to schedule their summer vacations so as to keep the office appropriately staffed. Who decides first?

_____ 5. As chair of the social committee, you are responsible for determining the theme for the company ball. How do you do so?

_____ 6. You have an opportunity to buy or rent an important piece of equipment for your company. After gathering all the facts, how do you make the choice?

_____ 7. The office is being redecorated. How do you decide on the color scheme?

_____ 8. Along with your associates you are taking a visiting dignitary to dinner. How do you decide what restaurant to go to?

Scoring

1. Count the number of situations to which you responded by marking *A*. This is your *delegating* score.
2. Count the number of situations to which you responded by marking *B*. This is your *participating* score.
3. Count the number of situations to which you responded by marking *C*. This is your *selling* score.
4. Count the number of situations to which you responded by marking *D*. This is your *telling* score.

Discussion Questions

1. Based on this exercise, what was your most predominant leadership style? Is this consistent with what you would have predicted in advance?
2. According to situational leadership theory, in what kinds of situations would this style be most appropriate? Have you ever found yourself in such a situation, and if so, how well did you do?
3. Do you think that it would be possible for you to change this style if needed? What challenges would you confront in attempting to do so?

Group Exercise

IDENTIFYING GREAT LEADERS IN ALL WALKS OF LIFE

A useful way to understand the great person theory (as discussed beginning on p. 338) is to identify those individuals who may be considered great leaders and then to consider what it is that makes them so great. This exercise is designed to guide a class in this activity.

Directions

1. Divide the class into four equal-size groups, arranging each in a semicircle.
2. In the open part of the semicircle, one group member—the recorder—should stand at a flip chart, ready to write down the group's responses.
3. The members of each group should identify the ten most effective leaders they can think of—living or dead, real or fictional—in one of the following fields: business, sports, politics/government, or humanitarian endeavors. One group should cover each of these domains. If more than ten names come up, the group should vote on the ten best answers. The recorder should write down the names as they are identified.
4. Examining the list, group members should identify the traits and characteristics that those people have in common that distinguish them from others not on the list. In other words, what is it that makes these people so special? The recorder should write down the answers.
5. One person from each group should be selected to present his or her group's responses to members of the class. This should include both the names of the leaders identified and their special characteristics.

Discussion Questions

1. How did the traits identified in this exercise compare to those described in Table 11.2 (p. 339) as important determinants of leadership? Were they similar or different? Why?
2. To what extent were the traits identified in the various groups different or similar? In other words, were different characteristics associated with leadership success in different walks of life? Or, were the ingredients for leadership success universal?
3. Were some traits identified surprising to you, or were they all what you would have expected?

Notes

MAKING THE CASE NOTES

About Houlihan's. (2012). http://houlihans.com/faq.aspx. Paynter, B. (2010, March). Happy hour. *Fast Company*, p. 24p. Evans, L. (2008, May 9). Houlihan's (2010). A little bio action. *Houlihans.com*. http://houlihans.com/about.aspx. WOMMA WOMM-U: Jen Gulvik presents Houlihan's WOMM case study. *SearchMarketingGurus.com*. http://www.searchmarketinggurus.com/search_marketing_gurus/2008/05/womma-womm-u-je.html.

CHAPTER NOTES

1. Yukl, G. (2012). *Leadership in organizations* (8th ed.). Upper Saddle River, NJ: Prentice Hall. Lord, R. G. (2001). The nature of organizational leadership: Conclusions and implications. In S. J. Zaccaro & R. J. Klimoski (Eds.), *The nature of organizational leadership: Understanding the performance imperatives confronting today's leaders* (pp. 413–436). San Francisco, CA: Jossey-Bass.
2. House, R. J., & Podsakoff, P. M. (1995). Leadership effectiveness: Past perspectives and future directions for research. In J. Greenberg (Ed.), *Organizational behavior: The state of the science* (pp. 45–82). Hillsdale, NJ: Erlbaum.
3. Bennis, W. G. (2009). *On becoming a leader*. New York: Basic Books. Bennis, W. G., & Nanus, B. (1985). *Leaders: The strategies for taking charge*. New York: Harper & Row (quote, p. 4).

4. See Note 1.

5. Bennis, W. G. (2009). *On becoming a leader.* New York: Basic Books.

6. Yukl, G. (2000). Use power effectively. In E. A. Locke (Ed.), *The Blackwell handbook of principles of organizational behavior* (pp. 241–256). Oxford, England: Blackwell.

7. Geier, J. G. (1969). A trait approach to the study of leadership in small groups. *Journal of Communication, 17,* 316–323.

8. Kirkpatrick, S. A., & Locke, E. A. (1991). Leadership: Do traits matter? *Academy of Management Executive, 5,* 48–60 (quote, p. 58).

9. House, R. J., Shane, S. A., & Herold, D. M. (1996). Rumors of the death of dispositional research are vastly exaggerated. *Academy of Management Review, 21,* 203–224.

10. See Note 9.

11. Chan, K-Y., & Drasgow, F. (2001). Toward a theory of individual differences and leadership: Understanding the motivation to lead. *Journal of Applied Psychology, 86,* 481–498.

12. Avolio, B. J., & Gardner, W. L. (2005). Authentic leadership development: Getting to the root of positive forms of leadership. *The Leadership Quarterly, 16,* 315–338. Zaccaro, S. J., Foti, R. J., & Kenny, D. A. (1991). Self-monitoring and trait-based variance in leadership: An investigation of leader flexibility across multiple group situations. *Journal of Applied Psychology, 76,* 308–315.

13. George, B. (2007). *True north: Discovering your authentic leadership.* San Francisco: Jossey-Bass. Gardner, W. L., Avolio, B. J., & Walumbwa, F. O. (2005). *Authentic leadership theory and practice: Origins, effects, and development.* San Diego, CA: Elsevier/JAI.

14. Chemers, M. M. (2001). Efficacy and effectiveness: Integrating models of leadership and intelligence. In R. E. Riggio & S. E. Murphy (Eds.), *Multiple intelligences and leadership* (pp. 139–160). Mahwah, NJ: Erlbaum.

15. Offerman, L. R., & Phan, L. U. (2001). Culturally intelligent leadership for a diverse world. In R. E. Riggio & S. E. Murphy (Eds.), *Multiple intelligences and leadership* (pp. 187–214). Mahwah, NJ: Erlbaum.

16. Stein, N. (2000, October 2). Global most admired companies: Measuring people power. *Fortune,* pp. 273–288.

17. Bass, B. M. (1998). *Transformational leadership: Industry, military, and educational impact.* Mahwah, NJ: Erlbaum.

18. Turner, N., Barling, J., Epitropaki, O., Butcher, V., & Milner, C. (2002). Transformational leadership and moral reasoning. *Journal of Applied Psychology, 87,* 304–311.

19. Colvin, G. (1999, November 22). The ultimate manager. *Fortune,* pp. 185–187. Slater, R. (1999). *Jack Welch and the GE way.* New York: McGraw-Hill.

20. Tichy, N. M. (1993). *Control your destiny or someone else will.* New York: Doubleday Currency.

21. Colvin, C. (2000, December 18). America's best and worst wealth creators. *Fortune,* pp. 207–208, 210, 212, 214, 216.

22. Judge, T. A., & Bono, J. E. (2000). Five-factor model of personality and transformational leadership. *Journal of Applied Psychology, 85,* 751–765.

23. Hater, J. J., & Bass, B. M. (1988). Superiors' evaluations and subordinates' perceptions of transformational and transactional leadership. *Journal of Applied Psychology, 73,* 695–702.

24. Bass, B. M., Avolio, B. J., Jung, D. I., & Berson, Y. (2003). Predicting unit performance by assessing transformational and transactional leadership. *Journal of Applied Psychology, 88,* 207–218.

25. Grant, A. M. (2012). Leading with meaning: Beneficiary contact, prosocial impact, and the performance effects of transformational leadership. *Academy of Management Journal, 55,* 458–476.

26. Bass, B. M., & Riggio, R. E. (2008). *Transformational leadership.* Mahwah, NJ: Erlbaum.

27. Sagie, A., Zaidman, N., Amichai-Hamburger, Y., Te'Eni, D., & Schwartz, D. G. (2002). An empirical assessment of the loose-tight leadership model: Quantitative and qualitative analyses. *Journal of Organizational Behavior, 23,* 303–320.

28. Muczyk, J. P., & Reimann, B. C. (1987). The case for directive leadership. *Academy of Management Review, 12,* 637–647.

29. Chen, C. C., & Meindl, J. R. (1991). The construction of leadership images in the popular press: The case of Donald Burr and People Express. *Administrative Science Quarterly, 36,* 521–551.

30. Likert, R. (1961). *New patterns in management.* New York: McGraw-Hill. Stogdill, R. M. (1963). *Manual for the leader behavior description questionnaire, form XII.* Columbus, OH:

Ohio State University, Bureau of Business Research.

31. Weissenberg, P., & Kavanagh, M. H. (1972). The independence of initiating structure and consideration: A review of the evidence. *Personnel Psychology, 25,* 119–130.

32. See Note 1.

33. Band, W. A. (1994). *Touchstones.* New York: Wiley (quote, p. 247).

34. Blake, R. R., & Mouton, J. J. (1969). *Building a dynamic corporation through grid organizational development.* Reading, MA: Addison-Wesley.

35. Graen, G. B., & Wakabayashi, M. (1994). Cross-cultural leadership-making: Bridging American and Japanese diversity for team advantage. In H. C. Triandis, M. D. Dunnette, & L. M. Hough (Eds.), *Handbook of industrial and organizational psychology* (2nd ed., Vol. 4, pp. 415–466). Palo Alto, CA: Consulting Psychologists Press.

36. Phillips, A. S., & Bedian, A. G. (1994). Leader-follower exchange quality: The role of personal and interpersonal attributes. *Academy of Management Journal, 37,* 990–1001.

37. Dunegan, K. J., Duchon, D., & Uhl-Bien, M. (1992). Examining the link between leader-member exchange and subordinate performance: The role of task analyzability and variety as moderators. *Journal of Management, 18,* 59–76.

38. Duarte, N. T., Goodson, J. R., & Klich, N. R. (1993). How do I like thee? Let me appraise the ways. *Journal of Organizational Behavior, 14,* 239–249.

39. Deluga, R. J., & Perry, J. T. (1991). The relationship of subordinate upward influencing behaviour, satisfaction and perceived superior effectiveness with leader-member exchanges. *Journal of Occupational Psychology, 64,* 239–252.

40. Ferris, G. R. (1985). Role of leadership in the employee withdrawal process: A constructive replication. *Journal of Applied Psychology, 70,* 777–781.

41. Scandura, T. A., & Schriesheim, C. A. (1994). Leader-member exchange and supervisor career mentoring as complementary constructs in leadership research. *Academy of Management Journal, 37,* 1588–1602.

42. Sheard, A. G., & Kakabadse, A. P. (2001). Key roles of the leadership landscape. *Journal of Managerial Psychology, 17,* 129–144.

Zenger, J. H., Musselwhite, E., Hurson, K., & Perrin, C. (1994). *Leading teams: Mastering the new role.* Homewood, IL: Business One Irwin.

43. Baron, T. (2010). *The art of servant leadership: Designing your organization for the sake of others.* Tucson, AZ: Wheatmark. Spears, L. C., & Greenleaf, R. K. (2002). *Servant leadership: A journey into the nature of legitimate power and greatness. 25th anniversary edition.* Mahwah, NJ: Paulist Press.

44. See Note 43.

45. Labarre, P. (1999, June). Unit of one: Leaders. com. *Fast Company,* pp. 95–98, 100, 102, 104, 108, 110, 112.

46. Lashinsky, A. (2003, September 1). Meg and the machine. *Fortune,* pp. 68–72, 76, 78.

47. See Note 45 (quote, p. 96).

48. See Note 45 (quote, p. 100).

49. See Note 45 (quote, p. 104).

50. Fiedler, F. E. (1978). Contingency model and the leadership process. In L. Berkowitz (Ed.), *Advances in experimental social psychology* (Vol. 11, pp. 60–112). New York: Academic Press.

51. Hersey, P., & Blanchard, K. H. (1988). *Management of organizational behavior.* Englewood Cliffs, NJ: Prentice Hall.

52. Pernick, R. (2001). Creating a leadership development program: Nine essential tasks. *Public Personnel Management, 30,* 429–444.

53. Day, D. V. (2001). Leadership development: A review in context. *Leadership Quarterly, 11,* 581–613.

54. Atwater, L. E., Ostroff, C., Yammarino, F. J., & Fleenor, J. W. (1998). Self-other agreement: Does it really matter? *Personnel Psychology, 51,* 577–598.

55. London, M., & Smither, J. W. (1995). Can multi-source feedback change perceptions of goal accomplishments, self-evaluations, and performance related outcomes? Theory-based applications and directions for research. *Personnel Psychology, 48,* 803–839.

56. Thornton, G. C., III, & Rupp, D. E. (2005). *Assessment centers in human resources management: Strategies for prediction, diagnosis, and development.* Hillsdale, NJ: Erlbaum.

57. Walker, A. G., & Smither, J. W. (1999). A five-year study of upward feedback: What managers do with their results matters. *Personnel Psychology, 52,* 393–423.

58. Olivero, G., Bane, D. K., & Kopellman, R. E. (1997). Executive coaching as a transfer of training tool: Effects of productivity in a public agency. *Public Personnel Management, 26,* 461–469.

59. Giber, D., Carter, L., & Goldsmith, M. (1999). *Linkage: Inc.'s best practices in leadership development handbook.* Lexington, MA: Linkage Press.

60. Marquardt, M. J., & Revans, R. (1999). *Action learning in action.* Palo Alto, CA: Davies-Black.

61. Pedler, M. (1997). Interpreting action learning. In J. Burgoyne & M. Reynolds (Eds.), *Management learning: Integrating perspectives in theory and practice* (pp. 248–264). London: Sage.

62. Dotlich, D. L., & Noel, J. L. (1998). *Action learning: How the world's top companies are recreating their leaders and themselves.* San Francisco, CA: Jossey-Bass.

63. See Note 62.

PART

IV

ORGANIZATIONAL PROCESSES

12 ORGANIZATIONAL CULTURE, CREATIVITY, AND INNOVATION

LEARNING OBJECTIVES

After reading this chapter, you will be able to:

1. **DEFINE** organizational culture and **IDENTIFY** its core characteristics.
2. **DESCRIBE** the major types of organizational culture identified in the competing values framework.
3. **IDENTIFY** the factors responsible for creating organizational culture, for transmitting it, and for getting it to change.
4. **DEFINE** creativity and **DESCRIBE** the basic components of individual and team creativity.
5. **DESCRIBE** various approaches to promoting creativity in organizations.
6. **IDENTIFY** the basic components of innovation, its various forms, and the stages of the innovation process.

THREE GOOD REASONS you should care about. . .

Organizational Culture, Creativity, and Innovation

1. Organizational culture exerts profound influences on employees, both positive and negative.
2. Managers play pivotal roles in developing, transmitting, and changing organizational culture.
3. Individual and team creativity is an important determinant of an organization's capacity to be innovative. This, in turn, plays an important role in determining organizational success.

Making the Case for. . .

Organizational Culture, Creativity, and Innovation

"Welcome to Google, Here's Your Desk"

"How many bread boxes can you fit in an airplane?" Nobody knows the answer, of course, but how you respond may reveal a great deal about your potential to thrive as a Google employee. So says Stacy Savides Sullivan, Google's director of human resources, who uses such questions to assess job candidates' creativity and capacity to address the question playfully. In her additional role as "chief culture officer," Sullivan takes seriously the fit of potential employees with the company's highly collaborative culture, in which openly sharing non-traditional ideas is encouraged while also having a little fun along the way. Founders Larry Page and Sergey Brin created this keeper-of-the-culture position because they feared that Google's astronomical growth would derail it from these core values that made the company so successful.

Google has come a long way since 1996, when Page and Brin formed the company in their Stanford University dorm room on the strength of their search engine. Their business model was simple. Anyone could perform incredibly fast and accurate Internet searches for free, but advertisers would pay the company a fee each time someone accessed a page on which they had placed an ad. Today, Google is a diversified company with successful products under its belt, such as the Chrome Web browser, the YouTube video sharing service, and the successful Android cell phone, among many others.

Googlers, the name for Google employees (and there are 18,500 of them around the world) are convinced that the company's successful innovations have been driven by an organizational culture that embraces "rapid experimentation." This has meant seeing how the market responds to new products instead of having managers give a yea or nay to ideas, which Page and Brin are convinced snuffs creativity. Google's culture keeps innovations flowing by tapping software developers' expertise and encouraging them to do their own things. In fact, Google engineers are free to spend as much as 20 percent of their workdays on projects of their own choosing.

This self-seeking aspect of Google's culture is reflected in a widely shared anecdote about a new employee's first day on the job. "Welcome to Google," he was told, "here's your desk." This was pretty much the extent of the guidance the engineer received. Instead of getting plugged into some projects, as he had expected, he was told to figure out what his job is. "We don't have a job for you. You have a paycheck but we actually aren't going to tell you what your role is."

As it worked out, this engineer was able to cultivate ideas and initiate projects with fellow Googlers he met in the company cafeteria, where gourmet meals are provided for free. Not simply a sign of the company's generous employee perks (Google has consistently placed at the top of *Fortune* magazine's list of "best companies to work for"), there's a good reason for the free meals: it brings people together and keeps them from leaving the building for lunch. And if there's any hope of promoting collaboration by assembling employees shoulder-to-shoulder, there's nothing like food to do the trick.

Online search engines already existed before Google came on the scene, but it proved to do a far superior job, making it the proverbial "better mousetrap." Behind the company's success were founders who demonstrated considerable *creativity* in the computer code they wrote. Of course, coming up with a creative idea and bringing it to fruition are two different things. And just as some individuals are more creative than others, some companies—3M, General Electric, and Rubbermaid, for example—are particularly adept at routinely doing the nonroutine. They take new ideas and turn them into cutting-edge solutions, making them highly *innovative*. Considering the importance of creativity and innovation in today's rapidly changing, technologically oriented business environment, I examine these topics in this chapter.

When thinking about why some organizations are more innovative than others, it's tempting to speculate that because people have different personalities, the companies in which they work are likely to vary as well. However, when you consider that entire organizations are often so consistently different from one another, it's apparent that there's more involved than simply the personalities of the employees. Even companies where employees are constantly changing do not reinvent themselves. If you've held jobs in different organizations, you probably recognize that they have unique styles and ways of operating and that employees have to adapt to them. For example, some are more formal while others are more casual; some are more high-pressured and others are more laid-back, and so on. In other words, organizations have stable existences of their own that make them unique, and these go beyond the composition of employees at any given time. This is the idea behind the important concept known as *organizational culture*.[1]

Because it provides much of the foundation for individual creativity and an organization's tendency toward innovation, I begin this chapter by examining organizational culture. Specifically, I describe the basic nature of organizational culture—its role in organizations, the processes through which it is formed and maintained, its effects on individual and organizational functioning, and finally, how culture is subject to change. With this foundation in place, I shift attention to creativity and innovation. This includes a discussion of not only their fundamental characteristics, but also specific tips and suggestions on how to bring out your own creativity and how to make your own organization more innovative.

ORGANIZATIONAL CULTURE: ITS BASIC NATURE

To appreciate organizational culture fully, we have to understand its basic qualities. With this in mind, I now examine fundamental aspects of organizational culture, including its nature and form. I begin, however, by presenting a definition that makes it clear precisely what this term means.

Organizational Culture: A Definition

When scientists speak of **organizational culture**, they are referring to something very specific—namely, a cognitive framework consisting of attitudes, values, behavioral norms, and expectations shared by members of an organization.[2] You may think of it as a set of basic assumptions about an organization that are accepted widely by its members. (Please note that organizational culture sometimes is referred to as *corporate culture,* and if you see that term someplace, its meaning is the same. However, because a company doesn't have to be designated legally as a corporation to have a culture, organizational culture is the more appropriate term.)

Some management experts have likened organizational culture to the roots of trees. What roots do for the lives of trees, culture does for organizations. Roots provide stability and nourishment for trees; culture provides stability and nourishment for organizations. Culture supports and feeds everything that goes on inside an organization. As one expert put it, "The strength of a firm's 'root system' ultimately shapes and determines its ability to perform in the marketplace."[3] With this in mind, the importance of organizational culture cannot be emphasized too strongly.[4]

Core Cultural Characteristics

Fundamental to any organization's culture is a set of six core characteristics that are valued collectively by its members.[5]

SENSITIVITY TO OTHERS   Years ago, the culture at UPS was relatively rigid and inflexible with respect to customer needs. With some arrogance, it operated however it thought best, and forced customers to adjust to its ways. No more. Today, UPS's culture places high value on service and satisfaction. UPS now strives to suit the needs of its customers; changes are driven by better opportunities to serve.[6]

INTEREST IN NEW IDEAS   Walt Disney Co. employees—or "cast members," as they are called—traditionally have had lengthy orientation programs to ensure that they know exactly what to say and how to behave toward guests.[7] For the most part, their behavior is scripted. By contrast, people working at Southwest Airlines are encouraged to be unique and to bring fresh ideas to their work. In fact, company founder Herb Kelleher is so adamant about this that managerial training is geared toward hiring people who bring to the job an orientation toward openness and fun.[8]

WILLINGNESS TO TAKE RISKS   At some companies, such as the Bank of America, the culture is very conservative, and employees make only the safest investments. By contrast, buyers at Limited Brands (parent company of The Limited chain of women's clothing stores) are discouraged from making too many "safe" choices. Taking risks in the purchasing of fashion merchandise is valued.[9]

THE VALUE PLACED ON PEOPLE   Some companies consider their employees as valuable only insofar as they contribute to production, much as they view machinery. Such organizations, where people do not feel valued, are considered to have **toxic organizational cultures**. A survey found that 48 percent of people believe they work in toxic organizational cultures.[10] Organizations like these tend to lose good employees, and struggle to be profitable as a result.

By contrast, organizations that treat people well and that inspire employees—said to have **healthy organizational cultures**—tend to have very low turnover, and generally thrive.[11] What, exactly, makes for a healthy organizational culture? How do you know one when you see it? The characteristics identified in Table 12.1 play large roles.[12]

OPENNESS OF AVAILABLE COMMUNICATION OPTIONS   At some companies, such as Yahoo!, employees are expected to make decisions freely and to communicate with whomever they need to in order to get the job done—even if it means going directly to the CEO.[13] At IBM, however, the traditional culture has called for working within the proper communication channels and to vest power in the hands of only a few key individuals. (This has been changing, however, in recent years.[14])

TABLE 12.1	Healthy Organizational Culture: What Does It Look Like?

Would you know a *healthy organizational culture* if you experienced one? These are characterized by the qualities described here.

Characteristic	Description
Everyone in the organization is open and humble.	• Arrogance is not to be found. This is good because it encourages people to learn from everyone else.
Individuals are held accountable and accept personal responsibility for their actions.	• Denial, blame, and excuses are absent. By accepting responsibility, conflict is lowered and opportunities for success are raised.
Within appropriate limits, people are free to take risks.	• Neither reckless risk-taking nor stiflingly high levels of control are found. Hence, freedom exists to follow new ideas (this is the case at Google, as described in this chapter's Making the Case on p. 367).
The commitment to doing things well is very high.	• Mediocrity is not tolerated. Everyone is expected to do things appropriately, not taking shortcuts to quality.
Mistakes are tolerated because they are considered learning opportunities.	• Attempts at innovation help the organization, but some failures are inevitable. These are accepted because they provide opportunities to learn how to improve things next time.
Integrity is unquestioned.	• Dishonesty undermines trust, which is essential to success. As a result, efforts to promote integrity, such as being transparent about decisions and following up on promises, are considered essential.
Collaboration and integration between units is ongoing.	• Turf wars and narrow thinking are discouraged. Instead, people work together in open, friendly, collaborative environments.
Courage and persistence are encouraged.	• Work often is challenging. In healthy cultures everyone is encouraged to persist even in the face of failure, as long as they remain realistic about what can be accomplished.

FRIENDLINESS AND CONGENIALITY At some companies, such as Nokia Corp., the employees tend to get along well. Friendships often run deep, and employees see each other outside of work.[15] At the toymaker Mattel, however, the culture has been depicted as being far more cutthroat and competitive.[16]

Strength of Organizational Culture: Strong and Weak

As I have been suggesting, organizations differ in many key facets of culture. They also vary in the degree to which their cultures impact employees. In some companies, there is widespread agreement concerning the elements of organizational culture I just described (i.e. sensitivity to others, willingness to take risks, etc.), and when this occurs, culture exerts a major influence on the behavior of individuals in those organizations. An organization of this type may be said to have a **strong culture**. By contrast, in other organizations, there may be less agreement with respect to the various cultural elements, thereby leading culture to have a more limited impact on the way people behave. Such an organization is said to have a **weak culture**.

In organizations with a strong cultures, core values are held intensely and shared widely. The more members accept these values and the greater their commitment to those concepts, the stronger the culture is considered to be. Specifically, organizations with strong cultures are characterized in the following ways:

- A clear philosophy exists about how business is to be conducted.
- Considerable time is spent communicating values and beliefs.
- Explicit statements are made that describe the organization's values.
- A set of values and norms exists that is shared widely and rooted deeply.
- New employees are screened carefully to ensure fit with the culture.

Research has shown that stronger organizational cultures are likely to be found in companies that are relatively new and small in size.[17] A key reason for this is that as organizations grow older and add more employees, the effects of culture become diffused. This would be the case, for example, as the influence of a company founder weakens because his or her impact is felt less in a maturing organization. This research finding and others suggest that strong cultures shape the preferences and actions of people in the organizations that have them.

Cultures Within Organizations: One or Many?

The discussion thus far has implied that each organization has only a single, uniform culture—one set of shared values, beliefs, and expectations. However, this rarely is the case. Instead, organizations, particularly large ones, typically have *several* cultures operating within them.

People generally have attitudes and values that are more in common with others in their own fields or work units than they do with those in other parts of their organizations. These various groups may be said to have several different **subcultures**—cultures existing within parts of organizations rather than entirely through them. These typically are distinguished with respect to either functional differences (i.e., the type of work done) or geographic distances (i.e., the physical separation between people).

Indeed, research suggests that several subcultures based on occupational, professional, or functional divisions usually exist within any large organization. So, for example, we might find that the subculture of an organization's accounting department differs from the subculture of its research and development unit although both groups work in the same organization. This would reflect the different norms and traditions of each professional group.

At the same time, however, there also is likely to be a **dominant culture** in effect. This refers to a distinctive, overarching "personality" of an organization, the kind of culture to which I have been referring. An organization's dominant culture reflects its **core values**, the prevailing perceptions that are generally shared throughout the organization. Typically, members of subcultures who share additional sets of values also accept the core values of their organizations as a whole. Thus, subcultures should not be thought of as a bunch of totally separate cultures but, rather, as "mini" cultures operating within a larger, dominant one.

The Role of Organizational Culture

It would be reasonable to think of organizations as unique because of the various cultural forces that shape them. Indeed, culture plays several important roles in organizations, and I now make these explicit (for a summary, see Figure 12.1).

CULTURE PROVIDES A SENSE OF IDENTITY The more clearly an organization's shared perceptions and values are defined, the more strongly people can associate with its mission and feel as they are a vital part of it. For example, employees at Southwest Airlines feel special because

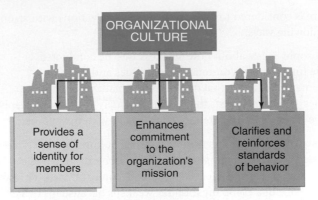

FIGURE 12.1 The Basic Functions of Organizational Culture
Organizational culture serves the three major functions summarized here.

of their company's emphasis on having fun and joking around on the job, a widespread practice initiated by founder Herb Kelleher.[18] Southwest's employees feel strongly connected to the company, believing that they belong there. As a result, they only infrequently resign to take other positions in the airline industry.

CULTURE GENERATES COMMITMENT TO AN ORGANIZATION'S MISSION   Sometimes it's difficult for people to go beyond thinking of their own interests (i.e., how will this affect me?). When there is a strong, overarching culture, however, people feel that they are part of that larger, well-defined whole and that they are involved in the entire organization's work. Bigger than any one individual's interests, culture reminds people of what their organization is all about.

CULTURE CLARIFIES AND REINFORCES STANDARDS OF BEHAVIOR   Culture guides employees' words and deeds, making it clear what they should do or say in a given situation, which is especially useful to newcomers. In this sense, culture provides stability to behavior, with respect to both what an individual might do at different times, and what various employees may do at the same time.

For example, in a company with a culture that strongly supports customer service, workers will have clear guidance as to how they are expected to behave: doing whatever it takes to please the customer. This is the case at the Walt Disney Company, which is committed to ensuring that employees strive to make guests feel at home. To ensure that all employees embrace this strong commitment to customer satisfaction, the company thoroughly indoctrinates them in this aspect of organizational culture as part of its ongoing training programs.[19]

Forms of Organizational Culture: The Competing Values Framework

As you might imagine, just as there are many different organizations, there also are many different organizational cultures. Although organizations may be unique in several ways, underlying cultural similarities have been noted by scientists, who developed useful ways of organizing and identifying these cultures. One of the most popular approaches is known as the **competing values framework**.[20] According to this approach, the cultures of organizations differ with respect to two sets of opposite values (hence, the name):

- Valuing *flexibility* and *discretion* as opposed to stability, order, and control.
- Valuing *internal affairs* as opposed to what's going on in the external environment.

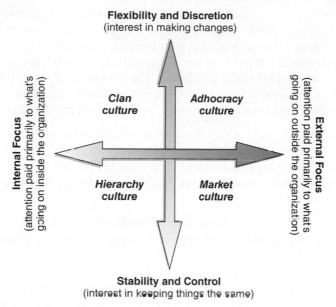

FIGURE 12.2 The Competing Values Framework

According to the *competing values framework*, the cultures of organizations can be distinguished in terms of the two opposite dimensions identified here. Combining these two sets of competing values results in the four types of organizational cultures shown.
Source: Adapted from Cameron & Quinn, 2011; see Note 20.

By combining both dimensions, scientists have identified the four unique types of organizational culture shown in Figure 12.2, which I now describe.

HIERARCHY CULTURE Organizations described as having a **hierarchy culture** (shown in the lower-left corner of Figure 12.2) have an internal focus and emphasize stability and control. Here, the most effective leaders are good coordinators of projects and emphasize smooth-running procedures, often relying on formal rules and policies to do so.

Governmental agencies and large corporations tend to fall into this category. At McDonald's, for example, key values center on maintaining efficient and reliable production, and to ensure this, both the equipment used and the procedures followed—described in a 350-page manual—are designed with this in mind. Sometimes, because organizations with hierarchy cultures are so attuned to internal concerns at the expense of external ones and so focused on stability as opposed to making necessary changes (which often are necessary; see Chapter 14), serious problems result.

Not surprisingly, as a large government agency, the National Aeronautics and Space Administration (NASA) has a hierarchy culture.[21] In the past, its sharp focus on stability created a culture that was blind to the threat posed by foam debris on its space shuttles. Furthermore, its attention to internal as opposed to external matters reinforced employees' convictions that the agency was far more attuned to making decisions based on safety than was truly the case. According to the Columbia Accident Investigation Board, flawed organizational culture was among the factors that led to the tragic explosion of the space shuttle *Columbia* on February 1, 2003. Although not all hierarchy cultures are doomed to fail, of course, this incident represents an extreme example of what may occur when they do.

MARKET CULTURE The term **market culture** describes organizations that are concerned with stability and control but are external in their orientation (see the lower-right corner of Figure 12.2).

In such organizations, the core values emphasize competitiveness and productivity, focusing on bottom-line results. They do this by carefully identifying the markets in which they are going to compete and then taking a very hard-driving, results-oriented approach to getting things done.

A classic example of a market culture is General Electric (GE) during the two decades (1981–2001) when it was led by CEO Jack Welch. The culture called for making each GE business unit either first or second in its respective market. Otherwise, the mandate from Welch was clear—fix, sell, or close the unsuccessful business.[22] He explained this as follows:

> When you're number four or five in a market, when number one sneezes, you get pneumonia. When you're number one, you control your destiny. The number fours keep merging; they have difficult times. That's not the same if you're number four, and that's your only business. Then you have to find strategic ways to get stronger. But, GE had a lot of number ones.[23]

Welch's approach to market success involved making major changes quickly rather than small, incremental changes slowly. In this respect, GE operates more like a small company than the enormous one it is.

CLAN CULTURE   An organization is said to have a **clan culture** when it has a strong internal focus along with a high degree of flexibility and discretion (see the upper-left corner of Figure 12.2). With goals that are highly shared by members of the organization and high levels of cohesiveness (see Chapter 9), such organizations feel more like extended families than economic entities. Given their highly friendly nature, it's not surprising that most people prefer clan cultures to any of the other forms of organizational culture.[24]

In the clan culture, the predominant focus is on flexibility when it comes to external needs. This is attained by concentrating on the excellence of the employees, which reflects the internal focus. An example of a company that fits the clan culture is the Finnish conglomerate Nokia, best known for its cellular phones. At this company, the well-being of employees is a top priority. In contrast to the attention-grabbing element of most high-tech firms, Nokia's emphasis is on collegiality.[25]

ADHOCRACY CULTURE   Organizations that have an **adhocracy culture** emphasize flexibility while also paying a great deal of attention to the external environment (see upper-right corner of Figure 12.2). An **adhocracy** is a form of organization that cuts across normal bureaucratic lines to capture opportunities, solve problems, and get results.[26] The term *adhocracy* is a reference to the absence of hierarchy, making it the opposite of *bureaucracy* (see Chapters 1 and 13). Commonly found in contemporary companies, which often have to make rapid changes in the way they operate (see Chapter 14), the adhocracy culture is characterized by recognition that, to succeed, organizations need to be highly innovative (a concept I will describe later in this chapter, beginning on p. 388) and constantly assess what the future requires for survival, let alone growth.

Adhocracy cultures thrive in organizations where research and development is essential. This is the case, for example, at 3M, the large American company that has been producing innovative products (currently, some 55,000 of them) for more than 100 years. To promote the innovative spirit at 3M, one of its earliest presidents, William McKnight, recognized the importance of a culture in which people were respected and felt free to take risks.[27] Consider the three principles he articulated back in 1948, which describe an adhocracy culture (although he didn't refer to it as such):[28] (1) delegate responsibility to encourage people to take initiative; (2) expect mistakes to be made, so be tolerant of them; and (3) criticize in a constructive, not destructive, manner.

CREATING, TRANSMITTING, AND CHANGING ORGANIZATIONAL CULTURE

Now that I have described the basic nature and forms of organizational culture, I shift attention to three additional issues of importance: how culture is created initially, how it is transmitted, and when and how it changes.

How Is Organizational Culture Created?

Two key factors contribute to the emergence of organizational culture. One of these, the impact of company founders, reflects the influential nature of particular individuals. The other, experiences with the external environment, focuses on critical events that shaped organizational history.

COMPANY FOUNDERS Organizational culture may be traced, at least in part, to the founders of the company.[29] These individuals often possess dynamic personalities, strong values, and clear visions of how their businesses should operate. Since they are on the scene first and play a key role in hiring initial staff, their attitudes and values are readily transmitted to new employees. As a result, founders' views become the accepted ones in the organization and persist as long as they are on the scene—and often, long afterward. For a summary of the four major steps involved in this process, see Figure 12.3.

A good example of this process in operation may be seen at Microsoft, where the culture dictates working exceptionally long hours, in large part because that's what cofounder Bill Gates always did. This remains the case today even though Gates is no longer involved with the company's daily operations. In fact, the influence of founders sometimes is felt even when those founders are no longer alive. We see this, for example, at McDonalds, where founder Ray Kroc's emphasis on offering tasty food at a good value served in clean, family-oriented surroundings remains intact today, some thirty years after his passing.

EXPERIENCES WITH THE EXTERNAL ENVIRONMENT As critical events occur in organizations based on their experiences with the external environment, it's not surprising that their effects contribute to the development of the culture. It's as if companies learn from these events and the memories are passed along from person to person, contributing to the development of the cultural framework. In this connection, the term **organizational memory** is used to describe information from an organization's history that its leaders draw upon later as needed.[30] That information is stored through the recollections of these events and their shared interpretations by key individuals in the organization who pass it along to others.[31]

Let's consider an example from the competitive world of consumer electronics. In particular, I point to Sony's experience with its Betamax format for home videocassette tapes. Introduced in 1975, Betamax competed with the VHS format introduced by JVC the following year. If you're thinking that you've heard of VHS, but not Betamax, that's indeed the story. Sony made two critical errors. First, unlike JVC, which permitted open sharing of its technology, Sony licensed its technology, which made it less popular among equipment manufacturers. Second, Sony failed to anticipate the demand for prerecorded movies, leading studios to release films on VHS instead. As a result, Sony's product never captured the market. In 1988, Sony gave up, abandoning Betamax, and began making VHS-format video cassette recorders.

In the aftermath of this incident, it appeared that Sony executives had learned an important lesson about what it takes to win a battle of formats. From 2006 to 2008, Sony once again found itself in a battle over format dominance. This time it was over high-definition DVDs, and its competitor

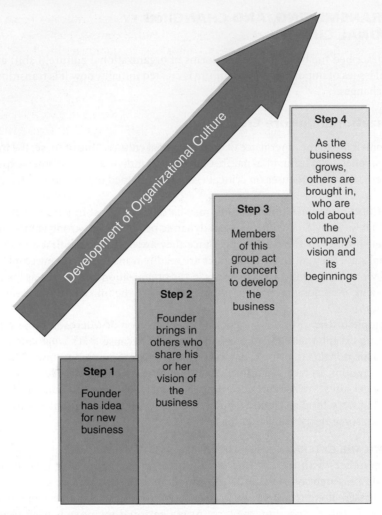

FIGURE 12.3 How Do Founders Influence Organizational Culture?
The cultures of organizations are affected by their founders. This tends to occur over time, generally according to the four steps summarized here.

was Toshiba. Having lost the videotape battle, Sony was more aggressive this time in making strategic decisions (see Chapter 8). It signed up more movie studios (including its own, Sony Pictures Studio) to its Blu-ray Disc (BD DVD) format than Toshiba did for its High Definition DVD (HD DVD) format, and it also promoted sales by making its popular PS3 game units compatible with Blu-ray. This time around, Sony won, and without a protracted battle. Toshiba threw in the towel after only two years. It cannot be said that Sony executives failed to learn from the Betamax fiasco. Indeed, bitter feelings about this experience lingered in Sony's organizational culture, and their resurrection helped the company avoid repeating mistakes from its past.

Tools for Transmitting Organizational Culture

How are cultural values transmitted between people? In other words, how do employees come to learn about their organizations' cultures? I now describe various ways in which this occurs.

SYMBOLS: OBJECTS THAT SAY MORE THAN MEETS THE EYE   To transmit organizational culture, companies often rely on **symbols**—material objects that connote meanings that extend beyond their intrinsic content. For example, some companies use impressive buildings to convey their strength and significance, signifying that they are large, stable places. In addition, the way an organization is furnished provides useful insight into its culture. Specifically, research has shown that companies whose decor includes lots of plants and flower arrangements are perceived as friendly, person-oriented cultures, whereas those whose waiting areas are adorned with awards and trophies are perceived as focusing on achieving success.[32] These findings suggest that material symbols are potent tools for sending messages about organizational culture. (To demonstrate this phenomenon for yourself, complete the Group Exercise on p. 396.)

SLOGANS: PHRASES THAT CAPTURE ORGANIZATIONAL CULTURE   When you think of the catchy phrases that companies use to call attention to their products and services, you may dismiss them as merely advertising gimmicks. It should be noted, however, that many slogans also communicate important aspects of an organization's culture, both to the public at large and to the company's own employees. For some examples of such slogans and what they communicate about organizational culture, see Table 12.2. As you peruse this list, you will see that these words help convey important information about an organization's culture, such as what the company stands for and what it values.

JARGON: THE SPECIAL LANGUAGE THAT DEFINES A CULTURE   In Chapter 8, I noted that the *jargon*, or specialized words or phrases used by members of a particular professional group can be a barrier to communication when used with individuals outside these groups. At the same

---

TABLE 12.2	Slogans That Reflect Organizational Culture

Corporate *slogans* often send messages about the cultures of the organizations that use them. The slogans they use allow customers, employees, and prospective employees to learn about the cultures of the companies listed here. Can you think of other slogans that reflect the culture of the businesses with which they are associated?

Company	Registered Slogan	Message
Staples	*That was easy.*	The office products we sell make your life easier, and purchasing from us is a pleasurable experience.
Gillette	*The best a man can get.*	The company's products are superior and/or they give men confidence
Walmart	*Save money. Live better.*	You can count on us to offer low prices on items that will improve your quality of life.
McDonald's	*I'm lovin' it.*	You will enjoy eating here.
Apple	*There's an app for that.*	You can download a broad range of applications for your iPhone, iPod, or iPad.
Microsoft Windows 7	*Your PC, simplified.*	This operating system is easy to use.
State Farm	*Like a good neighbor, State Farm is there.*	You can count on friendly and reliable service when you need it.

Sources: Registered slogans appear on the Web sites of the companies identified.

time, however, the uniqueness of the language used helps define membership in a group. Using the jargon transmits and reinforces aspects of its culture.

Illustrating this, for many years employees at IBM referred to disk drives as "hard files" and circuit boards as "planar boards," terms that reflected the insulated nature of the company's culture.[33] Today's jargon continues to predominate in the high-tech world. For example, within the information technology (IT) community, the term "geek keys" is used to refer to a loose deck of electronically encoded pass cards that are used to gain access to restricted areas.[34] Over time, as departments, organizations, or professional groups develop unique language, their terms, although strange to newcomers, serve as a common factor that brings together individuals belonging to an organizational culture or subculture.

CEREMONIES: SPECIAL EVENTS THAT COMMEMORATE CORPORATE VALUES   Organizations do a great deal to sustain their cultures by conducting various types of **ceremonies**. If you want to know what a company values, just attend its award ceremonies. Whatever it is that gets someone up to the stage to receive a plaque is what's valued. Award ceremonies may be seen as celebrations of an organization's basic values and assumptions. Just as a wedding ceremony symbolizes a couple's mutual commitment and a presidential inauguration marks the beginning of a new presidential term, various organizational ceremonies also celebrate some important accomplishment. These events have importance that go beyond the individuals involved—in this example, the bride and groom, and the new president and vice president. They send clear messages about the institutions of marriage and the presidency to all who participate in or view the ceremony. In this manner, it's easy to see how they function as important transmitters of organizational culture.

STORIES: "IN THE OLD DAYS, WE USED TO . . . "   Organizations also transmit information about culture by virtue of the *stories* that are told, both formally and informally. Stories illustrate key aspects of an organization's culture, and telling them can effectively introduce or reaffirm underlying values to employees.[35] It is important to note that these anecdotes need not involve some great event, such as someone who saved the company with a single wise decision, but may be less dramatic tales that become legends because they communicate a message so effectively. An example may be found at Nike, where employees are told stories about how the company was founded in an effort to help athletes (see Table 12.3).[36]

STATEMENTS OF PRINCIPLE: DEFINING CULTURE IN WRITING   Organizational culture also may be transmitted directly using written **statements of principle**. Some companies have explicitly written their principles for all to see. For example, as the online retailer Zappos.com grew from a small to a large company (from no sales to $1 billion in sales in its first ten years), it became useful to specify its core values, describing what it stands for. These involve: giving outstanding customer service, creating a fun atmosphere, promoting personal growth, and being open and honest with others.[37]

Although Zappos.com was acquired by Amazon.com in November 2009, it operates independently and has its own culture. Zappos.com CEO Tony Hsieh takes these principles seriously, as do employees. In fact, at the company's Web site, where its principles are described in detail, the organizational culture is identified as the company's "greatest asset."

Why and How Does Organizational Culture Change?

My comments about the relative stability of organizational culture may have left you wondering why and how culture ever changes. In other words, why isn't culture simply

TABLE 12.3	The Nike Story: Just Tell It—and Keep It Alive

New employees at Nike are told stories that transmit the company's underlying cultural values. The themes of some of the most important ones are summarized here, along with several of the ways the company helps keep its heritage alive.

New employees are told the following . . .

- Founder Phil Knight was a middle-distance runner who started the business by selling shoes out of his car.
- Knight's running coach and company cofounder, Bill Bowerman, developed the famous "waffle sole" by pouring rubber into the family waffle iron.
- The late Steve Prefontaine, coached by Bowerman, battled to make running a professional sport and was committed to helping athletes.

To ensure that these tales of Nike's heritage are kept alive, the company . . .

- Takes new hires to the track where Bowerman coached and to the site of Prefontaine's fatal car crash.
- Has created a "heritage wall" in its Eugene, Oregon, store.
- Requires salespeople to tell the Nike story to employees of the retail stores that sell its products.

Source: Based on information in Ransdell, 2000; see Note 36.

passed down from one generation of organizational members to the next in unchanging fashion? The answer lies in the fact that the worlds in which organizations operate are in a constant state of flux (see Chapter 14). Shifts in market conditions, new competitors, emerging technologies, altered government policies, and many other factors necessitate changing how companies operate, and with it, their cultures. I now consider several factors that promote changes in organizational culture.

COMPOSITION OF THE WORKFORCE Over time, the people entering an organization may differ in important ways from those already in it, and these differences may impinge on the existing culture of the organization. For example, people from different ethnic or national backgrounds may have contrasting views about various aspects of behavior at work. They may hold dissimilar views about style of dress, the importance of being on time (or even what constitutes "on-time" behavior), the level of deference one should show to higher-status people, and even what foods should be served in the company cafeteria. When people have different views, existing cultural norms are likely to be challenged. And when this occurs, changes in organizational culture can be expected to follow suit.

It's important to note that any such effects may be slow in coming. For the most part, individuals adapt to the cultures of their organizations as forces lead them in this manner. What I am saying here is that people also may affect the culture somewhat, but such changes tend to be gradual (e.g., eventually changing the cafeteria menu) and are unlikely to influence the organization's core ideas. With some effort, top executives may be able to change the culture, but an influx of new people generally will have little or no immediate impact on the core values of an organization. This is in keeping with the idea that organizational culture is relatively stable.

MERGERS AND ACQUISITIONS   Another, and even more dramatic, source of cultural change is *mergers* (two companies join forces as relative equals) and *acquisitions* (one organization purchases or otherwise acquires another).[38] When these events occur, there is likely to be a careful analysis of the financial and material assets of the acquired company. However, it is unusual for any consideration to be given to the acquired organization's culture. This is unfortunate, since several high-profile cases over the years have illustrated how the merger of two organizations with conflicting cultures leads to serious problems.[39] These are referred to as **culture clashes**.

Interestingly, just as some newlywed couples have problems due to their differing styles of spending money, so too have some newly merged companies. For example, Time Warner's 2001 merger with AOL was short-lived in large part because AOL's free-spending executives never saw eye-to-eye with their financially conservative counterparts from Time Warner. It was the same story in the 1998 merger between Chrysler and Daimler-Benz. After the new DaimlerChrysler was created, former Chrysler officials traveled to meetings in minivans and flew economy class while Daimler-Benz officials showed up in Mercedes sedans and flew first class. It took six months of attempting to iron out the differences in their corporate cultures before realizing they were at an impasse. Divorces resulted in both cases.

STRATEGIC CULTURAL CHANGE   Sometimes, company officials deliberately decide to change organizational culture as a means of adjusting to evolving conditions—even positive ones, such as rapid growth. It's probably not too surprising that the culture of a small organization has to change as the company grows in size. What once worked for a small company may no longer be successful as it becomes a much larger one.

This was the situation Robert Nardelli inherited when he took over as The Home Depot's CEO in 2000.[40] When The Home Depot first opened its doors in 1978, it was a small business, complete with a small-company culture that reflected the personality of one of its cofounders, Bernie Marcus. It had a high-spirited, entrepreneurial way of doing things. Employees were willing to take risks and showed a passionate commitment to customers, colleagues, and the company as a whole. Anything bureaucratic was rejected. However, things had to change. As Nardelli put it, "What so effectively got [The] Home Depot from zero to $50 billion in sales wasn't going to get it to go to the next $50 billion."[41]

As 1978 slipped into 2000, the small-company culture that had once worked still existed, but it was strangling an enormous enterprise with 1,000 stores. Nardelli introduced more formal operations in which the processes were centralized and data-driven instead of intuitive. The culture shift was abrupt, making some key executives so uncomfortable that they resigned. However, the change was overdue and came not a minute too soon. Only five years after Nardelli's orchestrated cultural changes were in place, The Home Depot's financial picture was much brighter. It now had a culture that was appropriate for its size. (For an example of a way to change organizational culture strategically, see the Winning Practices section on p. 381.)

RESPONDING TO THE INTERNET   There can be no doubt that the Internet is a major influence on organizational culture these days. Compared to traditional "brick-and-mortar" businesses, where things move slowly and in which people look at change skeptically, the culture of Internet businesses is agile, fast paced, and receptive to new solutions.[42] Information sharing is key, as such organizations not only accept, but also embrace, the expansion of communication networks and business relationships across organizational boundaries. When traditional, brick-and-mortar

Winning Practices

Organizational Culture for Sale

Companies that desire to make strategic changes in their own organizational cultures now have an interesting opportunity available to them. Zappos.com, the successful online retailer, conducts seminars in which staff members teach other companies how to re-create the essence of its own customer service–driven culture.[43]

Specifically, training sessions, referred to as "Zappos Insights Live Events" are held at the company's Henderson, Nevada, headquarters in three different forms.[44] Several times a month, the company offers the "Silver Package," where, for $797 per person, a half-day session gives trainees opportunities to see, among other things, the Zappos family culture in action and have question-and-answer sessions with the Zappos Insights Team. Once a month, the day-long "Gold Package" is offered, for $1,797 per person. Session attendees receive the Silver Package as well as meet with members of the sales force, referred to as the Customer Loyalty Team, and with people involved in recruiting and training new employees. Finally, for $4,997 per person, there's a two-day "Boot Camp" offered six times per year. This package provides a "full immersive experience" in which trainees not only learn about the Zappos culture but get to live it firsthand.

One of the key takeaways from these sessions is the emphasis on coddling customers. Although 95 percent of Zappos customers place Web orders, the 5 percent who call are looking for special treatment—and they get it. Instead of reading from a script, Zappos.com's sales agents—members of the Customer Loyalty Team—are empowered to "wing it" with customers. They may chat with them for hours, write them notes, or recommend other Web sites for them to visit. It's all okay. In an industry in which employees at call centers are regularly measured in terms of their hourly call counts and sales figures, Zappos.com's "extreme customer service" culture clearly is quite unique.

Although immersion in the Zappos culture sounds like it may be a valuable (and fun) way to pick up some tips, it's reasonable to wonder whether this unique organizational culture would work as well elsewhere. Can it be transplanted successfully into existing cultures, especially those that are more rigid? There's surely reason to be skeptical. Even when strategic changes to organizational culture are made, the process does not occur overnight. Wanting organizational culture to be different, even if you have a clear model of what it should be like, doesn't make it so.

However, the Zappos Insight Live Events would appear to be great launching points for inspiring cultural changes. In fact, the thousands of people who have been trained in the Zappos culture have come away from the experiences with useful ideas that may be adapted to their own organizational cultures. From this perspective, it would appear safe to regard training in Zappos' distinctive organizational culture to be wise investments for many companies.

companies expand into e-commerce (in which case they are known as "click-and-mortar" companies), changes in their organizational cultures follow suit. We see this, for example, at the investment firm Merrill Lynch, which launched a Web site for trading stock in an effort to compete with other brokerage firms, such as E*Trade, which do business online only. The previously stodgy organizational culture at the venerable Merrill Lynch has become more fast paced after adapting to the realities of today's Internet economy.

To conclude, it is clear that although organizational culture is generally stable, it is not immutable. In fact, culture often evolves in response to outside forces (e.g., changes in workforce composition and information technology) as well as deliberate attempts to change the design of organizations (e.g., through mergers and corporate restructuring). An important quality that an organization frequently strives to alter is the degree to which it approaches problems in creative and innovative ways. With this in mind, I now turn attention to the topics of *creativity* and *innovation* in organizations.

CREATIVITY IN INDIVIDUALS AND WORK TEAMS

Although you probably have no difficulty recognizing creativity when you see it, defining it can be a bit more challenging. Scientists define **creativity** as the process by which individuals or teams produce novel and useful ideas.[45] With this definition as a guide, I will explain how this process operates and outline several ways to enhance your own creativity.

Components of Individual and Team Creativity

Creativity in individuals and teams is composed of three basic components—*domain-relevant skills, creativity-relevant skills,* and *intrinsic task motivation* (see Figure 12.4).[46]

DOMAIN-RELEVANT SKILLS Whether it's the manual dexterity required to play the piano or use a computer keyboard, or the sense of rhythm and knowledge of music needed to conduct an orchestra, specific skills and abilities are necessary to perform certain tasks. In fact, any task you might undertake requires certain talents, knowledge, or skills. The skills and abilities that we already have constitute the raw materials needed for creativity to occur. After all, without the capacity to perform a certain task at even a basic level, one has no hope of demonstrating creativity in that task. For example, before he or she can begin to create dramatic automotive stunts, a stunt driver must have the basic skills of dexterity and eye–hand coordination required to drive a car.

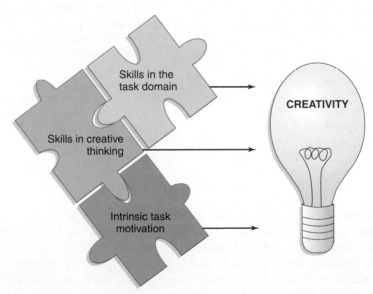

FIGURE 12.4 Components of Creativity
Scientists claim that people will be at their most creative when they exhibit high levels of the three factors shown here.
Source: Adapted from Amabile & Fisher, 2009; see Note 46.

CREATIVITY-RELEVANT SKILLS   Being creative requires more than just task know-how; it calls for special abilities that help people approach the things they do in novel ways. Specifically, when fostering creativity, it helps to be able to do the following:

- *Break mental sets in order to gain new perspectives*—Creativity is enhanced when people do not limit themselves to their usual way of doing things. Restricting oneself to the past can inhibit creativity. Take a fresh look at even the most familiar things. This involves what is known as **divergent thinking**—the process of reframing familiar problems in unique ways, producing multiple or alternative answers from available information. Divergent thinking requires creating unexpected combinations, recognizing associations between things, and transforming information into unexpected forms. Often, the result of divergent thinking is something novel and surprising, something that never before has existed.[47] For some examples of ways to promote divergent thinking, see Table 12.4. To practice this yourself, see the Self-Assessment Exercise on pp. 395–396.
- *Understand complexities*—Instead of making things overly simplistic, don't be afraid to consider the complex ways in which ideas may be interrelated.
- *Keep options open and avoid premature judgments*—Creative people are willing to consider all options. To do so, they examine all the angles and avoid reaching conclusions prematurely. People are particularly good at this when they are new to an organization and, therefore, don't know enough to accept everything the way it is. With this in mind, some companies actually prefer hiring executives from outside their industries.
- *Follow creativity heuristics*—People sometimes follow certain strategies, known as **creativity heuristics**, to come up with creative new ideas. These are rules that people follow to approach tasks in novel ways. They may involve such techniques as: (1) going out of your way to pause and notice things, (2) considering counterintuitive solutions to problems, and (3) approaching problems by examining analogies.
- *Use productive forgetting*—Sometimes, our creativity is inhibited by becoming fixated on certain ideas that we just can't get out of our heads. With this in mind, it helps to practice **productive forgetting**—abandoning unproductive ideas and temporarily putting aside stubborn problems until new approaches can be considered.

To help individuals and teams become more creative, many organizations are inviting employees to participate in training exercises designed to promote some of these skills. Although

---

TABLE 12.4   Ways of Triggering Divergent Thinking

To encourage divergent thinking, exercises often are conducted in which people are asked open-ended questions to which there are no correct answers. Responses are free to fall outside normal ways of thinking. The following are typical examples:

- List various uses for a hat other than wearing it.
- Make as many sentences as you can that include the following words: *melon, consider, flower, paper.*
- How could you turn a cardboard box into a temporary tent for use on a camping trip in the woods?
- Think carefully about a stone. Then indicate what you believe to be its hidden meanings.
- If you were going to host a party for a group of elves, what would you serve (in addition to those cookies they make)?
- Your car is stuck in a ditch along a deserted road and you do not have a cell phone. Using only the things likely to be found in and around the car, how could you summon help?

the results are not assessed scientifically, several companies have reported anecdotal success using these techniques to boost creativity in the workplace.[48]

INTRINSIC TASK MOTIVATION   The first two components of creativity, domain-relevant skills and creativity-relevant skills, focus on what people are *capable* of doing. However, the third component, *intrinsic task motivation*, refers to what people are *willing* to do. The idea is simple: for someone to be creative, he or she must be interested in performing the task in question. In other words, there must be a high degree of **intrinsic task motivation**—that is, the motivation to do work because it is interesting, engaging, or challenging in a positive way. People who have the capacity to be creative but are so bored with a task that they aren't motivated to do what it takes to produce novel outcomes certainly wouldn't become creative.[49]

PUTTING IT ALL TOGETHER   As you might imagine, the components of creativity are important insofar as they paint a picture of when creativity will occur. Specifically, people will be at their most creative when they have high amounts of all three of the components shown in Figure 12.4.

It has been claimed that there is a multiplicative relationship among these three components. Thus, higher degrees of each contributes to higher degrees of creativity. The multiplicative relationship also implies that people will not be creative at all if any one of these elements is at zero (i.e., if it is missing completely). After all, you would be unlikely to be creative at a job if you didn't have the skills needed to do it, regardless of how motivated you were to be creative and how well practiced you were at coming up with new ideas. Likewise, creativity would be nonexistent if either creativity-relevant skills or intrinsic task motivation was zero. The practical implications are clear: to be as creative as possible, people must strive toward attaining high levels of *all three* facets of creativity.

A Model of the Creative Process

Although it isn't always obvious how people come up with creative ideas, scientists have developed a model that outlines the general steps in this process.[50] Specifically, the model summarized in Figure 12.5 specifies that the process of creativity adheres to the following four steps:

1. *Prepare to be creative.* Although we often believe that our most creative ideas come "out of thin air," this is untrue. Instead, people are at their most creative when they have made suitable preparations. This involves gathering the appropriate information (e.g., statistics, prototypes, photos). and finding or creating an environment in which they can concentrate on the problem.
2. *Allow ideas to incubate.* Because ideas take time to develop, creativity can be enhanced by putting the problem out of our conscious minds and allowing it to incubate. If you've ever been successful at coming up with a fresh approach to a problem by putting it aside and working on something else, you know what I am describing. The phrase "sleep on it" captures this stage of the process.
3. *Document insight.* At some point during the first two stages, you are likely to come up with a unique idea. However, that idea may be lost if it is not documented. With this in mind, many people carry small notebooks that allow them to jot down their ideas before they become lost in a maze of other thoughts. Likewise, writers keep diaries, artists keep sketch pads, and songwriters keep digital recorders handy to capture ideas whenever inspiration strikes.
4. *Verify ideas.* Coming up with an idea is one thing but ensuring that it's a good idea is quite another. Assessing the usefulness of an idea requires consciously thinking about it and verifying its quality, such as by seeing what others have to say about it. In other words,

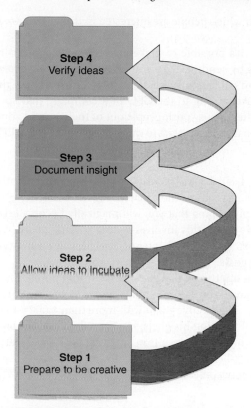

FIGURE 12.5 Steps in the Creative Process
Scientists have proposed that the creative process follows the four steps outlined here.
Source: Kabanoff & Rossiter, 1994; see Note 51.

you want to see if those ideas that came to you in a moment of inspiration in the middle of the night still make sense in the morning.

Knowing about the creative process is particularly useful because it can be applied to promoting individual and team productivity. I now examine this process.

PROMOTING CREATIVITY IN ORGANIZATIONS

Highly creative people are an asset to any organization. But what exactly do companies do to promote creativity within their ranks? In general terms, the answer lies in things that we can do as individuals and that organizations can do as a whole. I now describe two major approaches.

Training People to Be Creative

Although some people are by nature more creative than others, anyone can develop skills that help them become more creative, and this involves training.[51] Many good ideas go undeveloped because they are not in keeping with current ways of doing things.

THINK OUTSIDE THE BOX Becoming more creative requires allowing oneself to be open to new ideas, or as it is often described, *thinking outside the box*. Some people are by nature more open to new experiences than others. In fact, **openness to experience** is a personality variable that reflects the degree to which people are interested in things that are new and different and get excited by new ideas.

At the same time, it's possible to make anyone more open to new experiences. In fact, some companies do this by sending their employees on *thinking expeditions*—trips specifically designed to put people in challenging situations in an effort to help them think differently and become more creative. According to the CEO of a company that specializes in running such expeditions for clients, these trips "push people out of their 'stupid zone'—a place of mental and physical normalcy—so that they can start to think differently." The CEO adds, "It's an accelerated unlearning experience."[52]

SET CREATIVE GOALS   Learning to be creative is like learning any other skills; it takes practice. And among other things, it requires the discipline to set creativity goals and to strive to attain them. So, instead of simply hoping that you will magically become creative one day, you should work toward this end. However, this involves setting specific goals (recall the discussion of the motivational power of goal setting in Chapter 6). Specifically, creativity is enhanced when people strive to attain creativity goals.

Thomas A. Edison appears to have appreciated this point. The famous inventor set the goal of having a minor invention every ten days and a major invention every six months. This kept Edison focused on being creative—and with more than 1,000 patents in his name, he clearly did an outstanding job of meeting his goals. Importantly, I am not talking about strict external pressure to be creative, which rarely results in anything positive. Creativity is aided when people strive to meet their own challenging goals for achieving creativity.[53] Aim to be creative instead of merely hoping that creativity comes about.

Developing Creative Work Environments

Thus far, I have identified ways of making people more creative that focus on things they can do as individuals. It also is useful for organizations to take steps to change work environments in ways that bring out people's creativity.[54] Several such approaches are suggested by research.[55]

PROVIDE AUTONOMY   It has been established that people are especially creative when they are given the freedom to control their own behavior—that is, when they have *autonomy* (see Chapter 6) and are *empowered* to make decisions (see Chapter 10). At the Japanese video game manufacturer Nintendo, creativity is so important that people are empowered to determine how to spend their time so as to bring out that creativity. As a result, no one considers it odd when designers leave work to go see a movie or a play. Indeed, the high levels of creativity at Nintendo led to the development of its enormously successful Wii game console.

PROVIDE EXPOSURE TO OTHER CREATIVE PEOPLE   It is widely assumed that workers are likely to be creative when they are surrounded by other creative individuals. After all, being around creative people is inspirational. Moreover, one can learn creativity-relevant skills from these individuals. Although this is true under some circumstances, research suggests that the picture is not so simple. Specifically, the effect of having creative coworkers on a person's creativity depends on the extent to which that individual is closely monitored by his or her supervisor.

A researcher conducting a study on this topic administered questionnaires to a group of employees to assess the extent to which they believed they were surrounded by creative coworkers and their beliefs about how closely they were monitored by their supervisors.[56] In addition, supervisors who were familiar with these employees were asked to rate the degree of creativity they demonstrated in their work. The results showed that the presence of creative coworkers promoted creativity when supervisory monitoring was low, but that it actually discouraged creativity when supervisory monitoring was high.

These findings suggest that workers who feel that they are constantly being watched, evaluated, and controlled by their bosses are reluctant to take the chances required to behave in a creative fashion for fear of doing something that is considered inappropriate. As a result, they tend to "play it safe" by simply imitating what others are doing, thereby demonstrating less creativity than they are capable of showing. By contrast, employees who are not closely monitored by their supervisors are likely to be more willing to experiment with new ideas, thereby reaping the benefits of having creative coworkers around them.

ENCOURAGE IDEAS TO CROSS-POLLINATE   When people work on only one project they may get stale, but when they work on several, they are likely to come into contact with wider varieties of people and perspectives. This makes it possible for them to apply to one project ideas they picked up while working on another one. By assigning engineers to multiple projects at the same time, the design firm IDEO seeks to enhance the potential for such cross-pollination to occur. For example, suggestions about how to make comfortable handles for scooters were inspired by enhancements engineers developed while creating a more comfortable computer mouse.

As you might imagine, conditions don't always allow the cross-pollination of ideas to occur. For example, because of the upheaval that results when companies are downsizing, ideas are unlikely to cross-pollinate. It is, therefore, not surprising that creativity tends to be considerably lower at such times.[57]

MAKE JOBS INTRINSICALLY INTERESTING   As I described earlier, people are inclined to be creative when they are intrinsically interested in the work they do. After all, nobody will want to invest the effort it takes to be creative at a task that is boring. How, then, can jobs be made more interesting to people? One possibility is to capitalize on the fact that by nature, some people are more interested than others in performing various tasks. Thus, wherever possible workers should be assigned to jobs that match their interests.

Another way to enhance people's interest in their jobs involves changing the nature of jobs themselves—that is, designing jobs such that people find them engaging and interesting. In Chapter 6 I described several ways in which this may be done (e.g., by emphasizing the importance of jobs performed to the organization's mission, and by holding people accountable for the outcomes of their work) and explained that such tactics are effective at boosting motivation. I now add that the benefit of designing jobs that people find intrinsically interesting also extends to enhancing creativity. Considering these dual benefits, a strong case can be made for making jobs interesting to the people who perform them.

At some companies, this is taken to the extreme by turning work into play. This approach is used routinely at a marketing agency in Richmond, Virginia, appropriately named "Play." Instead of coming up with ideas by sitting in boring meetings, staff members are encouraged to play. For example, in creating a new marketing campaign for the Weather Channel, Play employees spent time developing costumes for superheroes. According to Play's cofounder Andy Stefanovich, the idea is simple: "When you work in a place that encourages people to be themselves, have fun, and take risks, you fuel and unleash their creativity. The best ideas come from playful minds. And the way to tap into that playfulness is to play—together."[58]

SUPPORT CREATIVITY AT HIGH ORGANIZATIONAL LEVELS Nobody in an organization is going to go out of his or her way to be creative if it is not welcomed by the bosses. Supervisors, team leaders, and top executives must encourage employees to take risks if they are to have any chance of being creative. At the same time, this involves accepting any failures that result. This idea was embraced by Livio D. DeSimone, a former CEO of 3M, who helped make it one of the most creative companies in the world. "Failure is not fatal," he has said, noting that success requires taking chances, "and when you take a chance, there is always the possibility of a failure."[59]

PROMOTE DIVERSITY When companies are staffed by people from diverse ethnic and cultural groups, those employees are likely to think differently about the situations they face. And, as I noted earlier, divergent thinking is a key element of creativity. Therefore, companies with ethnically diverse workforces are inclined to have cultures that allow creativity to flourish. In fact, some high-tech experts attribute the highly creative ideas emanating from California's Silicon Valley to the fact that more than one-third of its resident engineers and scientists come from countries throughout the world.[60]

Many of today's most successful multinational corporations attribute their successes to the fact that the adjustments they have made in the course of getting different kinds of people to work together in harmony have had a beneficial, if sometimes unintended by-product—namely, boosting creativity. Although having a diverse population does not ensure creativity, to be sure, it is safe to say that *not* having one can limit creativity. Today's multinational corporations are unwilling to be denied this benefit. One hotel executive expressed this well when referring to his "principle of the United Nations" when it comes to recruiting—hiring the best people in the world, regardless of their nationality.[61]

THE PROCESS OF INNOVATION

Having examined creativity, I now extend my analysis to situations in which people implement their creative skills for the sake of improving their organizations. This is the process of *innovation* to which I referred earlier. Specifically, **innovation** may be defined as the process of making changes to something already established by introducing something new. Put differently, innovation is the successful implementation of creative ideas within an organization. Thus, whereas creativity involves coming up with new ideas, innovation involves putting them into action.

To understand the nature of innovation, it helps to identify the companies considered most innovative and to examine some of the special things they do. With this in mind, see the overview in Table 12.5 of the five companies currently considered the most innovative ones in the world.[62] It's striking, but not surprising, that all of these happen to be in the high-tech industry. This reflects the fact that rapid advances in technology have driven innovation in high-tech firms.

This is all well and good, you may be thinking, but why do companies care about innovation? The answer is clear: innovation pays off on the bottom line. Take the top fifty most innovative companies (the first five of which are identified in Table 12.5), for example. These organizations have enjoyed increases in annual profit margin that are considerably higher than those of the average Standard & Poor's Global 1200 companies. In observing the financial successes of highly innovative companies over the years, one consultant noted that, "Innovation is allowing companies to grow faster [and to] have a richer product mix."[63] As you read about some of the innovative things companies are doing in the remainder of this chapter, you probably will find it easy to understand the positive financial impact of innovative practices.

TABLE 12.5	The Five Most Innovative Companies in the World

Highly innovative companies do not get that way by accident. As summarized here, the world's most innovative companies, as identified by *Fast Company* magazine in 2012, engage in a variety of practices to help promote innovation.

Rank	Company	Innovative Practices and Results
1	Apple	With iTunes, Apple has revolutionized the way we buy music; with the iPhone, it introduced the world to things that can be done with handheld devices; with the iPad, it launched an entirely new market in tablet computing.
2	Facebook	Facebook has created a compelling and ever-widening Web-based platform through which people, for free, can share information with everyone in the world.
3	Google	Thanks to YouTube, Chrome (the second most popular Web browser), and the highly regarded Android smartphones, Google has emerged from a single product company (its diversified search engine) to a multiproduct Internet giant that has transformed the things we do online (see this chapter's Making the Case on p. 367).
4	Amazon	After adding video streaming to its product line, Amazon introduced the first major successful reading device, the "Kindle," into which over a million books can be downloaded wirelessly from anyplace in the world. Amazon.com is still the gold standard for the Internet commerce interface.
5	Square	This small company developed a tiny device that plugs into iPhones that allows merchants to swipe customers' credit cards so that purchase transactions can be completed from just about anywhere.

Source: Fast Company, 2012; see Note 62.

Major Forms of Innovation

Innovation takes several different forms. These come to light in the process of distinguishing between contrasting types of innovation (for a summary comparison, see Figure 12.6).

IMPACT ON EXISTING BUSINESS Over the years, wireless networking standards have changed to allow increasingly faster transmissions of data through the air. First there was 802.11a, then the faster 802.11b, followed by 802.11g, and still faster networking standards such as today's 802.11n. An improvement of this type is referred to as a **sustaining innovation** because it allows companies to approach their markets in the same manner.[64] It gives existing customers better performance. A sustaining innovation is, quite simply, the proverbial "better mousetrap."

Sustaining innovations may be contrasted with others that bring significant changes to the market. For example, before it introduced its personal computer (PC), IBM was in the market of selling minicomputers, and before that, mainframe computers. The mini disrupted the market for the mainframe and the PC disrupted the market for the mini. As this description suggests, an innovation of this type, which completely changes the market, is known as a **disruptive innovation**.

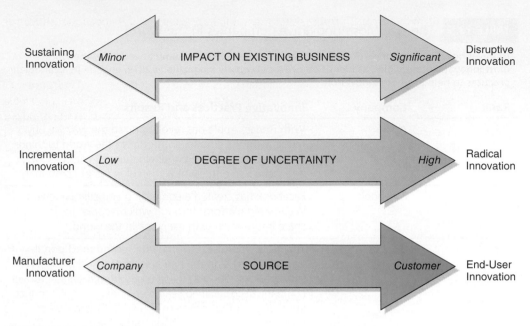

FIGURE 12.6   Forms of Innovation
Various forms of innovation may be distinguished with respect to the three dimensions summarized here.

Despite what the name suggests, a disruptive innovation is desirable for the company that produces it—although, of course, it is meant to be highly disruptive to competitors. One of the most dramatic examples of this may be seen in Apple's game-changing iPhone. This wildly popular multi-function device revolutionized what people were able to accomplish with a single handheld tool. The iPhone killed-off the Palm Pilot from U.S. Robotics and it put a serious dent into a market once dominated by a device with more limited functionality, RIM's once ubiquitous BlackBerry.

DEGREE OF UNCERTAINTY   Another way to categorize innovation is with respect to the degree of uncertainty involved. On some occasions, organizations face conditions in which things have evolved slowly, making it clear what may be done. Moving ahead with innovation isn't particularly risky because the future is relatively certain. This slow-and-steady approach to innovation is known as **incremental innovation**. Companies engaging in incremental innovation exploit existing technology and operate under conditions in which uncertainty about the future is low. In other words, you can pretty much figure out what the future will be.

   Former GE CEO Jack Welch didn't favor the incremental approach to innovation. Instead, he was inclined to do the opposite, shocking his competitors by making quantum leaps in innovation. This approach is known as **radical innovation**. In contrast to companies making incremental innovations, those making radical innovations explore new technology and operate under highly uncertain conditions.[65] Instead of making continuous, linear changes that are slow and steady, radical innovation involves a trajectory that is sporadic and discontinuous. And when it works, the payoffs of radical innovation tend to be huge. For example, radical innovations resulted in the Colgate-Palmolive Company's development of Colgate Total, a newly formulated germ-fighting toothpaste that unseated Crest as the world's leading toothpaste brand.

SOURCE OF INNOVATION   Traditionally, the source of innovation is the company itself. This process, known as **manufacturer innovation**, occurs when an individual or organization develops an innovation for the purpose of selling it. Intel, for example, develops faster processor chips, which it sells to customers demanding more powerful computers.

Although manufacturer innovation has been going on for some time, many of today's organizations are finding inspiration from the individuals who use their goods or services. This process, known as **end-user innovation**, is very popular today because users of products provide useful guidance with respect to what is needed.[66] Companies seeking feedback from the users of its products about what features they desire in the future are likely to be focusing on end-user innovation. Microsoft's Windows 7 operating system is said to be the result of this process. A much lower-tech example may be seen in the introduction of organic and fair-trade tea in China, the motherland of tea.[67] As customer interest in these products emerged, some enterprising new tea merchants were quick to corner the market for these premium products, hoping to change tastes that developed over many centuries.

Targets of Innovation

If innovation involves introducing changes to activities that already are established, it makes sense to ask: What business activities are the foci of innovation? In general, companies can be innovative with respect to just about anything. However, most innovation falls into one or more of the following seven categories, each of which may be considered a target of innovation.[68]

- **Product innovation**—Introducing goods that are new or substantially improved (e.g., easier-to-use software)
- **Service innovation**—Introducing services that are new or substantially improved (e.g., faster overnight delivery of packages)
- **Process innovation**—Creating a new or significantly improved production or delivery method (e.g., an easier and more accurate order taking system for call center operators)
- **Marketing innovation**—Coming up with new and/or improved marketing methods, such as those involving product design or packaging, product promotion, or pricing[69]
- **Supply chain innovation**—Developing quicker and more accurate ways to get products from suppliers into the hands of customers
- **Business model innovation**—Revising the basic way business is done (e.g., focusing on high volume and low prices or on offering extremely high-quality goods to exclusive clients)
- **Organizational innovation**—Changing key organizational practices, such as those presented in this book (e.g., how the organization is structured; see Chapter 13)

As you might imagine, companies attempting to be innovative tend to follow more than one of these practices at a time. For example, consider a financial investment firm that is trying to be more innovative. This may involve developing new financial products (e.g., new money market funds) and services (e.g., new interest-bearing checking accounts) for clients, combining basic financial attributes (e.g., risk sharing, liquidity, credit) in innovative ways, and finding legal ways to minimize clients' income tax liabilities. Not only does this require creating new products and services, but also new business models, improved business processes, and so on. In other words, innovation often involves multiple activities that are followed in concert.

Conditions Required for Innovation to Occur

Creativity is necessary for innovation to occur, but it is not sufficient. What other factors, then, are required for innovation to occur? As it works out, the answer lies in the same basic components that are essential for creativity to occur, albeit in different ways—motivation, resources, and skills.

MOTIVATION TO INNOVATE Just as individual creativity requires that people be motivated to do what it takes to be creative, organizational innovation requires that companies have the kinds of cultures that encourage innovation. When top executives fail to promote a vision of innovation and accept the status quo, change is unlikely. However, at organizations such as Google, where leaders envision innovation as being part of the natural order of things, it is not surprising that innovative efforts are constantly underway (see this chapter's Making the Case on p. 367).

RESOURCES TO INNOVATE   Again, a parallel to individual creativity is in order. Just as people must have certain basic skills to be creative, so too must organizations possess certain basic resources that make innovation possible. For example, to be innovative, at the very least, organizations must have what it takes in terms of human and financial resources. After all, unless the necessarily skilled people and deep pockets are available to do what it takes to innovate, stagnation is likely to result.

SKILLS TO MANAGE INNOVATION   Finally, just as individuals must hone special skills needed to be creative, so too must organizations develop special ways of managing people so as to encourage innovation—that is, *skills in innovation management.* Most notable in this regard is the matter of *balance.* Specifically, managers help promote innovation when they show balance with respect to three key matters: goals, reward systems, and time pressure.

- Organizational innovation is promoted when *goals* are linked carefully to the corporate mission. However, they should not be so specific as to tie the hands of those who put them into practice. Innovation is unlikely when such restrictions are imposed.
- *Reward systems* should recognize one's contributions generously and fairly, but they should not be so specific as to connect literally every move to a bonus or some type of monetary reward. To do so discourages people from taking the kinds of risks that make innovation possible.
- Innovation management requires carefully balancing the *time pressures* under which employees are placed. If pressures are too great, people may be unimaginative and offer routine solutions. By the same token, if pressure is too weak, employees may have no sense of time urgency and believe that a particular project is too unimportant to warrant any creative attention on their part.

Stages of the Organizational Innovation Process

Any CEO who snaps her fingers one day and expects her troops to be innovative on command surely will be in for disappointment. Innovation does not happen all at once. Rather, innovation occurs gradually, through a series of stages. I now describe these (see the summary in Figure 12.7).[70]

STAGE 1: SETTING THE AGENDA   The first stage of the process of innovation begins by setting the agenda for innovation. This involves creating a **mission statement**—a document describing an organization's overall direction and general goals. The component of innovation that is most involved here is *motivation* (see Chapter 6). After all, the highest-ranking officials of the organization must be highly committed to innovation before they will initiate a push toward it.

STAGE 2: SETTING THE STAGE   Once an organization's mission has been established, it is prepared to set the stage for innovation. This may involve narrowing down certain broad goals into more specific tasks and gathering the resources to meet them. It may also involve assessing the environment, both outside and inside the organization, searching for anything that either may support or inhibit later efforts to "break the rules" by being creative. Setting the stage for innovation most effectively requires using the skills necessary for innovation management as well as full use of the organization's human and financial resources.

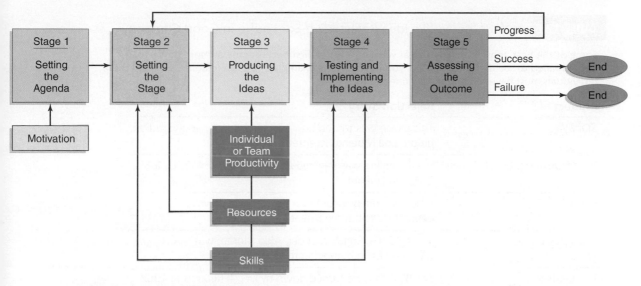

FIGURE 12.7 The Process of Innovation
The innovation process consists of the various components, and follows the steps, shown here.
Source: Adapted from Amabile et al., 2002; see Note 70.

STAGE 3: PRODUCING THE IDEAS   This stage of the process involves coming up with new ideas and testing them. It is in this third stage that individual and group creativity enters the picture. As a result, all of the components of individual creativity mentioned earlier are involved. What's more, these may combine in important ways with various organizational factors. For example, an individual who has the skills and motivation to be highly creative might find his motivation waning as he attempts to introduce novel ideas in an organization that is not committed to innovation and that fails to make the necessary resources available. By contrast, the highly innovative nature of a company may bring out the more creative side of an individual who may not have been especially creative.

STAGE 4: TESTING AND IMPLEMENTING THE IDEAS   This is the stage where implementation occurs. Now, after an initial group of individuals has developed an idea, other parts of the organization get involved. For example, a prototype product may be developed and tested, and market research may be conducted. In short, input from the many functional areas of the organization is provided. As you might imagine, resources in the task domain are important at this stage. After all, unless adequate amounts of money, personnel, material systems, and information are provided, the idea will be unlikely to survive.

Interestingly, even a good idea and resources are not enough to bring innovation to life. Skills in innovation management are critical, because for good ideas to survive it is necessary for them to be "nourished" and supported throughout the organization. Even the best ideas may be "killed off" if people in some parts of the company are not supportive. For some remarkable examples of this, see Table 12.6.[71] When you see all the great ideas that didn't quite make it at first, you come to realize that you are in excellent company if your own ideas are rejected.

STAGE 5: ASSESSING THE OUTCOME   The final stage of the process involves evaluating the new idea that arises. What happens to that concept depends on the results of the assessment.

| TABLE 12.6 | Is Your Innovative Idea Rejected? If So, You're in Good Company |

Some of the best, most innovative ideas were rejected at first because one or more powerful people failed to see their merit. When you look at these examples, you can imagine how bad these individuals must have felt about "the one that got away."

Product	Rejection Story
Star Wars	This movie was turned down by twelve Hollywood studios before finally being accepted.
Photocopying process	Photocopying was rejected as a viable technology by IBM, GM, and DuPont.
Velcro	American entrepreneur Victor Kiam turned down an opportunity to buy the patent for $25,000.
Transistor radio	In the 1950s, Sony's founder, Akio Morita, was unsuccessful in marketing this idea.
The Beatles	The Beatles were turned down by Decca Records in 1962 because it was believed that "groups with guitars are on the way out."
Movies with soundtracks	In 1927, Harry Warner, president of the Warner Brothers motion picture studio, said "nobody wants to hear actors talk."

Sources: Based on information reported by Davila et al., 2005; Ricchiuto, 1997; see Note 71.

Three outcomes are possible. If the resulting idea (e.g., a certain product or service) has been a total success, it will be accepted and carried out in the future. This ends the process. Likewise, the process is over if the idea has been a complete failure. In this case, there is no good reason to continue. However, if the new idea shows promise and makes some progress toward the organization's objectives, but still has problems, the process restarts at stage 2.

This five-stage process may not account for all innovations you may find in organizations. Still, this general model does a good job of identifying the major steps through which most innovations pass as they move from a specific organizational need to a product or service that meets that need.

Back to the Case

Answer the following questions based on this chapter's Making the Case (p. 367) to illustrate insights you have derived from the material in this chapter.

1. How would you characterize the organizational culture at Google? What particular aspects of that culture appear to drive the highly creative nature of the employees and innovative aspects of the company's products?
2. What might be done to promote still higher levels of creativity among Google engineers and software developers?
3. How do various aspects of the business and economic environment contribute to Google's capacity to be innovative?

You Be the Consultant

Promoting a Creative Organizational Culture

The president of your organization, a small manufacturing company, has been complaining that sales are stagnant. A key problem, you discover, is that the market for the products your firm makes is fully developed—and, frankly, the products themselves are not very exciting. No one seems to care about doing anything innovative. Instead, the employees seem more interested in doing things the way they have always done them. Answer the following questions based on the material in this chapter.

1. What factors do you suspect are responsible for the way the culture in this organization has developed over the years?
2. What do you recommend should be done to enhance the creativity of this company's employees?
3. What could be done to help make the company's products more innovative?

Self-Assessment Exercise

WHO'S MOST LIKE A GIRAFFE?

A highly effective way of "getting your creative juices flowing" is by thinking about things in unusual ways. (This is the concept of *divergent thinking* described on p. 396.) This opens you up to considering new approaches. And this, in turn, is key to promoting creative thinking. This exercise is designed to get this process going.

Directions

1. In the left-hand column of the following table is a list of animals. For each one, think of a famous person (a celebrity from any walk of life, such as a well-known performer, politician, athlete, etc.), alive or dead, who you believe is most similar to it in one way or another. The match can be based on a physical similarity, personality, whatever, so long as you think there's some strong similarity. Write that person's name on the corresponding line in the "Celebrity" column.
2. For each of the celebrities, think of one particular food that you associate with that person for one reason or another. Write the name of that food on the corresponding line in the "Food" column.

Animal	Celebrity	Food
Giraffe		
Snake		
Tiger		
Rat		
Panda		
Moose		
Monkey		
Flamingo		
Crab		
Grasshopper		
Cougar		
Parrot		

Discussion Questions

1. Was completing this exercise helpful in getting you to think about things in unusual ways? Why or why not?
2. Do you believe that thinking about things from unusual perspectives will help you think more creatively in other ways, such as in your job? If so, for how long do you think this will last?
3. In what ways do you think that being more creative will help you on your current job? How about in a job you hope to have someday? Might there be any ways in which being especially creative will be a hindrance?
4. So, who's most like a giraffe, anyway?

Group Exercise

WHAT DOES YOUR WORKSPACE SAY ABOUT YOUR ORGANIZATIONAL CULTURE?

Newcomers' impressions of an organization's culture depend greatly on the visual images of that organization they first see. Even without knowing anything about an organization, just seeing the workplace sends a message, intentional or unintentional, about what that organization is like. The following exercise is designed to demonstrate this phenomenon.

Directions

1. Each member of the class should take several photographs of his or her workplace and select the three that best capture, in his or her own mind, the essence of what that organization is like.
2. One member of the class should identify the company depicted in his or her photos, describe the type of work it does, and present the photos to the rest of the class.
3. Members of the class should then rate the organization shown in the photos using the following dimensions. Circle the number that comes closest to your feelings about the company shown.

unfamiliar	: 1 : 2 : 3 : 4 : 5 : 6 : 7 :	familiar
unsuccessful	: 1 : 2 : 3 : 4 : 5 : 6 : 7 :	successful
unfriendly	: 1 : 2 : 3 : 4 : 5 : 6 : 7 :	friendly
unproductive	: 1 : 2 : 3 : 4 : 5 : 6 : 7 :	productive
not innovative	: 1 : 2 : 3 : 4 : 5 : 6 : 7 :	innovative
uncaring	: 1 : 2 : 3 : 4 : 5 : 6 : 7 :	caring
conservative	: 1 : 2 : 3 : 4 : 5 : 6 : 7 :	risky
closed	: 1 : 2 : 3 : 4 : 5 : 6 : 7 :	open

4. Take turns sharing your individual reactions to each set of photos. Compare the responses of the student whose company pictures were examined with those of the students who were seeing the photos for the first time.
5. Repeat this process using the photos of other students' organizations.

Discussion Questions

1. For each set of photos examined, how much agreement or disagreement was there within the class about the companies rated?
2. For each set of photos examined, how close did the descriptions of members of the class come to the photographers' assessments of their own companies? In other words, how well did the photos capture the culture of the organization as perceived by an "insider"?
3. As a whole, were people more accurate in assessing the culture of companies with which they were already familiar than those they didn't already know? If so, why do you think this occurred?

Notes

MAKING THE CASE NOTES

CNNMoney. (2012). 100 best companies to work for. *Fortune*. http://money.cnn.com/magazines/fortune/best-companies/2012/full_list/. Hongkiat.Com. (2012). 14 interesting facts about Google. http://www.hongkiat.com/blog/interesting-facts-about-google/. Mills, E. (2007, April 27). Newsmaker: Meet Google's culture czar. *CNet*. http://news.cnet.com/Meet-Googles-culture-czar/2008-1023_3-6179897.html. Carr, A. (2010, September 16). How to unleash your human potential. *Fast Company*. http://www.fastcompany.com/1689433/how-to-unleash-your-employees-potential.

CHAPTER NOTES

1. Schein, E. H. (2010). *Organizational culture and leadership: A dynamic view* (4th ed.). San Francisco, CA: Jossey-Bass. Schneider, B. (1990). *Organizational climate and culture*. San Francisco, CA: Jossey-Bass.

2. Schein, E. H. (2010). *Organizational culture and leadership: A dynamic view* (4th ed.). San Francisco, CA: Jossey-Bass.

3. Knight, T. (2004, October). Build a strong foundation: High performance begins with culture. *CPA Leadership Report*. http://www.cpareport.com/Newsletter%20Articles/2004%20Articles/BuildaStrongFoundation_Oct_2004.htm

4. Consumer Reports (2010, February 22). Toyota reportedly worked with feds to save $199 million in recalls. *Cars Blog*. http://blogs.consumerreports.org. Liker, J. (2008). *Toyota culture: The heart and soul of the Toyota way*. New York: McGraw-Hill.

5. Cameron, K. S., & Quinn, R. E. (2011). *Diagnosing and changing organizational culture* (3rd ed.). San Francisco, CA: Jossey-Bass. Martin, J. (1996). *Cultures in organizations*. New York: Oxford University Press.

6. Perna, J. (2001, July 15). Reinventing how we do business. *Vital Speeches of the Day, 67*(19), 587–591.

7. The Disney Institute & Eisner, M. D. (2001). *Be our guest: Perfecting the art of customer service*. New York: Hyperion.

8. Barrett, C. (2006, January). Coleen's corner: Managers in training. *Spirit Magazine*, p. 12. http://www.southwest.com/about_swa

9. Nash, G. D. (1992). *A. P. Giannini and the Bank of America*. Norman, OK: University of Oklahoma Press.

10. Connors, R. & Smith, T. (2011). *Change the culture, change the game*. New York: Portfolio Hardcover. Anonymous. (1999, April). Toxic shock? *Fast Company*, p. 38.

11. Healthy Companies International. (2012). http://www.healthycompanies.com/. Rosen, R. H., & Berger, L. (1992). *Healthy company: Eight strategies to develop people, productivity, and profits*. New York: J. P. Tarcher.

12. Institute for Business, Technology, and Ethics. (2004). Eight traits of a healthy organizational culture. http://www.ethix.org/8%20traits.pdf. Barry, L. L. (1999). *Discovering the soul of service: Nine drivers of sustainable business success*. New York: The Free Press.

13. Driskill, G. W. (2010). *Organizational culture in action*. Thousand Oaks, CA: Sage. Vlamis, A., & Smith, B. (2001). *Do you? Business the Yahoo! way*. New York: Capstone.

14. Garr, D. (2000). *IBM redux: Lou Gerstner and the business turnaround of the decade*. New York: HarperCollins.

15. Merdidden, T. (2001). *Big shots: Business the Nokia way*. New York: Capstone.

16. Florea, G., & Phinney, G. (2001). *Barbie talks!: An expose of the first talking Barbie doll*. New York: Hyperion.

17. Tsui, A. S., Zhang, Z.-X., Wang, H., Xin, K. R., & Wu, J. B. (2006). Unpacking the relationship between CEO leadership behavior and organizational culture. *Leadership Quarterly, 17*, 113–137.

18. Freiberg, K., Freiberg, J., & Peters, T. (1998). *Nuts! Southwest Airlines' crazy recipe for business and personal success*. New York: Bantam Doubleday Dell.

19. Morrow, P. (2000, August 2). Eight keys to creating a customer service culture. *Inc.* http://www.inc.com/articles/2000/08/20028.html

20. Cameron, K. S., & Quinn, R. E. (2011). *Diagnosing and changing organizational culture: Based on the competing values framework* (3rd ed.). San Francisco, CA: Jossey-Bass.

21. Kauffman, J. (2005). Lost in space: A critique of NASA's crisis communications in the Columbia disaster. *Public Relations Review, 31*, 263–275.

22. Welch, J. (2005). *Winning*. New York: HarperCollins.

23. Welch, J. (1995, February). Interview with Jack Welch. *Business Today*. http://www.1000ventures.com/business_guide/mgmt_new-model_25lessons-welch.html

24. Berrio, A. A. (2003). An organizational culture assessment using the competing values framework: A profile of Ohio State University extension. *Journal of Extension, 41*(2). http://www.joe.org/joe/2003april/a3.shtml

25. Baker, S., Crockett, R. O., & Gross, N. (1998, August 10). Can CEO Ollila keep the cellular superstar flying high? *BusinessWeek*, pp. 55–57, 59. http://www.businessweek.com/1998/32/b3590001.htm

26. Waterman, R. J., Jr. (1993). *Adhocracy*. New York: W. W. Norton.

27. 3M. (2010). A culture of innovation. St. Paul, MN: Author. http://solutions.3m.com/3MContentRetrievalAPI/BlobServlet?lmd=1321384592000&locale=en_WW&assetType=MMM_Image&assetId=1319209959040&blobAttribute=ImageFile

28. Deering, A., Dilts, R., & Russell, J. (2003, Spring). Leadership cults and cultures. *Leader to Leader, 28*, 36–43.

29. Martin, J., Sitkin, S. B., & Boehm, M. (1985). Founders and the elusiveness of a cultural legacy. In P. J. Frost, L. F. Moore, M. R. Louis, C. C. Lundberg, & J. Martin (Eds.), *Organizational culture* (pp. 99–124). Beverly Hills, CA: Sage.

30. Lemon, M., & Sahota, P. S. (2004). Organizational culture as a knowledge repository for increased innovative capacity. *Technovation, 24*, 484–498. Walsh, J. P., & Ungson, G. R. (1991). Organizational memory. *Academy of Management Review, 16*, 873–896.

31. Reitman, J. (1998). *Bad blood: Crisis in the American Red Cross*. New York: Pinnacle Books.

32. Ornstein, S. L. (1986). Organizational symbols: A study of their meanings and influences on perceived psychological climate. *Organizational Behavior and Human Decision Processes, 38*, 207–229.

33. Carroll, P. (1993). *Big blues: The unmaking of IBM*. New York: Crown.

34. Branwyn, G. (1997). *Jargon watch: A pocket dictionary for the jitterati*. San Francisco, CA: Hardwired.

35. Martin, J. (1982). Stories and scripts in organizational settings. In A. Hastorf & A. Isen (Eds.), *Cognitive social psychology* (pp. 255–306). New York: Elsevier-North Holland.

36. Ransdell, E. (2000, January–February). The Nike story? Just tell it. *Fast Company*, pp. 44, 46.

37. Zappos.com. (2012). Zappos family core values. http://about.zappos.com/our-unique-culture/zappos-core-values

38. Walter, G. A. (1985). Culture collisions in mergers and acquisitions. In P. J. Frost, L. F. Moore, M. R. Louis, C. C. Lundberg, & J. Martin (Eds.), *Organizational culture* (pp. 301–314). Beverly Hills, CA: Sage.

39. Vlasic, B., & Stertz, B. A. (2001). *Taken for a ride: How Daimler-Benz drove off with Chrysler*. New York: Harper Business. Naughton, K. (2000, December 11). A mess of a merger. *Newsweek*, pp. 54–57. Elkind, P. (1998, November 9). A merger made in hell. *Fortune*, pp. 134–138, 140, 142, 144, 146, 149, 150. Burrough, B., & Helyar, J. (1990). *Barbarians at the gate*. New York: Harper Collins. Muller, J. (1999, November 29). Lessons from a casualty of the culture wars. *BusinessWeek*, p. 198. Muller, J. (1999, November 15). The one-year itch at DaimlerChrysler. *BusinessWeek*, p. 42.

40. Charan, R. (2006, April). Home Depot's blueprint for culture change. *Harvard Business Review*, pp. 60–70.

41. See Note 40 (quote, p. 64).

42. Fischer, I., & Frontczak, D. (1999, September). Culture club. *Business 2.0*, pp. 196–198.

43. Now for sale, the Zappos culture. (2010, January 11). *BusinessWeek*, p. 57.

44. Zappos Insights. (2012) Train onsite with the Zappos family. http://www.zapposinsights.com/training

45. Amabile, T. M. (1988). A model of creativity and innovation in organizations. In B. M. Staw & L. L. Cummings (Eds.), *Research in organizational behavior* (Vol. 10, pp. 123–167). Greenwich, CT: JAI Press.

46. Amabile, T. M., & Fisher, C. M. (2009). Stimulate creativity by fueling passion. In E. A. Locke (Ed.), *The Blackwell handbook of principles of organizational behavior* (2nd ed., pp. 481–497). Oxford, England: Blackwell.

47. Runco, M. A. (1991). *Divergent thinking*. Westport, CT: Greenwood.

48. The Drucker Foundation, Hesselbein, F., & Johnston, R. (2002). *On creativity, innovation, and renewal: A leader-to-leader guide.* New York: Wiley.

49. See Note 48.

50. Kabanoff, B., & Rossiter, J. R. (1994). Recent developments in applied creativity. In C. Cooper & I. T. Robertson (Eds.), *International review of industrial and organizational psychology* (Vol. 9, pp. 283–324). London: Wiley.

51. Kabanoff, B., & Bottiger, P. (1991). Effectiveness of creativity training and its reaction to selected personality factors. *Journal of Organizational Behavior, 12,* 235–248.

52. Muoio, A. (2000, January–February). Idea summit. *Fast Company,* pp. 151–156, 160, 162, 164 (quote, p. 152).

53. Shalley, C. E. (1991). Effects of productivity goals, creativity goals, and personal discretion on individual creativity. *Journal of Applied Psychology, 76,* 179–185.

54. Amabile, T. M., Conti, R., Coon, H., Lazenby, J., & Herron, M. (1996). Assessing the work environment for creativity. *Academy of Management Journal, 39,* 1154–1184.

55. Oldham, G. R., & Cummings, A. (1996). Employee creativity: Personal and contextual factors at work. *Academy of Management Journal, 39,* 607–634.

56. Zhou, J. (2003). When the presence of creative coworkers is related to creativity: The role of supervisor close monitoring, developmental feedback, and creative personality. *Journal of Applied Psychology, 88,* 413–422.

57. Amabile, T. M., & Conti, R. (1999). Changes in the work environment for creativity during downsizing. *Academy of Management Journal, 42,* 630–640.

58. Dahle, C. (2000, January–February). Mind games. *Fast Company,* pp. 169–173, 176, 178–179.

59. Sutton, R. I., & Hargadon, A. (1996). Brainstorming groups in context: Effectiveness in a product design firm. *Administrative Science Quarterly, 41,* 685–718 (quote, p. 702).

60. Zachary, P. C. (2000, July). Mighty is the mongrel. *Fast Company,* pp. 270–272, 276, 278, 280, 282, 284.

61. Zachary, G. P. (2000). *The global me: New cosmopolitans and the competitive edge.* New York: Public Affairs Books.

62. Fast Company Staff. (2012, March). The world's 50 most innovative companies. *Fast Company.* http://www.fastcompany.com/most-innovative-companies/2012/full-list

63. See Note 61 (quote, p. 66).

64. Christensen, C. M., & Raynor, M. E. (2003). *The innovator's solution.* Boston, MA: Harvard Business School.

65. Tucker, R. B. (2002). *Driving growth through innovation.* San Francisco, CA: Berrett-Koehler.

66. Von Hippel, E. (2005). *Democratizing innovation.* Cambridge, MA: MIT Press.

67. Nerenberg, J. (2010, August 16). Innovation in China's tea industry. *Fast Company.* http://www.fastcompany.com/1682155/while-not-the-same-as-in-england-the-united-states-demands-tea-but-with-an-organic-fair-trad

68. Davila, T., Epstein, M. J., & Shelton, R. (2006). *Making innovation work: How to manage it, measure it, and profit from it.* Upper Saddle River, NJ: Prentice Hall. Chakravorti, B. (2003). *The slow pace of fast change: Bringing innovations to market in a connected world.* Boston, MA: Harvard Business School Press. Chesbrough, H. W. (2003). *Open innovation: The new imperative for creating and profiting from technology.* Boston, MA: Harvard Business School Press.

69. Bernard, S. (2005, April 18). The perfect prescription: How the pill bottle was remade—sensibly and beautifully. *New York.* http://newyorkmetro.com/nymetro/health/features/11700/index.html

70. Amabile, T., Hadley, C. N., & Kramer, S. J. (2002). Creativity under the gun. *Harvard Business Review, 80*(8), 52–61.

71. Davila, T., Epstein, M., & Shelton, R. (2005). *Making innovation work: How to manage it, measure it, and profit from it.* Upper Saddle River, NJ: Prentice Hall. Ricchiuto, J. (1997). *Collaborative creativity.* New York: Oakhill.

13 DESIGNING EFFECTIVE ORGANIZATIONS

LEARNING OBJECTIVES

After reading this chapter, you will be able to:

1. **DEFINE** organizational structure and **DISTINGUISH** among aspects of organizational structure that are typically represented in an organization chart.
2. **DISTINGUISH** among the three types of departmentalization: functional organizations, product organizations, and matrix organizations.
3. **DEFINE** organizational design and **DISTINGUISH** between classical and neoclassical approaches to organizational design.
4. **DESCRIBE** the contingency approach to organizational design.
5. **IDENTIFY** emerging approaches to organizational design.
6. **DISTINGUISH** between conglomerates and strategic alliances as two types of interorganizational designs.

THREE GOOD REASONS you should care about. . .

Designing Effective Organizations

1. To understand how organizations function, you must know about their structural elements— their basic building blocks.
2. The design of organizations has profound effects on how they function.
3. The way organizations are designed has been changing in recent years and promises to continue changing in the years ahead.

Making the Case for...

Designing Effective Organizations

Verizon and McAfee Head for "the Cloud" Together

For three decades, companies purchased computers to run software that enabled them to be productive, and they connected them in networks to facilitate communication. This model served them well, although the investments in hardware, software, and networking infrastructure were enormous and keeping everything up and running was an ongoing battle. Today, there's a better option. Many organizations are finding it far easier, less expensive, and more efficient to give up all this and simply plug into "the cloud." This refers to an array of computer services accessed via the Internet (akin to the way you may be storing media files, such as when using Apple's iCloud).

As a business model, it works in a similar way to utilities. We don't own sources of electricity, but we can get all we want by plugging into outlets fed by our local electric companies. They provide the service, maintain it, and upgrade it to meet demands. Cloud computing operates the same way. As organizations grow, shrink, move in new directions, open facilities abroad, and join forces with others, their computing needs change accordingly.

By using cloud computing, companies can focus their resources on their core businesses instead of investing in the technology and enormous IT (information technology) staffs that support it. For cloud computing to succeed, two ingredients are essential: there must be an incredibly sophisticated and powerful hardware and software infrastructure in place that readily meets the needs of clients, and it must be perfectly secure. If the system breaks down or is compromised by hackers, that cloud will burst, triggering a massive storm of angry users.

As you might expect, organizations will reach for the cloud only when they feel assured that they can count on it to meet their needs effectively and securely. Making this a reality often requires the expert resources of more than one company. It was with this in mind that Verizon Business, a major provider of communication and IT solutions for businesses throughout the world, joined forces with McAfee, the world's largest dedicated security technology company. In announcing their strategic alliance, company officials explained that their objective was "to provide integrated security solutions to businesses and government agencies worldwide."

Beyond using this arrangement as a springboard for tomorrow's cloud computing business, it also enhances each company's capacity to serve today's customers. For example, Verizon now is able to offer McAfee's full range of enterprise security solutions to clients. It also will tap McAfee's secure technology, which makes it economically feasible to process credit card payments for companies with fewer than 1 million annual transactions, about a third of all business. At McAfee's end, the alliance gives it access to the vast distribution capabilities of Verizon and its army of 1,200 security specialists who provide onsite, "feet on the street" service to business customers.

These current benefits are only just the beginning of a more ambitious plan. Both companies hope that their deal will soon serve as a springboard to dominance in the rapidly emerging cloud computing business.

Although the complete story has not yet been written, McAfee and Verizon Business are counting on its happy ending, and they're investing considerable resources to see that it does. In today's complex and rapidly changing business environment it's not unusual for companies to join forces. Sometimes they do this to gain competitive advantages in the marketplace. Other times, however, companies must join forces so they can secure new capacities that enable them just to remain in business. At the core of the matter is the issue of how companies can best organize themselves to accomplish their objectives. This example focuses on external forms of organization, but this is a relatively new phenomenon. Traditionally, companies have examined ways of coordinating their efforts internally, organizing themselves into separate units that make them most effective. The question of how to do this is a venerable one for organizations—and, as I explain in this chapter, the answer has far-reaching implications.

OB scholars have provided considerable insight into this matter by studying what is called *organizational structure*—the way individuals and groups are arranged with respect to the tasks they perform—and *organizational design*—the process of coordinating these structural elements in the most effective fashion.[1] As you may suspect, finding the best way to structure and design organizations is no simple task. However, because understanding the structure and design of organizations is key to appreciating their functioning fully—and, ultimately, their success—scientists have devoted considerable attention to this topic.

I describe these efforts in this chapter. Specifically, I examine how these structural elements can be most effectively combined into productive organizational designs. In so doing, I cover the traditional ways of designing organizations as well as several of today's rapidly emerging organizational forms. Finally, I conclude by presenting designs that bring together multiple organizations. Before getting to this, however, I begin by examining the basic structural dimensions of organizations—the various qualities that characterize what they're like.

ORGANIZATIONAL STRUCTURE: THE BASIC DIMENSIONS OF ORGANIZATIONS

Think about how a simple house is constructed. Typically, it is composed of a wooden frame positioned atop a concrete slab covered by a roof and siding materials. Within this basic structure are separate systems operating to provide electricity, water, and telephone services. Similarly, the structure of the human body is composed of a skeleton surrounded by various systems of organs, muscle, and tissue serving bodily functions such as respiration, digestion, and the like. Although you may not have thought about it much, we also can identify the structure of an organization in a similar fashion.

Consider, for example, the college or university you attend. It probably is composed of various groupings of people and departments working together to serve special functions. Individuals and groups are dedicated to tasks such as teaching, providing financial aid, maintaining the physical facilities, and so on. Of course, within each group, even more distinctions can be found between the jobs people perform. For example, it's unlikely that the instructor for your organizational behavior course also is teaching seventeenth-century French literature. Clearly, organizations are not haphazard collections of people, but meaningful combinations of groups and individuals working together to achieve the goals of the organization.[2] The term **organizational structure** refers to the formal configuration between individuals and groups with respect to the allocation of tasks, responsibilities, and authority within organizations.[3]

Strictly speaking, one cannot see the structure of an organization; it is an abstract concept. However, the connections between various clusters of functions of which an organization is composed can be represented in the form of a diagram known as an *organization chart* (which I also described in conjunction with communication in Chapter 8). In other words, an organization chart can be considered a representation of a company's internal structure. As you might imagine, organization charts are useful tools for avoiding confusion regarding how various tasks or functions are interrelated.

Organization charts provide information about the various tasks performed within a company and the formal lines of authority between them. For example, look at the chart depicting part of a hypothetical manufacturing organization shown in Figure 13.1 (on p. 404). In this and any other organization chart there are boxes and lines. A box represents a specific job as prescribed formally by the organization—that is, the formal responsibilities associated with the particular post. A line connecting boxes reveals the formally prescribed *reporting relationships* between the individuals performing those jobs. In other words, it reveals "who answers to whom." To organizational scientists, such diagrams reveal a great deal more. Specifically, they reveal five basic dimensions of organizational structure, to which I now turn.

Hierarchy of Authority: Up and Down the Organizational Ladder

Among the first things you see when examining an organization chart is the distinction between higher-level individuals (toward the top) and lower-level individuals (toward the bottom) in what is referred to as a **hierarchy of authority**. The diagram reveals which particular lower-level employees are required to report to which particular individuals immediately above them in the hierarchy. In the hypothetical example in Figure 13.1, the various regional salespeople (at the bottom of the hierarchy and the bottom of the diagram) report to their respective regional sales directors, who report to the vice president of sales, who reports to the president, who reports to the chief executive officer, who reports to the board of directors. As we trace these reporting relationships, we work our way up the organization's hierarchy. In this case, the organization has seven levels.

Even before today's widespread practice of eliminating jobs as a cost-saving measure, organizations have, since the mid-1980s, been restructuring their workforces, seeking to eliminate waste by flattening them out.[4] This is the practice of **downsizing** that has received so much attention in the press. Sometimes, it's referred to as "rightsizing," "delayering," or "retrenching," but whatever it may be called, it essentially refers to the same thing—eliminating entire layers of organizational structure (I will return to this topic in Chapter 14).[5]

Typically, when jobs are lost through restructuring, they are positions found in the middle layers of organizational hierarchies. To a great extent, this follows from the trend toward getting work done through teams (see Chapter 9). As this occurs, tall organizational hierarchies become unnecessary. The underlying assumption is that fewer layers reduce waste and enable people to make better decisions (by moving decision-making authority into the hands of the individuals who are closer to the problems at hand), thereby leading to greater profitability. "Doing more with less" is the mantra of proponents of delayering.

Span of Control: Breadth of Responsibility

Over how many individuals should a manager have responsibility? The earliest management theorists and practitioners alike (even the Roman legions) addressed this question.[6] When you look at an organization chart, the number of people formally required to report to each individual manager is immediately clear. This number constitutes what is known as a manager's **span of control**.

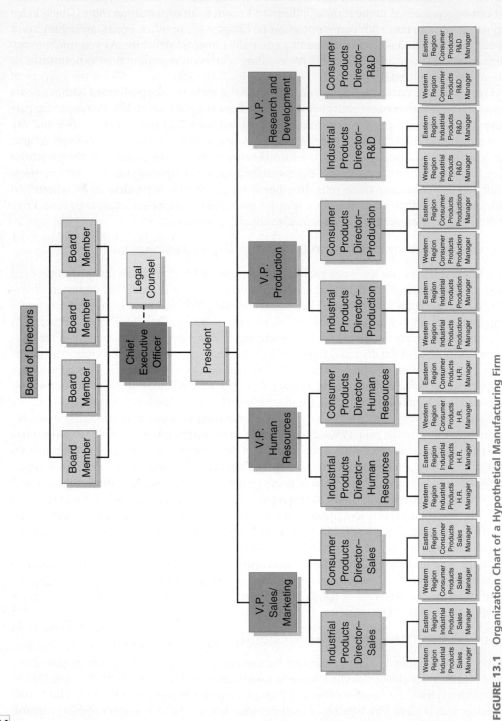

FIGURE 13.1 Organization Chart of a Hypothetical Manufacturing Firm

An organization chart, such as this one, identifies the various functions performed within an organization and the lines of authority between the individuals performing those functions.

Supervisors responsible for many individuals are said to have a *wide* (or *broad*) span of control, whereas those responsible for fewer are said to have a *narrow* span of control.

In the organization chart in Figure 13.2 (on p. 406), note how the managers in the top portion of this diagram have relatively narrow spans of control (only two workers), whereas the ones in the bottom have relatively broader spans of control (twice as many people). In real companies, some managers have spans of control so broad that they may be responsible for dozens of subordinates.

Figure 13.2 shows something important about the relationship between the tallness of a hierarchy and the span of control of its supervisory personnel. Generally speaking, when a manager's span of control is wide, the organization itself tends to have a flat hierarchy. In contrast, when a manager's span of control is narrow, the organization tends to have a tall hierarchy. Specifically, notice that in the "Tall Organization" (at the top of the diagram), there are many levels in the hierarchy and that the span of control is relatively narrow (i.e., the number of people supervised is low). By contrast, in the "Flat Organization" (at the bottom of the diagram), there are only a few levels in the hierarchy, and the span of control is relatively wide. Both organizations depicted here have thirty-one positions, but these are arranged quite differently, as you can see.

It is not readily possible to specify the "ideal" span of control that should be sought. Instead, it makes better sense to consider what form of organization is best suited to various purposes. For example, because supervisors in a military unit must have tight control over subordinates and get them to respond quickly and precisely, a narrow span of control is likely to be effective. As a result, military organizations tend to have extremely tall hierarchies (in the army, for example, ranging in rank from private to four-star general). In contrast, people working in a research and development lab must have an open exchange of ideas and typically require little managerial guidance to be successful. Units of this type tend to have very flat structures. (What is the span of control like in various organizations you may know? The Group Exercise on p. 432 will help you answer this question.)

Division of Labor: Carving Up the Work to Be Done

The standard organization chart makes clear that the many tasks to be performed within a company are divided into specialized jobs, a process known as the **division of labor**. The more that tasks are divided into separate jobs, the more those jobs are *specialized* and the narrower the range of activities that job incumbents are required to perform. In theory, the fewer tasks a person performs, the better he or she may be expected to execute them, freeing others to do the tasks at which they excel. Taken together, an entire organization is composed of people performing a collection of specialized jobs. This is one of the most obvious feature that can be seen in an organization chart.

As you might imagine, the degree to which employees perform specialized jobs is likely to depend on the size of the organization. The larger the organization, the more opportunities for specialization are likely to exist. For example, an individual working in a large advertising agency may get to specialize in a very narrow field, such as writing jingles for radio and TV spots for automobiles. By contrast, someone employed at a much smaller agency may be required to do all writing of print and broadcast ads in addition to helping out with the artwork, meeting with clients, and even making coffee for the office.

Obviously, large organizations are in a good position to reap the benefits of using the talents of employees efficiently (a natural result of an extensive division of labor). As companies downsize, however, many jobs become less specialized. For example, at General Electric, quite a few middle-management positions have been eliminated in recent years. As a consequence, the

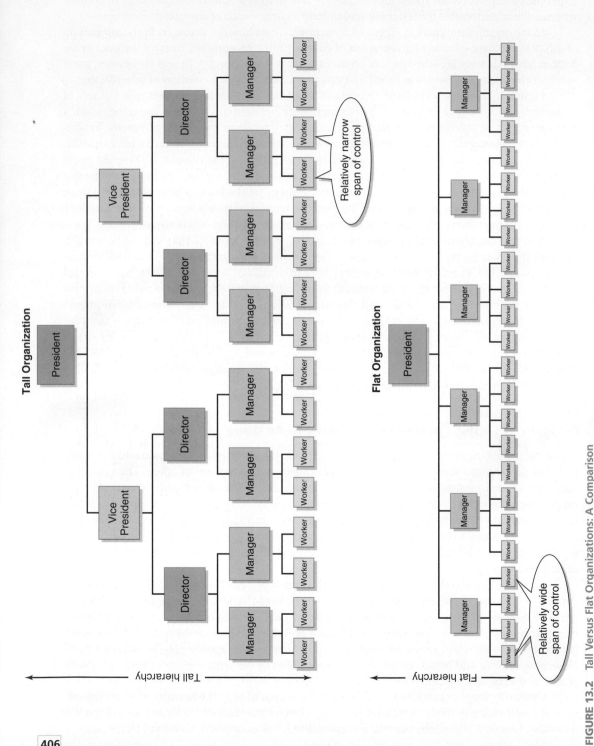

FIGURE 13.2   Tall Versus Flat Organizations: A Comparison

In tall organizations, the hierarchy has many layers, and managers have a narrow span of control (i.e., they are responsible for few subordinates). However, in flat organizations, the hierarchy has few layers, and managers have a wide span of control (i.e., they are responsible for many workers). Both of the organizations depicted here have thirty-one members, although each one is structured differently.

	Division of Labor	
TABLE 13.1 Division of Labor: A Summary		

Low and high levels of division of labor can be characterized with respect to the three dimensions shown here.

	Division of Labor	
Dimension	**Low**	**High**
Degree of specialization	General tasks	Highly specialized tasks
Typical organizational size	Small	Large
Economic efficiency	Inefficient	Highly efficient

remaining managers must perform a wider variety of jobs, making their own jobs less specialized.[7] You can see this relationship in the summary in Table 13.1.

Line Versus Staff Positions: Decision Makers Versus Advisers

The organization chart shown in Figure 13.1 (on p. 404) reveals an additional distinction that deserves to be highlighted—that between *line positions* and *staff positions*. People occupying **line positions** (e.g., the various vice presidents and managers) have decision-making power. However, the individual shown in the dotted box set off to the right—the legal counsel—cannot make decisions, but provides advice and recommendations to be used by the line managers. Such individuals are said to have **staff positions**. In this particular case, the legal counsel may help corporate officials decide whether a certain product name can be used without infringing on copyright restrictions. However, it's the occupants of line positions who make the actual decisions.

In many of today's organizations, human resource managers occupy staff positions, providing specialized services regarding testing and interviewing procedures as well as information about the latest laws on personnel discrimination. Various assistants also fall into this category, holding staff positions. For an example from a large government agency, see Figure 13.3.

Sociologists have reported that staff managers tend to be younger, better educated, and more committed to their fields than to the organizations employing them.[8] Line managers might feel more committed not only because of the greater opportunities they have to exercise decisions, but also because they are more likely to perceive themselves as being part of a company rather than an independent specialist (whose identity lies primarily within his or her specialty area).

Decentralization: Delegating Power Downward

During the first half of the twentieth century, as companies grew in size, they shifted power and authority into the hands of a few upper-echelon administrators—executives whose decisions influenced the many people below them in the organizational hierarchy. In fact, it was during the 1920s that Alfred P. Sloan, Jr., president of General Motors at the time, introduced the notion of a "central office"—the place where a few individuals made policy decisions for the entire company.[9] As part of Sloan's plan, decisions regarding the day-to-day operation of the company were pushed further down the organizational hierarchy, allowing those individuals who were most affected to make the decisions. This process of delegating power from higher to lower levels within organizations is known as **decentralization**. It is the opposite, of course, of **centralization**, the tendency for just a few powerful individuals or groups to hold most of the decision-making power.

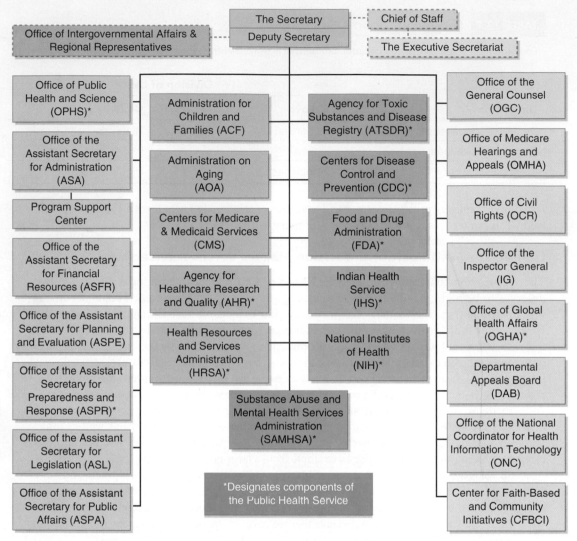

FIGURE 13.3   Line Versus Staff Positions in the U.S. Department of Health and Human Services
The upper echelons of the U.S. Department of Health and Human Services are organized as shown here. Note how the chief of staff, the executive secretariat, and the Office of Intergovernmental Affairs and Regional Representatives are staff positions (designated by broken lines), whereas all others on this organization chart are line positions (designated by solid lines).
Source: U.S. Department of Health and Human Services, 2012.

Earlier, I mentioned that flattening hierarchies has made it possible to streamline organizations by eliminating many middle-management jobs. This is in keeping with the tendency toward decentralization. After all, as people become empowered to make their own decisions, it's unnecessary for them to report to as many supervisors. As a result, organization charts flatten out as decision-making authority is pushed farther down the hierarchy. We see this today as many companies are moving toward decentralization to promote managerial efficiency and to improve employee satisfaction (the result of giving people greater opportunities to take responsibility for their own actions).

TABLE 13.2	Centralization Versus Decentralization: A Matter of Trade-Offs

Various benefits are associated with low decentralization (high centralization) and high decentralization (low centralization) within organizations.

Low Decentralization (High Centralization)	High Decentralization (Low Centralization)
• Eliminates the additional responsibility not desired by people performing routine jobs	• Can eliminate levels of management, making a leaner organization—one that is better equipped to make changes required to adapt to market demands and opportunities (see Chapter 14).
• Permits crucial decisions to be made by individuals who have the "big picture"	• Promotes greater opportunities for decisions to be made by people closest to problems

It is important to note that decentralization is *not* always an ideal way for organizations to be structured. In fact, for some types of jobs, it may be a serious hindrance to productivity. Consider production-oriented positions. In a classic study, researchers found that decentralization improved the performance on some jobs—notably, the work of employees in a research lab. However, decentralization interfered with the performance of people doing more routine, assembly-line jobs.[10] These findings make sense once you consider that people working in research and development positions are inclined to enjoy the autonomy to make decisions that decentralization allows, whereas people working on production jobs are likely to be less interested in taking responsibility for decisions and actually may welcome *not* having to take such responsibility. For a summary of the relative advantages and disadvantages of centralization, see Table 13.2.

DEPARTMENTALIZATION: WAYS OF STRUCTURING ORGANIZATIONS

Thus far, I have been referring to "the" organization chart of a company. Typically, such charts, like the one shown in Figure 13.1 (on p. 404), divide an organization into different units based on the particular functions they perform. However, as I will describe in this section, this is only one option. Organizations also may be structured in other ways, such as with respect to their products, the markets they serve, or combinations of these factors. I now will take a closer look at these various ways of organizing companies into coherent units—a process known as **departmentalization**.

Functional Organizations: Departmentalization by Task

Because it is the form organizations usually take when they are first created, and because it is how we usually think of businesses, the *functional organization* can be considered the most basic approach to departmentalization. Essentially, **functional organizations** departmentalize individuals according to the nature of the tasks they perform, with people who perform similar jobs assigned to the same department. For example, a manufacturing company might consist of separate departments devoted to basic functions such as production, sales, research and development, and accounting (see Figure 13.4).

ADVANTAGES AND DISADVANTAGES Naturally, as organizations grow and become more complex, additional departments may be added or deleted as the need arises. As certain functions become centralized, resources can be saved by avoiding duplication of effort, resulting in a higher level of efficiency. Not only does this type of structure take advantage of *economies of scale* (by

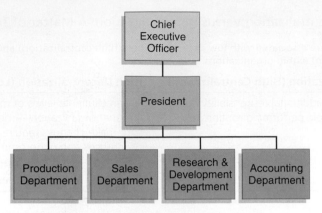

FIGURE 13.4 Functional Organization of a Typical Manufacturing Firm
Functional organizations are ones in which departments are formed on the basis of common tasks performed. In the hypothetical manufacturing firm shown in this simplified organization chart, four typical departments are identified. In specific organizations, the actual functions may differ.

allowing employees performing the same jobs to share facilities and not duplicating functions), but it also allows individuals to specialize, thereby performing only those tasks at which they are most expert. The result is a highly skilled workforce, a direct benefit to the organization.

Partly offsetting these advantages, however, are several potential limitations. The most important of these stems from the fact that functional organizational structures encourage separate units to develop their own narrow perspectives and to lose sight of overall organizational goals. For example, in a manufacturing business, an engineer might see the company's problems in terms of the reliability of its products and lose sight of other key considerations, such as market trends, overseas competition, and so on. Such narrow-mindedness is the inevitable result of functional specialization—the downside of people seeing the company's operations through a narrow lens.

A related problem is that functional structures discourage innovation (see Chapter 12) because they channel individual efforts toward narrow, functional areas instead of encouraging coordination and cross-fertilization of ideas between areas. As a result, such organizations are slow to respond to the challenges and opportunities they face from the environment (such as the need for new products and services). In summary, although functional organizations certainly are logical in nature and have proven useful in many contexts, they are by no means the perfect way to departmentalize people.

Product Organizations: Departmentalization by Type of Output

Organizations—at least successful ones—do not stand still; they change constantly in size and scope. As they develop new products and seek new customers, they might find that a functional structure doesn't work as well as it once did. Manufacturing a wide range of products using a variety of different methods, for example, might put a strain on the manufacturing division of a functional organization. Similarly, keeping track of the varied tax requirements for different types of businesses (e.g., restaurants, farms, real estate, manufacturing) might pose quite a challenge for a single financial division of a company. In response to such strains, a **product organization** might be created. This type of departmentalization creates self-contained divisions, each of which is responsible for everything to do with a certain product or group of products. (For a look at the structure of a product organization, see Figure 13.5.)

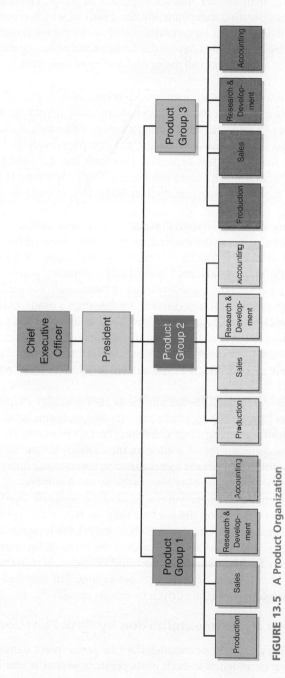

FIGURE 13.5 A Product Organization

In a *product organization*, separate units are established to handle different products or product lines. Each of these divisions contains all of the departments necessary for operating as an independent unit.

When organizations are departmentalized by products, separate divisions are established, each of which is devoted to a certain product or group of products. Each unit contains all the resources needed to develop, manufacture, and sell its particular goods. The organization is composed of separate divisions operating independently, the heads of which report to top management. Although some functions might be centralized within the parent company (e.g., human resources management or legal staff), on a day-to-day basis, each division operates autonomously as a separate company or, as accountants call them, *cost centers* of their own.

ADVANTAGES AND DISADVANTAGES   Such arrangements allow companies to benefit from a marketing perspective, as many auto companies are aware. Take Toyota, for example. In 1989, it introduced its Lexus line of luxury cars. By creating a separate division, manufactured in separate plants and sold by a separate network of dealers, the company made its higher-priced cars look special and avoided making its less expensive cars look less appealing by putting them together with superior products on the same showroom floors. Applying the same reasoning to a completely different market, Toyota launched its Scion line in 2003 to appeal to younger car buyers.

Product organizations also have several drawbacks. The most obvious of these is the loss of economies of scale stemming from the duplication of various departments within operating units. For example, if each unit carries out its own research and development functions, the need for costly equipment, facilities, and personnel is multiplied. Another problem associated with product designs involves the organization's ability to attract and retain talented employees. Since each department within operating units is necessarily smaller than a single, combined one would be, opportunities for advancement and career development are limited. This, in turn, may pose a serious problem with respect to the long-term retention of talented employees. Finally, problems of coordination across product lines may arise. In fact, in extreme cases, actions taken by one operating division may have adverse effects on the outcomes of one or more others.

CASE IN POINT: HP   Hewlett-Packard (better known as HP) provides a clear example of such problems.[11] For most of its history, HP adopted a product design. It consisted of scores of small, largely autonomous divisions, each producing and selling certain products. As it grew—merging with Compaq in 2002—the company found itself in an increasingly untenable situation in which sales representatives from different divisions sometimes attempted to sell different lines of equipment, often to be used for the same basic purposes, to the same customers.

To address this problem, top management reorganized the company into four sectors—what they called "business groups"—based on the markets they serve: the Enterprise Systems Group (which provides information technology hardware for businesses), the Imaging and Printing Group (which focuses on printers for businesses and consumers), the Personal Systems Group (which focuses on personal computers for home and office use), and HP Services (which offers information technology services).[12] In short, driven by market considerations, HP switched from a traditional product organization to an internal structure driven by market considerations.

Matrix Organizations: Departmentalization by Both Function and Product

When the aerospace industry was first developing, the U.S. government demanded that a single manager in each company be assigned to each of its projects so that it was immediately clear who was responsible for the progress of each project. In response to this requirement, the large aerospace company TRW established a "project leader" for each project, someone who shared

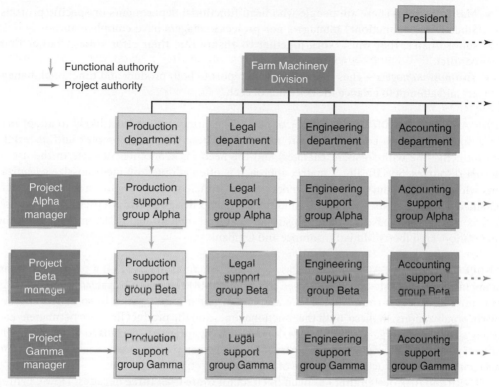

FIGURE 13.6   A Typical Matrix Organization
In a *matrix organization,* a portion of which is depicted here, a product structure is superimposed on a basic functional structure. This results in a dual system of authority in which some managers report to two bosses—a project (or product) manager and a functional (departmental) manager.

authority with the leaders of the existing functional departments.[13] This temporary arrangement later evolved into what is called a **matrix organization**, the type of organization in which an employee is required to report to both a functional (or division) manager and the manager of a specific project (or product). In essence, they developed a complex type of structure that combines both the function and product forms of departmentalization.[14] To better understand matrix organizations, examine the partial organization chart shown in Figure 13.6.

TYPES OF BOSSES   Employees in matrix organizations have two bosses (or, more technically, they are under *dual authority*). One line of authority, shown by each vertical axis on Figure 13.6, is *functional*, managed by vice presidents in charge of various functional areas. The other, shown by each horizontal axis, is *product* (or it may be a specific project or temporary business), managed by specific individuals in charge of certain products (or projects).

In matrix designs, there are three major kinds of bosses. These are as follows:

- *Top leaders*—These are individuals who have authority over both lines (the one based on function and the one based on product or project). Top leaders are responsible for facilitating coordination between functional and product managers and for maintaining an appropriate balance of power between them.

- *Matrix bosses*—These are people who head functional departments or specific projects. Since neither functional managers nor project managers have complete authority over subordinates, they must work together to ensure that their efforts mesh rather than conflict.
- *Two-boss managers*—These are people who report to both product and functional managers and attempt to balance the demands of each.

WHEN ARE MATRIX ORGANIZATIONS USED?   Organizations are most likely to adopt matrix designs when they confront certain conditions. These include a complex and uncertain environment (one with frequent changes) and the need for economies of scale in the use of internal resources. Specifically, a matrix approach is often adopted by medium-size organizations with several product lines that do not possess sufficient resources to establish fully self-contained operating units. Under such conditions, a matrix design provides a useful compromise. Some companies that have adopted this structure, at least on a limited basis, in portions of the organization, are Liberty Mutual Insurance and Citibank.[15]

DEGREE OF PERMANENCE   In some cases, matrix structures are used on a permanent basis. An organization is considered to have used a **permanent overlay** when its project teams are kept going after a project is completed. There also is a degree of permanence in so-called, **mature matrix** organizations. In these, both the functional lines and the product lines are permanent and equally strong in the organization. Finally, it's also possible for matrix designs to be temporary in nature. Specifically, a **temporary overlay** is said to exist when projects are crossed with functions on a short-term basis, such as in the case of a special project.

With a matrix design that has been in effect for more than three decades, Dow Corning is an example of a mature matrix organization.[16] At this company, each functional representative reports to the leaders of his or her own department, while also contributing to the design and operation of the particular product line for which he or she is responsible. Because people working in this fashion have two bosses, they must have sufficient freedom to attain their objectives. As you might imagine, a fair amount of coordination, flexibility, openness, and trust is essential for such a design to work, suggesting that not everyone adapts well to such a system.

ADVANTAGES AND DISADVANTAGES   Several key advantages offered by matrix designs may be identified.[17] First, they permit flexible use of an organization's human resources. Individuals within functional departments can be assigned to work on specific products or projects as the need arises and then return to their regular duties when this task is completed. Such arrangements allow project costs to be shared because it reduces the number of full-time employees required. Second, matrix designs offer organizations an efficient means of responding quickly to a changing, unstable environment. Third, such designs often enhance communication among managers. Indeed, they require matrix bosses to discuss and agree on many matters.

Disadvantages of such designs include the frustration and stress faced by two-boss managers. By reporting to two different supervisors, there's a danger that one of the two authority systems (functional or project) will overwhelm the other, along with the consistently high levels of cooperation required from the people involved for the organization to succeed.[18] In situations where organizations must stretch their financial and human resources to meet challenges from the external environment or take advantage of new opportunities, however, matrix designs often can play a useful role.

ORGANIZATIONAL DESIGN: COORDINATING THE STRUCTURAL ELEMENTS OF ORGANIZATIONS

Earlier in this chapter, I likened the structure of an organization to the structure of a house. Now I am prepared to extend that analogy for purposes of introducing the concept of *organizational design*. Just as a house is designed in a particular fashion by combining its structural elements in various ways, so too can an organization be designed by combining its basic elements in different ways. Accordingly, **organizational design** refers to the process of coordinating the structural elements of organizations in a particular manner.

As you might imagine, this is no easy task. Although I might describe some options that sound neat and rational on the next few pages, in reality this is hardly ever the case. Even the most thoughtfully designed organizations will face the need to change at one time or another, adjusting to the realities of technological changes, political pressures, accidents, and so on. Organizational designs also might be changed intentionally, as may occur when companies enter new businesses, when they merge with others, or simply just because they seek a higher level of operating efficiency. In recent decades, concerns about waste and inefficiency have driven many efforts at redesigning organizations, especially among U.S. government agencies, where the need to streamline has been considerable.

My point is that because organizations operate within a changing world, their own designs must be flexible. Those organizations that are either poorly designed or inflexible cannot survive. If you consider the large number of banks and airlines that have gone out of business in the last few years because of their inability to deal with rapid changes brought about by deregulation and a shifting economy, you'll get a good idea of the ultimate consequences of ineffective organizational design.

Classical and Neoclassical Approaches: The Quest for the One Best Design

The earliest theorists interested in organizational design did not operate out of awareness of the point I just made regarding the need for organizations to be flexible. Instead, they approached the task of designing organizations as a search for "the one best way." Although today we are more attuned to the need to adapt organizational designs to various economic and social conditions, theorists in the early and middle part of the twentieth century sought to establish the ideal form for all organizations under all conditions—that is, the universal design.

In Chapter 1, I described the efforts of the earliest organizational scholars such as Max Weber and Frederick Taylor. These theorists believed that effective organizations were ones that had a formal hierarchy, a clear set of rules, specialization of labor, highly routine tasks, and a highly impersonal working environment. You may recall that Weber referred to this form as a *bureaucracy*. Such **classical organizational theory**, as it is known, has fallen into disfavor because it is insensitive to human needs and is not suited to a changing environment. Unfortunately, the "ideal" form of an organization, according to Weber, did not take into account the realities of the world within which it operates. Apparently, what is ideal is not necessarily what is realistic.

In response to these conditions, and with inspiration from the Hawthorne studies, the classical approach of the bureaucratic model gave way to more of a human relations orientation. Organizational scholars such as McGregor, Argyris, and Likert attempted to improve upon the classical model—which is why their approach is labeled **neoclassical organizational theory**. These theorists argued that economic effectiveness is not the only goal of an industrial organization, but also employee satisfaction.

Specifically, Douglas McGregor was an organizational theorist who objected to the rigid hierarchy imposed by Weber's bureaucratic form because it was based on negative assumptions about people—primarily that they lacked ambition and wouldn't work unless coerced (the *Theory X* approach described in Chapter 1).[19] In contrast, McGregor argued that people desire to achieve success by working and that they seek satisfaction by behaving responsibly (the *Theory Y* approach also described in Chapter 1).

Another neoclassical theorist, Chris Argyris, expressed similar ideas.[20] Specifically, he argued that managerial domination of organizations blocks basic human needs to express oneself and to accomplish tasks successfully. This results in feelings of dissatisfaction, he argued, that encourage turnover and lead to poor performance.

An additional neoclassical theorist, Rensis Likert, shared these perspectives, arguing that organizational performance is enhanced not by rigidly controlling people's actions, but by actively promoting their feelings of self-worth and their importance to the organization.[21] An effective organization, Likert proposed, is one in which individuals would have a great opportunity to participate in making organizational decisions—what he called a *System 4* organization. Doing this, he claimed, would enhance employees' personal sense of worth, motivating them to succeed. Likert called the opposite type of organization *System 1*, the traditional form in which power is distributed in the hands of a few top managers who tell lower-ranking people what to do. (*System 2* and *System 3* are intermediate forms between the System 1 and System 4 extremes.)

The organizational design implications of these neoclassical approaches are clear. In contrast to the classical approach, calling for organizations to be designed with a rigid, tall hierarchy with a narrow span of control (allowing managers to maintain close supervision over their subordinates), the neoclassical approach argues for designing organizations with flat hierarchies (minimizing managerial control over workers) and a high degree of decentralization (encouraging employees to make their own decisions). (For a summary of these differences, see Figure 13.7.) Indeed, such design features may well serve the underlying neoclassical philosophy.

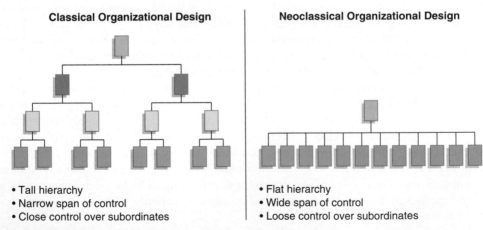

Classical Organizational Design

- Tall hierarchy
- Narrow span of control
- Close control over subordinates

Neoclassical Organizational Design

- Flat hierarchy
- Wide span of control
- Loose control over subordinates

FIGURE 13.7 Classical Versus Neoclassical Designs: A Summary
The *classical approach* to designing organizations assumed that managers needed to have close control over their subordinates. As such, it called for designing organizations with tall hierarchies and narrow spans of control. In contrast, the *neoclassical approach* to designing organizations assumed that managers did not have to carefully monitor their workers. As such, it called for designing organizations with flat hierarchies and wide spans of control.

Like the classical approach, the neoclassical approach also may be faulted on the grounds that it has been promoted as "the one best approach" to organizational design. Although the benefits of flat, decentralized designs may be many, to claim that this represents the universal, ideal form for all organizations would be naive. In response to this criticism, more contemporary approaches to organizational design have given up on finding the one best way in favor of finding designs that are most appropriate to various circumstances and contexts within which companies operate. I now turn to such approaches.

The Contingency Approach: Design According to Environmental Conditions

The idea that the best design for an organization depends on the nature of the environment in which it is operating lies at the heart of the modern **contingency approach to organizational design.** I use the term *contingency* here in a manner similar to how I used it when discussing leadership (see Chapter 11). But rather than considering the best approach to leadership for a given situation, I now discuss the best way to design an organization given the environment within which it functions.

THE EXTERNAL ENVIRONMENT: ITS CONNECTION TO ORGANIZATIONAL DESIGN It is widely accepted that the most appropriate type of organizational design depends on its *external environment.* In general, the **external environment** is the sum of all the forces impinging on an organization with which it must deal effectively if it is to survive.[22] These forces include general work conditions, such as the economy, geography, and natural resources, as well as the specific task environment within which the company operates—notably, its competitors, customers, workforce, and suppliers.

Banks represent a good example. Financial institutions operate within an environment that is highly influenced by the economy (e.g., interest rates and government regulations) as well as by competition that makes customers sensitive to other banks' products (e.g., types of accounts), fees (e.g., charges for ATM transactions and overdrafts), and services (e.g., drive-through hours, sophistication of online banking services). Banking is also affected by the availability of trained personnel (e.g., individuals suitable for entry-level positions) in addition to the nature of suppliers providing goods and services (e.g., automated teller equipment, surveillance equipment, computer workstations). These have been the standard environmental factors affecting banks for many years. However, since 2008, additional factors have emerged as the subprime mortgage crisis has made banks more sensitive than ever to the creditworthiness of the customers to whom they issue loans.

Although many features of the environment may be taken into account when considering how an organization should be designed, a classic investigation provides some useful guidance.[23] Scientists interviewed people in twenty industrial organizations in the United Kingdom to determine the relationship between managerial activities and the external environment. In so doing, they distinguished between businesses that operated in highly *stable*, unchanging environments, and those that operated in highly *unstable*, turbulent ones. For example, a rayon company in their sample operated in a highly stable environment: The demands were predictable, people performed the same jobs in the same ways for a long time, and the organization had clearly defined lines of authority that helped get the job done. (Not too many organizations can be characterized this way today.) In contrast, a new electronics development company in their sample operated in a highly turbulent environment: Conditions changed on a daily basis, jobs were not well defined, and no clear organizational structure existed.

The researchers noted that many of the organizations studied tended to be described in ways that were appropriate for their environments. For example, when the environment is stable, people can do the same tasks repeatedly, allowing them to perform highly specialized jobs. However, in turbulent environments, many different jobs may have to be performed, and such specialization should not be designed into the jobs. Clearly, a strong link exists between the stability of working conditions and the proper organizational form. It was the researchers' conclusion that two different approaches to management existed and that these are largely based on the degree of stability within the external environment. These two approaches are known as *mechanistic organizations* and *organic organizations*. A **mechanistic organization** is one that is stable in nature, where people perform jobs that do not change much over the years. In contrast, an **organic organization** is one that changes frequently, making it likely that people will have to alter the nature of the jobs they perform over the years.

MECHANISTIC VERSUS ORGANIC ORGANIZATIONS: DESIGNS FOR STABLE VERSUS TURBU-LENT CONDITIONS   If you've ever worked at a McDonald's restaurant, you probably know how highly standardized each step of the most basic operations must be.[24] Boxes of fries are to be stored two inches from the wall, in stacks one inch apart. Making those fries is another matter— one that requires nineteen distinct steps, each clearly laid out in a training video shown to new employees. The process is the same, whether it's done in Melbourne, Florida, or Melbourne, Australia. This is an example of a highly mechanistic task. Organizations can be highly mechanistic when conditions don't change. Although the fast-food industry has changed a great deal in recent years (with the introduction of healthier choices, $1 menu items, gourmet coffee drinks, and the like), the making of fries at McDonald's has changed very little. The key to mechanization is the lack of change. If the environment doesn't change, a highly mechanistic organizational form can be very efficient.

An environment is considered stable whenever there is little or no unexpected change in product, market demands, or technology. Examples are hard to come by these days, but if you've ever seen bottles of Dickinson's witch hazel (used to cleanse the skin surrounding a wound) in drugstores, you've found one. Despite changing ownership on several occasions and relocating facilities (although remaining in eastern Connecticut), the company has been making the product following the same distillation process since 1866, suggesting that it certainly is operating in a relatively stable manufacturing environment.[25] As I described earlier, stability affords the luxury of high employee specialization. Without change, people easily can specialize. When change is inevitable, however, this is impractical.

Mechanistic organizations can be characterized in several additional ways (for a summary, see Table 13.3). Not only do mechanistic organizations allow for a high degree of specialization, but they also impose many rules. Authority is vested in a few people located at the top of a hierarchy who give direct orders to their subordinates. Mechanistic organizational designs tend to be most effective under conditions in which the external environment is stable and unchanging.

Now, let's consider the other extreme by thinking about high-technology industries, such as those dedicated to telecommunications, aerospace, and biotechnology. Their environmental conditions are changing all the time. These industries are so prone to change that as soon as a new way of operating is introduced, it sometimes has to be altered. It isn't only technology, however, that makes an environment turbulent. Turbulence also can be high in industries in which adherence to rapidly changing regulations is essential. For example, times were turbulent in the nuclear power industry when governmental regulations dictated the introduction of many new standards

| TABLE 13.3 | Mechanistic Versus Organic Designs: A Summary |

Mechanistic designs and *organic designs* differ along the key dimensions identified here. These represent extremes; organizations can be relatively organic, relatively mechanistic, or somewhere in between.

| | Structure | |
Dimension	Mechanistic	Organic
Stability	Change unlikely	Change likely
Specialization	Many specialists	Many generalists
Formal rules	Rigid rules	Considerable flexibility
Authority	Centralized, vested in a few top people	Decentralized, diffused throughout the organization

that had to be followed. Times also were turbulent in the hospital industry when new Medicaid legislation was passed. Today's renewed interest in further developing nuclear power capabilities and in completely rebuilding the health-care system in the United States is already beginning to make these industries more turbulent once again.

The pure organic form of organization may be characterized in several different ways (see Table 13.3). The degree of job specialization possible is very low; instead, a broad knowledge of many different jobs is required. Very little authority is exercised from the top. Rather, self-control is expected, and an emphasis is placed on coordination between peers. As a result, decisions tend to be made in a highly democratic, participative manner. Be aware that the mechanistic and organic types of organizational structure described here are ideal forms. The mechanistic–organic distinction should be thought of as opposite poles along a continuum rather than as completely distinct options for organizations. Certainly, organizations can be relatively organic or relatively mechanistic compared with others, but may not be located at either extreme. (Which type of organization, mechanistic or organic, do you prefer? To help you answer this question, complete the Self-Assessment Exercise on pp. 431–432.)

It is important to note that organizational effectiveness is related to the degree to which an organization's structure (mechanistic or organic) is matched to its environment (stable or turbulent). In a classic study, researchers evaluated four departments in a large company—two of which manufactured containers (a relatively stable environment at the time), and two of which dealt with communications research (a highly unstable one).[26] One department in each pair was evaluated as being more effective than the other. It was found that for the container manufacturing departments, the more effective unit was the one structured in a highly mechanistic form (roles and duties were clearly defined). In contrast, the more effective communications research department was structured in a highly organic fashion (roles and duties were vague). Additionally, the other, less effective departments were structured in the opposite manner (i.e., the less effective manufacturing department was organically structured, and the less effective research department was mechanistically structured; see Figure 13.8).

Taken together, the results made it clear that departments were most effective when their organizational structures fit their environments. This question of "Which design is best under which conditions?" lies at the heart of the modern orientation—the contingency approach—to organizational structure. Rather than specifying *which* structure is best, the contingency approach specifies *when* each type of organizational design is most effective.

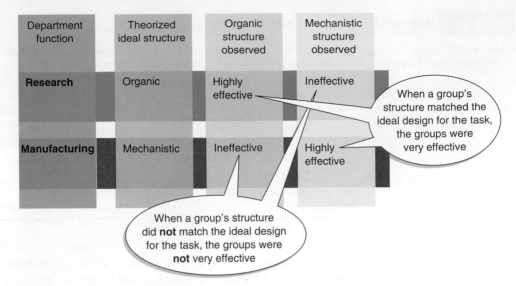

FIGURE 13.8 Matching Organizational Design and Industry: The Key to Effectiveness
In a classic study, researchers evaluated the performance of four departments in a large company. The most effective units were ones in which the way the group was structured (mechanistic or organic) matched the most appropriate form for the type of task performed (i.e., organic for research work and mechanistic for manufacturing work).
Source: Based on suggestions by Morse & Lorsch, 1970; see Note 26.

Mintzberg's Framework: Five Organizational Forms

Although the distinction between mechanistic and organic designs is important, it is not terribly specific with respect to exactly how organizations can be designed. Filling this void, however, is the work of contemporary organizational theorist Henry Mintzberg.[27] Specifically, Mintzberg claims that organizations are composed of five basic elements, or groups of individuals, any of which may predominate in an organization. The one that does will determine the most effective design in that situation. The five basic elements are as follows:

- *The* **operating core**—Employees who perform the basic work related to the organization's product or service. Examples include teachers (in schools) and chefs and waiters (in restaurants).
- *The* **strategic apex**—Top-level executives responsible for running the entire organization. Examples include the entrepreneur who runs her own small business and the general manager of an automobile dealership.
- *The* **middle line**—Managers who transfer information between the strategic apex and the operating core. Examples include middle managers, such as regional sales managers (who connect top executives with the sales force) and the chair of an academic department in a college or university (an intermediary between the dean and the faculty).
- *The* **technostructure**—Those specialists responsible for standardizing various aspects of the organization's activities. Examples include accountants, auditors, and computer systems analysts.
- *The* **support staff**—Individuals who provide indirect support services to the organization. Examples include consultants on technical matters and corporate attorneys.

TABLE 13.4	Mintzberg's Five Organizational Forms: A Summary

Mintzberg has identified five distinct organizational designs, each of which is likely to occur in organizations in which certain groups are in power.

Design	Description	Dominant Group	Example
Simple structure	Simple, informal, authority centralized in a single person	Strategic apex	Small, entrepreneurial business
Machine bureaucracy	Highly complex, formal environment with clear lines of authority	Technostructure	Government office
Professional bureaucracy	Complex, decision-making authority is vested in professionals	Operating core	University
Divisional structure	Large, formal organizations with several separate divisions	Middle line	Multidivisional business, such as General Motors
Adhocracy	Simple, informal, with decentralized authority	Support staff	Software development firm

Source: Based on suggestions by Mintzberg, 1983, 2009; see Note 27.

What organizational designs best fit under conditions in which each of these five groups dominate? Mintzberg has identified five specific designs: *simple structure, machine bureaucracy, professional bureaucracy, divisionalized structure,* and *adhocracy.* I describe these below and summarize them in Table 13.4.

SIMPLE STRUCTURE Imagine that you open an antique shop and hire a few people to help you out in the store. You have a small, informal organization in which there is a single individual with ultimate power. There is little in the way of specialization or formalization, and the overall structure is organic in nature. The hierarchy is quite flat, and all decision-making power is vested in a single individual—you. An organization so described, simple in nature, with the power residing at the strategic apex, is referred to by Mintzberg as having a **simple structure**.

As you might imagine, organizations with simple structures can respond quickly to the environment and be very flexible. For example, the chef-owner of a small, independent restaurant can change the menu to suit the various tastes of customers whenever needed, without first consulting anyone else. The downside to this, however, is that the success or failure of the entire enterprise is dependent on the wisdom and health of the individual in charge. Not surprisingly, organizations with simple structure are risky ventures.

MACHINE BUREAUCRACY If you've ever worked for your state's department of motor vehicles, you probably found it to be a very large place, with numerous rules and procedures for employees to follow. The work is highly specialized (e.g., one person gives the vision tests, and another completes the registration forms), and decision making is concentrated at the top (e.g., you need to get permission from your supervisor to do anything other than exactly what's expected). This type of work environment is highly stable and does not have to change. An organization so characterized, where power resides with the technostructure, is referred to as a **machine bureaucracy**.

Although machine bureaucracies can be highly efficient at performing standardized tasks, they tend to be dehumanizing and very boring for the employees who work in them.

PROFESSIONAL BUREAUCRACY   Suppose you are a doctor working at a large city hospital. You are a highly trained specialist with considerable expertise in your field. You don't need to check with anyone else before authorizing a certain medical test or treatment for your patient: you make the decisions as they are needed, when they are needed. At the same time, the environment is highly formal (e.g., there are lots of rules and regulations for you to follow). Of course, you do not work alone; you also require the services of other highly qualified professionals, such as nurses and laboratory technicians. Organizations of this type—and these include universities, libraries, and consulting firms as well as hospitals—maintain power with the operating core, and are called **professional bureaucracies**. Such organizations can be highly effective because they allow employees to practice those skills for which they are best qualified. However, sometimes specialists become so overly narrow that they fail to see the "big picture," leading to errors and potential conflict between employees.

DIVISIONAL STRUCTURE   When you think of large organizations, such as General Motors, DuPont, Xerox, and IBM, the image that comes to mind is probably closest to what Mintzberg describes as **divisional structure**. Such organizations consist of a set of autonomous units coordinated by a central headquarters (i.e., they rely on departmental structure). In such organizations, because the divisions are autonomous (e.g., a General Motors employee at Cadillac does not have to consult with another at Chevrolet to do his or her job), division managers (the *middle line* part of Mintzberg's basic elements) have considerable control. Such designs preclude the need for top-level executives to think about the day-to-day operations of their companies and free them to concentrate on larger scale, strategic decisions. At the same time, companies organized into separate divisions frequently tend to have high duplication of effort (e.g., separate order processing units for each division). Having operated as separate divisions for about a century, General Motors is considered the classic example of divisional structure.[28] Although the company has undergone significant periods of growth and decline, in recent years, it has maintained much of its divisional structure (see Table 13.5).

ADHOCRACY   After graduating from college, where you spent years learning how to program computers, you take a job at a small software company. Compared to your friends who found positions at large accounting firms, your professional life is much less formal. You work as a member of a team developing a new time-management software product. There are no rules, and schedules are made to be broken. You all work together, and although there is someone who is "officially" in charge, you'd never know it. Using Mintzberg's framework, you work for an **adhocracy**—an organization in which all members have the authority to make decisions that fall within their areas of specialization.

The term adhocracy is constructed from "ad hoc" and "bureaucracy." This, of course, is a contradiction in terms, given that bureaucracies are highly formal rather than unstructured in the way decisions are made. Thus, you may think of an adhocracy as the opposite of a bureaucracy. Essentially, an adhocracy is the epitome of the organic structure identified earlier. Specialists coordinate with each other not because of their shared functions (e.g., accounting, manufacturing), but as members of teams working on specific projects.

The primary benefit of the adhocracy is that it fosters innovation. Some large companies, such as Johnson & Johnson (J&J), nest within their formal divisional structures units that operate as adhocracies. In the case of J&J, it's the New Products Division, a unit that has been churning

TABLE 13.5	GM Reorganization: 2007–Present

General Motors (GM) has maintained a divisional structure for more than a century. In response to mounting financial losses in 2008, however, GM dropped some product lines and organized others into four "sales channels." The following year, as part of its bankruptcy reorganization plan, some brands were sold or dismantled, leaving only four divisions. Although GM has maintained its potentially inefficient, decentralized divisional structure, by devoting its more limited resources into divisions representing fewer, more successful brands, GM has regained its dominance in the auto business. (Note that this information is limited to automotive operations for brands sold in the United States. The overall organizational design of GM is far more complex.)

"Old GM" (Through 2007)	"Streamlined GM" (2008)	"New GM" (2009-Present; Postbankruptcy)
Nine divisions:	• Seven divisions in four channels:	• Four divisions:
• Chevrolet	*Chevrolet Channel*	• Chevrolet
	• Chevrolet	
• Pontiac	*Buick-Pontiac Channel*	
	• Pontiac	
• Buick	• Buick	• Buick
• Cadillac	*Premium Channel*	• Cadillac
	• Cadillac	
• Hummer	• Hummer	
• Saab	• Saab	
• Oldsmobile		
• Saturn	*Saturn Channel*	
	• Saturn	
• GMC		• GMC

out an average of forty products per year.[29] As in the case of all other designs, there are disadvantages. In this case, the most serious limitations are their high levels of inefficiency (they are the opposite of machine bureaucracies in this regard) and their considerable potential for disruptive conflict (see Chapter 7).

The Vertically Integrated Organization

For many years, Ford has owned its own steel mills and its own financing company. The steel mills have presupplied customers as Ford purchases the steel to manufacture cars. The financing company also has built-in business as Ford dealers rely on it to finance purchases for their customers. Organizations that own their own suppliers and/or their own customers who purchase their products are said to be relying on **vertical integration**.

By contrast, other companies only assemble products that they buy from outside suppliers and sell to customers. Companies of this type are not vertically integrated. Dell presents a good example because it purchases computer components from other companies and assembles them into finished computers for customers who have ordered them configured in certain ways. For a comparison between vertically integrated companies and non–vertically integrated companies, see Figure 13.9.

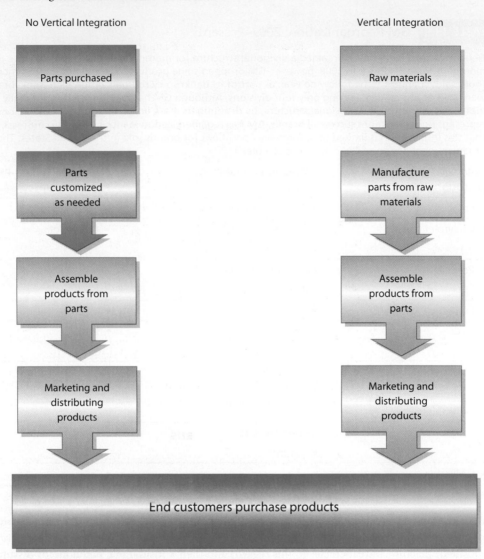

FIGURE 13.9 The Vertically Integrated Organization
A vertically integrated organization, like the one summarized on the right, owns the suppliers and/
or the customers with whom it does business. It even may own the sources of the raw materials it
requires. Because it is involved only in the assembly and selling products, the organization summarized
on the left is not considered vertically integrated.

The fact that companies don't have to worry about attracting customers would appear to be
a big advantage for vertical integration. Although this is true, there also are challenges associated
with vertical integration.[30] For one, because the company's suppliers are internal, they don't face
competition to keep their prices down, potentially resulting in higher costs for the company.
Also, if the various parts of the organization are tightly interconnected, it is very difficult to
respond to changes, such as developing new products. Because this would involve changes in supplies, manufacturing, and sales, the vertically integrated company faces more challenges than its
non–vertically integrated counterpart when it comes to making such changes.

Team-Based Organizations

The organizational designs I have described thus far have been around for a long time, and because they are so well known and often so effective, they are not likely to fade away anytime soon. However, based on the growing popularity of work teams (see Chapter 9), it's not surprising that many of today's organizations rely on teams as their basic organizing structure. These are referred to as *team-based organizations*. Specifically, **team-based organizations** are organizations in which autonomous work teams are organized in parallel fashion such that each performs many different steps in the work process.

The underlying idea is simple. Instead of organizing jobs in the traditional, hierarchical fashion by having a long chain of groups or individuals perform parts of a task (e.g., one group that sells the advertising job, another that plans the ad campaign, and yet another that produces the ads), team-based organizations have flattened hierarchies. Essentially, this approach calls for designing organizations around *processes* instead of tasks (see Figure 13.10).[31] For example, members of an advertising team may combine their different skills and expertise and become responsible for all aspects of advertising.

INTERORGANIZATIONAL DESIGNS: JOINING MULTIPLE ORGANIZATIONS

All the organizational designs examined thus far have concentrated on the arrangement of units within one organization—what may be termed **intraorganizational designs**. However, sometimes parts of different organizations come together to operate jointly, coordinating efforts on projects. When this is the case, businesses must create **interorganizational designs**, plans by which two or more organizations come together. I now examine several such designs.

Boundaryless Organizations: Eliminating Walls

Often, when today's organizations join forces, it's done in ways that give them considerable flexibility, allowing them to respond to rapidly changing conditions in the business environment. Keenly aware of the need for successful organizations to turn on a dime, Jack Welch, the former CEO of General Electric, introduced the **boundaryless organization**. This refers to a type of organization in which chains of command are eliminated, spans of control are unlimited, and rigid departments give way to empowered teams. The idea is that replacing rigid distinctions between people with roles that are fluid, intentionally ambiguous, and ill defined, makes it much easier to be flexible. Welch's vision was that GE would operate like a family grocery store (albeit a $60-billion one)—one in which barriers that separate employees from one another would be eliminated.[32]

This part of Welch's idea focuses on breaking down boundaries within organizations. However, he also advocated eliminating external boundaries so that organizations could join forces quickly and as needed to take advantage of opportunities. With this in mind, two popular forms of externally oriented boundaryless organizations have emerged, which I now describe.[33]

MODULAR (OR NETWORKED) ORGANIZATIONS Businesses that outsource noncore functions to other companies while focusing on their own core business are referred to as **modular (or networked) organizations**. Such organizations are organized around a central hub that is surrounded by networks of outside specialists that can be added or subtracted as needed.[34]

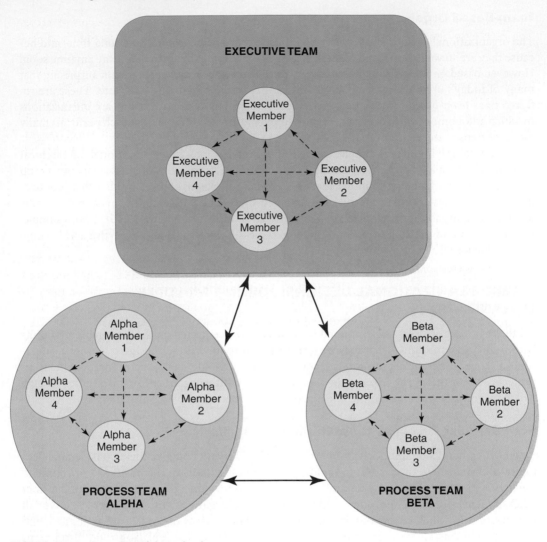

FIGURE 13.10 Team-Based Organizations
Instead of arranging individuals and tasks in hierarchical fashion, *team-based organizations* are designed with respect to the processes performed by various teams and the interconnections between them. *Source:* Adapted from Mohrman et al., 1997; see Note 31.

Reebok is a good example of a modular organization. It focuses on designing and marketing athletic shoes and apparel but outsources all production to companies in Taiwan and South Korea that specialize in manufacturing. This allows the company to concentrate on what it does best—tapping the changing tastes of its customers.[35]

VIRTUAL ORGANIZATIONS Organizations composed of a continually evolving network of companies linked together to share skills, costs, and access to markets are known as **virtual organizations**. They form a partnership to capitalize on their existing talents, pursuing common objectives. In most cases, after these objectives have been met, the organizations disband.[36]

This arrangement allows each participating company to contribute only its core competencies (i.e., its areas of greatest strength), resulting in products that no one company could have created on its own.

Corning, the giant glass and ceramics manufacturer, is a good example of a company that builds upon itself by developing partnerships with other companies (including Siemens, the German electronics firm, and Vitro, the largest glass manufacturer in Mexico). In fact, Corning officials see their company not as a single entity, but as "a network of organizations."[37] Many other organizations also have "gone virtual" in some of their operations, including Sun Microsystems, NEC, and Microsoft. These practices, however, should not be taken as an indication that going virtual is always appropriate. (For a discussion of the conditions under which organizations should go virtual, see the Winning Practices section on p. 428.)

Conglomerates: Diversified "Megacorporations"

When an organization diversifies by adding an entirely unrelated business or product to its organizational design, it may be said to have formed a **conglomerate**. Some of the world's largest conglomerates may be found in Asia. For example, in South Korea, companies such as Samsung and Hyundai produce home electronics, automobiles, textiles, and chemicals in large, unified conglomerates known as *chaebols*.[38] These are all separate companies overseen by leaders in the same parent company. In Japan, the same type of arrangement is known as a *keiretsu*.[39] A good example of a keiretsu is the Matsushita Group.[40] This enormous conglomerate consists of a bank (Asahi Bank), a consumer electronics company (Panasonic), and several insurance companies (e.g., Sumitomo Life, Nippon Life). Conglomerates are not unique to Asia. Indeed, many large U.S.-based corporations, such as IBM and Tenneco, also are conglomerates.

Companies form conglomerates for several reasons. First, as an independent business, the parent company can enjoy the benefits of diversification. Thus, as one industry languishes, another may excel, allowing for a stable economic outlook for the parent company. In addition, conglomerates may provide built-in markets and access to supplies, since companies typically support other organizations within the conglomerate. For example, General Motors's cars and trucks are fitted with Delco radios, and Ford cars and trucks have engines with Autolite spark plugs, separate companies that are owned by their respective parent companies. In this manner conglomerates can benefit by providing a network of companies that are dependent on each other for products and services, thereby creating considerable advantages.

Strategic Alliances: Joining Forces for Mutual Benefit

A **strategic alliance** is a type of organizational design in which two or more separate firms join their competitive capabilities to operate a specific business. The goal of a strategic alliance is to provide benefits to each individual organization that could not be attained if they operated separately. They are low-risk ways of diversifying (adding new business operations) and entering new markets. Some companies, such as GE and Ford, have strategic alliances with many others. Although some alliances last only a short time, others have remained in existence for well over thirty years and are still going strong.[41]

THE CONTINUUM OF ALLIANCES A study of thirty-seven strategic alliances from throughout the world identified three types of cooperative arrangements between organizations.[42] These may

Winning Practices

When Is It Time to Go Virtual?

More and more of today's companies are finding it useful to "go virtual," downscaling their hierarchies and networking with other companies on an ad hoc basis. Doing so allows them to move more quickly, standing a better chance of improving in a highly competitive environment. However, virtual organizations are far from perfect. Because people from different companies may not share common values, interpersonal conflicts are likely to occur, and coordination is often challenging. This raises an important question: When should companies organize in a virtual manner?

The answer depends on how organizations fare with respect to two considerations: the type of capabilities organizations need and the type of change that will be made.[43] Specifically, organizational changes may be either *autonomous* or *systemic*. **Autonomous change** is made independently of other changes. For an example, an auto company that develops a new type of upholstery may do so without revising the rest of the car. **Systemic change**, in contrast, is such that change in one part of an organization requires changes in another part of that same organization. For example, Nikon's development of digital photography required changes in both lens and battery technologies.

A second key distinction involves the capabilities needed to complete the project. In some cases, outside capabilities are required. For example, in the early 1980s, IBM was able to develop its first personal computer in only fifteen months because it went outside the company for expertise (e.g., buying chips from Intel and an operating system from Microsoft). Other times, capability can be found inside the company. For example,

Ford traditionally develops many of the components used in its cars, making it less dependent on other companies (although in the wake of financial problems in the auto industry in recent years, the company now does far less of this than it used to).[44]

By combining these factors, it becomes clear when companies should "go virtual" and when they should work exclusively within their own walls. *Virtual organizations work best for companies considering autonomous changes using technologies that exist only outside their walls*. For example, Motorola has developed virtual organizations with several battery manufacturers for its cell phones. In so doing, it can focus on its core business—the delivery of wireless communication—while ensuring it has the battery power to make such devices work.

In contrast, *companies should keep their focus inward when changes are systemic in nature and involve capabilities the company either already has or can create*. Under such conditions, relying on outside help may be far too risky—and unnecessary. For example, these days Intel is making extensive investments to enhance its current and future capacities.

Finally, for conditions that fall between these extremes (i.e., when systemic changes are being made using capabilities that come only from outside the company, and when autonomous changes are being made using capabilities that must be created), virtual alliances should be created with extreme caution. Clearly, the virtual organization has a key place in today's organizational world. The trick, however, lies in understanding precisely what that place is. These principles described here represent useful guidance in that respect.

be arranged along a continuum from those alliances that are weak and distant, at one end, to those that are strong and close, at the other end (see Figure 13.11).

At the weak end of the continuum are strategic alliances known as **mutual service consortia**. These are arrangements between two similar companies from the same or similar industries to pool their resources to receive a benefit that would be too difficult or expensive for either to obtain alone. Often, the focus is some high-tech capacity, such as an expensive piece of

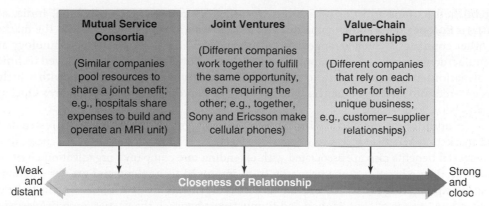

FIGURE 13.11 Strategic Alliances: A Continuum of Interorganizational Relationships
The three types of strategic alliances identified here may be distinguished with respect to their location along a continuum ranging from weak and distant to strong and close.
Source: Based on suggestions by Kanter, 1994; see Note 41.

diagnostic equipment that might be shared by two or more small, rural hospitals (e.g., a magnetic resonance imaging, or MRI unit).

At the opposite end of the scale are the strongest and closest type of collaborations, referred to as **value-chain partnerships**. These are alliances between companies in different industries that have complementary capabilities. Customer–supplier relationships are a prime example. In such arrangements one company buys necessary goods and services from another so that it can do business. Because each company greatly depends on the other, each party's commitment to their mutual relationship is high. As noted earlier, Toyota has a vast network of suppliers with whom it regularly does business. The relationship between Toyota and these various companies represent value-chain partnerships.

Between these two extremes are **joint ventures**. These are arrangements, either temporary or permanent, in which companies work together to fulfill opportunities that require the capabilities of the other. For example, two companies might enter into a joint venture if one has a valuable technology and the other has the marketing knowledge to help transform that technology into a viable commercial product.

Joint ventures have been especially popular between organizations from different nations. One such joint venture with which you are probably familiar is Sony Ericsson, a joint venture created in 2001 to make cellular phones. This company combined the consumer electronics expertise of the Japanese company, Sony, with telecommunications expertise of the Swedish company, Ericsson. Joint ventures between international partners have been particularly popular in the oil and gas industry. For example, over the years, Royal Dutch Shell has been involved in quite a few joint ventures with foreign partners. In most cases, companies from different nations form joint ventures voluntarily. However, in some cases, companies that wish to enter markets in another country—China, in particular—discover that they are required to do so by way of finding joint venture partners in those countries.

STRATEGIC ALLIANCES IN THE GLOBAL ECONOMY It is not just joint ventures but strategic alliances in general that have become popular between companies from different nations. In particular, strategic alliances have been popular between companies in established nations and those with transforming economies (such as China, India, and Eastern Europe). This allows companies from richer nations to gain entry into the markets of other countries.[45] Such arrangements also may allow for an exchange of technology and manufacturing services. For example, over the years, Korea's Daewoo has received technical information and has been paid to manufacture automobiles for companies with which it has entered into strategic alliances, such as General Motors, as well as Germany's Opel and Japan's Isuzu and Nissan.[46]

In addition to the financial incentives (circumventing trade and tariff restrictions) and marketing benefits (access to internal markets) associated with strategic alliances, direct managerial benefits also are associated with extending one company's organization chart into another's. These benefits come primarily from improved technology and greater economies of scale (e.g., sharing functional operations across organizations). For these benefits to be derived, a high degree of coordination and fit must exist between the parties, each delivering on its promise to the other.

Finally, it is noteworthy that strategic alliances with companies in nations with transforming economies provide good opportunities for those nations' economies to develop.[47] Given the rapid move toward globalization of the economy, we may expect to see many companies seeking strategic alliances in the future as a means for gaining or maintaining a competitive advantage.[48]

THE SPINOFF: AN ALTERNATIVE TO THE JOINT VENTURE   Although forming joint ventures with other organizations is a popular way for companies to grow in new directions, it is not the only way. An alternative that has been popular in many companies has been to create a **spinoff**—that is, an entirely new company that is separate from the original parent organization, one with its own identity, a new board of directors, and a different management team. The idea is that instead of looking around for a suitable partner, a rich and powerful company can create its own partner.

Consider, for example, the development of Expedia, Microsoft's online travel service. In 1996, Expedia was launched as just another Microsoft product.[49] As it became more successful, Expedia was set up as a separate operating unit. Then, in November 1999, Expedia was "spun off" into a separate publicly traded company (i.e., it can be purchased by anyone on the stock market). This raised $84 million for Microsoft, and because the company retains 85 percent of Expedia's stock, it promises to make still more money in the future.

Back to the Case

Answer the following questions based on this chapter's Making the Case (p. 401) to illustrate insights you have derived from the material in this chapter.

1. What type of organizational design appears to describe the relationship between Verizon and McAfee? Explain the basis for your answer.
2. What are the advantages and disadvantages of this type of organizational design?
3. What alternative organizational designs might have been used to combine the special areas of expertise of Verizon and McAfee?

You Be the Consultant

Designing a Rapidly Growing Company

The president of a small but rapidly growing software company asks you to consult with him about an important matter. As the company expands, several options for designing the company's operations are being considered, and your job is to help him make a decision about which route to take. Answer the following questions relevant to this situation based on the material in this chapter.

1. What would you recommend with respect to the following structural variables: hierarchy of authority (tall or flat), division of labor (specialized or not), span of control (wide or narrow), and degree of centralization (highly centralized or highly decentralized)? Explain the reasons behind your recommendations.

2. How do you think the company should be departmentalized—by task (functional), by output (product), or both task and output (matrix)? What are the reasons for these conclusions?

3. If the company were thinking about entering into a strategic alliance with another, what factors would have to be considered? What kind of company would be an effective partner in an alliance with this software firm?

Self-Assessment Exercise

WHICH DO YOU PREFER—MECHANISTIC OR ORGANIC ORGANIZATIONS?

Because mechanistic and organic organizations are so different, it is reasonable to expect that people will tend to prefer one of these organizational forms over the other. This questionnaire is designed to help you identify your own preferences (and, in so doing, to help you learn about the different forms themselves).

Directions

Each of the following questions deals with your preferences for various conditions that may exist where you work. Answer each one by checking the one alternative that better describes your feelings.

Scale

1. When I have a job-related decision to make, I usually prefer to:
   _____ a. make the decision myself.
   _____ b. have my boss make it for me.
2. I usually find myself more interested in performing:
   _____ a. a highly narrow, specialized task.
   _____ b. many different types of tasks.
3. I prefer to work in places in which working conditions:
   _____ a. change a great deal.
   _____ b. generally remain the same.
4. When a lot of rules are imposed on me, I generally feel:
   _____ a. very comfortable.
   _____ b. very uncomfortable.

5. I believe that governmental regulation of industry is:
   _____ a. usually best for all.
   _____ b. rarely good for anyone.

Scoring and Interpretation

1. Give yourself one point each time you answered as follows: 1 = b; 2 = a; 3 = b; 4 = a; 5 = a. This score is your preference for *mechanistic organizations.*
2. Subtract this score from 5. This score is your preference for *organic organizations.*
3. Interpret your scores as follows: Higher scores (closer to 5) reflect stronger preferences and lower scores (closer to 0) reflect weaker preferences.

Discussion Questions

1. How did you score? That is, which organizational form, mechanistic or organic, did this exercise suggest that you prefer?
2. Think back over the jobs you've had. For the most part, have these been in organizations that were mechanistic or organic?
3. Do you think you were any more committed to organizations in which you worked whose designs matched your preferences as compared to those in which there was a mismatch?

Group Exercise

COMPARING SPAN OF CONTROL IN ORGANIZATION CHARTS

One of the easiest things to determine about a company by looking at its organization chart is its span of control. This exercise will allow you to learn about and compare span of control within different companies.

Directions

1. Divide the class into four equal size groups.
2. Assign one of the following industry types to each group: (a) manufacturing companies, (b) financial institutions, (c) public utilities, and (d) charities.
3. Within the industry assigned to each group, identify one company per student. It helps to consider larger organizations inasmuch as these are more likely to have formal organization charts. For example, if there are five students in the "financial institutions" group, name five different banks or savings and loan institutions.
4. Each student should get a copy of the organization chart (or at least a portion of it) for the company assigned to him or her in step 3. You may be able to get this information from various companies' Web sites and/or by consulting their annual reports (which may be found online as well as in many libraries). If all else fails, you may have to ask someone you know who works at a given company to show you its organization chart.
5. Meet as a group to discuss the spans of control of the organizations in your sample.
6. Gather as a class to compare the findings of the various groups.

Discussion Questions

1. How easy or difficult was it to find the organization charts? Did the class report differences in this regard (e.g., organization charts were readily available in some cases but not others)? If so, why do you think this may have been the case?
2. Did you find that there were differences with respect to span of control?
3. Were spans of control different at different organizational levels or for different industry groups? In what ways were they similar and different?

Notes

MAKING THE CASE NOTES

Greene, T. (2010, March 5). Cloud security, cyber war loom over RSA conference. *InfoWorld.* http://www.infoworld.com/d/cloud-computing/cloud-security-cyber-war-loom-over-rsa-conference-734. Cloud computing and the tech giants. (2009, October 15). *The Economist.* http://www.economist.com/displaystory.cfm?story_id-14637206. McAfee. (2009, October 8). Press release: Verizon Business and McAfee form strategic alliance. http://newsroom.mcafee.com/article_display.cfm?article_id=3579. Strategic alliance between McAfee and Verizon Business aims for the clouds. (2009, October 9). *Twilight in the Valley of the Nerds.* http://nerdtwilight.wordpress.com/2009/10/08/strategic-alliance-between-mcafee-and-verizon-business-aims-for-the-clouds. Gubbins, E. (2009, June 3). Verizon debuts cloud computing service. *Connected Planet.* http://connectedplanetonline.com/business_services/news/verizon-cloud-computing-0603.

CHAPTER NOTES

1. Daft, R. L. (2007). *Essentials of organization theory and design* (9th ed.). Cincinnati, OH: Thomson South-Western.
2. Miller, D. (1987). The genesis of configuration. *Academy of Management Review, 12,* 686–701.
3. Galbraith, J. R. (1987). Organization design. In J. W. Lorsch (Ed.), *Handbook of organizational behavior* (pp. 343–357). Englewood Cliffs, NJ: Prentice Hall.
4. Hendricks, C. F. (1992). *The rightsizing remedy.* Homewood, IL: Business One Irwin.
5. Swoboda, F. (1990, May 28–June 3). For unions, maybe bitter was better. *Washington Post National Weekly Edition,* p. 20.
6. Urwick, L. F. (1956, May–June). The manager's span of control. Harvard Business Review, 34, pp. 39–47.
7. Speen, K. (1988, September 12). Caught in the middle. *BusinessWeek,* pp. 80–88.
8. Dalton, M. (1950). Conflicts between staff and line managerial officers. *American Sociological Review, 15,* 342–351.
9. Chandler, A. (1962). *Strategy and structure.* Cambridge, MA: MIT Press.
10. Lawrence, P., & Lorsch, J. (1967). *Organization and environment.* Boston, MA: Harvard University Press.
11. Anders, G. (2003). *Perfect enough: Carly Fiorina and the reinvention of Hewlett-Packard.* Middlesex, England: Portfolio.
12. Hewlett-Packard: About us. (2003). http://www.hp.com/hpinfo/abouthp
13. Mee, J. F. (1964). Matrix organizations. *Business Horizons, 7*(2), 70–72.
14. Bartlett, C. A., & Ghoshal, S. (1990, May–June). Matrix management: Not a structure, a frame of mind. *Harvard Business Review, 68,* pp. 138–145.
15. See Note 14.
16. Goggin, W. (1974, January–February). How the multidimensional structure works at Dow Corning. *Harvard Business Review, 56,* pp. 33–52.
17. Ford, R. C., & Randolph, W. A. (1992). Cross-functional structures: A review and integration of matrix organization and project management. *Journal of Management, 18,* 267–294.
18. See Note 17.
19. McGregor, D. (1960). *The human side of enterprise.* New York: McGraw-Hill.
20. Argyris, C. (1964). *Integrating the individual and the organization.* New York: Wiley.
21. Likert, R. (1961). *New patterns of management.* New York: McGraw-Hill.
22. Duncan, R. (1979, Winter). What is the right organization structure? *Organizational Dynamics,* pp. 59–69.
23. Burns, T., & Stalker, G. M. (1961). *The management of innovation.* London: Tavistock.
24. Deveney, K. (1986, October 13). Bag those fries, squirt that ketchup, fry that fish. *BusinessWeek,* pp. 57–61.
25. Kerr, P. (1985, May 11). Witch hazel still made the old-fashioned way. *New York Times,* pp. 27–28.
26. Morse, J. J., & Lorsch, J. W. (1970, May–June). Beyond Theory Y. *Harvard Business Review, 48,* pp. 61–68.
27. Mintzberg, H. (2009). *Managing.* San Francisco, CA: Berrett-Koehler. Mintzberg, H. (1983). *Structure in fives: Designing effective organizations.* Englewood Cliffs, NJ: Prentice Hall.

28. Livesay, H. C. (1979). *American made: Men who shaped the American economy*. Boston, MA: Little, Brown.

29. See Note 1.

30. Harrigan, K. R. (2003). *Vertical integration, outsourcing, and corporate strategy*. Frederick, MD: Beard Group.

31. Mohrman, S. A., Cohen, S. G., & Mohrman, A. M., Jr. (1997). *Designing team-based organizations*. San Francisco, CA: Jossey-Bass.

32. GE: Just your average everyday $60 billion family grocery store. (1994, May 2). *Industry Week*, pp. 13–18.

33. Dees, G. D., Rasheed, A. M. A., McLaughlin, K. J., & Priem, R. L. (1995). The new corporate architecture. *Academy of Management Executive, 9*, 7–18.

34. See Note 33.

35. Tully, S. (1993, February 3). The modular corporation. *Fortune*, pp. 106–108, 110.

36. Byrne, J. (1993, February 8). The virtual corporation. *BusinessWeek*, pp. 99–103.

37. Sherman, S. (1992, September 21). Are strategic alliances working? *Fortune*, pp. 77–78 (quote, p. 78).

38. Nakarmi, L., & Einhorn, B. (1993, June 7). Hyundai's gutsy gambit. *BusinessWeek*, p. 48.

39. Gerlach, M. L. (1993). *Alliance capitalism: The social organization of Japanese business*. Berkeley, CA: University of California Press.

40. Miyashita, K., & Russell, D. (1994). *Keiretsu: Inside the Japanese conglomerates*. New York: McGraw-Hill.

41. Kanter, R. M. (1994, July–August). Collaborative advantage: The art of alliances. *Harvard Business Review*, pp. 96–108.

42. See Note 41.

43. See Note 37.

44. Nooteboom, B. (2004). *Inter-firm collaboration, networks and strategy: An integrated approach*. London: Routledge.

45. Fletcher, N. (1988, December 10). U.S., China form joint venture to manufacture helicopters. *Journal of Commerce*, p. 58.

46. Bransi, B. (1987, January 3). South Korea's carmakers count their blessings. *The Economist*, p. 45.

47. Newman, W. H. (1992). Focused joint ventures in transforming economies. *The Executive, 6*, 67–75.

48. Lewis, J. (1990). *Partnerships for profit: Structuring and managing strategic alliances*. New York: Free Press.

49. Albrinck, J., Irwin, G., Neilson, G., & Sasina, D. (2000, third quarter). From bricks to clicks: The four stages of e-volution. *Strategy and Business*, pp. 63–66, 68–72.

14

MANAGING ORGANIZATIONAL CHANGE: STRATEGIC PLANNING AND ORGANIZATIONAL DEVELOPMENT

LEARNING OBJECTIVES

After reading this chapter, you will be able to:

1. **DISTINGUISH** among the three major targets of organizational change.
2. **IDENTIFY** the major sources of unplanned organizational change.
3. **DESCRIBE** what is meant by strategic planning and **IDENTIFY** the steps in the strategic planning process.
4. **DESCRIBE** why people are resistant to change in organizations and ways in which this resistance may be overcome.
5. **DEFINE** organizational development (OD) and **DESCRIBE** five OD techniques.
6. **DESCRIBE** how OD is affected by national culture and **EXPLAIN** the ethical concerns that have been voiced about using OD techniques.

THREE GOOD REASONS you should care about. . .

Managing Organizational Change

1. The success—or even the survival—of companies depends on the extent to which they effectively adapt to change.
2. Overcoming people's resistance to change is a key determinant of organizational effectiveness.
3. Organizational development techniques can be effective tools for getting people to adapt to change.

Making the Case for...

Managing Organizational Change

Saving Campbell's from the Soup

With its iconic red and white cans a staple on grocers' shelves for a century and a half, no one would have suspected that the Campbell Soup Company was struggling. But that was exactly the case a decade ago, when the venerable organization, which sells a range of packaged foods in 120 different countries, admittedly suffered what was called "a precipitous decline in market value and employee engagement."

Engineering a turnaround was the challenge Douglas R. Conant faced in January 2001, when he assumed the reins as the company's eleventh president and CEO. A decade later, all accounts suggest that he did precisely this, revitalizing the company by winning back customers, retaining employees, and developing new products. Even when the 2008 recession hit the consumer packaged goods industry hard, slashing investors' earnings by 25 percent, Campbell Soup Company investors' earnings rose 7 percent.

Conant's recipe for success focused on promoting changes from the inside out: "You can't win in the marketplace unless you win first in the workplace." And in an industry where "you evolve and grow or you die," as he says, this approach has served the company well. At the heart of Conant's approach to driving change has been an emphasis on building trust, which, he empathizes, has made it possible for people to work together to do amazing things. As he explains it, the more management delivers on its commitments, the more people are inspired to execute with excellence, creating what he refers to as a "flywheel of performance."

Conant went about this in several ways. To begin, during his first 30 months on the job, he replaced 300 of the company's top 350 executives, individuals who he believed were underperforming. Not only were these high-ranking leaders unproductive, but many contributed to what appeared to be a toxic work environment that was poisoning the 20,000 other employees in the workplace who looked up to them. Half were replaced with people from outside the company, and the rest were insiders with exciting new ideas who were hungry to put them into place.

To ensure that these problems weren't going to reoccur—and to encourage just the opposite—Conant vowed to keep his finger on the pulse of the company's culture. He has been doing this by annually assessing "employee engagement" with a questionnaire developed by the Gallup Organization. These metrics have allowed him to track how emotionally committed Campbell's 580 managers are feeling and to compare the results with the levels of engagement found in managers from other organizations. The first time Campbell's administered the questionnaire, the results were off the chart—in the negative direction. A harsh picture was painted of an organization in which managers simply didn't care—far worse than conditions found in other *Fortune* 500 companies.

Sensing urgency, Conant developed a process in which managers became more actively involved in everything. Their voices were heard, they were held accountable for results, and they developed action plans aimed at turning things around. The very next year, there was a marked improvement, along with increases in performance at all levels. Conant believes that this is so important that each year he presents employees' engagement scores in Campbell's annual report.

This case depicts a talented leader who stepped in heroically to rescue his company. Although not all efforts are equally successful, you can be sure that officials in most organizations are, in one way or another, striving to bring about changes and to make them work. When you consider rapid advances in technology, a volatile economic environment, new government regulations, and competition from companies around the world, it's easy to recognize that organizational change is inevitable, making it the rule rather than the exception. Formally defined, **organizational change** refers to planned or unplanned transformations in an organization's structure, technology, and/or people.

Because of its prevalence and importance, I devote this chapter to organizational change. To help you fully understand this topic, I examine it from several key perspectives. I begin by describing the general nature of the change process, considering the forces for change operating in the business environment. Then I shift my focus to changes that are deliberate in nature, describing what is known as *strategic planning*. This involves deliberately making radical changes in the way an organization operates.

As you might imagine, people get used to doing things in certain ways and are often reluctant to accept changes in their organizations. But because changes are often necessary, it's essential for people to accept new ways of operating. With this in mind, I will describe various reasons people are resistant to change and how to overcome them. Specifically, social scientists have developed various methods, known collectively as *organizational development* techniques, which are designed to implement needed organizational change in a manner that is acceptable to employees and that enhances the effectiveness of the organizations involved. I conclude this chapter by reviewing such techniques and then raising key questions about them.

THE PREVALENCE OF CHANGE IN ORGANIZATIONS

A century ago, advances in machine technology made farming so highly efficient that fewer hands were needed to plant and reap the harvest. Displaced laborers fled to nearby cities, seeking jobs in newly opened factories, opportunities created by some of the same technologies that sent them from the farm. The economy shifted from agrarian to manufacturing, and the *industrial revolution* was underway. With it came drastic shifts in where people lived, how they worked, how they used their leisure time, how much money they made, and how they spent it.

Fast-forward 100 years to another industrial revolution. This one is driven by a new wave of global economic forces and rapid technological transformation. As one observer put it, "This workplace revolution . . . may be remembered as a historic event, the Western equivalent of the collapse of Communism."[1] And, like the revolution that occurred when the nineteenth century rolled into the twentieth, transition into the twenty-first century has brought broad changes in the workplace to which we all must adapt.

Today's business leaders readily acknowledge that the pace of change in organizations is more rapid than ever. When asked why this is so, they identify a variety of reasons. As shown in Figure 14.1, most prominent among these are innovations in products, services, or business models, and greater ease of obtaining information.[2] Indeed, I have already highlighted the importance of these factors elsewhere in this book (see Chapters 8 and 12).

The Message Is Clear: Change or Disappear!

Remember Douglas Conant's admonition (in Making the Case, on p. 436) that "you evolve and grow or you die"? As harsh as it may seem, this Darwinian (survival of the fittest) notion is reality for more than just the packaged foods industry.[3] Take auto manufacturing as an illustration.

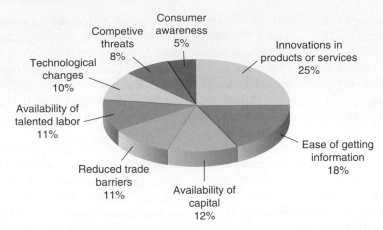

FIGURE 14.1 Why Are Things Changing So Rapidly?
A large group of executives was asked to identify one factor that contributes most to the accelerating pace of change in today's global business environment. The percentage of respondents who named various factors is summarized here.
Source: McKinsey & Company, 2006; see Note 2.

Several automakers have been forced to sell some of their brands to other companies in recent decades. For example, Ford purchased the struggling British luxury car company Jaguar in 1989 but facing its own financial difficulties, Ford sold Jaguar to the large Indian company Tata Motors (only a few years later). With no buyers on the horizon, other auto companies had to take more extreme measures, liquidating brands that suddenly began to fail. In 2010, for example, GM closed down Hummer and Ford shuttered its venerable Mercury brand.

With these examples in mind, it shouldn't be surprising that support for organizational change among senior managers is a characteristic that distinguishes the most successful organizations from their less successful counterparts. Specifically, research has revealed that leaders of successful organizations support change 94 percent of the time, whereas all others support change only 76 percent of the time.[4] Although this alone does not mean that support for change directly causes success, of course, the sizable difference surely suggests that it may be a factor. This is important because business failure is the rule rather than the exception: fully 62 percent of new ventures fail to last as long as 5 years, and only 2 percent make it as long as 50 years.[5]

Change Is a Global Phenomenon

It is important to note that the forces for organizational change are not unique to the United States, but rather, they are global in nature. This point is illustrated in a study in which more than 12,000 managers from twenty-five different countries were asked to identify the major changes that their organizations had encountered in the previous two years.[6] The most-cited factors turned out to be large restructurings, mergers, divestitures and acquisitions, reductions in employment, and international expansion. Furthermore, these same factors emerged in all twenty-five countries, suggesting that organizational change is a worldwide phenomenon.

This makes sense if you think about it from an economic perspective. Because it's not unusual for banks from one nation to carry the debt from companies and governments of other nations, it's easy to see how one country's "financial cold" can be experienced as "financial pneumonia" by the time it crosses the ocean. An all-too-clear example of this may be seen in the crisis that rocked

European banks in recent years. As financially overextended governments struggled to repay loans, changes in taxes and benefits were enacted that required greater sacrifices from citizens, and austerity among customers harmed companies in Europe and its trading partners all around the world. Despite my highly oversimplified depiction of a complex financial situation, I hope that my underlying point is clear: change is an inevitable fact of organizational life all around the world.

THE NATURE OF THE CHANGE PROCESS

Given that change is so prevalent, it is important to understand the basic nature of the process. With this in mind, I turn my attention to two key questions: (1) What, exactly, happens when organizational change occurs? and (2) What forces are responsible for unplanned organizational change?

Targets: What, Exactly, Is Changed?

Imagine that you are a facilities manager responsible for overseeing a large office building. The property owner has noted a dramatic increase in the use of heat in the building, leading operating costs to skyrocket. As such, a need for change exists—specifically, doing something that results in reducing the heating bills. You cannot get the power company to lower its rates, of course, so it's up to you to take action. What can you do?

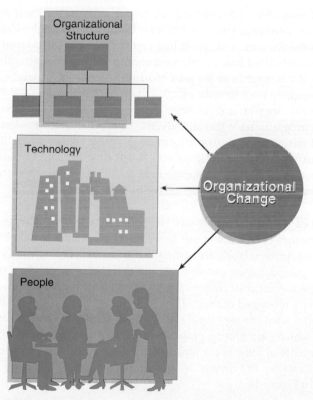

FIGURE 14.2 Organizational Change Targets: Structure, Technology, People
To create change in organizations, one can rely on altering organizational structure, technology, and/or people. Changing any one of these areas may impact the others.

As in many cases of organizational change, the options focus on three prospective targets—changes in *organizational structure,* in *technology,* and/or in *people* (see Figure 14.2). In describing each one, let's consider how it might be applied to the heat usage example.

CHANGES IN ORGANIZATIONAL STRUCTURE   In Chapter 13, I described the key characteristics of organizational structure. Here, I note that altering the structure of an organization can be an effective way of responding to a need for change. In the example, the structural solution to the heat-regulation problem would be to rearrange job responsibilities so that only maintenance personnel can adjust thermostats. Essentially, this involves moving from a decentralized system (in which anyone can make adjustments) to a centralized one (in which only maintenance personnel are permitted to reset the temperature). Where this is done in office buildings, you tend to find lockboxes covering thermostats with only authorized personnel holding keys. Putting it differently, the people with the keys control the power.

In other situations, structural shifts may take different forms. For example, changes may be made in an organization's span of control, altering the number of employees over which supervisors are responsible. Structural changes may also take the form of revising the basis for creating departments—such as from product-based departments to functional ones. Other structural changes may be much simpler, such as clarifying someone's job description or the written policies and procedures to be followed.

CHANGES IN TECHNOLOGY   In many organizational settings, the most straightforward way to make changes is by introducing new technology. Essentially, technology dictates the way jobs must be done, thereby ensuring change. When computers were introduced into offices in the mid-1980s, they revolutionized how people went about creating, storing, and transmitting documents. Typewriters became relics as the jobs of administrative staff members changed and entirely new ways of working were introduced.

How could technology be used to drive change in the thermostat example? One solution would be to install programmable thermostats that adjust temperatures (lowering them in cool winter months and raising them during the summer) to save energy when the building is not in use. Combining this with the structural solution I just described, a centralized, multiple-zone system could be used in which sensors appear in several different locations but the mechanisms for making adjustments appear only in one centralized locked office.

CHANGES IN PEOPLE   You've probably seen stickers next to light switches in hotel rooms asking guests to turn off the lights when not in use. Something of this nature could be done in the example. Very inexpensive, printed labels requesting that occupants not adjust the thermostats could be affixed to them. Indeed, asking people to change their behavior can be a very straightforward way of introducing organizational change. The problem is that it doesn't always work: individuals don't always do what's requested of them. If you said to yourself, "If I'm cold—I'm going to turn up the heat, no matter what the sign says," then you know exactly what I mean.

The point at which I am hinting probably comes as no surprise: changing people isn't easy. Indeed, it lies at the core of most of the topics discussed in this book. Despite unique differences found in various situations, in one way or another, the process of changing people involves the three steps shown in Figure 14.3.

- *Unfreezing*—This is the process of recognizing that the current state of affairs is undesirable. Realizing that change is needed may be the result of some serious organizational crisis or threat (e.g., a serious financial loss, a strike, an accident, or a major lawsuit) or simply

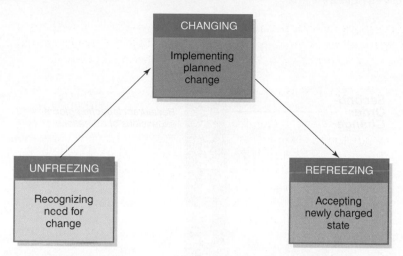

FIGURE 14.3   Changes Involving People: A Three-Step Process   Many organizational changes require people to do things differently. For this to occur it's necessary to follow the three general steps outlined here. As you will see later in this chapter, there are several specific ways in which this may be carried out.

becoming aware that current conditions are unacceptable (e.g., antiquated equipment, inadequately trained employees, etc.). To bring this about, managers sometimes create a sense of urgency in employees by introducing the idea that there is an impending crisis. This approach, referred to as **doomsday management**, effectively unfreezes people, stimulating change before it's too late to do any good. The practice of emphasizing potentially troublesome aspects of a situation may help create a sense of urgency that triggers action.

- *Changing*—Following unfreezing, the stage is set for changes to be made that create more desirable states for organizations and the individuals who work in them. As I describe below, these changes may range from ones that are highly ambitious in nature (e.g., an organization wide restructuring that follows from a merger) to ones that are far more modest in scope (e.g., a revision in the training schedule).
- *Refreezing*—Once changes are incorporated into employees' new ways of thinking and the organizations' ways of operating, refreezing occurs. That is, the new attitudes and behaviors become a new part of life in the organization. Inevitably, these new threads in the organizational fabric are likely to become targets of subsequent organizational change efforts at some time in the future.

Magnitude: How Much Is Changed?

The changes that organizations make differ in magnitude. Whereas some are limited in scope and complexity (e.g., the addition of a new sales rep to an already large sales force), others are more extensive in nature (e.g., the acquisition of a new firm).

Change that is continuous in nature and involves no major shifts in the way an organization operates is known as **first-order change**. This is apparent in the very deliberate, incremental changes that Lexus has been making in continuously improving the environmentally friendly nature of its production process.[7] Similarly, a restaurant may be seen as making first-order changes as it gradually adds new items to its menu and gauges their success before completely revamping its concept.

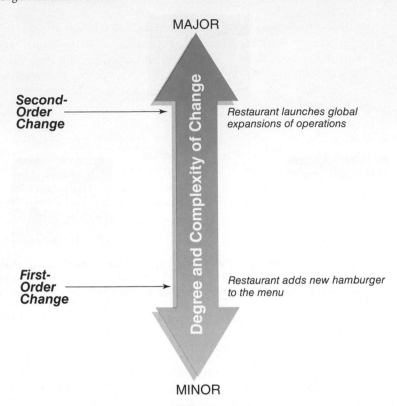

FIGURE 14.4   Comparing First-Order and Second-Order Change
Changes occurring in organizations differ with respect to scope and complexity. A change that is relatively minor is referred to as *first-order change,* whereas one that is more major is referred to as a *second-order change.* One example of each is shown here.

As you might imagine, however, other types of change are far more complex and dramatic. **Second-order change** is the term used to refer to more radical change, major shifts involving many different levels of the organization and many different aspects of business.[8] (For a comparison between these two forms of change, see Figure 14.4.) Citing only some of the most publicized examples of second-order change from recent years, General Electric and Tenneco have radically altered the ways they operate, the cultures they promote, the technologies they use, the structures they create, and the nature of their relations with employees.[9]

Environmental Forces: Why Does Unplanned Change Occur?

As organizations encounter forces in the environments in which they operate, they face formidable challenges to adapt. Indeed, as I noted earlier, businesses must be responsive to **unplanned changes**. I now examine key forces that lead to unplanned change.

SHIFTING EMPLOYEE DEMOGRAPHICS   It is easy to see how, even within your own lifetime, the composition of the workforce has changed. As noted in Chapters 1 and 5, the racial and ethnic makeup of the American workforce is now more highly diversified than ever. To people concerned with the long-term operation of organizations, these are not simply curious sociological trends but shifting conditions that require adjustments.

Human resources experts need to know how the workforce is changing so they can compensate. For example, in recent years, the growth of minority groups in the United States has been considerable. Among other things, this has made it possible to hire people from different ethnic groups. This, in turn, allows companies to capitalize on the varied perspectives that such individuals bring to the workplace. It also provides opportunities for service providers with ethnically diverse customer bases to expose their customers to company representatives with whom they share common language and cultural backgrounds.[10]

Besides requiring familiarity with different languages, growing ethnic diversity has led many businesses to incorporate diversity management programs. As I described in Chapter 5, these practices are designed to help employees from different backgrounds not only get along with one another but to create "inclusive" conditions—ones that enable all employees to feel valued and appreciated for who they are. Sometimes, the changes are small but make a big difference. For example, changing the menu in the company cafeteria to accommodate the varied tastes of people from different ethnic groups can make a big difference to employees, who feel at home as a result.

PERFORMANCE GAPS If you've ever heard the phrase, "If it's not broken, don't fix it," you already have a feel for one of the most potent sources of unplanned internal changes in organizations—*performance gaps*. A product line that isn't moving, a vanishing profit margin, a level of sales that isn't up to corporate expectations—these are gaps between real and expected levels of organizational performance.

Few things force change more than sudden and unexpected information about poor performance. Organizations usually stay with a winning course of action and change in response to failure. Indeed, a performance gap is one of the key factors providing impetus for organizational innovation (for an example, see this chapter's Making the Case section on p. 436). Those organizations that are best prepared to mobilize in response to unexpected downturns are inclined to be the ones that succeed.

GOVERNMENT REGULATION Some of the most commonly witnessed unplanned organizational changes stem from government regulations. Consider, for example, rulings imposed on the auto industry. The U.S. federal government has set restrictions that limit the emission of greenhouse gases from vehicles, that reduce the levels of damage to bumpers resulting from impacts at different speeds, and that raise the fuel economy of vehicles in company fleets. Banks also have made changes in response to governmental regulations. These include changes in over-limit fees for credit cards and limits to the length of time checks can be held before clearing.

Industries also experience change when regulations are removed. Again, let's consider banking, where today's financial institutions may compete against one another in determining the interest they pay depositors—a feature that used to be regulated. Likewise, deregulation has also occurred over the years in airline ticket pricing and long-distance telephone services. As a result, these are some of the most competitively priced (and highly taxed) services available to consumers today.

GLOBAL COMPETITION It happens every day—someone builds a better mousetrap, or at least a less expensive one. Consequently, companies must often fight to maintain their shares of the market, such as by advertising more effectively and lowering their costs. This kind of economic competition not only forces organizations to change but also requires that they do so effectively if they are to survive. Although competition has always been crucial to organizational success, competition comes from all over the world today. As it has become increasingly less expensive to transport materials globally, industrialized countries have found themselves competing with one another for shares of the world's marketplace.

A good illustration is found in the auto industry. In the later part of the twentieth century, globalization led American auto companies to respond to the growing international market for smaller, more fuel-efficient, higher-quality vehicles. They proved unable to innovate accordingly, however and were unprepared to meet this challenge. This opened the door for Japanese competitors to satisfy the market's eager demand, and they took the lead in this large market segment. Having learned a hard lesson, American automakers used the occasion of their reorganization (at the end of the first decade of the 2000s; see Chapter 13) to reverse this trend: they delivered vehicles that were more responsive to the global market. Surely, this trend reflects these companies' recognition of the do-or-die positions in which they found themselves.

FLUCTUATING ECONOMIC CONDITIONS   The ever-changing economy has been very challenging for organizations in recent years. A prolonged recession beginning in 2008 hit many companies hard, forcing them to reduce their workforces—sometimes, dramatically. In fact, the unemployment rate in the United States more than doubled between December 2007 and October 2009.[11] Of course, as people lose their jobs, they have less money to spend, leading to more economic woes. Although the unemployment rate has improved since its 2009 historic high (about 10 percent), it remains far higher than economists consider healthy. This volatile cycle, as economists tell us, is challenging because it limits the accuracy of economic forecasts. Clearly, this roller-coaster economy is a major source of unplanned organizational change.

Economic downturns result in more than lost jobs: individuals who remain employed also encounter disruptions stemming from changes in their work schedules. In many cases, this takes the form of cuts in work hours (attempting to save expenses when forestalling layoffs) while also requiring greater productivity from surviving employees, who scramble to assume the responsibilities of those who were laid off. Not surprisingly, feelings of inequity (Chapter 6) and the stress associated with it (Chapter 4) take their toll on people.

ADVANCES IN TECHNOLOGY   As you know, advances in technology have produced changes in the way organizations operate. Senior scientists and engineers, for example, can probably tell you how their work was drastically altered in the mid-1970s, when their ubiquitous plastic slide rules gave way to pocket calculators. Things changed again only a decade later, when calculators were supplanted by powerful desktop microcomputers, which have revolutionized the way documents are prepared, transmitted, and filed in an office. Today, powerful handheld devices, such as smartphones and tablet computers, make portable, wireless communication a reality, further changing the way work is done.

Companies that in the late 1980s and early 1990s may have considered jumping on the technology bandwagon to gain an advantage over their competitors quickly found out that doing so wasn't an option needed to get ahead—but rather, a requirement just to stay in the game. In the late 1990s, technology made it possible for people to develop new, Web-based businesses with only limited start-up capital. Businesses started by *Internet entrepreneurs* became commonplace, although vast numbers of these went bust by 2000. Today, although the Internet is no longer seen as a path to instant riches, it is clear that its technology has transformed the way many people work. For a summary of ways in which computer technology has changed the way we work, see Table 14.1.

STRATEGIC PLANNING: DELIBERATE CHANGE

Thus far, I have been describing unplanned organizational change. However, not all changes that companies make fall into this category. Organizations also make changes that are very carefully planned and deliberate. This is the idea behind **strategic planning**, which I define as the process

TABLE 14.1	How Has Computer Technology Changed the Way We Work?

Advances in computer technology have revolutionized many of the ways in which we work. Key changes are summarized here.

Area of Change	Old Way	New Technology Examples
Use of machines	Materials were moved by hand, with the aid of mechanical devices (e.g., pulleys and chains).	*Automation* is prevalent—the process of using machines to perform tasks that otherwise might be done by people. For example, computer-controlled machines manipulate materials and perform complex functions, a process known as *industrial robotics* (IR).
Work by employees with disabilities	People with various physical or mental disabilities either were relegated to the simplest jobs, or they didn't work at all.	*Assistive technology* is widespread—devices and other solutions that help individuals with physical or mental problems perform the various actions needed to do their jobs. For example, *telephone handset amplifiers* make it possible for people with hearing impediments to use the telephone and *voice recognition systems* read to people with visual impairments.
Monitoring employees	Supervisors used to enter the offices of employees at work and observe them from afar.	*Computerized performance monitoring* systems are in widespread use, which allow supervisors to access their subordinates' computers for purposes of assessing how well they are performing their jobs—and even if they are doing them at all.
Customer service	Individual service providers did things to help employees, customizing goods and services as time and skill allowed.	*Personalized service* is likely to take the form of greeting visitors to one's Web page with information customized to match the goods and services in which they expressed interest in their last visit (e.g., Amazon.com does this).
Environmental friendliness	Products at the end of their lives were buried in landfills, often polluting the earth.	*Design for disassembly* (DFD) is the process of designing and building products so that their parts can be reused several times and then disposed of at the end of the product's life without harming the environment.

of formulating, implementing, and evaluating changes that enable an organization to achieve its objectives.[12]

Basic Assumptions About Strategic Planning

To understand clearly the nature of strategic plans used in organizations today, it is important to highlight three fundamental assumptions about them.[13]

- *Strategic planning is deliberate*—When organizations make strategic plans, they make conscious decisions to alter fundamental aspects of themselves. These changes tend to be radical in nature (e.g., changing the major goods and services offered by a business), as opposed to minor (e.g., changing the color of the office walls).[14]

- *Strategic planning occurs when current objectives can no longer be met*—For the most part, when a company's current strategy is already bringing about the desired results, change is unlikely to occur. In other words, companies follow the "don't mess with success" rule. However, when it becomes clear that current objectives can no longer be met, companies may formulate new strategies to turn things around.
- *New organizational objectives require new strategic plans*—Whenever a company takes steps to move in a completely different direction, it establishes new objectives—and designs a strategic plan to meet them. Acknowledging that the various parts of an organization are all interdependent, the new plan is likely to involve all functions and levels of the organization. Moreover, the plan will require adequate resources from throughout the organization to bring it to fruition.

To illustrate how these assumptions come to life, I now present examples of the kinds of issues about which companies tend to make strategic plans.

About What Do Companies Make Strategic Plans?

As you might imagine, organizations can make strategic plans to change just about anything. However, most of the plans we see these days involve a change in products and services or in organizational structure.

PRODUCTS AND SERVICES   Imagine that you and a friend have a small janitorial business. The two of you divide the duties, each doing some cleaning, buying supplies, and performing some administrative work. Before long, the business grows, leading you to add additional employees to accommodate your new customers. At this point, you're merely doing more of the same thing. Then, suppose that in response to inquiries about window cleaning from many of your commercial clients, you and your partner decide to expand into that business as well. This decision to take a different direction with the business, to add a new, specialized service, will require a bit of organizational change. Not only will you need new equipment and supplies, but you will have to hire and train new personnel, purchase additional insurance, and secure new accounts. In short, you made a strategic decision to add to the company's line of services, and this necessitates organizational change.

Organizations are required to make these kinds of changes all the time. History reveals that some have done it more successfully than others, however. For example, Canon, Minolta, and Nikon, dominant players in the film camera market, responded to the digital revolution of the 1990s by adding digital cameras to their product mix. By contrast, Polaroid, the longtime leader in instant film-based photography, was slow to jump on the digital photography bandwagon.[15] Because Polaroid executives stuck to their beliefs about the relative benefits of their instant-film products, which proved to be unfounded, the company ultimately was forced to declare bankruptcy.

ORGANIZATIONAL STRUCTURE   It is not only changes in products and services that prompt companies to make strategic changes. As I noted in Chapter 13, organizations also make strategic plans to change their structures. For example, consider IBM's 2004 decision to reorganize by selling its personal computer division to the China-based Lenovo Group.[16] Although IBM was the world's third largest PC maker (behind market leaders Dell and HP), company officials made a strategic decision to strengthen its focus on the company's core business—developing information technology for corporate customers. This, of course, represented a significant departure for

IBM because it was the original leader of the personal computer revolution with the release of the first IBM PC in August 1981—four months before *Time* magazine named the personal computer its "man of the year."[17]

Another way organizations are restructuring is by completely eliminating parts of their businesses that focus on noncore sectors and hiring outside firms to perform these functions instead—a practice known as **outsourcing**. For example, companies like ServiceMaster, which provides janitorial services, and ADP, which provides payroll processing services, make it possible for other organizations to concentrate on the business functions most central to their missions, thereby freeing them from having to attend to peripheral support functions.

Outsourcing is particularly popular in various high-tech businesses, as when firms contract with other, specialized companies to provide such services as data storage or disaster recovery. Another widely outsourced function in computer-related businesses is customer service. Although this has been changing in recent years, the vast majority of these services are provided by companies in other countries, in specialized facilities. The practice of using outsourcing services of overseas companies is known as **offshoring** (short for *offshore outsourcing*).[18] Typically, this practice allows companies to take advantage of lower labor costs and to leverage the expertise of workers in other parts of the world.[19] Three popular types of offshoring are summarized in Table 14.2.

Critics have expressed concerns that outsourcing represents a "hollowing out" of companies—a reduction of functions that weakens organizations by making them more dependent on others. The counterargument is that outsourcing makes sense when the outsourced work is not highly critical to competitive success (e.g., janitorial services) or when it is so highly critical that the only way to succeed requires outside assistance. If you think that outsourcing is an unusual occurrence, guess again. A survey has found that 81 percent of companies outsource multiple functions, and 57 percent indicate that they have increased outsourcing in response to

---

TABLE 14.2 Major Forms of Offshoring

So as to remain focused on their core competencies, many organizations contract with companies in other countries to provide necessary goods and services instead of developing these themselves. This practice, known as offshoring, takes the three major forms summarized here.

Name	Description	Examples
Product offshoring	Relocating the manufacturing of existing products to new locations in countries where conducting business is less expensive.	Electronic components are often made in Costa Rica; clothing and toys frequently are made in China.
Services offshoring	Telecommunications technology is used to provide services for clients.	People working in large call centers in the Philippines and India provide technical support services for some computer companies.
Innovation offshoring	Specialized companies in other nations are used to develop and test innovative new products (see Chapter 13).	Technical experts working in labs in India and China contract with high-tech firms to develop innovative new products, bringing them to market more rapidly than otherwise possible.

the economic downturn.[20] One-third of all outsourcing occurs in the field of information technology, and one-quarter in the field of human resources. The remaining outsourced jobs are in the areas of customer service (22 percent), procurement (14 percent), and finance (6 percent).

The Strategic Planning Process: Making Change Happen

The process of strategic planning typically follows the ten ordered steps described below.[21] Although these steps are not immutable and are not always followed in the exact order specified, they do a reasonably good job of describing the way companies go about planning change strategically. As you consider these ten steps, you may find it useful to follow along with the summary in Figure 14.5.

1. *Define goals.* A strategic plan must begin with a stated goal. Typically, goals involve a company's market (e.g., to gain a certain position in the product market) and/or its financial standing (e.g., to achieve a certain return on equity). Organizational goals also involve society (e.g., to benefit certain groups or the environment) or organizational culture (e.g., to make the workplace more pleasant). (Recall the discussion of the motivational quality of goals in Chapter 6.)
2. *Define the scope of products or services.* For a strategic plan to be effective, company officials must clearly define their organization's *scope*—that is, the businesses in which it already

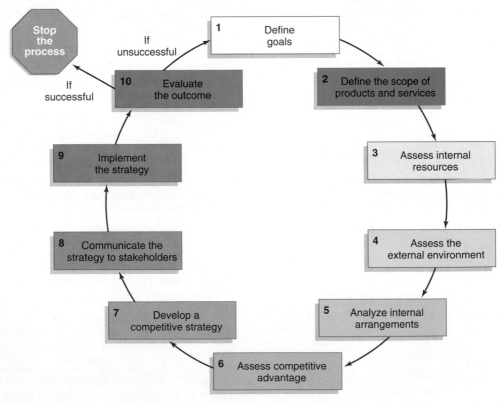

FIGURE 14.5 **Strategic Planning: A Ten-Step Process**
Strategic planning—the process of formulating, implementing, and evaluating decisions that enable an organization to achieve its objectives—generally follows the ten steps summarized here.
Sources: Based on suggestions by Beven, 2011, and Christensen, 1994; see Note 21.

operates and the new ones in which it aims to participate. If scope is defined too narrowly, the company will overlook opportunities; if it is defined too broadly, the effectiveness of its plan will be diluted.

3. *Assess internal resources.* An essential question to be answered is: What resources does the company have available to plan and implement its strategy? The ones in question involve funds (e.g., money to make purchases), physical assets (e.g., required space), and human assets (e.g., knowledge and skills of the workforce).

4. *Assess the external environment.* The extent to which the environment either helps or hinders a company's growth (or even its existence) depends on several key factors. Specifically, a company has a competitive advantage over others when its resources (a) cannot be easily imitated by others, (b) will not depreciate anytime soon, and (c) are better than those its competitors might have.[22]

5. *Analyze internal arrangements.* By "internal arrangements," I am referring to the nature of the organization itself as identified by the characteristics described in this book. For example, are the employees paid in a way that motivates them to strive for corporate goals (Chapter 6)? Does the culture of the organization encourage people to be innovative and to make changes, or does it encourage them to be stagnant (see Chapter 12)? Do people communicate with each other clearly (Chapter 8) and cooperate with one another sufficiently well (Chapter 7) to accomplish their goals? These and other basic questions must be answered to formulate an effective plan for change. After all, unless the organization is operating properly in these key respects, even the best strategic plans may not pan out.

6. *Assess competitive advantage.* A company is said to have a **competitive advantage** over another to the extent that customers perceive its products or services as being superior and offered at an equal or lower price. Superiority may be assessed in terms of such factors as quality, price, breadth of product line, reliability of performance, styling, service, and company image.

7. *Develop a competitive strategy.* A competitive strategy is the means by which an organization achieves its goal. Based on a careful assessment of a company's standing in the factors described earlier (e.g., the company's available resources, its competitive advantage, etc.), a decision is made about how to go about achieving its goal. Organizations can follow many different strategies, some of which I outlined in Chapter 13 because of their links to organizational structure. Here, in Table 14.3, I identify some additional strategies that are widely adopted by today's organizations.

8. *Communicate the strategy to stakeholders.* The term **stakeholder** is used to describe an individual or group in whose interest an organization is run. In other words, these are entities that have a special stake, or claim, on the company. The most important stakeholders include employees at all levels, boards of directors, stockholders, and customers. It is essential to communicate a firm's strategy to stakeholders very clearly so they can contribute to its success, either actively (e.g., employees who pitch in to help meet goals) or passively (e.g., investors who pour money into the company). Without stakeholders' full understanding and acceptance of a firm's strategy, a firm is unlikely to receive the full support it needs to accomplish its goals.

9. *Implement the strategy.* Once a strategy has been formulated and communicated, it is time for it to be implemented. When this occurs, there is likely to be some upheaval as people scramble to adjust to new ways of doing things. As I describe in the next section of this chapter, people tend to be reluctant to make changes in the way they work. However, as I also note, several steps can be taken to ensure that the people who are responsible for making changes will embrace rather than reject them.

TABLE 14.3	Varieties of Competitive Strategies

Some of the most popular competitive strategies used by today's organizations are summarized here.

Strategy	Description
Market-share increasing strategies	Developing a broader share of an existing market, such as by widening the range of products, or by forming a joint venture (see Chapter 13) with another company that already has a presence in the market of interest
Profit strategies	Attempting to derive more profit from existing businesses, such as by training employees to work more efficiently or salespeople to sell more effectively
Market concentration strategies	Withdrawing from markets where the company is less effective and instead concentrating resources in markets where the company is likely to be more effective
Turnaround strategies	Attempting to reverse a decline in business by moving to a new product line or by radically restructuring operations
Exit strategies	Withdrawing from a market, such as by liquidating assets

10. *Evaluate the outcome.* Finally, after a strategy has been implemented, it is crucial to determine whether the goals have been met. If so, then new goals may be sought. If not, then different goals may be defined or different strategies followed so as to achieve success the next time.

(Now that you have read about how to develop a strategic plan, you may be wondering what it's like to actually participate in this process. For some experience in this regard, complete the Self-Assessment exercise on p. 464.)

RESISTANCE TO CHANGE: MAINTAINING THE STATUS QUO

Even if people are unhappy with the state of affairs in their organizations, they may be afraid that change will be disruptive and only make things worse. Indeed, fear of new conditions is quite real, and it creates unwillingness to accept change. For this reason, people may react to organizational change quite negatively. Then again, if the process is managed effectively, people may respond in a very enthusiastic manner. Scientists have summarized the nature of people's reactions to organizational change as falling along a continuum ranging from acceptance, through indifference and passive resistance, to active resistance.[23] For a summary of the various forms these reactions may take, see Figure 14.6.

As you might imagine, for an organization to make the changes needed to remain competitive, it must tackle the problem of **resistance to change** head on. With this in mind, I discuss the issue of readiness for change and examine both its individual and organizational barriers. I conclude this section of the chapter by identifying specific steps that organizations can take to overcome resistance to change.

Individual Barriers to Change

People resist changes in organizations for a variety of reasons stemming from their own individual concerns, qualities, and interests.[24] Key reasons are as follows:

- *Economic insecurity*—Because any changes on the job have the potential to threaten one's livelihood—by either the loss of a job or reduced pay—some resistance to change is inevitable.

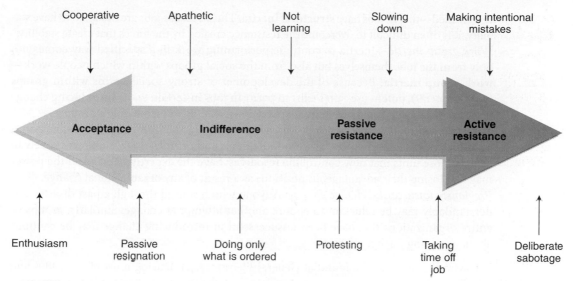

FIGURE 14.6 A Continuum of Reactions to Organizational Change
People's reactions to organizational change can range from acceptance (left) to active resistance (right). Some of the specific forms these reactions might take are indicated here.
Sources: Based on suggestions by Burke, 2010, Goldstein, 2001, and Judson, 1991; see Note 22.

- *Fear of the unknown*—Employees derive a sense of security from doing things the same way, knowing who their coworkers will be, and knowing to whom they will answer from day to day. Disrupting these comfortably established patterns creates unfamiliar conditions, a state of affairs that is often rejected. It is not unusual for such fears to be based on adjustments required to adapt to the use of new technology.
- *Threats to social relationships*—As people continue to work within organizations, they form strong bonds with their coworkers. Many changes (e.g., the reassignment of job responsibilities) threaten the integrity of friendship groups that provide valuable social rewards.
- *Habit*—Jobs that are well learned and become habitual are easy to perform. The prospect of changing the way jobs are done challenges people to develop new job skills. Doing this is clearly more difficult than continuing to perform the job as it was originally learned.
- *Failure to recognize need for change*—Unless employees can recognize and fully appreciate the need for changes in organizations, any vested interests they may have in keeping things the same may overpower their willingness to accept change. Using the terminology of Figure 14.3 (on p. 441), unfreezing is necessary before change can occur.

Organizational Barriers to Change

In addition to individual factors, resistance to change also stems from conditions associated with organizations themselves.[25] Several such factors are as follows:

- *Structural inertia*—Organizations are designed to promote stability. To the extent that employees are carefully selected and trained to perform certain jobs, and rewarded for doing them well, the forces acting on individuals to work in certain ways are very powerfully determined—that is, jobs have **structural inertia**. Thus, because jobs are designed to have stability, it is often difficult to overcome the resistance created by the forces that create stability.

- *Work group inertia*—Inertia to continue performing work in a specified way comes not only from the jobs themselves but also from the social groups within which people work—**work group inertia**. Because of the development of strong social norms within groups (see Chapter 9), potent pressures exist to perform jobs in certain ways. Introducing change disrupts these established normative expectations, leading to formidable resistance.
- *Threats to existing balance of power*—If changes are made with respect to who's in charge, a shift in the balance of power between individuals and organizational subunits is likely to occur. Those units that now control the resources, have the expertise, and wield the power may fear losing their advantageous positions as a result of any organizational change.
- *Previously unsuccessful change efforts*—Anyone who has lived through a past disaster understandably may be reluctant to endure another attempt at change. Similarly, groups or entire organizations that have been unsuccessful in introducing change may be cautious about accepting further attempts.

A classic example may be found at General Electric (GE). During most of the 1980s and 1990s, this company underwent a series of widespread changes in its basic strategy, organizational structure, and relationships with employees. In this process, it experienced several of the barriers identified above. For example, GE managers had mastered a set of bureaucratic traditions that kept their habits strong and their inertia moving straight ahead. The prospect of doing things differently was scary for those who were strongly entrenched in doing things the "GE way." In particular, the company's interest in globalizing triggered many fears of the unknown.

Resistance to change at GE was also strong because it threatened to strip power from those units that traditionally had possessed most of it (e.g., the Power Systems and Lighting Division). Changes also were highly disruptive to GE's "social architecture"; friendship groups were broken up and scattered throughout the company. In all, GE has been a living example of many different barriers to change rolled into a single company. (How attuned are you to people's resistance to organizational change? To answer this question, complete the Group Exercise on pp. 464–465.)

When Will Organizational Change Occur?

As you might imagine, there are times when organizations are likely and less likely to change. In general, change is inclined to occur when the people involved believe that the benefits associated with making a change outweigh the costs.[26] The factors contributing to the benefits of making a change are as follows:

- *Dissatisfaction with current conditions*—Change is most likely when dissatisfaction with the status quo is high.
- *Availability of a desirable alternative*—Change is most likely when clearly desirable alternatives are recognized.
- *A plan for achieving that alternative*—Change is most likely when it is clear how an alternative may be made to come about.

When assessing the benefits of making a change, these three factors are assumed to combine multiplicatively (see Figure 14.7). This suggests that if the value of any one of these factors is zero, change will not occur. If you think about it, this makes sense. After all, people are unlikely to initiate change if they are not dissatisfied, if they don't have any desirable alternative in mind, or if they fail to recognize a way of attaining that alternative if they do have one in mind. Of course,

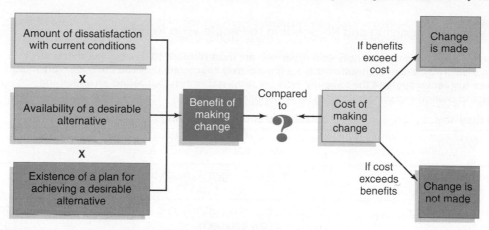

FIGURE 14.7   Organizational Change: When Will It Occur?
Whether or not an organizational change will take place depends on people's beliefs regarding its relative benefits and costs. The benefits are reflected by three considerations reviewed here.
Source: Based on suggestions by Beer, 1980; see Note 26.

for change to occur, the expected benefits must outweigh the likely costs involved (e.g., disruption, uncertainties).

How Can Resistance to Organizational Change Be Overcome?

Because organizational change is inevitable, managers should be sensitive to its barriers so that resistance can be overcome. This is of course easier said than done. However, several useful approaches have been suggested, including the key ones summarized here.[27]

GAIN LEADERSHIP SUPPORT   For change to be accepted, it is often useful (if not absolutely necessary) to win the support of the most powerful and influential individuals in the company. Doing so builds a critical internal mass of support for change. Clearly demonstrating that key organizational leaders endorse change is an effective way to get others to go along with it. This may be because they share the leader's vision or because they fear his or her retaliation. Either way, their support will facilitate acceptance of change.

IDENTIFY AND NEUTRALIZE CHANGE RESISTERS   An important way of supporting change initiatives involves neutralizing the efforts of those who resist change. Often, resistance occurs because people publicly express their fears and organizational officials fail to respond. An offhand remark that conveys concerns and fears about impending change can be contagious, spreading fear into the workplace. Not saying anything to counter such statements is to support that concern tacitly. As such, it is important for individuals promoting organizational change to identify and neutralize those who resist it. Several statements reflecting a fear of change and ways of responding to them are identified in Table 14.4.[28]

EDUCATE THE WORKFORCE   Often, people are reluctant to change because they fear what the future has in store for them. Fears about economic security, for example, may be put to rest with a few reassuring words from leaders. As part of educating employees about what organizational changes may mean for them, top management must show a considerable amount of emotional

TABLE 14.4	Recognizing and Responding to People Who Resist Change

It generally is not difficult to identify employees who are most resistant to change. The things they say give them away. Unless such statements are immediately countered, they run the risk of spreading resistance further throughout the company. Here are some statements that reflect an underlying resistance to change and some guidelines for responding to them.

When they say . . .	You should counter by saying . . .
That seems risky.	Yes, but the risk is worth taking. After all, it is even riskier to do nothing.
Let's get back to basics.	The world has changed so much that what once seemed appropriate because it was "basic" no longer works today.
It worked in the past.	Maybe so, but as conditions have changed, so there is reason to consider a new approach.
Things are okay as they are.	Possibly, but unless we take action, things are unlikely to be okay in the future.
I don't see any threat.	There's always a threat. Just because you don't see any compelling threat doesn't mean that one doesn't exist.
That's not our core competence.	Just because a particular area used to be an organization's core competence doesn't mean that it shouldn't be.
The numbers don't work.	In the new Internet-based economy, new rules of accounting may be considered.
Once we start down that road, we can never go back.	Don't be afraid of relinquishing control. We can stop anything that doesn't work.
There will be unforeseen consequences.	This is always the case. In fact, that is precisely why it is necessary to consider making changes.

Sources: Based on suggestions by Harvey & Brolyes, 2010, and Reich, 2000; see Note 28.

sensitivity. Doing so makes it possible for the people affected by change to help make it work. Some companies have found that simply answering the question, "What's in it for me?" can help allay fears. Although it may go without saying, it's important to emphasize that openness and honesty are important when addressing this issue.

"SELL" THE NEED FOR CHANGE   For organizational change to occur, top management must accept the idea that change is required. And quite often, it's lower-level supervisors, those who toil daily in the trenches, who offer the best ideas. For these ideas to be accepted and implemented, however, leaders must be convinced that the ideas are worthwhile.

INVOLVE EMPLOYEES IN THE CHANGE EFFORTS   People who participate in making a decision tend to be more committed to its outcomes than are those who are not involved. Accordingly, employees who participate in responding to unplanned change or who are made part of the team charged with planning a needed organizational change may be expected to put up very little resistance to change. As a manager at Hewlett-Packard once put it, "I don't think people really enjoy change, but if they can participate in it and understand it, it can become a positive [experience] for them."[29]

REWARD CONSTRUCTIVE BEHAVIORS   One rather obvious, and quite successful, mechanism for facilitating organizational change, as I noted in Chapter 3, is to reward people for behaving in the desired fashion. Changing operations may require a change in the kinds of behaviors that need to be rewarded by an organization. This is especially critical when a company is in the transition period of introducing the change. For example, employees who must learn to use new equipment should be praised for their successful efforts along the way. Feedback on how well they are doing not only provides a great deal of useful assurance to uncertain workers, but also helps shape the desired behavior.

CREATE A "LEARNING ORGANIZATION"   Although all organizations change, whether they want to or not, some do so more effectively than others. Those that have developed the capacity to adapt and change continuously are known as **learning organizations**.[30] In learning organizations, people set aside old ways of thinking, freely share ideas with others, form a vision of the organization, and work together on a plan for achieving that goal. As a result, learning organizations are said to transform themselves. Examples of learning organizations include Ford, General Electric, Walmart, Xerox, and Motorola.

As you might imagine, becoming a learning organization is no simple feat. In fact, it involves implementing many of the principles of organizational behavior described throughout this book. Specifically, for a firm to become a continuous learner, management must take the following steps:

- *Establish commitment to change*—Unless all employees clearly see that top management is committed strongly to altering and improving the organization, they will be unlikely to make the changes necessary to bring about improvements.
- *Adopt an informal organizational structure*—Change is more readily accepted when organizational structures (described in Chapter 13) are flat, cross-functional teams are created (see Chapter 9), and the formal boundaries between people are eliminated.
- *Develop an open organizational culture*—As I described in Chapter 12, managers play a key role in forming organizational culture. To adapt effectively to changes in their environments, organizations should have cultures that embrace risk-taking, openness, and growth. Companies whose leaders are reluctant to confront the chance of failure will be unlikely to grow and develop.

Although these suggestions may be easier to state than to implement, efforts at following them will be well rewarded. Given the many forces that make employees resistant to change, managers should keep these guidelines in mind. (For some suggestions as to how some effective organizations promote change, see the Winning Practices section on p. 456.)

ORGANIZATIONAL DEVELOPMENT INTERVENTIONS: IMPLEMENTING PLANNED CHANGE

Now that I've shed light on the basic issues surrounding organizational change, I will review systematic ways of implementing it—collectively known as techniques of **organizational development (OD)**. Formally defined, organizational development refers to a set of social science techniques designed to plan and implement change in work settings for purposes of enhancing the personal development of individuals and improving the effectiveness of organizational functioning.

Over the years, many different strategies for implementing planned organizational change (referred to as *OD interventions*) have been used by specialists known as *OD practitioners*.[31] All

Winning Practices

Making Changes Stick: How Three Successful Organizations Do It

If you want to understand change, it makes sense to look at successful organizations that have been around for a while. To have made it for more than 100 years, a company must be managing change quite effectively. This clearly applies to three of the world's largest organizations—Royal Dutch Shell, Sears, and the U.S. Army. By analyzing what they have done to manage change effectively, it's possible to identify several practices that are worth emulating.[32]

1. *Fully incorporate employees into challenges faced by the organization.* This means more than simply involving employees in an organization's operations, but engaging them actively in the problems it faces. Officials from Shell Malaysia had long been unsuccessful in getting employees to work together to beat the competition. They were far too complacent, and the competition was rapidly gaining market share. In response to this, Shell officials called together all 260 managers and put the problem of the rapidly encroaching competition before them. They emerged with a firm plan that was put into place. Back on the job, regular follow-up meetings were held to make sure the plan was implemented. Because employees took ownership of the problem, Shell was successful in changing the way it operated.

2. *Lead in a way that stresses the urgency of change.* It's not unusual for company officials to get in a rut, becoming lazy and complacent about the way they operate—even when it's necessary to take decisive action. This is *almost* what happened to Sears a few years ago. The retailing giant was losing customers rapidly as officers sat by, merely lowering sales goals. That's when CEO Arthur Martinez lit a fire under everyone by stressing the importance of turning things around—or else! He generated a sense of urgency by setting very challenging goals (e.g., increasing customer satisfaction by 15 percent). Although Martinez didn't have all the answers to Sears's problems, he provided something even more important—straightforward, honest talk about the company's problems, creating a sense of urgency that got everyone moving in the right direction.

3. *Create relentless discomfort with the status quo.* Following military maneuvers, the U.S. Army thoroughly debriefs all participants in what is called an "After Action Review." In these sessions, careful feedback is given about what soldiers did well and where they stand to improve. By focusing in a relentless, detailed manner on work that needs to be done, officers eventually get soldiers to internalize the need for excellence. Soldiers are encouraged to consider how they can do something better (faster, cheaper, or more accurately), or if there is a new and more effective approach that could be taken. In short, the status quo is the enemy; current performance levels are never good enough; things can always be better. Army brass liken this commitment to continuous improvement to painting a bridge: the job is never over because as soon as one side is done, the other side needs to be repainted.

Although these measures may be challenging to implement, they certainly warrant careful consideration. After all, their effectiveness has been demonstrated in some of the most successful organizations in the world.

the major methods of organizational development attempt to produce some kind of change in individual employees, work groups, and/or entire organizations. This is the goal of the five OD interventions I review here.

Management by Objectives: Clarifying Organizational Goals

In Chapter 7, I discussed the motivational benefits of setting specific goals. As you might imagine, not only individuals, but entire organizations also stand to benefit from this. For example, an executive may express interest in "raising productivity" and "improving the quality" of her company's goods or services. These objectives, well intentioned though they may be, are not as useful as more specific ones, such as, "increase production of widgets by 15 percent" or "lower the failure rate of widgets by 25 percent." After all, as the old saying goes, "It's usually easier to get somewhere if you know where you're going." The late management expert Peter Drucker was well aware of this idea while consulting for General Electric during the early 1950s and is credited with promoting the benefits of specifying clear organizational goals—a technique known as **management by objectives (MBO)**.

As summarized in Figure 14.8, the MBO process consists of four basic steps. First, goals are selected that employees will try to attain to best serve the needs of the organization. These should be determined by managers and their subordinates working together and not simply imposed on subordinates by managers. Further, these goals should be directly measurable and have some time frame attached to them. Goals that cannot be measured (e.g., "make the company better"), or that have no time limits, are useless. By contrast, as the saying goes, "what gets measured gets done."

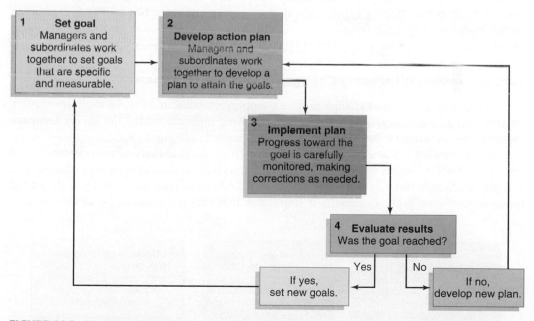

FIGURE 14.8 **Management by Objectives: Developing Organizations Through Goal Setting**
The organizational development technique of *management by objectives* requires managers and their subordinates to work together on setting and trying to achieve important organizational goals. The basic steps of the process are outlined here.

In step two, managers and their subordinates work together to plan ways of attaining the goals they have selected—developing what is known as an *action plan*. Specifically, an **action plan** is a carefully specified set of guidelines indicating exactly what needs to be done to attain desired results.

Once goals are set and action plans have been developed to accomplish them, the third step calls for *implementation*—carrying out the plan and regularly assessing its progress. Is the plan working? Are the goals being approximated? Are there any problems being encountered in attempting to meet the goals? Such questions need to be considered while implementing an action plan. If the plan is failing, a midcourse correction is in order—changing the plan, the way it's carried out, or even the goal itself.

Finally, after monitoring progress toward the goal, the fourth step may be instituted: *evaluation*—assessing goal attainment. Were the organization's goals reached? If so, what new ones should be set to improve things still further? If not, what new plans can be initiated to help meet the goals? Because the ultimate assessment of the extent to which goals are met helps determine the selection of new goals, MBO is a continuous process.

MBO represents a potentially effective source of planning and implementing strategic change for organizations. Systematic efforts to meet organizational goals get individual employees and their organizations working together toward common ends. When this happens, system-wide change results. Of course, for MBO to work, everyone involved has to buy into it. Because MBO programs typically require a great deal of participation by lower-level employees, top managers must be willing to accept and support the cooperation and involvement of all.

Making MBO work also requires a great deal of time—anywhere from three to five years. Hence, MBO may be inappropriate in organizations that do not have the appropriate time to commit to the process. Despite these considerations, MBO has become one of the most widely used techniques for affecting organizational change in recent years. Not only is it used on an ad hoc basis by many organizations, but it also constitutes an ingrained element of the organizational culture in some companies, such as Hewlett-Packard and Intel.

Survey Feedback: Inducing Change by Sharing Information

For effective organizational change to occur, employees must understand their companies' current strengths and weaknesses. That's the underlying rationale behind the **survey feedback** method. This technique follows the three steps summarized in Figure 14.9.

First, data are collected that provide information about matters of general concern to employees, such as organizational culture (see Chapter 12), leadership style (see Chapter 11), and job satisfaction (see Chapter 5). This may take the form of intensive interviews, structured questionnaires, or both. Because it is important that this information be as unbiased as

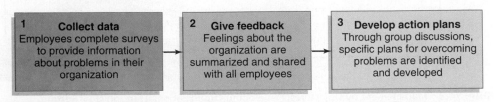

FIGURE 14.9   Survey Feedback: An Overview
The *survey feedback* technique of organizational development follows the three steps outlined here: collecting data, giving feedback, and developing action plans.

possible, employees providing feedback should be assured that their responses will be kept confidential. For this reason, this process is usually conducted by outside consultants who keep the responses of individual employees from management.

The second step calls for reporting the information obtained back to the employees during small group meetings. Typically, this consists of summarizing the average scores on the information assessed in the survey. Profiles are created of feelings about the organization, its leadership, the work done, and related topics. Discussions also focus on why the scores are as they are, and what problems are revealed by the feedback.

The final step involves analyzing problems dealing with communication, decision making, and other organizational processes to make plans for dealing with them. Such discussions are usually most effective when they are documented carefully and a specific plan of implementation is made, with someone put in charge of carrying it out.

Survey feedback is used widely as an organizational development technique. This is not surprising in view of the advantages it offers. It is efficient, allowing a great deal of information to be collected relatively quickly. Also, it is very flexible and can be tailored to the needs of different organizations facing a variety of problems. However, the technique can be no better than the quality of the questionnaire used—it must measure the things that really matter to employees. Of course, to derive the maximum benefit from survey feedback, it must have the support of top management. The plans developed by the small discussion groups must be capable of being implemented with the full approval of the organization's leaders. When these conditions are met, survey feedback has proven to be a very effective OD technique.

Appreciative Inquiry

Although survey feedback and MBO are highly regarded OD techniques, they focus only on deficiencies, such as negative feedback and unmet goals. By contrast, a relatively new approach to organizational development known as *appreciative inquiry* helps organizations focus on the positive and the possible.[33] Specifically, **appreciative inquiry (AI)** is an OD intervention that focuses attention away from an organization's shortcomings and toward its capabilities and its potential. It is based on the assumption that members of organizations already know the problems they face and that they stand to benefit more by focusing on what is possible.

As currently practiced, the process of appreciative inquiry involves assembling small groups of people from an organization and guiding them through four straightforward steps. These are as follows:[34]

1. *Discovery.* The discovery step involves identifying the positive aspects of the organization, the best of "what is." This frequently is accomplished by documenting the positive reactions of customers or people from other organizations.
2. *Dreaming.* Through the process of discovering the organization's strengths, it is possible to begin dreaming by envisioning "what might be." By discussing dreams for a theoretically ideal organization, employees are free to reveal their ideal hopes.
3. *Designing.* The designing stage involves having a dialogue in which participants discuss their ideas about "what should be." The underlying idea is that by listening to others in a highly receptive manner, it is possible to understand others' ideas and to come to a common understanding of what the future should look like.
4. *Delivering.* After having jointly discussed the ideal state of affairs, members of the organization are ready to begin instituting a plan for delivering their ideas. Specifically, this involves establishing specific objectives and directions regarding "what will be."

Although appreciative inquiry is a newer approach to OD than the others I've discussed, it has been used a great deal and with considerable success.[35]

Action Labs

Usually, bringing about change is a very slow process. At a typical large company, it involves painstakingly analyzing and planning ideas and then rolling out only small changes in a deliberate sequence. However, in today's rapidly moving world, this pace is likely to be far too slow. To accelerate the change process, a technique known as the *action lab* has been introduced in recent years. The action lab is meant to be a "greenhouse" in which change can be created by insulating a group of decision makers from daily operations and getting them to focus on a business problem. Specifically, an **action lab** is an OD intervention in which teams of participants work off-site to develop and implement new ways of solving organizational problems by focusing on the ineffectiveness of current methods.[36]

One of the unique features of action labs is that the participants are in contact with one another for such extended periods of time (e.g., every day for four weeks) that they eventually find it impossible to cling to their established ways. For example, in one particular action lab, participants faced a frustrating few days in which bold proposals were constantly shot down. Inevitably, an executive would find some flaw and the idea was dropped in an attempt to avoid conflict. Soon, however, team members realized that despite the aim of treating everyone as equals, they inevitably retreated to the safety of the company's established practice of pleasing the bosses. Eventually, the lab participants figured out that the very forces that were blocking changes in the company were also present within the lab. They were more concerned with avoiding conflict than with getting new ideas out into the open. With this new insight, however, the team was now able to develop innovative ideas.

Quality of Work Life Programs: Humanizing the Workplace

When you think of work, do you think of drudgery? Although many people believe these two terms go together naturally, it has grown increasingly popular to systematically improve the quality of life experienced on the job. As more people demand satisfying and personally fulfilling places to work, OD practitioners have attempted to create work situations that enhance employees' motivation, satisfaction, and commitment—factors that contribute to high levels of organizational performance (as demonstrated in Chapters 5 and 6).

Such efforts are known collectively as **quality of work life (QWL) programs**. These programs are a way to increase organizational output and improve quality by involving employees in the decisions that affect them on their jobs. Typically, QWL programs support highly democratic treatment of employees at all levels and encourage their participation in decision making (see Chapter 10). Although many approaches to improving the quality of work life exist, they all share a common goal: humanizing the workplace.

A popular approach to improving the quality of work life involves using **quality circles (QCs)**. These are small groups of volunteers (about ten) who meet regularly (usually weekly) to identify and solve problems related to the quality of the work they perform and the conditions under which they work. An organization may have several QCs operating at once, each dealing with a particular work area about which it has the most expertise. To help them work effectively, the members of the circle usually receive some form of training in problem solving.

Although QCs originated in Japan and have been used extensively there, many large American companies also have included QCs as part of their QWL efforts. Groups have dealt with issues such as how to reduce vandalism, how to create safer and more comfortable working environments, and how to improve product quality. Research has shown that although quality circles are very effective at bringing about short-term improvements in quality of work life (i.e., those lasting up to eighteen months), they are less effective at creating more permanent changes.

THREE CRITICAL QUESTIONS ABOUT ORGANIZATIONAL DEVELOPMENT

No discussion of organizational development would be complete without addressing the three important questions I raise in this final section of the chapter.

Is Organizational Development Inherently Unethical?

By its very nature, OD represents an attempt to change attitudes and behavior. Because of this, some people have claimed over the years that its practice is inherently unethical. They have argued that forcing people to change in ways they might not want to change is manipulative and inappropriate.[37]

For example, it has been suggested that OD techniques impose the values of the organization on the individual without taking the person's own attitudes into account. OD is a very one sided approach, reflecting the imposition of the more powerful organization on the less powerful employee. A related claim is that OD fails to provide workers with free choice. As a result, it may be seen as *coercive*. When faced with a "do it, or else" situation, employees are forced to allow themselves to be manipulated, a potentially degrading prospect.

Despite these considerations, many professionals (the author, included) do not agree that OD is inherently unethical. Such a claim, it has been countered, is to say that the practice of management is itself unethical. After all, the very act of going to work for an organization requires one to submit to both the company's and society's values. One cannot help but face life situations in which others' ideals are imposed. This is not to say that organizations have opportunities to impose unethical values on people for the purpose of making a profit (e.g., stealing from customers). Indeed, because they have the potential to abuse their power, organizations have a special obligation to refrain from doing so.

Although abuses of organizational power are all too common, OD itself is not necessarily the culprit. Indeed, like any other tool (even a gun!), OD is not inherently good or evil. Instead, many proponents argue that how the tool is used will depend upon the individual wielding it. With this in mind, the ethical use of OD interventions requires that they be supervised by professionals in an organization that places a high value on ethics. In fact, today's OD practitioners subscribe to a code of ethics that holds them to clear standards with respect to ensuring the benefits to organizations and the well-being of all employees.[38]

Does OD Really Work?

Because OD requires a considerable amount of time, money, and effort, it is appropriate to ask if this investment is worthwhile. In other words, does OD really work? Given the popularity of OD in organizations, this question is very important.

In general, the news is good. Most of the studies show the effects of the various OD interventions to be beneficial—particularly when it comes to improving organizational functioning.[39] This said, however, I must note that any conclusions about the effectiveness of OD should be qualified in several important ways.

- *OD interventions tend to be more effective among blue-collar employees than among white-collar employees*—This likely occurs for a simple reason—namely, that most OD techniques are focused on changing the behavior of front-line people in operative roles rather than higher-level decision makers.
- *The beneficial effects of OD are enhanced by using a combination of several techniques (e.g., two or more together) instead of any single technique*—Given that the various techniques have strengths and weaknesses, it is not surprising that using one approach to offset the limitations of another is quite helpful.
- *The effectiveness of OD techniques depends on the degree of support they receive from top management*—The more programs are supported from the top, the more successful they tend to be. I have already made this point in conjunction with QWL programs, but it is applicable to all OD interventions. If management is not fully supportive of such efforts, they are doomed to fail.

Overall, the conclusion is positive. Despite some limitations, organizational development techniques have considerable capacity to benefit both organizations and the individuals working within them. And, as you may recall from Chapter 1, these are among the fundamental objectives of the field of OB.

Is OD Affected by National Culture?

For organizational development to be effective, people must be willing to share their ideas candidly with others, accept uncertainty, and show concern for others, especially members of their own teams. However, not all people are comfortable doing these things; this pattern better characterizes the people from some countries than others. For example, this profile closely describes people from Scandinavian countries, suggesting that OD may be most effective in such nations. However, people from Latin American nations are much the opposite, suggesting that OD interventions will be less successful when conducted there.[40] For a summary of the extent to which the basic assumptions of OD fit with the cultural styles of people from various nations, see Figure 14.10.[41]

Although the predominant cultural values of people from the United States place it in the middle region of the diagram in Figure 14.10, this is not to say that OD is doomed to be ineffective in American companies. Not all OD techniques are alike with respect to their

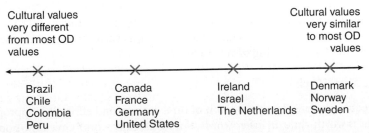

FIGURE 14.10   Organizational Development: Its Fit with National Values
Organizational development (OD) techniques tend to be successful when the underlying values of the technique match the cultural values of the nations in which it is used. General OD values tend to conform more to the cultural norms of some nations, shown on the right (where OD is more likely to be accepted), than others, shown on the left (where OD is less likely to be accepted).
Sources: Based on suggestions by Livermote, 2009, and Jaeger, 1986; see Note 41.

underlying cultural values.[42] For example, MBO has become a very popular OD technique in the United States in large part because it promotes the American values of willingness to take risks and working aggressively at attaining high performance. However, because MBO also encourages superiors and subordinates to negotiate freely with each other, the technique has been generally unsuccessful in France, where the higher levels of authority of others are well accepted.[43] Reasoning similarly, one may expect survey feedback to be unsuccessful in the Southeast Asian nation of Brunei, where the prevailing cultural value is such that problems are unlikely to be confronted openly.

These examples illustrate a key point: the effectiveness of OD techniques will depend, in part, on the extent to which the values of the technique match the underlying values of the national culture in which it is employed. As such, OD practitioners must appreciate fully the cultural norms of the nations in which they are operating. Failure to do so not only may make OD interventions unsuccessful, but they may even yield unintended negative consequences.

Back to the Case

Answer the following questions based on this chapter's Making the Case (p. 436) to illustrate insights you have derived from the material in this chapter.

1. What particular types or categories of organizational change occurred at Campbell's? What were the major drivers of these changes?
2. What factors may have led to resistance to change at Campbell's? How might these have been overcome?
3. How might OD techniques have been used to facilitate the changes that Campbell's CEO Douglas Conant tried to introduce? What one particular technique do you believe would be most effective? Why?

You Be the Consultant

Promoting Organizational Change

Things have been rough for the former employees at Small Town S&L ever since their institution was bought by First National Mega Bank. First National's procedures were more formal than those at Small Town. The CEO of First National is concerned about the employees' negative reactions to the change and calls on you for help. Answer the following questions relevant to this situation based on the material in this chapter.

1. Besides new operating procedures, what other planned and unplanned changes would you suspect are responsible for the employees' negative responses?
2. What barriers to change are likely to be encountered in this situation, and what steps would you propose to overcome them?
3. Do you think that an OD intervention would help in this case? If so, which one (or ones) do you propose, and why?

Self-Assessment Exercise

DEVELOPING A STRATEGIC PLAN

Developing a strategic plan is not an easy matter. In fact, doing it right requires a great deal of information and lots of practice. This exercise will give you a feel for some of the challenges involved in developing such a plan.

Directions

1. Suppose that you are the president of a small software development firm that has for years sold a utility that adds functionality to the operating system used in most computers. Now, you suddenly face a serious problem: Microsoft has changed its operating system such that your product no longer serves any purpose.
2. Using the ten steps outlined in Figure 14.5 (on p. 448), develop a strategic plan to keep your company alive. Make any assumptions you need to develop your plan and state them in the process of describing it.

Discussion Questions

1. How easy or difficult was it for you to develop this strategic plan? What would have made the process easier or more effective?
2. Which of the ten steps do you imagine would be easiest to implement? Which do you think would be most challenging? Explain your answers.
3. What special challenges, if any, would the employees of your company face as they attempted to implement this plan? How would you attempt to overcome these challenges?

Group Exercise

RECOGNIZING IMPEDIMENTS TO CHANGE—AND HOW TO OVERCOME THEM

To confront the reality of organizational change, one of the most fundamental steps involves recognizing the barriers to change. Then, once these impediments have been identified, consideration can be given to ways of overcoming them. This exercise is designed to help you practice thinking along these lines while working in groups.

Directions

1. Divide the class into groups of approximately six and gather each group in a circle.
2. All groups should consider each of the following situations.

   - *Situation A.* A large hospital is doing away with keeping patients' records on charts, or even on computers rolled around on carts. Now, doctors and nurses are being issued handheld, tablet computers on which they access the information they need, record new information, and even attach devices that allow them to record patients' vital signs.
   - *Situation B.* A very popular employee who's been with the company for many years is retiring. He will be replaced by a completely new employee from the outside, whom no one has met before.

3. For each situation, discuss three major impediments to change.
4. Identify a way of overcoming each of these impediments.
5. Have someone from the group record the answers and present them to the class for a discussion session.

Discussion Questions

1. For each of the situations, were the impediments to change similar or different?
2. Were the ways of overcoming the impediments similar or different?
3. How might the nature of the situation confronted dictate the types of change barriers confronted and the ease with which these may be overcome?

Notes

MAKING THE CASE NOTES

Campbell Soup Company. (2012) About us: The world's leading maker of soup. http://www.campbellsoup.com/Resources/AboutUs. When Campbell was in the soup. (2010, March 4). *Gallup Management Journal.* http://gmj.gallup.com/content/126278/Campbell-Soup.aspx. Saving Campbell Soup Company. (2010, February 11). *Gallup Management Journal.* http://gmj.gallup.com/content/125687/Saving-Campbell-Soup-Company.aspx. Campbell's Soup Company. (2010). Our company: Executive team. http://www.campbellsoupcompany.com/bio_conant.asp.

CHAPTER NOTES

1. Burke, W. W. (2011). Organizational change: Theory and practice (3rd ed.). Thousand Oaks, CA: Sage. Dawson, P. (2004). *Understanding organizational change: The contemporary experience of people at work.* Thousand Oaks, CA: Sage. Sherman, S. (1993, December 13). How will we live with the tumult? *Fortune,* pp. 123–125.
2. McKinsey & Company. (2006, April). An executive take on the top business trends: A McKinsey Global Survey. *McKinsey Quarterly.* https://www.mckinseyquarterly.com/An_executive_take_on_the_top_business_trends__A_McKinsey_Global_Survey_1754
3. Haveman, H. A. (1992). Between a rock and a hard place: Organizational change and performance under conditions of fundamental environmental transformation. *Administrative Science Quarterly, 37,* 48–75.
4. Smith, D. (1998, May). Invigorating change initiatives. *Management Review,* pp. 45–48.
5. Senior, B., & Swailes, S. (2011). *Organizational change* (4th ed.). Englewood Cliffs, NJ: Prentice Hall. Nystrom, P. C., & Starbuck, W. H. (1984, Spring). To avoid organizational crises, unlearn. *Organizational Dynamics,* 44–60.
6. Kanter, R. M. (1991, May–June). Transcending business boundaries: 12,000 world managers view change. *Harvard Business Review,* pp. 151–164.
7. Lexus. (2008, September 2). Lexus committed to sustainable transportation and business. http://www.lexus.com/articles/print/2008/9/20080902_1.html
8. Levy, A. (1986). Second-order planned change: Definition and conceptualization. *Organizational Dynamics, 16*(1), 4–20.
9. A master class in radical change. (1993, December 13). *Fortune,* pp. 82–84, 88, 90.
10. Woodyard, C. (2005, February 21). Multilingual staff can drive up auto sales. *USA Today.* http://www.usatoday.com/money/autos/2005-02-21-ethnic-cars-usat_x.htm?POE=click-refer
11. Bureau of Labor Statistics. (2010, March 5). News release: The employment situation, February 2010. http://www.bls.gov/news/release/pdf/empsit.pdf
12. Cameron, E., & Green, M. (2004). Making sense of change management. London: Kogan Page. David, F. R. (1993). *Concepts of strategic management.* New York: Macmillan.
13. Mead, R. (1998). *International management* (2nd ed.). Malden, MA: Blackwell.
14. Lewis, L. K. (2011). *Organizational change: Creating change through strategic communication.* Malden, MA: Blackwell. Taylor, B. (1995). The new strategic leadership—driving change, getting results. *Long Range Planning, 28*(5), 71–81.
15. Tripas, M., & Favetti, G. (2000). Capabilities, cognition, and inertia: Evidence from digital imaging. *Strategic Management Journal, 21,* 1147–1161.
16. Spooner, J. G., & Kanellos, M. (2004, December 8). IBM sells PC group to Lenovo. *CNET News.* http://news.com.com/IBM+sells+PC+group+to+Lenovo/2100-1042_3-5482284.html

17. Bellis, M. (2006). Inventors of the modern computer. http://inventors.about.com/library/weekly/aa031599.htm

18. Kennedy, R. E., & Sharma, A. (2009). *The services shift: Seizing the ultimate offshore opportunity.* Upper Saddle River, NJ: Pearson Education.

19. Travis, L. (2004, December 15). *India offshore outsourcing frees up $30B domestically.* Boston, MA: AMR Research. http://www.amrresearch.com/Content/View.asp?pmillid=17845

20. Conference Board. (2009). *The 2009 strategic outsourcing conference: Maximizing outsourcing strategies in current times.* New York: Author. http://www.conference-board.org/pdf_free/TCB_CK-009_StratOutsourcing.pdf

21. Beven, R. (2011). *Change making: Tactics and resources for managing organizational change.* Seattle, WA: CreateSpace Press. Christensen, H. K. (1994). Corporate strategy: Managing a set of businesses. In L. Fahley & R. M. Randall (Eds.), *The portable MBA in strategy* (pp. 53–83). New York: Wiley.

22. Collis, D. J., & Montgomery, C. A. (1995, July–August). Competing on resources: Strategy in the 1990s. *Harvard Business Review, 73,* 118–128.

23. Burke, W. W. (2010). *Organizational change: Theory and practice,* 3rd ed. Thousand Oaks, CA: Sage. Goldstein, A. P. (2001). *Reducing resistance: Methods for enhancing openness to change.* Champaign, IL: Research Press. Judson, A. S. (1991). *Changing behavior in organizations: Minimizing resistance to change.* Cambridge, MA: Basil Blackwell.

24. Nadler, D. A. (1987). The effective management of organizational change. In J. W. Lorsch (Ed.), *Handbook of organizational behavior* (pp. 358–369). Englewood Cliffs, NJ: Prentice Hall.

25. Katz, D., & Kahn, R. L. (1978). *The social psychology of organizations* (2nd ed.). New York: Wiley.

26. Beer, M. (1980). *Organizational change and development: A systems view.* Glenview, IL: Scott Foresman.

27. Nadler, D. A. (1987). The effective management of organizational change. In J. W. Lorsch (Ed.), *Handbook of organizational behavior* (pp. 358–369). Englewood Cliffs, NJ: Prentice Hall.

28. Harvey, T. R. & Broyles, E. A. (2010). *Resistance to change: A guide.* Lanham, MD: Rowan & Littlefield. Reich, R. B. (2000, October). Your job is change. *Fast Company,* pp. 140–148, 150, 152, 154, 156, 158.

29. Huey, J. (1993, April 5). Managing in the midst of chaos. *Fortune,* pp. 38–41, 44, 46, 48.

30. Senge, P. M. (1990). *The fifth discipline.* New York: Doubleday.

31. Collarelli, S. M. (1998). Psychological interventions in organizations. *American Psychologist, 53,* 1044–1056.

32. Pascale, R., Millemann, M., & Gioja, L. (1997, November–December). Changing the way we change. *Harvard Business Review,* pp. 127–139.

33. Whitney, D., & Sachau, C. (1998, Spring). Appreciative inquiry: An innovative process for organization change. *Employment Relations Today, 25,* pp. 11–21.

34. Bushe, G. R., & Coetzer, G. (1995). Appreciative inquiry as a team-developed intervention: A controlled experiment. *Journal of Applied Behavioral Science, 31,* 13–30.

35. Sugarman, H. C. (2006). The United States Navy: A case study in leadership development. http://appreciativeinquiry.case.edu/uploads/Navy%20-%20mini%20case%20summary.doc

36. See Note 35.

37. The International Organization Development Code of Ethics. (2006). *Organizational Development Network: Organization and human systems development credo.* http://hometown.aol.com/odinst/ethics.htm

38. Jaeger, A. M. (1986). Organizational development and national culture: Where's the fit? *Academy of Management Review, 11,* 178–190.

39. White, L. P., & Wotten, K. C. (1983). Ethical dilemmas in various stages of organizational development. *Academy of Management Review, 8,* 690–697.

40. Kedia, B. L., & Bhagat, R. S. (1998). Cultural constraints on transfer of technology across nations: Implications for research in

international and comparative management. *Academy of Management Review, 13,* 559–571.

41. Livermote, D. (2009). *Leading with cultural intelligence.* New York: AMACOM. Jaeger, A. M. (1986). Organizational development and national culture: Where's the fit? *Academy of Management Review, 11,* 178-190.

42. Trepo, G. (1973, Autumn). Management style *a la française. European Business, 39,* 71–79.

43. Blunt, P. (1988). Cultural consequences for organization change in a Southeast Asian state: Brunei. *Academy of Management Executive, 2,* 235–240.

COMPANY INDEX

Note: Page numbers followed by "*f*" or "*t*" refer to "figures" or "tables" respectively.

NAME INDEX

Note: Page numbers followed by "*f*" or "*t*" refer to "figures" or "tables" respectively.

SUBJECT INDEX

Note: Page numbers followed by "*f*" or "*t*" refer to "figures" or "tables" respectively.